MAJOR ARCHAEOLOGICAL SITES

Understanding Physical Anthropology and Archaeology

NINTH EDITION

Barry Lewis

University of Illinois at Urbana-Champaign

Robert Jurmain

Professor Emeritus, San Jose State University

Lynn Kilgore

Colorado State University

THOMSON
—™—
WADSWORTH

Australia • Canada • Mexico • Singapore • Spain
United Kingdom • United States

THOMSON

WADSWORTH

Understanding Physical Anthropology and Archaeology, **Ninth Edition**
Barry Lewis, Robert Jurmain, and Lynn Kilgore

Anthropology Editor: *Lin Marshall*
Development Editor: *Julie Cheng*
Assistant Editor: *Leata Holloway*
Editorial Assistant: *Danielle Yumol*
Technology Project Manager: *Dee Dee Zobian*
Marketing Manager: *Caroline Concilla*
Marketing Assistant: *Teresa Jensen*
Marketing Communications Manager: *Linda Yip*
Project Manager, Editorial Production: *Emily Smith*
Creative Director: *Rob Hugel*
Art Director: *Maria Epes*
Print Buyer: *Karen Hunt*
Permissions Editor: *Joohee Lee*

Production Service: *Patti Zeman, Hespenheide Design*
Text Designer: *Yvo Riezebos Design*
Photo Researcher: *Hespenheide Design*
Copy Editor: *Christianne Thillen*
Illustrator: *Alexander Productions; DLF Group; Graphic World; Hespenheide Design, Randy Miyake; Paragon 3; Sue Sellars; Cyndie Wooley*
Compositor: *Hespenheide Design*
Cover Designer: *Eric Handel*
Cover Image: *Courtesy of the Illinois State Museum: Photographer, Gary Andrashko*
Text and Cover Printer: *Courier Corporation/Kendallville*

Library of Congress Control Number: 2006924999

ISBN 0-534-62396-4

Thomson Higher Education
10 Davis Drive
Belmont, CA 94002-3098
USA

For more information about our products, contact us at:
Thomson Learning Academic Resource Center
1-800-423-0563

For permission to use material from this text or product, submit a request online at **http://www.thomsonrights.com.**
Any additional questions about permissions can be submitted by e-mail to **thomsonrights@thomson.com.**

BRIEF CONTENTS

CONTENTS

Lynn Kilgore

Chapter 4
Modern Human Variation and Adaptation

Chapter 5
Macroevolution: Processes of Vertebrate and Mammalian Evolution

Fred Jacobs

Fred Jacobs

PRIMATES

Chapter 6
An Overview of the Primates

Chapter 7
Primate Behavior

PALEOANTHROPOLOGY/ FOSSIL HOMINIDS

Chapter 8

Understanding the Past: Archaeological and Paleoanthropological Methods

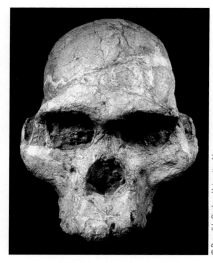

© Russell L. Ciochon, University of Iowa

Chapter 9

Hominid Origins

William L. Rathja

Chapter 10
The Earliest Dispersal of the Genus *Homo:*
Homo erectus and Contemporaries

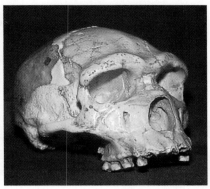

H. DeLumley

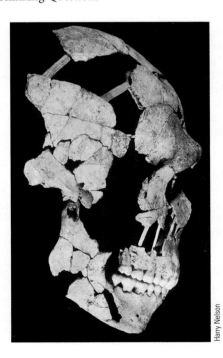

Harry Nelson

Chapter 11
Premodern Humans

Harry Nelson

Chapter 12
The Origin and Dispersal of Modern Humans

ARCHAEOLOGY

Chapter 13
Early Holocene Hunters and Gatherers

Chapter 14
Food Production

Chapter 15
The First Civilizations

Barry Lewis

Chapter 16
New World Civilizations

Barry Lewis

PREFACE

So, a new edition! New cover, new layout, lots of new pictures and graphs, and many, many pages of new text . . . and, yes, there's more: We even have a new coauthor. With the retirement of William Turnbaugh, who ably contributed to this book through eight editions, Barry Lewis, an archaeologist with extensive field experience in North America and South Asia, joins the author team.

But why a new edition? Our biology is still the same, our primate cousins haven't perceptibly changed, and both the fossil record and archaeological record of the human past are still in the past. So what's the big deal? Why not trundle on with the same edition? The answer's simple—we learn so much more about the world with each passing year. The new discoveries, fresh theories, new methods and technologies force changes, sometimes fundamental changes, in the *understanding* of how the world around us works.

Consider this: There are probably more physical anthropologists and archaeologists at work right now than in all the preceding generations combined. The sheer number, diversity, and global distribution of their research projects would have been unthinkable to scholars 60–70 years ago and laughably improbable in the eyes of researchers just a century ago (when physicists speculated that their field would likely soon disappear because there was so little left to discover!). The net result of the scale of recent research is that our understanding of the world around us, not just in physical anthropology and archaeology, but in all scientific disciplines, unfolds with fresh perspectives at an increasing rate year after year.

The ninth edition of *Understanding Physical Anthropology and Archaeology* stays true to our 25-year tradition of providing introductory students and their instructors with a current and comprehensive understanding of human biological and cultural development from an evolutionary point of view. Fresh perspectives and new discoveries will be found in nearly every part of this book. To mention only a few important examples (see the next section, "What's New in the Ninth Edition," for detailed highlights), recent advances in molecular biology are having profound effects on the biological understanding of the human past. The implications of these advances are so fundamental that they even impact archaeology, where the emerging subdiscipline of "archeogenetics" is now defining itself! New archaeological discoveries around the world also are driving major theoretical changes. For example, at the 23,000-year-old campsite of Ohalo II in the Near East, archaeologists have found abundant, well-preserved evidence of extensive dependence on plant foods more than 10,000 years older than the oldest known cases when the eighth edition of this text went to press. Critical finds such as Ohalo II often poke holes in major theories and send researchers back to their workbenches to hammer out fresh ideas.

Today's learning environment is also changing. Although every edition of *Understanding Physical Anthropology and Archaeology* is committed to providing up-to-date subject content for students and their instructors, we authors are also teachers and even sometimes students ourselves. We know that instructional software, the Internet, multimedia, new teaching approaches, and a host of other factors (including technologically adept students!) are reshaping classrooms and the ways in which students and instructors engage the course material. To meet the pedagogical challenges of today's classrooms, we work hard to enhance each edition with in-chapter learning aids (see the appropriately titled "In-Chapter Learning Aids" section below) to help ensure that learning (and teaching) the course material continues to be a positive and productive experience.

What's New in the Ninth Edition

Since the eighth edition of this text went to press in Spring 2001 much in the world around us has changed—in many cases disconcertingly so. When the prior edition came out, the September 11th terrorist attacks hadn't yet occurred, iPods hadn't been invented, reality TV didn't exist, the United States briefly enjoyed its second largest budget surplus in history, and approximately 450 million fewer people were living on the planet. In science and in our world, so much has happened that it's no surprise that the ninth edition of *Understanding Physical Anthropology and Archaeology* is the most dramatically revised new version of this text since its first appearance a quarter century ago.

First, as noted, we have a new lead author, archaeologist Barry Lewis. Second, there have been several major organizational changes. The number of chapters has been reduced from 18 to 16. The two chapters in the eighth edition on modern human variation have been combined into one chapter (Chapter 4); likewise, the two chapters dealing with methods of understanding the past from paleoanthropological and archaeological perspectives have been combined into an integrated single chapter (Chapter 8). A new chapter order will also be evident, with the earlier placement of the chapter (Chapter 5) on macroevolutionary processes. We believe this organization will work better since the broad evolutionary processes influencing vertebrates, and more specifically, mammals, are now discussed prior to the materials on primates.

Another obvious change from the eighth edition is found in the between-chapter features. While in the prior edition we had several photo essays, in this one we have focused on short and, we hope engaging, discussions of the latest "cutting edge" research in physical anthropology and archaeology.

And, of course, the content of the book has been updated throughout with new information derived from molecular studies of DNA and exciting, in some cases even shocking, accounts of new finds of early human fossils from Africa, Asia, and Europe. To show how these two kinds of new data can blend together, there've been several remarkable new determinations of ancient human DNA from fossils as much as 70,000 years old (which we discuss in Chapters 11 and 12 and the "Cutting Edge Research" feature between these chapters). Discussion of the entry of the first humans into the New World (Chapter 13) takes a broader perspective, both in time depth and spatial coverage, and examines the three main competing hypotheses and their strengths and weaknesses. The theoretical perspectives on the origins of agriculture (Chapter 14) and the origins of the first civilizations (Chapter 15) have been completely rewritten to consider fresh views on these crucial developments in the human past.

Students will be glad to know there are also several new learning aids in every chapter to help them master more easily the sometimes complex material. These include focus questions at the beginning of each chapter, "At a Glance" boxes summarizing key concepts through a simple visual presentation, and thought-provoking critical thinking questions at the end of each chapter. And, lastly, the photos and artwork have been substantially expanded and updated, not just to make the book more visually appealing, but also to provide a better sense of what physical anthropologists and archaeologists do, and why they enjoy doing it!

FEATURES

Cutting Edge Research boxes are major between-chapter features, highlighting some of the newest and most innovative research in physical anthropology and archaeology. Five areas of research are covered, including:

- Molecular Applications in Forensic Anthropology (following Chapter 3)
- Molecular Applications in Primatology (following Chapter 6)
- Reconstructing the Diets of Earlier Humans (following Chapter 8)
- Ancient DNA (following Chapter 11)
- Geomatics: Analyzing Spatial Patterns of the Past (following Chapter 14)

Boxed highlights titled **"Digging Deeper"** are high-interest features found throughout the book. They expand on the topic under discussion in the chapter by providing a more in-depth perspective.

IN-CHAPTER LEARNING AIDS

- **Chapter outlines**, at the beginning of each chapter list all major topics covered.
- **Focus Questions**, a new feature that appears at the beginning of each chapter, highlight the central topic of that chapter.
- A **running glossary** in the margins provides definitions of important terms on the page where the term is first introduced. A **full glossary** is provided in the back of the book.
- **At a Glance**, a new feature for the ninth edition, briefly summarizes complex or controversial material in a visually simple fashion.
- **Figures**, including numerous photographs, line drawings, and maps, most in full color, are carefully selected to clarify text materials and are placed to directly support discussion in the text.
- **Critical Thinking Questions** at the end of each chapter have been completely revised to reinforce key concepts and encourage students to think critically about what they have read.
- Two new features, **Most Significant Fossil Discoveries Discussed in This Chapter** and **Most Significant Sites Discussed in This Chapter,** are included at the end of relevant chapters to help students as they review the chapter material.
- **Full bibliographic citations** throughout the entire book provide sources from which the materials are drawn. This type of documentation guides students to published source materials and illustrates for them the proper use of referencing; all cited sources are listed in the comprehensive bibliography at the back of the book.
- A **"Click" Icon** at the beginning of most chapters directs students to the media relevant to that chapter. One or more of the following media will be listed when appropriate: *Virtual Laboratories in Physical Anthropology CD-ROM, Third Edition* (an online version is also available), *Basic Genetics for Anthropology CD-ROM: Principles and Applications,* and *Hominid Fossils CD-ROM: An Interactive Atlas.*

ACKNOWLEDGMENTS

Over the years many friends and colleagues have assisted us with our books. For this edition we are especially grateful to the reviewers who so carefully commented on the manuscript and made such helpful suggestions:

Kenneth Kelly, University of South Carolina
Kenneth E. Lewis, Michigan State University
Timothy G. Roufs, University of Minnesota Duluth
Elizabeth Salter, University of Texas at Dallas
Michael Shott, University of Northern Iowa

We also wish to thank at Wadsworth Publishing Lin Marshall, Senior Acquisitions Editor for Anthropology; Leata Holloway, Assistant Editor; Danielle Yumol, Editorial Assistant; Julie Cheng, Developmental Editor; Dee Dee Zobian, Technology Product Manager; Caroline Concilla, Executive Marketing Manager; Emily Smith, Content Project Manager; Eve Howard, Vice President and Editor-in-Chief; Sean Wakely, President, Thomson Higher Education, Arts and Sciences; and Susan Badger, CEO of Thomson Higher Education. Moreover, for their unflagging expertise and patience, we are grateful to our copy editor, Christianne Thillen, and our production coordinator, Gary Hespenheide and his skilled staff at Hespenheide Design: Patti Zeman, production coordinator, and Bridget Neumayr, proofreader/editor.

To the many friends and colleagues who have generously provided photographs, comments, and criticism, we are greatly appreciative: Gary Andrashko, Cecilia Ayala, Colin Betts, Dana Blount, C. K. Brain, Günter Bräuer, Russ Ciochon, Desmond Clark, Ron Clarke, Robert Clouse, Raymond Dart, Jean deRousseau, James Dixon, Tom Emerson, Denis Etler, Andy Fortier, Diane France, David Frayer, Kathleen Galvin, Joshua Gruber, Michael Hargrave, Eve Hargrave, David Haring, Nancy Hawkins, Ellen Ingmanson, Fred Jacobs, Peter Jones, Leslie Knapp, Laura Kozuch, Arlene Kruse, Carol Kussman, Clark Larsen, Richard Leakey, Craig Lee, Hannah Lewis, Susan Lewis, Carol Lofton, William Manley, Margaret Maples, Terry Martin, Lorna Moore, John Oates, Carolina Orsini, Bonnie Pedersen, Lorna Pierce, David Pilbeam, Dolores Piperno, William Pratt, Paul J. Ray, Jr., Judith Regensteiner, Debra Rich, James Rogers, Sastrohamijoyo Sartono, Eugenie Scott, Kirk Scott, Rose Sevick, Helaine Silverman, Elwyn Simons, Meredith Small, Fred Smith, Judy Suchey, Heather Thew, Li Tianyuan, Philip Tobias, William Turnbaugh, Shane Vanderford, Richard VanderHoek, Alan Walker, Milford Wolpoff, and Xinzhi Wu.

Barry Lewis
Robert Jurmain
Lynn Kilgore

SUPPLEMENTS

Understanding Physical Anthropology and Archaeology comes with a strong supplements program to help instructors create an effective learning environment both inside and outside the classroom and to aid students in mastering the material.

Supplements for Instructors

Instructor's Manual with Test Bank   The Instructor's Manual offers detailed chapter outlines, lecture suggestions, key terms and student activities such as *InfoTrac College Edition* exercises and Internet exercises. In addition, each chapter offers over 50 test questions including multiple-choice, true/false, fill-in-the-blank, short-answer, and essay.

ExamView Computerized and Online Testing   Create, deliver, and customize tests and study guides (both print and online) in minutes with this easy to use assessment and tutorial system. ExamView offers both a Quick Test Wizard and an Online Test Wizard that guide you step-by-step throughout the process of creating tests, while its unique "WYSWYG" capability allows you to see the test you are creating on screen exactly as it will print or display online. You can build tests of up to 250 questions using up to 12 question types. Using ExamView's complete word processing capabilities, you can enter an unlimited number of new questions or edit existing questions.

JoinIn on TurningPoint   The anthropology discipline at Thomson Wadsworth is pleased to offer **JoinIn**™ (clicker) content for Audience Response Systems tailored to many of our anthropology texts. Use the program by posing your own questions and display students' answers instantly within the Microsoft® PowerPoint® slides of your existing lecture. Or, utilize any or all of the following content that will be included with your Anthropology JoinIn product:

- **Opinion polls** on issues important to each Anthropology chapter (5 questions per chapter). Students may feel uncomfortable talking about sensitive subjects such as sexuality or religion. JoinIn gives students complete anonymity and helps students feel connected to the issues.

- **Conceptual quiz questions** for each chapter. Give students a quick quiz during or after the chapter lecture and determine if they have understood the material.

- Plus, **pre-assembled PowerPoint lecture slides** for each chapter of your book are included with the material above integrated into the slides. All of the work integrating clicker questions into the chapter lecture slides has been done for you!

The program can be used simply to take roll, or it can assess your students' progress and opinions with in-class questions. Enhance how your students interact with you, your lecture, and each other. *Contact your local Thomson representative to learn more.*

Multimedia Manager for Anthropology: A Microsoft PowerPoint Link Tool   This new CD-ROM contains digital media and Microsoft PowerPoint presentations for all of Wadsworth's 2007 introductory anthropology texts, placing images, lectures and video clips at your fingertips. This CD-ROM includes preassembled Microsoft PowerPoint presentations, charts, graphs, maps and line art from all Wadsworth anthropology texts. You can add your own lecture notes and images to create a customized lecture presentation. Also included are videos and an Earth Watch Institute Research Expedition feature that offers even more images.

Wadsworth Anthropology Video Library   Qualified adopters may select full-length videos from an extensive library of offerings drawn from such excellent educational video sources as *Films for the Humanities and Sciences.*

ABC Anthropology Video Series   This exclusive video series was created jointly by Wadsworth and ABC for the anthropology course. Each video contains approximately 45 minutes of footage originally broadcast on ABC within the past several years. The videos are broken into short two- to seven-minute segments, perfect for classroom use as lecture launchers or to illustrate key anthropological concepts. An annotated table of contents accompanies each video, providing descriptions of the segments and suggestions for their possible use within the course.

Online Resources for Instructors and Students

Premium Companion Site for *Understanding Physical Anthropology and Archaeology*
Go to http://thomsonedu.com/anthropology and click on the *Physical Anthropology and Archaeology* link to reach the website that accompanies this book.

This premium companion website offers an in-depth and interactive study experience that will help students make their grade. Some of the chapter resources include:

- **Learning Modules** on key anthropology concepts, such as Remote Sensing and Foraging to Farming Subsistence

- **Animations** that help students understand anthropology ideas, including Stratigraphy

- **Interactive Exercises** that require students to identify Hominids, taxonomy categories, skeletal anatomy, and much more

- **Map Exercises** that show statistics throughout the world and ask students to interact with the data

- **Video Exercises** with questions that can be answered and e-mailed to instructors

- **Tutorial Quizzes** with feedback – 30 per chapter

- **Essay Questions** that can be answered and e-mailed to instructors

- **Instructor resources** such as PowerPoint lecture slides.

Access to this rich resource is free when packaged with new books.

Anthropology Resource Center This online center offers a wealth of information and useful tools for both instructors and students in all four fields of anthropology. It includes interactive maps, learning modules, video exercises and breaking news in anthropology. To get started with the Anthropology Resource Center, students are directed to http://thomsonedu.com where they can create an account through 1Pass. Access to this rich resource is free when packaged with new books.

Thomson InSite for Writing and Research—With Turnitin Originality Checker InSite features a full suite of writing, peer review, online grading, and e-portfolio applications. It is an all-in-one tool that helps instructors manage the flow of papers electronically and allows students to submit papers and peer reviews online. Also included in the suite is Turnitin, an originality check that offers a simple solution for instructors who want a strong deterrent against plagiarism, as well as encouragement for students to employ proper research techniques. Access is available for packaging with each copy of this book. For more information, visit http://insite.thomson.com

InfoTrac College Edition InfoTrac College Edition is an online library that offers full-length articles from thousands of scholarly and popular publications. Among the journals available are American Anthropologist, Current Anthropology, and Canadian Review of Sociology and Anthropology. To get started with InfoTrac, students are directed to http://thomsonedu.com where they can create an account through 1Pass.

Supplements for Students

Basic Genetics for Anthropology CD-ROM: Principles and Applications (Stand Alone Version), by Jurmain and Kilgore This student CD-ROM expands on the biological concepts covered in the book, focusing on biological inheritance (genes, DNA sequencing, etc.) and its applications to modern human populations at the molecular level (human variation and adaptation, i.e., to disease, diet, growth and development). Interactive animations and simulations will bring these important concepts to life for students so they can fully understand the essential biological principles required for Physical Anthropology. Also available are quizzes and interactive flashcards for further study.

Hominid Fossils CD-ROM: An Interactive Atlas, by James Ahern The interactive atlas CD-ROM includes over 75 key fossils important for a clear understanding of human evolution. The QuickTime Virtual Reality (QTVR) "object" movie format for each fossil enables students to have a near-authentic experience of working with these important finds, by allowing them to rotate the fossil 360 degrees. Unlike some VR media, QTVR objects are made using actual photographs of the real objects and thus better preserve details of color and texture. The fossils used are high-quality research casts and real fossils. The organization of the atlas is non-linear, with three levels and multiple paths, enabling students to see how the fossil fits into the map of human evolution in terms of geography, time, and evolution. The CD-ROM offers students an inviting, authentic, learning environment, one that also contains a dynamic quizzing feature that will allow students to test their knowledge of fossil and species identification, as well as provide more detailed information about the fossil record. Available packaged at a discount with the text upon request.

Virtual Laboratories for Physical Anthropology CD-ROM, 4th edition, by John Kappelman The new edition of this full-color, interactive CD-ROM provides students with a hands-on computer component for completing lab assignments at school or at home. Through the use of video clips, 3-D animations, sound, and digital images, students can actively participate in 12 labs as part of their physical anthropology and archaeology course. The labs and assignments teach students how to formulate and test hypotheses with exercises that include how to measure, plot, interpret, and evaluate a variety of data drawn from osteological, behavioral, and fossil materials. Also available online.

Readings and Case Studies

Case Studies in Archaeology, edited by Jeffrey Quilter These engaging accounts of cutting-edge archaeological techniques, issues and solutions—as well as studies discussing the collection of material remains—range from site-specific excavations to types of archaeology practiced.

Modules in Physical Anthropology Each free-standing module is actually a complete text chapter, featuring the same quality of pedagogy and illustration contained in Thomson Wadsworth's physical anthropology texts.

Primate Evolution Module by Robert Jurmain Robert Jurmain examines primate evolution as it has developed over the last 60 million years, helping students understand the ecological adaptations and evolutionary relationships of fossil forms to each other and to contemporary primates. Using what they know about primate anatomy and social behavior, students will learn to "flesh out" the bones and teeth that make up the evolutionary record of primate origins.

Forensics Anthropology Module: A Brief Review by Diane France Diane France explores the myths and realities of the search for human remains in crime scenes, what should be expected from a forensic anthropology expert in the courtroom, some of the special challenges in mass fatality incident responses (such as plane crashes and terrorist acts) and what students should consider if they want to pursue a career in forensic anthropology.

Molecular Anthropology Module by Leslie Knapp Leslie Knapp explores how molecular genetic methods are used to understand the organization and expression of genetic information in humans and nonhuman primates. Students will learn about the common laboratory methods used to study genetic variation and evolution in molecular anthropology. Examples are drawn from up-to-date research on human evolutionary origins and comparative primate genomics to demonstrate that scientific research is an ongoing process with theories frequently being questioned and re-evaluated.

Human-Environment Interactions: New Directions in Human Ecology by Kathleen A. Galvin Kathleen Galvin looks at the fundamental concepts in human ecology, how those concepts have changed and been added to through time, and how this approach is used to answer important questions of a global nature.

ABOUT THE AUTHORS

Barry Lewis has joined Robert Jurmain and Lynn Kilgore to write the ninth edition of *Understanding Physical Anthropology and Archaeology*. While the authors have their particular areas of expertise and have made distinct contributions to the text, their effort has truly been a collaborative one!

Barry Lewis

Barry Lewis received his Ph.D. from the University of Illinois at Urbana-Champaign, where he is currently Professor of Anthropology. His teaching focuses on introductory archaeology, quantitative methods in archaeology, geographic information systems, and social science research methods. He has published extensively on his research concerning late prehistoric Native American towns and villages in the southeastern United States. His recent research centers on the archaeology and history of early modern kingdoms and chiefdoms in South India.

Robert Jurmain

Robert Jurmain received an A.B. in anthropology from UCLA, and a Ph.D. in biological anthropology from Harvard. He taught at San Jose State University from 1975–2004 and is now a Professor Emeritus. During his teaching career he taught courses in all major branches of physical anthropology including osteology and human evolution, with the greatest concentration in general education teaching for introductory students. His areas of research interest are skeletal biology of humans and non-human primates; paleopathology; and paleoanthropology. In addition to his three textbooks, which together have appeared in 25 editions, he is author of numerous articles in research journals as well as the book, *Stories from the Skeleton: Behavioral Reconstruction in Human Osteology* (1999, Gordon & Breach Publishers).

Lynn Kilgore

Lynn Kilgore earned her Ph.D. from the University of Colorado, Boulder, and holds an affiliate faculty position at Colorado State University. Her primary research interests are osteology and paleopathology. She has taught numerous undergraduate and graduate courses in human osteology, primate behavior, human heredity and evolution, and general physical anthropology. Her research focuses on developmental defects, disease, and trauma in human and great ape skeletons.

ANTHROPOLOGY

CHAPTER 1

Introduction to Anthropology

FOCUS QUESTIONS

What is anthropology, and what can it tell us about our past, present, and future?

How does anthropological research work?

Introduction

Go to the following CD-ROMs for interactive activities and exercises on topics covered in this chapter:

- Virtual Laboratories for Physical Anthropology CD-ROM, Third Edition
- Genetics in Anthropology: Principles and Applications CD-ROM, First Edition
- Hominid Fossils: An Interactive Atlas CD-ROM, First Edition

anthropology The field of inquiry that studies human culture and evolutionary aspects of human biology; includes cultural anthropology, archaeology, linguistics, and physical anthropology.

biocultural evolution The mutual, interactive evolution of human biology and culture; the concept that biology makes culture possible and that developing culture further influences the direction of biological evolution; a basic concept in understanding the unique components of human evolution.

culture All aspects of human adaptation, including technology, traditions, language, religion, and social roles. Culture is a set of learned behaviors ; it is transmitted from one generation to the next through learning and not by biological or genetic means.

A trip along the northern coast of New Guinea would be high adventure for most of us. We'd be treated to great natural beauty, welcoming people, and at least one remarkable observation that we probably wouldn't anticipate—the northern coast holds an extraordinary diversity of local languages. The inhabitants of villages separated by only a few miles may speak different languages. Language diversity is nearly as great in the rest of New Guinea; on an island only a little bigger than the state of Texas, more than 800 languages are spoken—or roughly 15 percent of the world's languages (Wurm, 1994, p. 93).

But why should anyone care how many languages are spoken on the island of New Guinea? Mostly because language diversity is a good rough measure of cultural diversity, and humans exhibit an enormous range of cultural diversity. But biologically, human populations from around the world are very similar to each other. In fact, regardless of their extraordinary cultural diversity, humans show less genetic variation than can be found in a group of wild chimpanzees (Pagel and Mace, 2004).

The main points of this example are, first, that modern humans are cultural *and* biological organisms, and they cannot be adequately understood without examining them from both perspectives. Secondly, human beings are probably unique among other animals because they alone have the capacity to ask the question, "why?" These points illustrate fundamental motivations for the field of anthropology and for this book as an introduction to the biocultural perspective of human evolution.

Anthropology addresses the entire scope of the human experience, past and present, and deliberately brings multiple perspectives to bear on research. Such a broad focus encompasses all topics related to behavior, including social relationships (for example, kinship and marriage patterns), religion, ritual, technology, subsistence techniques, and economic and political systems. Anthropology is also concerned with the numerous biological and evolutionary dimensions of our species, such as genetics, anatomy, skeletal structure, adaptation to disease and other environmental factors, growth, nutrition, and ultimately, all the evolutionary processes that have resulted in the development of modern humans. In short, then, anthropology is a holistic discipline that studies all aspects of what it is to be human.

In contrast, an economist, for example, might study market systems—the production, distribution, and consumption of goods—and only rarely, if ever, consider the effects of genetics, evolutionary factors, religion, or kinship on economic systems. But anthropology's holistic approach recognizes that many factors contribute to whatever we humans do, even including economic transactions. Indeed, anthropologists incorporate findings from many academic fields (for example, psychology, biology, history, and religious studies) as they seek to understand and explain what being human is all about. In a practical sense, however, no single anthropologist can hope to encompass the entire discipline.

In keeping with anthropology's commitment to a holistic perspective, aspects of this discipline rest firmly both in science, because anthropologists answer many questions by applying the scientific method in their research, and in the humanities, because they also apply interpretive methods to achieve an understanding of such human qualities as love, individual or group identity, compassion, and ethnicity.

The Biocultural Approach

The concept of **biocultural evolution** helps give all anthropologists a shared perspective. Humans are the product of the combined influences of biology and **culture** that have shaped our evolutionary history over the last several million years. It is by tracing the changing interaction between biology and culture and understanding *how* the process worked in the past, and how it continues to work today, that we are able to come to grips scientifically with what we are and how we came to be.

As we'll emphasize in this book, humans have occupied center stage in only one short scene of life's evolutionary play. Our role is fascinating; but because of cultural factors, we have also become a threat to many life-forms, including ourselves. Culture is therefore an extremely important concept, not only as it pertains to modern humans but also in terms of its critical role in human evolution.

Viewed in evolutionary perspective, human culture can be described as the strategy people use in adapting to the natural and social environments in which we live. Culture includes technologies that range from stone tools to computers; subsistence patterns ranging from hunting and gathering to agribusiness on a global scale; housing types from thatched huts to skyscrapers; and clothing from animal skins to synthetic fibers (Fig. 1–1). Because religion,

FIGURE **1–1**

(a) An early stone tool from East Africa. This type of tool was used there about 1.5 million years ago. (b) Assortment of implements available today in a modern hardware store. (c) A Samburu woman building a simple, traditional dwelling of stems, plant fibers, and mud. (d) A modern high-rise apartment complex, typical of industrialized cities.

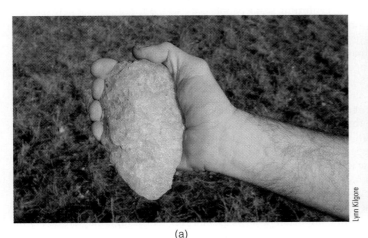

(a)

(b)

(c)

(d)

values, social organization, language, kinship, marriage rules, gender roles, and so on are all aspects of culture, each culture shapes people's perceptions of the external environment, or worldview, in particular ways that distinguish that culture from all others. One fundamental point to remember is that culture is *learned* and not biologically determined. Consequently, culture is transmitted from generation to generation independently of biological factors (that is, genes).

For example,* if a young South Indian girl is raised in New Orleans by Italian American parents, she'll acquire, through the process called **enculturation**, all those aspects of growing up in the Big Easy, including a distinctive dialect of American English, a sense of surprise when she discovers that Mardi Gras is not a national holiday, how to make a roux, and the understanding that red beans go with Monday and a choupic court bouillon is a joke. Alternatively, an Italian American girl raised in Mysore by South Indian parents will just as likely grow up speaking Kannada as her first language, experience a sense of surprise when she learns that the chili pepper is not native to India, know all the latest and best Kannada and Hindi filmi gana, and understand that onion sambar goes with idli. In short, both girls' perspectives will be strongly shaped by their respective enculturation experiences, not their genetic ancestry. We are all products of the culture in which we are socialized, and since most human behavior is learned, it clearly is also culturally patterned.

But as biological organisms, humans are subject to the same evolutionary forces as all other species. On hearing the term **evolution**, many people think of the appearance of new **species**. Certainly, new species formation is one consequence of evolution; however, biologists see evolution as an ongoing process with a precise genetic meaning. Quite simply, *evolution* is a change in the genetic makeup of a population from one generation to the next. It is the accumulation of such changes, over considerable periods of time that can result in the appearance of a new species. So, evolution can be defined and studied at two different levels. At one level there are genetic alterations *within* populations. Although this kind of change may not lead to the development of new species, it frequently does result in variation between populations with regard to the frequency of certain traits. Evolution at this level is referred to as *microevolution*. The other level involves long-term genetic change that does lead to the appearance of a new species, by a process sometimes termed *macroevolution* or *speciation*. Evolution at both these levels will be addressed in this textbook.

In the course of human evolution, biocultural interactions have resulted in such anatomical, biological, and behavioral changes as increased brain size, reorganization of neurological structures, decreased tooth size, and development of language, to list a few. Biocultural interactions are still critically important today and, among other things, they are changing patterns of disease worldwide. As one example, rapid culture change (for example, in Africa) and changing social and sexual mores may have influenced evolutionary rates of HIV, the virus that causes AIDS. Certainly, these cultural factors influenced the spread of HIV throughout populations in both developed and developing countries.

The study of many of the biological aspects of humankind, including **adaptation** and evolution, could certainly be the purview of biologists; and in fact, it frequently is. However, when such research also considers the role of cultural factors, in the United States it is placed within the discipline of anthropology. This approach recognizes that the human predisposition to assimilate a culture and to function within it is influenced by biological factors. But in the course of human evolution, as you'll see, the role of culture has increasingly assumed an added importance. In this respect, humans are unique among biological organisms.

enculturation   The process by which individuals, generally as children, learn the values and beliefs of the family, peer groups, and society in which they are raised.

evolution   A change in the genetic structure of a population from one generation to the next. The term is also frequently used to refer to the appearance of a new species.

species   A group of organisms that can interbreed to produce fertile offspring. Members of one species are reproductively isolated from members of all other species (i.e., they can't mate with them to produce fertile offspring).

adaptation   Functional response of organisms or populations to the environment. Adaptation results from evolutionary change (specifically, as a result of natural selection).

---

*These examples draw upon two very different enculturation experiences to illustrate what enculturation is all about. If, like most readers, you didn't grow up in these cultural webs, you may find them impenetrable because you're an outsider. It's okay. The big differences that result from enculturation experiences are much of the point we want to make here. Need a quick guide to some of the terms? In New Orleans (aka "The Big Easy"), red beans and rice are a traditional Monday dish; a roux is flour browned in oil and used as the base for many South Louisiana dishes; many people view the choupic as a "trash fish" and won't eat it; a court bouillon is a fish stew, often made with redfish. In Mysore, a city in South India, Kannada is a Dravidian language of southern India; *filmi gana* is Hindi for "movie music," an extremely popular music genre throughout South Asia; and idli is a steamed cake made of fermented rice or *rava* (farina) and typically served with onion sambar, a spicy dal soup.

What Is Anthropology?

Stated ambitiously but simply, anthropology is the study of humankind. The term itself is derived from the Greek words *anthropos*, meaning "human," and *logos*, meaning "word" or "study of." Clearly, anthropologists aren't the only scientists who study humans, and the goals of anthropology are shared by other disciplines within the social, behavioral, and biological sciences. As we noted earlier, the main difference between anthropology and other related fields is anthropology's holistic perspective, which integrates the findings of many disciplines, including sociology, economics, history, psychology, and biology.

In the United States, anthropology comprises three main subfields: cultural or social anthropology, archaeology, and physical or biological anthropology. Additionally, many universities include linguistic anthropology as a fourth subfield. Each of these subdisciplines, in turn, is divided into more specialized areas of interest. The following is a brief discussion of the main subdisciplines of anthropology.

CULTURAL ANTHROPOLOGY

Cultural anthropology is the study of all aspects of human behavior. It could reasonably be argued that cultural anthropology began in the fourth century B.C. with the Greek philosopher Aristotle, or even earlier. But for practical purposes, the beginnings of cultural anthropology are rooted in the **Enlightenment** of the eighteenth century, which exerted considerable influence on how Europeans viewed the place of humans in nature, questioned the extent to which there exists a knowable order to the natural world, and introduced fresh concepts of "primitive" or traditional societies. These changes in political and social philosophy were particularly felt in the spread of European colonial powers between 1500 and 1900.

The interest in traditional societies led many early anthropologists to study and record lifeways that are now mostly extinct. These studies yielded descriptive **ethnographies** that later became the basis for comparisons between cultures. Early ethnographies were encyclopedic descriptive narratives emphasizing such phenomena as religion, ritual, myth, use of symbols, subsistence and dietary preferences, technology, gender roles, child-rearing practices, taboos, medical practices, and how kinship was reckoned.

The focus of cultural anthropology changed considerably with the global social, political, and economic upheavals of the twentieth century. Researchers using traditional ethnographic methods still spend months or years living in and studying various societies, but the nature of the study groups has changed. For example, in recent decades, ethnographic techniques have been applied to the study of diverse subcultures and their interactions with one another in contemporary metropolitan areas. The subfield of cultural anthropology that deals with issues of inner cities is appropriately called *urban anthropology*. Among the many issues addressed by urban anthropologists are relationships among various ethnic groups, those aspects of traditional cultures that are maintained by immigrant populations, poverty, labor relations, homelessness, access to health care, and problems facing the elderly.

Medical anthropology is the subfield of cultural anthropology that explores the relationship between various cultural attributes and health and disease. Areas of interest include how different groups view disease processes, and how these views affect treatment or the willingness to accept treatment. When medical anthropologists focus on the social dimensions of disease, they may collaborate with physicians and physical anthropologists. Indeed, many medical anthropologists have received much of their training in physical anthropology.

Economic anthropologists are concerned with factors that influence the distribution of goods and resources within and between cultures. Areas of interest include such topics as division of labor (by gender and age), factors that influence who controls resources and wealth, and trade practices and regulations.

Many cultural anthropologists are involved in *gender studies*. Such studies may focus on gender norms, how such norms are learned, and the specific cultural factors that lead to individual development of gender identity. It is also valuable to explore the social consequences when gender norms are violated.

There is also increasing interest in the social aspects of development and aging. This field is particularly relevant in industrialized nations, where the proportion of elderly individuals

enlightenment An eighteenth-century philosophical movement in western Europe that assumed a knowable order to the natural world and the interpretive value of reason as the primary means of identifying and explaining this order.

ethnographies Detailed descriptive studies of human societies. In cultural anthropology, *ethnographies* are traditionally studies of non-Western societies.

is higher than ever before. As populations age, the needs of the elderly, particularly in the area of health care, become social issues that require more and more attention.

Many subfields of cultural anthropology (for example, medical anthropology) have practical applications and are pursued by anthropologists working both within and outside the university setting. This approach is aptly termed *applied anthropology*. Although most applied anthropologists regard themselves as cultural anthropologists, the designation is also sometimes used to describe the activities of archaeologists and physical anthropologists. Indeed, the various fields of anthropology, as they are practiced in the United States, overlap to a considerable degree—after all, that was the rationale for combining them under the umbrella of anthropology in the first place.

PHYSICAL ANTHROPOLOGY

As we've already said, *physical anthropology* is the study of human biology within the framework of evolution and with an emphasis on the interaction between biology and culture. This subdiscipline is also referred to as *biological anthropology*, and you will find the terms used interchangeably. *Physical anthropology* is the original term, and it reflects the initial interests of anthropologists in describing human physical variation. The American Association of Physical Anthropologists, its journal, many college courses, and numerous publications retain this term. The designation *biological anthropology* reflects the shift in emphasis to more biologically oriented topics, such as genetics, evolutionary biology, nutrition, physiological adaptation, and growth and development. This shift has occurred largely due to advances in the field of genetics since the late 1950s. Although we have continued to use the traditional term in the title of this textbook, you will find that all the major topics in physical anthropology pertain to biological issues.

The origins of physical anthropology are found in two main areas of interest among nineteenth-century scholars. First, there was increasing concern among many scientists (at the time called *natural historians*) regarding the mechanisms by which modern species had come to be. In other words, they were beginning to doubt the literal, biblical interpretation of creation. Although most scientists weren't actually prepared to believe that humans had evolved from earlier forms, discoveries of several Neandertal fossils in the 1800s raised questions about the origins and antiquity of the human species.

The sparks of interest in biological change over time were fueled into flames by the publication of Charles Darwin's *On the Origin of Species* in 1859. Today, **paleoanthropology**, or the study of human evolution, particularly as revealed in the fossil record, is a major subfield of physical anthropology (Fig. 1–2). There are now thousands of specimens of human ancestors housed in research collections. Taken together, these fossils cover a span of at least 4 million years of human prehistory; and although incomplete, they provide us with significantly more knowledge than was available just 10 years ago. The ultimate goal of paleoanthropological research is to identify the various early **hominid** species, establish a chronological sequence of relationships among them, and gain insights into their adaptation and behavior. Only then will there emerge a clear picture of how and when humankind came into being.

Observable physical variation was a second nineteenth-century interest that had direct relevance to anthropology. Enormous effort was aimed at describing and explaining the biological differences among human populations. Although some endeavors were misguided and even racist, they gave birth to literally thousands of body measurements that could be used to compare people. Physical anthropologists use many of the techniques of **anthropometry** today, not only to study living groups but also to study skeletal remains from archaeological sites (Fig. 1–3). Moreover, anthropometric tech-

paleoanthropology   The interdisciplinary approach to the study of earlier hominids—their chronology, physical structure, archaeological remains, habitats, etc.

hominid   Colloquial term for member of the family Hominidae, the classificatory group to which humans belong; also includes other, now extinct, bipedal relatives.

anthropometry   Measurement of human body parts. When osteologists measure skeletal elements, the term *osteometry* is often used.

FIGURE 1–2
Paleoanthropological research at Omo, Ethiopia. This is the hominid ulna excavation site.

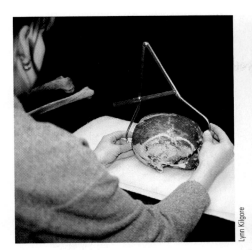

Lynn Kilgore

FIGURE 1–3

This anthropology student is measuring the length of a human cranium with spreading calipers.

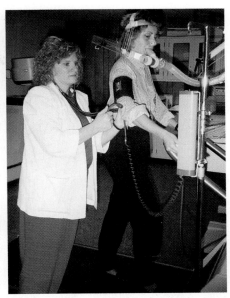

Judith Regensteiner

FIGURE 1–4

Researcher using a treadmill test to assess a subject's heart rate, blood pressure, and oxygen consumption.

genetics The study of gene structure and action and of the patterns of inheritance of traits from parent to offspring. Genetic mechanisms are the underlying foundation for evolutionary change.

primate A member of the order of mammals Primates (pronounced "pry-may´-tees"), which includes prosimians, monkeys, apes, and humans.

FIGURE 1–5

Kathleen Galvin measures upper arm circumference in a young Maasai boy in Tanzania. Data derived from various body measurements, including height and weight, were used in a health and nutrition study of groups of Maasai cattle herders.

niques have considerable application in the design of everything from airplane cockpits to office furniture.

Today, anthropologists are concerned with human variation partly because of its *adaptive significance* and because they want to identify the evolutionary factors that have produced variability. In other words, some traits evolved as biological adaptations to local environmental conditions, including infectious disease. Others may simply be the results of geographical isolation or the descent of populations from small founding groups.

Some physical anthropologists examine other aspects of human variation, including how various groups respond physiologically to different kinds of environmentally induced stress (Fig. 1–4). Examples of such stresses include high altitude, cold, and heat. Others conduct nutritional studies, investigating the relationships between various dietary components, cultural practices, physiology, and certain aspects of health and disease (Fig. 1–5). Investigations of human fertility, growth, and development are closely related to the topic of nutrition and are fundamental to studies of adaptation in modern human populations.

It would be impossible to study evolutionary processes without an understanding of genetic principles. For this reason and others, **genetics** is a crucial field for physical anthropologists. Modern physical anthropology wouldn't exist as an evolutionary science if not for rapidly developing advances in the understanding of genetic mechanisms.

Molecular anthropologists use cutting-edge technologies to investigate evolutionary relationships between human populations as well as between humans and nonhuman **primates**. To do this, they examine similarities and differences in DNA sequences among individuals, populations, and species. In addition, by extracting DNA from

Kathleen Galvin

FIGURE 1–6

Cloning and DNA sequencing methods are frequently used to identify genes in humans and nonhuman primates. This graduate student identifies a genetically modified bacterial clone.

Robert Jurmain

Bonnie Pedersen/Arlene Kruse

FIGURE 1–7

Yahaya Alamasi, a member of the senior field staff at Gombe National Park, Tanzania. Alamasi is recording behaviors in free-ranging chimpanzees.

primatology The study of the biology and behavior of nonhuman primates (prosimians, monkeys, and apes).

osteology The study of skeletal material. Human osteology focuses on the interpretation of the skeletal remains of past groups. Some of the same techniques are used in paleoanthropology to study early hominids.

paleopathology The branch of osteology that studies the traces of disease and injury in human skeletal (or, occasionally, mummified) remains.

certain fossils, they've contributed to our understanding of relationships between extinct and living species. As genetic technologies continue to improve, molecular anthropologists will play a key role in explaining human evolution, adaptation, and our biological relationships with other species (Fig. 1–6).

Primatology, the study of nonhuman primates, has become increasingly important since the late 1950s (Fig. 1–7). Behavioral studies, especially when conducted in the wild, have implications for numerous scientific disciplines. Because nonhuman primates are our closest living relatives, the identification of underlying factors related to social behavior, communication, infant care, reproductive behavior, and so on, helps us develop a better understanding of the natural forces that have shaped so many aspects of modern human behavior.

But an even more important reason to study nonhuman primates is that most species are threatened or seriously endangered. Only through research will scientists be able to recommend policies that can better ensure the survival of many nonhuman primates and thousands of other species as well.

Primate paleontology, the study of the primate fossil record, has implications not only for nonhuman primates but also for hominids. Virtually every year, fossil-bearing beds in North America, Africa, Asia, and Europe yield important new discoveries. In fact, in late 2004 the discovery of a new hominid species on an island near Java stunned physical anthropologists around the world. (This fossil is discussed on page 287.) By studying fossil primates and comparing them with anatomically similar living species, primate paleontologists can learn a great deal about such things as diet or locomotion in earlier life-forms. They can also make assumptions about social behavior in some extinct primates and attempt to clarify what we know about evolutionary relationships between extinct and living species, including ourselves.

Osteology, the study of the skeleton, is central to physical anthropology. In fact, it's so important that when many people think of biological anthropology, the first thing that comes to mind is bones. The emphasis on osteology is due partly to the importance of fossil analysis, which requires a thorough knowledge of the structure and function of the skeleton.

Bone biology and physiology are of major importance to many other aspects of physical anthropology. Many osteologists specialize in studies that emphasize various measurements of skeletal elements. This type of research is essential, for example, to the identification of stature and growth patterns in archaeological populations.

One subdiscipline of osteology is the study of disease and trauma in skeletons from archaeological sites. **Paleopathology** is a prominent subfield that investigates the prevalence of trauma, certain infectious diseases (such as syphilis and tuberculosis), nutritional deficiencies, and many other conditions that may leave evidence in bone (Fig. 1–8). This research tells

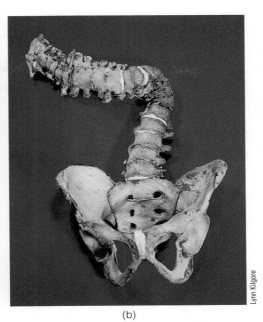

(a)   (b)

Lynn Kilgore

Lynn Kilgore

FIGURE 1–8

(a) A partially healed fracture of the femur (thigh bone) from a child's skeleton (estimated age at death is 6 years). Cause of death was probably an infection resulting from this injury. (b) Very severe congenital scoliosis in an adult male from Nubia. The curves are due to several developmental defects that affect individual vertebrae. (This is not the most common form of scoliosis.)

us a great deal about the lives of individuals and populations in the past. Paleopathology also provides information pertaining to the history of certain disease processes, making it of interest to scientists in biomedical fields.

Forensic anthropology is directly related to osteology and paleopathology. Technically, this approach is the application of anthropological (usually osteological and sometimes archaeological) techniques to legal issues (Fig. 1–9). Forensic anthropologists are routinely called on to help identify skeletal remains in cases of mass disaster or other situations where a human body has been found.

Forensic anthropologists have been involved in numerous cases having important legal, historical, and human consequences. These scientists played a prominent role in identifying the skeletons of most of the Russian imperial family, whose members were executed in 1918. Forensic anthropologists also participated in the process of identifying missing American soldiers in Southeast Asia. And more recently, many forensic anthropologists participated in the

Lorna Pierce/Judy Suchey

FIGURE 1–9

Physical anthropologists Lorna Pierce (left) and Judy Suchey (center) working as forensic consultants. The dog has just located a concealed human cranium during a training session.

forensic anthropology   An applied anthropological approach dealing with legal matters. Forensic anthropologists work with coroners and law enforcement agencies in the recovery, analysis, and identification of human remains.

FIGURE 1–10
Dr. Linda Levitch teaching a human anatomy class at the University of North Carolina School of Medicine.

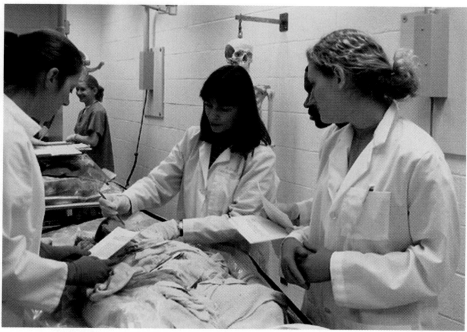

Linda Levitch

overwhelming task of trying to identify human remains in the aftermath of the September 11, 2001, terrorist attacks in the United States.

Anatomical studies are another area of interest for physical anthropologists. In living organisms, bones and teeth are intimately linked to the muscles and other tissues that surround and act on them. Consequently, a thorough knowledge of soft tissue anatomy is essential to the understanding of biomechanical relationships involved in movement. Knowledge of such relationships is fundamental to the accurate interpretation of the structure and function of limbs and other structures in extinct animals now represented only by fossilized remains. For such reasons, many physical anthropologists specialize in anatomical studies. In fact, several physical anthropologists hold professorships in anatomy departments at universities and medical schools (Fig. 1–10).

ARCHAEOLOGY

Stripped to its basics, archaeology is a body of methods designed to understand the human past through the examination and study of its material remains. Its primary data are the **artifacts** and other **material culture**, associations, and contextual information created by past peoples and preserved to the extent that they can be reliably identified and interpreted by modern researchers. From this, it should be clear that archaeologists don't study the fossils of non-primate species such as dinosaurs or mammoths, a field properly claimed by **paleontologists**.

Given that archaeology is just a body of methods, you won't be surprised to learn that there are lots of different kinds of archaeology. For example, *classical archaeologists* study the Mediterranean world's "classical" civilizations, such as those created by the Romans and Greeks (Fig. 1–11). These archaeologists tend to be found in departments of art history, classics, and architecture rather than anthropology. To these examples, we could also add battlefield archaeology, industrial archaeology, underwater archaeology (Fig. 1–12), and many more; but you get the picture.

Anthropological archaeology, which is the kind of archaeology dealt with in this book, refers to the application of archaeological methods by anthropologists to the understanding of the origins and diversity of modern humans. As such, its domain covers the entire span of the **archaeological record**—from the earliest identifiable hominid tools, and the **sites** in which these implements were deposited, to the trash cans in our kitchens.

Archaeology exists as a discipline because researchers can justify a key assumption: many human activities and their by-products tend to enter the archaeological record in patterned,

artifacts   Objects or materials made or modified for use by hominids. The earliest artifacts tend to be tools made of stone or, occasionally, bone.

material culture   The physical manifestations of human activities, such as tools, art, and structures. As the most durable aspects of culture, material remains make up the majority of archaeological evidence of past societies.

paleontologists   Scientists whose study of ancient life-forms is based on fossilized remains of extinct animals and plants.

archaeological record   The material remains of the human past and the physical contexts of these remains (e.g., stratigraphic relationships, association with other remains).

sites   Locations of past human activity, often associated with artifacts and features.

FIGURE 1-11
Classical archaeologists study architectural details at the Roman marketplace built by the emperor Trajan in the first century A.D.

knowable ways that reflect the behaviors, values, and beliefs of the individuals who created them. Given this assumption, archaeologists can study events and processes that are far removed in time from the modern world and interpret developments in the human past that happened at rates ranging from months to millennia. This perspective of the human past is unique to archaeology.

Archaeology is a historical science, much like geology and evolutionary biology. It is scientific because it answers many research questions by applying the scientific method, and it is inherently historical because its primary data can't be divorced from their context in space and time. The past, as the late paleontologist and evolutionary biologist Stephen Jay Gould (1989) liked to remind us, happened, and it won't happen again. Consequently, archaeology differs in several fundamental aspects from research in such fields as physics and chemistry, where primary data are not anchored firmly in time and space (Dunnell, 1982).

As we've mentioned, archaeology is also firmly rooted in the humanities. Archaeology in general—and anthropological archaeology in particular—tries to answer many questions about the past that go beyond the search for explanations of general trends and patterns. Understanding certain cognitive and symbolic aspects of the past requires additional interpretive tools from such fields as history, art history, architecture, and comparative literature.

Anthropological archaeologists (from here on, simply called "archaeologists") traditionally differ from other anthropologists in their emphasis on the archaeological record as their primary data source. But the boundaries between anthropological subfields are not sharply drawn. Some archaeologists mainly study cultures that existed before the invention of writing (the era commonly known as **prehistory**).

FIGURE 1-12
Underwater archaeologists map the wooden framing and ballast of a British vessel that sank off the Bermuda coast about 200 years ago.

prehistory   The several million years between the emergence of bipedal hominids and the availability of written records.

Archaeologists expose the foundation of a nineteenth-century farmstead in Illinois.

Illinois Transportation Archaeological Research Program, University of Illinois

William Turnbaugh; painting by Gilbert Stuart

FIGURE 1–14
Thomas Jefferson conducted early archaeological excavations before becoming president of the United States.

historical archaeology Archaeology supplemented by contemporary written documents.

ethnoarchaeologists Archaeologists who use ethnographic methods to study modern peoples so that they can better understand and explain patterning in the archaeological record.

antiquarian Relating to an interest in things and texts of the past.

Other specialists, sometimes called **historical archaeologists**, also examine the archaeological and documentary record of past cultures that left written evidence (Fig. 1–13). And **ethnoarchaeologists** blur the past-present dichotomy between archaeology and cultural anthropology by conducting ethnographic research with modern peoples in projects designed to achieve archaeological objectives.

Like the other anthropological subfields, modern archaeology largely grew out of the Enlightenment in Europe. Although European awareness of the past can be traced to Roman times, it wasn't until the eighteenth and nineteenth centuries that some scholars began to accept evidence that the existence of living things, including humans, must be considerably older than previously thought. They also began to devise instruments for measuring time as it's reflected in the archaeological and fossil records. Once these factors came together with emerging evolutionary ideas in the mid-nineteenth century, the stage was set for the development of archaeology as the primary means by which the human past can be discovered.

Although the rise of American archaeology was greatly influenced by events in western Europe, it didn't develop along precisely the same lines. In North America, early **antiquarian** interests were fueled by the desire to explain the relationship between contemporary Native Americans and the archaeological record. Although this relationship seems obvious to us in the twenty-first century, it was by no means equally clear to colonists from the Old World or their descendants, even into the early twentieth century. In the United States, curiosity about the possible solution to this problem motivated what is generally agreed to be the earliest systematically conducted archaeological excavation, conducted in 1782 by Thomas Jefferson (Fig. 1–14). He excavated a prehistoric burial mound on his property in Virginia not to find artifacts, but to discover how it was constructed. Therefore, he took careful notes on what he found and on the stratigraphic relationships. He then published an account of his work and concluded that the mound had been constructed by the ancestors of modern Native Americans.

Few of Jefferson's contemporaries on either side of the Atlantic took such care in their excavations, which is hardly surprising: For most early archaeologists, the questions that motivated their excavations were nearly as crude as their methods. By the early twentieth century, this situation had changed; archaeologists began to exploit the patterned nature of the archaeological record as a way to measure the relative sequence of events in the human past and to explain how and why past cultures changed.

Archaeology reached a certain methodological maturity in the second half of the twentieth century. This process was greatly facilitated by the development of various dating techniques such as radiocarbon and by new technological possibilities created by the advent of cheap computing power in the 1960s and '70s. The breadth of questions asked of the archaeological record also expanded greatly throughout the twentieth century in response to theoretical changes in anthropology as a whole. In 1900, many archaeologists were satisfied simply to describe what their excavations revealed and perhaps to arrange these remains in time and space frameworks. By 2000, they also were seeking to understand how the people who created these sites lived. They asked how or why these people differed culturally from one another, what similarities they shared, and even why they held particular beliefs about themselves, each other, and the cosmos—all this while simultaneously controlling for time and space in the archaeological record.

In addition to the social science perspective of anthropology, archaeology established itself as a scientific endeavor in the twentieth century, and it maintains strong ties with the natural and physical sciences. Contemporary archaeological research often involves the specialized expertise of many disciplines. Remote-sensing technology, including everything from GPS (global positioning satellite) handhelds to ground-penetrating radar, may be used to locate or define sites. Geologists, soil scientists, **palynologists**, and others assist in determining a site's ancient environment. In the subfield of *archaeometry*, archaeologists work with physicists, chemists, engineers, and other scientists to apply the methods and techniques of their respective fields to the analysis of ancient materials. Recall that physical anthropologists, specializing in osteology, examine human skeletal remains for the overall health status, diet, and physical traits of ancient individuals; when these anthropologists are working closely with archaeologists, this integrated specialization is called *bioarchaeology* (Fig. 1–15). Many archaeology students also combine their studies with training that prepares them to conduct specialized analyses of ancient plant and animal remains (called *archaeobotany* and *archaeozoology*, respectively), GIS (geographic information systems) spatial data, stable isotopes, ceramics, textiles, and other materials from the archaeological record.

In the late twentieth century, the emergence of a comprehensive **public archaeology** program was an important development in American archaeology. This field includes efforts to reach out to communities and involve wider audiences through education and the media. Most public archaeologists have been engaged in cultural resource management (CRM) and other heritage management programs. As mandated by government environmental legislation since the 1970s, archaeologists in these fields are contracted to evaluate sites that may be threatened with damage from development and construction on public lands and in connection with private land projects that receive federal funds or are licensed or regulated by a federal agency (Fig. 1–16). CRM work utilizes a wide range of archaeological expertise, including prehistorians, historical archaeologists, field technicians, archaeological illustrators and writers, and laboratory specialists. Many archaeologists in the CRM field are affiliated with environmental study firms in the private sector, and others are employed by state or federal agencies or by educational institutions. About 40 percent of the respondents in a 1994 membership survey conducted by the Society for American Archaeology fill such positions (Zeder, 1997), and the long-term trend is for this part of archaeology to continue to grow.

A commitment to the scientific method is also evident in the field of *experimental archaeology*, where researchers attempt to replicate ancient techniques and processes under controlled conditions so that they can better understand the past. Using these approaches, archaeologists have reproduced the entire range of ancient stone tools and employed them in many tasks that replicate the tool wear and breakage patterns on similar tools made and used by prehistoric peoples.

Archaeology's goals also continue to broaden as anthropology changes and as we learn more about the past. Today, anthropological archaeology has several primary goals. The first goal is to reconstruct culture history: This task orders the archaeological record in time and space and creates the archaeological equivalent of the chronologies of history. The second goal is to reconstruct and describe ancient lifeways, and the third is to understand the general

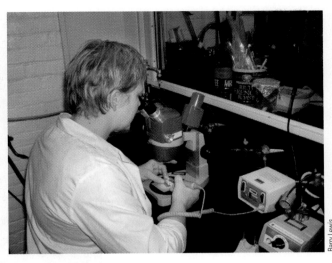

FIGURE 1–15
Bioarchaeologist Kris Hedman processing a bone sample for analysis of strontium levels in prehistoric human skeletons.

palynologists Scientists who identify ancient plants from pollen samples unearthed at archaeological sites.

public archaeology A broad term that covers archaeological research conducted for the public good as part of cultural resource management and heritage management programs; a major growth area of world archaeology.

FIGURE 1–16

Archaeological field crew excavates the remains of late prehistoric houses (the outlines of which are marked by lines of white dots in the excavation) and other village features in advance of highway construction. The St. Louis, Missouri, skyline can be seen in the distance.

Illinois Transportation Archaeological Research Program, University of Illinois

processes of culture change and explain how and why past cultures changed in patterned ways. Finally, as an emerging area of research, archaeologists aim to examine and interpret the cognitive and symbolic aspects of past cultures.

As we should expect of any field in which basic goals continue to unfold, archaeologists are engaged in an ongoing negotiation of the discipline's research priorities, the bodies of theory that motivate research, and even the philosophical underpinnings of these theories. No single approach commands a clear consensus in archaeology; but this is a good sign of a healthy, growing, scholarly discipline, not an implication that something is broken. Every option—from ways of knowing about the past to the inevitable conflict between what C. P. Snow (1965) characterized as the "Two Cultures" of science and humanism—is on the table, and the early twenty-first century is an exciting time to be an archaeologist.

LINGUISTIC ANTHROPOLOGY

Linguistic anthropology is the study of human speech and language, including the origins of language in general as well as specific languages. By examining similarities between contemporary languages, linguists have been able to trace historical ties between languages and groups of languages; in this way, linguistic anthropologists can identify language families and perhaps past relationships between human populations.

There is also much interest in the relationship between language and culture: how language reflects the way members of a society perceive phenomena, and how the use of language shapes perceptions in different cultures. For example, language dialects can encode many meanings, including geographical origins, identity, and social class. Such encoded meanings influence how a person is treated by those who do or do not speak the same dialects of this or a closely related language. For example, a teacher who speaks Southern American English with the slow cadence or drawl of Vicksburg, Mississippi, may not be taken seriously by students in Minneapolis or Chicago, where the stereotypical image of the speakers of such dialects is that of hillbillies. However, in Southampton, England, or Adelaide, Australia, the same teacher's voice may simply be viewed as wonderfully exotic, the main difference being cultural—in this case, the social meanings associated with the tones and cadence of speech.

Because the spontaneous acquisition and use of language is a uniquely human characteristic, this topic holds considerable interest for linguistic anthropologists, who, along with specialists in other fields, study the process of language acquisition in infants. Because insights into this process may well have implications for the development of language skills in human evolution, as well as in growing children, it is also an important subject to physical anthropologists.

The Scientific Method

Science is a process of understanding phenomena through observation, generalization, verification, and refutation. By this we mean that there is an **empirical** approach to gaining information through the use of systematic and explicit techniques. Because physical anthropologists and archaeologists are engaged in scientific pursuits, they adhere to the principles of the **scientific method**, whereby a research question is identified and information is subsequently gathered to provide an answer.

The gathering of information is referred to as **data** collection, and when researchers use a rigorously controlled approach, they can precisely describe their techniques and results in a manner that facilitates comparisons with the work of others. For example, when scientists collect data on tooth size in hominid fossils, they must specify precisely which teeth are being measured, how they are measured, and what the results of the measurements are (expressed numerically, or **quantitatively**). Subsequently, it's up to the investigators to draw inferences about the meaning and significance of their measurements. This body of information then becomes the basis of future studies—possibly by other researchers, who can compare their own results with those already obtained. The eventual outcome of this type of inquiry may be the acceptance or rejection of certain proposed explanations.

Once facts have been established, scientists attempt to explain them. First, a **hypothesis**, or provisional explanation of phenomena, is developed. To be analytically useful, a hypothesis must be tested by means of data collection and analysis. Indeed, the testing of hypotheses with the possibility of proving them false is the very basis of the scientific method. Everything that a scientist accepts as true is always a "working" or "conditional" truth, because subsequent testing may demonstrate it to be false.

In anthropology, the **scientific testing** of hypotheses may take several years or longer and may involve researchers who weren't connected with the original work. In subsequent studies, other investigators may achieve results comparable to the original study or fail to replicate these outcomes. For example, the archaeologist V. Gordon Childe argued in the early 1950s that the earliest prehistoric Near Eastern plant and animal domestication events took place soon after the end of the last Ice Age around the oases or waterholes of the region (Childe, 1928). Later, Robert Braidwood (Braidwood and Howe, 1960) tested Childe's hypothesis in the field and found that the oldest evidence of Near Eastern plant domestication was actually to be found not around the oases, as Childe's hypothesis predicted, but in village sites scattered among the foothills of the Zagros Mountains in Iraq and Iran. Braidwood's research effectively refuted Childe's hypothesis (just as Braidwood's tentative explanation was itself refuted by subsequent research, which is a story that we'll take up in more detail in Chapter 14). The main point is that although it's easier to repeat original studies conducted in laboratory settings, it's no less important to verify research results based on data collected outside of tightly controlled laboratory situations.

If a hypothesis cannot be falsified when examined against empirical evidence, researchers accept it as a **theory** or a working explanation of the relationship between those phenomena under examination. In common everyday usage, the word *theory* often means nothing more than a hunch or speculation. But in scientific terms, a theory is a statement of relationships that relevant empirical evidence doesn't (at least, as yet) falsify. As such, a given theory not only helps organize current knowledge, but ideally, it also predicts how new facts may fit into the established pattern.

Use of the scientific method allows for the development and testing of hypotheses, and it also permits various types of *bias* to be addressed and controlled. It's important to realize that bias occurs in all studies. Sources of bias include the researcher's personal values; dishonesty; how the investigator was trained and by whom; what particular questions interest the researcher; what specific skills and talents he or she possesses; what earlier results (if any) have been established in this realm of study and by whom (for example, the researcher, close colleagues, or those with rival approaches or even rival personalities); and what sources of data are available (for example, accessible countries or museums) and thus what samples can be collected (at all, or at least conveniently).

Bias cannot be entirely eliminated from research, but it's possible to minimize its effects through careful research design, in which the researcher consciously works to identify and

science A body of knowledge gained through observation and experimentation; from the Latin *scientia*, meaning "knowledge."

empirical Relying on experiment or observation; from the Latin *empiricus*, meaning "experienced."

scientific method A research method whereby a problem is identified, a hypothesis (or hypothetical explanation) is stated, and that hypothesis is tested through the collection and analysis of data. If the hypothesis is tested many times and not rejected, it becomes a theory.

data (*sing.*, datum) Facts from which conclusions can be drawn; scientific information.

quantitatively (quantitative) Pertaining to measurements of quantity and including such properties as size, number, and capacity.

hypothesis (*pl.*, hypotheses) A provisional explanation of a phenomenon. Hypotheses require repeated testing.

scientific testing The precise repetition of an experiment or expansion of observed data to provide verification; the procedure by which hypotheses and theories are verified, modified, or discarded.

theory A broad statement of scientific relationships or underlying principles that has been at least partially verified.

control for possible bias effects. Anthropologists, like all good researchers, strive to minimize bias in their research outcomes as well as in the articles and books they write.

Science is an approach—indeed, a *tool*—used to minimize bias, enable the replication of relevant tests by other researchers, and maximize the validity and reliability of the results. Application of the scientific method thus requires constant vigilance by all who practice it. The goal isn't to establish "truth" in any absolute sense, but rather to generate ever more accurate and consistent explanations of phenomena in our universe. At its very heart, scientific methodology is an exercise in rational thought and critical thinking.

The development of critical thinking skills is an important and lasting benefit of a college education. Such skills enable people to evaluate, compare, analyze, critique, and synthesize information so they won't accept everything they hear at face value. Perhaps the most glaring need for critical thinking is in how we evaluate advertising claims. For example, people spend billions of dollars every year on "natural" dietary supplements, basing their purchasing decisions on marketing claims that in fact may not have been tested. So when a salesperson tells you that, for example, echinacea helps prevent colds, you should ask if that statement has been scientifically tested—and if so, how, when, and by whom it was tested. Similarly, when politicians make claims in 30-second sound bites, check those claims before you accept them as truth. Be skeptical. And if you do check on the validity of advertising and political statements, you'll find that they're frequently misleading or just plain wrong.

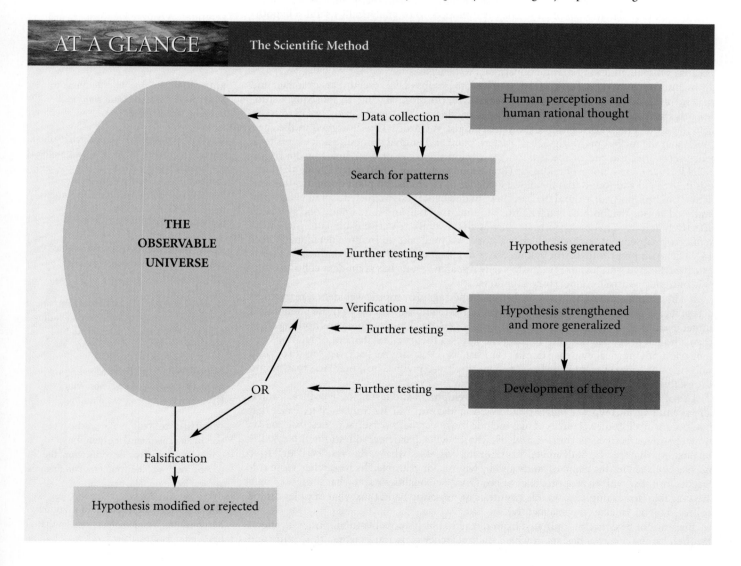

AT A GLANCE   The Scientific Method

The Anthropological Perspective

Perhaps the most important benefit you will derive from this textbook (and the course of which it is a part) is a wider appreciation of the human experience. To better understand human beings and how our species came to be, it's necessary to broaden our viewpoint across space (comparing individuals, populations, and even species) and through time (considering the past, with special emphasis on evolutionary factors). In their own ways, all branches of anthropology seek to do this in an approach we call the *anthropological perspective*.

From the overview presented in this chapter, we can see that physical anthropologists focus on varied aspects of the biological nature of *Homo sapiens*, and that archaeologists discover and interpret the cultural evidence of hominid (including modern human) behavior from sites ranging in age from over 2 million years old up to the present day. Modern humans are products of the same forces that produced all life on earth. As such, we represent one contemporary component of a vast biological continuum at one point in time. In this regard, we're simultaneously just another animal as well as an extraordinary form of life. Like many other organisms, we have been biologically successful when viewed across the depths of evolutionary time. Unlike other organisms, we are conscious of that fact, aware of the responsibilities our success engenders, and feel compelled to learn more about how and why it happened.

This question—*how* and *why* did humans become so successful?—is the main motivation for this textbook. Humans are the only species to develop complex culture as a means of buffering the challenges posed by nature, and we are the only species that spontaneously acquires and uses spoken language as a very complex form of communication. Consequently, physical anthropologists are keenly interested in how humans differ from and are similar to other animals, especially nonhuman primates. For example, in Chapters 4 and 14, we will discuss how aspects of human nutrition have been influenced by evolutionary factors. Today, most of the foods people eat are derived from domesticated plants and animals; but these dietary items were unavailable prior to the development of agriculture more than 10,000 years ago. However, human physiological mechanisms for chewing and digesting, as well as the types of foods humans are predisposed to eat, are variations of patterns that had been well established in nonhuman primate ancestors long before 10,000 years ago. Indeed, these adaptive complexes probably go back millions of years.

In addition to differences in diet prior to the development of agriculture, earlier hominids might well have differed from modern humans in average body size, metabolism, and activity patterns. How, then, does the basic evolutionary "equipment" (that is, physiology) inherited from our hominid and prehominid forebears accommodate our modern diets? Clearly, the way to understand such processes is not simply to look at contemporary human responses, but to place them within the context of evolution and adaptation through time. Indeed, throughout this book, we will focus on the biocultural interactions that came about after the development of agriculture, an event that was one of the most fundamental revolutions in all of human prehistory. By studying human behavior and anatomy from the broader perspective provided by an evolutionary context, we are better able to understand the factors leading to the development of the human species.

Archaeologists trace the evolution of culture and its ever-expanding role in human affairs over the past 2.5 million years. Information from archaeological research is frequently combined with biological data to elucidate how cultural and biological factors interacted in the past to produce variations in human adaptive response, disease patterns, and even the genetic diversity that we see today. From such a perspective, we can begin to appreciate the diversity of the human experience and, in so doing, more fully understand human constraints and potentials. Furthermore, by extending the breadth of our knowledge, it's easier to avoid the **ethnocentric** pitfalls inherent in a more limited view of humanity, a view that isolates modern humans from other human groups and places them outside the context of evolution.

We hope that the following pages will help you develop an increased understanding of the similarities we share with other biological organisms as well as of the biocultural processes that have shaped the traits that make us unique. We live in what may well be the most crucial period for our planet in the last 65 million years. We are members of the one species that,

ethnocentric Viewing other cultures from the inherently biased perspective of one's own culture. Ethnocentrism often results in other cultures being seen as inferior to one's own.

through the very agency of culture, has wrought such devastating changes in ecological systems that we must now alter our technologies or face potentially disastrous consequences. In such a time, it's vital that we attempt to gain the best possible understanding of what it means to be human. We believe that the study of physical anthropology and archaeology is one endeavor that aids in this attempt, and that is indeed the goal of this text.

Summary

In this chapter, we introduce the fields of physical anthropology and archaeology and place them within the overall context of anthropology, a social science discipline that also includes cultural anthropology and linguistics as major subfields.

Physical anthropology studies aspects of human biology (emphasizing evolutionary perspectives), the study of nonhuman primates, and the study of the hominid fossil record. Physical anthropologists are interested in how hominids came to possess culture and how this process influenced the direction of human evolution. Especially in regard to the study of early hominids (as incorporated within the interdisciplinary field of *paleoanthropology*), physical anthropologists work in close collaboration with many other scientists from the fields of archaeology, geology, chemistry, and so forth.

Archaeology provides time depth for our understanding of humans as biocultural organisms. Systematic examination of the archaeological record provides the basis for archaeologists' interpretations of extinct lifeways as well as the construction of cultural chronologies, explanations for observable cultural changes, and interpretations of the cognitive and symbolic patterns that mark our past. As with paleoanthropology (of which prehistoric archaeology is a key component), archaeological research also involves input from many related disciplines. This collaborative examination of the archaeological record yields nearly all we know, if not all we are likely to ever know, about prehistoric human behavior and activities.

Critical Thinking Questions

1. Why does American anthropology describe itself as a three- (often four-) field discipline that includes cultural or social anthropology, physical or biological anthropology, and archaeology?
2. Is it important to you, personally, to know about human evolution? Why or why not?
3. Why is the biocultural perspective important to understanding human evolution?
4. What fundamental assumption about the relationship between human behavior and the archeological record makes archaeology's study of the human past possible? Can archaeology exist as a valid and reliable source of understanding about the past if this assumption is true only sometimes or only under certain conditions?
5. Do you think that understanding the scientific method and developing critical thinking skills can benefit you personally? Why?

HEREDITY AND EVOLUTION

CHAPTER

2

The Development of Evolutionary Theory

FOCUS QUESTIONS

What are the basic premises of natural selection?

What were the technological and philosophical changes that led people to accept notions of evolutionary change?

Go to the following CD-ROMs for interactive activities and exercises on topics covered in this chapter:

- Virtual Laboratories for Physical Anthropology CD-ROM, Third Edition
- Genetics in Anthropology: Principles and Applications CD-ROM, First Edition

Introduction

Has anyone ever asked you, "If humans evolved from monkeys, then why do we still have monkeys?" Or maybe you've heard this one: "If evolution happens, then why don't we ever see new species?" These are the kinds of questions asked by people who have no understanding of evolutionary processes and who usually don't even believe those processes exist. The fact that anyone today, given the overwhelming evidence for biological evolution, would ask such questions is a depressing reflection of the poor quality of education. Evolution is one of the most fundamental of biological processes, and it's also one of the most misunderstood. This is partly because the topic is commonly avoided in primary and secondary schools so students aren't exposed to it. And at colleges and universities, evolution is covered only in classes that directly relate to it. Indeed, if you're not an anthropology or biology major and you're taking a class in biological anthropology mainly to fill a science requirement, you'll probably never study evolution again.

By the end of this course, you'll know the answers to the questions that opened the previous paragraph. Briefly, no one who studies evolution would ever say that humans evolved from monkeys, because they didn't. They didn't evolve from chimpanzees, either. The earliest human ancestors evolved from a species that lived some 5 to 8 million years ago (mya). That ancestral species was the *last common ancestor* we share with chimpanzees. In turn, the lineage that led to the apes and ourselves separated from a monkey-like ancestor some 20 mya, and monkeys are still around because as lineages diverged from a common ancestor, each group went its separate way. Over time, some of these groups became extinct while others evolved into the species we see today. Therefore, each living species is the current product of processes that go back millions of years. Because evolution takes time, and lots of it, we rarely witness the appearance of new species except in microorganisms. But we do see *microevolutionary* changes in many species.

The subject of evolution is controversial especially in the United States, because some religious views hold that evolutionary statements run counter to biblical teachings. Indeed, as you are probably aware, there is strong opposition to the teaching of evolution in public schools.

People who deny that evolution happens often say that "evolution is only a theory," implying that evolution is mere supposition. Actually, referring to a concept as "theory" supports it. As we discussed in Chapter 1, theories are hypotheses that have been tested and subjected to verification through accumulated evidence. Evolution *is* a theory, one that has increasingly been supported by a mounting body of genetic evidence. It's a theory that has stood the test of time, and today it stands as the most fundamental unifying force in biological science.

Because physical anthropology is concerned with all aspects of how humans came to be and how we adapt physiologically to the external environment, understanding the details of the evolutionary process is crucial. Therefore, it's beneficial to know how the mechanics of the process came to be discovered. Also, if we want to appreciate the nature of the controversy that still surrounds the issue, we need to see how social and political events influenced the discovery of evolutionary principles.

A Brief History of Evolutionary Thought

The discovery of evolutionary principles first took place in western Europe and was made possible by advances in scientific thinking that date back to the sixteenth century. Having said this, we must recognize that western science borrowed many of its ideas from other cultures, especially the Arabs, Indians, and Chinese. In fact, intellectuals in these cultures and in ancient Greece had notions of biological evolution (Teresi, 2002), but they never formulated them into a cohesive theory.

Charles Darwin was the first person to explain the basic mechanics of the evolutionary process. But while he was developing his theory of **natural selection**, a Scottish naturalist named Alfred Russel Wallace independently reached the same conclusion. The fact that natural selection, the single most important force of evolutionary change, should be proposed at more or less the same time by two British men in the mid-nineteenth century may seem like a strange coincidence. But, if Darwin and Wallace hadn't made their simultaneous discoveries, someone else soon would have, and that someone would probably have been British or French. That's because the groundwork had already been laid in Britain and France, and many scientists there were prepared to accept explanations of biological change that would have been unacceptable even 25 years before.

Like other human endeavors, scientific knowledge is usually gained through a series of small steps rather than giant leaps, and just as technological change is based on past achievements, scientific knowledge builds on previously developed theories. For this reason, it's informative to examine the development of ideas that led Darwin and Wallace to independently develop the theory of evolution by natural selection.

Throughout the Middle Ages, one predominant feature of the European worldview was that all aspects of nature, including all forms of life and their relationships to one another, never changed. This view was partly shaped by a feudal society that was itself a hierarchical, rigid class system that hadn't changed much for centuries. It was also influenced by an extremely powerful religious system, in which the teachings of Christianity were taken literally. Consequently, it was generally accepted that all life on earth had been created by God exactly as it existed in the present, and the belief that life-forms couldn't change came to be known as **fixity of species**.

The plan of the entire universe was viewed as God's design. In what is called the "argument from design," anatomical structures were engineered to meet the purpose for which they were required. Wings, arms, eyes, and so on fit the functions they performed, and nature was a deliberate plan of the Grand Designer. Also, pretty much everybody believed that the Grand Designer had completed his works fairly recently. An Irish archbishop named James Ussher (1581–1656) analyzed the "begat" chapter of Genesis and determined that the earth was created in 4004 B.C. Archbishop Ussher wasn't the first person to suggest a recent origin of the earth, but he was the first to propose a precise date for it.

The prevailing notion of the earth's brief existence, together with fixity of species, provided a huge obstacle to the development of evolutionary theory because evolution requires time, and the idea of immense geological time, which today we take for granted, simply didn't exist. In fact, until the concepts of fixity and time were fundamentally altered, it was impossible to conceive of evolution by means of natural selection.

THE SCIENTIFIC REVOLUTION

So, what transformed centuries-old beliefs in a rigid, static universe to a view of worlds in continuous motion? How did the earth's brief history become an immense expanse of incomprehensible time? How did the scientific method as we know it today develop? These are important questions, but it would be equally appropriate to ask why it took so long for Europe to break from the constraints of traditional belief systems when Arab and Indian scholars had developed concepts of planetary motion centuries earlier.

For Europeans, the discovery of the New World and circumnavigation of the globe in the fifteenth century overturned some very basic ideas about the planet. For one thing, the earth could no longer be thought of as flat. Also, as Europeans began to explore the New World,

natural selection The most critical mechanism of evolutionary change, first articulated by Charles Darwin; refers to genetic change or changes in the frequencies of certain traits in populations due to differential reproductive success between individuals.

fixity of species The notion that species, once created, can never change; an idea diametrically opposed to theories of biological evolution.

their awareness of biological diversity was greatly expanded as they encountered plants and animals previously unknown to them.

There were other attacks on traditional beliefs. In 1514, a Polish mathematician named Copernicus challenged the notion, proposed more than 1,500 years earlier by Aristotle, that the earth, circled by the sun, moon, and stars, was the center of the universe. In fact, in India, scholars had figured this out long before Copernicus did; but Copernicus is generally credited with removing the earth as the center of all things by proposing a sun-centered solar system.

Copernicus' theory didn't attract much attention at the time; however, in the early 1600s, it was restated by an Italian mathematician named Galileo Galilei. To his misfortune, Galileo came into confrontation with the Catholic Church over his publications and, consequently, he spent the last nine years of his life under house arrest. Still, in intellectual circles, the universe had changed from an earth-centered to a solar-centered one, and from one of fixity to one of motion.

Throughout the sixteenth and seventeenth centuries, European scholars developed methods and theories that revolutionized scientific thought. Their technological advances, such as the invention of the telescope, permitted investigations of natural phenomena and opened up entire new worlds for discoveries such as never before had been imagined. But even with these advances the idea that, over time, living forms could change simply didn't occur to people.

PRECURSORS TO THE THEORY OF EVOLUTION

Before early naturalists could begin to understand the many forms of organic life, it was necessary to list and describe them. And as research progressed, scholars were increasingly impressed with the amount of biological diversity they saw.

John Ray   It wasn't until the seventeenth century that John Ray (1627–1705), a minister educated at Cambridge University, developed the concept of species. He was the first person to recognize that groups of plants and animals could be distinguished from other groups by their ability to mate with one another and produce offspring. He placed such groups of reproductively isolated organisms into a single category, which he called the *species* (*pl.*, species). Thus, by the late 1600s, the biological criterion of reproduction was used to define species, much as it is today (Young, 1992).

Ray also recognized that species frequently shared similarities with other species, and he grouped these together in a second level of classification he called the *genus* (*pl.*, genera). He was the first to use the labels *genus* and *species* in this way, and they're the terms we still use today. But he also strongly believed in the fixity of species, and he wrote his 1691 publication, *The Wisdom of God Manifested in the Works of Creation*, to show how nature reflected God's plan.

Carolus Linnaeus   Swedish naturalist Carolus Linnaeus (1707–1778) is best known for developing a method of classifying plants and animals. In his famous work, *Systema Naturae* (Systems of Nature), first published in 1735 (Fig. 2–1), he standardized Ray's use of genus and species terminology and established the system of **binomial nomenclature**. He also added two more categories: class and order. Linnaeus' four-level system became the basis for **taxonomy**, the system of classification we continue to use today.

Another of Linnaeus' innovations was to include humans in his classification of animals, placing them in the genus *Homo* and species *sapiens*. Including humans in this scheme was controversial because it defied contemporary thought that humans, made in God's image, should be considered unique and separate from the animal kingdom.

Linnaeus also believed in fixity of species, although in later years, faced with mounting evidence to the contrary, he came to question it. Indeed, fixity was being challenged on many fronts, especially in France, where voices were being raised in

binomial nomenclature (*binomial*, meaning "two names") In taxonomy, the convention established by Carolus Linnaeus whereby genus and species names are used to refer to species. For example, *Homo sapiens* refers to human beings.

taxonomy The branch of science concerned with the rules of classifying organisms on the basis of evolutionary relationships.

FIGURE 2–1
Linnaeus developed a classification system for plants and animals.

favor of a universe based on change—and, more to the point, in favor of a biological relationship between similar species based on descent from a common ancestor.

Count Georges-Louis Leclerc de Buffon

Buffon (1707–1788) was Keeper of the King's Gardens in Paris (Fig. 2–2). Unlike others, he recognized the dynamic relationship between the external environment and living forms. In his *Natural History*, first published in 1749, he repeatedly stressed the importance of change in the universe and in the changing nature of species.

Buffon believed that when groups of organisms migrated to new areas, they would gradually be altered as a result of adaptation to a somewhat different environment. Buffon's recognition of the external environment as an agent of change in species was an important innovation; however, he rejected the idea that one species could give rise to another.

Erasmus Darwin Today, Erasmus Darwin (1731–1802) is best known for being Charles Darwin's grandfather (Fig. 2–3). But, he was also a physician, inventor, naturalist, philosopher, poet, and leading member of a well-known intellectual community in Lichfield, England. Living in the English midlands, the birthplace of the industrial revolution—which was in full swing—Darwin counted among his friends some of the leading figures of this time of rapid technological and social change.

During his lifetime, Erasmus Darwin became famous as a poet. His most famous work was a medical book of over 500,000 words written entirely in verse. In this book (which, admittedly, few of us would read today), he publicly expressed his views that life had originated in the seas and that all species had descended from a common ancestor. Thus he introduced many of the ideas that would be proposed 56 years later by his grandson. These concepts include vast expanses of time for life to evolve, competition for resources, and the importance of the environment in evolutionary processes. From letters and other sources, we know that Charles Darwin read his grandfather's writings; but the degree to which his theories were influenced by Erasmus isn't known.

Jean-Baptiste Lamarck Neither Buffon nor Erasmus Darwin attempted to *explain* the evolutionary process. The first scientist to do this was a French naturalist named Jean-Baptiste Lamarck (1744–1829). Lamarck (Fig.2–4) suggested a dynamic relationship between species and the environment such that if the external environment changed, an animal's activity patterns would also change to accommodate the new circumstances. This would result in the increased or decreased use of certain body parts, and consequently, those body parts would be modified. According to Lamarck, these physical changes would occur in response to bodily "needs," so that if a particular part of the body felt a certain need, "fluids and forces" would be directed to that point and the structure would be modified. Because the alteration would make the animal better suited to its habitat, the new trait would be passed on to offspring. This theory is known as the *inheritance of acquired characteristics,* or the *use-disuse* theory.

One of the most frequently given hypothetical examples of Lamarck's theory is that of the giraffe, which, having stripped all the leaves from the lower branches of a tree (environmental change), tries to reach leaves on upper branches. As "vital forces" move to tissues of the neck, it becomes slightly longer, and the giraffe can reach higher. The longer neck is then transmitted to offspring, with the eventual result that all giraffes have longer necks than their predecessors had (Fig. 2–5a). Thus, according to this theory, *a trait acquired by an animal during its lifetime can be passed on to offspring.* Today we know that this explanation is incorrect, because only those traits that are influenced by genetic information contained within sex cells (eggs and sperm) can be inherited (see Chapter 3).

FIGURE 2–2
Buffon recognized the influence of the environment on life-forms.

FIGURE 2–3
Erasmus Darwin, grandfather of Charles Darwin, believed in species change.

FIGURE 2–4
Lamarck believed that species change was influenced by environmental change. He is best known for his theory of the inheritance of acquired characteristics.

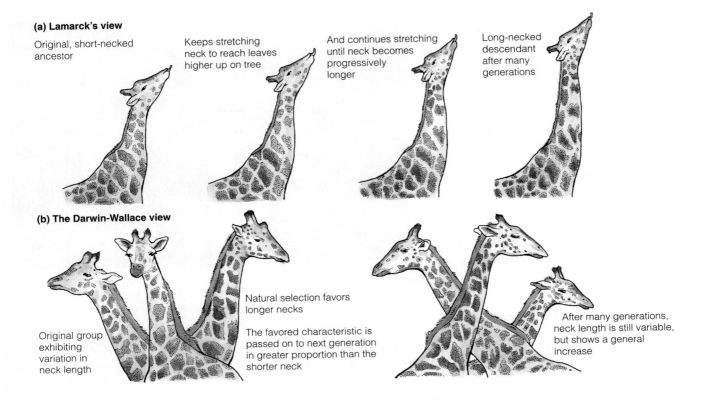

(a) Lamarck's view

Original, short-necked ancestor

Keeps stretching neck to reach leaves higher up on tree

And continues stretching until neck becomes progressively longer

Long-necked descendant after many generations

(b) The Darwin-Wallace view

Original group exhibiting variation in neck length

Natural selection favors longer necks

The favored characteristic is passed on to next generation in greater proportion than the shorter neck

After many generations, neck length is still variable, but shows a general increase

Dept. of Library Services, American Museum of Natural History

FIGURE 2–5

Contrasting ideas about the mechanism of evolution. (a) According to Lamarck's theory, acquired characteristics can be passed to subsequent generations. Thus, short-necked giraffes stretched their necks to reach higher into trees for food, and, according to Lamarck, this acquired trait was passed on to offspring, which were born with longer necks. (b) According to the Darwin-Wallace theory of natural selection, among giraffes there is variation in neck length. If having a longer neck provides an advantage for feeding, this trait will be passed on to a greater number of offspring, leading to an increase in the length of giraffe necks over many generations.

Because Lamarck's explanation of species change isn't genetically correct, it's sometimes made fun of and dismissed. But actually, Lamarck deserves a lot of credit because he was the first person to emphasize the importance of interactions between organisms and the external environment in the evolutionary process. And, incidentally, he also coined the term *biology* to refer to studies of living organisms.

Georges Cuvier

Georges Cuvier (1769–1832), the most vehement opponent of Lamarck, was a French vertebrate paleontologist who introduced the concept of extinction to explain the disappearance of animals represented by fossils (Fig. 2–6). Although a brilliant anatomist, Cuvier never grasped the dynamic concept of nature, and he insisted on the fixity of species. So, rather than assume that similarities between certain fossil forms and living species indicated evolutionary relationships, he suggested a variation of a theory known as **catastrophism**.

Catastrophism was the belief that the earth's geological features are the results of sudden, worldwide cataclysmic events like the Noah flood. Cuvier's version of catastrophism suggested that a series of regional disasters had destroyed most or all of the plant and animal life in various places. These areas were then restocked with new, similar forms that migrated in from unaffected regions. But, since he needed to be consistent with the emerging fossil evidence indicating that organisms had become more complex over time, Cuvier proposed that after each disaster, the incoming migrants had a more modern appearance because they were the results of more recent creation events. (The last of these creations was the one described in Genesis.) So Cuvier's explanation of increased complexity over time avoided any notion of evolution while still being able to account for the evidence for change that was preserved in the fossil record.

FIGURE 2–6

Cuvier explained the fossil record as the result of a succession of catastrophes followed by new creation events.

catastrophism   The view that the earth's geological landscape is the result of violent cataclysmic events. This view was promoted by Cuvier, especially in opposition to Lamarck.

Thomas Malthus   In 1798, Thomas Malthus (1766–1834), an English clergyman and economist, wrote *An Essay on the Principle of Population,* which inspired both Charles Darwin and Alfred Wallace in their separate discoveries of natural selection (Fig. 2–7). In his essay, Malthus said that human populations could double in size every 25 years if they weren't kept in check by limited food supplies. That is, population size increases exponentially while food supplies remain relatively stable.

Malthus, who was arguing for limits to population growth, focused on humans because we can increase food supplies artificially and therefore reduce constraints on population size. However, the same logic could be applied to nonhuman organisms, and both Darwin and Wallace later extended Malthus' principles to all organisms. They did this in recognition of the fact that, in nature, the tendency for populations to increase is always checked by resource availability; and this situation results in constant competition for food and other resources.

Charles Lyell   Charles Lyell (1797–1875), the son of Scottish landowners, is considered the founder of modern geology (Fig. 2–8). He was a barrister, a geologist, and for many years, Charles Darwin's friend and mentor. Before meeting Darwin in 1836, Lyell had earned acceptance in Europe's most prestigious scientific circles, thanks to his highly praised *Principles of Geology,* first published during the years 1830–1833.

In this immensely important work, Lyell argued that the geological processes observed in the present are the same as those that occurred in the past. This theory, called **uniformitarianism**, didn't originate entirely with Lyell, having been proposed by James Hutton in the late 1700s. Even so, it was Lyell who demonstrated that such forces as wind, water erosion, local flooding, frost, decomposition of vegetable matter, volcanoes, earthquakes, and glacial movements had all contributed in the past to produce the geological landscape that exists in the present. What's more, the fact that these processes still occurred indicated that geological change was still happening and that the forces driving such change were consistent, or *uniform,* over time. In other words, although various aspects of the earth's surface (for example, climate, plants, animals, and land surfaces) are variable through time, the *underlying processes* that influence them are constant.

The theory of uniformitarianism flew in the face of Cuvier's catastrophism. Additionally, Lyell emphasized the obvious: namely, that for such slow-acting forces to produce momentous change, the earth would have to be far older than anyone had previously suspected. By providing an immense time scale and thereby altering perceptions of earth's history from a few thousand to many millions of years, Lyell changed the framework within which scientists viewed the geological past. Thus, the concept of "deep time" (Gould, 1987) remains one of Lyell's most significant contributions to the discovery of evolutionary principles. The immensity of geological time permitted the necessary time depth for the inherently slow process of evolutionary change.

THE DISCOVERY OF NATURAL SELECTION

Charles Darwin   Having already been introduced to Erasmus Darwin, you shouldn't be surprised that his grandson Charles grew up in an educated family with ties to intellectual circles. Charles Darwin (1809–1882) was one of six children of Dr. Robert and Susanna Darwin (Fig. 2–9). Being the grandson not only of Erasmus Darwin but also of the wealthy Josiah Wedgwood (of Wedgwood china fame), Charles grew up enjoying the comfortable lifestyle of the landed gentry in rural England.

As a boy, he had a keen interest in nature and spent his days fishing and collecting shells, birds' eggs, and rocks. However, this interest in natural history didn't dispel the generally held view of family and friends that he was in no way remarkable. In fact, his performance at school was no more than ordinary.

After the death of his mother when he was eight years old, Darwin was raised by his father and his older sisters. Because he showed little interest in anything except hunting, shooting, and perhaps science, his father sent him to Edinburgh University to study medicine. It was there that Darwin first became acquainted with the evolutionary theories of Lamarck and others.

During that time (the 1820s), notions of evolution were becoming feared in England and elsewhere. Anything identifiable with postrevolutionary France was viewed with suspicion by the established order in England. Lamarck, partly because he was French, was especially vilified by British scientists.

FIGURE 2–7
Thomas Malthus' *Essay on the Principle of Population* led both Darwin and Wallace to the principle of natural selection.

FIGURE 2–8
Lyell, the father of geology, stated the theory of uniformitarianism in his *Principles of Geology.*

uniformitarianism   The theory that the earth's features are the result of long-term processes that continue to operate in the present as they did in the past. Elaborated on by Lyell, this theory opposed catastrophism and contributed strongly to the concept of immense geological time.

FIGURE 2–9
Charles Darwin, photographed 5 years before the publication of *Origin of Species*.

transmutation   The change of one species to another. The term *evolution* did not assume its current meaning until the late nineteenth century.

FIGURE 2–10
The route of the HMS *Beagle*.

It was also a time of growing political unrest in Britain. The Reform Movement, which sought to undo many of the wrongs of the traditional class system, was under way; and like most social movements, this one had a radical faction. Because many of the radicals were atheists and socialists who also supported Lamarck's ideas, many people came to associate evolution with atheism and political subversion. Such was the growing fear of evolutionary ideas that many believed that, if they were generally accepted, "the Church would crash, the moral fabric of society would be torn apart, and civilized man would return to savagery" (Desmond and Moore, 1991, p. 34). It's unfortunate that some of the most outspoken early proponents of **transmutation** were so vehemently anti-Christian, because their rhetoric helped establish the entrenched suspicion and misunderstanding of evolutionary theory that persists today.

While at Edinburgh, young Darwin studied with professors who were outspoken supporters of Lamarck. Therefore, although he hated medicine and left Edinburgh after two years, his experience there was a formative period in his intellectual development.

Even though Darwin was fairly indifferent to religion, he next went to Christ's College, Cambridge, to study theology. It was during his Cambridge years that he seriously cultivated his interests in natural science, immersing himself in botany and geology. It's no wonder that following his graduation in 1831, he was invited to join a scientific expedition that would circle the globe. And so it was that Darwin set sail aboard the HMS *Beagle* on December 17, 1831. The famous voyage of the *Beagle* would take almost five years and would forever change not only the course of Darwin's life but also the history of biological science.

Darwin went aboard the *Beagle* believing in fixity of species. But during the voyage, he privately began to have doubts. For example, he came across fossils of ancient giant animals that, except for size, looked very much like species that still lived in the same vicinity, so he wondered if the fossils represented ancestors of those living forms.

During the famous stopover at the Galápagos Islands (Fig. 2–10), Darwin noted that the vegetation and animals (especially birds) shared many similarities with those on the mainland of South America. But they weren't identical to them. What's more, the birds of one island were somewhat different from those living on another. Darwin collected 13 different

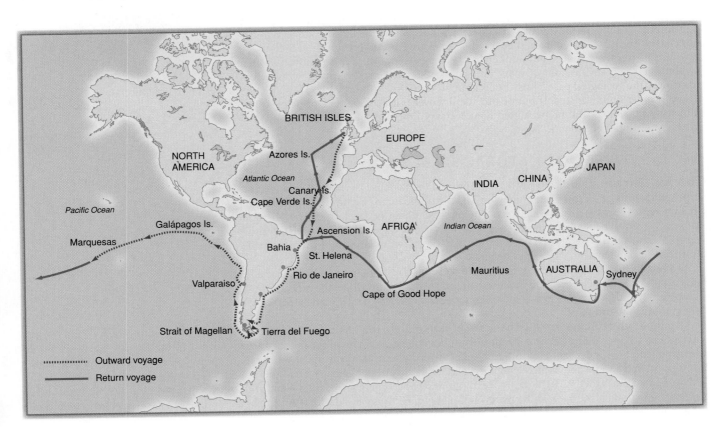

varieties of Galápagos finches, and it was clear that they represented a closely affiliated group; but they differed with regard to certain physical traits, particularly the shape and size of their beaks (Fig. 2–11). He also collected finches from the mainland, and these appeared to represent only one group, or species.

The insight that Darwin gained from the finches is legendary. He recognized that the various Galápagos finches had all descended from a common, mainland ancestor and had been modified over time in response to different island habitats and dietary preferences. But actually, it wasn't until *after* he returned to England that he recognized the significance of the variation in beak structure. In fact, during the voyage, he had paid little attention to the finches. It was only later that he considered the factors that could lead to the modification of one species into 13 (Gould, 1985; Desmond and Moore, 1991).

Darwin arrived back in England in October 1836 and was immediately accepted into the most prestigious scientific circles. He married his cousin, Emma Wedgwood, and moved to the village of Down, near London, where he spent the rest of his life writing on topics ranging from fossils to orchids. But the question of species change was his overriding passion.

At Down, Darwin began to develop his views on what he called *natural selection*. This concept was borrowed from animal breeders, who choose or "select" as breeding stock those animals that possess certain traits they want to emphasize in offspring. Animals with undesirable traits are "selected against," or prevented from breeding. A dramatic example of the effects of selective breeding can be seen in the various domestic dog breeds shown in Fig. 2–12. Darwin applied his knowledge of domesticated species to naturally occurring ones, recognizing that in undomesticated organisms, the selective agent was nature, not humans.

By the late 1830s, Darwin had realized that biological variation within a species (that is, differences among individuals) was crucial. Furthermore, he recognized that sexual reproduction increased variation, although he didn't know why. Then, in 1838, he read Malthus' essay, and there he found the answer to the question of how new species came to be. He accepted from Malthus that populations increase at a faster rate than do resources, and he recognized that in nonhuman animals, increase in population size is continuously restricted by limited food supplies. He also accepted Lyell's observation that in nature there is a constant

(a) Ground finch
   Main food: seeds
   Beak: heavy

(b) Tree finch
   Main food: leaves, buds,
   blossoms, fruits
   Beak: thick, short

(c) Tree finch (called
   woodpecker finch)
   Main food: insects
   Beak: stout, straight

(d) Ground finch (known as
   warbler finch)
   Main food: insects
   Beak: slender

FIGURE 2–11
Beak variation in Darwin's Galápagos finches.

Wolf: John Giustina/Getty Images   Dogs surrounding wolf: Lynn Kilgore and Lin Marshall

FIGURE 2–12
All domestic dog breeds share a common ancestor, the wolf. The extreme variation that dog breeds exhibit today has been achieved in a relatively short period of time through artificial selection. In this situation, humans allow only certain dogs to breed because they possess specific characteristics that humans want to emphasize. (We should note that not all traits deemed desirable by human breeders are advantageous to the dogs themselves.)

"struggle for existence." The idea that in each generation more offspring are born than survive to adulthood, coupled with the notions of competition for resources and biological diversity, was all Darwin needed to develop his theory of natural selection. He wrote: "It at once struck me that under these circumstances favourable variations would tend to be preserved, and unfavourable ones to be destroyed. The result of this would be the formation of a new species" (F. Darwin, 1950, pp. 53–54). Basically, this quotation summarizes the entire theory of natural selection.

By 1844 Darwin had written a short summary of his views on natural selection, but he didn't think he had enough data to support his hypothesis, so he continued his research without publishing. He also had other reasons for not publishing what he knew would be, to say the least, a highly controversial work. He was deeply troubled by the fact that his wife, Emma, saw his ideas as running counter to her strong religious convictions (Keynes, 2001). Also, as a member of the established order, he knew that many of his friends and associates were concerned with threats to the status quo, and evolutionary theory was viewed as a very serious threat. So he waited.

Alfred Russel Wallace Unlike Darwin, Alfred Russel Wallace (1823–1913) was born into a family of modest means (Fig. 2–13). He went to work at the age of 14, and with little formal education, he moved from one job to the next. He became interested in collecting plants and animals, and in 1848 he joined an expedition to the Amazon, where he acquired firsthand knowledge of many natural phenomena. Then, in 1854, he sailed for Southeast Asia and the Malay Peninsula to collect bird and insect specimens.

In 1855, Wallace published a paper suggesting that species were descended from other species and that the appearance of new species was influenced by environmental factors. The Wallace paper caused Lyell and others to urge Darwin to publish, but still he hesitated.

Then, in 1858, Wallace sent Darwin another paper, "On the Tendency of Varieties to Depart Indefinitely from the Original Type." In it, Wallace described evolution as a process driven by competition and natural selection. When he received Wallace's paper, Darwin feared that Wallace might get credit for a theory (natural selection) that he himself had developed. He quickly wrote a paper presenting his ideas, and the papers of both men were read before the Linnean Society of London. Neither author was present. Wallace was out of the country, and Darwin was mourning the recent death of his young son.

The papers received little notice at the time; but when Darwin completed and published his greatest work, *On the Origin of Species,** in December 1859, the storm broke, and it still hasn't abated. Although public opinion was negative, there was much scholarly praise for the book, and scientific opinion gradually came to Darwin's support. The riddle of species was now explained: Species were mutable, not fixed; and they evolved from other species through the mechanism of natural selection.

FIGURE 2–13
Alfred Russel Wallace independently discovered the key to the evolutionary process.

Down House and The Royal College of Surgeons of England

NATURAL SELECTION

Early in his research, Darwin had realized that natural selection was the key to evolution. With the help of Malthus' ideas, he saw *how* selection in nature could be explained. In the struggle for existence, those *individuals* with favorable variations would survive and reproduce, but those with unfavorable variations wouldn't. For Darwin, the explanation of evolution was simple. The basic processes, as he understood them, are as follows:

1. All species are capable of producing offspring at a faster rate than food supplies increase.
2. There is biological variation within all species. (Today we know that, except for identical twins, no two individuals are genetically the same.)

---

*The full title is *On the Origin of Species by Means of Natural Selection, or the Preservation of Favoured Races in the Struggle for Life.*

3. Since in each generation more offspring are produced than can survive, and owing to limited resources, there is competition between individuals. (*Note:* This statement doesn't mean that there is constant fierce fighting.)

4. Individuals who possess favorable variations or traits (for example, speed, resistance to disease, protective coloration) have an advantage over those who don't have them. In other words, favorable traits increase the likelihood of survival and reproduction.

5. The environmental context determines whether or not a trait is beneficial. What is favorable in one setting may be a liability in another. Consequently, the traits that become most advantageous are the result of a natural process.

6. Traits are inherited and passed on to the next generation. Because individuals who possess favorable traits contribute more offspring to the next generation than others do, over time, such characteristics become more common in the population; less favorable ones aren't passed on as frequently, and they become less common, or they are "weeded out." Individuals who produce more offspring in comparison to others are said to have greater **reproductive success**.

7. Over long periods of geological time, successful variations accumulate in a population, so that later generations may be distinct from ancestral ones. Thus, in time, a new species may appear.

8. Geographical isolation also contributes to the formation of new species. As populations of a species become geographically isolated from one another, for whatever reasons, they begin to adapt to different environments. Over time, as populations continue to respond to different **selective pressures** (that is, different ecological circumstances), they may become distinct species. The 13 species of Galápagos finches are presumably all descended from a common ancestor on the South American mainland, and they provide an example of the role of geographical isolation.

Before Darwin, individual members of species weren't considered important, so they weren't studied. But as we've seen, Darwin recognized the uniqueness of individuals and realized that variation among them could explain how selection occurred. Favorable variations were selected, or chosen, for survival by nature; unfavorable ones were eliminated. *Natural selection operates on individuals,* favorably or unfavorably, but *it's the population that evolves.* The unit of natural selection is the individual; the unit of evolution is the population, because individuals don't change genetically, but over time, populations do.

Natural Selection in Action

The most frequently cited example of natural selection documents changes in the coloration of "peppered" moths around Manchester, England. In recent years, the moth story has come under some criticism; but the basic premise remains valid, so we use it to illustrate how natural selection works.

Before the nineteenth century, the most common variety of the peppered moth was a mottled gray color. During the day, as moths rested on lichen-covered tree trunks, their coloration provided camouflage (Fig. 2–14). There was also a dark gray variety of the same species, but since the dark moths were uncamouflaged, they were eaten by birds more frequently and so they were less common. (In this example, the birds are the *selective agent,* and they apply *selective pressures* on the moths.) Therefore, the dark moths produced fewer offspring than the camouflaged moths. Yet, by the end of the nineteenth century, the common gray form had been almost completely replaced by the darker one.

The cause of this change was the changing environment of industrialized nineteenth-century England. Coal dust from factories and fireplaces settled on trees, turning them dark gray and killing the lichen. The moths continued to rest on the trees, but the light gray ones became more conspicuous as the trees became darker, and they were increasingly targeted by birds. Since fewer of the light gray moths were living long enough to reproduce, they contributed fewer genes to the next generation than the darker moths did, and the proportion of lighter moths decreased while the dark moths became more common. A similar color shift had also occurred in North America. But as clean air acts in both Britain and the United States reduced the amount of air pollution (at least from coal), the predominant color of the

reproductive success   The number of offspring an individual produces and rears to reproductive age; an individual's genetic contribution to the next generation.

selective pressures   Forces in the environment that influence reproductive success in individuals.

(a)

(b)

FIGURE 2–14
Variation in the peppered moth. (a) The dark form is more visible on the light, lichen-covered tree. (b) On trees darkened by pollution, the lighter form is more visible.

peppered moth once again became the light mottled gray. This kind of evolutionary shift in response to environmental change is called *adaptation*.

Another example of natural selection is provided by the medium ground finch of the Galápagos Islands. In 1977, drought killed many of the plants that produced the smaller, softer seeds favored by these birds. This forced a population of finches on one of the islands to feed on larger, harder seeds. Even before 1977, some birds had smaller, less robust beaks than others (that is, there was variation); and during the drought, because they were less able to process the larger seeds, more smaller-beaked birds died than larger-beaked birds. Therefore, although overall population size declined, average beak thickness in the survivors and their offspring increased, simply because thicker-beaked individuals were surviving in greater numbers and producing more offspring. In other words, they had greater reproductive success. But during heavy rains in 1982–1983, smaller seeds became more plentiful again and the pattern in beak size reversed itself, demonstrating how reproductive success is related to environmental conditions (Grant, 1986; Grant and Grant, 2002; Ridley, 1993).

The best illustration of natural selection, however, and certainly one with potentially grave consequences for humans, is the recent increase in resistant strains of disease-causing microorganisms. When antibiotics were first introduced in the 1940s, they were seen as the end of bacterial disease. But that optimistic view didn't take into account the fact that bacteria, like other organisms, possess genetic variability. Consequently, whereas an antibiotic will kill most bacteria in an infected person, any bacterium with an inherited resistance to that particular therapy will survive. Subsequently, the survivors reproduce and pass their drug resistance to future generations so that eventually, the population is mostly made up of bacteria that don't respond to treatment. What's more, because bacteria produce new generations every few hours, antibiotic-resistant strains are continuously being produced. As a result, many types of infection no longer respond to treatment. For example, tuberculosis was once thought to be well controlled, but it has seen a resurgence in recent years because the bacterium that causes it is now resistant to many antibiotics.

These three examples provide the following insights into the fundamentals of evolutionary change produced by natural selection:

1. *A trait must be inherited if natural selection is to act on it.* A characteristic that isn't hereditary (such as a temporary change in hair color produced by the hairdresser) won't be passed on to succeeding generations. In finches, for example, beak size is a hereditary trait.

2. *Natural selection can't occur without population variation in inherited characteristics.* If, for example, all the peppered moths had initially been gray (you will recall that some dark forms were always present) and the trees had become darker, the survival and reproduction of all moths could have been so low that the population might have become extinct. *Selection can work only with variation that already exists.*

3. **Fitness** *is a relative measure that changes as the environment changes.* Fitness is simply *differential reproductive success.* In the initial stage, the lighter moths were more fit because they produced more offspring. But as the environment changed, the dark gray moths became more fit, and a further change reversed the adaptive pattern. Likewise, the majority of Galápagos finches will have larger or smaller beaks, depending on external conditions. So it should be obvious that statements regarding the "most fit" mean nothing without reference to specific environments.

4. *Natural selection can act only on traits that affect reproduction.* If a characteristic isn't expressed until later in life, after organisms have reproduced, then natural selection can't influence it. This is because the inherited components of the trait have already been passed on to offspring. Many forms of cancer and cardiovascular disease are influenced by hereditary factors, but because these diseases usually affect people after they've had children, natural selection can't act against them. By the same token, if a condition usually kills or compromises the individual before he or she reproduces, natural selection acts against it because the trait won't be passed on.

So far, our examples have shown how different death rates influence natural selection (for example, moths or finches that die early leave fewer offspring). But mortality isn't the complete picture. Another important aspect of natural selection is fertility, because an animal that gives birth to more young passes its genes on at a faster rate than one that bears fewer off-

fitness   Pertaining to natural selection, a measure of *relative* reproductive success of individuals. Fitness can be measured by an individual's genetic contribution to the next generation compared to that of other individuals. The terms *genetic fitness, reproductive fitness,* and *differential reproductive success* are also used.

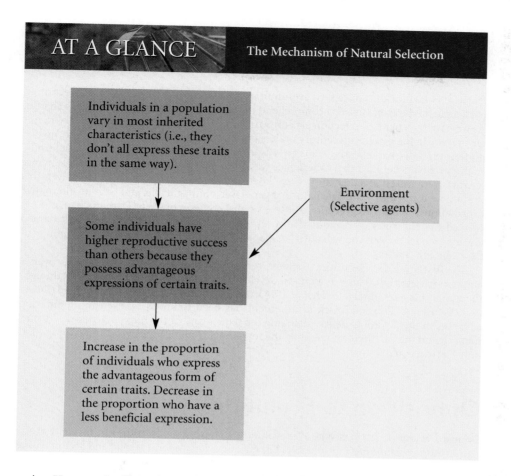

spring. However, fertility isn't the entire story either, because the crucial element is the number of young raised successfully to the point at which they themselves reproduce. We call this *differential net reproductive success.* The way this mechanism works can be demonstrated through another example.

In swifts (small birds that resemble swallows), data show that producing more offspring doesn't necessarily guarantee that more young will be successfully raised. The number of eggs hatched in a breeding season is a measure of fertility. The number of birds that mature and are eventually able to leave the nest is a measure of net reproductive success, or offspring successfully raised. The following table shows the correlation between the number of eggs hatched (fertility) and the number of young that leave the nest (reproductive success), averaged over four breeding seasons (Lack, 1966):

Number of eggs hatched (fertility)	2 eggs	3 eggs	4 eggs
Average number of young raised (reproductive success)	1.92	2.54	1.76
Sample size (number of nests)	72	20	16

As you can see, the most efficient number of eggs is three, because that number yields the highest reproductive success. Raising two offspring is less beneficial to the parents since the end result isn't as successful as with three eggs. Trying to raise more than three is actually detrimental, since the parents may not be able to provide enough nourishment for any of the offspring. Offspring that die before reaching reproductive age are, in evolutionary terms, equivalent to never being born. Actually, death of an offspring can be a minus to the parents, because before it dies, it drains parental resources. It may even inhibit their ability to raise other offspring, thereby reducing their reproductive success even further. Selection favors those genetic traits that yield the maximum net reproductive success. If the number of eggs laid is a genetic trait in birds (and it seems to be), natural selection in swifts should act to favor the laying of three eggs as opposed to two or four.

Constraints on Nineteenth-Century Evolutionary Theory

Darwin argued for the concept of evolution in general and the role of natural selection in particular, but he didn't entirely comprehend the exact mechanisms of evolutionary change. As we have seen, natural selection acts on *variation* within species. But neither Darwin nor anyone else in the nineteenth century understood the actual source of variation. Also, no one understood how parents pass traits to offspring. Almost without exception, nineteenth-century scholars believed that inheritance was a *blending* process in which parental characteristics were mixed together to produce intermediate expressions in offspring. Given this notion, we can see why the true nature of genes was unimaginable, and with no alternative explanations, Darwin accepted it. As it turns out, a contemporary of Darwin's had actually worked out the rules of heredity. However, the work of this Augustinian monk named Gregor Mendel (whom you will meet in Chapter 3) wasn't recognized until the beginning of the twentieth century.

The first three decades of the twentieth century saw the merger of Mendel's discoveries and natural selection. This was a crucial development because until then, scientists thought these concepts were unrelated. Then, in 1953, the structure of **deoxyribonucleic acid (DNA)** was discovered. This landmark achievement has been followed by even more amazing advances in the field of genetics, including the sequencing of the human **genome**. We may finally be on the threshold of revealing the remaining secrets of the evolutionary process. If only Darwin could know!

Opposition to Evolution

Almost 150 years later, the debate over evolution is far from over. For the vast majority of scientists today, evolution is indisputable. The genetic evidence for it is solid and accumulating daily. Anyone who appreciates and understands genetic mechanisms can't avoid the conclusion that populations and species evolve. What's more, the majority of Christians don't believe that biblical depictions should be taken literally. But at the same time, some surveys show that about half of all Americans don't believe that evolution occurs. There are a number of reasons for this.

The mechanisms of evolution are complex and don't lend themselves to simple explanations. Understanding them requires some familiarity with genetics and biology—a familiarity that most people don't have. What's more, many people who haven't been exposed to scientific training want definitive, clear-cut answers to complex questions. But as you learned in Chapter 1, scientific research doesn't always provide definitive answers to questions, nor does it establish absolute truths. Another thing to consider is that regardless of their culture, most people are raised in belief systems that don't emphasize **biological continuity** between species.

The relationship between science and religion has never been easy (remember Galileo). Even though both systems serve, in their own ways, to explain various phenomena, scientific explanations are based in data analysis, hypothesis testing, and interpretation. Religion, meanwhile, is a system of beliefs based in faith, and it isn't amenable to scientific testing. Religion and science concern different aspects of the human experience; still, we should remember that they aren't inherently mutually exclusive approaches. Belief in God doesn't exclude the possibility of biological evolution; and acknowledgement of evolutionary processes doesn't preclude the existence of God. What's more, not all forms of Christianity and other religions are opposed to evolutionary concepts. Some years ago, the Vatican hosted an international conference on human evolution; and in 1996, Pope John Paul II issued a statement that "fresh knowledge leads to recognition of the theory of evolution as more than just a hypothesis." Today, the official position of the Catholic Church is that evolutionary processes do occur, but that the human soul is of divine creation and not subject to evolutionary processes. Likewise, mainstream Protestants don't generally see a conflict.

deoxyribonucleic acid (DNA) The double-stranded molecule that contains the genetic code.

genome The entire genetic makeup of an individual or species.

biological continuity Refers to a biological continuum—that organisms are related through common ancestry and that traits present in one species are also seen to varying degrees in others. When expressions of a phenomenon continuously grade into one another so that there are no discrete categories, they exist on a continuum. Color is one such phenomenon, and life-forms are another.

Unfortunately, those who believe absolutely in a literal interpretation of the bible (called fundamentalists) accept no form of compromise.

In 1925, a law banning the teaching of evolution in public schools was passed in Tennessee. To test the validity of the law, the American Civil Liberties Union persuaded a high school teacher named John Scopes to allow himself to be arrested and tried for teaching evolution. The subsequent trial (called the Scopes Monkey Trial) was a 1920s equivalent of current celebrity trials, and in the end, Scopes was convicted and fined $100. In the more than 80 years since the trial, Christian fundamentalists have continued with their attempts to remove evolution from public school curricula. Known as "creationists" because they explain the existence of the universe as the result of a sudden creation event, they are determined either to eliminate the teaching of evolution or to introduce antievolutionary material into public school classes. In the past 20 years, creationists have insisted that what they used to call "creation science" is as valid a scientific endeavor as is the study of evolution. They argue that in the interest of fairness, a balanced view should be offered: If evolution is taught as science, then creationism should also be taught as science. Sounds fair, doesn't it? But "creation science" isn't science at all, for the simple reason that creationists insist that their view is absolute and infallible. Consequently, creationism isn't a hypothesis that can be tested, nor is it amenable to falsification. Because hypothesis testing is the basis of all science, creationism, by its very nature, cannot be considered science. It is religion.

Still, creationists remain active in state legislatures, promoting laws that mandate the teaching of creationism in public schools. In 1981, the Arkansas state legislature passed one such law; it was overturned in 1982. In his ruling against the state, the judge justifiably stated that "a theory that is by its own terms dogmatic, absolutist and never subject to revision is not a scientific theory." And, he added, "Since creation is not science, the conclusion is inescapable that the only real effect of [this law] is the advancement of religion." In 1987, the United States Supreme Court struck down a similar law in Louisiana.

So far, these and similar laws have been overturned because they violate the principle of separation of Church and State as provided in the First Amendment to the U.S. Constitution. (Basically, this means that money derived from taxes can't be used to promote religion. It was initially proposed to ensure that the government could neither promote nor restrict any particular religious view, as it did in England at the time the Constitution was written.) But this hasn't stopped the creationists, who encourage teachers to claim "academic freedom" to teach creationism. They've also dropped the word *creationism* in favor of the less religious-sounding term *intelligent design theory*, which harkens back to the argument from design (see p. 22). The term *intelligent design* is based on the notion that most biological functions and anatomical traits (for example, the eye) are too complex to be explained by a theory that doesn't include the presence of a creator or designer. To avoid objections based on the guarantee of separation of Church and State, proponents of intelligent design claim that they don't emphasize any particular religion. But this argument still doesn't speak to the essential point that teaching *any* religious views, in a way that promotes them in publicly funded schools, constitutes a violation of the U.S. Constitution.

Antievolution feeling also remains very strong among many politicians, particularly those with strong support from Christian fundamentalists. The president of the United States (as of this writing) has publicly supported teaching intelligent design in public schools; and in 1999, one very powerful U.S. congressman (now under indictment) went so far as to state that the teaching of evolution is one of the factors behind violence in America today! Now, that's a stretch!

Summary

Our current understanding of evolutionary processes is directly traceable to developments in intellectual thought in western Europe over the last 300 years. Many people contributed to this shift in perspective, and we've named only a few. Linnaeus placed humans in the same taxonomic scheme as all other animals. Importantly, Lamarck and Buffon both recognized that species could change in response to environmental circumstances, but Lamarck also attempted to explain *how* the changes occurred. He proposed the idea of *inheritance of acquired characteristics*, which was later discredited. Lyell, in his theory of uniformitarianism, provided the necessary expanse of time for evolution to occur, and Malthus discussed how population size is kept in check by the availability of resources. Darwin and Wallace, influenced by their predecessors, independently recognized that because of competition for resources, individuals with favorable characteristics would tend to survive and pass those traits on to offspring. Those lacking beneficial traits would produce fewer offspring, if they survived to reproductive age at all. That is, they would have lower reproductive success and reduced fitness. Thus, over time, advantageous characteristics accumulate in a population (because they have been selected for) while disadvantageous ones are eliminated (selected against). This, in a nutshell, is the theory of evolution by means of natural selection.

Critical Thinking Questions

1. After having read this chapter, how would you respond to the question, "If humans evolved from monkeys, why do we still have monkeys?"
2. Do you, personally, object to the idea that humans are closely related to chimpanzees? (By closely related, we mean that the two species are extremely similar genetically and that they share a recent common ancestor.) Explain your answer.
3. What are selective agents? Can you think of some examples we didn't discuss? Why did Darwin look at domesticated species as models for natural selection, and what is the selective agent in artificial selection? List some examples of artificial selection that we didn't discuss.
4. Given what you've read about the scientific method, how would you explain the differences between science and religion as methods of explaining natural phenomena? Do you personally see a conflict between evolutionary and religious explanations of how species came to be?

CHAPTER 3

Heredity and Evolution

FOCUS QUESTIONS

How would you say that knowing about the mechanisms of heredity helps to understand how human beings fit into a biological continuum?

Why is it important to know the basic mechanisms of inheritance to understand the processes of evolution?

Introduction

Go to the following CD-ROM for interactive activities and exercises on topics covered in this chapter:

- Genetics in Anthropology: Principles and Applications CD-ROM, First Edition

Have you ever seen a cat with five, six, or even seven toes? Or, maybe you've known someone with an extra finger or toe, because it's not unheard of in people. Anne Boleyn, mother of England's Queen Elizabeth I and the first of Henry VIII's wives to lose her head, apparently had an extra little finger. (Of course, this had nothing to do with her early demise— that's another story.)

Having extra fingers or toes (digits) is called polydactyly, and it's fairly certain that one of Anne Boleyn's parents was also polydactylous. It's also likely that any polydactylous cat has a parent with extra toes. But how do we know this? Actually, it's fairly simple. Polydactyly is a Mendelian trait, meaning that its pattern of inheritance follows principles discovered almost 150 years ago by a monk named Gregor Mendel. And, by the time you finish reading this chapter, you'll know these principles and be able to explain how we know that polydactylous cats and people probably have a polydactylous parent, even if we've never seen their parents.

For at least 10,000 years, beginning with the domestication of plants and animals, people have tried to explain how offspring inherit characteristics from their parents. One common belief was that traits of offspring resulted from the blending of parental characteristics. We know now that this isn't true, and in fact, thanks to genetic research, mostly in the twentieth century, we actually know a lot about how traits are inherited.

As you already know, this book is about human evolution and adaptation, both of which are intimately linked to life processes that involve cells, the replication and decoding of genetic information, and the transmission of this information between generations. So, to present human evolution and adaptation in the broad sense, we need to examine the fundamental principles of genetics. Genetics is the study of how traits are transmitted from one generation to the next, and even though many physical anthropologists don't actually specialize in genetics, it is genetics that ultimately links the various subdisciplines of biological anthropology.

The Cell

In order to discuss genetic and evolutionary principles, we first need to know how cells function. Cells are the basic units of life in all living things. In some forms, such as bacteria, a single cell constitutes the entire organism. However, more complex *multicellular forms*, such as plants, insects, birds, and mammals, are composed of billions of cells. Indeed, an adult human is made up of perhaps as many as 1,000 billion (1,000,000,000,000) cells, all functioning in complex ways to promote the survival of the individual.

Life on earth can be traced back at least 3.7 billion years, in the form of *prokaryotic* cells. Prokaryotes are single-celled organisms, represented today by bacteria and blue-green algae. Structurally more complex cells appeared approximately 1.2 billion years ago, and these are referred to as *eukaryotic* cells. Because eukaryotic cells are found in all multicellular organisms, they're the focus of the remainder of this discussion. Despite the numerous differences between various life-forms and the cells that constitute them, it's important to understand that the cells of all living organisms share many similarities because they share a common evolutionary past.

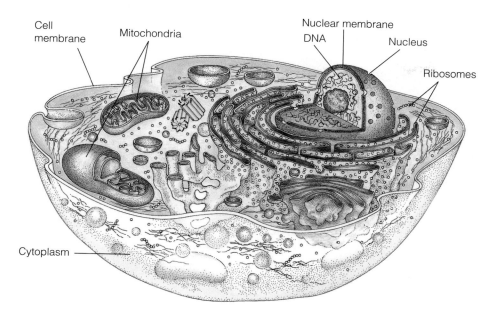

Cell membrane · Mitochondria · Nuclear membrane · DNA · Nucleus · Ribosomes · Cytoplasm

FIGURE 3–1

Structure of a generalized eukaryotic cell, illustrating the cell's three-dimensional nature. Although various organelles are shown, for the sake of simplicity only those we discuss are labeled.

nucleus A structure (organelle) found in all eukaryotic cells. The nucleus contains chromosomes (nuclear DNA).

molecules Structures made up of two or more atoms. Molecules can combine with other molecules to form more complex structures.

deoxyribonucleic acid (DNA) The double-stranded molecule that contains the genetic code. DNA is a main component of chromosomes.

ribonucleic acid (RNA) A molecule, similar in structure to DNA. Three single-stranded forms of RNA are essential to protein synthesis.

cytoplasm The portion of the cell contained within the cell membrane, excluding the nucleus. The cytoplasm consists of a semifluid material and contains numerous structures involved with cell function.

proteins Three-dimensional molecules that serve a wide variety of functions through their ability to bind to other molecules.

protein synthesis The assembly of chains of amino acids into functional protein molecules. The process is directed by DNA.

somatic cells Basically, all the cells in the body except those involved with reproduction.

gametes Reproductive cells (eggs and sperm in animals) developed from precursor cells in ovaries and testes.

zygote A cell formed by the union of an egg and a sperm cell. It contains the full complement of chromosomes (in humans, 46) and has the potential of developing into an entire organism.

nucleotides Basic units of the DNA molecule, composed of a sugar, a phosphate, and one of four DNA bases.

complementary Referring to the fact that DNA bases form base pairs in a precise manner. For example, adenine can bond only to thymine. These two bases are said to be *complementary* because one requires the other to form a complete DNA base pair.

In general, a eukaryotic cell is a three-dimensional entity composed of *carbohydrates, lipids, nucleic acids,* and *proteins*. It contains a variety of structures, called organelles, enclosed within a *cell membrane* (Fig. 3–1). One of these organelles is the **nucleus** (*pl.,* nuclei), a discrete unit surrounded by a thin nuclear membrane. Within the nucleus are two acids that contain the genetic information that controls the cell's functions. These two important **molecules** are **deoxyribonucleic acid (DNA)** and **ribonucleic acid (RNA)**. The nucleus is surrounded by a gel-like fluid called the **cytoplasm**, which contains several other types of organelles. These organelles are involved in various activities, such as breaking down nutrients and converting them to other substances (*metabolism*), storing and releasing energy, eliminating waste, and manufacturing **proteins** (**protein synthesis**).

There are basically two types of cells: **somatic cells** and **gametes**. Somatic cells are the cellular components of body tissues, such as muscle, bone, skin, nerve, heart, and brain. Gametes, or sex cells, on the other hand, are specifically involved in reproduction and aren't structural components of the body. There are two types of gametes: *ova,* or egg cells, produced in the ovaries in females; and *sperm,* which develop in male testes. The sole function of a sex cell is to unite with a gamete from another individual to form a **zygote**, which has the potential to develop into an entire new individual. In this way, gametes transmit genetic information from parent to offspring.

DNA Structure and Function

As already mentioned, cellular functions are directed by DNA. If we want to understand these functions and how traits are inherited, we must first know something about the structure and function of DNA.

The DNA molecule is composed of two chains of even smaller molecules called **nucleotides**. A nucleotide, in turn, is made up of three components: a sugar molecule (deoxyribose), a phosphate, and one of four bases (Fig. 3–2). In DNA, nucleotides are stacked on one another to form a chain that is bonded along its bases to another **complementary** nucleotide chain. Together the two twist to form a spiral, or helical, shape. The resulting DNA molecule, then, is two-stranded and is described as forming a *double helix* that resembles a twisted ladder. If we follow the twisted ladder analogy, the sugars and phosphates represent the two sides, while the bases and the bonds that join them form the rungs.

The four bases are the key to how DNA works. These bases are named *adenine, guanine, thymine,* and *cytosine,* but they're usually referred to by their initial letters, A, G, T, and C. In

FIGURE 3–2

Part of a DNA molecule. The illustration shows the two DNA strands with the sugar and phosphate backbone and the bases extending toward the center.

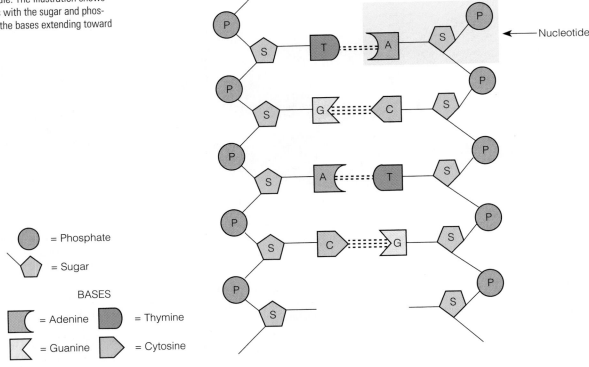

Strand 1

Strand 2

← Nucleotide

= Phosphate

= Sugar

BASES

= Adenine   = Thymine

= Guanine   = Cytosine

the formation of the double helix, one type of base can pair or bond with only one other type. Therefore, base pairs can form only between adenine and thymine and between guanine and cytosine (Fig. 3–3). This specificity is essential to the DNA molecule's ability to **replicate**, or make an exact copy of itself.

DNA REPLICATION

In order for organisms to develop and grow, and for injured tissues to be repaired, cells have to multiply. And, in order to multiply, they divide in a way that insures that each new cell receives a full complement of genetic material. This is a crucial point, since a cell can't function properly without the appropriate amount of DNA, and for new cells to receive the essential amount of DNA, the DNA must first replicate.

Prior to cell division, **enzymes** break the bonds between bases in the DNA molecule, leaving the two previously joined strands of nucleotides with their bases exposed (see Fig. 3–3). The exposed bases then attract unattached nucleotides, which are free-floating in the cell nucleus. Because one base can be joined to only one other, the attraction between bases occurs in a complementary fashion. Consequently, each of the two previously joined parental nucleotide chains serve as models, or *templates*, for the formation of a new strand of nucleotides. As each new strand is formed, its bases are joined to the bases of an original strand. When the process is completed, there are two double-stranded DNA molecules exactly like the original, and each new molecule consists of one original nucleotide chain joined to a newly formed one (see Fig. 3–3).

PROTEIN SYNTHESIS

The most important function of DNA is to direct the manufacture of proteins (protein synthesis) within the cell. Proteins are complex, three-dimensional molecules that function through their ability to bind to other molecules. For example, the protein **hemoglobin**, found in red blood cells, is able to bind to oxygen which it transports to cells throughout the body.

replicate   To duplicate. The DNA molecule is able to make copies of itself.

enzymes   Specialized proteins that initiate and direct chemical reactions in the body.

hemoglobin   A protein molecule that occurs in red blood cells and binds to oxygen molecules.

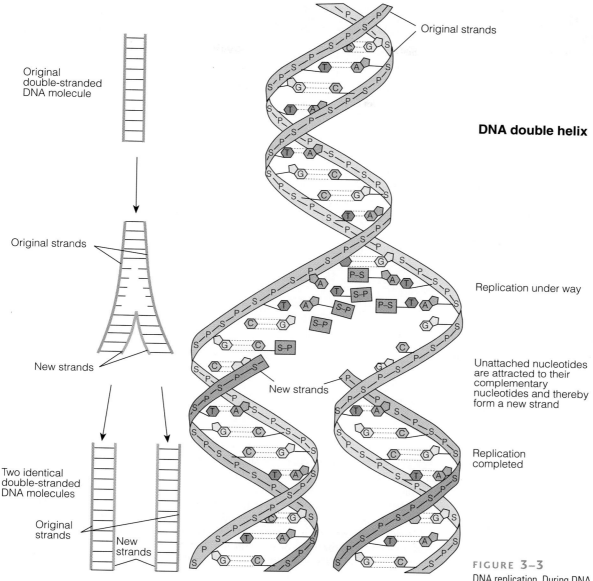

Original double-stranded DNA molecule

Original strands

New strands

Two identical double-stranded DNA molecules

Original strands

New strands

Original strands

DNA double helix

Replication under way

Unattached nucleotides are attracted to their complementary nucleotides and thereby form a new strand

Replication completed

FIGURE 3–3

DNA replication. During DNA replication, the two strands of the DNA molecule are separated, and each strand serves as a template for the formation of a new strand. When replication is complete, there are two DNA molecules. Each molecule consists of one new and one original DNA strand.

Proteins function in countless ways. Some are structural components of tissues. Collagen, for example, is the most common protein in the body and it's a major component of all connective tissues. Aside from minerals, it's the most abundant structural material in bone. Enzymes are also proteins, and they initiate and enhance chemical reactions. One example is the digestive enzyme *lactase*, which breaks down *lactose* (milk sugar) into two simpler sugars. Another class of proteins includes many kinds of **hormones**. Specialized cells produce and release hormones into the bloodstream to circulate to other areas of the body, where they produce specific effects in tissues and organs. Insulin is a good example of this type of protein. Insulin, which is produced by cells in the pancreas, causes cells in the liver and certain types of muscle tissue to absorb glucose (sugar) from the blood. Lastly, there are many kinds of proteins that can actually enter a cell's nucleus and attach directly to the DNA. These proteins are called regulatory proteins or molecules because, when they bind to the DNA, they can switch genes on and off, thereby influencing how the genes act. As you can see, proteins make us what we are, so it's critical that protein synthesis occurs accurately. If it doesn't, physiological development and activities can be disrupted or even prevented.

hormones   Substances (usually proteins) that are produced by specialized cells and that travel to other parts of the body, where they influence chemical reactions and regulate various cellular functions.

TABLE 3–1	The Genetic Code		
Amino Acid Symbol	**Amino Acid**	**mRNA Codon**	**DNA Triplet**
Ala	Alanine	GCU, GCC, GCA, GCG	CGA, CGG, CGT, CGC
Arg	Arginine	CGU, CGC, CGA, CGG, AGA, AGG	GCA, GCG, GCT, GCC, TCT, TCC
Asn	Asparagine	AAU, AAC	TTA, TTG
Asp	Aspartic acid	GAU, GAC	CTA, CTG
Cys	Cysteine	UGU, UGC	ACA, ACG
Gln	Glutamine	CAA, CAG	GTT, GTC
Glu	Glutamic acid	GAA, GAG	CTT, CTC
Gly	Glycine	GGU, GGC, GGA, GGG	CCA, CCG, CCT, CCC
His	Histidine	CAU, CAC	GTA, GTG
Ile	Isoleucine	AUU, AUC, AUA	TAA, TAG, TAT
Leu	Leucine	UUA, UUG, CUU, CUC, CUA, CUG	AAT, AAC, GAA, GAG, GAT, GAC
Lys	Lysine	AAA, AAG	TTT, TTC
Met	Methionine	AUG	TAC
Phe	Phenylalanine	UUU, UUC	AAA, AAG
Pro	Proline	CCU, CCC, CCA, CCG	GGA, GGG, GGT, GGC
Ser	Serine	UCU, UCC, UCA, UCG, AGU, AGC	AGA, AGG, AGT, AGC, TCA, TCG
Thr	Threonine	ACU, ACC, ACA, ACG	TGA, TGG, TGT, TGC
Trp	Tryptophan	UGG	ACC
Tyr	Tyrosine	UAU, UAC	ATA, ATG
Val	Valine	GUU, GUC, GUA, GUG	CAA, CAG, CAT, CAC
Terminating triplets		UAA, UAG, UGA	ATT, ATC, ACT

amino acids Small molecules that are the components of proteins.

gene A sequence of DNA bases that specifies the order of amino acids in an entire protein or, in some cases, a portion of a protein. A gene may be made up of hundreds or thousands of DNA bases.

mutation A change in DNA. Technically, mutation refers to changes in DNA bases as well as changes in chromosome number and/or structure.

Proteins are made up of chains of smaller molecules called **amino acids**. In all, there are 20 amino acids, which are combined in different amounts and sequences to produce potentially millions of proteins. What makes proteins different from one another is the number of amino acids involved and the *sequence* in which they are arranged. This means that a protein can't function correctly unless its amino acids are arranged in the proper order.

DNA serves as a recipe for making a protein, because it's the sequence of DNA bases that ultimately determines the order of amino acids in a protein molecule. In the DNA instructions, a *triplet*, or group of three bases, specifies a particular amino acid. For example, if a triplet includes the bases cytosine, guanine, and adenine (CGA), it specifies the amino acid *alanine*. If the next triplet in the chain contains guanine, thymine, and cytosine (GTC), it refers to another amino acid—*glutamine*. So, a DNA recipe might look like this: AGA CGA ACA ACC TAC TTT TTC CTT AAG GTC, and so on, as it instructs the cell how to make proteins (Table 3–1).

Protein synthesis is a little more complicated than the last paragraph suggests, and it involves an additional molecule similar to DNA called RNA (ribonucleic acid). While DNA provides the instructions for protein synthesis, it's RNA that reads the instructions and actually assembles amino acids to form proteins.

The entire sequence of DNA bases responsible for the synthesis of a protein or, in some cases, part of a protein, is referred to as a **gene**. Or, to put it another way, a gene is a segment of DNA that dictates the sequence of amino acids in a particular protein. A gene may consist of only a few hundred bases, or it may be composed of thousands. If the sequence of DNA bases is altered through **mutation**, some proteins may not be manufactured, and the cell (or indeed the organism) may not function properly, if at all.

This definition of a gene is a functional one, and it's technically correct. But it's important to emphasize that gene action is complex and only partly understood. For example, the DNA segments that ultimately are translated into amino acids are called *exons*. But most of the DNA in a gene isn't expressed during protein synthesis, and these unexpressed segments

AT A GLANCE   Coding and "Noncoding" DNA

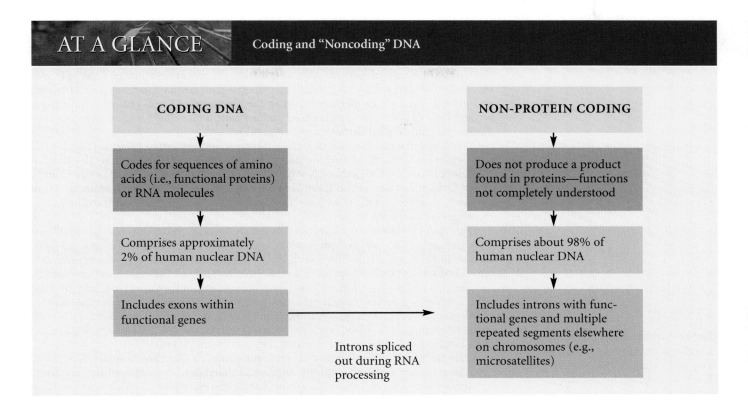

CODING DNA

Codes for sequences of amino acids (i.e., functional proteins) or RNA molecules

↓

Comprises approximately 2% of human nuclear DNA

↓

Includes exons within functional genes

→ Introns spliced out during RNA processing

NON-PROTEIN CODING

Does not produce a product found in proteins—functions not completely understood

↓

Comprises about 98% of human nuclear DNA

↓

Includes introns with functional genes and multiple repeated segments elsewhere on chromosomes (e.g., microsatellites)

---

are called *introns* (Fig. 3–4). Even though introns aren't instrumental in protein manufacture, they may have other functions, and it's the combination of introns and exons interspersed along a DNA strand that makes up the unit we call a gene.

We usually think of genes as coding for the production of proteins that make up bodily tissues. But some genes, called *regulatory genes*, direct the production of the regulatory proteins that bind to DNA. Obviously, regulatory genes are critical for individual organisms, and they also play an important role in evolution. For example, some of the anatomical differences between humans and chimpanzees are probably the results of evolutionary changes in regulatory genes in both lineages.

All somatic cells contain the same genetic information, but in any given cell, only a fraction of the DNA is actually involved in protein synthesis. For example, bone cells carry the same DNA that directs the production of digestive enzymes produced by cells in the stomach lining. But bone cells don't produce digestive enzymes. Instead, they make collagen, the major organic component of bone. The reason bone cells don't produce digestive enzymes is that, during early embryonic development, cell lines differentiate (that is, bone cells become distinct from skin cells or nerve cells). During this process, cells undergo changes in form, their functions become specialized, and most of their DNA is permanently deactivated through the action of regulatory genes.

A final point is that the genetic code is universal because, at least on earth, DNA is the genetic material in all forms of life. The DNA of all organisms, from bacteria to oak trees to human beings, is composed of the same molecules using the same kinds of instructions. Consequently, the DNA triplet CGA, for example, specifies the amino acid alanine, regardless of species. These similarities imply biological relationships among, and an ultimate common ancestry for, all forms of life. What makes oak trees different from humans isn't differences in their DNA material, but differences in how that material is arranged.

FIGURE 3–4
Diagram of a DNA sequence being transcribed. The introns are deleted from the pre-mRNA before it leaves the cell nucleus. The remaining mature mRNA contains only exons.

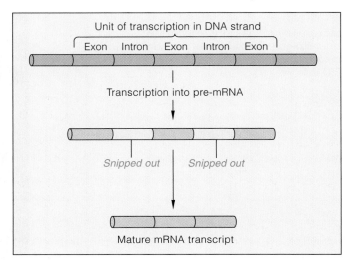

Cell Division: Mitosis and Meiosis

Throughout much of a cell's life, its DNA exists as an uncoiled, threadlike substance. (Incredibly, the nuclei of every one of your somatic cells contain an estimated 6 feet of DNA!) However, at various times in the life of most types of cells, normal functions are interrupted and the cell divides. Cell division results in the production of new cells and, during this process, the DNA becomes tightly coiled and is visible under a light microscope as a set of discrete structures called **chromosomes** (Fig. 3–5).

A chromosome is composed of a DNA molecule and associated proteins (Fig. 3–6). If chromosomes were visible during normal cell function, they would appear as single-stranded structures. However, during the early stages of cell division, they are made up of two strands, or two DNA molecules, joined together at a constricted area called the **centromere**. There are two strands because the DNA molecules have *replicated*. Therefore, one strand of a chromosome is an exact copy of the other.

Every species is characterized by a specific number of chromosomes in somatic cells (Table 3–2). In humans there are 46 chromosomes, organized into 23 pairs. Chimpanzees and gorillas have 48, or 24 pairs. This difference in chromosome number doesn't necessarily mean that humans have less DNA; it only indicates that the DNA is packaged differently in the three species.

One member of each chromosomal pair is inherited from the father (paternal), and the other member is inherited from the mother (maternal). Members of chromosomal pairs are alike in size and position of the centromere, and they carry genetic information for the same traits (for example, ABO blood type). This doesn't mean that partner chromosomes are genetically identical; it just means that the traits they govern are the same.

There are two basic types of chromosomes: **autosomes** and **sex chromosomes**. Autosomes carry genetic information that governs all physical characteristics except primary sex determination. The two sex chromosomes are the X and Y chromosomes. The Y chromosome carries genes that are directly involved with determining maleness. Although the X chromosome is called a "sex chromosome," it really functions more like an autosome since it isn't involved in primary sex determination, but it does influence a number of other traits. Among mammals, all genetically normal females have two X chromosomes (XX), and they are female simply because the Y chromosome is absent. (You could say that femaleness is the default setting.) All genetically normal males have one X and one Y chromosome (XY).

It is extremely important to note that *all* autosomes occur in pairs. Normal human somatic cells have 22 pairs of autosomes and one pair of sex chromosomes. It's also important to know that abnormal numbers of autosomes, with few exceptions, are fatal to the individual—usually soon after conception. Although abnormal numbers of sex chromosomes are not usually fatal, they may result in sterility and frequently have other consequences as well. This means that to function normally, it's essential for a human cell to possess both members of each chromosomal pair, or a total of 46 chromosomes.

chromosomes   Discrete structures, composed of DNA and protein, found only in the nuclei of cells. Chromosomes are visible only under magnification during certain stages of cell division.

centromere   The constricted portion of a chromosome. After replication, the two strands of a double-stranded chromosome are joined at the centromere.

autosomes   All chromosomes except the sex chromosomes.

sex chromosomes   The X and Y chromosomes. The Y chromosome determines maleness and, in its absence, an embryo develops as a female.

FIGURE 3–5
Scanning electron micrograph of human chromosomes during cell division. Note that these chromosomes are composed of two strands, or two DNA molecules.

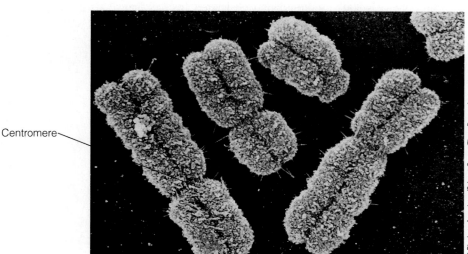

Centromere

© Biophoto Associates/Science Source/Photo Researchers

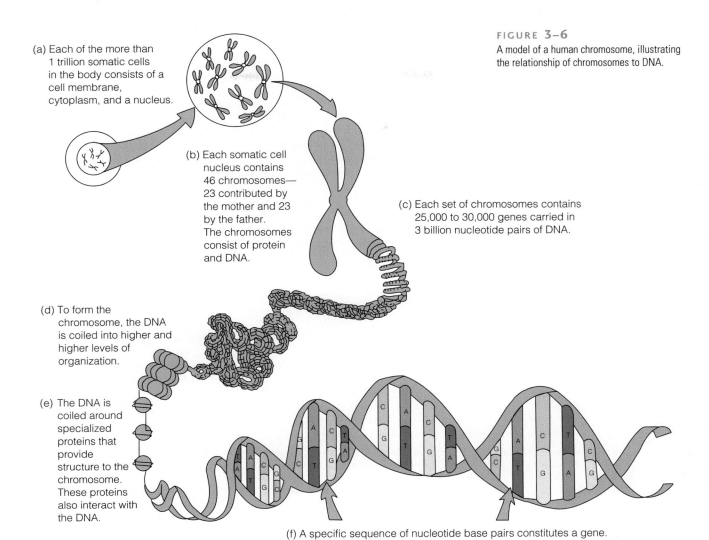

FIGURE 3-6
A model of a human chromosome, illustrating the relationship of chromosomes to DNA.

(a) Each of the more than 1 trillion somatic cells in the body consists of a cell membrane, cytoplasm, and a nucleus.

(b) Each somatic cell nucleus contains 46 chromosomes— 23 contributed by the mother and 23 by the father. The chromosomes consist of protein and DNA.

(c) Each set of chromosomes contains 25,000 to 30,000 genes carried in 3 billion nucleotide pairs of DNA.

(d) To form the chromosome, the DNA is coiled into higher and higher levels of organization.

(e) The DNA is coiled around specialized proteins that provide structure to the chromosome. These proteins also interact with the DNA.

(f) A specific sequence of nucleotide base pairs constitutes a gene.

TABLE 3-2	Standard Chromosomal Complement in Various Organisms	
Organism	Chromosome Number in Somatic Cells	Chromosome Number in Gametes
Human (*Homo sapiens*)	46	23
Chimpanzee (*Pan troglodytes*)	48	24
Gorilla (*Gorilla gorilla*)	48	24
Dog (*Canis familiaris*)	78	39
Chicken (*Gallus domesticus*)	78	39
Frog (*Rana pipiens*)	26	13
Housefly (*Musca domestica*)	12	6
Onion (*Allium cepa*)	16	8
Corn (*Zea mays*)	20	10
Tobacco (*Nicotiana tabacum*)	48	24

Source: Cummings, 1991, p. 16.

mitosis   Simple cell division; the process by which somatic cells divide to produce two identical daughter cells.

MITOSIS

Cell division in somatic cells is called **mitosis**. Mitosis occurs during growth of the individual. It also permits healing of injured tissues and replaces older cells with newer ones. In short, it's the way somatic cells reproduce.

In the early stages of mitosis, the cell contains 46 double-stranded chromosomes, which line up in random order along the center of the cell (Fig. 3–7). As the cell wall begins to constrict at the center, the chromosomes split apart at the centromere, so that the two strands are separated. Once the two strands are apart, they pull away from each other and move to opposite ends of the dividing cell. At this point, each strand is now a distinct chromosome, *composed of one DNA molecule.* Following the separation of chromosome strands, the cell wall pinches in and becomes sealed, so that two new cells are formed, each with a full complement of DNA, or 46 chromosomes.

Mitosis is referred to as "simple cell division" because a somatic cell divides one time to produce two daughter cells that are genetically identical to each other and to the original cell. In mitosis, the original cell possesses 46 chromosomes, and each new daughter cell inherits

FIGURE 3–7
Mitosis.

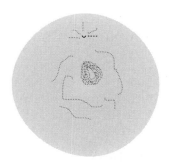
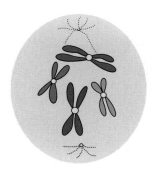
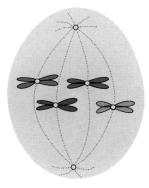

(a) The cell is involved in metabolic activities. DNA replication occurs, but chromosomes are not visible.

(b) The nuclear membrane disappears, and double-stranded chromosomes are visible.

(c) The chromosomes align themselves at the center of the cell.

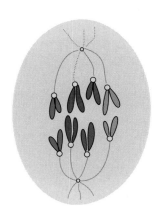

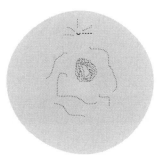
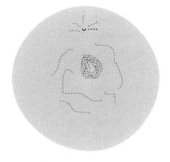

(d) The chromosomes split at the centromere, and the strands separate and move to opposite ends of the dividing cell.

(e) The cell membrane pinches in as the cell continues to divide. The chromosomes begin to uncoil (not shown here).

(f) After mitosis is complete, there are two identical daughter cells. The nuclear membrane is present, and chromosomes are no longer visible.

an exact copy of all 46. This precise arrangement is made possible by the ability of the DNA molecule to replicate. Thus, DNA replication ensures that the amount of genetic material remains constant from one generation of cells to the next.

MEIOSIS

Mitosis produces new cells, but **meiosis** may lead to the development of new individuals, since it produces reproductive cells, or gametes. Although meiosis is another form of cell division and shares some similarities with mitosis, it's a more complicated process (Fig. 3–8).

meiosis   Cell division in specialized cells in ovaries and testes. Meiosis involves two divisions and results in four daughter cells, each containing only half the original number of chromosomes. These cells can develop into gametes.

FIGURE 3–8
Meiosis.

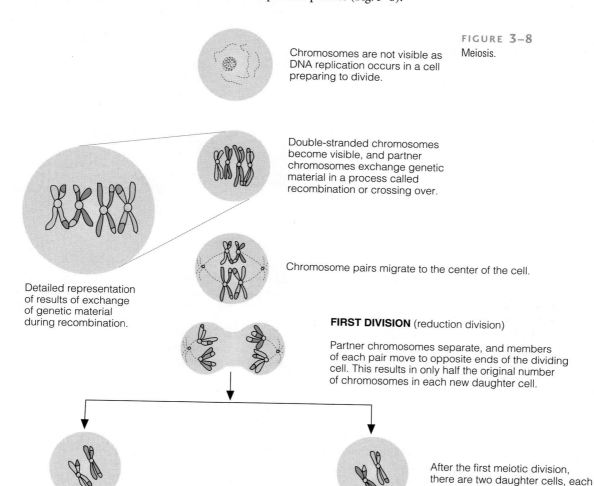

Chromosomes are not visible as DNA replication occurs in a cell preparing to divide.

Double-stranded chromosomes become visible, and partner chromosomes exchange genetic material in a process called recombination or crossing over.

Detailed representation of results of exchange of genetic material during recombination.

Chromosome pairs migrate to the center of the cell.

FIRST DIVISION (reduction division)

Partner chromosomes separate, and members of each pair move to opposite ends of the dividing cell. This results in only half the original number of chromosomes in each new daughter cell.

After the first meiotic division, there are two daughter cells, each containing only one member of each original chromosomal pair, or 23 nonpartner chromosomes.

SECOND DIVISION

In this division, the chromosomes split at the centromere, and the strands move to opposite sides of the cell.

After the second division, meiosis results in four daughter cells. These may mature to become functional gametes, containing only half the DNA in the original cell.

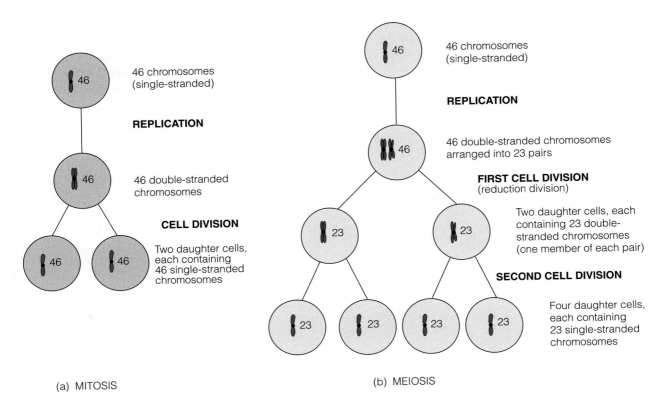

(a) MITOSIS

(b) MEIOSIS

FIGURE 3–9

Mitosis and meiosis compared. In mitosis, one division produces two daughter cells, each of which contains 46 chromosomes. Meiosis is characterized by two divisions. After the first, there are two cells, each containing only 23 chromosomes (one member of each original chromosome pair). Each daughter cell divides again, so that the final result is four cells, each with only half the original number of chromosomes.

During meiosis, specialized cells in male testes and female ovaries divide and develop, eventually to produce sperm or egg cells. Meiosis is characterized by *two divisions* that result in *four daughter cells*, each of which contains only 23 chromosomes, or half the original number.

Reduction of chromosome number is a critical feature of meiosis, because the resulting gamete, with its 23 chromosomes, may eventually unite with another gamete that also carries 23 chromosomes. The product of this union is a *zygote*, or fertilized egg, which in humans receives a total of 46 chromosomes. In other words, the zygote inherits the full complement of DNA it needs (half from each parent) to develop and function normally. If it weren't for reduction division (the first division) in meiosis, it wouldn't be possible to maintain the correct number of chromosomes from one generation to the next.

During the first division of meiosis, partner chromosomes come together to form pairs of double-stranded chromosomes. Then, the *pairs* of chromosomes line up along the cell's equator (see Fig. 3–8). Pairing of partner chromosomes is extremely important because, while they are together, members of pairs exchange genetic information in a critical process called **recombination** or *crossing over*. Pairing is also important because it facilitates the accurate reduction of chromosome number by ensuring that each new daughter cell receives only one member of each pair.

As the cell begins to divide, the chromosomes themselves remain intact (that is, double-stranded), *but members of pairs* separate and migrate to opposite ends of the cell. After the first division, there are two new daughter cells, but they aren't identical to each other or to the parental cell. They're different because each cell contains only one member of each chromosome pair and therefore only 23 chromosomes. And, all the chromosomes still have two strands (see Fig. 3–8).

The second meiotic division proceeds in much the same way as cell division in mitosis. In the two newly formed cells, the 23 double-stranded chromosomes align themselves at the cell's center, and as in mitosis, the strands of each chromosome separate at the centromere and move apart. Once this second division is completed, there are four daughter cells, each with 23 single-stranded chromosomes. (For a diagrammatic representation of the differences between mitosis and meiosis, see Fig. 3–9.)

recombination   The exchange of DNA between paired chromosomes during meiosis; also called *crossing over*.

The Evolutionary Significance of Meiosis Meiosis occurs in all sexually reproducing organisms, and it's an extremely important evolutionary innovation, since it increases genetic variation in populations at a faster rate than mutation alone can do. Individual members of sexually reproducing species aren't genetically identical **clones** of other individuals. Rather, they result from the contribution of genetic information from two parents. As a result, each individual represents a unique combination of genes that, in all likelihood, has never occurred before and will never occur again. The genetic uniqueness of individuals is further enhanced by recombination between partner chromosomes during meiosis, since recombination ensures that chromosomes aren't transmitted intact from one generation to the next. Instead, in every generation, parental contributions are reshuffled in an almost infinite number of combinations, altering the genetic composition of chromosomes even before they are passed on.

Genetic diversity is therefore considerably enhanced by meiosis. As we mentioned in Chapter 2, natural selection acts on genetic variation in populations. If all individuals in a population are genetically identical over time, then natural selection (and evolution) cannot occur. Although there are other sources of variation (mutation being the only source of *new* variation), sexual reproduction and meiosis are of major evolutionary importance because they contribute to the role of natural selection in populations.

The Genetic Principles Discovered by Mendel

It wasn't until Gregor Mendel (1822–1884) addressed the question of heredity that it began to be resolved (Fig. 3–10). Mendel was a monk living in an abbey at Brno in what is now the Czech Republic. At the time he began his research, he had already studied botany, physics, and mathematics at the University of Vienna, and he had performed various experiments in the monastery gardens. These experiments led him to explore the various ways in which physical traits, such as color or height, could be expressed in plant **hybrids**.

Mendel worked with garden peas, concentrating on seven different traits, each of which could be expressed in two different ways (Fig. 3–11). We want to emphasize that the principles Mendel discovered apply to all biological organisms, not just peas. We discuss Mendel's pea experiments only to illustrate the basic rules of inheritance.

MENDEL'S PRINCIPLE OF SEGREGATION

Mendel began by crossing parent (P) plants that produced only tall plants with others that produced only short ones (Fig. 3–12). Blending theories of inheritance would have predicted that the hybrid offspring of the initial crosses (called the F_1 plants) would be intermediate in height, but they weren't. Instead, they were all tall.

Next, he allowed the F_1 plants to self-fertilize and produce a second generation (the F_2 generation). But this time, only about 3/4 of the offspring were tall, and the remaining 1/4 were short. One expression (shortness) of the trait (height) had completely disappeared in the F_1 plants and reappeared in the second generation (the F_2 plants). Moreover, the expression that was present in all members of the F_1 generation was more common in the F_2 generation, occurring in a ratio of approximately 3:1, or three tall plants for every short one.

These results suggested that different expressions of a trait were controlled by discrete *units* or particles (we would call them genes), which occurred in pairs, and that offspring inherited one unit from each parent. Mendel realized that the members of a pair of units controlling a trait somehow separated into different sex cells and were again united with another member during fertilization of the egg. This discovery was the basis of Mendel's *first principle of inheritance*, known as the **principle of segregation**.

Today we know that meiosis explains Mendel's principle of segregation. You will remember that during meiosis, paired chromosomes, and the genes they carry, separate from each other and are distributed to different gametes. However, in the zygote, the full complement of chromosomes is restored, and both members of each chromosome pair are present in the offspring.

Raychel Ciemma and Precision Graphics

FIGURE 3–10
Portrait of Gregor Mendel.

clones Plural for clone, an organism that is genetically identical to another organism. The term may also be used to refer to genetically identical DNA segments and molecules.

hybrids Offspring of mixed ancestry; heterozygotes.

principle of segregation Genes (alleles) occur in pairs (because chromosomes occur in pairs). During gamete production, the members of each gene pair separate, so that each gamete contains one member of each pair. During fertilization, the full number of chromosomes is restored, and members of gene or allele pairs are reunited.

FIGURE 3–11
The traits Mendel studied in peas.

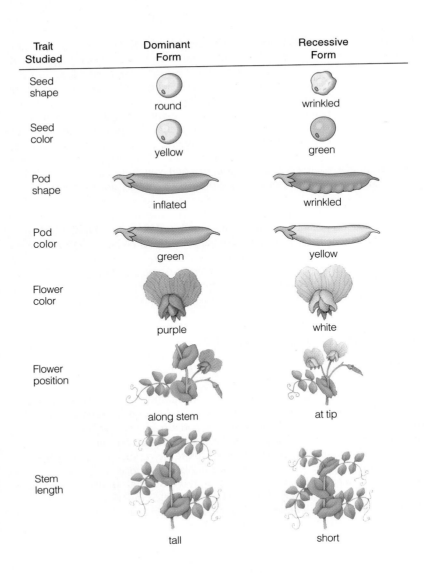

FIGURE 3–11
The traits Mendel studied in peas.

Trait Studied	Dominant Form	Recessive Form
Seed shape	round	wrinkled
Seed color	yellow	green
Pod shape	inflated	wrinkled
Pod color	green	yellow
Flower color	purple	white
Flower position	along stem	at tip
Stem length	tall	short

recessive   Describing a trait that is not expressed in heterozygotes; also refers to the allele that governs the trait. For a recessive allele to be expressed, there must be two copies of the allele (that is, the individual must be homozygous).

dominant   Describing a trait governed by an allele that can be expressed in the presence of another, different allele (that is, in heterozygotes). Dominant alleles prevent the expression of recessive alleles in heterozygotes. (This is the definition of *complete* dominance.)

locus   (*pl.,* loci) (lo´-kus, lo-sigh´) The position on a chromosome where a given gene occurs. The term is sometimes used interchangeably with *gene.*

alleles   Alternate forms of a gene. Alleles occur at the same locus on paired chromosomes and thus govern the same trait. However, because they are different, their action may result in different expressions of that trait. The term *allele* is often used synonymously with *gene.*

DOMINANCE AND RECESSIVENESS

Mendel also realized that the expression that was absent in the first generation hadn't actually disappeared at all. It had remained present, but somehow it was masked and couldn't be expressed. He described the trait that seemed to disappear as **recessive**, and he called the expressed trait **dominant**. With this fact in mind, Mendel developed the important principles of *recessiveness* and *dominance*, and they are still important concepts in the field of genetics.

As you already know, a *gene* is a segment of DNA that directs the production of a specific protein, part of a protein, or any functional element. Each gene has a specific location on a chromosome, and that position is called its **locus** (*pl.,* loci). At numerous genetic loci, however, there may be more than one possible form of the gene, and these variations of genes at specific loci are called **alleles** (Fig. 3–13). Simply stated, alleles are different versions of a gene, each of which can direct the cell to make a slightly different form of the same protein and, ultimately, a different expression of a trait.

As it turns out, plant height in garden peas is controlled by two different alleles at one genetic locus. The allele that determines that a plant will be tall is dominant to the allele for short. (It's worth mentioning that height isn't governed this way in all plants.) In Mendel's experiments, all the parent (P) plants had two copies of the same allele, either dominant or recessive, depending on whether they were tall or short. When two copies of the same allele

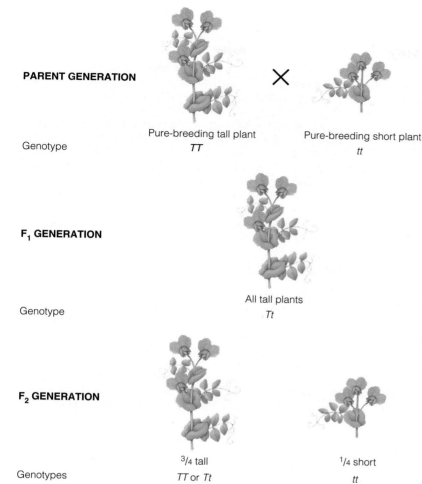

FIGURE 3–12
Results of crosses when only one trait at a time is considered.

PARENT GENERATION

Pure-breeding tall plant
TT

Pure-breeding short plant
tt

Genotype

F₁ GENERATION

All tall plants
Tt

Genotype

F₂ GENERATION

³/₄ tall
TT or *Tt*

¹/₄ short
tt

Genotypes

homozygous Having the same allele at the same locus on both members of a chromosome pair.

heterozygous Having different alleles at the same locus on members of a chromosome pair.

genotype The genetic makeup of an individual. Genotype can refer to an organism's entire genetic makeup or to the alleles at a particular locus.

FIGURE 3–13
As this diagram illustrates, alleles are located at the same locus on paired chromosomes, but they aren't always identical. For the sake of simplicity, they are shown here as single-stranded chromosomes.

Pair of homologous chromosomes, one from a male parent and its partner from a female parent

Gene locus, the location for a specific gene on a specific type of chromosome

Pair of alleles. Although they influence the same characteristic, their DNA varies slightly, so they produce somewhat different expressions of the same trait.

Three pairs of alleles (at three loci on this pair of homologous chromosomes). Note that at two loci the alleles are identical (homozygous), and at one locus they are different (heterozygous).

are present, the individual is said to be **homozygous**. Thus, all the tall parent plants were homozygous for the dominant allele, and all the short parent plants were homozygous for the recessive allele. (This explains why tall plants crossed with tall plants produced only tall offspring, and short plants crossed with short plants produced only short offspring; they were all homozygous, and they lacked genetic variation at this locus.) However, all the hybrid F₁ plants had inherited one allele from each parent plant, and therefore, they all possessed two different alleles at specific loci. Individuals that possess two different alleles at a locus are **heterozygous**.

Figure 3–12 illustrates the crosses that Mendel initially performed. Uppercase letters refer to dominant alleles (or dominant traits), and lowercase letters refer to recessive alleles (or recessive traits). Therefore,

T = the allele for tallness
t = the allele for shortness

The same symbols are combined to describe an individual's actual genetic makeup, or **genotype**. The term *genotype* can be used to refer to an organism's entire genetic makeup or to the alleles at a specific genetic locus. Thus, the genotypes of the plants in Mendel's experiments were

TT = homozygous tall plants
Tt = heterozygous tall plants
tt = homozygous short plants

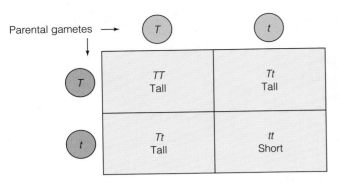

Parental gametes →

FIGURE **3–14**

Punnett square representing possible genotypes and phenotypes and their proportions in the F₂ generation. The circles across the top and at the left of the Punnett square represent the gametes of the F₁ parents. The four squares illustrate that $\frac{1}{4}$ of the F₂ plants can be expected to be homozygous tall (*TT*); another $\frac{1}{2}$ also can be expected to be tall but will be heterozygous (*Tt*); and the remaining $\frac{1}{4}$ can be expected to be short (*tt*). Thus, $\frac{3}{4}$ can be expected to be tall and $\frac{1}{4}$ to be short.

Figure 3–14 is a *Punnett square*. It represents the different ways the alleles can be combined when the F₁ plants are self-fertilized to produce an F₂ generation. In this way, the figure shows the genotypes that are possible in the F₂ generation, and it also demonstrates that approximately $\frac{1}{4}$ of the F₂ plants are homozygous dominant (*TT*); $\frac{1}{2}$ are heterozygous (*Tt*); and the remaining $\frac{1}{4}$ are homozygous recessive (*tt*).

The Punnett square also shows the proportions of F₂ **phenotypes**, or the observed physical manifestations of genes, and it illustrates why Mendel saw three tall plants for every short plant in the F₂ generation. By examining the Punnett square, you can see that $\frac{1}{4}$ of the F₂ plants will be tall because they have the *TT* genotype. An additional half of the plants, which are heterozygous (*Tt*), will also be tall because *T* is dominant to *t* and will therefore be expressed in the phenotype. The remaining $\frac{1}{4}$ are homozygous recessive (*tt*), and they will be short because no dominant allele is present. It's important to note that the *only* way a recessive allele can be expressed is if it occurs with another recessive allele—that is, if the individual is homozygous recessive at the particular locus in question.

MENDEL'S PRINCIPLE OF INDEPENDENT ASSORTMENT

Mendel also showed that traits aren't necessarily inherited together by demonstrating that plant height and seed color are independent of each other. That is, he proposed that any tall plant had a 50-50 chance of producing either yellow or green seeds (peas). This relationship, called the **principle of independent assortment**, says that the units (genes) that code for different traits assort independently of one another during gamete formation. Today we know that this happens because the genes that control plant height and seed color are located on different chromosomes, and during meiosis, the chromosomes travel to newly forming cells independently of one another. But if Mendel had used just *any* two traits, his results would have sometimes been different. For example, if the two traits in question were influenced by genes located on the same chromosome, then they would be more likely to be inherited together; and if so, they wouldn't conform to Mendel's ratios. The ratios came out as he predicted because the loci governing most of the traits he chose were carried on different chromosomes. Even though Mendel didn't know about chromosomes, he was certainly aware that all traits weren't independent of one another in the F₂ generation, so he appears to have reported only on those characteristics that did in fact illustrate independent assortment.

In 1866, Mendel's results were published, but their methodology and statistical nature were beyond the thinking of the time, and the significance of his work wasn't appreciated. However, by the end of the nineteenth century, several investigators had made important contributions to the understanding of chromosomes and cell division. These discoveries paved the way for the acceptance of Mendel's work by 1900, when three different groups of scientists came across his paper. Unfortunately, Mendel had died 16 years earlier and never saw his work substantiated.

phenotypes   The observable or detectable physical characteristics of an organism; the detectable expressions of genotypes.

principle of independent assortment   The distribution of one pair of alleles into gametes does not influence the distribution of another pair. The genes controlling different traits are inherited independently of one another.

Mendelian traits   Characteristics that are influenced by alleles at only one genetic locus. Examples include many blood types, such as ABO. Many genetic disorders, including sickle-cell anemia and Tay-Sachs disease, are also Mendelian traits.

Mendelian Inheritance in Humans

Mendelian traits (also referred to as *discrete traits* or *traits of simple inheritance*) are controlled by alleles at *one* genetic locus). The most comprehensive listing of Mendelian traits in humans is V. A. McKusick's (1998) *Mendelian Inheritance in Man*. This volume, as well as its continuously updated online version (www.ncbi.nlm.nih.gov/omim/), currently lists over 16,000 human characteristics that are inherited according to Mendelian principles.

Although some Mendelian traits have a visible phenotypic expression, most don't. Most are biochemical in nature, and many genetic disorders (some of which do produce visible phenotypic abnormalities) result from harmful alleles inherited in Mendelian fashion (Table 3–3). So if it seems like textbooks overemphasize genetic disease when they discuss Mendelian traits, it's because many of the known Mendelian characteristics are the results of harmful alleles.

TABLE 3-3	Some Mendelian Traits in Humans		

Dominant Traits		Recessive Traits	
Condition	Manifestations	Condition	Manifestations
Achondroplasia	Dwarfism due to growth defects involving the long bones of the arms and legs; trunk and head size usually normal.	Cystic fibrosis	Among the most common genetic (Mendelian) disorders among European Americans; abnormal secretions of the exocrine glands, with pronounced involvement of the pancreas; most patients develop obstructive lung disease. Until the recent development of new treatments, only about half of all patients survived to early adulthood.
Brachydactyly	Shortened fingers and toes.		
Familial hyper-cholesterolemia	Elevated cholesterol levels and cholesterol plaque deposition; a leading cause of heart disease, with death frequently occurring by middle age.		
		Tay-Sachs disease	Most common among Ashkenazi Jews; degeneration of the nervous system beginning at about 6 months of age; lethal by age 2 or 3 years.
Neurofibromatosis	Symptoms range from the appearance of abnormal skin pigmentation to large tumors resulting in gross deformities; can, in extreme cases, lead to paralysis, blindness, and death.	Phenylketonuria (PKU)	Inability to metabolize the amino acid phenylalanine; results in mental retardation if left untreated during childhood; treatment involves strict dietary management and some supplementation.
Marfan syndrome	The eyes and cardiovascular and skeletal systems are affected; symptoms include greater than average height, long arms and legs, eye problems, and enlargement of the aorta; death due to rupture of the aorta is common. (Abraham Lincoln may have had Marfan syndrome.)	Albinism	Inability to produce normal amounts of the pigment melanin; results in very fair, untannable skin, light blond hair, and light eyes; may also be associated with vision problems. (Albinism can have different forms.)
Huntington disease	Progressive degeneration of the nervous system accompanied by dementia and seizures; age of onset variable but commonly between 30 and 40 years.	Sickle-cell anemia	Caused by an abnormal form of hemoglobin (HbS) that results in collapsed red blood cells, blockage of capillaries, reduced blood flow to organs, and, without treatment, death.
Camptodactyly	Malformation of the hands whereby the fingers, usually the little finger, is permanently contracted.		
Hypodontia of upper lateral incisors	Upper lateral incisors are absent or only partially formed (peg-shaped). Pegged incisors are a partial expression of the allele.	Thalassemia	A group of disorders characterized by reduced or absent alpha or beta chains in the hemoglobin molecule; results in severe anemia and, in some forms, death.
Cleft chin	Dimple or depression in the middle of the chin; less prominent in females than males.	Absence of permanent dentition	Failure of the permanent dentition to erupt. The primary dentition is not affected.
PTC tasting	The ability to taste the bitter substance phenylthiocarbamide (PTC). Tasting thresholds vary, suggesting that alleles at another locus may also exert an influence.		

TABLE 3–4	ABO Genotypes and Associated Phenotypes	
Genotype	**Antigens on Red Blood Cells**	**ABO Blood Type (Phenotype)**
AA, AO	A	A
BB, BO	B	B
AB	A and B	AB
OO	None	O

The blood groups, like the ABO system, provide some of the best examples of Mendelian traits in humans. The ABO system is governed by three alleles, *A*, *B*, and *O*, found at the ABO locus on the ninth chromosome. Although three alleles are present in populations, an individual can possess only two. These alleles determine which ABO blood type a person has by coding for the production of special substances, called **antigens**, on the surface of red blood cells. If only antigen A is present, the blood type (phenotype) is A; if only B is present, the blood type is B; if both are present, the blood type is AB; and when neither is present, the blood type is O (Table 3–4).

Dominance and recessiveness are clearly illustrated by the ABO system. The *O* allele is recessive to both *A* and *B*; therefore, if a person has type O blood, he or she must be homozygous (*OO*) for the *O* allele. Since both *A* and *B* are dominant to *O*, an individual with blood type A can have one of two genotypes: *AA* or *AO*. The same is true of type B, which results from the genotypes *BB* and *BO*. However, type AB presents a slightly different situation and is an example of **codominance**.

Codominance is seen when two different alleles occur in heterozygotes, but instead of one having the ability to mask the expression of the other, the products of *both* are expressed in the phenotype. So, when both *A* and *B* alleles are present, both A and B antigens can be detected on the surface of red blood cells and the blood type is AB.

Some genetic disorders are inherited as dominant traits (see Table 3–3). This means that if a person inherits only one copy of a harmful dominant allele, the condition it causes will be present, regardless of the existence of a different, recessive allele on the corresponding chromosome.

Recessive conditions (see Table 3–3) are commonly associated with the lack of a substance, usually an enzyme. For a person actually to have a recessive disorder, he or she must have *two* copies of the recessive allele that causes it. Heterozygotes who have only one copy of a harmful recessive allele are unaffected, but they're sometimes called carriers.

Although carriers don't actually have the recessive condition they carry, they can pass the allele that causes it to their children. (Remember, half their gametes will carry the recessive allele.) If the carrier's mate is also a carrier, then it's possible for them to have a child who has two copies of the allele, and that child will be affected. In fact, in a mating between two carriers, the risk of having an affected child is 25 percent (see Fig. 3–14).

Misconceptions Regarding Dominance and Recessiveness

Traditional methods of teaching genetics have led to some misunderstanding of dominance and recessiveness. Thus, virtually all introductory students (and most people in general) have the impression that these phenomena are all-or-nothing situations. This misconception especially pertains to recessive alleles, and the general view is that when these alleles occur in heterozygotes (that is, carriers), they have absolutely no effect on the phenotype. Certainly, this is how it appeared to Gregor Mendel, and until the last two or three decades, to most geneticists.

antigens   Large molecules found on the surface of cells. Several different loci governing antigens on red and white blood cells are known. (Foreign antigens provoke an immune response in individuals.)

codominance   The expression of two alleles in heterozygotes. In this situation, neither is dominant or recessive, so that both influence the phenotype.

However, modern biochemical techniques have shown that recessive alleles actually do have some effect on the phenotype, although these effects aren't always apparent through simple observation. It turns out that in heterozygotes, many recessive alleles act to reduce, but not eliminate, the gene products they influence. In fact, it's now clear that our *perception* of recessive alleles greatly depends on whether we examine them at the directly observable phenotypic level or the biochemical level.

Scientists now know of several recessive alleles that produce phenotypic effects in heterozygotes. Consider Tay-Sachs disease, a lethal condition that results from the inability to produce an enzyme called hexosaminidase A (see Table 3–3). This inability, seen in people who are homozygous for a recessive allele (*ts*), invariably results in death by early childhood. Carriers don't have the disease, and practically speaking, they aren't affected. However, in 1979 it was shown that Tay-Sachs carriers, although functionally normal, have only about 40 to 60 percent of the amount of the enzyme seen in normal people. In fact, there are now voluntary tests to screen carriers in populations at risk for Tay-Sachs disease.

Similar misconceptions also relate to dominant alleles. Most people see dominant alleles as somehow "stronger" or "better," and there is always the mistaken notion that dominant alleles are more common in populations. These misconceptions undoubtedly stem from the label "dominant" and some of its connotations. But in genetic usage, those connotations are misleading. If dominant alleles were always more common, then a majority of people would have such conditions as achondroplasia and Marfan syndrome (see Table 3–3). But, as you know, most people don't.

As you can see, the relationships between recessive and dominant alleles and their functions are more complicated than they first appear to be. Previously held views of dominance and recessiveness were guided by available technologies. And, as genetic technologies continue to change, new theories will emerge—and, as they do, our perceptions will be further altered. Therefore, it's entirely possible that one day the concepts of dominance and recessiveness, as they have traditionally been taught, will be obsolete.

Polygenic Inheritance

Mendelian traits are said to be *discrete*, or *discontinuous*, because their phenotypic expressions don't overlap; instead, they fall into clearly defined categories (Fig. 3–15a). For example, Mendel's pea plants were either short or tall, but none was intermediate in height. In the ABO system, the four phenotypes are completely distinct from one another; that is, there is no

FIGURE **3–15**

(a) This histogram shows the discontinuous distribution of a Mendelian trait (ABO blood type) in a hypothetical population. The expression of the trait is described in terms of frequencies. (b) This histogram represents the continuous expression of a polygenic trait (height) in a large group of people. Note that the percentage of extremely short or tall individuals is low; the majority of people are closer to the mean (or average) height, represented by the vertical line at the center of the distribution.

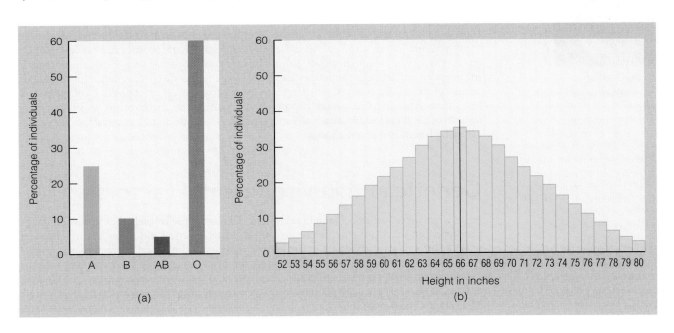

(a)

(b)

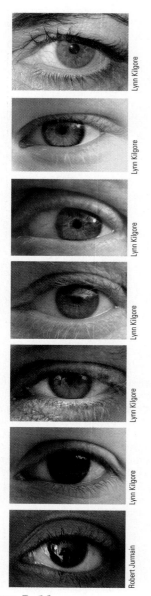

Lynn Kilgore

Lynn Kilgore

Lynn Kilgore

Lynn Kilgore

Lynn Kilgore

Lynn Kilgore

Robert Jurmain

FIGURE 3–16

Examples of the continuous variation seen in human eye color.

intermediate form between type A and type B to represent a gradation between the two. In other words, Mendelian traits don't show *continuous* variation.

However, many traits do have a wide range of phenotypic expressions that form a graded series. These are called **polygenic**, or *continuous*, traits (Fig. 3–15b). While Mendelian traits are governed by only one genetic locus, polygenic characteristics are governed by two or more loci, with each locus making a contribution to the phenotype. For example, one of the most frequently cited examples of polygenic inheritance in humans is skin color, and the single most important factor influencing skin color is the amount of the pigment melanin that is present.

Melanin production is believed to be influenced by between three and six genetic loci, with each locus having at least two alleles, neither of which is dominant. There are perhaps six loci and at least 12 alleles, so there are many ways in which these alleles can combine in individuals. A person who inherits mostly reduced-pigmentation alleles will have lighter skin color, while someone who has mostly darker-pigmentation alleles will be darker. So, human skin color varies because in this system, as in some other polygenic systems, there is an *additive effect*. Each allele that codes for melanin production makes a contribution to increased melanization (although for some characteristics, the contributions of the alleles are not all equal). Likewise, each allele coding for less melanin production contributes to reduced pigmentation. So, the effect of multiple alleles at several loci is to produce continuous variation from very dark to very fair skin within the species. (Skin color is also discussed in Chapter 4.)

Polygenic traits actually account for most of the readily observable phenotypic variation seen in humans, and they have traditionally served as a basis for racial classification (see Chapter 4). In addition to skin color, polygenic inheritance in humans is seen in hair color, weight, stature, eye color (Fig. 3–16), shape of face, shape of nose, and fingerprint pattern. Because they exhibit continuous variation, most polygenic traits can be measured on a scale made up of equal increments (see Fig. 3–15b). For example, height (stature) is measured in feet and inches (or meters and centimeters). If we were to measure height in a large number of individuals, the distribution of measurements would continue uninterrupted from the shortest extreme to the tallest. That's what is meant by the term *continuous traits*.

Because polygenic traits usually lend themselves to metric analysis, biologists, geneticists, and physical anthropologists treat them statistically. (Incidentally, *all* physical traits measured and discussed in fossils are polygenic.) By using simple summary statistics, such as the *mean* (average) or *standard deviation* (a measure of variation within a group), scientists can create basic descriptions of, and make comparisons between, populations. For example, a researcher might be interested in average height in two different populations and whether any differences between the two are significant, and if so, why. However, the types of statistical tests that would be used in such a study can't be used to examine Mendelian traits, because those traits can't be measured in the same way. They are either present or they aren't. Or, they're expressed one way or another. Nevertheless, Mendelian characteristics can be described in terms of frequency within populations, and this permits between-group comparisons regarding prevalence. Mendelian traits can also be analyzed for mode of inheritance (dominant or recessive). Finally, for many Mendelian traits, the approximate or exact positions of genes have been identified, and this makes it possible to examine the mechanisms and patterns of inheritance at these loci. Because polygenic characters are influenced by several loci, they can't, as yet, be traced to a specific locus.

Genetic and Environmental Factors

From what we've just said, it might seem that the phenotype is solely the expression of the genotype, but that's not true. (Here we use the terms *genotype* and *phenotype* in a broader sense to refer to an individual's entire genetic makeup and physical characteristics, respectively.) The genotype sets limits and potentials for development, but it also interacts with the environment, so this genetic-environmental interaction influences many aspects of the phenotype. However, it's usually not possible to identify which specific environmental factors are affecting the phenotype.

polygenic   Referring to traits that are influenced by genes at two or more loci. Examples of such traits are stature, skin color, and eye color. Many polygenic traits are also influenced by environmental factors.

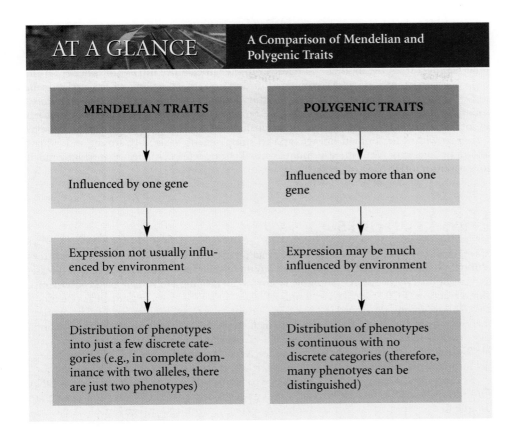

AT A GLANCE A Comparison of Mendelian and Polygenic Traits

MENDELIAN TRAITS	POLYGENIC TRAITS
Influenced by one gene	Influenced by more than one gene
Expression not usually influenced by environment	Expression may be much influenced by environment
Distribution of phenotypes into just a few discrete categories (e.g., in complete dominance with two alleles, there are just two phenotypes)	Distribution of phenotypes is continuous with no discrete categories (therefore, many phenotyes can be distinguished)

Many polygenic traits are obviously influenced by environmental factors. Adult height, for example, is strongly affected by the quality of an individual's diet (that is, nutrition) during growth and development. Other important environmental factors that affect various phenotypes include exposure to sunlight, altitude, temperature, and, unfortunately, increasing levels of exposure to toxic waste and airborne pollutants. All these, and many more, contribute in complex ways to the continuous phenotypic variation seen in characteristics governed by multiple loci.

Mendelian traits are less likely to be influenced by environmental factors. For example, ABO blood type is determined at fertilization and remains fixed throughout the individual's lifetime, regardless of diet, exposure to ultraviolet radiation, temperature, and so forth.

Mendelian and polygenic inheritance produce different kinds of phenotypic variation. In the former, variation occurs in discrete categories, while in the latter, it's continuous. However, it's important to understand that even for polygenic characteristics, Mendelian principles still apply at individual loci. In other words, if a trait is influenced by genes at seven loci, each one of those loci may have two or more alleles, with one perhaps being dominant to the other or with the alleles being codominant. It's the combined action of the alleles at all seven loci, interacting with the environment, that results in observable phenotypic expression.

Mitochondrial Inheritance

Another component of inheritance involves cellular organelles called **mitochondria**. All cells contain hundreds of these oval-shaped structures that convert energy (derived from the breakdown of nutrients) into a form that can be used by the cell.

Each mitochondrion contains several copies of a DNA molecule. While **mitochondrial DNA (mtDNA)** is distinct from the DNA found within cell nuclei, its molecular structure and

mitochondria (*sing.*, mitochondrion) (my´-tow-kond´-dree-uh) Structures contained within the cytoplasm of eukaryotic cells that convert energy, derived from nutrients, into a form that is used by the cell.

mitochondrial DNA (mtDNA) DNA found in the mitochondria that is inherited only through the maternal line.

functions are the same. The entire molecule has been sequenced and is known to contain around 40 genes that direct the conversion of energy within the cell.

Like nuclear DNA, mtDNA is subject to mutations; but unlike nuclear DNA, mtDNA is inherited only from the mother and never from the father. Since mtDNA is inherited from only one parent, meiosis and recombination don't occur. Therefore, all the variation in mtDNA between individuals is the result of mutation alone, which makes mtDNA extremely useful for studying genetic change over time. So far, geneticists have used rates of mutation in mtDNA to investigate evolutionary relationships between species, to trace ancestral relationships within the human lineage, and to study genetic variability among individuals and/or populations. While these techniques are still being refined, it's clear that we have much to learn from mtDNA.

New Frontiers

Since the discovery of DNA structure and function in the 1950s, the field of genetics has revolutionized biological science and reshaped our understanding of inheritance, genetic disease, and evolutionary processes. For example, scientists can now use a technique called **polymerase chain reaction (PCR)** to make thousands of copies of a DNA sample as small as one molecule. This technique, developed in 1986, is important since DNA samples obtained from crime scenes or from fossils are frequently too small to permit a reliable analysis of nucleotide sequences. Using PCR, scientists have been able to examine nucleotide sequences in, for example, Neandertal fossils and Egyptian mummies. As you can imagine, PCR has limitless potential for many disciplines, including forensic science, medicine, and evolutionary biology.

By examining multiplied DNA samples, provided by PCR, scientists can identify DNA *fingerprints*, so called because they appear as patterns of repeated DNA sequences that are unique to each individual. For example, one person might have a segment of six bases—such as ATTCTA—repeated three times, and another might have the same segment repeated ten times. DNA fingerprinting is perhaps the most powerful tool available for human identification (Fig. 3–17). Scientists have used it to identify hundreds of unidentified remains, including members of the Russian royal family who were murdered in 1918 as well as victims of the terrorist attacks on September 11, 2001. The technique has also been used to exonerate innocent people who were wrongly convicted of crimes and even imprisoned for years.

Over the last two decades, using the techniques of recombinant DNA, scientists have been able to transfer genes from the cells of one species into those of another. The most common method has been to insert genes that direct the production of various proteins into bacterial cells. The altered bacteria can then produce human gene products such as insulin. For example, until the early 1980s, diabetic patients had to rely on insulin derived from nonhuman animals. However, this insulin wasn't plentiful, and some patients developed allergies to it. But since 1982, abundant supplies of human insulin, produced by bacteria, have been available; and bacteria-derived insulin doesn't cause allergic reactions.

In recent years, genetic manipulation has become increasingly controversial owing to questions related to product safety, environmental concerns, and animal welfare, among others. For example, the insertion of bacterial DNA into certain crops has made them toxic to leaf-eating insects, which reduces the need for pesticide use. And cattle and pigs are commonly treated with genetically engineered growth hormones to increase growth rates. Although there isn't any current evidence that humans are susceptible to the insect-repelling bacterium or adversely affected by the consumption of meat and dairy products from animals treated with growth hormone, there are concerns over the unknown effects of such long-term exposure.

But regardless of how controversial these new techniques may be, **cloning** is one of the most hotly debated issues. In 1997, a sheep clone named Dolly became famous worldwide because of innovative techniques used to produce her (Wilmut et al., 1997). But cloning isn't as new as you might think. Anyone who has ever taken a cutting from a plant and rooted it to grow a new plant has produced a clone. Cloning does have many useful applications, including allowing animal breeders to better control how traits are expressed in livestock. Objections to cloning are raised because many people fear that some individuals will clone loved ones or even themselves, and they consider this to be unethical. And antiabortion groups are partic-

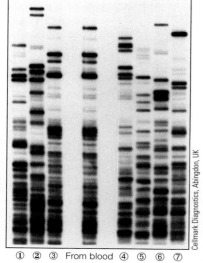

① ② ③ From blood ④ ⑤ ⑥ ⑦
at crime
scene

Cellmark Diagnostics, Abingdon, UK

FIGURE 3–17

Eight DNA fingerprints, one of which is from a blood sample left at an actual crime scene. The other seven are from suspects. By comparing the banding patterns, it's easy to identify the guilty person.

polymerase chain reaction (PCR)
A method of producing copies of a DNA segment using the enzyme DNA polymerase.

cloning The process of producing a clone.

ularly opposed to the cloning of human embryos for use in research. The list of cloned mammals now includes mice, rats, rabbits, a cat, a dog, a horse, sheep, cattle, and a mule. Primates have been difficult to clone, although two groups of scientists have successfully produced clones of monkey embryos. But, as of this writing, no live birth of any primate has resulted from cloning. No one knows how successful cloning may be. Studies have yet to show whether cloned animals live out their normal life span, but some evidence in mice suggests that they don't. And, Dolly was euthanized at the age of 6 after developing health problems.

As exciting as these innovations are, probably the single most important advance in genetics has been the sequencing of the human **genome**, which consists of some 3 billion bases comprising approximately 30,000 to 40,000 genes. This project was completed in 2003 by an international effort called the **Human Genome Project**. But scientists are still several years away from sorting out which DNA segments operate as functional genes and which don't. It will also be years before we know the identity and function of many of the proteins produced by newly identified genes. In other words, it's one thing to know the chemical makeup of a gene, but quite another to know what that gene does. Nevertheless, the magnitude and importance of the achievement can't be overstated, because it will ultimately transform biomedical and pharmaceutical research, and it will change forever how doctors diagnose and treat many human diseases.

Meanwhile, as scientists were sequencing human genes, the genomes of other organisms were also being studied. As of late 2004, the genomes of over 600 species, including mice and dogs, had been sequenced. In September 2005, the Chimpanzee Sequencing and Analysis Consortium announced the completion of a draft of the chimpanzee genome. This is particularly important because it's now possible to directly compare the human and chimpanzee genomes. Also, the sequencing of the gorilla, orangutan, and rhesus macaque genomes is under way. We already know that about 98 percent of human and chimpanzee DNA is the same and that humans also share genes with other species (68 percent with mice, for example). Just what these similarities (and the differences) mean isn't yet known, but comparative genome research is absolutely crucial for studies of evolutionary relationships among species. Scientists hope that through comparative genomics, they will finally be able to identify the genetic changes that occurred in the human lineage and in turn led to the differences between ourselves and other species. Given the potential for this research, it's no exaggeration to say that this is the most exciting time in the history of evolutionary biology since Darwin published *On the Origin of Species*.

Modern Evolutionary Theory

By the beginning of the twentieth century, the foundations for evolutionary theory had already been developed. Darwin and Wallace had described natural selection 40 years earlier, and the rediscovery of Mendelian genetics in 1900 contributed the other major component—a mechanism for inheritance. We might expect that these two basic contributions would have been combined into a consistent theory of evolution, but they weren't. For the first 30 years of the twentieth century, some scientists argued that mutation was the main factor in evolution, while others emphasized natural selection. What they really needed was a merger of both views (not an either-or situation), but that didn't happen until the mid-1930s.

THE MODERN SYNTHESIS

In the 1920s and early 1930s, biologists realized that mutation and natural selection weren't opposing processes and that both actually contributed to biological evolution. The two major foundations of the biological sciences had thus been brought together in what a scientist named Julian Huxley called the Modern Synthesis. From such a "modern" (that is, the middle of the twentieth century onward) perspective, we define evolution as a two-stage process:

1. The production and redistribution of **variation** (inherited differences among organisms)
2. *Natural selection* acting on this variation, whereby inherited differences, or variation, among individuals differentially affect their ability to successfully reproduce

genome   The entire genetic makeup of an individual or species. In humans, it is estimated that each person possesses approximately 3 billion DNA nucleotides.

Human Genome Project   An international effort aimed at sequencing and mapping the entire human genome.

variation   (genetic) Inherited differences among individuals; the basis of all evolutionary change.

A CURRENT DEFINITION OF EVOLUTION

As we discussed in Chapter 2, Darwin saw **evolution** as the gradual unfolding of new varieties of life from previous forms over long periods of time. And this is indeed one result of the evolutionary process. But these long-term effects can come about only through the accumulation of many small genetic changes occurring over generations; and today, we can show how evolution works by examining some of these intergenerational genetic changes. And, from this modern genetic perspective, we define *evolution* as a change in **allele frequency** from one generation to the next.

Allele frequencies are indicators of the genetic makeup of an interbreeding group of individuals known as a **population**. To show how allele frequencies change, we'll use a simplified example of an inherited characteristic, again the ABO blood groups (see p. 52). (*Note:* In addition to ABO, several other blood type systems are controlled by many other loci.)

Let's assume that the students in your anthropology class represent a population, an interbreeding group of individuals, and that we've determined the ABO blood type of each member. (To be considered a population, individuals must choose mates more often from *within* the group than from outside it. Obviously, your class won't meet this requirement, but we'll overlook this point for now.) The proportions of the *A*, *B*, and *O* alleles are the allele frequencies for this trait. Therefore, if 50 percent of all the ABO alleles in your class are *A*, 40 percent are *B*, and 10 percent are *O*, then the frequencies of these alleles are *A* = .50, *B* = .40, and *O* = .10.

Since the frequencies for these alleles represent only proportions of a total, it's obvious that allele frequencies can refer only to groups of individuals—that is, populations. Individuals don't have allele frequencies; they have either *A*, *B*, or *O* in any combination of two. Also, from conception onward, a person's genetic composition is fixed. If you start out with blood type A, you'll always have type A. Therefore, only a population can evolve over time; individuals can't.

Assume that 25 years from now, we calculate the frequencies of the ABO alleles for the children of our classroom population and find the following: *A* = .30, *B* = .40, and *O* = .30. We can see that the relative proportions have changed: *A* has decreased, *O* has increased, and *B* has remained the same. This wouldn't really be a big deal, but in a biological sense, these kinds of apparently minor changes constitute evolution. Over the short span of just a few generations, such changes in inherited traits may be very small; but if they continue to happen, and particularly if they go in one direction as a result of natural selection, they can produce new adaptation and even new species.

Whether we're talking about the short-term effects (as in our classroom population) from one generation to the next, which is sometimes called **microevolution**, or the long-term effects through time, called speciation or **macroevolution**, the basic evolutionary mechanisms are similar. But how do allele frequencies change? Or, to put it another way, what causes evolution? As we've already seen, evolution is a two-stage process. Genetic variation must first be produced by mutation, and then it can be acted on by natural selection.

evolution   (modern genetic definition) A change in the frequency of alleles from one generation to the next.

allele frequency   In a population, the percentage of all the alleles at a locus accounted for by one specific allele.

population   Within a species, a community of individuals where mates are usually found.

microevolution   Small changes occurring within species, such as a change in allele frequencies.

macroevolution   Changes produced only after many generations, such as the appearance of a new species.

Factors That Produce and Redistribute Variation

We've emphasized the importance of genetic variation to the process of evolution and pointed out that mutation is the only source of new variation, because when a gene is changed, a new allele is produced. We've also mentioned natural selection several times. But, in order to really understand how evolution works, we need to consider these two factors in greater detail; and we also have to consider a few other mechanisms that contribute to the process.

MUTATION

You've already learned that a change in DNA is one kind of mutation. Many genes can occur in one of several alternative forms, which we've defined as alleles (*A*, *B*, or *O*, for example). If one allele changes to another—that is, if the gene itself is altered—a mutation has occurred.

In fact, alleles are the results of mutation. Even the substitution of one single DNA base for another, called a *point mutation*, can cause the allele to change. But point mutations have to occur in sex cells if they're going to be important to the evolutionary process. This is because evolution is a change in allele frequencies *between* generations and mutations that occur in somatic cells, but not in gametes, aren't passed on to offspring. If, however, a genetic change occurs in the sperm or egg of one of the students in our classroom (*A* mutates to *B*, for instance), the offspring's blood type will be different from that of the parent, causing a minute shift in the allele frequencies of the next generation.

Actually, it would be rare to see evolution occurring by mutation alone, except in microorganisms. Mutation rates for any given trait are usually low, so we wouldn't really expect to see a mutation at the ABO locus in so small a population as your class. In larger populations, mutations might be observed in, say, 1 individual out of 10,000; but by themselves, the mutations wouldn't affect allele frequencies. However, when mutation is combined with natural selection, evolutionary changes not only can occur, they can occur more rapidly.

It's important to remember that mutation is the basic creative force in evolution, since it's the *only* way to produce *new* genes (that is, variation). Its role in the production of variation is the key to the first stage of the evolutionary process.

GENE FLOW

Gene flow is the exchange of genes between populations. The term *migration* is also frequently used; but strictly speaking, migration means movement of people, whereas gene flow refers to the exchange of *genes* between groups, and this can happen only if the migrants interbreed. Also, even if individuals move temporarily and mate in a new population (thus leaving a genetic contribution), they don't necessarily remain in the population. For example, the offspring of U.S. soldiers and Vietnamese women (born during the Vietnam War) represent gene flow, even though the fathers returned to their native population.

Population movements (particularly in the last 500 years) have reached unprecedented levels, and few breeding isolates remain. Although not at current levels, significant population movements also occurred in the past. Migration between populations has been a consistent feature of hominid evolution since the first dispersal of our genus, and gene flow between populations (even though sometimes limited) helps explain why, in the last million years, speciation has been rare.

An interesting example of how gene flow influences microevolutionary changes in modern human populations is seen in African Americans. African Americans in the United States are largely of West African descent, but there has also been considerable genetic admixture with European Americans. By measuring allele frequencies for specific genetic loci, we can estimate the amount of migration of European alleles into the African American **gene pool**. Data from northern and western U.S. cities (including New York, Detroit, and Oakland) have shown the migration rate (that is, the proportion of *non*-African genes in the African American gene pool) at 20 to 25 percent (Cummings, 2000). However, more restricted data from the southern United States (Charleston and rural Georgia) have suggested a lower degree of gene flow (4 to 11 percent).

Gene flow doesn't require large-scale movements of entire groups. In fact, significant changes in allele frequencies can come about through long-term patterns of mate selection whereby members of a group obtain mates from one or more other groups. If mate exchange consistently moves in one direction (for example, village A obtains mates from village B, but not vice versa) over a long period of time, allele frequencies in village A will eventually change.

GENETIC DRIFT AND FOUNDER EFFECT

Genetic drift is the random factor in evolution, and it's directly related to population size. *Drift occurs because the population is small.* If an allele is rare in a population comprised of, say, a few hundred individuals, then there is a chance it simply may not be passed on to offspring. In this type of situation, such an allele can eventually disappear altogether from the population (Fig. 3–18a). This may seem like a minor thing, but in effect, genetic variability in this population has been reduced.

gene flow   Exchange of genes between populations.

gene pool   The total complement of genes shared by the reproductive members of a population.

genetic drift   Evolutionary changes—that is, changes in allele frequencies—produced by random factors. Genetic drift is a result of small population size.

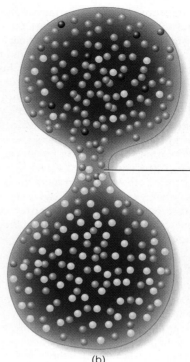

Time

A small population with considerable genetic variability. Note that the dark green and blue alleles are less common than the other alleles.

After just a few generations, the population is approximately the same size but genetic variation has been reduced. Both the dark green and blue alleles have been lost. Also, the red allele is less common and the frequency of the light green allele has increased.

(a)

Original population with considerable genetic variation

A small group leaves to colonize a new area, or a bottleneck occurs, so that population size decreases and genetic variation is reduced.

Population size restored but the dark green and purple alleles have been lost. The frequencies of the red and yellow alleles have also changed.

(b)

FIGURE 3–18
Small populations are subject to genetic drift where rare alleles can be lost because, just by chance, they weren't passed to offspring. Also, although more common alleles may not be lost, their frequencies may change for the same reason. The first diagram (a) represents 6 alleles (different colored dots) that occur at one genetic locus in a small population. You can see that, in a fairly short peiod of time, e.g., 3 or 4 generations, rare alleles can be lost and genetic diversity is consequently reduced. The second diagram (b) is an illustration of founder effect, a form of genetic drift, where diversity is lost because a large population is drastically reduced in size and it consequently passes through a genetic "bottleneck." Those individuals that survive, and the alleles they carry, represent only a sample of the variation that was present in the original population. And, future generations, all descended from the survivors (founders) will therefore have less variability.

One particular kind of genetic drift is called **founder effect**, and we can see its results today in many modern human and nonhuman populations. Founder effect can occur when a small migrant band of "founders" leaves its parent group and forms a new colony somewhere else. Over time, a new population will be established, and as long as mates are chosen only from within this population, all of its members will be descended from the small group of founders. In effect, all the genes in the expanding group will have come from a few original colonists. In such a case, an allele that was rare in the founders' parent population, but that is carried by even one of the founders, can eventually become common in succeeding generations. This is because a high proportion of members of later generations are all descended from that one founder (Fig. 3–18b).

Colonization isn't the only way founder effect can happen. Small founding groups may consist of a few survivors of a large group that, at some time in the past, was decimated by famine, war, disease, or some other disaster. The small founder population (the survivors) possesses only a sample of all the alleles that were present in the original group. Just by chance alone, some alleles may be completely removed from the gene pool. Other alleles may become the only allele at a locus that previously had two or more. Whatever the cause, the outcome is a reduction of genetic diversity, and the allele frequencies of succeeding generations may be substantially different from those of the original large population. The loss of genetic diversity in this type of situation is called a *genetic bottleneck,* and its effects can be very detrimental to a species (Fig. 3–18b).

There are many known examples of species or populations that have passed through genetic bottlenecks. Genetically, cheetahs (Fig. 3–19) are an extremely uniform species, and

founder effect   A type of genetic drift in which allele frequencies are altered in small populations that are taken from, or are remnants of, larger populations.

biologists believe that at some point in the past, these magnificent cats suffered a catastrophic decline in numbers. For reasons we don't know, but that are related to the species-wide loss of numerous alleles, male cheetahs produce a high percentage of defective sperm compared to other cat species.

Decreased reproductive potential, greatly reduced genetic diversity, and other factors (including human hunting) have combined to jeopardize the continued existence of this species. Other examples include California elephant seals, sea otters, and condors. Indeed, our own species is genetically uniform, compared to chimpanzees, and it appears that all modern human populations are the descendants of a few small groups (see Chapter 12).

Many examples of founder effect in human populations have been documented in small, usually isolated populations (for example, island groups or small agricultural villages in New Guinea or South America). Even larger populations that are descended from fairly small groups of founders can show the effects of genetic drift many generations later. For example, French Canadians in Quebec, who currently number close to 6 million, are all descended from about 8,500 founders who left France during the sixteenth and seventeenth centuries. Because the genes carried by the initial founders represented only a sample of the gene pool from which they were derived, just by chance a number of alleles now occur in different frequencies from those of the current population of France. These differences include an increased presence of several harmful alleles (see Table 3–3), including cystic fibrosis, a variety of Tay-Sachs, thalassemia, and PKU (Scriver, 2001).

In small populations, drift plays a major evolutionary role because fairly sudden fluctuations in allele frequency occur solely because of small population size. Throughout much of human evolution (at least the last 4 to 5 million years), hominids probably lived in small groups, and drift would have had significant impact.

While drift has caused evolutionary change in certain circumstances, the effects have been irregular and nondirectional. (Remember, drift is *random* in nature.) Certainly, the pace of evolutionary change could have been accelerated if many small populations were isolated and thus subject to drift. By modifying the genetic makeup of such populations, drift can provide significantly greater opportunities for natural selection, the only truly directional force in evolution.

As we've seen, both gene flow and genetic drift can produce some evolutionary changes by themselves. However, these changes are usually *microevolutionary* ones; that is, they produce changes within species over the short term. To have the kind of evolutionary changes that ultimately result in entire new groups (for example, the diversification of the first primates or the appearance of the hominids), natural selection would be necessary. But natural selection can't operate independently of the other evolutionary factors—mutation, gene flow, and genetic drift.

RECOMBINATION

As we saw earlier in this chapter, in sexually reproducing species both parents contribute genes to offspring. Thus, the genetic information is reshuffled every generation. By itself, recombination doesn't change allele frequencies (that is, cause evolution). However, it does produce different combinations of genes that natural selection may be able to act on. In fact, the reshuffling of chromosomes during meiosis can produce literally trillions of gene combinations, making every human being genetically unique.

Natural Selection Acts on Variation

The evolutionary factors just discussed—mutation, gene flow, genetic drift, and recombination—interact to produce variation and to distribute genes within and between populations. But there is no long-term *direction* to any of these factors. So how do populations adapt? The answer is natural selection. Natural selection provides directional change in allele frequency relative to *specific environmental factors*. As we've already seen, if the environment changes, then the selection pressures also change. Such a functional shift in allele frequencies is what we mean by *adaptation*. If there are long-term environmental changes in a consistent direction, then

FIGURE 3–19

Cheetahs, like many other species, have passed through a genetic bottleneck. Consequently, as a species they have little genetic variation.

TABLE 3–5   Levels of Organization in the Evolutionary Process

Evolutionary Factor	Level	Evolutionary Process	Technique of Study
Mutation	DNA	Storage of genetic information; ability to replicate; influences phenotype by production of proteins	Biochemistry, electron microscope, recombinant DNA
Mutation	Chromosomes	A vehicle for packaging and transmitting genetic material (DNA)	Light or electron microscope
Recombination (sex cells only)	Cell	The basic unit of life that contains the chromosomes and divides for growth and for production of sex cells	Light or electron microscope
Natural selection	Organism	The unit, composed of cells, that reproduces and which we observe for phenotypic traits	Visual study, biochemistry
Drift, gene flow	Population	A group of interbreeding organisms; changes in allele frequencies between generations; it's the population that evolves	Statistical analysis

allele frequencies should also shift gradually in each generation. The levels of organization in the evolutionary are summarized in Table 3–5.

In Chapter 2, we discussed the general principles underlying natural selection and gave some nonhuman examples. The best-documented example of natural selection in humans involves hemoglobin S, an abnormal form of hemoglobin that results from a point mutation in the gene that produces part of the hemoglobin molecule. The allele for hemoglobin S, Hb^S, is recessive to the allele for normal hemoglobin, Hb^A. People who are homozygous for the Hb^A allele produce normal hemoglobin. Heterozygotes (whose genotype is Hb^A/Hb^S) have a condition called sickle-cell trait. Although some of their hemoglobin is abnormal, enough of it is normal to enable them to function normally under most circumstances. But people who inherit the recessive allele from both parents (that is, they are homozygous with the genotype Hb^S/Hb^S) have sickle-cell anemia.

There are many manifestations of sickle-cell anemia, but basically, the abnormal hemoglobin reduces the ability of red blood cells to transport oxygen. When the body has an increased demand for oxygen (as during exercise or at high altitude), the red blood cells collapse and form a shape similar to a sickle (Fig. 3–20). As a result, they can't carry normal amounts of oxygen, and they also clump together and block small capillaries, depriving vital organs of oxygen. Even with treatment, life expectancy in the United States today is less than 45 years for patients with sickle-cell anemia. Worldwide, sickle-cell anemia causes an estimated 100,000 deaths each year; in the United States, approximately 40,000 to 50,000 individuals, mostly of African descent, suffer from this disease.

FIGURE 3–20

(a) Scanning electron micrograph of a normal, fully oxygenated red blood cell. (b) Scanning electron micrograph of a collapsed, sickle-shaped red blood cell that contains Hb^S.

© Dr. Stanley Flegler / Visuals Unlimited

© Dr. Stanley Flegler / Visuals Unlimited

(a)

(b)

Hb^S is a mutation that occurs occasionally in all human populations, but it's usually rare. In some populations, however, it's more common, and this is especially true in western and central Africa, where its frequency approaches 20 percent. The frequency of the allele is also moderately high in parts of Greece and India (Fig. 3–21). Given the devastating effects of Hb^S in homozygotes, how do we explain its higher prevalence in some populations? The answer to this question is malaria, an infectious disease that currently kills an estimated 1 to 3 million people a year worldwide.

Malaria is caused by a single-celled organism that is transmitted to humans by mosquitoes. Very briefly, after an infected mosquito bite, these parasites invade red blood cells, where they get the oxygen they need for reproduction. The consequences of this infection to the human host include fever, chills, headache, nausea, vomiting, and frequently death. In parts of western and central Africa, where malaria is always present, children bear the burden of the disease; as many as 50 to 75 percent of 2- to 9-year-olds are afflicted.

The geographical correlation between malaria and the distribution of the sickle-cell allele is indirect evidence of a biological relationship (Figs. 3–21 and 3–22). In the 1950s, a British biologist named A. C. Allison showed that individuals with one Hb^S allele (that is, those with sickle-cell trait) and therefore some hemoglobin S had greater resistance to malaria than the homozygous "normals" had. Later, scientists learned that heterozygotes resist infection because their red blood cells don't provide a suitable environment for the parasite to reproduce. So in areas where malaria is always present, individuals with sickle-cell trait have higher reproductive success than do those with normal hemoglobin. Those with sickle-cell anemia, of course, have the lowest reproductive success—without treatment, most of these individuals die before reaching adulthood.

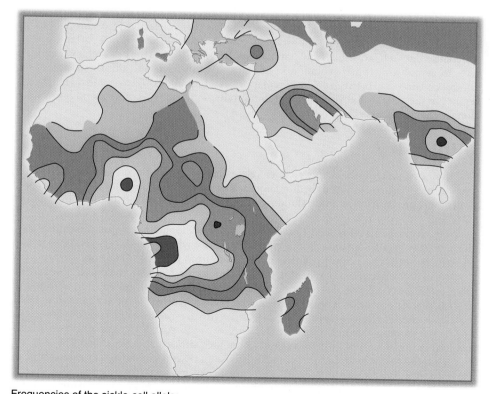

FIGURE 3–21
A frequency map of the sickle-cell distribution in the Old World.

Frequencies of the sickle-cell allele:

Greater than .14

.12–.14

.10–.12

.08–.10

.06–.08

.04–.06

.02–.04

.00–.02

FIGURE 3–22
Malaria distribution in the Old World.

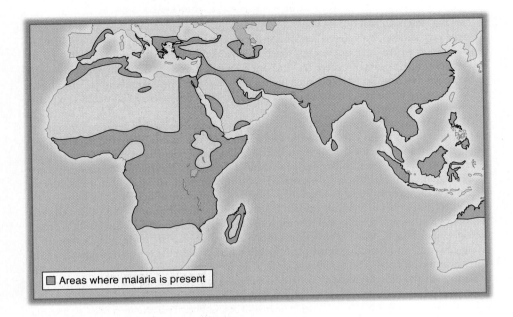

FIGURE 3–22
Malaria distribution in the Old World.

□ Areas where malaria is present

The relationship between malaria and Hb^S provides one of the best examples we have of natural selection in contemporary humans. In this case, natural selection has favored the heterozygous phenotype, thus increasing the frequency of Hb^S, an allele that in homozygotes causes severe disease and early death.

There are many other examples of how disease has been a selective force throughout the course of human evolution and how it has contributed to small, but important, genetic differences between individuals and populations. But, sickle-cell is the best single example we have to demonstrate microevolution in humans. If you understand this discussion of the complex relationship between environmental factors (mosquitoes), disease, and one slight difference in the gene that governs hemoglobin production, you will comprehend how evolutionary change occurs.

Summary

The topics we've covered in this chapter relate almost entirely to discoveries made after Darwin and Wallace described the fundamentals of natural selection. But all the issues presented here are basic to an understanding of biological evolution, adaptation, and human variation.

We have shown that cells are the fundamental units of life and that they are essentially classified into two types. Somatic cells make up body tissues, while gametes (eggs and sperm) are reproductive cells that transmit genetic information from parent to offspring.

Genetic information is contained in the DNA molecule, found in the nuclei of cells. The DNA molecule is capable of replication, or making copies of itself, and, during mitosis and meiosis, this feature makes it possible for daughter cells to receive the correct amount of DNA that allows them to function properly. DNA also controls protein synthesis by directing cells to arrange amino acids in the proper sequence for each particular type of protein. Also involved in the process of protein synthesis is another, similar molecule called RNA.

Cells multiply by dividing, and during cell division, DNA is visible under a microscope in the form of chromosomes. In humans, there are 46 chromosomes, or 23 pairs.

Somatic cells divide during growth or tissue repair or to replace old or damaged cells. Somatic cell division is called mitosis. During mitosis, a cell divides one time to produce two daughter cells, each possessing a full and identical set of chromosomes.

Sex cells are produced when specialized cells in the ovaries and testes divide during meiosis. Unlike mitosis, meiosis is characterized by two divisions that produce four nonidentical daughter cells, each having only half the amount of DNA (23 chromosomes) contained within the original cell.

We've also discussed how Gregor Mendel discovered the principles of segregation, independent assortment, and dominance and recessiveness by doing experiments with pea plants. Characteristics that are influenced by only one genetic locus are called Mendelian traits, and the ABO blood type system is one example of a human Mendelian trait. In contrast, many characteristics such as stature and skin color are said to be polygenic, or continuous, because they are influenced by more than one genetic locus and show a continuous range of expression.

Building on fundamental nineteenth-century contributions by Charles Darwin and the rediscovery of Mendel's work in 1900, advances in genetics throughout the twentieth century contributed to contemporary evolutionary thought. In particular, the combination of natural selection with Mendel's principles of inheritance and experimental evidence concerning the nature of mutation have all been synthesized into a modern understanding of evolutionary change, appropriately termed the Modern Synthesis. In this, the central contemporary theory of evolution, evolutionary change is seen as a two-stage process. The first stage is the production and redistribution of variation. The second stage is the process whereby natural selection acts on the accumulated genetic variation.

Mutation is crucial to all evolutionary change because it's the only source of completely new genetic material (which increases variation). Natural selection is the crucial factor that influences the long-term direction of evolutionary change. How natural selection works can best be explained as differential reproductive success—that is, how successful individuals are in producing offspring for succeeding generations. Genetic drift (the random loss of alleles due to small population size) and gene flow (the exchange of genes between populations) are also very important to evolutionary change.

The expression of all biological traits is, to varying degrees, under genetic control. Genes, then, can be said to set limits and potentials for human growth, development, and achievement. However, these limits and potentials aren't written in stone, so to speak, because many characteristics are also very much influenced by such environmental factors as temperature, diet, and sunlight. So ultimately, it's the interaction between genetic and environmental factors that produces phenotypic variation and evolutionary change in all species, including *Homo sapiens.*

Critical Thinking Questions

1. Before you read this chapter, were you aware that the DNA in your body is structurally the same as in all other organisms? How do you see this fact as having potential to clarify some of the many questions we still have regarding biological evolution?
2. How would you describe genes and their functions? Has this chapter changed your understanding of genetics, and if so, how?
3. Now that you've read this chapter, do you understand evolutionary processes more completely? Explain your answer.
4. Many people have the misconception that sickle-cell anemia affects only people of African descent. Why is this not true?
5. Give some examples of how selection, gene flow, genetic drift, and mutation have acted on populations or species in the past. Try to think of at least one human and one nonhuman example. Why do you think genetic drift might be important today to endangered species?
6. Did the discussion of misconceptions about dominance and recessiveness change your perceptions of these phenomena? If so, how?
7. What is mitochondrial DNA? What is its primary function? Explain why it is useful for studying relationships between two different populations of the same species.
8. What is the Human Genome Project, and why is it important? Do you think that you personally will be affected by this research in your lifetime? Explain your answer.

Molecular Applications in Forensic Anthropology

No doubt, you know of instances where DNA analysis is used in forensic circumstances to identify a criminal. You've probably also heard of cases where mistakenly imprisoned individuals have been released when DNA evidence cleared them of various crimes—sometimes several years after their conviction.

Since the 1980s, molecular applications have greatly assisted law enforcement agencies. In fact, immediately following development of the polymerase chain reaction (PCR) technique in the mid-1980s, the first widely applied examples of precise DNA genotyping were for forensic purposes.

Forensic anthropologists, from the outset, have been central contributors in these molecular applications. It's important to understand that forensic science is a coordinated *team effort*. Thus, forensic anthropologists work in close collaboration with law enforcement agencies, medical examiners, forensic odontologists (that is, dental experts), entomologists, and DNA identification laboratories.

The standard methods used in these laboratories include PCR and DNA fingerprinting (see p. 56). Both mitochondrial and nuclear DNA are used to identify individuals. PCR makes it possible to reliably identify individuals from exceedingly small samples of tissue—for example, blood, semen, teeth, and bone. So, even in cases where the remains have deteriorated badly over time or were crushed or burned in a mass disaster, proper collection and precise laboratory controls can often yield useful results. For example, forensic scientists can take a small scrap of bone and identify a person who's been missing for several years if the DNA fingerprint can be matched with that of a close relative. Anthropologists provide crucial assistance in the identification process because their initial analysis of the skeleton's physical attributes (for example, age, sex, stature) can greatly narrow the range of possibilities, so that fewer potential relatives need to be tested for a match. The data banks existing today are insufficient to accomplish the task without such initial corroborating clues.

To successfully make a positive genetic ID, the DNA must be (1) extracted from bone, by cutting a small section with a saw; (2) purified to remove chemicals that interfere with PCR; (3) amplified, that is, replicated millions of times by PCR; and (4) sequenced, usually via "fingerprinting," that is, characterizing for particular chromosomal regions, unique repeated arrays of small DNA segments.

One renowned case of DNA identification from skeletal remains was that of the last tsar of Russia, Nicholas II. As many people know, Nicholas and his entire immediate family were executed in July 1918. The bodies were long thought to have been completely destroyed, but the true location of the graves of the Russian royal family was discovered several years ago. Only

FIGURE 1

Forensic anthropologist Bill Maples examining the cranium of Tsar Nicholas II (inset).

after the fall of communism, however, were the skeletal remains finally exhumed in 1991.

A team led by the late William Maples was permitted to examine the remains and try to establish the exact identities of all the individuals. This was no easy task, because more than 1,000 bone fragments were mixed together (Fig. 1). Anthropological analysis of the skeletons suggested that five members of the royal family were represented among the remains: Tsar Nicholas, Empress Alexandra, and their three oldest daughters. In agreement with documents from the time of the execution, the two youngest children—Anastasia and Alexei—were missing because they had been buried elsewhere.

In 1992 the first DNA testing was done on small bone samples taken to England. Molecular results agreed with the anthropological findings (Gill et al., 1994), except that some lingering

Molecular Applications in Forensic Anthropology CONTINUED

questions remained concerning the identification of the tsar's mtDNA. To provide absolute confirmation, additional bone and tooth samples were taken, and further DNA analysis was done at the Armed Forces DNA Identification Laboratory (AFDIL) in Washington, D.C. What's more, because the DNA thought to come from the tsar's skeleton showed a highly unusual pattern, permission was given by the Russian Orthodox Church to exhume the body of his younger brother (who had died in 1899) and compare his DNA with that taken from the presumed tsar's skeleton. The results showed beyond any doubt that the skeleton was indeed that of the executed tsar, Nicholas II (Ivanov et al., 1996).

Scenes of mass disaster—such as fires, earthquakes, tsunamis, or plane crashes—are another context in which both forensic anthropology and DNA analysis play crucial roles. To respond quickly and effectively to such disasters, the federal government has organized regional disaster reaction work groups called DMORT (Disaster Mortuary Operational Response Team). These teams all include a forensic anthropologist, who is sometimes the team leader. In fact, following the tragic events of September 11, 2001, Paul Sledzik—a forensic anthropologist then at the Armed Forces Institute of Pathology—was the DMORT leader at the Pennsylvania crash site of United Flight 93.

During the recovery, the team followed strict procedures in collecting and analyzing the human remains and other evidence. It's important to remember that besides being a site of immense personal tragedy, this was also a crime scene. As in all such circumstances, close interaction with law enforcement agencies is essential; in this case, the FBI led the criminal investigation. (For a detailed documentation of the procedures followed at the Flight 93 crash site, see the website provided with other sources at the end of this feature.)

Forensic anthropologists also assisted in the recovery of human remains at the World Trade Center. There, procedures differed, because millions of tons of debris had to be sifted through; and the few human remains that were present were extremely fragmentary and severely burned.

In Pennsylvania, although broken and burned, the remains of victims were much more complete. The DMORT staff was thus able to select the material most likely to provide the best DNA results. Moreover, clothing and other personal items found with the remains could provide an exact identification, which could be further corroborated through basic anthropological observations of age, sex, and so on. Where identification was unambiguous, DNA analysis was not required.

At the World Trade Center disaster site, few remnants of associated clothing or personal effects were found. Also, since the

bone and tooth fragments were so small and were often altered by intense heat, few of the standard anthropological skeletal observations were possible. As a result, basically all the presumed bone and dental remains are being analyzed for DNA.

More recently, forensic anthropologists assisted in identifying remains of individuals killed during the tsunami that struck southern Asia in December 2004. Teams came from several countries, and up-to-date information on the tsunami assistance as well as forensic technical advances can be seen on the Environmental Sciences and Research (ESR) website (see Sources).

Major tragedies leading to large numbers of civilian deaths also occur during wars and ethnic conflicts. Forensic anthropologists are often asked to assist in these circumstances as well, since victims of atrocities sometimes are left in mass graves. When possible, these graves are intensively investigated, often revealing decomposed bodies as well as partial skeletons. Sadly, such work has become more commonplace, keeping pace with the increase in brutality seen throughout the world. (Consider, for example, the tragedies of Argentina, Guatemala, Rwanda, the Balkans, and Iraq.)

Recovery efforts are concerned first with identifying the victims. Successful personal identification allows family members to learn the fate of missing loved ones. Second, the evidence obtained can be used in legal proceedings in which perpetrators are tried for genocide or other crimes against humanity; such trials are now being conducted in Africa, Iraq, and at the World Court.

As with the circumstances at the 9/11 disaster sites, DNA analyses are sometimes required; but in other cases, accurate personal identification can be done more quickly and more economically using standard anthropological criteria and from associated personal items that have been corroborated by relatives of the deceased. Such methods are especially important in very poor, war-torn regions, which can't afford large-scale DNA testing (Baraybar, 2004). However, international agencies have recently stepped up aid; for example, in Bosnia and Herzegovina, the International Commission on Missing Persons is overseeing large-scale DNA testing (Drukier et al., 2004; Klanowski, 2004). A similar approach is also being implemented in the United States to identify bodies of hundreds of immigrants who died while trying to cross the Mexican–U.S. border (Baker and Baker, 2004).

In addition to the field collection and analysis contexts we've just discussed, forensic anthropologists are becoming directly involved in molecular research in the laboratory. Several anthropologists working in cooperation with molecular biologists are investigating how to refine procedures to make DNA sequencing more accurate (Kontanis, 2004; Latham, 2004). For example,

Molecular Applications in Forensic Anthropology

Craig King, Armed Forces DNA Identification Laboratory

FIGURE 2

DNA analyst Heather Thew prepares a bone sample at the Armed Forces DNA Identification Laboratory.

at AFDIL, anthropologist Heather Thew is a DNA analyst. She's directly involved in all steps of sample preparation and molecular analysis. Because much of her work concerns mtDNA testing of the physical remains of military personnel, some of whom have been missing since World War II, they consist only of very fragmented bone pieces. Thew credits her anthropology training in human skeletal analysis and modern population biology as providing her with both a solid background and specialized skills that allow her to better perform many of the laboratory duties at AFDIL (Fig. 2).

SOURCES:

Baker, Lori E., and Erich Baker. 2004. "Reuniting Families: Using Phenotypic and Genotypic Forensic Evidence to Identify Unknown Immigrant Remains." Paper presented at Annual Meetings of the American Academy of Forensic Sciences, Dallas, February 2004.

Environmental Sciences and Research (ESR). See website: www.esr.cri.nz/competencies/forensicscience/dna/

Flight 93 Morgue Protocols. See website: www.dmort.org/FilesforDownload/Protocol_flight_93.pdf

Gill, P., P. L. Ivanov, and C. Kimpton et al. 1994. "Identification of the Remains of the Romanov Family by DNA Analysis." *Nature Genetics* 6:130–135.

Ivanov, Pavel L., Mark J. Wadhams, and Rhonda K. Roby et al. 1996. "Mitochondrial DNA Sequence Heteroplasmy in the Grand Duke of Russia Georgij Romanov Establishes the Authenticity of the Remains of Tsar Nicholas II." *Nature Genetics* 12:417–420.

Klanowski, Eva. 2004. "Exhumation—and What After? ICMP Model in Bosnia and Herzegovina." Paper presented at Annual Meetings of the American Academy of Forensic Sciences, Dallas, February 2004.

Kotanis, Elias J. 2004. "Using Real-Time PCR Quantifications of Nuclear and Mitochondrial DNA to Develop Degradation Profiles for Various Tissues." Paper presented at Annual Meetings of the American Academy of Forensic Sciences, Dallas, February 2004.

Latham, Krista E. 2004. "The Ability to Amplify Skeletal DNA After Heat Exposure Due to Maceration." Paper presented at Annual Meetings of the American Academy of Forensic Sciences, Dallas, February 2004.

HEREDITY AND EVOLUTION

CHAPTER

4

Modern Human
Variation and
Adaptation

FOCUS QUESTION

How does the contemporary evolutionary-based approach to understanding human diversity differ from the traditional nineteenth-century approach?

Introduction

At some time or other, you have probably been asked to specify your "race" or "ethnic identity" on an application or census form. What did you think about that question? How comfortable were you answering it? Usually, you can choose from a variety of racial/ethnic categories. Was it easy to pick one? What about your parents and grandparents? Where would they fit in?

Notions about human diversity have for centuries played a large role in human relations, and they still influence political and social perceptions. While it would be comforting to believe that informed views have become almost universal, the gruesome tally of genocidal/ethnic cleansing atrocities in recent years tells us tragically that worldwide, as a species, we have a long way to go before tolerance becomes the norm.

Most people don't seem to understand the nature of human diversity, and worse yet, many seem quite unwilling to accept what science has to contribute on the subject. Many of the misconceptions, especially those regarding how *race* is defined and categorized, are no doubt rooted in cultural history over the last few centuries. Although many cultures have attempted to come to grips with these issues, for better or worse, the most influential of these perspectives were developed in the Western world (that is, Europe and North America). The way many individuals still view themselves and their relationship to other peoples is a legacy of the last four centuries of racial interpretations.

In Chapter 3 we saw how physical characteristics are influenced by the DNA in our cells. We went on to discuss how individuals inherit genes from parents, and how variations in genes (alleles) can produce different expressions of traits. We also focused on how the basic principles of inheritance are related to evolutionary change.

In this chapter, we'll continue to discuss topics that directly relate to genetics, namely biological diversity in humans and how humans adapt physically to environmental challenges. After discussing historical attempts at explaining human phenotypic diversity and racial classification, we examine contemporary methods of interpreting diversity. In recent years, several new techniques have emerged that permit direct examination of the DNA molecule, revealing differences between individuals even at the level of single nucleotides. But even as discoveries of different levels of diversity emerge, geneticists have also revealed that our species is remarkably uniform genetically, particularly when compared with other species.

Later in the chapter, we'll consider human phenotypic variation in the context of adaptation to specific environmental contexts. We examine how populations and individuals differ in their adaptive response to such factors as ultraviolet radiation, heat, cold, and high altitude. Finally, we consider the significant role of infectious disease in human evolution and adaptation.

Historical Views of Human Variation

The first step toward understanding natural phenomena is the ordering of variation into categories that can then be named, discussed, and perhaps studied. Historically, when different groups of people came into contact with one another, they tried to account for the physical differences they saw. Because skin color was so noticeable, it was one of the more frequently explained traits, and most systems of racial classification were based on it.

Go to the following CD-ROMs for interactive activities and exercises on topics covered in this chapter:

- Virtual Laboratories for Physical Anthropology CD-ROM, Third Edition
- Genetics in Anthropology: Principles and Applications CD-ROM, First Edition

As early as 1350 B.C., the ancient Egyptians had classified humans on the basis of skin color: red for Egyptian, yellow for people to the east, white for those to the north, and black for sub-Saharan Africans (Gossett, 1963). In the sixteenth century, after the discovery of the New World, Europe embarked on a period of intense exploration and colonization in both the New and Old Worlds. One result of this contact was an increased awareness of human diversity.

Throughout the eighteenth and nineteenth centuries, European and American scientists concentrated primarily on describing and classifying the biological variation in humans as well as in nonhuman species. The first scientific attempt to describe the newly discovered variation between human populations was Linnaeus' taxonomic classification (see p. 22), which placed humans into four separate categories (Linnaeus, 1758). Linnaeus assigned behavioral and intellectual qualities to each group, with the least complimentary descriptions going to black Africans. This ranking was typical of the period and reflected the almost universal European ethnocentric view that Europeans were superior to all other peoples.

Johann Friedrich Blumenbach (1752–1840), a German anatomist, classified humans into five races. Although Blumenbach's categories came to be described simply as white, yellow, red, black, and brown, he also used criteria other than skin color. Moreover, he emphasized that racial categories based on skin color were arbitrary and that many traits, including skin color, weren't discrete phenomena. Blumenbach pointed out that to attempt to classify all humans using such a system would be to omit completely all those who didn't neatly fall into a specific category. Blumenbach and others also recognized that traits such as skin color showed overlapping expression between groups.

In 1842 Anders Retzius, a Swedish anatomist, developed the *cephalic index* as a method of describing the shape of the human head. The cephalic index, derived by dividing maximum head breadth by maximum length and multiplying by 100, gives the ratio of head breadth to length. (The cephalic index does not measure actual head size.) The cephalic index is still used to assess head shape in individual skulls, but in the nineteenth century, it was viewed as a precise scientific technique that could be used to categorize groups of people. In addition, because people could be quickly categorized by a single number, the index provided a superficial but easy method for describing variation. Individuals with an index of less than 75 had long, narrow heads and were labeled "dolichocephalic." "Brachycephalic" individuals, with broad heads, had an index of over 80; and those whose indices were between 75 and 80 were "mesocephalic." Northern Europeans tended to be dolichocephalic, while southern Europeans were brachycephalic. Not surprisingly, these results led to heated and nationalistic debate over whether one group was superior to another.

By the mid-nineteenth century, populations were ranked essentially on a scale based on skin color (along with size and shape of the head), with sub-Saharan Africans at the bottom. What's more, the Europeans themselves were also ranked, so that northern, light-skinned populations were considered superior to their southern, somewhat darker-skinned neighbors.

To many Europeans, the fact that non-Europeans weren't Christian suggested that these "foreigners" were "uncivilized" and implied an even more basic inferiority of character and intellect. This view was rooted in a concept called **biological determinism**, which in part holds that there is an association between physical characteristics and such attributes as intelligence, morals, values, abilities, and even social and economic condition. In other words, cultural variations are *inherited* in the same way that biological variations are. It follows, then, that there are inherent behavioral and cognitive differences between groups and that some groups are *by nature* superior to others. Following this logic, it's a simple matter to justify the persecution and even enslavement of other peoples simply because their appearance differs from what is familiar.

After 1850, biological determinism was a constant theme underlying common thinking as well as scientific research in Europe and the United States. Most people—including such notable figures as Thomas Jefferson, Georges Cuvier, Benjamin Franklin, Charles Lyell, Abraham Lincoln, Charles Darwin, and Oliver Wendell Holmes—held deterministic (and what we today would call racist) views. Commenting on this usually de-emphasized characteristic of notable historical figures, the late evolutionary biologist Stephen J. Gould (1981, p. 32) remarked that "all American culture heroes embraced racial attitudes that would embarrass public-school mythmakers."

Francis Galton (1822–1911), a cousin of Charles Darwin, shared an increasingly common fear among nineteenth-century Europeans that "civilized society" was being weakened by the

biological determinism The concept that phenomena, including various aspects of behavior (e.g., intelligence, values, morals) are governed by biological (genetic) factors; the inaccurate association of various behavioral attributes with certain biological traits, such as skin color.

failure of natural selection to completely eliminate "unfit" and "inferior" members (Greene, 1981, p. 107). Galton wrote and lectured on the necessity of "race improvement" and suggested government regulation of marriage and family size, an approach he called **eugenics**. Although eugenics had its share of critics, its popularity flourished throughout the 1930s. Nowhere was it more attractive than in Germany, where the viewpoint took a horrifying turn: The false idea of pure races was increasingly extolled as a means of reestablishing a strong and prosperous state. Eugenics was seen as scientific justification for purging Germany of its "unfit," and many of Germany's scientists continued to support the policies of racial purity and eugenics during the Nazi period (Proctor, 1988, p. 143), when these policies served as justification for condemning millions of people to death.

But at the same time, many scientists were turning away from racial typologies and classification in favor of a more evolutionary approach. No doubt for some, this shift in direction was motivated by their growing concerns over the goals of the eugenics movement. Probably more important, however, was the synthesis of genetics and Darwin's theories of natural selection during the 1930s. As discussed in Chapter 3, this breakthrough influenced all the biological sciences, and some physical anthropologists soon began to apply evolutionary principles to the study of human variation.

The Concept of Race

All contemporary humans are members of the same **polytypic** species, *Homo sapiens*. A polytypic species is one composed of local populations that differ in the expression of one or more traits. Even *within* local populations, there's a great deal of genotypic and phenotypic variation between individuals.

In discussions of human variation, people have traditionally clumped together various attributes, such as skin color, face shape, nose shape, hair color, hair form (curly or straight), and eye color. People who have particular combinations of these and other traits have been placed together in categories associated with specific geographical localities. Such categories are called *races*.

We all think we know what we mean by the word *race*, but in reality, the term has had various meanings since the 1500s, when English speakers first commonly used it. *Race* has been used synonymously with *species*, as in "the human race." Since the 1600s, *race* has also referred to various culturally defined groups, and this meaning is still common. For example, you'll hear people say, "the English race" or "the Japanese race," when they actually mean nationality. Another phrase you've probably heard is "the Jewish race," where the speaker is really talking about a particular ethnic and religious identity.

So, even though *race* is usually a term with biological connotations, it also has enormous social significance. And there's still a widespread perception that certain physical traits (skin color, in particular) are associated with numerous cultural attributes (such as language, occupational preferences, or even morality). As a result, in many cultural contexts a person's social identity is strongly influenced by the way that he or she expresses those physical traits traditionally used to define "racial groups." Characteristics such as skin color are highly visible, and they make it easy to immediately and superficially group people into socially defined categories. However, so-called racial traits aren't the only phenotypic expressions that contribute to social identity. Sex and age are also critically important. But aside from these two variables, an individual's biological and/or ethnic background is still inevitably a factor that influences how he or she is initially perceived and judged by others.

References to national origin (for example, African, Asian) as substitutes for racial labels have become more common in recent years, both within and outside anthropology. Within anthropology, the term *ethnicity* was proposed in the early 1950s in order to avoid the more emotionally charged term *race*. Strictly speaking, ethnicity refers to cultural factors, but the fact that the words *ethnicity* and *race* are used interchangeably reflects the social importance of phenotypic expression and demonstrates once again how phenotype is mistakenly associated with culturally defined variables.

In its most common biological usage, the term *race* refers to geographically patterned phenotypic variation within a species. By the seventeenth century, naturalists had begun to

eugenics The philosophy of "race improvement" through the forced sterilization of members of some groups and increased reproduction among others; an overly simplified, often racist view that is now discredited.

polytypic Referring to species composed of populations that differ with regard to the expression of one or more traits.

describe races in plants and nonhuman animals, because they recognized that when populations of a species occupied different regions, they sometimes differed from one another in the expression of one or more traits. But even today, there are no established criteria by which races of plants and animals, including humans, are assessed.

Prior to World War II, most studies of human variation focused on visible phenotypic variation between large, geographically defined populations, and these studies were largely descriptive. Since World War II, the emphasis has shifted to examining the differences in allele frequencies within and between populations, as well as considering the adaptive significance of phenotypic and genotypic variation. This shift in focus occurred partly because of the Modern Synthesis in biology and partly because of advances in genetics.

In the twenty-first century, the application of evolutionary principles to the study of modern human variation has replaced the superficial nineteenth-century view of race *based solely on observed phenotype*. Additionally, the genetic emphasis has dispelled previously held misconceptions that races are fixed biological entities that don't change over time and that are composed of individuals who all conform to a particular *type*.

Clearly, there are phenotypic differences between humans, and some of these differences roughly correspond to particular geographical locations. But certain questions must be asked. Is there any adaptive significance attached to observed phenotypic variation? Is genetic drift a factor? What is the degree of underlying genetic variation that influences phenotypic variation? These questions place considerations of human variation within a contemporary evolutionary framework.

Although, in part, physical anthropology has its roots in attempts to explain human diversity, no contemporary scholar subscribes to pre-Darwinian and pre–Modern Synthesis concepts of races (human or nonhuman) as fixed biological entities. Also, anthropologists generally recognize that race isn't a valid concept, especially from a genetic perspective, because the amount of genetic variation accounted for by differences *between* groups is vastly exceeded by the variation that exists *within* groups. But given these considerations, some anthropologists continue to view variations in outwardly expressed phenotype as having the potential to yield information about population adaptation, genetic drift, mutation, and gene flow.

Forensic anthropologists, in particular, find the phenotypic criteria associated with race to have practical applications because they are frequently called on by law enforcement agencies to assist in identifying human skeletal remains. Because unidentified human remains are often those of crime victims, identification must be as accurate as possible. The most important variables in such identification are the individual's sex, age, stature, and ancestry or "racial" and ethnic background. Using metric and nonmetric criteria, forensic anthropologists employ various techniques for establishing broad population affinity, and generally their findings are accurate about 80 percent of the time.

On the flip side of this issue are the numerous physical anthropologists who argue that race is a meaningless concept when applied to humans. They see race as an outdated creation of the human mind that attempts to simplify biological complexity by organizing it into categories. Thus, human races are a product of the human tendency to impose order on complex natural phenomena. Classification may have been an acceptable approach some 150 years ago, but it's no longer valid given the current state of genetic and evolutionary science.

Objections to racial taxonomies have also been raised because classification schemes are *typological*, meaning that categories are discrete and based on stereotypes or ideals that comprise a specific set of traits. So in general, typologies are inherently misleading, because in any grouping there are always many individuals who don't conform to all aspects of a particular type.

In any so-called racial group, there will be individuals who fall into the normal range of variation for another group with regard to one or several characteristics. For example, two people of different ancestry might vary with regard to skin color, but they could share any number of other traits, such as height, shape of head, hair color, eye color, or ABO blood type. In fact, they could easily share more similarities with each other than they do with many members of their own populations.

To further blur this picture, the characteristics that have traditionally been used to define races are *polygenic*; that is, they are influenced by several genes and therefore exhibit a continuous range of expression. So it's difficult, if not impossible, to draw distinct boundaries between populations with regard to many traits. This limitation becomes clear if you ask yourself, "At what point is hair color no longer dark brown but medium brown, or no longer light brown but blond?"

The scientific controversy over race will diminish as we increase our understanding of the genetic diversity (and uniformity) of our species. Given the rapid changes in genome studies and the fact that very few genes contribute to outward expressions of phenotype, dividing the human species into racial categories isn't a biologically meaningful way to look at human variation. But among the general public, variations on the theme of race will undoubtedly continue to be the most common view of human biological and cultural variation. Keeping all this in mind, it falls to anthropologists and biologists to continue exploring the issue so that, to the best of our abilities, accurate information regarding human variation is available to anyone who seeks informed explanations of complex phenomena.

Racism

Racism is based on the previously mentioned false belief that such factors as intellect and various cultural attributes are inherited along with physical characteristics. Such beliefs also commonly rest on the assumption that one's own group is superior to other groups.

Since we've already alluded to certain aspects of racism, such as the eugenics movement and persecution of people based on racial or ethnic misconceptions, we won't belabor the point here. However, it's important to point out that racism is hardly a thing of the past, nor is it restricted to Europeans and Americans of European descent. Racism is a cultural phenomenon, and it's found worldwide.

We end this brief discussion of racism with an excerpt from an article, "The Study of Race," by the late Sherwood Washburn, a well-known physical anthropologist who taught at the University of California, Berkeley. Although written many years ago, the statement is as fresh and applicable today as it was then:

> Races are products of the past. They are relics of times and conditions which have long ceased to exist. Racism is equally a relic supported by no phase of modern science. We may not know how to interpret the form of the Mongoloid face, or why Rh is of high incidence in Africa, but we do know the benefits of education and of economic progress. We . . . know that the roots of happiness lie in the biology of the whole species and that the potential of the species can only be realized in a culture, in a social system. It is knowledge and the social system which give life or take it away, and in so doing change the gene frequencies and continue the million-year-old interaction of culture and biology. Human biology finds its realization in a culturally determined way of life, and the infinite variety of genetic combinations can only express themselves efficiently in a free and open society. (Washburn, 1963, p. 531)

Intelligence

As we have shown, belief in the relationship between physical characteristics and specific behavioral attributes is popular even today, but there is no scientific evidence to show that personality or any other behavioral trait differs genetically *between* human groups. Most scientists would agree with this last statement, but one question that has produced controversy both inside scientific circles and among laypeople is whether population affinity and **intelligence** are associated.

Both genetic and environmental factors contribute to intelligence, although it's not possible to measure accurately the percentage each contributes. What can be said is that IQ scores and intelligence aren't the same thing. IQ scores can change during a person's lifetime, and average IQ scores of different populations overlap. Such differences in average IQ scores that do exist between groups are difficult to interpret, given the problems inherent in the design

intelligence Mental capacity; ability to learn, reason, or comprehend and interpret information, facts, relationships, and meanings; the capacity to solve problems, whether through the application of previously acquired knowledge or through insight.

of the IQ tests. Moreover, complex cognitive abilities, however measured, are influenced by multiple loci and are thus polygenic.

Innate factors set limits and define potentials for behavior and cognitive ability in any species. In humans, the limits are broad and the potentials aren't fully known. Individual abilities result from complex interactions between genetic and environmental factors. One product of this interaction is learning, and the ability to learn is influenced by genetic and other biological components. Undeniably, there are differences between individuals regarding these biological components. However, it's probably not possible to determine what proportion of the variation in test scores is due to biological factors. Besides, innate differences in abilities reflect individual variation *within* populations, not inherent differences *between* groups. Comparing populations on the basis of IQ test results is a misuse of testing procedures, and there's no convincing evidence *whatsoever* that populations vary with regard to cognitive abilities, regardless of the assertions in some popular books. Unfortunately, despite the lack of evidence of mental inferiority of some populations and mental superiority of others, and despite the questionable validity of intelligence tests, racist attitudes toward intelligence continue to flourish.

Contemporary Interpretations of Human Variation

Since the physical characteristics (such as skin color and hair form) used to define race are *polygenic*, precisely measuring the genetic influence on them hasn't been possible. So, physical anthropologists and other biologists who study modern human variation have largely abandoned the traditional perspective of describing superficial phenotypic characteristics in favor of examining differences in allele frequencies.

Beginning in the 1950s, studies of modern human variation focused on the various components of blood as well as other aspects of body chemistry. Such traits as the ABO blood types are *phenotypes*, but they are *direct* products of the genotype. (Recall that genes code for proteins, and the antigens on blood cells and many components of blood serum are partly composed of proteins; Fig. 4–1). During the twentieth century, this perspective met with a great deal of success as eventually dozens of loci were identified and the frequency data of many specific alleles obtained from numerous human populations. Nevertheless, in all these cases, it was the phenotype that was observed, and information about the underlying genotype remained largely unobtainable. Beginning in the 1990s, however, with the development of genomic studies, a drastic shift in techniques has taken place. Using precise DNA sequencing, genotypes can now be ascertained directly. And as specific differences in DNA within and between human populations are studied, we will dramatically increase our knowledge of human variation.

FIGURE 4–1

(a) A blood sample is drawn. (b) To determine an individual's blood type, a few drops of blood are treated with specific chemicals. Presence of A and B blood type, as well as Rh, can be detected by using commercially available chemicals. The glass slides below the blue- and yellow-labeled bottles show reactions for the ABO system. The blood on the top slide (at left) is type AB; the middle is type B; and the bottom is type A. The two samples to the right depict Rh-negative blood (top) and Rh-positive blood (bottom).

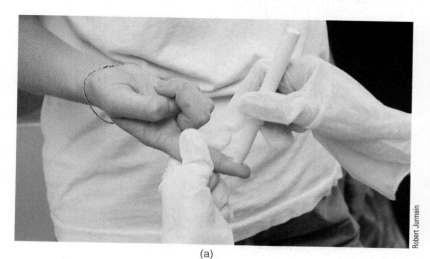
(a)

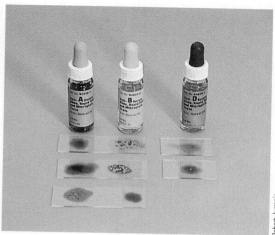
(b)

HUMAN POLYMORPHISMS

As you know, traits such as the ABO blood groups and the various genetic conditions presented in Chapter 3 are Mendelian traits because they can be linked to the action of single, identified loci. Consequently, these simple genetic mechanisms are much more easily studied than are the polygenic characteristics usually associated with traditional racial studies (for example, skin color, hair form, and face shape) because the loci that govern these complex traits haven't been identified. But new technologies are emerging that will, in the near future, permit the detailed analysis of loci associated with polygenic traits.

The most useful traits to examine in studies of contemporary human variation are those that differ in expression among various populations and between individuals. Such characteristics with different phenotypic expressions are called **polymorphisms**. A genetic trait is *polymorphic* if the locus that governs it has two or more alleles. (Refer to p. 52 for a discussion of the ABO blood group system governed by three alleles at one locus.)

Understanding polymorphisms requires evolutionary explanations, and geneticists use polymorphisms as a principal tool to understand evolutionary processes in modern populations. Additionally, by using these polymorphisms to compare allele frequencies between different populations, we can begin to reconstruct the evolutionary events that link human populations with one another.

By the 1960s, the study of *clinal distributions* of individual polymorphisms had become a popular alternative to the racial approach to human diversity. A **cline** is a gradual change in the frequency of a trait or allele in populations dispersed over geographical space. In humans, the various expressions of some polymorphic traits exhibit a more or less continuous distribution from one region to another, and most of these traits are Mendelian. The distribution of the *A* and *B* alleles in the Old World provides a good example of a clinal distribution (Fig. 4–2). Clinal distributions are generally thought to reflect microevolutionary influences of natural selection and/or gene flow. Consequently, clinal distributions are explained in evolutionary terms.

The ABO system is interesting from an anthropological perspective because the frequencies of the *A*, *B*, and *O* alleles vary tremendously among humans. In most groups, *A* and *B*

polymorphisms   Loci with more than one allele. Polymorphisms can be expressed in the phenotype as the result of gene action (as in ABO), or they can exist solely at the DNA level within noncoding regions.

cline   A gradual change in the frequency of genotypes and phenotypes from one geographical region to another.

FIGURE 4–2
Distribution of the *B* allele in the indigenous populations of the world. (After Mourant et al., 1976.)

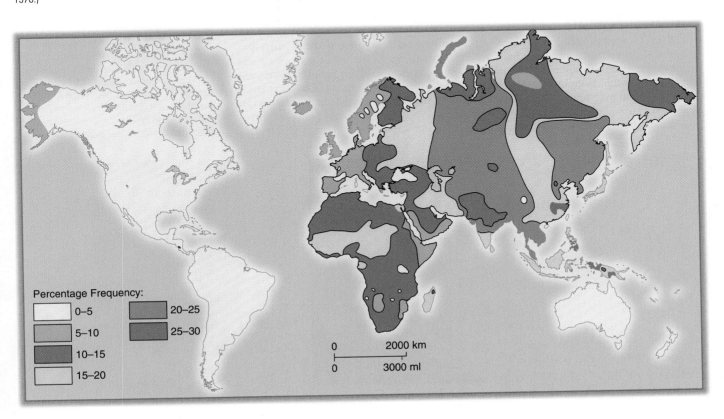

are rarely found in frequencies greater than 50 percent, and usually, their frequencies are much lower. Still, most human groups are polymorphic for all three alleles; but there are exceptions. For example, in native South American Indians, frequencies of the *O* allele reach 100 percent, and this allele is said to be "fixed" in these populations. Exceptionally high frequencies of *O* are also found in northern Australia, and some islands off the Australian coast show frequencies exceeding 90 percent. In these populations, the high frequencies of the *O* allele are probably due to genetic drift (founder effect), although the influence of natural selection can't be entirely ruled out.

Examining single traits can yield information regarding potential influences of natural selection or gene flow. This approach, however, is limited when we try to sort out population relationships, since the study of single traits, by themselves, can lead to confusing interpretations regarding likely population relationships. A more meaningful approach is to study several traits simultaneously.

POLYMORPHISMS AT THE DNA LEVEL

The techniques used in the Human Genome Project have facilitated the direct study of both mitochondrial DNA and chromosomal (nuclear) DNA. Using these new technologies, molecular biologists have recently discovered previously unknown variability in various regions of the genome. For example, scattered throughout the human genome are hundreds of sites where DNA segments are repeated—in some cases, just a few times, and in other cases, many hundreds of times. These areas of nucleotide repetition are called *microsatellites*, and they vary tremendously from person to person. In fact, each person has their own unique arrangement that defines their distinctive DNA "fingerprint" (see p. 56).

Researchers are also now mapping patterns of variation at individual nucleotide sites. As you have already learned, geneticists have studied point mutations (p. 40) for years and have used some of them (for example, the sickle-cell allele) to examine how natural selection has acted in the past to produce genetic variation among populations. But now we know that point mutations also frequently occur in "noncoding" DNA segments such as introns (see p. 41). These sites, together with those in coding regions of DNA, are all referred to as *single nucleotide polymorphisms* (*SNPs*). Already, more than a million such sites, dispersed throughout the genome, have been recognized (96 percent of them are in noncoding DNA), and these SNPs are extraordinarily variable (the International SNP Map Working Group, 2001). So, at the beginning of the twenty-first century, geneticists have gained access to a vast biological "library," documenting the population patterning and genetic history of our species.

Another fruitful area of recent research holds great promise for future advances. Our knowledge of the genetic makeup of polygenic traits has been woefully inadequate. However, by identifying specific loci at the DNA level (or using these highly variable regions as "markers" for sequencing ever-smaller areas of chromosomes), geneticists will soon be able to isolate particular gene variants that contribute to skin color, stature, hypertension, and a host of other previously enigmatic human phenotypic traits.

As you can see, the recently developed tools now used by geneticists permit the study of human genetic variation at a level never before conceived, and our views of human variation will be profoundly altered as our focus continues to shift away from observable phenotypic differences toward underlying genetic factors. And, through the use of these new techniques, the broader history of *Homo sapiens* is coming under closer genetic scrutiny.

Human Biocultural Evolution

We've defined culture as the human strategy of adaptation. Humans live in cultural environments that are continually modified by their own activities; thus, evolutionary processes are understandable only within this *cultural* context. You may recall that natural selection pressures operate within specific environmental settings. For humans and many of our hominid ancestors, this means an environment dominated by culture. For example, you learned in Chapter 3 that the altered form of hemoglobin called Hb^S confers resistance to malaria. But the sickle-cell allele has not always been an important genetic factor in human

slash-and-burn agriculture A traditional land-clearing practice involving the cutting and burning of trees and vegetation. In many areas, fields are abandoned after a few years and clearing occurs elsewhere.

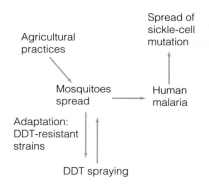

FIGURE 4–3
Evolutionary interactions affecting the frequency of the sickle-cell allele.

TABLE 4–1	Frequencies of Lactose Intolerance
Population Group	Percent
U.S. whites	2–19
Finnish	18
Swiss	12
Swedish	4
U.S. blacks	70–77
Ibos	99
Bantu	90
Fulani	22
Thais	99
Asian Americans	95–100
Native Americans	85

Source: Lerner and Libby, 1976, p. 327.

populations. Before the development of agriculture, humans rarely, if ever, lived close to mosquito-breeding areas for long periods of time. But with the spread in Africa of **slash-and-burn agriculture**, perhaps in just the last 2,000 years, penetration and clearing of tropical rain forests occurred. As a result, rain water was left to stand in open, stagnant pools that provided prime mosquito-breeding areas in close proximity to human settlements. DNA analyses have further confirmed such a recent origin and spread of the sickle-cell allele in a population from Senegal, in West Africa. One recent study estimates the origin of the Hb^S mutation in this group at between 1,250 and 2,100 ya (Currat et al., 2002). So it appears that, at least in some areas, malaria began to have an impact on human populations only recently. But once it did, this disease very rapidly became a powerful selective force.

No doubt humans tried to adjust culturally to these circumstances, and numerous biological adaptations also probably came into play. The sickle-cell trait is one of these biological adaptations. However, there is a definite cost involved with such an adaptation. Carriers have increased resistance to malaria and presumably higher reproductive success, but some of their offspring may be lost through sickle-cell anemia. So there is a counterbalancing of selective forces with an advantage for carriers *only* in malarial environments. The genetic patterns of recessive traits such as sickle-cell anemia are discussed in Chapter 3.

Following World War II, extensive and systematic DDT spraying by the World Health Organization began to control mosquito-breeding areas in the tropics. Forty years of DDT spraying killed many mosquitoes; but natural selection, acting on these insect populations, produced several DDT-resistant strains (Fig. 4–3). Accordingly, malaria is again on the rise, with several hundred thousand new cases reported annually in India, Africa, and Central America.

Lactose intolerance, a condition involving an individual's ability to digest fresh milk, is another example of human biocultural evolution. In all human populations, infants and young children are able to digest milk, an obvious necessity for any young mammal. One ingredient of milk is the sugar *lactose*, which is broken down in humans and other mammals by the enzyme *lactase*. In most mammals, including many humans, the gene that codes for lactase production "switches off" in adolescence. Once this happens, the lactose ferments in the large intestine, leading to diarrhea and severe gastrointestinal upset. Among many African and Asian populations (a majority of humankind today), most adults are lactose intolerant (Table 4–1).

Why do we see variation in lactose tolerance among human populations? Throughout most of hominid evolution, milk was unavailable after weaning. Perhaps, in such circumstances, the continued action of an unnecessary enzyme might inhibit digestion of other foods. Therefore, there *may* be a selective advantage for the gene coding for lactase production to switch off. So why can some adults (the majority in some populations) tolerate milk? The distribution of lactose-tolerant populations may provide an answer to this question, and it suggests a probable cultural influence on this trait.

Europeans, who are generally lactose tolerant, are partially descended from Middle Eastern populations. Often economically dependent on pastoralism, these groups raised cows and/or goats and probably drank considerable quantities of milk. In such a cultural environment, strong selection pressures would favor lactose tolerance, and modern European descendants of these populations apparently retain this ancient ability. Very interesting genetic evidence from northern Europe has recently supported this interpretation. In fact, analyses of both cattle *and* human DNA suggest both species have coevolved, leading to cattle that produce high-quality milk and humans with the genetic capacity to digest it (Beja-Pereira et al., 2003).

Just as informative is the distribution of lactose tolerance in Africa, where most people are lactose intolerant. But groups such as the Fulani and Tutsi, who have been pastoralists perhaps for thousands of years, have much higher rates of lactose tolerance than nonpastoralists do. Presumably, like their European counterparts, these groups have retained the ability to produce lactase because of their continued consumption of fresh milk. Within Africa, the population pattern has become somewhat complicated, however, perhaps as a result of recent gene flow (Powell et al., 2003).

As we've seen, the geographical distribution of lactose tolerance is related to a history of cultural dependence on fresh milk products. There are, however, some populations that rely on dairying but don't have high rates of lactose tolerance (Fig. 4–4). It's been suggested that such populations have traditionally consumed milk in the form of cheese and yogurt, in which the lactose has been broken down by bacterial action (Durham, 1981).

FIGURE 4–4
Natives of Mongolia rely heavily on milk products from goats and sheep, but mostly consume these foods in the form of cheese and yogurt.

The interaction of human cultural environments and changes in lactose tolerance among human populations is another example of biocultural evolution. In the last few thousand years, cultural factors have initiated specific evolutionary changes in human groups. Such cultural factors have probably influenced the course of human evolution for at least 3 million years, and today they are of paramount importance.

Population Genetics

Physical anthropologists today use the approach of **population genetics** to interpret microevolutionary patterns of human variation. As we defined it in Chapter 3, a *population* is a group of interbreeding individuals. More precisely, a population is the group within which one is most likely to find a mate. As such, a population is marked by a degree of genetic relatedness and shares a common gene pool.

In theory, this is a straightforward concept. In every generation, the genes (alleles) are mixed by recombination and rejoined through mating. What emerges in the next generation is a direct product of the genes going into the pool, which in turn is a product of who is mating with whom.

In practice, however, describing human populations is difficult. The largest population of *Homo sapiens* that could be described is the entire species. All members of a species are *potentially* capable of breeding with one another, but are incapable of fertile breeding with members of other species. The problem arises not in describing who potentially can interbreed, but in isolating exactly the pattern of those individuals who are doing so.

Factors that determine mate choice are geographical, ecological, and social. If people are isolated on a remote island in the middle of the Pacific, there isn't much chance they'll find a mate outside the immediate vicinity. Such **breeding isolates** are fairly easily defined and are a favorite target of microevolutionary studies. Geography plays a dominant role in producing these isolates by rather strictly determining the range of available mates. But even within these limits, cultural rules can easily play a deciding role by prescribing which mate is the most appropriate among those who are potentially available.

Human population segments within the species are defined as groups with relative degrees of **endogamy** (marrying/mating within the group). These are, however, not totally closed systems. Gene flow often occurs between groups, and individuals may choose mates from distant localities. With the modern advent of rapid transportation, greatly accelerated rates of **exogamy** (marrying/mating outside the group) have emerged.

population genetics   The study of the frequency of alleles, genotypes, and phenotypes in populations from a microevolutionary perspective.

breeding isolates   Populations that are clearly isolated geographically and/or socially from other breeding groups.

endogamy   Mating with individuals from the same group.

exogamy   Mating pattern whereby individuals obtain mates from groups other than their own.

Most humans today aren't so clearly defined as members of particular populations as they would be if they belonged to a breeding isolate. Inhabitants of large cities may appear to be members of a single population, but within the city are social, ethnic, and religious boundaries that crosscut in a complex fashion to form smaller population segments. In addition to being members of these highly open local population groupings, we are simultaneously members of overlapping gradations of larger populations—the immediate geographical region (a metropolitan area or perhaps a state), a section of the country, a nation, and ultimately, the entire species.

Once specific human populations have been identified, the next step is to ascertain what evolutionary forces, if any, are operating on them. To determine whether evolution is occurring at a given locus, population geneticists measure allele frequencies for specific traits and compare these observed frequencies with a set predicted by a mathematical model called the **Hardy-Weinberg equilibrium** equation. Just how the equation is used is illustrated in Appendix C. The Hardy-Weinberg formula provides a tool to establish whether allele frequencies in a human population are indeed changing. In Chapter 3, we discussed several factors that act to change allele frequencies, including

1. New variation (that is, *mutation*)
2. Redistributed variation (that is, *gene flow* or *genetic drift*)
3. Selection of "advantageous" allele combinations that promote reproductive success (that is, *natural selection*)

The Adaptive Significance of Human Variation

Today, biological anthropologists view human variation as the result of the evolutionary factors we have just listed: mutation, genetic drift/founder effect, gene flow, and natural selection (the latter especially seen in adaptations to environmental conditions, both past and present). As emphasized, cultural adaptations have also played an important role in the evolution of *Homo sapiens*, and although in this discussion we're primarily concerned with biological issues, we still have to consider the influence of cultural practices on human adaptive response.

All organisms must maintain the normal functions of internal organs, tissues, and cells in order to survive, and they must do so in the context of an ever-changing environment. Even during the course of a single, seemingly uneventful day, there are numerous fluctuations in temperature, wind, solar radiation, humidity, and so on. Physical activity also places **stress** on physiological mechanisms. The body has to accommodate all these changes by compensating in some way to maintain internal constancy, or **homeostasis**, and all life-forms have evolved physiological mechanisms that, within limits, achieve this goal.

Physiological response to environmental change is, to some degree, influenced by genetic factors. We've already defined adaptation as a functional response to environmental conditions in populations and individuals. In a narrower sense, adaptation refers to *long-term* evolutionary (that is, genetic) changes that characterize all individuals within a population or species.

Examples of long-term adaptations in *Homo sapiens* include some physiological responses to heat (sweating) and deeply pigmented skin in tropical regions. Such characteristics are the results of evolutionary change in species or populations, and they don't vary due to short-term environmental change. For example, the ability to sweat isn't lost in people who spend their entire lives in predominantly cool areas. Likewise, individuals born with deeply pigmented skin won't become pale, even if they're never exposed to intense sunlight.

Short-term physiological response to environmental change is called **acclimatization**. Tanning, which can occur in almost everyone, is a form of acclimatization. Another example is the very rapid increase in hemoglobin production that occurs when lowland natives travel to higher elevations. This increase provides the body with more oxygen in an environment where oxygen is less available. In both examples, the physiological change is tem-

Hardy-Weinberg equilibrium   The mathematical relationship expressing—under ideal conditions—the predicted distribution of alleles in populations; the central theorem of population genetics.

stress   In a physiological context, any factor that acts to disrupt homeostasis; more precisely, the body's response to any factor that threatens its ability to maintain homeostasis.

homeostasis   A condition of balance, or stability, within a biological system, maintained by the interaction of physiological mechanisms that compensate for changes (both external and internal).

acclimatization   Physiological responses to changes in the environment that occur during an individual's lifetime. Such responses may be temporary or permanent, depending on the duration of the environmental change and when in the individual's life it occurs. The *capacity* for acclimatization may typify an entire species or population, and because it is under genetic influence, it is subject to evolutionary factors such as natural selection or genetic drift.

porary. Tans fade once exposure to sunlight is reduced; and hemoglobin production drops to original levels following a return to lower altitudes.

In the following discussion, we'll present some examples of how humans respond to environmental challenges. Some of these examples illustrate adaptations that characterize the entire species. Others illustrate adaptations seen in only some populations. And still others illustrate the more short-term process of acclimatization.

SOLAR RADIATION, VITAMIN D, AND SKIN COLOR

Skin color is often cited as an example of adaptation and natural selection in human populations. In general, prior to European contact, skin color in populations followed a largely predictable geographical distribution, especially in the Old World. Populations with the greatest amount of pigmentation are found in the tropics, while lighter skin color is associated with more northern latitudes, particularly the inhabitants of northwestern Europe.

Skin color is mostly influenced by the pigment *melanin*, a granular substance produced by specialized cells called *melanocytes* that are found in the epidermis. All humans appear to have approximately the same number of melanocytes. It's the amount of melanin and the size of the melanin granules that vary.

Melanin has the capacity to absorb the potentially dangerous ultraviolet (UV) rays present (although not visible) in sunlight. Therefore, it provides protection from overexposure to ultraviolet radiation, which can cause genetic mutations in skin cells. These mutations may ultimately lead to skin cancer, which if left untreated can eventually spread to other organs and result in death.

As we mentioned earlier, exposure to sunlight triggers a protective mechanism in the form of tanning, the result of temporarily increased melanin production (acclimatization). This response occurs in all humans except albinos, who carry a genetic mutation that prevents their melanocytes from producing melanin (Fig. 4–5). But even humans who do produce melanin differ in their ability to tan. For instance, many people of northern European descent have very fair skin, blue eyes, and light hair. Their cells obviously produce small amounts of melanin, but when exposed to sunlight, these people have little ability to increase production. And in all populations, women tend not to tan as deeply as men do.

Natural selection has favored dark skin in areas nearest the equator, where the sun's rays are most direct and thus where exposure to UV light is most intense and constant. In considering the cancer-causing effects of UV radiation from an *evolutionary* perspective, keep in mind these three points:

1. Early hominids lived in the tropics, where solar radiation is more intense than in temperate areas to the north and south.
2. Unlike modern city dwellers, early hominids were always outdoors.
3. Early hominids didn't wear clothing that would have protected them from the sun.

Given these conditions, UV radiation was probably a powerful agent selecting for varied levels of melanin production in early humans, especially as they left the tropics.

As hominids migrated out of Africa into Europe and Asia, selective pressures changed. Not only were they moving away from the tropics, where UV rays were most direct, but they were also moving into areas where it was cold and cloudy during winter. Bear in mind, too, that physiological adaptations weren't sufficient to meet the demands of living in colder climates. Therefore, we assume that these populations had adopted certain cultural practices, such as wearing animal skins or other types of clothing. Although clothing would have added necessary warmth, it also would have blocked sunlight. Consequently, the advantages provided by deeply pigmented skin in the tropics were no longer important, and selection for melanin production may have been relaxed (Brace and Montagu, 1977).

However, relaxed selection favoring dark skin may not adequately explain the very depigmented skin seen especially in some northern Europeans. Perhaps another factor, the need for adequate amounts of vitamin D, was also critical. The theory concerning the possible role of vitamin D, known as the *vitamin D hypothesis*, offers the following explanation.

Vitamin D is produced in the body partly because of the interaction between UV radiation and a substance similar to cholesterol. It's also available in some foods, including liver, fish oils, egg yolk, butter, and cream. Vitamin D is necessary for normal bone growth and

FIGURE 4–5

An African albino. This young man has a greatly increased likelihood of developing skin cancer compared to the man on the right.

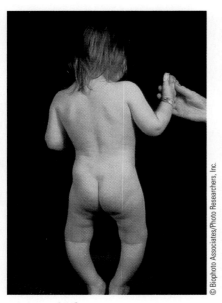

FIGURE **4–6**
A child with rickets.

mineralization, and some exposure to UV radiation is therefore essential. Insufficient amounts of vitamin D during childhood result in *rickets*, which often leads to bowing of the long bones of the legs and deformation of the pelvis (Fig. 4–6). Pelvic deformities are of particular concern for women, since they can lead to a narrowing of the birth canal, which, in the absence of surgical intervention, frequently results in the death of both mother and infant during childbirth.

This explanation illustrates the potential for rickets as a significant selective factor favoring less-pigmented skin in regions where climate and other factors reduce exposure to UV radiation. It's obvious how reduced exposure to sunlight could have been detrimental to dark-skinned individuals in more northern latitudes (Fig. 4–7). In these individuals, melanin would have blocked absorption of the already reduced amounts of available UV radiation required for vitamin D synthesis. Therefore, selection pressures would have shifted over time to favor individuals with lighter skin. There is substantial evidence, both historically and in contemporary populations, to support this theory.

During the last decades of the nineteenth century in the United States, African Americans living in northern cities suffered a higher incidence of rickets than whites did. Northern African Americans were also more commonly affected than were those living in the South, where exposure to sunlight is greater. (The supplementation of milk with vitamin D was initiated to alleviate this problem.) Another example is seen in Britain, where darker-skinned East Indians and Pakistanis show a higher incidence of rickets than do people with lighter skin (Molnar, 1983).

Jablonski (1992) and Jablonski and Chaplin (2000) offer an additional explanation for the distribution of skin color, one that focuses on the role of UV radiation in the degradation of folate. Folate is a B vitamin that isn't stored in the body and must be replenished through

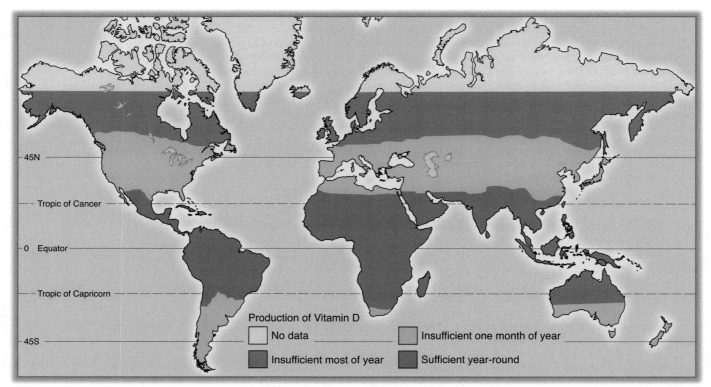

FIGURE **4–7**
Populations indigenous to the tropics (green band) receive sufficient UV radiation for vitamin D synthesis (year-round). The orange band represents areas where people with moderately melanized skin do not receive sufficient UV light for vitamin D synthesis for one month of the year. The purple band represents an area where even light skin does not receive enough UV light for vitamin D synthesis on a yearly basis. (Adapted from Jablonski and Chaplin, 2000, 2002.)

dietary sources. Folate deficiencies in pregnant women are associated with numerous complications, including maternal death, and in children they can lead to growth retardation and other serious conditions. Folate also plays a crucial role in **neural tube** development very early in embryonic development, and in this context, deficiencies can lead to defects that include various expressions of **spina bifida**. The consequences of severe neural tube defects can include pain, infection, paralysis, and even death. It goes without saying that neural tube defects can dramatically reduce the reproductive success of affected individuals.

Studies have shown that UV radiation rapidly depletes folate serum levels both in laboratory experiments and in light-skinned individuals. These findings have implications for pregnant women and children as well as for the evolution of dark skin in hominids. Jablonski and Chaplin suggest that the earliest hominids may have had light body skin covered with dark hair, as is seen in chimpanzees and gorillas. (Both have darker skin on exposed body parts.) But as loss of body hair in hominids occurred, dark skin evolved rather quickly as a protective response to the damaging effects of UV radiation on folate.

Perhaps more social importance has been attached to variation in skin color than to any other single human biological trait. But aside from its probable adaptive significance relative to UV radiation, skin color is no more important physiologically than many other biological characteristics. Still, from an evolutionary perspective, it's a good example of how the forces of natural selection have produced geographically patterned variation due to at least three selective forces: the need for protection from overexposure to UV radiation; the competing necessity for adequate UV exposure to promote vitamin D synthesis; and the need for protection against folate loss.

THE THERMAL ENVIRONMENT

Mammals and birds have evolved complex mechanisms to maintain a constant internal body temperature. While reptiles rely on exposure to external heat sources to raise their body temperature and energy levels, mammals and birds have physiological mechanisms that, within certain limits, increase or reduce the loss of body heat. The optimum internal body temperature for normal cellular functions is species-specific, and for humans it's approximately 98.6°F.

Homo sapiens is found in a wide variety of habitats, with temperatures ranging from over 120°F to less than –60°F. In these extremes, human life wouldn't be possible without cultural innovations. But even accounting for the artificial environments in which we live, such external conditions place the human body under enormous stress.

Response to Heat All available evidence suggests that the earliest hominids evolved in the warm-to-hot woodlands and savannas of East Africa. The fact that humans cope better with heat than they do with cold is testimony to the long-term adaptations to heat that evolved in our ancestors.

In humans, as well as in certain other species such as horses, sweat glands are distributed throughout the skin. This wide distribution of sweat glands makes it possible to lose heat at the body surface through evaporative cooling, a mechanism that has evolved to the greatest degree in humans.

The capacity to dissipate heat by sweating is seen in all humans to an almost equal degree, with the average number of sweat glands per individual (approximately 1.6 million) being fairly constant. However, there is some variation since people who aren't generally exposed to hot conditions do experience a period of acclimatization that initially involves significantly increased perspiration rates (Frisancho, 1993). Another factor that enhances the cooling effects of sweating is increased exposure of the skin through reduced amounts of body hair. We don't know when in our evolutionary history we began to lose body hair, but it was an important species-wide adaptation because heat reduction through evaporation can be expensive, and indeed dangerous, in terms of water and sodium loss.

Yet another mechanism for radiating body heat is **vasodilation**, which takes place when capillaries near the skin's surface widen to permit increased blood flow to the skin. The visible effect of vasodilation is flushing—or increased redness of the skin, particularly of the face—accompanied by warmth. But the physiological effect is to permit heat, carried by the blood from the interior of the body, to be emitted from the skin's surface to the surrounding

neural tube In early embryonic development, the anatomical structure that develops to form the brain and spinal cord.

spina bifida A condition in which the arch of one or more vertebrae fails to fuse and form a protective barrier around the spinal cord.

vasodilation Expansion of blood vessels, permitting increased blood flow to the skin. Vasodilation permits warming of the skin, and it facilitates radiation of warmth in order to cool the skin. Vasodilation is an involuntary response to warm temperatures, various drugs, and even emotional states (blushing).

FIGURE 4–8

(a) This African woman has the linear proportions characteristic of many inhabitants of sub-Saharan Africa. (b) By comparison, the Inuit woman is short and stocky. These two individuals serve as good examples of Bergmann's and Allen's rules.

(a)　　　(b)

air. (Some drugs, including alcohol, also produce vasodilation, which accounts for the increased redness and warmth of the face some people experience after a drink or two.)

Body size and proportions are also important in regulating body temperature. Indeed, there seems to be a general relationship between climate and body size and shape in birds and mammals. In general, within a species, body size (weight) increases as distance from the equator increases. In humans, this relationship holds up fairly well, but there are numerous exceptions. Two rules concerning the relationship between body size, body proportions, and climate are *Bergmann's rule* and *Allen's rule.*

1. *Bergmann's rule (considers the relationship of body mass or volume to surface area)*: In mammalian species, body size tends to be greater in populations that live in colder climates. This occurs because as mass increases, the relative amount of surface area decreases proportionately. Because heat is lost at the surface, it follows that increased mass allows for greater heat retention and reduced heat loss.
2. *Allen's rule (considers shape of the body, especially appendages)*: In colder climates, shorter appendages, with increased mass-to-surface ratios, are adaptive because they're more effective at preventing heat loss. Conversely, longer appendages, with increased surface area relative to mass, are more adaptive in warmer climates because they promote heat loss.

According to these rules, the most suitable body shape in hot climates is linear, with long arms and legs. In a cold climate, a more suitable body type is stocky, with shorter limbs. Considerable data gathered from several human populations generally conform to these principles. In colder climates, body mass tends, on average, to be greater and characterized by a larger trunk relative to arms and legs (Roberts, 1973). People living in the Arctic tend to be short and stocky, while many sub-Saharan Africans, especially East African pastoralists, are on average tall and linear (Fig. 4–8). But there's a great deal of variability regarding human body proportions, and not all populations conform so readily to Bergmann's and Allen's rules.

Response to Cold Human physiological responses to cold combine factors that increase heat retention with those that enhance heat production. Of the two, heat retention is more efficient because it requires less energy. This is an important point because energy is derived from dietary sources. Unless food is abundant, and in winter it frequently isn't, any factor that conserves energy can have adaptive value.

Short-term responses to cold include increased metabolic rate and shivering, both of which generate body heat, at least for a short time. **Vasoconstriction**, another short-term response, restricts heat loss and conserves energy. In addition, humans have a subcutaneous (beneath the skin) fat layer that provides insulation throughout the body. Behavioral modifications include increased activity, wearing warmer clothing, increased food consumption, and even curling up into a ball.

Increases in metabolic rate (the rate at which cells break up nutrients into their components) release energy in the form of heat. Shivering also generates muscle heat, as does voluntary exercise. But these methods of heat production are expensive because they require an increased intake of nutrients to provide energy. (This might explain why we tend to have a heartier appetite during the winter, and why we also tend to increase our intake of fats and carbohydrates, the very sources of energy our bodies require.)

In general, people exposed to chronic cold (meaning much or most of the year) maintain higher metabolic rates than do those living in warmer climates. The Inuit (Eskimo) people living in the Arctic maintain metabolic rates between 13 and 45 percent higher than those observed in non-Inuit control subjects (Frisancho, 1993). Moreover, the highest metabolic rates are seen in inland Inuit, who are exposed to even greater cold stress than coastal populations are. Traditionally, the Inuit had the highest animal protein and fat diet of any human population in the world. Such a diet, necessitated by the available resource base, helped maintain the high metabolic rates required by exposure to chronic cold.

Vasoconstriction restricts capillary blood flow to the surface of the skin, thus reducing heat loss at the body surface. Because it's more economical to retain body heat than to create it, vasoconstriction is very efficient, as long as temperatures don't drop below freezing. However, if temperatures do fall below freezing, continued vasoconstriction can be detrimental because the skin temperature can drop to the point of frostbite or worse.

Long-term responses to cold vary among human groups. For example, in the past, desert-dwelling indigenous Australian populations were subjected to wide temperature fluctuations from day to night. Because they wore no clothing and didn't build shelters, their only protection against temperatures that hovered only a few degrees above freezing was provided by sleeping fires. Throughout the night, these people experienced continuous vasoconstriction, which cooled their skin to an extent that most people would find extremely uncomfortable. But, since temperatures stayed above freezing, there was no threat of frostbite, and continued vasoconstriction helped to prevent excessive internal heat loss.

By contrast, the Inuit experience intermittent periods of vasoconstriction and vasodilation. This response is a compromise that causes periodic warming of the skin and helps prevent frostbite in below-freezing temperatures. At the same time, because vasodilation is intermittent, energy loss is restricted so that more heat is retained at the body's core.

These examples are just two of the many ways human populations adapt to cold. Although all humans respond to cold stress in much the same way, we manifest our adaptation and acclimatization in different ways.

HIGH ALTITUDE

Studies of high-altitude residents have greatly contributed to our understanding of physiological adaptation. As you would expect, altitude studies have focused on inhabited mountainous regions, particularly in the Himalayas, Andes, and Rocky Mountains. Of these three areas, permanent human habitation probably has the longest history in the Himalayas (Moore et al., 1998). Today, perhaps as many as 25 million people live at altitudes above 10,000 feet. In Tibet, permanent settlements exist above 15,000 feet, and in the Andes, they can be found as high as 17,000 feet (Fig. 4–9).

Because the mechanisms that maintain homeostasis in humans evolved at lower altitudes, they are compromised by the conditions at higher elevations. At high altitudes, many factors produce stress on the human body. These include **hypoxia** (reduced available oxygen), more intense solar radiation, cold, low humidity, wind (which amplifies cold stress), a reduced nutritional base, and rough terrain. Of these, hypoxia exerts the greatest amount of stress on human physiological systems, especially the heart, lungs, and brain.

Hypoxia results from reduced barometric pressure. It's not that there is less oxygen overall in the atmosphere at high altitudes; rather, it's less concentrated. This means that to obtain

vasoconstriction Narrowing of blood vessels to reduce blood flow to the skin. Vasoconstriction is an involuntary response to cold and reduces heat loss at the skin's surface.

hypoxia Lack of oxygen. Hypoxia can refer to reduced amounts of available oxygen in the atmosphere (due to lowered barometric pressure) or to insufficient amounts of oxygen in the body.

William Pratt

L. G. Moore

(a)

(b)

FIGURE 4–9

(a) La Paz, Bolivia, at just over 12,000 feet above sea level, is home to more than 1 million people. (b) A household in northern Tibet, situated at an elevation of over 15,000 feet above sea level.

the same amount of oxygen at 9,000 feet as at sea level, people must make certain physiological alterations aimed at increasing the body's ability to transport and efficiently use the oxygen that is available.

At high altitudes, reproduction is particularly affected, as shown by increased rates of infant mortality, miscarriage, low birth weights, and premature birth. An early study (Moore and Regensteiner, 1983) reported that in Colorado, infant deaths are almost twice as common at above 8,200 feet as at lower elevations. One cause of fetal and maternal death is preeclampsia, a severe elevation of blood pressure that can occur in pregnant women after the twentieth gestational week.

People born at lower altitudes and high-altitude natives differ somewhat in how they adapt to hypoxia. Upon exposure to high altitude, people born at low elevation become acclimatized. The responses may be short-term modifications, depending on duration of stay, but they begin within hours of the altitude change. These changes include an increase in respiration rate, heart rate, and production of red blood cells. (As we mentioned in Chapter 3, red blood cells contain hemoglobin, the protein responsible for transporting oxygen to organs and tissues.)

A more permanent, developmental acclimatization occurs in high-altitude natives during growth and development. This type of acclimatization is present only in people who grow up in high-altitude areas, not in those who moved there as adults. Compared with populations at lower elevations, lifelong residents of high altitudes display slowed growth and maturation. Other differences include larger chest size, associated in turn with greater lung volume and larger heart. In addition to greater lung capacity, people born at high altitudes are more efficient than migrants are at diffusing oxygen from blood to body tissues. Developmental acclimatization to high-altitude hypoxia serves as a good example of physiological plasticity by illustrating how, within the limits set by genetic factors, development can be influenced by environment.

There is evidence that entire *populations* have also genetically adapted to high altitudes. Indigenous peoples of Tibet who have inhabited regions higher than 12,000 feet for around 25,000 years may have made genetic (that is, evolutionary) accommodations to hypoxia. Altitude doesn't appear to affect reproduction in these people to the degree it does in other populations. Infants have birth weights as high as those of lowland Tibetan groups and higher than those of recent (20 to 30 years) Chinese immigrants. This fact may be the result of alterations in maternal blood flow to the uterus during pregnancy (Moore et al., 1994, 1999).

Another line of evidence concerns how the body processes glucose (blood sugar). Glucose is critical because it's the only source of energy used by the brain, and it's also used, although not exclusively, by the heart. Both highland Tibetans and the Quechua (inhabitants of high-altitude regions of the Peruvian Andes) burn glucose in a way that permits more efficient use of oxygen. This implies the presence of genetic mutations in the mitochondrial DNA (mtDNA directs how cells use glucose). It also implies that natural selection has acted to increase the frequency of these advantageous mutations in these groups.

As yet, there's no certain evidence that Tibetans and Quechua have made evolutionary changes to accommodate high-altitude hypoxia (since specific genetic mechanisms that underlie these populations' unique abilities have not been identified). But current data strongly suggest that selection has operated to produce evolutionary change in these two groups. If further study supports these findings, we have an excellent example of evolution in action producing long-term adaptation at the population level.

INFECTIOUS DISEASE

Infection, as opposed to other disease categories, such as degenerative or genetic disease, includes pathological conditions caused by microorganisms (viruses, bacteria, and fungi). Throughout the course of human evolution, infectious disease has exerted enormous selective pressures on populations and consequently has influenced the frequency of certain alleles that affect the immune response. In fact, it would be difficult to overemphasize the importance of infectious disease as an agent of natural selection in human populations. But as important as infectious disease has been, its role in this regard isn't very well documented.

The effects of infectious disease on humans are mediated culturally as well as biologically. Innumerable cultural factors, such as architectural styles, subsistence techniques, exposure to domesticated animals, and even religious practices, all affect how infectious disease develops and persists within and between populations.

Until about 10,000 to 12,000 years ago, all humans lived in small nomadic hunting and gathering groups. And since these groups rarely remained in one location more than a few days at a time, they had minimal contact with refuse heaps that house disease **vectors**. But with the domestication of plants and animals, people became more sedentary and began living in small villages. Gradually, villages became towns, and towns, in turn, developed into densely crowded, unsanitary cities.

As long as humans lived in small bands, there was little opportunity for infectious disease to have much impact on large numbers of people. Even if an entire local group were wiped out, the effect on the overall population in a given area would have been negligible. Besides, a disease can't become **endemic** in a population unless sufficient numbers of people are present. For these reasons, small bands of hunter-gatherers weren't faced with continuous exposure to endemic disease.

With the advent of settled living and close proximity to domesticated animals, opportunities for humans to contract disease greatly increased. As sedentary life permitted larger group size, it became possible for several diseases to become permanently established in some populations. Routine exposure to domestic animals, such as cattle and fowl, provided an opportune environment for the spread of **zoonotic** diseases, such as tuberculosis and SARS (severe acute respiratory disease), and avian flu. (As we are now aware, there is international concern over the potential of a particularly virulent strain of the avian flu virus to mutate to a form that can be transmitted from one human to another.) Humans have no doubt always contracted some diseases from the animals they hunted; but when they began to live with domesticated animals, they were faced with an entire array of new infectious conditions (see Chapter 14 for a further discussion of the biocultural effects of domestication). Also, the crowded, unsanitary conditions that characterized parts of all cities until the late nineteenth century, and that persist in much of the world today, further added to the disease burden borne by human inhabitants.

AIDS (acquired immune deficiency syndrome) provides an excellent, but indirect, example of the influence of human infectious disease as a selective agent. In the United States, the first cases of AIDS were reported in 1981. Since then, perhaps as many as 1.5 million Americans have been infected by HIV (human immunodeficiency virus), the agent that causes AIDS. However, most of the burden of AIDS is borne by developing countries, where

vectors   Agents that serve to transmit disease from one carrier to another. Mosquitoes are vectors for malaria, just as fleas are vectors for bubonic plague.

endemic   Continuously present in a population.

zoonotic   (zoh-oh-nah´-tic) Pertaining to a zoonosis (pl., zoonoses), a disease that is transmitted to humans through contact with nonhuman animals.

95 percent of all HIV-infected people live. By the end of 2005, an estimated 37 to 45 million people worldwide were living with HIV infection, and at least 25 million had died (UNAIDS/WHO AIDS Epidemic Update, 2005).

HIV is transmitted from person to person through the exchange of bodily fluids, usually blood or semen. It is not spread through casual contact with an infected person. Within six months of infection, most infected people test positive for anti-HIV antibodies, meaning that their immune system has recognized the presence of foreign antigens and has responded by producing antibodies. However, serious HIV-related symptoms may not appear for years. HIV is a "slow virus" that may persist in a person's body for several years before the onset of severe illness. This asymptomatic state is called a latency period, and the average latency period in the United States is more than 11 years.

Like all viruses, HIV must invade certain types of cells and change the activities of those cells in order to produce more virus particles in a process that eventually leads to cell destruction. (HIV does this in a different way from that of many other viruses.) HIV can attack various types of cells, but it especially targets so-called T4 helper cells, which are major components of the immune system. As HIV infection spreads and T4 cells are destroyed, the patient's immune system begins to fail. Consequently, he or she develops symptoms caused by various **pathogens** that are commonly present but usually kept in check by a normal immune response. When an HIV-infected person's T cell count drops to a level indicating that immunity has been suppressed, and when symptoms of "opportunistic" infections appear, the patient is said to have AIDS.

By the early 1990s, scientists were aware of several patients who had been HIV positive for 10 to 15 years, but who continued to show few if any symptoms. This awareness led researchers to suspect that some individuals are naturally immune or resistant to HIV infection. This was shown to be true in late 1996 with the publication of two different studies (Dean et al., 1996; Samson et al., 1996) that demonstrated a mechanism for resistance to HIV.

These two reports describe a genetic mutation that involves a major protein "receptor site" on the surface of certain immune cells, including T4 cells. (Receptor sites are protein molecules that enable HIV and other viruses to invade cells.) Because of the mutation, the receptor site doesn't function properly and HIV is unable to bind to the cell. Current evidence suggests that people who are homozygous for a particular (mutant) allele may be completely resistant to many types of HIV infection. In heterozygotes, infection may still occur, but the course of HIV disease is slowed.

Interestingly, and for unknown reasons, the mutant allele occurs mainly in people of European descent, among whom its frequency is about 10 percent. Samson and colleagues (1996) reported that in the Japanese and West African groups they studied, the mutation was absent, but Dean and colleagues (1996) reported an allele frequency of about 2 percent among African Americans. They speculated that the presence of the allele in African Americans may be entirely due to genetic admixture (gene flow) with European Americans. They further suggested that this polymorphism exists in Europeans as a result of selective pressures favoring an allele that originally occurred as a rare mutation. But we should point out that the original selective agent was *not* HIV. Instead it was some other pathogen, not yet identified, that uses the same receptor site as HIV, and some researchers (Lalani et al., 1999) have suggested that it may have been the virus that causes smallpox.

Without a doubt, the best-known epidemic in history was the Black Death (bubonic plague) in the mid-fourteenth century. Bubonic plague is caused by a bacterium that is transmitted from rodents to humans by fleas. In just a few years, this deadly disease had spread (following trade routes and facilitated by rodent-infested ship cargoes) from the Caspian Sea throughout the Mediterranean area to northern Europe. During the initial exposure to this disease, as many as one-third of the inhabitants of Europe died.

A lesser-known but even more devastating example was the influenza **pandemic** that broke out in 1918 at the end of World War I. This was actually one of a series of influenza outbreaks, but it has remained notable for its still unexplained virulence and the fact that it accounted for the deaths of over 21 million people worldwide.

Even though we have no clear-cut evidence of a selective role for bubonic plague or influenza, that doesn't mean there isn't one. The tremendous mortality that these diseases (and others) are capable of causing certainly increases the likelihood that they influenced the development of human adaptive responses in ways we haven't yet discovered.

pathogens   Any agents, especially microorganisms such as viruses, bacteria, or fungi, that infect a host and cause disease.

pandemic   An extensive outbreak of disease affecting large numbers of individuals over a wide area; potentially a worldwide phenomenon.

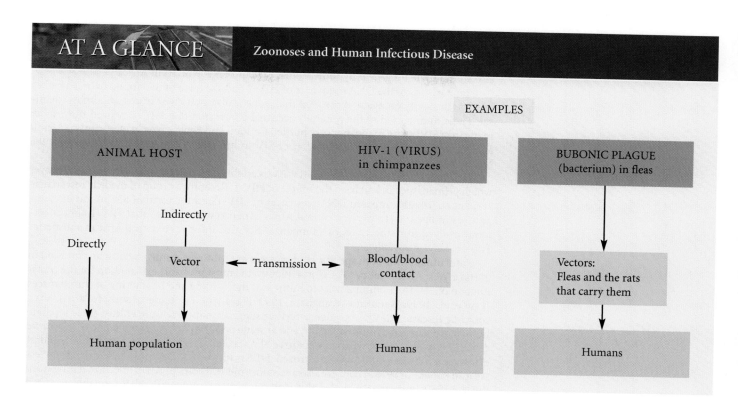

AT A GLANCE — Zoonoses and Human Infectious Disease

EXAMPLES

ANIMAL HOST → Directly → Human population

ANIMAL HOST → Indirectly → Vector → Human population

Vector ← Transmission → Blood/blood contact

HIV-1 (VIRUS) in chimpanzees → Blood/blood contact → Humans

BUBONIC PLAGUE (bacterium) in fleas → Vectors: Fleas and the rats that carry them → Humans

The Continuing Impact of Infectious Disease

It's important to understand that humans and pathogens exert selective pressures on each other, creating a dynamic relationship between disease organisms and their human (and non-human) hosts. Just as disease exerts selective pressures on host populations to adapt, microorganisms also evolve and adapt to various pressures exerted on them by their hosts.

Evolutionarily speaking, it's to the advantage of any pathogen not to be so virulent as to kill its host too quickly. If the host dies soon after becoming infected, the virus or bacterium may not have time to reproduce and infect other hosts, so it will be eliminated along with its host. Thus, selection sometimes acts to produce resistance in host populations and/or to reduce the virulence of disease organisms, to the benefit of both. However, members of populations exposed for the first time to a new disease frequently die in huge numbers. This type of exposure was a major factor in the decimation of indigenous New World populations after they came in contact with Europeans, who introduced smallpox into Native American groups. And this has also been the case with the current worldwide spread of HIV.

Of the known disease-causing organisms, HIV provides the best-documented example of evolution and adaptation in a pathogen. It's also one of several examples of interspecies transfer of infection. HIV is the most mutable and genetically variable virus known. The type of HIV responsible for the AIDS epidemic is HIV-1, which in turn is divided into three major subtypes (Hu et al., 1996; Gao, 1999). Another far less common type is HIV-2, which is present only in populations of West Africa. HIV-2 also exhibits a wide range of genetic diversity, and while some strains cause AIDS, others are far less virulent.

Since the late 1980s, researchers have been comparing the DNA sequences of HIV and a closely related retrovirus called *simian immunodeficiency virus (SIV)*. SIV is found in chimpanzees and several African monkey species. Like HIV, SIV is genetically variable, and each strain appears to be specific to a given species and even subspecies of primate. SIV produces no symptoms in the African monkeys and chimpanzees that are its traditional hosts, but when injected into Asian monkeys, it eventually causes AIDS-like symptoms and death. These findings indicate that the various forms of SIV have shared a long evolutionary history (perhaps several hundred thousand years) with a number of African primate species and that the latter are able to accommodate this virus, which is deadly to their Asian relatives. These results also substantiate long-held hypotheses that SIV and HIV evolved in Africa.

Comparisons of the DNA sequences of HIV-2 and the form of SIV found in one monkey species (the sooty mangabey) revealed that, genetically, these two viruses are almost identical. These findings led to the generally accepted conclusion that HIV-2 evolved from sooty mangabey SIV. Sooty mangabeys are hunted for food and kept as pets in west-central Africa, and it's probable that the transmission of SIV to humans occurred through bites and the butchering of monkey carcasses.

But although the likely origin of HIV-2 was established, there was continuing debate over which primate species had been the source of HIV-1. Recently, a group of medical researchers (Gao et al., 1999) compared DNA sequences of HIV-1 and the form of SIV found in chimpanzees indigenous to western central Africa. Their results showed that HIV-1 almost certainly evolved from the strain of chimpanzee SIV that infects the central African subspecies *Pan troglodytes troglodytes*.

Unfortunately for both species, chimpanzees are routinely hunted by humans for food in parts of West Africa (see p. 137). Consequently, the most probable explanation for the transmission of SIV from chimpanzees to humans is the hunting and butchering of chimpanzees (Gao et al., 1999; Weiss and Wrangham, 1999; Fig. 4–10). For these reasons, HIV/AIDS is a zoonotic disease. The DNA evidence further suggests that there were at least three separate human exposures to chimpanzee SIV, and at some point the virus was altered to the form we call HIV. No one knows when chimpanzee SIV was first transmitted to humans. The oldest evidence of human infection is a frozen HIV-positive blood sample taken from a West African patient in 1959. There are also a few documented cases of AIDS infection dating from the late 1960s and early 1970s. So, although human exposure to SIV/HIV probably occurred many times in the past, the virus didn't become firmly established in humans until the latter half of the twentieth century.

Severe acute respiratory syndrome (SARS) is another contemporary example of zoonotic transmission of disease. In early 2003, an outbreak of SARS in southern China surprised the world health community by quickly spreading through much of Asia and then to North America (especially Canada), South America, and Europe.

When compared to diseases such as HIV/AIDS, tuberculosis, influenza, and malaria, SARS poses a relatively minor threat. Nevertheless, it can be fatal, especially in the elderly. Scientists don't know the exact mode of SARS transmission in humans, but most believe that it's spread through close contact by means of infected droplets (that is, when people cough or sneeze). Many health officials think that it was initially transmitted to humans through contact with domesticated animals or wild animals, such as civet cats, sold in Asian markets for food. Indeed, many of the influenza strains that frequently arise in China seem to originate in pigs and fowl that live in very close contact with humans.

How did SARS spread so quickly around the world, even though it has a fairly low transmission rate? The answer is travel. If modern technology didn't exist, this infection would have been confined to one or a few villages, and perhaps a small number of people would have died. But overall, it would have been a fairly unremarkable event, and it certainly wouldn't have become widely known. In fact, this and many other similar scenarios have undoubtedly been repeated countless times throughout the course of human history.

In 2003 and 2004, in addition to SARS, there were several outbreaks of a severe influenza in poultry in China and seven other Asian countries (Li et al., 2004). These outbreaks were caused by a particularly virulent

FIGURE 4–10
These people, selling butchered chimpanzees, may not realize that by handling this meat they could be exposing themselves to HIV or the Ebola virus.

Karl Ammann

virus called H5N1. Several influenza viruses commonly infect wild birds, but most of them don't cause serious illness. Typically, these viruses are present in the saliva and feces of infected birds and are spread when noninfected birds have contact either with infected birds or with contaminated surfaces. But, the H5N1 virus is usually fatal to birds (domestic and wild) and it has sporadically spread to humans. As of this writing, all the people who contracted the virus had been in close contact with domestic fowl and are believed to have been infected while handling and slaughtering poultry or coming into contact with contaminated cages.

The first known outbreak in humans was in Hong Kong in 1997. As of January, 2006, 156 people in Asia (particularly Viet Nam) had been infected, and approximately half had died. There were also human cases in Turkey and Iraq; the virus was also detected in wild bird carcasses in Africa, and as far west as Britain. The virus is spreading along migration routes of wild birds, and it can also spread through the shipping of live poultry and, possibly, uncooked poultry products.

Among scientists, there is considerable debate over whether or not the H5N1 virus poses a serious threat to humans (Butler, 2006). The main concern is that the virus might mutate to a form that could be spread from human to human—and, considering its virulence, that it could cause an influenza pandemic similar to the one in 1918. The concern is significant enough that hundreds of millions of chickens and ducks have been slaughtered and millions more have been vaccinated. Results of laboratory studies indicate that there are a few already available medications that should be effective in treating human H5N1 infection, as long as the virus doesn't become resistant. And, scientists are working to develop an effective vaccine for humans—but as of this writing, none is available.

From these three examples (HIV, SARS, and H5N1) you can appreciate how, by adopting various cultural practices, humans have radically altered patterns of infectious disease. In the past, the interaction of cultural and biological factors influenced microevolutionary change in humans (as in the example of sickle-cell anemia) to accommodate altered relationships with disease organisms. And, as you can see, infectious disease in humans continues to be a highly significant consequence of cultural practices today. It remains to be seen whether it will produce microevolutionary change.

Until the twentieth century, infectious disease was the number one cause of death in all human populations. Even today, in many developing countries, infectious disease causes as many as half of all deaths. This compares to only about 10 percent in the United States. For example, malaria is a disease of the poor in developing nations. Annually, there are an estimated 1 million deaths due to malaria. Ninety percent of these deaths occur in sub-Saharan Africa, where 5 percent of children die of malaria before age 5 (Greenwood and Mutabingwa, 2002; Weiss, 2002). In the United States and other developed nations, with better living conditions and sanitation and especially with the widespread use of antibiotics and pesticides beginning in the late 1940s, infectious disease has given way to heart disease and cancer as the leading causes of death.

Optimistic predictions held that infectious disease would be a thing of the past in developed countries and, with the introduction of antibiotics and better living standards, in developing nations too. But between 1980 and 1992, the number of deaths in the United States in which infectious disease was the underlying cause rose from 41 to 65 per 100,000, an increase of 58 percent (Pinner et al., 1996).

Obviously, HIV/AIDS contributed substantially to the increase in infectious disease in the United States between 1980 and 1992. Still, even when subtracting the effect of AIDS in mortality rates, there was a 22 percent increase in mortality rates due to infectious disease between 1980 and 1992 (Pinner et al., 1996).

This increase may partly be due to the overuse of antibiotics. It's estimated that half of all antibiotics prescribed in the United States are used to treat viral conditions such as colds and flu. Because antibiotics are completely ineffective against viruses, such therapy is not only useless, but may also have dangerous long-term consequences. There is considerable concern in the biomedical community over the indiscriminate use of antibiotics and pesticides since the 1950s. Antibiotics have exerted selective pressures on bacterial species that have, over time, developed antibiotic-resistant strains (an excellent example of natural selection). Consequently, the past few years have seen the *reemergence* of many bacterial diseases, including influenza, pneumonia, cholera, and tuberculosis, in forms that are less responsive to treatment.

The World Health Organization now lists tuberculosis as the world's leading killer of adults (Colwell, 1996). Notably, the number of tuberculosis cases has risen 28 percent worldwide since the mid-1980s, with an estimated 10 million people infected in the United States alone. Although not all infected persons develop active disease, in the 1990s, an estimated 30 million persons worldwide were believed to have died from TB. One very troubling aspect of the increase in tuberculosis infection is that newly developed strains of *Mycobacterium tuberculosis,* the bacterium that causes TB, are resistant to antibiotics and other treatments.

Various treatments for nonbacterial conditions have also become ineffective. One such example is the appearance of chloroquin-resistant malaria, which has rendered chloroquin (the traditional preventive medication) virtually useless in some parts of Africa. And many insect species have also developed resistance to commonly used pesticides.

In addition to threats posed by resistant strains of pathogens, there are other factors that may contribute to the emergence (or reemergence) of infectious disease. Political leaders (aside from most in the United States) and an overwhelming majority of scientists worldwide are becoming increasingly concerned over the potential for global warming to expand the geographical range of numerous tropical disease vectors, such as mosquitoes. And the destruction of natural environments not only contributes to global warming but also has the potential of causing disease vectors formerly restricted to local areas to spread to new habitats.

One other factor associated with the rapid spread of disease and directly related to technological change is the mixing of people at an unprecedented rate. Indeed, an estimated 1 million people per day cross national borders by air (Lederberg, 1996)! In addition, new road construction and wider availability of motor-driven vehicles allow more people (armies, refugees, truck drivers, etc.) to travel farther and faster than ever before.

Fundamental to all these factors is human population size, which, as it continues to soar, causes more environmental disturbance and, through additional human activity, adds further to global warming. Moreover, in developing countries, where as much as 50 percent of mortality is due to infectious disease, overcrowding and unsanitary conditions increasingly contribute to increased rates of communicable illness. It's hard to conceive of a better set of circumstances for the appearance and spread of communicable disease, and it remains to be seen if scientific innovation and medical technology can meet the challenge.

Summary

In this chapter, we investigated some of the ways that humans differ from one another, both within and between populations. First, we explored how this variation was approached in the past, in terms of racial typologies. Then we discussed contemporary approaches that describe simple genetic polymorphisms for which allele frequencies may be calculated, and we emphasized new techniques in which genetic data are obtained from direct analyses of mitochondrial and nuclear DNA. We also reviewed the theoretical basis of the population genetics approach, the subdiscipline of physical anthropology that seeks to measure genetic diversity among humans. Data on polymorphic traits can be used to understand aspects of human microevolution. For humans, of course, culture also plays a crucial evolutionary role, so we've taken a biocultural perspective in discussing the sickle-cell trait and lactose intolerance.

In this chapter we also considered how populations vary in their physiological adaptations to different environmental conditions, including solar radiation, heat, cold, and high altitude. We then focused on how infectious disease influences evolutionary processes, and we particularly emphasized AIDS/HIV and the dynamic relationship between pathogens and human hosts.

The topic of human variation is very complicated, and the biological and cultural factors that have contributed to it in the past, and continue to do so today, are manifold. Still, it is from an explicitly evolutionary perspective, including the investigation of changes in allele frequencies in response to environmental conditions, that we are able to understand the diverse adaptive potential that characterizes our species.

Critical Thinking Questions

1. Imagine you and three of your friends are discussing human diversity and the number of races. One friend says that there are three clearly defined races. A second disagrees, claiming there are five, while the third is positive that there are actually nine races. Would you agree with any of these views? Why or why not?

2. For the same group of friends mentioned in question 1 (none of whom have had a course in biological anthropology), how would you explain why scientific knowledge does not support their preconceived notions about human races?

3. Why can we say that variations in human skin color are the result of natural selection in different environments? Why is less-pigmented skin a result of conflicting selective factors?

4. Do you think that infectious disease has played an important role in human evolution? Do you think it plays a *current* role in human adaptation?

5. How have human cultural practices influenced the patterns of infectious disease seen today? Provide as many examples as you can, including some not discussed in this chapter.

HEREDITY AND EVOLUTION

CHAPTER 5

Macroevolution: Processes of Vertebrate and Mammalian Evolution

FOCUS QUESTION

In what ways do humans fit into a biological continuum (as vertebrates and as mammals)?

Introduction

Many people think of paleontology as pretty boring, a subject that's interesting only to overly serious academics. But have you ever been to a natural history museum—or perhaps to one of the larger, more elaborate toy stores? If so, you may have seen a full-size mock-up of *Tyrannosaurus rex,* one that might even have moved its head and arms and screamed threateningly. These displays are usually encircled by flocks of noisy children who seem anything but bored.

The study of the history of life on earth is full of mystery and adventure. The bits and pieces of fossils are the remains of once living, breathing animals (some of them extremely large and dangerous). Searching for these fossils in remote corners of the globe is not a task for the faint of heart. Piecing together the tiny clues and ultimately reconstructing what *Tyrannosaurus* (or for that matter, a small, 50-million-year-old primate) looked like and how it might have behaved are really much like detective work. Sure, it can be serious; but it's also a lot of fun.

In this chapter, we review the evolution of vertebrates and, more specifically, of mammals. It's important to understand these more general aspects of evolutionary history so that we can place our species in its proper biological context. *Homo sapiens* is only one of millions of species that have evolved. More than that, humans have been around for just an instant in the vast expanse of time that life has existed, and we want to know where we fit in this long and complex story of life on earth. To discover how humans relate in this continuum of evolving life on earth, we also discuss some contemporary issues relating to evolutionary theory. In particular, we emphasize concepts that relate to large-scale evolutionary processes, that is, *macroevolution* (in contrast to the microevolutionary focus of Chapters 3 and 4). The fundamental perspectives reviewed here concern geological history, principles of classification, and modes of evolutionary change, and they serve as a basis for topics covered throughout much of the remainder of this book.

Go to the following CD-ROMs for interactive activities and exercises on topics covered in this chapter:

- Virtual Laboratories for Physical Anthropology CD-ROM, Third Edition

The Human Place in the Organic World

There are millions of species living today; if we were to include microorganisms, the total would likely exceed tens of millions. And if we added in the multitudes of species that are now extinct, the total would be staggering—perhaps hundreds of millions!

How do we deal scientifically with all this diversity? Biologists, being human, approach complexity by simplifying it. One way to do this is to develop a system of **classification** that organizes diversity into categories and, at the same time, indicates evolutionary relationships.

Organisms that move about and ingest food (but don't photosynthesize, as do plants) are called animals. More precisely, the multicelled animals are placed within the group called the **Metazoa** (Fig. 5–1). Within the Metazoa there are more than 20 major groups termed *phyla* (*sing.,* phylum). One of these phyla is the **Chordata**, animals with a nerve cord, gill slits (at some stage of development), and a supporting cord along the back. In turn, most chordates are called **vertebrates**, because they have a vertebral column. Vertebrates also have a developed brain and paired sensory structures for sight, smell, and balance.

The vertebrates themselves are subdivided into six classes: bony fishes, cartilaginous fishes, amphibians, reptiles, birds, and mammals. We'll discuss mammalian classification later in this chapter.

classification In biology, the ordering of organisms into categories, such as orders, families, and genera, to show evolutionary relationships.

Metazoa Multicellular animals; a major division of the animal kingdom.

Chordata The phylum of the animal kingdom that includes vertebrates.

vertebrates Animals with segmented, bony spinal columns; includes fishes, amphibians, reptiles, birds, and mammals.

FIGURE **5-1**

Classification chart, modified from Linnaeus. All animals are placed in certain categories based on structural similarities. Not all members of categories are shown. For example, there are up to 20 orders of placental mammals (8 are depicted). A more comprehensive classification of the primate order is presented in Chapter 6.

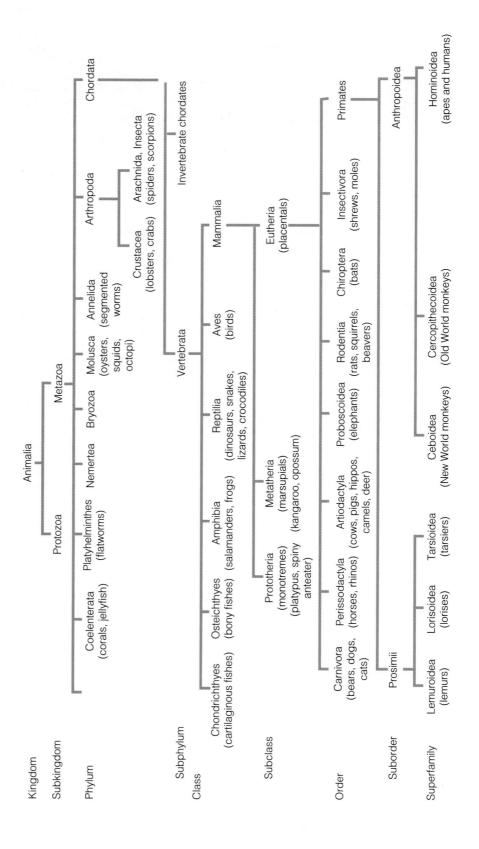

By putting organisms into increasingly narrow groupings, this hierarchical arrangement organizes diversity into categories. It also makes statements about evolutionary and genetic relationships between species and groups of species. Further dividing mammals into orders makes the statement that, for example, all carnivores (Carnivora) are more closely related to each other than they are to any species placed in another order. Consequently, bears, dogs, and cats are more closely related to each other than they are to cattle, pigs, or deer (Artiodactyla). At each succeeding level (suborder, superfamily, family, subfamily, genus, and species), finer distinctions are made between categories until, at the species level, only those animals that can interbreed and produce viable offspring are included.

Principles of Classification

Before going any further, we need to discuss the basis of animal classification. The field that specializes in establishing the rules of classification is called *taxonomy*. Organisms are classified first, and most traditionally, based on their physical similarities. Such was the basis of the first systematic classification devised by Linnaeus in the eighteenth century (see Chapter 2).

Today, basic physical similarities are still considered a good starting point, but in order for them to be useful, they *must* reflect evolutionary descent. For example, the bones of the forelimb of all terrestrial air-breathing vertebrates are so similar in number and form (Fig. 5–2) that the obvious explanation for the striking resemblance is that all four kinds of air-breathing vertebrates ultimately derived their forelimb structure from a common ancestor.

The way such seemingly major evolutionary modifications in structure could occur likely begins with only relatively minor genetic changes. For example, recent research shows that forelimb development in all vertebrates is directed by just a few regulatory genes (see p. 41), (Shublin et al., 1997; Riddle and Tabin, 1999). A few mutations among early vertebrates in certain regulatory genes led to the basic limb structure seen in all subsequent vertebrates. Additional small mutations in these genes could produce the varied structures that make up

FIGURE 5–2
Homologies. The similarities in the forelimb bones of these animals can be most easily explained by descent from a common ancestor.

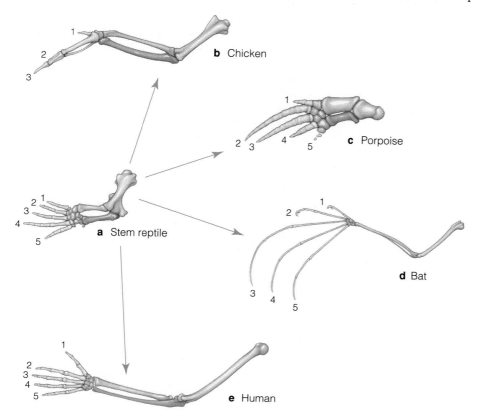

the wing of a chicken, the flipper of a porpoise, or the upper limb of a human. You should recognize that *basic* genetic regulatory mechanisms are highly conserved in animals; that is, they've been maintained relatively unchanged for hundreds of millions of years. Like a musical score with a basic theme, small variations on the pattern can produce the different "tunes" that distinguish one organism from another. This is the essential genetic foundation for most macroevolutionary change, telling us that large anatomical modifications don't always require major genetic alterations.

Structures that species share based on their descent from a common ancestor are called **homologies**. Homologies alone are reliable indicators of evolutionary relationship. But we have to be careful not to draw hasty conclusions from superficial similarities. For example, both birds and butterflies have wings, but they shouldn't be grouped together on the basis of this single characteristic; butterflies (as insects) differ dramatically from birds in a number of other, even more fundamental ways. (For example, birds have an internal skeleton, central nervous system, and four limbs. Insects don't.)

What has happened in evolutionary history is that starting from quite distant ancestors, both butterflies and birds have developed wings *independently*. So, their superficial similarities are a product of separate evolutionary response to roughly similar functional demands. These kinds of similarities, based on independent functional adaptation and not on shared evolutionary descent, are called **analogies**. The process that leads to the development of analogies (also called analogous structures) such as wings in birds and butterflies is termed **homoplasy**. In the case of butterflies and birds, the homoplasy has occurred in evolutionary lines that share only very remote ancestry. Here, homoplasy has produced analogous structures that are in no way homologous. In some cases, however, homoplasy can occur in lineages that are more closely related and therefore share considerable homology as well. Examples of homoplasy in closely related lineages are evident among the primates (for example, among New and Old World monkeys and among the great apes; see Chapter 6).

CONSTRUCTING CLASSIFICATIONS AND INTERPRETING EVOLUTIONARY RELATIONSHIPS

To interpret evolutionary relationships and produce classifications, evolutionary biologists use two major approaches. The first of these, called **evolutionary systematics**, is a more traditional approach, whereas the second approach, called **cladistics** (favored by most anthropologists) has emerged primarily in the last 20 years.

Before we discuss the differences between these two approaches, it is first helpful to note the features that they share. First, both trace evolutionary relationships and construct classifications that reflect these relationships. Second, they both recognize that organisms must be compared for specific features (called *characters*) and that some of these characters are more informative than others. Third (and deriving directly from the previous two points), both approaches focus exclusively on homologies.

However, these approaches also differ significantly in terms of how characters are chosen, which groups are compared, and how the results are interpreted and eventually incorporated into evolutionary schemes and classifications. The primary difference is that cladistics more rigorously defines the kinds of homologies that provide the most useful information. For example, at a very basic level, all life-forms (except for some viruses) share DNA as the molecule underlying all biological processes. However, beyond implying that all life most likely derives from a single origin (a most intriguing point), the presence of DNA tells us nothing else about more specific relationships among different kinds of life-forms. To draw further conclusions, we need to look at particular characters that certain groups share as the result of more recent ancestry.

This perspective emphasizes an important point: Some homologous characters are much more informative than others. We saw earlier that all terrestrial vertebrates share homologies in the number and basic arrangement of bones in the forelimb. While these similarities are broadly useful in showing that these large evolutionary groups (reptiles, birds, and mammals) are all related through a distant ancestor, they don't provide any usable information that lets us distinguish one from another (a reptile from a mammal, for example). Such characters (also called traits) that are shared through a very remote ancestry are said to be **primitive**, or **ancestral**. We prefer the term *ancestral* because it doesn't have a negative connotation regarding the evolutionary value of the character in question. So, in physical anthropology,

homologies   Similarities between organisms based on descent from a common ancestor.

analogies   Similarities between organisms based strictly on common function, with no assumed common evolutionary descent.

homoplasy   (*homo*, meaning "same," and *plasy*, meaning "growth") The separate evolutionary development of similar characteristics in different groups of organisms.

evolutionary systematics   A traditional approach to classification (and evolutionary interpretation) in which presumed ancestors and descendants are traced in time by analysis of homologous characters.

cladistics   An approach to classification that attempts to make rigorous evolutionary interpretations based solely on analysis of certain types of homologous characters (those considered to be derived characters).

ancestral (primitive)   Referring to characters inherited by a group of organisms from a remote ancestor and thus not diagnostic of groups (lineages) that diverged after the character first appeared.

Evolutionary Systematics	Cladistics
Similarities	
Both: Compare specific characters (traits)	
Both: Construct classifications to show evolutionary relationships	
Both: Focus on homologies	
Differences	
Might use any homologous character	Use only explicitly defined derived characters
Attempts, where possible, to make ancestor-descendant links (stated as hypotheses)	No attempt is made to make conclusions regarding ancestor-descendant relationships
Attempts, where possible, to place fossils in a chronological framework	All members of an evolutionary group (both fossil and living) are interpreted in one dimension (i.e., no timeframe is used)
Goal	
Construction of a phylogenetic tree	Construction of a cladogram

the term *primitive* or *ancestral* simply means that a character seen in two organisms is inherited in both of them from a distant ancestor.

In most circumstances, analyzing ancestral characters does not give biologists enough information to make accurate evolutionary interpretations about relationships between different groups. In fact, misinterpretation of ancestral characters can easily lead to quite inaccurate evolutionary conclusions! Cladistics focuses on traits that are far more informative—those that distinguish particular evolutionary lineages. Such characters are said to be **derived**, or **modified**. So, even though the general ancestral bony pattern of the forelimb in land animals with backbones doesn't allow us to distinguish among them, the further modification in certain groups (as hooves, flippers, or wings, for instance) does.

Among vertebrates, *only* birds have feathers and *only* mammals have fur. In comparing mammals with other vertebrates, presence of fur is a *derived* characteristic. Similarly, in describing birds, feathers are derived only in this group.

So how do we know which kind of characteristics to use? That depends on which group we are describing and what we're comparing it to. For the most part, it's best to use characteristics that reflect more specific evolutionary adaptations; in other words, derived characteristics are the most useful. Moreover, we should group two forms together (say, a bat with a mouse, both as mammals) *only* when they show **shared derived** characteristics (here, both possessing fur). (See Fig. 5–1 and look ahead to Fig. 6–8 for examples of classifications of animals.)

One last point needs to be mentioned. Traditional evolutionary systematics illustrates the hypothesized evolutionary relationships using a *phylogeny,* more properly called a **phylogenetic tree**. Strict cladistic analysis, however, shows relationships in a **cladogram**. A phylogenetic tree incorporates the dimension of time. (Numerous examples can be found in this and subsequent chapters.) But a cladogram doesn't indicate time, because all forms (fossil and modern) are indicated along one dimension. Phylogenetic trees usually attempt to make hypotheses regarding ancestor-descendant relationships. Cladistic analysis (through cladograms) makes no

derived (modified)   Referring to characters that are modified from the ancestral condition and thus *are* diagnostic of particular evolutionary lineages.

shared derived   Relating to specific character states shared in common between two life-forms and considered the most useful for making evolutionary interpretations.

phylogenetic tree   A chart showing evolutionary relationships as determined by evolutionary systematics. It contains a time component and implies ancestor-descendant relationships.

cladogram   A chart showing evolutionary relationships as determined by cladistic analysis. It is based solely on interpretation of shared derived characters. It contains no time component and does *not* imply ancestor-descendant relationships.

attempt at all to identify ancestor-descendant relationships. In fact, strict cladists are quite skeptical that the evidence really permits such specific evolutionary hypotheses to be scientifically confirmed, since there are many more extinct species than living ones.

In practice, most physical anthropologists (and other evolutionary biologists) use cladistic analysis to identify and assess the utility of traits and to make testable hypotheses regarding the relationships between groups of organisms. While some strict practitioners of cladistics wouldn't fully agree, most evolutionary biologists still will frequently extend this basic cladistic methodology to further hypothesize likely ancestor-descendant relationships shown relative to a time scale (that is, in a phylogenetic tree). In this way, aspects of both traditional evolutionary systematics and cladistic analyses are combined to produce a more complete picture of evolutionary history.

Definition of Species

Whether biologists are doing a cladistic or more traditional phylogenetic analysis, they're comparing groups of organisms—that is, different species, genera (pl. of *genus*), families, orders, and so forth. Fundamental to all these levels of classification is the most basic, the species.

It's appropriate, then, to ask just how biologists define species. We addressed this issue briefly in Chapter 1, where we applied the most common definition, which emphasizes interbreeding and reproductive isolation. While it's not the only definition of species (we'll discuss some others shortly), this view, called the **biological species concept** (Mayr, 1970), is the one most zoologists prefer.

The best way to understand what species are, then, is to consider how they come about in the first place—what Darwin called "origin of species." Today, this most fundamental of macroevolutionary processes is called **speciation**. According to the biological species concept, the way new species are first produced involves some form of isolation. Picture a single species (baboons, for example) composed of several populations distributed over a wide geographical area. But if a geographical barrier, such as a river, mountain range, or even just a large distance, effectively separates these populations, then gene exchange between them (gene flow) will be limited. This extremely important form of isolating mechanism is called *geographical isolation*.

If one baboon population (A) is separated from another baboon population (B) by a mountain range, members of population A won't mate with members of B (Fig. 5–3). As time passes (several generations), genetic differences will accumulate in both populations. And if group sizes are small, genetic drift may cause allele frequencies to change in both populations. What's more, since drift is *random* in nature, we wouldn't expect the effects to be the same. Consequently, the two populations will begin to diverge.

As long as gene exchange is limited, the populations can only become more genetically different with time. We can expect even further difference if the baboon groups live in slightly different habitats. In other words, additional genetic differences will come about through natural selection. Certain individuals in population A would be most reproductively fit in their

biological species concept   A depiction of species as groups of individuals capable of fertile interbreeding, but reproductively isolated from other such groups.

speciation   The process by which a new species evolves from a prior species. Speciation is the most basic process in macroevolution.

FIGURE 5–3

FIGURE 5–3
A speciation model. This model of speciation is called branching evolution, or cladogenesis.

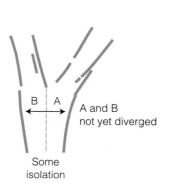

Some isolation

B | A   A and B not yet diverged

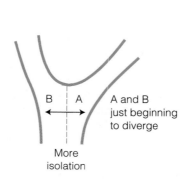

More isolation

B | A   A and B just beginning to diverge

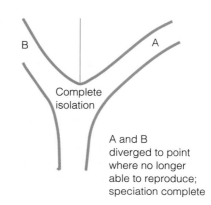

B   A

Complete isolation

A and B diverged to point where no longer able to reproduce; speciation complete

own environment, but they would show less reproductive success in the environment occupied by population B. So over time, allele frequencies will shift further, resulting in additional genetic differences between the two groups.

With the cumulative effects of genetic drift and natural selection acting over many generations, the result will be two populations that, even if they were to come back into geographical contact, could no longer interbreed. And at this point, more than just geographical isolation might come into play. For instance, there may be behavioral differences that interfere with courtship. This is an example of what we call *behavioral isolation*. Using our *biological* definition of species, we now would recognize two distinct species where initially only one existed.

While most biologists today accept the biological species concept as the most workable definition of species (see, for example, Wilson, 2002), they still don't completely agree on the best approach for defining species. Some biologists have thus proposed alternative definitions, two of which are most relevant to our discussion. One of these definitions emphasizes mate recognition and breeding, while the other is based on ecological separation. It's important to remember, however, that these varied approaches to defining species are not mutually exclusive. Indeed, aspects of all three concepts could potentially interact in the formation of new species. For example, some species isolation could *begin* the process of speciation and then be further reinforced by selective breeding (that is, mate recognition) as well as ecological separation.

INTERPRETING SPECIES AND OTHER GROUPS IN THE FOSSIL RECORD

Throughout much of this text, we'll be using various taxonomic terms for fossil primates, including fossil hominids; consequently, you will be introduced to such terms as *Proconsul, Sivapithecus, Australopithecus,* and *Homo.* Of course, *Homo* is still a living primate. But it's especially difficult to make these types of designations from remains of animals that are long dead (and only partially preserved as skeletal remains). So, what do such names mean in evolutionary terms when we apply them to extinct species?

Our goal when applying species, genus, or other taxonomic labels to groups of organisms is to make meaningful biological statements about the variation that is present. When looking at populations of living or long-extinct animals, we'll certainly see some variation. The situation is true of *any* sexually reproducing organism. For example, as a result of recombination (see Chapter 3), every individual organism is a unique combination of genetic material, and the uniqueness is usually reflected to some extent in the phenotype.

In addition to such *individual variation,* there are other kinds of variation in all biological populations. *Age changes* alter overall body size as well as shape in many mammals. One pertinent example for studies of fossil hominids and our closest primate relatives is the change in number, size, and shape of teeth from deciduous (milk) teeth (only 20 present) to the permanent dentition (32 present). It would be an obvious error to differentiate fossil forms solely on the basis of such age-dependent criteria. If one individual were represented just by milk teeth and another (seemingly very different) individual were represented just by adult teeth, they could simply be different-aged individuals from the *same* population. Variation due to sex also plays an important role in influencing differences among individuals. Differences in physical characteristics between males and females of the same species are called **sexual dimorphism** (see p. 130), and these can result in marked variation in body size and proportions in adults of the same species.

Recognition of Fossil Species   Keeping in mind all the types of variation present within interbreeding groups of organisms, the minimum biological category we would like to define in fossil primate samples is the *species.* As already defined (according to the biological species concept), a species is a group of interbreeding or potentially interbreeding organisms that is reproductively isolated from other such groups. In modern organisms, this concept is theoretically testable by observations of reproductive behavior. In animals long extinct, such observations are obviously impossible. Our only way, then, of getting a handle on the variation we see in fossil groups is to refer to living animals.

We know without doubt that variation is present. The question is, What is its biological significance? Two immediate answers come to mind. Either the variation is accounted for by

sexual dimorphism   Differences in physical characteristics between males and females of the same species. For example, humans are slightly sexually dimorphic for body size, with males being taller, on average, than females of the same population.

individual, age, and sex differences seen within every biological species (that is, it is **intra-specific**) or the variation represents differences between reproductively isolated groups (it is **interspecific**). How do we decide which answer is correct? To do this, we have to look at contemporary species.

If the amount of morphological variation observed in fossil samples is comparable to that seen today *within species of closely related forms*, then we shouldn't "split" our sample into more than one species. We must, however, be careful in choosing modern analogues, because rates of morphological evolution vary among different groups of mammals. So, for example, when studying extinct primates, we need to compare them with well-known species of modern primates.

Nevertheless, studies of living groups have shown that defining exactly where species boundaries begin and end is often difficult. In dealing with extinct species, the uncertainties are even greater. In addition to the overlapping patterns of variation *over space,* variation also occurs *through time.* In other words, even more variation will be seen in **paleospecies**, since individuals may be separated by thousands or even millions of years. Applying strict Linnaean taxonomy to such a situation presents an unavoidable dilemma. Standard Linnaean classification, designed to take account of variation present at any given time, describes a static situation. However, when we deal with paleospecies, the time frame is expanded, and the situation can be dynamic (that is, later forms might be different from earlier ones). In such a dynamic situation, taxonomic decisions (where to draw species boundaries) are ultimately going to be somewhat arbitrary.

Because the task of interpreting paleospecies is so difficult, paleoanthropologists have sought various solutions. Most researchers today define species using clusters of derived traits (identified cladistically). But, owing to the ambiguity of how many derived characters are required to identify a fully distinct species (as opposed to a subspecies), the frequent mixing of characters into novel combinations, and the always difficult problem of homoplasy, there continues to be disagreement. A good deal of the dispute is driven by philosophical orientation. Exactly how much diversity should one *expect* among fossil primates, especially among fossil hominids?

Some researchers, called "splitters," claim that speciation occurred frequently during hominid evolution, and they often identify numerous fossil hominid species in a sample being studied. Others, called "lumpers," assume that speciation was less common and see much variation as being intraspecific; consequently, fewer hominid species are identified, named, and eventually plugged into evolutionary schemes. As you'll see in the following chapters, debates of this sort pervade paleoanthropology, perhaps more than in any other branch of evolutionary biology.

Recognition of Fossil Genera   The next, and broader, level of taxonomic classification, the **genus**, presents another problem. To have more than one genus, we obviously must have at least two species (reproductively isolated groups), and the species of one genus must differ in a basic way from the species of another genus. A genus is therefore defined as a group of species composed of members more closely related to each other than they are to species from any other genus.

Grouping species together into genera can be quite subjective and is often much debated by biologists. One possible test for contemporary animals is to check for results of hybridization between individuals of different species—rare in nature but quite common in captivity. If members of two normally separate species interbreed and produce live, though not necessarily fertile, offspring, the two parental species probably are not too different genetically and should therefore be grouped together in the same genus. A well-known example of such a cross is horses with donkeys (*Equus caballus* × *Equus asinus*), which normally produces live but sterile offspring (mules).

As previously mentioned, we can't perform breeding experiments with extinct animals, but another definition of genus becomes highly relevant. Species that are members of the same genus share the same broad adaptive zone. What this represents is a general ecological lifestyle more basic than the narrower ecological niches characteristic of individual species. This ecological definition of genus can be an immense aid in interpreting fossil primates. Teeth are the most frequently preserved parts, and they often can provide excellent general ecological inferences. In addition, cladistic analysis also provides assistance in making judg-

intraspecific   Within species; refers to variation seen within the same species.

interspecific   Between species; refers to variation beyond that seen within the same species to include additional aspects seen between two different species.

paleospecies   Species defined from fossil evidence, often covering a long time span.

genus   A group of closely related species.

ments about evolutionary relationships. That is, members of the same genus should all share derived characters not seen in members of other genera.

As a final comment, we should emphasize that classification by genus is not always a straightforward decision. For instance, many current researchers (Wildman et al., 2003), pointing to the very close genetic similarities between humans (*Homo sapiens*) and chimpanzees (*Pan troglodytes*), place both in the same genus (*Homo sapiens, Homo troglodytes*). When it gets this close to home, it frequently becomes difficult to remain objective!

Vertebrate Evolutionary History: A Brief Summary

In addition to the staggering array of living and extinct life-forms, biologists must also contend with the vast amount of time that life has been evolving on earth. Again, scientists have devised simplified schemes—but in this case to organize *time,* not biological diversity.

Geologists have formulated the **geological time scale** (Fig. 5–4), in which very large time spans are organized into eras and periods. Periods, in turn, can be broken down into epochs.

ERA	PERIOD	(Began mya)	EPOCH	(Began mya)
CENOZOIC	Quaternary	1.8	Holocene Pleistocene	0.01 1.8
	Tertiary	65	Pliocene Miocene Oligocene Eocene Paleocene	5 23 34 55 65
MESOZOIC	Cretaceous	136		
	Jurassic	190		
	Triassic	225		
PALEOZOIC	Permian	280		
	Carboniferous	345		
	Devonian	395		
	Silurian	430		
	Ordovician	500		
	Cambrian	570		
PRE-CAMBRIAN				

FIGURE 5–4
Geological time scale.

geological time scale The organization of earth history into eras, periods, and epochs; commonly used by geologists and paleoanthropologists.

DIGGING DEEPER

Deep Time

The vast expanse of time during which evolution has occurred on earth staggers the imagination. Indeed, this fundamental notion of what John McPhee has termed "deep time" is not really understood or, in fact, widely believed. Of course, as we have emphasized beginning in Chapter 1, *belief*, as such, is not part of science. But observation, theory building, and testing are. Nevertheless, in a world populated mostly by nonscientists, the concept of deep time, crucial as it is to geology and anthropology, is resisted by many people. This situation is really not surprising; as an idea that can be truly understood (that is, internalized and given some personal meaning), deep time is in many ways counterintuitive. As individuals, human beings measure their existence in months, years, or in the span of human lifetimes.

But what are these durations, measured against geological or galactic phenomena? In a real sense, these vast time expanses are beyond human comprehension. We can reasonably fathom the reaches of human history, stretching to about 5,000 years ago. In a leap of imagination, we can perhaps even begin to grasp the stretch of time back to the cave painters of France and Spain, approximately 17,000 to 25,000 years ago. How do we relate, then, to a temporal span that's 10 times this one, back to 250,000 years ago, about the time of the earliest *Homo sapiens*—or to 10 times this span to 2,500,000 years ago (about the time of the appearance of our genus, *Homo*)? We surely can respond that any of these time blocks are vast—and then *more* vast. But multiply this last duration another 1,000 times (to 2,500,000,000), and we're back to a time of fairly early life-forms. And we'd have to reach still further into earth's past, another 1.5 billion years, to approach the *earliest* documented life.

The dimensions of these intervals are humbling, to say the least. The discovery in the nineteenth century of deep time (as we documented in Chapter 2) in what the late Stephen Jay Gould called "geology's greatest contribution to human thought" plunged one more dagger into humanity's long-cherished special view of itself. Astronomers had previously established how puny our world was in the physical expanse of space, and then geologists showed that even on our own small planet, we were but residues dwarfed within a river of time "without a vestige of a beginning or prospect of an end" (from James Hutton, a founder of modern geology and one of the discoverers of deep time). It's no wonder that people resist the concept of deep time; it not only stupefies our reason, but implies a sense of collective meaninglessness and reinforces our individual mortality.

Geologists, astronomers, and other scholars have struggled for over a century, with modest success, to translate the tales told in rocks and hurtling stars in terms that everyone can understand. Various analogies have been attempted—metaphors, really—drawn from common experience. Among the most successful of these attempts is a "cosmic calendar" devised by eminent astronomer Carl Sagan in his book *Dragons of Eden* (1977). In this version of time's immensity, Sagan likens the passage of geological time to that of one calendar year. The year begins on January 1 with the "Big Bang," the cosmic explosion marking the beginning of the universe and the beginning of time. In this version, the Big Bang is set at 15 billion years ago,* with some of the major events in the geological past as follows:

For the time span encompassing vertebrate evolution, there are three eras: the Paleozoic, the Mesozoic, and the Cenozoic. The first vertebrates are present in the fossil record dating to early in the Paleozoic at 500 mya, and their origins probably go back considerably further. It is the vertebrate capacity to form bone that accounts for their more complete fossil record *after* 500 mya.

During the Paleozoic, several varieties of fishes (including the ancestors of modern sharks and bony fishes), amphibians, and reptiles appeared. In addition, at the end of the Paleozoic, close to 250 mya, several varieties of mammal-like reptiles were also diversifying. It's generally thought that some of these forms ultimately gave rise to the mammals.

The evolutionary history of vertebrates and other organisms during the Paleozoic and Mesozoic was profoundly influenced by geographical events. We know that the positions of the earth's continents have dramatically shifted during the last several hundred million years. This process, called **continental drift**, is explained by the geological theory of *plate tectonics*, which states that the earth's crust is a series of gigantic moving and colliding plates. Such massive geological movements can induce volcanic activity (as, for example, all around the Pacific rim), mountain building (for example, the Himalayas), and earthquakes. Living on the juncture of the Pacific and North American plates, residents of the Pacific coast of the United States are acutely aware of some of these consequences, as illustrated by the explosive volcanic eruption of Mt. St. Helens and the frequent earthquakes in Alaska and California.

While reconstructing the earth's physical history, geologists have established the prior, much altered, positions of major continental landmasses. During the late Paleozoic, the

continental drift   The movement of continents on sliding plates of the earth's surface. As a result, the positions of large landmasses have shifted drastically during the earth's history.

TIME UNIT CONVERSIONS USING THE COSMIC CALENDAR

1 year = 15,000,000,000 years
1 month = 1,250,000,000 years
1 day = 41,000,000 years

1 hour = 1,740,000 years
1 minute = 29,000 years
1 second = 475 years

		December 31 Events	
Big Bang	January 1		
Formation of the earth	September 14	Appearance of early hominoids (apes and humans)	12:30 P.M.
Origin of life on earth (approx.)	September 25	First hominids	9:30 P.M.
Significant oxygen atmosphere begins to develop	December 1	Extensive cave painting in Europe	11:59 P.M.
		Invention of agriculture	11:59:20 P.M.
Precambrian ends; Paleozoic begins; invertebrates flourish	December 17	Renaissance in Europe: Ming Dynasty in China; emergence of scientific method	11:59:59 P.M.
Paleozoic ends and Mesozoic begins	December 25	Widespread development of science and technology; emergence of a global culture; first steps in space exploration	NOW: the first second of the New Year
Cretaceous period: first flowers; dinosaurs become extinct	December 28		
Mesozoic ends; Cenozoic begins; adaptive radiation of placental mammals	December 29		

*Recent evidence gathered by the Hubble Space Telescope has questioned the established date for the Big Bang. However, even the most recent data are somewhat contradictory, suggesting a date from as early as 16 billion years ago (indicated by the age of the oldest stars) to as recent as 8 billion years ago (indicated by the rate of expansion of the universe). Here, we will follow the conventional dating of 15 billion years; if you apply the most conservative approximation (8 billion years), the calibrations shift as follows: 1 day = 22,000,000 years; 1 hour = 913,000 years; 1 minute = 15,000 years. Using these calculations, for example, the first hominids appear on December 31 at 7:37 P.M., and modern *Homo sapiens* are on the scene at 11:42 P.M.

continents came together to form a single colossal landmass called *Pangea*. (In reality, the continents had been drifting on plates, coming together and separating, long before the end of the Paleozoic around 225 mya.) During the early Mesozoic, the southern continents (South America, Africa, Antarctica, Australia, and India) began to split off from Pangea, forming a large southern continent called *Gondwanaland* (Fig. 5–5a). Similarly, the northern continents (North America, Greenland, Europe, and Asia) were consolidated into a northern landmass called *Laurasia*. During the Mesozoic, Gondwanaland and Laurasia continued to drift apart and to break up into smaller segments. By the end of the Mesozoic (about 65 mya), the continents were beginning to assume their current positions (Fig. 5–5b).

The evolutionary ramifications of this long-term continental drift were profound. Groups of land animals became effectively isolated from each other by oceans, and the distribution of reptiles and mammals was significantly influenced by continental movements. These movements continued in the Cenozoic and indeed are still happening, although without such dramatic results.

During most of the Mesozoic, reptiles were the dominant land vertebrates, and they exhibited a broad expansion into a variety of **ecological niches**, which included aerial and marine habitats. The most famous of these highly successful Mesozoic reptiles were the dinosaurs, which themselves evolved into a wide array of sizes and species and adapted to a variety of lifestyles. Dinosaur paleontology, never a boring field, has advanced several startling notions in recent years: that many dinosaurs were "warm-blooded" (see p. 108); that some varieties were quite social and probably also engaged in considerable parental care; that many forms

ecological niches The positions of species within their physical and biological environments, together making up the *ecosystem*. A species' ecological niche is defined by such components as diet, terrain, vegetation, type of predators, relationships with other species, and activity patterns, and each niche is unique to a given species.

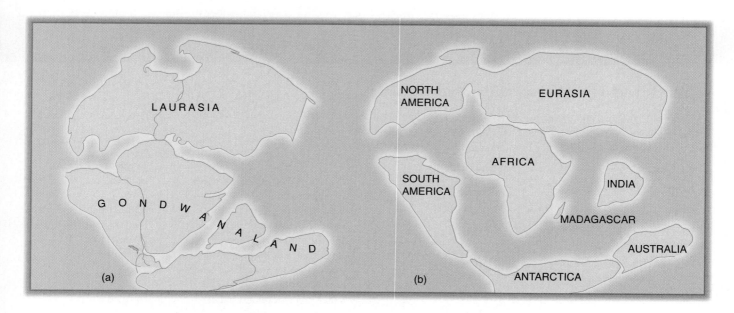

FIGURE 5–5

Continental drift. Changes in positions of the continental plates from late Paleozoic to the early Cenozoic. (a) The positions of the continents during the Mesozoic (c. 125 m.y.a.). Pangea is breaking up into a northern landmass (Laurasia) and a southern landmass (Gondwanaland). (b) The positions of the continents at the beginning of the Cenozoic (c. 65 mya).

FIGURE 5–6

Time line of major events in early vertebrate evolution.

became extinct as the result of major climatic changes to the earth's atmosphere from collisions with comets or asteroids; and finally, that not all dinosaurs became entirely extinct, with many descendants still living today (that is, all modern birds). (See Fig. 5–6 for a summary of major events in early vertebrate evolutionary history.)

The earliest mammals are known from traces of fossils from early in the Mesozoic, but the first **placental** mammals can't be positively identified until quite late in the Mesozoic, approximately 70 mya. This means that the highly successful mammalian diversification, portions of which we still see today, took place almost entirely within the most recent era of geological history, the Cenozoic.

The Cenozoic is divided into two periods, the Tertiary (about 63 million years duration) and the Quaternary, from about 1.8 mya up to and including the present. Paleontologists often refer to the next, more precise level of subdivision within the Cenozoic, the **epochs**. There are seven epochs within the Cenozoic: the Paleocene, Eocene, Oligocene, Miocene, Pliocene, Pleistocene, and Holocene, the last often referred to as the Recent.

PALEOZOIC							MESOZOIC		
Cambrian	Ordovician	Silurian	Devonian	Carbon-iferous	Permian		Triassic	Jurassic	Cretaceous
Trilobites abundant; also brachiopods, jellyfish, worms, and other invertebrates	First fishes; trilobites still abundant; graptolites and corals become plentiful; possible land plants	Jawed fishes appear; first air-breathing animals; definite land plants	Age of Fish; first amphibians; first forests	First reptiles; radiation of amphibians; modern insects diversify	Reptile radiation; mammal-like reptiles	Major extinction event	Reptiles further radiate; first dinosaurs; egg-laying mammals	Great Age of Dinosaurs; flying and swimming dinosaurs; first toothed birds	Placental and marsupial mammals appear; first modern birds	Major extinction event

570 mya   500 mya   430 mya   395 mya   345 mya   280 mya   225 mya   190 mya   136 mya   65 mya

Mammalian Evolution

Following the extinction of the dinosaurs and many other Mesozoic forms (at the end of the Mesozoic), a wide array of ecological niches became available, and this allowed the rapid expansion and diversification of mammals. The Cenozoic was an opportunistic time for mammals, and it is known as the Age of Mammals. Mesozoic mammals were small animals, about the size of mice, which they resembled superficially. The wide diversification of mammals in the Cenozoic saw the rise of the major lineages of all modern mammals. Indeed, mammals, along with birds, replaced reptiles as the dominant terrestrial vertebrates.

How do we account for the rapid success of the mammals? Several characteristics relating to learning and general flexibility of behavior are of prime importance. To process more information, mammals were selected for larger brains than those typically found in reptiles. In particular, the cerebrum became generally enlarged, especially the outer covering, the neocortex, which controls higher brain functions (Fig. 5–7). In some mammals, the cerebrum expanded so much that it came to comprise the majority of brain volume; moreover, the number of surface convolutions increased, creating more surface area and thus providing space for even more nerve cells (neurons). As we will see shortly (in Chapter 6), this is a trend even further emphasized among the primates.

For such a large and complex organ as the mammalian brain to develop, a longer, more intense period of growth is required. Slower development can occur internally (*in utero*) as well as after birth. While internal fertilization and internal development are not unique to mammals, the latter is a major innovation among terrestrial vertebrates. Other forms (birds, most fishes, and reptiles) incubate their young externally by laying eggs, while mammals, with very few exceptions, give birth to live young. Even among mammals, however, there is considerable variation among the major groups in how mature the young are at birth. As you will see, it is in mammals like ourselves, the *placental* forms, where *in utero* development goes farthest.

Another distinctive feature of mammals is seen in the dentition. While living reptiles consistently have similarly shaped teeth (called a *homodont* dentition), mammals have differently shaped teeth (Fig. 5–8). This varied pattern, termed a **heterodont** dentition, is reflected in the primitive (ancestral) mammalian array of dental elements, which includes 3 incisors, 1 canine, 4 premolars, and 3 molars in each quarter of the mouth. Since the upper and lower jaws are usually the same and are symmetrical for both sides, the "dental formula" is conventionally illustrated by dental quarter (see p. 120 for a more complete discussion of dental patterns as they apply to primates). Thus, with 11 teeth in each quarter of the mouth, the primitive (that is, ancestral) mammalian dental complement includes a total of 44 teeth. Such a heterodont arrangement allows mammals to process a wide variety of foods. Incisors can

placental   A type (subclass) of mammal. During the Cenozoic, placentals became the most widespread and numerous mammals and today are represented by upwards of 20 orders, including the primates.

epochs   Categories of the geological time scale; subdivisions of periods. In the Cenozoic, epochs include the Paleocene, Eocene, Oligocene, Miocene, and Pliocene (from the Tertiary) and the Pleistocene and Holocene (from the Quaternary).

heterodont   Having different kinds of teeth; characteristic of mammals, whose teeth consist of incisors, canines, premolars, and molars.

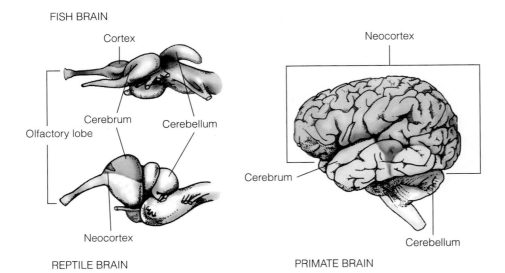

FIGURE 5–7
Lateral view of the brain. The illustration shows the increase in the cerebral cortex of the brain. The cerebral cortex integrates sensory information and selects responses.

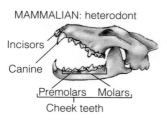

REPTILIAN (alligator): homodont

MAMMALIAN: heterodont

Incisors

Canine

Premolars   Molars
Cheek teeth

FIGURE 5–8
Reptilian and mammalian teeth.

endothermic   (*endo,* meaning "within" or "internal") Able to maintain internal body temperature through the production of energy by means of metabolic processes within cells; characteristic of mammals, birds, and perhaps some dinosaurs.

FIGURE 5–9
A wallaby with an infant in the pouch (marsupials).

J. C. Stevenson/Animals Animals

be used for cutting, canines for grasping and piercing, and premolars and molars for crushing and grinding.

A final point regarding teeth relates to their disproportionate representation in the fossil record. As the hardest, most durable portion of a vertebrate skeleton, teeth have the greatest likelihood of becoming fossilized (that is, mineralized). As a result, the vast majority of the available fossil data for most vertebrates, including primates, consists of teeth.

Another major adaptive complex that distinguishes contemporary mammals from reptiles is the maintenance of a constant internal body temperature. Also colloquially (and incorrectly) called warm-bloodedness, this crucial physiological adaptation is also seen in contemporary birds (and was also perhaps characteristic of many dinosaurs as well). In fact, many contemporary reptiles are able to approximate a constant internal body temperature through behavioral means (especially by regulating activity and exposing the body to the sun). In this sense, reptiles (along with birds and mammals) could be said to be *homeothermic.* So a more useful distinction is to see how the energy to maintain body temperature is produced and channeled. In reptiles, it's obtained directly from exposure to the sun; reptiles are thus said to be *ectothermic.* In mammals and birds, however, the energy is generated *internally* through metabolic activity (by processing food or by muscle action); for this reason, mammals and birds are referred to as **endothermic.**

The Emergence of Major Mammalian Groups

There are three major subgroups of living mammals: the egg-laying mammals, or monotremes, the pouched mammals, or marsupials (Fig. 5–9), and the placental mammals. The monotremes are extremely primitive and are considered more distinct from marsupials or placentals than these latter are from each other.

The most notable difference between marsupials and placentals concerns fetal development. In marsupials, the young are born extremely immature and must complete development in an external pouch. But placental mammals develop over a longer period of time inside the mother, and this is made possible by the evolutionary development of a specialized tissue (the placenta) that provides for fetal nourishment.

With a longer gestation period, the central nervous system develops more completely in the fetus. Moreover, after birth, the "bond of milk" between mother and young also allows more time for complex neural structures to form. It should also be emphasized that from a *biosocial* perspective, this dependency period not only allows for adequate physiological development but also provides for a wider range of learning stimuli. That is, the young mammalian brain receives a vast amount of information channeled to it through observation of the mother's behavior and through play with age-mates. It's not sufficient to have evolved a brain capable of learning. Collateral evolution of mammalian social systems has ensured that young mammal brains are provided with ample learning opportunities and are thus put to good use.

Processes of Macroevolution

As noted earlier, evolution operates at both microevolutionary and macroevolutionary levels. We discussed evolution primarily from a microevolutionary perspective in Chapters 3 and 4; in this chapter, our focus is on macroevolution. Macroevolutionary mechanisms operate more on the whole species than on individuals or populations, and they take much longer than microevolutionary processes to have a noticeable impact.

ADAPTIVE RADIATION

As we mentioned in Chapter 2, the potential capacity of a group of organisms to multiply is practically unlimited, but its ability to increase its numbers is regulated largely by the availability of resources (food, water, shelter, and space). As population size increases, access to resources decreases, and the environment will ultimately prove inadequate. Depleted resources induce some members of a population to seek an environment in which competition is reduced and the opportunities for survival and reproductive success are increased. This evolutionary tendency to exploit unoccupied habitats may eventually produce an abundance of diverse species.

This story has been played out countless times during the history of life, and some groups have expanded extremely rapidly. Known as **adaptive radiation**, this evolutionary process can be seen in the divergence of the stem reptiles into the profusion of different forms of the late Paleozoic and especially those of the Mesozoic. It's a process that takes place when a life-form rapidly takes advantage, so to speak, of the many newly available ecological niches.

The principle of evolution illustrated by adaptive radiation is fairly simple, but important. It may be stated in this way: *A species, or group of species, will diverge into as many variations as two factors allow: (1) its adaptive potential and (2) the adaptive opportunities of the available niches.*

In the case of reptiles, there was little divergence in the very early stages of evolution, when the ancestral form was little more than one among a variety of amphibian water dwellers. In reptiles, a more efficient egg than that of amphibians had developed (one that could incubate out of water). This new egg, with a hard, watertight shell, had great adaptive potential, but initially there were few zones to invade. When reptiles became fully terrestrial, however, a wide array of ecological niches became accessible to them. Once freed from their attachment to water, reptiles were able to exploit landmasses with no serious competition from any other animal. They moved into the many different ecological niches on land (and to some extent in the air and sea), and as they adapted to these areas, they diversified into a large number of species. This spectacular radiation burst forth with such evolutionary speed that it may well be termed an adaptive explosion.

Of course, the rapid expansion of placental mammals at the beginning of the Cenozoic is another excellent example of adaptive radiation.

GENERALIZED AND SPECIALIZED CHARACTERISTICS

Another aspect of evolution closely related to adaptive radiation involves the transition from generalized characteristics to specialized characteristics. These two terms refer to the adaptive potential of a particular trait. A trait that's adapted for many functions is said to be generalized, while one that is limited to a narrow set of functions is said to be specialized.

For example, a generalized mammalian limb has five fairly flexible digits, adapted for many possible functions (grasping, weight support, digging). In this respect, human hands are still quite generalized. On the other hand (or foot), there have been many structural modifications in our feet in order to make them suited for the specialized function of stable weight support in an upright posture.

The terms *generalized* and *specialized* are also sometimes used when speaking of the adaptive potential of whole organisms. Consider, for example, the aye-aye of Madagascar, an unusual primate species. The aye-aye is a highly specialized animal, structurally adapted to a narrow rodent/woodpecker-like econiche—digging holes with prominent incisors and removing insect larvae with an elongated bony finger.

It's important to note that only a generalized ancestor can provide the flexible evolutionary basis for rapid diversification. Only a generalized species with potential for adaptation to varied ecological niches can lead to all the later diversification and specialization of forms into particular ecological niches.

An issue that we have already raised also bears on this discussion: the relationship of ancestral and derived characters. While not always the case, ancestral characters *usually* tend to be more generalized. And specialized characteristics are almost always also derived ones.

adaptive radiation The relatively rapid expansion and diversification of life-forms into new ecological niches.

MODES OF EVOLUTIONARY CHANGE

Until fairly recently, the general consensus among evolutionary biologists was that microevolutionary mechanisms could be translated directly into the larger-scale macroevolutionary changes, especially the most central of all macroevolutionary processes, speciation. In the last two decades, this view has been seriously challenged. Many scientists now believe that macroevolution can't be explained solely in terms of accumulated microevolutionary changes. Consequently, these researchers are convinced that macroevolution is only partly understandable through microevolutionary models.

Gradualism vs. Punctuated Equilibrium   The traditional view of evolution has emphasized that change accumulates gradually in evolving lineages, an idea called phyletic gradualism. Accordingly, the complete fossil record of an evolving group (if it could be recovered) would display a series of forms with finely graded transitional differences between each ancestor and its descendant. The fact that such transitional forms are only rarely found is attributed to the incompleteness of the fossil record, or, as Darwin called it, "a history of the world, imperfectly kept, and written in changing dialect."

For more than a century, this perspective dominated evolutionary biology, but in the last 30 years, some biologists have called it into question. The evolutionary mechanisms operating on species over the long run aren't always gradual. In some cases species persist, basically unchanged, for thousands of generations. Then, rather suddenly, at least in evolutionary terms, a "spurt" of speciation occurs. This uneven, nongradual process of long stasis and quick spurts has been termed **punctuated equilibrium** (Gould and Eldredge, 1977).

What the advocates of punctuated equilibrium are disputing are the tempo (rate) and mode (manner) of evolutionary change as commonly understood since Darwin's time. Rather than a slow, steady tempo, this alternate view postulates long periods of no change (that is, equilibrium) punctuated only occasionally by sudden bursts. From this observation, many researchers concluded that the mode of evolution, too, must be different from that suggested by classical Darwinists. Rather than gradual accumulation of small changes in a single lineage, advocates of punctuated equilibrium believe that an additional evolutionary mechanism is required to push the process along. They thus postulate *speciation* as the major influence in bringing about rapid evolutionary change.

How well does the paleontological record agree with the predictions of punctuated equilibrium? Considerable fossil data do, in fact, show long periods of stasis punctuated by occasional quite rapid changes (taking from about 10,000 to 50,000 years). The best supporting evidence for punctuated equilibrium has come from marine invertebrate fossils. Intermediate forms are rare, not so much because the fossil record is poor but because the speciation events and longevity of these transitional species were so short that we shouldn't expect to find them very often.

And while some of the fossil evidence of other animals, including primates (Gingerich, 1985; Brown and Rose, 1987; Rose, 1991), doesn't fit the expectations of punctuated equilibrium, it would be a fallacy to assume that evolutionary change in these groups must therefore be of a completely gradual tempo. In all lineages, the pace assuredly speeds up and slows down due to factors that influence the size and relative isolation of populations. In addition, environmental changes that influence the pace and direction of natural selection must also be considered. Nevertheless, in general accordance with the Modern Synthesis, microevolution and macroevolution do not need to be "decoupled," as some evolutionary biologists have suggested.

Summary

In this chapter, we've surveyed the basics of vertebrate and mammalian evolution, emphasizing a macroevolutionary perspective. Given the huge amount of organic diversity displayed, as well as the vast amount of time involved, two major organizing perspectives prove indispensable: schemes of formal classification to organize organic diversity and the geological time scale to organize geological time. We reviewed the principles of classification in some detail, contrasting two differing approaches: evolutionary systematics and cladistics. Because

punctuated equilibrium   The concept that evolutionary change proceeds through long periods of stasis punctuated by rapid periods of change.

primates are vertebrates and, more specifically, mammals, we briefly reviewed these broader organic groups, emphasizing major evolutionary trends.

Theoretical perspectives relating to contemporary understanding of macroevolutionary processes (especially the concepts of species and speciation) are crucial to any interpretation of long-term aspects of evolutionary history, be it vertebrate, mammalian, or primate. Since genus and species designation is the common form of reference for both living and extinct organisms (and we use it frequently throughout the text), we discussed its biological significance in depth. From a more general theoretical perspective, evolutionary biologists have postulated two different modes of evolutionary change: gradualism and punctuated equilibrium. At present, even though the available fossil record does not conform entirely to the predictions of punctuated equilibrium, we should not conclude that evolutionary tempo was necessarily strictly gradual (which it certainly was not).

Critical Thinking Questions

1. What are the two goals of classification? What happens when meeting both goals simultaneously becomes difficult or even impossible?

2. Remains of a fossil mammal have been found on your campus. If you adopt a cladistic approach, how would you determine (a) that it is a mammal rather than some other kind of vertebrate (discuss specific characters), (b) what kind of mammal it is (again, discuss specific characters), and (c) how it *might* be related to one or more living mammals (again, discuss specific characters)?

3. For the same fossil find (and your interpretation) in question 2, draw an interpretive figure using cladistic analysis (that is, draw a cladogram). Next, using more traditional evolutionary systematics, construct a phylogeny. Lastly, explain the differences between the cladogram and the phylogeny (be sure to emphasize the fundamental ways the two schemes differ).

4. a. Humans are fairly generalized mammals. What do we mean by this, and what specific features (characters) would you select to illustrate this statement?

    b. More precisely, humans are *placental* mammals. How do humans, and generally all other placental mammals, differ from the other two major groups of mammals?

PRIMATES

CHAPTER

6

An Overview of the Primates

Introduction

Chimpanzees aren't monkeys. Gorillas and orangutans aren't either. They're apes, and there are many differences between monkeys and apes. Yet, how many times have you seen a greeting card with a picture of a chimpanzee and a phrase that goes something like, "Don't monkey around"? Or maybe you've noticed how people at zoos think primates are funny, particularly when they tease them. While these issues may seem trivial, they aren't, because they illustrate how ill-informed most people are about our closest relatives. This is extremely unfortunate, because by better understanding these relatives, not only can we better know ourselves, but we can also try to preserve the many primate species that are critically endangered.

One way to better understand any species is to compare its anatomy and behavior with those of other, closely related species. This comparative approach helps us explain how and why both physiological and behavioral systems evolved as adaptive responses. This statement applies to *Homo sapiens* just as it does to any other species, and if we want to identify the components that have shaped the evolution of our species, a good starting point is a comparison between humans and our closest living relatives, the approximately 230 species of nonhuman primates (**prosimians**, monkeys, and apes). (Groves, 2001b, suggests that there may be as many as 350 primate species.)

In this chapter we'll describe the physical characteristics that define the order Primates; give a brief overview of the major groups of living primates; and introduce some methods of comparing living primates through genetic data. (For a comparison of human and nonhuman skeletons, see Appendix A.) But before we go any further, we again want to call to your attention a few common misunderstandings about evolutionary processes.

Evolution is *not* a goal-directed process, so we can't conclude that just because prosimians evolved before **anthropoids**, prosimians "progressed" or "advanced" to become anthropoids. Living primate species aren't "superior" to their predecessors or to one another. Consequently, in discussions of major groupings of contemporary nonhuman primates, there is no implied superiority or inferiority of any of these groups. Each lineage or species has come to possess unique qualities that make it better suited to a particular habitat and lifestyle. Given that all contemporary organisms are "successful" results of the evolutionary process, it's best to avoid altogether the use of such loaded terms as *superior* and *inferior*. Finally, you shouldn't make the mistake of thinking that contemporary primates (including humans) necessarily represent the final stage or apex of a lineage. Actually, the only species that represent final evolutionary stages of particular lineages are the ones that become extinct.

Go to the following CD-ROMs for interactive activities and exercises on topics covered in this chapter:

- Virtual Laboratories for Physical Anthropology CD-ROM, Third Edition

Characteristics of Primates

All primates share numerous characteristics in common with other placental mammals (see Chapter 5). Some of these traits are body hair; a relatively long gestation period followed by live birth; mammary glands (thus the term *mammal*); different types of teeth (incisors, canines, premolars, and molars); the ability to maintain a constant internal body temperature through physiological means or *endothermy*; increased brain size; and a considerable capacity for learning and behavioral flexibility. So, in order to differentiate primates—as a group—from other mammals, we need to describe those characteristics that, taken together, set primates apart.

prosimians Members of a suborder of Primates, the *Prosimii* (pronounced "pro-sim´-ee-eye"). Traditionally, the suborder includes lemurs, lorises, and tarsiers.

anthropoids Members of a suborder of Primates, the *Anthropoidea* (pronounced "ann-throw-poid´-ee-uh"). Traditionally, the suborder includes monkeys, apes, and humans.

FIGURE 6–1

(a) A horse's front foot, homologous with a human hand, has undergone reduction from 5 digits to one. (b) While raccoons are capable of considerable manual dexterity and can readily pick up small objects with one hand, they have no opposable thumb. (c) Many monkeys are able to grasp objects with an opposable thumb, while others have very reduced thumbs. (d) Humans are capable of a "precision grip." (e) Chimpanzees with their reduced thumbs are also capable of a precision grip but they frequently use a modified form.

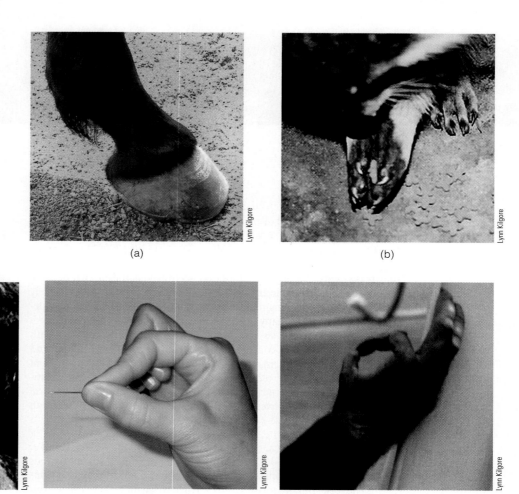

(a)   (b)

(c)   (d)   (e)

specialized   Evolved for a particular function; usually refers to a specific trait (e.g., incisor teeth), but may also refer to an organism's entire way of life.

primatologists   Scientists who study the evolution, anatomy, and behavior of nonhuman primates. Those who study behavior in free-ranging animals are usually trained as physical anthropologists.

Identifying single traits that define the primate order isn't easy because, compared to many mammals, primates have remained quite *generalized*. That is, primates have retained many ancestral or primitive mammalian traits that some other mammals have lost over time. In response to particular selective pressures, many mammalian groups have become increasingly **specialized**. For example, through the course of evolution, horses and cattle have undergone a reduction of the number of digits (fingers and toes) from the ancestral pattern of five to one and two respectively. In addition, these species have developed hard, protective coverings over their feet in the form of hooves (Fig. 6–1a). While this type of limb structure is adaptive in prey species, whose survival depends on speed and stability, it restricts the animal to only one type of locomotion. Moreover, limb function is limited entirely to support and movement, while the ability to manipulate objects is completely lost.

Primates can't be simply defined by one or even two traits they share in common, precisely because they *aren't* so specialized. As a result, anthropologists have pointed to a group of characteristics that, taken together, more or less characterize the entire order. But you should keep in mind that these are a set of *general* tendencies that aren't equally expressed in all primates. The following list is meant to give an overall structural and behavioral picture of the animals we call "primates," focusing on those characteristics that tend to distinguish primates from other mammals. Concentrating on certain retained (ancestral) mammalian traits along with more specific, derived ones has been the traditional approach of **primatologists**, and it's an approach still used today. In their limbs and locomotion, teeth and diet, senses, brain, and behaviors, primates reflect a common evolutionary history with adaptations to similar environmental challenges.

A. *Limbs and locomotion*
   1. *A tendency toward erect posture (especially in the upper body).* Present to some degree in all primates, this tendency is variously associated with sitting, leaping, standing, and, occasionally, bipedal walking.
   2. *A flexible, generalized limb structure allows most primates to practice a number of locomotor behaviors.* Primates have retained some bones (for example, the clavicle, or collarbone) and certain abilities (for example, rotation of the forearm) that have been lost in some more specialized mammals. Various aspects of hip and shoulder **morphology** also provide primates with a wide range of limb movement and function. Thus, by maintaining a generalized locomotor anatomy, primates aren't restricted to one form of movement, like many other mammals. Primate limbs are also used for activities other than locomotion.
   3. *Hands and feet with a high degree of* **prehensility** *(grasping ability).* Many species can manipulate objects, but not as skillfully as primates can (Fig. 6–1b). This ability is variably expressed and is enhanced by various characteristics, including:
      a. *Retention of five digits on hands and feet.* This trait varies somewhat throughout the order, and some species show marked reduction of the thumb or second digit (first finger).
      b. *An opposable thumb and, in most species, a divergent and partially opposable big toe.* Most primates are capable of moving the thumb so that it comes in contact (in some fashion) with the second digit or the palm of the hand (Fig. 6–1c through 6–1e).
      c. *Nails instead of claws.* This characteristic is seen in all primates except some New World monkeys. All prosimians also possess a claw on one digit.
      d. *Tactile pads enriched with sensory nerve fibers at the ends of digits.* This enhances the sense of touch.

B. *Diet and teeth*
   1. *Lack of dietary specialization.* This is typical of most primates, who tend to eat a wide assortment of food items. In general, primates are **omnivorous**.
   2. *A generalized dentition.* The teeth aren't specialized for processing only one type of food, a pattern related to the lack of dietary specialization.

C. *The senses and the brain*
   Primates (**diurnal** ones in particular) rely heavily on the visual sense and less on the sense of smell. This emphasis is reflected in evolutionary changes in the skull, eyes, and brain.
   1. *Color vision.* This is a characteristic of all diurnal primates.
   2. *Depth perception.* **Stereoscopic vision**, or the ability to perceive objects in three dimensions, is made possible through a variety of mechanisms, including:
      a. *Eyes positioned toward the front of the face (not to the sides).* This provides for overlapping visual fields, or **binocular vision** (Fig. 6–2).

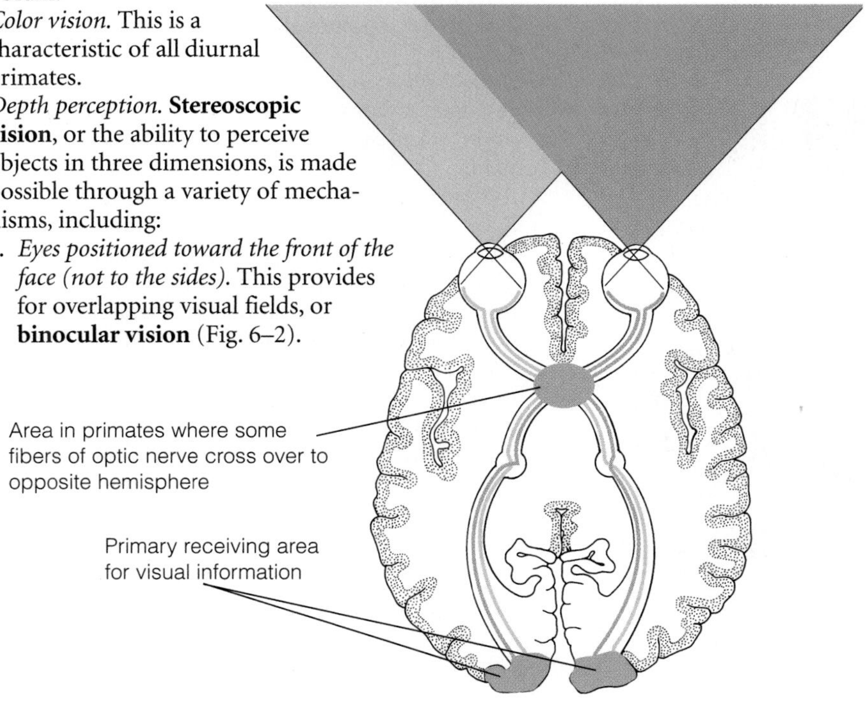

Area in primates where some fibers of optic nerve cross over to opposite hemisphere

Primary receiving area for visual information

morphology   The form (shape, size) of anatomical structures; can also refer to the entire organism.

prehensility   Grasping, as by the hands and feet of primates.

omnivorous   Having a diet consisting of many kinds of foods, such as plant materials (seeds, fruits, leaves), meat, and insects.

diurnal   Active during the day.

stereoscopic vision   The condition whereby visual images are, to varying degrees, superimposed on one another. This trait provides for depth perception, or the perception of the external environment in three dimensions. Stereoscopic vision is partly a function of structures in the brain.

binocular vision   Vision characterized by overlapping visual fields, provided for by forward-facing eyes. Binocular vision is essential to depth perception.

FIGURE **6–2**
Simplified diagram showing overlapping visual fields that permit binocular vision in primates and many predators with eyes positioned at the front of the face. (The green shaded area represents the area of overlap.) Stereoscopic vision (three-dimensional vision) is provided in part by binocular vision and in part by the transmission of visual stimuli from each eye to both hemispheres of the brain. (In nonprimate mammals, most, if not all, visual information crosses over to the hemisphere opposite the eye in which it was initially received.)

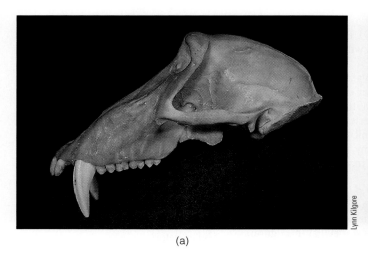

(a)

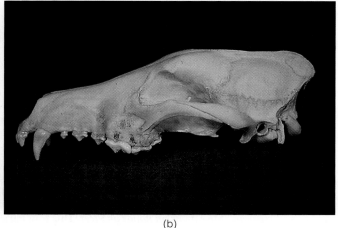

(b)

FIGURE 6–3

The skull of a male baboon (a) compared to that of a red wolf (b). Note the forward-facing eyes positioned above the snout in the baboon, compared to the lateral position of the eyes at the side of the wolf's face. Also, the baboon's large muzzle doesn't reflect a heavy reliance on the sense of smell. Rather, it supports the roots of the large canine teeth which curve back through the bone for as much as 1½ inches.

FIGURE 6–4

The skull of a gibbon (left) compared to that of a red wolf (right). Note that the absolute size of the braincase in the gibbon is slightly larger than that of the wolf, even though the wolf (at about 80 to 100 pounds) is six times the size of the gibbon (about 15 pounds).

Braincase

Postorbital bar

Eye socket   No postorbital bar

b. *Visual information from each eye transmitted to visual centers in both* **hemispheres** *of the brain.* In nonprimate mammals, most optic nerve fibers cross to the opposite hemisphere through a structure at the base of the brain. In primates, about 40 percent of the fibers remain on the same side (see Fig. 6–2).

c. *Visual information organized into three-dimensional images by specialized structures in the brain itself.* The capacity for stereoscopic vision is dependent on each hemisphere of the brain receiving visual information from both eyes and from overlapping visual fields.

3. *Decreased reliance on the sense of smell (olfaction).* This trend is seen in an overall reduction in the size of olfactory structures in the brain. Corresponding reduction of the entire olfactory apparatus has also resulted in a relatively smaller snout. Some primates, such as baboons, do have large muzzles; however, this isn't related to olfaction but rather to the presence of large teeth, especially the canines (Fig. 6–3).

4. *Expansion and increased complexity of the brain.* This is a general trend among placental mammals, but it's especially true of primates. In primates, this expansion is most evident in the visual and association areas of the neocortex (portions of the brain where information from different **sensory modalities** is integrated). Significant expansion in regions involved with the hand (both sensory and motor) is seen in many species, particularly humans (Fig. 6–4).

D. *Maturation, learning, and behavior*

1. *A more efficient means of fetal nourishment, longer periods of gestation, reduced numbers of offspring (with single births the norm), delayed maturation, and extension of the entire life span.*

2. *A greater dependence on flexible, learned behavior.* This trend is correlated with delayed maturation and consequently longer periods of infant and child dependency on the parent. As a result of both these trends, parental investment in each offspring is increased, so that although fewer offspring are born, they receive more intense and efficient rearing.

3. *The tendency to live in social groups and the permanent association of adult males with the group.* Except for some **nocturnal** species, primates tend to associate with other individuals. The permanent association of adult males with the group is uncommon in many mammals but widespread in primates.

4. *The tendency to diurnal activity patterns.* This is seen in most primates; only one monkey species and some prosimians are nocturnal.

Primate Adaptations

In this section, we'll consider how primate anatomical traits evolved as adaptations to environmental circumstances. It's important to remember that the term *environmental circumstances* includes a number of interrelated factors including climate, diet, habitat (woodland, grassland, forest, etc.), and predation.

EVOLUTIONARY FACTORS

Traditionally, the suite of characteristics shared by primates has been explained as the result of adaptation to **arboreal** living. While other placental mammals were adapting to various ground-dwelling lifestyles and even marine environments, the primates found their **adaptive niche** in the trees. Some other mammals were also adapting to arboreal living, but while many nested in trees, they continued to come to the ground to find food. But throughout the course of evolution, primates increasingly exploited foods (leaves, seeds, fruits, nuts, insects, and small mammals) in the branches themselves. Over time, this dietary shift enhanced the general trend toward increased *omnivory* and, along with this diet, the evolution of the primate generalized dentition.

This adaptive process is also reflected in how primates rely on vision. In a complex, three-dimensional environment with uncertain footholds, acute color vision with depth perception is, to say the least, extremely beneficial. Grasping hands and feet also reflect an adaptation to living in the trees. Obviously, animals like squirrels and raccoons can climb by digging in with claws. But primates adopted a technique of grasping branches with prehensile hands and feet, and their grasping abilities were further enhanced by the appearance of flattened nails instead of claws.

An alternative to this traditional **arboreal hypothesis**, called the *visual predation hypothesis* (Cartmill, 1972, 1992), emphasizes that predators such as cats and owls also have forward-facing eyes. What's more, forward-facing eyes, grasping hands and feet, and the presence of nails instead of claws didn't necessarily come about in a purely arboreal environment. So, primates may first have adapted to shrubby forest undergrowth and the lowest tiers of the forest canopy, where they hunted insects and other small prey primarily through stealth.

In a third scenario, Sussman (1991) suggests that the basic primate traits developed in conjunction with another major evolutionary occurrence, the appearance of flowering plants. Flowering plants provide numerous resources, including nectar, seeds, and fruits, and their diversification was accompanied by the emergence of ancestral forms of major groups of modern birds and mammals.

These hypotheses aren't mutually exclusive. The complex of primate characteristics might well have its origins in nonarboreal settings and certainly may have been stimulated by the new econiches provided by evolving flowering plants. But at some point, the primates did take to the trees, and that's where most of them still live today.

GEOGRAPHICAL DISTRIBUTION AND HABITATS

With just a couple of exceptions, primates are found in tropical or semitropical areas of the New and Old Worlds. In the New World, these areas include southern Mexico, Central America, and parts of South America. Old World primates are found in Africa, India, Southeast Asia, and Japan (Fig. 6–5).

Most primates are mainly arboreal and live in forest or woodland habitats, but some Old World monkeys (for example, baboons) have adapted to life on the ground in places where trees are sparsely distributed. The African apes (gorillas, chimpanzees, and bonobos) also spend a considerable amount of time on the ground in forested and wooded habitats. Even so, no nonhuman primate is adapted to a fully terrestrial lifestyle, and they all spend some time in the trees.

hemispheres   The two halves of the cerebrum that are connected by a dense mass of fibers. (The cerebrum is the large, rounded, outer portion of the brain.)

sensory modalities   Different forms of sensation (e.g., touch, pain, pressure, heat, cold, vision, taste, hearing, and smell).

nocturnal   Active during the night.

arboreal   Tree-living; adapted to life in the trees.

adaptive niche   The entire way of life of an organism: where it lives, what it eats, how it gets food, how it avoids predators, and so on.

arboreal hypothesis   The traditional view that primate characteristics can be explained as a consequence of primate diversification into arboreal habitats.

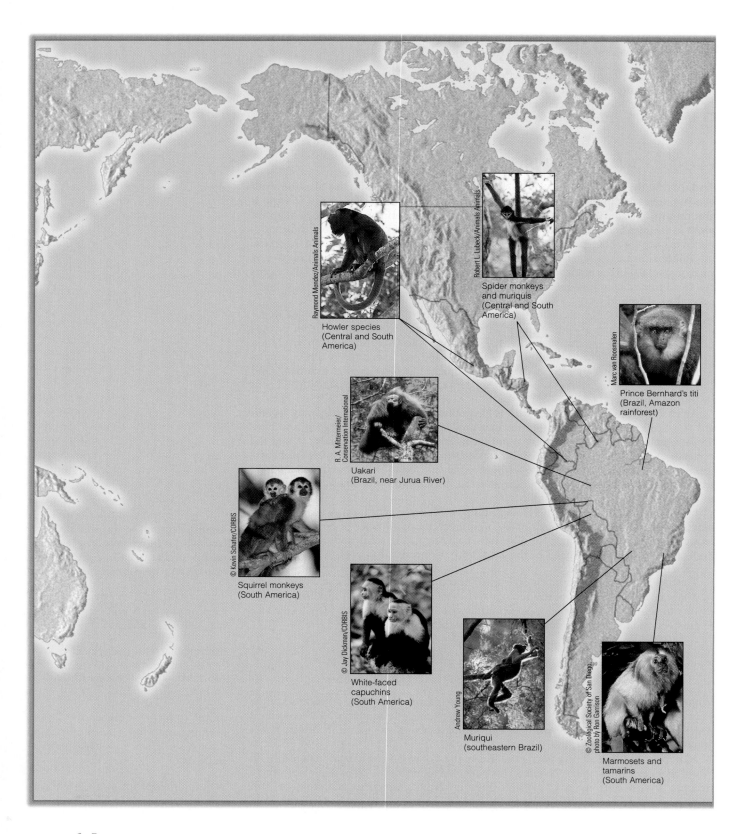

Howler species
(Central and South
America)

Spider monkeys
and muriquis
(Central and South
America)

Prince Bernhard's titi
(Brazil, Amazon
rainforest)

Uakari
(Brazil, near Jurua River)

Squirrel monkeys
(South America)

White-faced
capuchins
(South America)

Muriqui
(southeastern Brazil)

Marmosets and
tamarins
(South America)

FIGURE 6–5

Geographical distribution of living nonhuman primates. Much original habitat is now very fragmented.

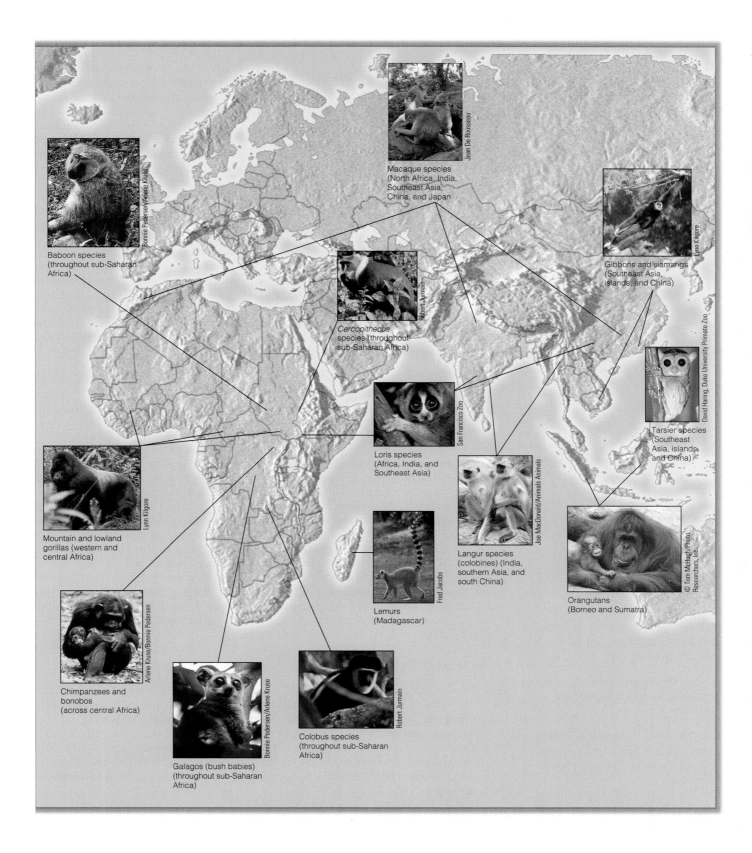

Macaque species
(North Africa, India,
Southeast Asia,
China, and Japan

Jean De Rousseau

Baboon species
(throughout sub-Saharan
Africa)

Bonnie Pedersen/Arlene Kruse

Gibbons and siamangs
(Southeast Asia,
islands, and China)

Lynn Kilgore

Cercopithecus
species (throughout
sub-Saharan Africa)

Robert Jurmain

Mountain and lowland
gorillas (western and
central Africa)

Lynn Kilgore

Loris species
(Africa, India, and
Southeast Asia)

San Francisco Zoo

Tarsier species
(Southeast
Asia, islands,
and China)

David Haring, Duke University Primate Zoo

Lemurs
(Madagascar)

Fred Jacobs

Langur species
(colobines) (India,
southern Asia, and
south China)

Joe MacDonald/Animals Animals

Orangutans
(Borneo and Sumatra)

© Tom McHugh/Photo
Researchers, Inc.

Chimpanzees and
bonobos
(across central Africa)

Arlene Kruse/Bonnie Pedersen

Galagos (bush babies)
(throughout sub-Saharan
Africa)

Bonnie Pedersen/Arlene Kruse

Colobus species
(throughout sub-Saharan
Africa)

Robert Jurmain

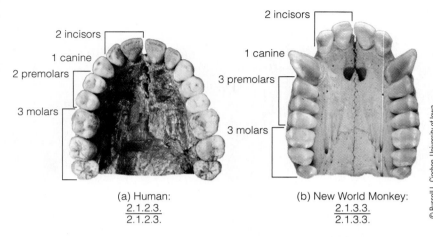

2 incisors

1 canine

2 premolars

3 molars

(a) Human:
2.1.2.3.
2.1.2.3.

2 incisors

1 canine

3 premolars

3 molars

(b) New World Monkey:
2.1.3.3.
2.1.3.3.

© Russell L. Ciochon, University of Iowa

FIGURE 6–6

The human maxilla (a) illustrates a dental formula of 2.1.2.3./2.1.2.3. characteristic of all Old World monkeys, apes, and humans. The *Cebus* maxilla (b) shows the 2.1.3.3./2.1.3.3. dental formula that is typical of most New World monkeys.

midline   An anatomical term referring to a hypothetical line that divides the body into right and left halves.

cusps   The elevated portions (bumps) on the chewing surfaces of premolar and molar teeth.

quadrupedal   Using all four limbs to support the body during locomotion; the basic mammalian (and primate) form of locomotion.

macaques   (muh-kaks´) Group of Old World monkeys comprising several species, including rhesus monkeys. Most macaque species live in India, other parts of Asia, and nearby islands.

DIET AND TEETH

Omnivory is one example of the overall lack of specialization in primates. Although the majority of primate species tend to emphasize some food items over others, most eat a combination of fruit, nuts, seeds, leaves, other plant materials, and insects. Many also get animal protein from birds and amphibians, and some occasionally kill and eat small mammals, including other primates. Others, such as African colobus monkeys and the leaf-eating monkeys (langurs) of India and Southeast Asia, have become more specialized and mostly eat leaves. Such a wide array of choices is highly adaptive, even in fairly predictable environments.

Like nearly all other mammals, most primates have four kinds of teeth: incisors and canines for biting and cutting, and premolars and molars for chewing. Biologists use a *dental formula* to describe the number of each type of tooth that typifies a species. A dental formula indicates the number of each type of tooth in each quarter of the mouth (Fig. 6–6). For example, all Old World *anthropoids* have two incisors, one canine, two premolars, and three molars on each side of the **midline** in both the upper and lower jaws, or a total of 32 teeth. This pattern is represented as a dental formula of

2.1.2.3 (upper)
2.1.2.3 (lower)

The dental formula for a generalized placental mammal is 3.1.4.3. (three incisors, one canine, four premolars, and three molars). Primates have fewer teeth than this ancestral pattern because there has been a general evolutionary trend toward reduction of the number of teeth in many mammal groups. Consequently, the number of each type of tooth varies between lineages. For example, in most of the New World monkeys, the dental formula is 2.1.3.3. (two incisors, one canine, three premolars, and three molars). Humans, apes, and all Old World monkeys have the same dental formula: 2.1.2.3.; that is, there is one less premolar than in New World monkeys.

The overall lack of dietary specialization in primates is also correlated with minimal specialization in the size and shape of the teeth. This is because tooth form is directly related to diet. For example, carnivores typically have premolars and molars with high pointed **cusps** adapted for tearing meat, while the premolars of herbivores, such as cattle and horses, have broad, flat surfaces suited to chewing tough grasses and other plant materials. Most primates have premolars and molars with low, rounded cusps, which allows them to process most types of foods. Thus, throughout their evolutionary history, the primates have developed a dentition adapted to a varied diet, and the capacity to exploit many foods has contributed to their overall success during the last 50 million years.

LOCOMOTION

Almost all primates are, at least to some degree, **quadrupedal**, meaning they use all four limbs to support the body during locomotion. However, most primates use more than one form of locomotion, and they're able to do this because of their generalized anatomy.

Although most of the quadrupedal primates are arboreal, terrestrial quadrupedalism is fairly common and is typical of some lemurs, baboons, and **macaques**. Typically, the limbs of terrestrial quadrupeds are approximately the same length, with forelimbs being 90 percent (or more) as long as hind limbs (Fig. 6–7a). In arboreal quadrupeds, forelimbs are somewhat shorter (Fig. 6–7b).

Vertical clinging and leaping, another form of locomotion, is characteristic of many prosimians and tarsiers. As the term implies, vertical clingers and leapers support themselves vertically by grasping onto trunks of trees while their knees and ankles are tightly flexed (Fig. 6–7c). Forceful extension of their long hind limbs allows them to spring powerfully away in either a forward or backward direction.

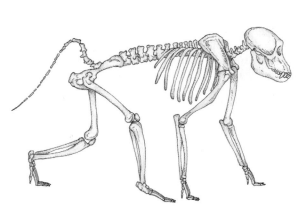

(a) Skeleton of a terrestrial quadruped (savanna baboon).

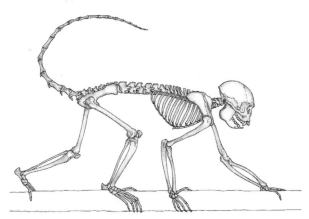

(b) Skeleton of an arboreal New World monkey (bearded saki).

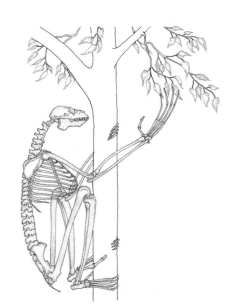

FIGURE 6–7
(a–d) Differences in skeletal anatomy and limb proportions reflect differences in locomotor patterns. (Redrawn from original art by Stephen Nash in John G. Fleagle, *Primate Adaptation and Evolution,* 2nd ed., 1999. Reprinted by permission of publisher and Stephen Nash.)

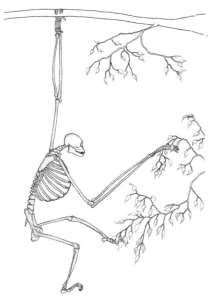

(c) Skeleton of a vertical clinger and leaper (indri).   (d) Skeleton of a brachiator (gibbon).

Brachiation, or arm swinging, is another type of primate locomotion where the body is alternatively supported under either forelimb. Because of anatomical modifications at the shoulder joint, apes and humans are capable of true brachiation. However, only the small gibbons and siamangs of Southeast Asia brachiate almost exclusively (Fig. 6–7d).

Species that brachiate tend to have arms that are longer than legs; a short, stable lower back; long, curved fingers; and reduced thumbs. Because these are traits seen in all the apes, it's believed that, although none of the great apes (orangutans, gorillas, bonobos, and chimpanzees) habitually brachiates today, they most likely inherited these characteristics from brachiating or perhaps climbing ancestors.

Some New World monkeys (for example, muriquis and spider monkeys) are called *semibrachiators*, because they practice a combination of leaping with some arm swinging. And in some New World species, arm swinging and other suspensory behaviors are enhanced by use of a *prehensile tail*, which in effect serves as a grasping fifth "hand." Prehensile tails are restricted to New World monkeys and aren't seen in any Old World primate species.

brachiation A form of locomotion in which the body is suspended beneath the hands and support is alternated from one forelimb to the other; arm swinging.

Primate Classification

The living primates are commonly categorized into their respective subgroups, as shown in Figure 6–8. This taxonomy is based on the system originally established by Linnaeus. (Remember that the primate order, which includes a diverse array of at least 230 species, belongs to a larger group, the class *Mammalia.*)

As you learned in Chapter 5, in any taxonomic system, animals are organized into increasingly specific categories. For example, the order *Primates* includes *all* primates. However, at the next level down—the *suborder*—the primates have conventionally been divided into two large categories, Prosimii (all the prosimians: lemurs, lorises, and, customarily, the tarsiers) and Anthropoidea (all the monkeys, apes, and humans). Therefore, the suborder distinction is more specific and narrower than the order.

At the level of the suborder, the prosimians are distinct as a group from all the other primates, and this classification makes the biological and evolutionary statement that all the prosimian species are more closely related to one another than they are to any of the anthropoids. Likewise, all anthropoid species are more closely related to one another than they are to the prosimians.

The taxonomy shown in Figure 6–8 is the traditional one, and it's based on physical similarities between species and lineages. But this approach isn't foolproof. For example, two species that resemble each other anatomically (for example, some New and Old World monkeys) may in fact not be closely related at all. By looking only at physical characteristics, it's possible to overlook the unknown effects of separate evolutionary history (see our discussion of homoplasy on p. 102). But genetic evidence avoids this problem and indeed shows that Old and New World monkeys are evolutionarily quite distinct.

Primate classification is currently in a state of transition, mainly because of genetic evidence that certain relationships, especially between humans and chimpanzees, are even closer than previously thought. Beginning in the 1970s, scientists began to apply genetic analysis to help identify biological and phylogenetic relationships between species.

Direct comparisons of the amino acid sequences of various proteins (products of DNA) are excellent indicators of shared evolutionary history. If two species are similar in their protein structure, we know that their DNA sequences are also similar. Also, if two species share similar DNA, it's probable that both inherited their blueprint from a common ancestor.

But, as useful as this technique has been, it's an *indirect* method of comparing DNA sequences between species. Now, however, the techniques of DNA sequencing used in the Human Genome Project make it possible to make direct between-species comparisons of DNA sequences. This approach is called *comparative genomics.*

A map of the chimpanzee genome was completed in 2005, and this was a major advance in human comparative genomics because human and chimpanzee genomes can now be directly compared. But even before that, molecular anthropologists had already compared the sequences of several chimpanzee and human genes or groups of genes. For example, Wildman et al. (2003) compared 97 human genes with their chimpanzee, gorilla, and orangutan counterparts and determined that humans are most closely related to chimpanzees and that genes of these two species are between 98.4 and 99.4 percent identical. They also calculated that humans and chimpanzees last shared a common ancestor with gorillas around 6–7 mya and that the chimpanzee and human lineages diverged sometime between 5 and 6 mya. These results are consistent with the findings of several other studies, and together, they've motivated many primatologists to consider changing how they classify the hominoids (Goodman et al., 1998; Wildman et al., 2003). Although there is no formal acceptance of suggested changes, there's a lot of support for placing all great apes in the family Hominidae along with humans. (We'll return to this important development in Chapter 8.)

Another area where changes have been suggested concerns tarsiers (see p. 126). Tarsiers are highly specialized animals that display several unique physical characteristics. Because they possess a number of prosimian traits, they've traditionally been classified as prosimians (with lemurs and lorises). But they also have certain anthropoid features, and biochemically they're more similar to the anthropoids (Dene et al., 1976).

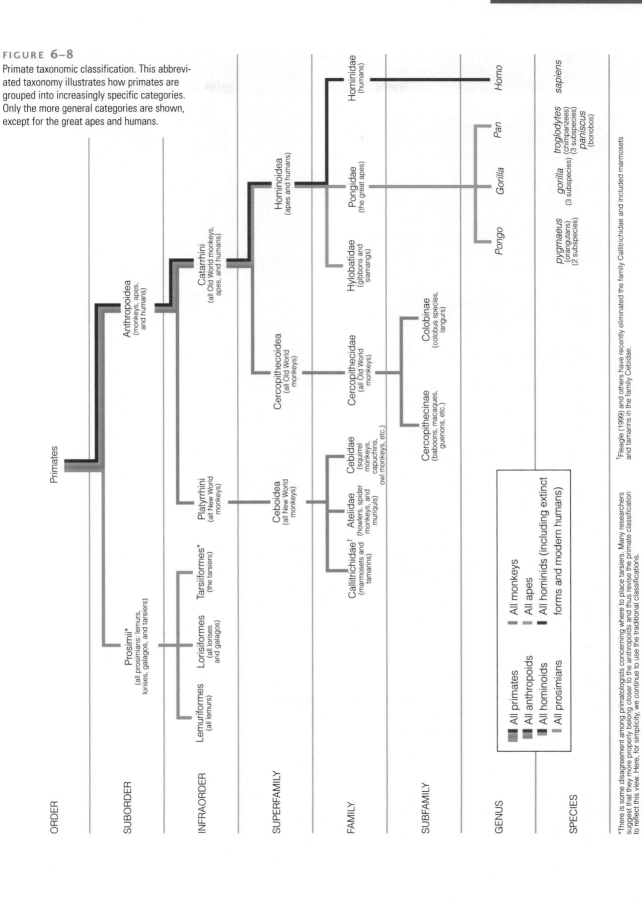

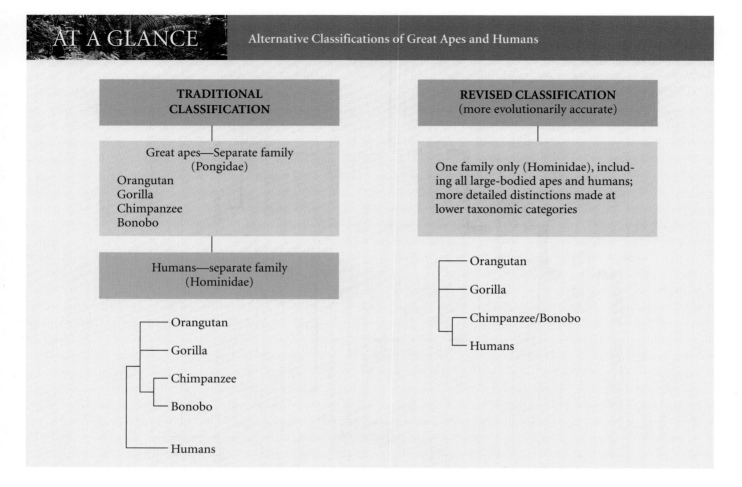

AT A GLANCE   Alternative Classifications of Great Apes and Humans

TRADITIONAL CLASSIFICATION

Great apes—Separate family (Pongidae)
Orangutan
Gorilla
Chimpanzee
Bonobo

Humans—separate family (Hominidae)

- Orangutan
- Gorilla
- Chimpanzee
- Bonobo
- Humans

REVISED CLASSIFICATION (more evolutionarily accurate)

One family only (Hominidae), including all large-bodied apes and humans; more detailed distinctions made at lower taxonomic categories

- Orangutan
- Gorilla
- Chimpanzee/Bonobo
- Humans

Today, most primatologists consider tarsiers to be more closely related to anthropoids than to prosimians. But instead of simply moving them into the suborder Anthropoidea, one scheme places lemurs and lorises in a different suborder, Strepsirhini (instead of Prosimii), while including tarsiers with monkeys, apes, and humans in another suborder, Haplorhini (Szalay and Delson, 1979) (Fig. 6–9). In this classification, the conventionally named suborders Prosimii and Anthropoidea are replaced by Strepsirhini and Haplorhini, respectively. This designation hasn't been universally accepted, but the terminology is now common, especially in technical publications. So if you see the term *strepsirhine*, you know the author is referring specifically to lemurs and lorises.

We've presented the traditional system of primate classification in this chapter, even though we acknowledge the need for change. Until the new designations are formally adopted, we think it's appropriate to use the standard taxonomy along with discussing some proposed changes. We also want to point out that even though specific details and names haven't yet been worked out, the vast majority of experts do accept the evolutionary implications of the revised groupings.

FIGURE 6–9

Revised partial classification of the primates. In this system, the terms *Prosimii* and *Anthropoidea* have been replaced by *Strepsirhini* and *Haplorhini*, respectively. The tarsier is included in the same suborder with monkeys, apes, and humans to reflect a closer relationship with these species than with lemurs and lorises. (Compare with Fig. 6–8.)

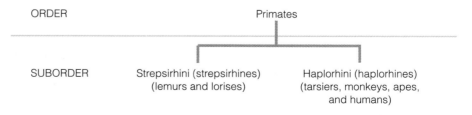

ORDER   Primates

SUBORDER   Strepsirhini (strepsirhines)   Haplorhini (haplorhines)
            (lemurs and lorises)   (tarsiers, monkeys, apes,
                                                   and humans)

A Survey of the Living Primates

In this section, we take a closer look at the major primate subgroups. It's beyond the scope of this book to cover any species in detail; so instead, we present a brief description of each grouping as an introduction to the Primate order.

PROSIMIANS (LEMURS AND LORISES)

The most primitive primates are the lemurs and lorises (we don't include tarsiers here). Remember that when we use the word "primitive," we mean that prosimians are more anatomically similar to their earlier mammalian ancestors than are the other primates (monkeys, apes, and humans). Prosimians thus tend to exhibit certain more ancestral characteristics, such as a more pronounced reliance on olfaction (sense of smell). Their greater olfactory capabilities (compared to other primates) are reflected in the presence of a moist, fleshy pad or **rhinarium** at the end of the nose and in a relatively long snout.

Many other characteristics distinguish lemurs and lorises from the anthropoids, including eyes placed more to the side of the face, differences in reproductive physiology, and shorter gestation and maturation periods. Lemurs and lorises also have a unique trait called a "dental comb" (Fig. 6–10). The dental comb is formed by forward-projecting lower incisors and canines, and together these modified teeth are used in grooming and feeding. Another characteristic that sets lemurs and lorises apart from anthropoids is the retention of a claw on the second toe.

Lemurs   Lemurs are found only on the island of Madagascar and nearby islands off the east coast of Africa (Fig. 6–11). As the only nonhuman primates on Madagascar, lemurs diversified into numerous and varied ecological niches without competition from monkeys and apes.

Lemurs range in size from the small mouse lemur, with a body length (head and trunk) of only 5 inches, to the indri, with a body length of 2 to 3 feet (Nowak, 1999). While the larger lemurs are diurnal and exploit a wide variety of dietary items, such as leaves, fruit, buds, bark, and shoots, the smaller species (mouse and dwarf lemurs) are nocturnal and insectivorous.

Lemurs display considerable variation regarding numerous other aspects of behavior. Some are mostly arboreal; but others, such as the ring-tailed lemur (Fig. 6–12), are more terrestrial. Some arboreal species are quadrupeds, and others (sifakas and indris) are vertical clingers and leapers (Fig. 6–13). Socially, several species (for example, ring-tailed lemurs and sifakas) are gregarious and live in groups of 10 to 25 animals composed of males and females of all ages. Others (the indris) live in family units composed of a mated pair and their offspring. And several nocturnal forms are mostly solitary.

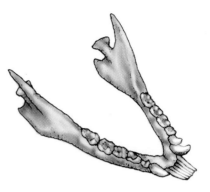

FIGURE **6–10**
Prosimian dental comb, formed by forward-projecting incisors and canines.

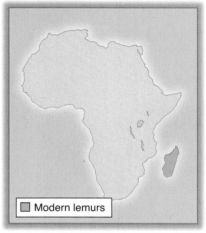

□ Modern lemurs

FIGURE **6–11**
Geographical distribution of modern lemurs.

FIGURE **6–12**
Ring-tailed lemur.

FIGURE **6–13**
Sifakas in their native habitat in Madagascar.

rhinarium   (rine-air´-ee-um) The moist, hairless pad at the end of the nose; seen in most mammals. The rhinarium enhances an animal's ability to smell.

FIGURE **6–14**
Slow loris.

FIGURE **6–15**
Galago, or "bush baby."

FIGURE **6–16**
Tarsier.

Tarsiers

FIGURE **6–17**
Geographical distribution of tarsiers.

Lorises   Lorises (Fig. 6–14), which resemble lemurs, were able to survive in mainland areas by adopting a nocturnal activity pattern at a time when most other prosimians became extinct. In this way, they were (and are) able to avoid competition with more recently evolved primates (the diurnal monkeys).

There are at least eight loris species, all of which are found in tropical forest and woodland habitats of India, Sri Lanka, Southeast Asia, and Africa. Also included in the same general category are six to nine (Bearder, 1987; Nowak, 1999) galago species (Fig. 6–15), which are widely distributed throughout most of the forested and woodland savanna areas of sub-Saharan Africa.

Locomotion in lorises is a slow, cautious climbing form of quadrupedalism. In contrast, all galagos are highly agile vertical clingers and leapers. Some lorises and galagos are almost entirely insectivorous; others supplement their diet with fruit, leaves, gums, and slugs. Lorises and galagos frequently forage for food alone, and females leave infants behind in nests until they are older. However, ranges overlap, and two or more females occasionally forage together or share the same sleeping nest.

TARSIERS

There are five recognized tarsier species (Nowak, 1999) (Fig. 6–16), all restricted to island areas in Southeast Asia (Fig. 6–17), where they inhabit a wide range of forest types, from tropical forest to backyard gardens. Tarsiers are nocturnal insectivores that leap onto prey (which may also include small vertebrates) from lower branches and shrubs. They appear to form stable pair bonds, and the basic tarsier social unit is a mated pair and their young offspring (MacKinnon and MacKinnon, 1980).

As we've already mentioned, tarsiers present a complex blend of characteristics not seen in other primates. They're unique in that their enormous eyes, which dominate much of the face, are immobile within their sockets. To compensate for the inability to move the eyes, tarsiers (like owls) are able to rotate their heads 180 degrees.

ANTHROPOIDS (MONKEYS, APES, AND HUMANS)

Although there is much variation among anthropoids, they share certain features that, when taken together, distinguish them as a group from prosimians (and most other placental mammals). Here's a partial list of these traits:

1. Generally larger body size
2. Larger brain (in absolute terms and relative to body weight)
3. Reduced reliance on the sense of smell, indicated by absence of rhinarium and other structures
4. Increased reliance on vision, with forward-facing eyes at the front of the face
5. Greater degree of color vision
6. Back of eye socket formed by a bony plate
7. Blood supply to brain different from that in prosimians

8. Fusion of the two sides of the mandible at the midline to form one bone (in prosimians and tarsiers, they are joined by fibrous tissue)
9. Less-specialized dentition, as seen in the absence of dental comb and some other features
10. Differences in female internal reproductive anatomy
11. Longer gestation and maturation periods
12. Increased parental care
13. More mutual grooming

Approximately 85 percent of all primates are monkeys (about 195 species). It's impossible to give precise numbers of species because the taxonomic status of some primates remains in doubt, and primatologists are still making new discoveries. Monkeys are divided into two groups separated by geographical area (New World and Old World), as well as by several million years of separate evolutionary history.

New World Monkeys The New World monkeys exhibit a wide range of size, diet, and ecological adaptation (Fig. 6–18). In size, they vary from the tiny marmosets and tamarins (about 12 ounces) to the 20-pound howler monkeys (Figs. 6–19 and 6–20). New World monkeys are almost exclusively arboreal, and some never come to the ground. They can be found

FIGURE **6–18**
New World monkeys.

Prince Bernhard's titi monkey (discovered in 2002)

Marc van Roosmalen

Squirrel monkeys

© Kevin Schafer/CORBIS

Male uakari

R. A. Mittermeier/Conservation International

White-faced capuchins

© Jay Dickman/CORBIS

Female muriqui with infant

Andrew Young

127

FIGURE 6-19
A pair of golden lion tamarins.

FIGURE 6-20
Howler monkeys.

FIGURE 6-21
Geographical distribution of modern New World monkeys.

Callitrichidae (kal-eh-trick´-eh-dee)

Cebidae (see´-bid-ee)

ischial callosities Patches of tough, hard skin on the buttocks of Old World monkeys and chimpanzees.

Cercopithecidae (serk-oh-pith´-eh-sid-ee) The family designation for all the Old World monkeys.

Cercopithecines (serk-oh-pith´-eh-seens) The subfamily of Old World monkeys that includes baboons, macaques, and guenons.

colobines (kole´-uh-beans) The subfamily of Old World monkeys that includes the African colobus monkeys and Asian langurs.

in a wide range of arboreal environments throughout most forested areas in southern Mexico and Central and South America (Fig. 6–21). Like Old World monkeys, all except one species (the owl monkey) are diurnal.

New World monkeys have traditionally been divided into two families: **Callitrichidae** (marmosets and tamarins) and **Cebidae** (all others). But molecular data along with recently reported fossil evidence indicate that a major regrouping of New World monkeys is in order (Fleagle, 1999).*

Of the roughly 70 New World monkey species, marmosets and tamarins are the smallest. They have claws instead of nails and, unlike other primates, usually give birth to twins. They are mostly insectivorous, although marmosets eat gums from trees, and tamarins eat fruit. Locomotion is quadrupedal, and they use their claws for climbing. These small monkeys usually live in social groups composed of a mated pair, or a female and two adult males, and their offspring. Marmosets and tamarins are among the few primate species in which males are extensively involved in infant care.

Cebids range in size from the squirrel monkey (body length 12 inches) to the howler (body length 24 inches). Diet varies, with most relying on a combination of fruit and leaves supplemented with insects. Most are quadrupedal, but some—for example, muriquis and spider monkeys (Fig. 6–22)—are semibrachiators. Muriquis, howlers, and spider monkeys also have powerful prehensile tails that are used not only in locomotion but also for suspension under branches while feeding. Socially, most cebids are found in groups of both sexes and all age categories. Some (for example, titis) form monogamous pairs and live with their subadult offspring.

Old World Monkeys   Except for humans, Old World monkeys are the most widely distributed of all living primates. They are found throughout sub-Saharan Africa and southern Asia, ranging from tropical jungle habitats to semiarid desert and even to seasonally snow-covered areas in northern Japan (Fig. 6–23).

Most Old World monkeys are quadrupedal and primarily arboreal, but some (for example, baboons) are also adapted to life on the ground. In general, they spend a good deal of time sleeping, feeding, and grooming. They also have areas of hardened skin on the buttocks (**ischial callosities**) that serve as sitting pads. All Old World monkeys are placed in one taxonomic family: **Cercopithecidae**. In turn, this family is divided into two subfamilies: the **cercopithecines** and **colobines**.

---

*One possibility is to include spider monkeys, howler monkeys, and muriquis (woolly spider monkeys) in a third family, Atelidae (see Fig. 6–9). Another is to eliminate the family Callitrichidae altogether and include marmosets and tamarins as a subfamily within the family Cebidae.

FIGURE 6–22

Spider monkey. Note the prehensile tail.

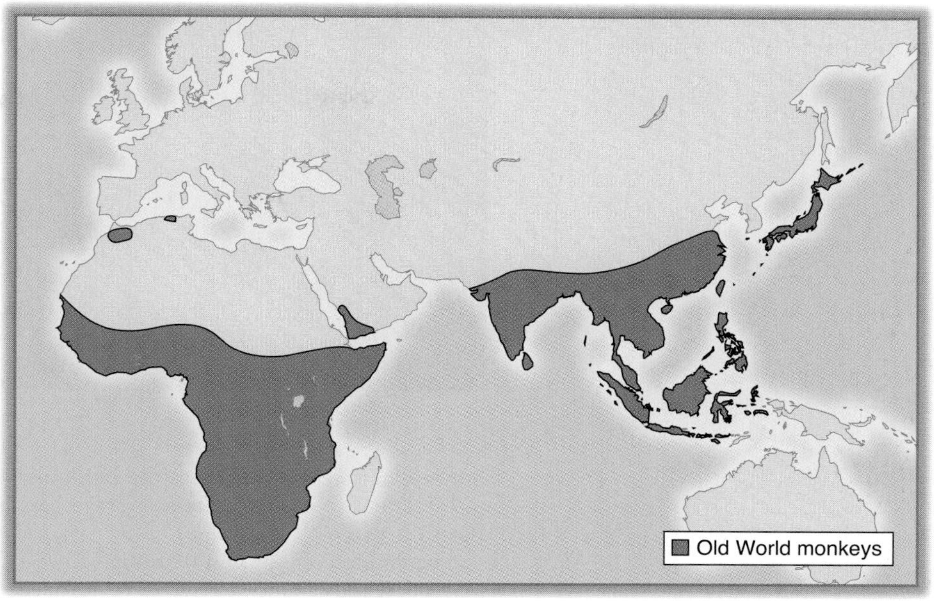

FIGURE 6–23

Geographical distribution of modern Old World monkeys.

Old World monkeys

The cercopithecines are the more generalized of the two groups, showing a more omnivorous dietary adaptation and cheek pouches for storing food. As a group, the cercopithecines eat almost anything, including fruit, seeds, leaves, grasses, tubers, roots, nuts, insects, birds' eggs, amphibians, small reptiles, and small mammals (the last seen in baboons).

The majority of cercopithecine species, such as the mostly arboreal guenons (Fig. 6–24) and the more terrestrial savanna (Fig. 6–25) and hamadryas baboons, are found in Africa. However, the several macaque species, which include the well-known rhesus monkey, are widely distributed in southern Asia and India.

Colobine species have a narrower range of food preferences and mainly eat mature leaves, which is why they're also called leaf-eating monkeys. The colobines are found mainly in Asia,

FIGURE 6–24

Adult male sykes monkey, one of several guenon species.

FIGURE **6–25**
Savanna baboons. (a) Male. (b) Female.

(a)   (b)

but both the red colobus and the black-and-white colobus are exclusively African (Fig. 6–26). Other colobines include several Asian langur species and the proboscis monkey of Borneo.

Locomotion among Old World monkeys includes arboreal quadrupedalism in guenons, macaques, and langurs; terrestrial quadrupedalism in baboons, patas, and macaques; and semibrachiation and acrobatic leaping in colobus monkeys.

Marked differences in body size or shape between the sexes, referred to as **sexual dimorphism**, are typical of some terrestrial species and are particularly pronounced in baboons and patas. In these species, male body weight (up to 80 pounds in baboons) may be twice that of females.

In several species (especially baboons and some macaques) females have pronounced cyclical changes of the external genitalia. These changes, including swelling and redness, are associated with **estrus**, a hormonally initiated period of sexual receptivity in female nonhuman mammals correlated with ovulation.

Old World monkeys live in a few different kinds of social groups, and there are uncertainties among primatologists regarding some species. In general, colobines tend to live in small groups, with only one or two adult males. Savanna baboons and most macaque species are found in large social units comprising several adults of both sexes and offspring of all ages. Monogamous pairing isn't common in Old World monkeys but is seen in a few langurs and possibly one or two guenon species.

FIGURE **6–26**
Black-and-white colobus monkey.

sexual dimorphism   Differences in physical characteristics between males and females of the same species. For example, humans are slightly sexually dimorphic for body size, with males being taller, on average, than females of the same population.

estrus   (ess´-truss) Period of sexual receptivity in female mammals (except humans), correlated with ovulation. When used as an adjective, the word is spelled *estrous*.

HOMINOIDS (APES AND HUMANS)

The other large grouping of anthropoids (the hominoids) includes apes and humans. The superfamily **Hominoidea** includes the small gibbons and siamangs in the family **Hylobatidae**; the great apes in the family **Pongidae** (orangutans, gorillas, bonobos, and chimpanzees); and humans in the family Hominidae.* Apes and humans differ from monkeys in several ways:

1. Generally larger body size, except for gibbons and siamangs
2. Absence of a tail
3. Shortened trunk (lumbar area shorter and more stable)
4. Differences in position and musculature of the shoulder joint (adapted for suspensory locomotion)
5. More complex behavior
6. More complex brain and enhanced cognitive abilities
7. Increased period of infant development and dependency

Gibbons and Siamangs   The eight gibbon species and the closely related siamangs are found in the southeastern tropical areas of Asia (Fig. 6–27). These are the smallest of the apes, with a long, slender body weighing around 13 pounds in gibbons (Fig. 6–28) and approximately 25 pounds in siamangs.

The most distinctive structural features of gibbons and siamangs are adaptations for brachiation. They have extremely long arms; long, permanently curved fingers; short thumbs; and powerful shoulder muscles. (Actually, in all ape species the arms are longer than the legs, but not to the extent seen in gibbons and siamangs.) These highly specialized adaptations may be related to feeding behavior while hanging beneath branches. The diet of both species is largely composed of fruit. Both (but especially siamangs) also eat a variety of leaves, flowers, and insects.

The basic social unit of gibbons and siamangs is an adult male and female with dependent offspring. Although they've been described as monogamous, in reality they sometimes do mate with other individuals. As in marmosets and tamarins, male gibbons and siamangs are very much involved in child rearing. Both males and females are highly territorial and protect their territories with elaborate whoops and siren-like "songs."

---

*Note that this classification is currently being revised. See pages 122 and 167 for further discussion.

FIGURE 6–27
Geographical distribution of modern Asian apes.

Lynn Kilgore

FIGURE 6–28
White-handed gibbon.

Hominoidea   The formal designation for the superfamily of anthropoids that includes apes and humans.

Hylobatidae   (high-lo-baht´-id-ee) The family designation of the gibbons and siamangs that live in parts of southeast Asia.

Pongidae   (ponj´-id-ee) The traditional family designation of the great apes (orangutans, chimpanzees, bonobos, and gorillas).

FIGURE 6–29
Orangutans. (a) Female. (b) Male.

Noel Rowe

Noel Rowe

(a)   (b)

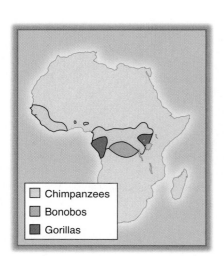

Chimpanzees
Bonobos
Gorillas

FIGURE 6–30
Geographical distribution of modern African apes.

FIGURE 6–31
Western lowland gorillas. (a) Male. (b) Female.

Orangutans   Orangutans (*Pongo pygmaeus*) (Fig. 6–29) are represented by two subspecies found today only in heavily forested areas on the Indonesian islands of Borneo and Sumatra (see Fig. 6–26). Due to poaching by humans and continuing habitat loss on both islands, orangutans are severely threatened by extinction in the wild.

Orangutans are slow, cautious climbers whose locomotor behavior can best be described as four-handed, since they tend to use all four limbs for grasping and support. Although they're almost completely arboreal, orangutans sometimes travel quadrupedally on the ground. Orangutans are also very large animals with pronounced sexual dimorphism (males may weigh 200 pounds or more and females less than 100 pounds).

In the wild, orangutans lead largely solitary lives, although adult females are usually accompanied by one or two dependent offspring. They are primarily **frugivorous** but may also eat bark, leaves, insects, and meat (on rare occasions).

Gorillas   The largest of all living primates, gorillas (*Gorilla gorilla*) are today confined to forested areas of western and eastern equatorial Africa (Fig. 6–30). There are three generally recognized subspecies. The western lowland gorilla is found in several countries of west-central Africa and is the most numerous of the three subspecies (Fig. 6–31). Doran and

Lynn Kilgore

Lynn Kilgore

frugivorous   (fru-give´-or-us) Having a diet composed primarily of fruit.

(a)   (b)

(a)

(b)

McNeilage (1998) reported an estimated population size of perhaps 110,000. However, a recently published report (Walsh et al., 2003) suggests that numbers may be far lower. The eastern lowland gorilla is found near the eastern border of the Democratic Republic of the Congo (DRC—formerly Zaire) and numbers about 12,000. Mountain gorillas (Fig. 6–32), the most extensively studied of the three subspecies, are found in the mountainous areas of central Africa in Rwanda, the DRC, and Uganda. Mountain gorillas have probably never been very numerous, and today they are among the more endangered primates, numbering only about 600.

Gorillas exhibit marked sexual dimorphism, with males weighing up to 400 pounds and females around 150 to 200 pounds. Because of their weight, adult gorillas, especially males, are primarily terrestrial and adopt a **knuckle-walking** posture on the ground.

Mountain gorillas live in groups consisting of one or sometimes two large silverback males, a variable number of adult females, and their subadult offspring. The term *silverback* refers to the saddle of white hair across the back of fully adult (at least 12 or 13 years of age) male gorillas. In his group, a silverback male may tolerate the presence of one or more young adult *blackback* males, probably his sons. Typically, but not always, both females and males leave their **natal group** as young adults. Females join other groups; and males, who appear to be less likely to emigrate, may either live alone for a while or join up with other males before eventually forming their own group.

Systematic studies of free-ranging western lowland gorillas weren't begun until the mid-1980s, and we don't know as much about them, even though they're the only gorillas you'll see in zoos. In general, it appears that their social structure is similar to that of mountain gorillas, but groups are smaller and somewhat less cohesive.

All gorillas are almost exclusively vegetarian. Mountain and western lowland gorillas concentrate primarily on leaves, pith, and stalks, but the latter eat more fruit. Also, western lowland gorillas, unlike mountain gorillas, frequently wade through swamps while foraging on aquatic plants.

Because of their large body size and enormous strength, gorillas have long been considered ferocious. But in reality, they're usually shy and gentle. However, this doesn't mean they're never aggressive. Among males, competition for females can be extremely violent. When threatened, males will attack and defend their group from any perceived danger, whether it's another male gorilla or a human hunter. Still, the reputation of gorillas as murderous beasts is the result of uninformed myth making and little else.

Chimpanzees   Although chimpanzees are probably the best known of all nonhuman primates (Fig. 6–33), they're often misunderstood because of zoo exhibits, television shows, and movies. The true nature of chimpanzees didn't become known until years of fieldwork with wild groups provided a reliable picture. Today, chimpanzees are found in equatorial Africa, in an area that stretches from the Atlantic Ocean in the west to Lake Tanganyika in

FIGURE 6–32
Mountain gorillas. (a) Male. (b) Female.

knuckle walking   A form of quadrupedal locomotion used by chimpanzees, bonobos, and gorillas wherein, the weight of the upper body is supported on the knuckles rather than on the palms of the hands.

natal group   The group in which animals are born and raised. (*Natal* pertains to birth.)

FIGURE 6–33
Chimpanzees. (a) Male. (b) Female.

(a)   (b)

the east. Unfortunately, within this large region their range is very patchy, and it's becoming even more so with continued forest clearing.

In many ways, chimpanzees are anatomically similar to gorillas, with corresponding limb proportions and upper-body shape. However, the ecological adaptations of chimpanzees and gorillas differ, with chimpanzees spending more time in the trees. Unlike gorillas, which are typically placid and quiet, chimpanzees are highly excitable, active, and noisy.

Chimpanzees are smaller than orangutans and gorillas, and although they are sexually dimorphic, sex differences aren't as pronounced. While male chimpanzees may weigh over 100 pounds, females can weigh at least 80.

In addition to quadrupedal knuckle walking, chimpanzees (particularly youngsters) may brachiate when in the trees. On the ground, they frequently walk bipedally for short distances if they're carrying food or other objects.

Chimpanzees eat a huge variety of foods, including fruits, leaves, insects, nuts, birds' eggs, berries, caterpillars, and small mammals. Both males and females also occasionally take part in group hunting efforts to kill small mammals such as red colobus, young baboons, bush-pigs, and antelope. When hunts are successful, group members share the prey.

Chimpanzees live in large, fluid communities of as many as 50 individuals or more. At the core of a chimpanzee community is a group of bonded males. Although relationships between them aren't always peaceful, these males nevertheless act as a group to defend their territory, and they're highly intolerant of unfamiliar chimpanzees, especially males.

Even though chimpanzees are said to live in communities, it's rare for all members to be together at the same time. Rather, they tend to come and go, so that the individuals they encounter vary from day to day. Adult females usually forage alone or in the company of their offspring, a grouping that might include several individuals since females with infants sometimes accompany their own mothers and their younger siblings. A female may also leave her group, either permanently to join another community or temporarily while she's in estrus. This behavior may reduce the risk of mating with close male relatives, because males apparently never leave the group in which they were born.

Chimpanzee social behavior is complex, and individuals form lifelong attachments with friends and relatives. If they continue to live in the same group, the bond between mothers and infants can remain strong until one or the other dies. This may be a considerable period, because many wild chimpanzees live into their mid-30s, and a few live well into their 40s.

Bonobos Bonobos (*Pan paniscus*) are found only in an area south of the Zaire River in the DRC (Fig. 6–34). Not officially recognized by European scientists until the 1920s, they remain among the least studied of the great apes. Although ongoing field studies have produced much information (Susman, 1984; Kano, 1992), research has been hampered by civil war. There are no accurate counts of bonobos; their numbers are believed to be between 10,000 and 20,000 (IUCN, 1996), and they're highly threatened by human hunting, warfare, and habitat loss.

FIGURE 6–34
Female bonobos with young.

Bonobos bear a strong resemblance to chimpanzees but, since they're slightly smaller, they've been called "pygmy chimpanzees." The main anatomical differences between bonobos and chimpanzees are that bonobos have a more linear body build, longer legs relative to arms, a relatively smaller head, a dark face from birth, and tufts of hair at the side of the face (see Fig. 6–33).

Bonobos are more arboreal and less excitable than chimpanzees. While aggression isn't unknown, it appears that physical violence both within and between groups is uncommon. Like chimpanzees, bonobos live in geographically based, fluid communities, and they eat many of the same foods, including occasional meat derived from small mammals (Badrian and Malinky, 1984). But bonobo communities aren't centered around a group of closely bonded males. Instead, male-female bonding is more important than in chimpanzees (and most other nonhuman primates), and females aren't peripheral to the group (Badrian and Badrian, 1984). This may be related to bonobo sexuality, which differs from that of other nonhuman primates in that copulation is very frequent and occurs throughout a female's estrous cycle.

HUMANS

Humans are the only living representatives of the habitually bipedal hominids (genus *Homo*, species *sapiens*). Our primate heritage is evident in our overall anatomy and genetic makeup and in many aspects of human behavior. Except for reduced canine size, human teeth are typical primate (especially ape) teeth. Our dependence on vision and decreased reliance on olfaction, as well as flexible limbs and grasping hands, are rooted in our primate, arboreal past. Humans can even brachiate, and playgrounds often accommodate this ability in children.

Humans in general are omnivorous, although all societies observe certain culturally based dietary restrictions. Nevertheless, as a species with a rather generalized digestive system, we are physiologically adapted to digest an extremely wide assortment of foods. Perhaps to our detriment, we also share with our relatives a fondness for sweets that originates from the importance of high-energy fruits in the diets of many nonhuman primates.

But quite obviously, humans are unique among primates and indeed among all animals. For example, no member of any other species has the ability to write or think about issues such as how they differ from other life-forms. This ability is rooted in the fact that human evolution, during the last 800,000 years or so, has been characterized by dramatic increases in brain size and other neurological changes.

Humans are also completely dependent on culture. Without cultural innovation, it would never have been possible for us to leave the tropics. As it is, humans inhabit every corner of the planet except Antarctica, and we've even established outposts there. And lest we forget, a fortunate few have even walked on the moon. None of the technologies and other aspects of culture that humans have developed over the last several thousand years would have been possible without the highly developed cognitive abilities that we alone possess. Nevertheless, the neurological basis for intelligence is rooted in our evolutionary past, and it's something we share with other primates. Indeed, research has demonstrated that several nonhuman primate species—most notably chimpanzees, bonobos, and gorillas—display a level of problem solving and insight that most people would have considered impossible 25 years ago (see Chapter 7).

Aside from cognitive abilities, the one other trait that sets humans apart from other primates is our unique (among mammals) form of *habitual* bipedal locomotion. This particular trait appeared early in the evolution of our lineage, and over time, we have become more efficient at it because of related changes in the musculoskeletal anatomy of the pelvis, leg, and foot (see Chapter 8). So, while it's certainly true that human beings are unique intellectually, and in some ways anatomically, we are still primates. In fact, humans are basically exaggerated African apes.

Endangered Primates

In September 2000, scientists announced that a subspecies of red colobus, named Miss Waldron's red colobus, had officially been declared extinct. This announcement came after a six-year search for the 20-pound monkey that had not been seen for 20 years (Oates, et al., 2000). Sadly, this species, indigenous to the West African countries of Ghana and the Ivory Coast, has the distinction of being the first nonhuman primate to be declared extinct in the twenty-first century. But it won't be the last. In fact, as of this writing, over half of all nonhuman primate species are now in jeopardy, and some face almost immediate extinction in the wild.

There are three basic reasons for the worldwide depletion of nonhuman primates: habitat destruction, hunting for food, and live capture for export or local trade. Underlying these three causes is one major factor: unprecedented human population growth, which is occurring at a faster rate in developing countries than in the developed world. The developing nations of Africa, Asia, and Central and South America are home to over 90 percent of all nonhuman primate species, and these countries, aided in no small part by the industrialized countries of Europe and the United States, are cutting their forests at a rate of about 30 million acres per year. Unbelievably, in the year 2002, deforestation of the Amazon increased by 40 percent over that of 2001. This increase was largely due to land clearing for the cultivation of soybeans. In Brazil, the Atlantic rain forest originally covered some 385,000 square miles. Today, an estimated 7 percent is all that remains of what was once home to countless New World monkeys and thousands of other species.

Much of the motivation behind the destruction of the rain forests is, of course, economic: the short-term gains from clearing forests to create immediately available (but poor) farmland or ranchland; the use of trees for lumber and paper products; and large-scale mining operations (with their necessary roads, digging, etc., all of which cause habitat destruction). And, of course, the demand for tropical hardwoods (for example, mahogany, teak, and rosewood) in the United States, Europe, and Japan continues unabated, creating an enormously profitable market for rain forest products.

In many areas, habitat loss has been, and continues to be, the single greatest cause of declining

FIGURE 6–35
Red-eared guenons (with red tails) and Preuss' guenons for sale in bushmeat market, Malabo, Equatorial Guinea.

John Oates

Karl Ammann

FIGURE **6–36**
These orphaned chimpanzee infants are being bottle-fed at a sanctuary near Pointe Noir, Congo. Probably, they will never be returned to the wild and they face a very uncertain future.

numbers of nonhuman primates. But increasingly, human hunting poses an even greater threat. During the 1990s, primatologists and conservationists became aware of a rapidly developing trade in *bushmeat,* or meat from wild animals in west and central Africa (Fig. 6–35). The current slaughter, which now accounts for the loss of thousands of nonhuman primates and other species annually, has been compared to the near extinction of the American bison in the nineteenth century.

Nonhuman primates have traditionally been a source of food for people. In the past, subsistence hunters didn't usually pose a serious threat to nonhuman primate populations, and certainly not to entire species. But now, hunters armed with shotguns and automatic rifles can wipe out an entire group of monkeys or gorillas in minutes.

One major factor in the development of the bushmeat trade has been logging. The construction of logging roads, mainly by French, German, and Belgian lumber companies, has opened up vast tracts of forest that were previously inaccessible to local hunters. Once the roads are cut, hunters hitch rides on logging trucks (for a fee paid from the proceeds of bushmeat sales). What has emerged is a profitable trade in bushmeat, a trade in which logging company employees and local governmental officials participate with hunters, villagers, market vendors, and smugglers who cater to growing overseas markets. In other words, the hunting of wild animals for food, particularly in Africa, has quickly shifted from a subsistence activity to a commercial enterprise of international scope.

It's impossible to know how many animals are killed each year. But estimates for monkeys and apes are in the thousands. In addition, hundreds of infants are orphaned and sold in markets as pets. Although a few of these traumatized orphans make it to sanctuaries, most die within days or weeks of capture (Fig. 6–36).

Although the slaughter may be most extreme in Africa, it's by no means limited to that continent. In South America, for example, hunting nonhuman primates for food is common. One report documents that in less than two years, a single family of Brazilian rubber tappers killed almost 500 members of various large-bodied species, including spider monkeys, woolly monkeys, and howler monkeys (Peres, 1990). Live capture and illegal trade in endangered primate species also continues unabated in China and Southeast Asia, where nonhuman primates are not only eaten but also funneled into the exotic pet trade. Primate body parts also figure prominently in traditional medicines, and with increasing human population size, the enormous demand for these products (and products from nonprimate species, such as tigers) has placed many species in extreme jeopardy.

Fortunately, steps are being taken to ensure the survival of some species. Many developing countries, such as Costa Rica and the Malagasy Republic (Madagascar), are designating national parks and other reserves for the protection of natural resources, including primates. Several private international efforts are aimed at curbing the bushmeat trade. It's only through such practices and through educational programs that many primate species have a chance of escaping extinction, at least in the immediate future.

Perhaps most encouraging is the establishment of the Great Ape Survival Project (GRASP) in 2000 by the United Nations Environmental Program. GRASP is an alliance of many of the world's major great ape conservation and research organizations. In 2003, GRASP appealed for $25 million to be used in protecting the great apes from extinction. The money (a paltry sum) would be used to enforce laws that regulate hunting and illegal logging. It goes without saying that GRASP and other organizations must succeed if the great apes are to survive in the wild for even 20 more years!

If you are in your twenties or thirties, you will most certainly live to hear about the extinction of some of our marvelously unique cousins. Many more will undoubtedly slip away unnoticed. Tragically, they will disappear, in most cases, before we've even gotten to know them. Each species on earth is the current result of a unique set of evolutionary events that, over millions of years, has produced a finely adapted component of a diverse ecosystem. When a species becomes extinct, that adaptation and that part of biodiversity are lost forever. What a tragedy it will be if, through our own mismanagement and greed, we awaken to a world without chimpanzees, mountain gorillas, or the tiny, exquisite lion tamarin. When that day comes, we truly will have lost a part of ourselves, and we will certainly be the poorer for it.

Summary

In this chapter we've introduced you to the primates, the mammalian order that includes prosimians, monkeys, apes, and humans. We discussed how primates, including humans, have retained a number of ancestral characteristics that have permitted them, as a group, to be generalized in terms of diet and locomotor patterns. You were also presented with a general outline of traits that differentiate primates from other mammals.

We also discussed primate classification and how primatologists are redefining relationships between some lineages. In particular, we mentioned that tarsiers will likely be removed from the suborder Prosimii and placed with the anthropoids in a grouping called the haplorhines. The lemurs and lorises would be kept together under the suborder distinction of strepsirhine. Also, chimpanzees, bonobos, and gorillas would be placed with humans in the family Hominidae. These changes reflect increasing knowledge of the genetic relationships between primate lineages and, particularly in the case of tarsiers, reconsideration of various anatomical characteristics.

You also became acquainted with the major groups of nonhuman primates, especially regarding their basic social structure, diet, and locomotor patterns. Most primates are diurnal and live in social groups. The only nocturnal primates are lorises, some lemurs, tarsiers, and owl monkeys. Nocturnal species tend to forage for food alone or with offspring and one or two other animals. Diurnal primates live in a variety of social groupings, including monogamous pairs as well as groups consisting of one male with several females and offspring or those composed of several males and females and offspring.

Finally, we talked about the precarious existence of most nonhuman primates today as they face hunting, capture, and habitat loss. These threats are all imposed by only one primate species, one that arrived fairly late on the evolutionary stage. Throughout the remainder of this textbook, you'll become better acquainted with this fairly recently evolved primate species, of which you are a member.

Critical Thinking Questions

1. How does a classification scheme reflect biological and evolutionary changes in a lineage? Can you give an example of suggested changes to the way primates are classified? What is the basis of these suggestions?

2. How do you think continued advances in genetic research will influence how we look at relationships between ourselves and nonhuman primates in 10 years' time?

3. What factors are threatening the existence of nonhuman primates in the wild? What can you do to help in the efforts to save nonhuman primates from extinction?

Molecular Applications in Primatology

Primatologists have recently used molecular biological techniques to compare the DNA sequences of a wide range of contemporary primates. From these data, they've gained new insights concerning sensory perception, physiology, social relationships, and evolutionary relationships.

One crucial source of information concerns the precise identification of kin relationships within primate societies. Recognizing maternity is almost always obvious—not only to primatologists studying primate social groups, but probably to the members of all these groups as well. Tracing paternity, however, has always been difficult. And without knowing who fathered individuals within the group, the testing of behavioral ecological hypotheses—such as those relating to kin selection, infanticide, and the selective advantage of dominance—has been severely hampered.

Recently, researchers have made great strides in overcoming these difficulties. Biologist Phillip Morin and anthropologist Jim Moore (of the University of California, San Diego) did the first molecular-based study on the Gombe chimpanzees (Morin et al., 1994). An important advantage of this research was that workers could obtain DNA samples without interfering with the animals themselves (Fig. 1). Previously, they had to capture the animals—usually by firing a sedative dart—retrieve a blood sample, and then release them. These procedures are dangerous for the animals, and they can seriously disrupt the social group.

What's more, due to the development of PCR techniques (see p. 56), primatologists can now use much smaller DNA samples. In this study, for example, Moore retrieved shed hairs from abandoned chimpanzee nests; if the hair follicle is present, there's usually enough DNA to analyze. Back in the laboratory, following PCR, researchers used DNA fingerprinting (see p. 56) to identify the individual and its close kin.

Researchers from the Max Planck Institute for Evolutionary Anthropology (MPIEA) recently did a more complete study on West African chimpanzees from the Tai Forest. The MPIEA, which was founded in Leipzig, Germany, in 1997, has quickly become the leading center for a variety of groundbreaking applications within anthropology. Its staff of molecular biologists, primatologists, and molecular anthropologists have contributed significantly to many aspects of molecular research discussed in this text (see Sources for the MPIEA website).

Led by primatologist Linda Vigilant, the researchers found that most of the chimpanzee offspring within the Tai Forest community were fathered by resident males (Vigilant et al., 2001). What's more, it appeared that the females might be bonded more closely and over longer time spans than previously recognized. Such a conclusion could force primatologists to revise the traditional view that male-male bonds are the most central cohesive influence on chimpanzee group structure.

Lastly, and supporting the more recent results from West Africa, a further study of the Gombe chimpanzees, using DNA

FIGURE 1
Physical anthropologist Jim Moore collecting hair samples from a chimpanzee sleeping nest at Gombe.

from both shed hair and fecal samples, found that *all* offspring were fathered by resident males (Constable et al., 2001). Detailed examination of social relationships within the Gombe community also showed that a variety of male strategies—such as dominance, possessiveness, opportunistic mating, and consortships—could lead to reproductive success. DNA can also be used to assess the degree of inbreeding. At Gombe, 13 of 14 offspring were not closely inbred; but in one case, a male had successfully mated with his mother.

Other primatologists have recently conducted similar molecular research on paternity and its social correlates in savanna

Molecular Applications in Primatology CONTINUED

FIGURE 2

Variation in DNA sequences can be studied using a variety of molecular genetic techniques. A graduate student at the University of Cambridge uses gradient gel electrophoresis (DGGE) to study variability in the chromosomal region involved in immune response (the area of DNA which helps provide protection against infection).

baboons (Buchan et al., 2003). Among groups of baboons in Kenya, males display paternal care by supporting their juvenile offspring in disputes with other baboons more than they support unrelated juveniles. Considering that baboon society is polygynous, and estrous females usually mate with more than one male, how could fathers distinguish their offspring from unrelated individuals? Clues to how nonhuman primates might recognize kin could come from new molecular-based research.

Led by Leslie Knapp, the Primate Immunogenetics and Molecular Ecology Research Group at Cambridge University is investigating aspects of human and nonhuman primate genetic mechanisms—and how these, in turn, might influence immunity, disease, and potentially social behavior as well. The focus of their investigations is a genetic system called the major histocompatibility complex, or more simply, the MHC (Grob et al., 1998). This group is currently examining MHC variation in chimpanzees, gorillas, mandrills, several New World monkeys, lemurs, and humans. Techniques of analysis include PCR and nucleotide sequencing (Fig. 2). Results are used to test hypotheses regarding the effects of natural selection on particular allele combinations, the antiquity of these genes in different primate groups, and possible influences on how individuals signal each

other information regarding their genotype—which, in turn, could facilitate kin recognition, mate choice, and inbreeding avoidance (Knapp, personal communication; Primate Immunogenetics and Molecular Ecology Research Group).

Members of the Cambridge research team work both in the laboratory and in the field, where they assist in collecting appropriate samples and collaborate in long-term behavioral studies. Such intensive investigations are necessary in this work—and for all the investigations discussed earlier. It's not very helpful to know, for example, that two chimpanzees are brothers if we don't have detailed long-term data on how they behave in relation to each other as compared to other members of the group.

Primatologists still don't fully understand how nonhuman primates detect information concerning kin. Some researchers propose that olfactory (smell) cues may be crucial in many circumstances, and they are currently testing this hypothesis. In the process they're discovering some fascinating genetic patterns that influence olfactory perception in contemporary primates—including humans.

Several genes and their protein products that directly control olfactory reception in mammals have recently been recognized. One of these directly influences a particular form of scent perception. This gene is present and fully active in most mammals and in some primates (prosimians and New World monkeys), but it's completely dysfunctional in all Old World anthropoids (Old World monkeys, apes, and humans). These observations were discovered separately by two pairs of investigators, one at the University of Southern California (Liman and Innan, 2003) and the other at the University of Michigan (Zhang and Webb, 2003). What's more, both research teams have reached the same conclusions regarding *when* in evolution such olfactory capabilities were lost and *why* it happened. The evolutionary timing of the genetic mutations that made this type of olfaction no longer possible is placed just before the divergence of Old World monkeys and hominoids (about 25–20 mya). In addition, the reason hypothesized for such altered selection in primate evolution is the parallel development of full color vision, which has also recently been investigated in different primates using molecular techniques. The researchers suggest that the advantages provided by full color vision relaxed the selection pressure that favored pheromone detection—eventually leading to deactivation of genes controlling that ability.

We know that the ability shown by many primates to recognize kin is partly influenced by olfactory detection, but we also know that it's not tied primarily to pheromone perception—at least not among Old World anthropoids. It may be that in many Old World monkeys and apes, other olfactory mechanisms are at work. Hundreds of other genes have been shown to directly influence olfactory reception, and in fact they constitute the largest gene family currently known within mammalian genomes. But there's one major exception—*Homo sapiens*.

In pioneering research, Yoav Gilad (formerly at MPIEA and now at the University of Chicago) has shown that humans have far fewer functional olfactory receptor genes than any other primate, including our closest African ape cousins (Gilad et al., 2003, 2005). It's not clear just when in hominid evolution this extreme reduction in olfactory ability occurred. But, at least for modern *H. sapiens*, we can add a reduced sense of smell to the list of characteristics distinguishing us from other primates.

SOURCES:

Buchan, Jason C., Susan Alberts, Joan B. Silk, and Jeanne Altman. 2003. "True Paternal Care in Multi-Male Primate Society." *Nature* 425:179–181.

Constable, Julie L., Mary V. Ashley, Jane Goodall, and Anne E. Pusey. 2001. "Noninvasive Paternity Assignment in Gombe Chimpanzees." *Molecular Ecology* 10:1279–1300.

Gilad, Yoav, Orna Man, and Gustavo Glusman. 2005. "A Comparison of the Human and Chimpanzee Olfactory Gene Repertoires." *Genome Research* 15:224–230.

Gilad, Yoav, Orna Man, Svante Paabo, and Doran Lancet. 2003. "Human Specific Loss of Receptor Genes." *Proceedings of the National Academy of Sciences*, 100:3324–3327.

Grob, B., L. A. Knapp, R. D. Martin, and G. Anzenberger. 1998. "The Major Histocompatibility Complex and Mate Choice: Inbreeding Avoidance and Selection of Good Genes." *Experimental and Clinical Immunogenetics* 15(3):119–129.

Liman, Emily R., and Hideki Innan. 2003. "Relaxed Selective Pressure on an Essential Component of Pheromone Transduction in Primate Evolution." *Proceedings of the National Academy of Sciences* 100:3328–3332.

Max Planck Institute for Evolutionary Anthropology website: www.eva.mpg.de

Morin, P.A., J. Wallis, J. Moore, and D. S. Woodruff. 1994. "Paternity Exclusion in a Community of Wild Chimpanzees Using Hypervariable Simple Sequence Repeats." *Molecular Evolution* 3:469–477.

Primate Immunogenetics and Molecular Ecology Research Group website: www-prime.bioanth.cam.ac.uk

Vigilant, Linda, Michael Hofreiter, Heike Siedel, and Christophe Boesch. 2001. "Paternity and Relatedness in Wild Chimpanzee Communities." *Proceedings of the National Academy of Sciences* 98:12890–12895.

Zhang, Jianzhi, and David Webb. 2003. "Evolutionary Deterioration of the Vomeronasal Pheromone Transduction Pathway in Catarrrhine Primates." *Proceedings of the National Academy of Sciences* 100:8337–8341.

PRIMATES

CHAPTER

7

Primate
Behavior

FOCUS QUESTION

How can behavior be a product of evolutionary processes, and what is one example of a behavior that has been influenced by evolution?

Introduction

Do you think cats are cruel when they play with mice before they kill them? Or, have you ever been tossed off a horse when she leaped aside because a breeze shook the leaves in a shrub? If so, did you think she was skittish and overeacting to the sound? These are commonly held views about cats and horses, and they illustrate how most people misunderstand nonhuman animal **behavior**.

Behavior (especially in mammals and birds) has been shaped over evolutionary time by interactions between genetic and environmental processes, and therefore, behavior is extremely complex. But most people don't give this concept much thought, and even those who do don't universally accept this basic premise. For example, while most social scientists agree that genetic factors influence nonhuman behavior, many object to the suggestion that they might also affect human behavior. This objection is due to concerns over implications that genetically influenced behaviors are fixed and can't be modified by experience (that is, learning).

Furthermore, most people assume there's a fundamental division between humans and all other animals. But at the same time, and in complete contradiction, they often judge other species as if their motives were entirely human (for example, cats are cruel). Of course, this isn't a valid thing to do, simply because other species aren't human. It's true that cats sometimes play with mice before they kill them because that's how, as kittens, they learn to hunt. But, cruelty doesn't enter into it, since the cat has no concept of cruelty and no idea of what it's like to be the mouse. Likewise, the horse inadvertently threw you off when she reacted in a perfectly natural way to a sudden noise. Her behavior has been shaped by thousands of generations of horse ancestors who jumped first and asked questions later. Horses evolved as prey animals, and their evolutionary history is littered with animals that didn't jump at a sound in a shrub. In many cases they learned, too late, that the sound wasn't caused by a breeze at all. This is a mistake prey animals don't usually survive, and those that don't leap first don't leave many descendants.

Of course, this chapter isn't about cats and horses. It's about what we know and hypothesize about the individual and social behaviors of nonhuman primates. But we began with the familiar examples of cats (predators) and horses (prey) because we want to point out that many basic behaviors have been shaped by the evolutionary histories of species. And the same factors that have influenced many behaviors in nonprimate animals also apply to primates. So, if we want to discover the underlying principles of behavioral evolution, including that of humans, we first need to identify the interactions between a number of environmental and physiological variables.

The Evolution of Behavior

Scientists study behavior in free-ranging primates from an **ecological** and evolutionary perspective, meaning that they focus on the relationship between behaviors, the natural environment, and various biological traits of the species in question. This approach is called **behavioral ecology**, and it's based on the underlying assumption that all of the components of ecological systems (animals, plants, and even microorganisms) evolved together. Therefore, behaviors are adaptations to environmental circumstances that existed in the past as well as in the present.

Go to the following CD-ROMs for interactive activities and exercises on topics covered in this chapter:

- Virtual Laboratories for Physical Anthropology CD-ROM, Third Edition

behavior Anything organisms do that involves action in response to internal or external stimuli; the response of an individual, group, or species to its environment. Such responses may or may not be deliberate, and they aren't necessarily the results of conscious decision making.

ecological Pertaining to the relationships between organisms and all aspects of their environment (temperature, predators, nonpredators, vegetation, availability of food and water, types of food, disease organisms, parasites, etc.)

behavioral ecology The study of the evolution of behavior, emphasizing the role of ecological factors as agents of natural selection. Behaviors and behavioral patterns have been favored because they increase the reproductive fitness of individuals (i.e., they are adaptive) in specific environmental contexts.

Briefly, the cornerstone of behavioral ecology is that since some behaviors are influenced by genes, they're subject to natural selection in the same way physical characteristics are. (Remember that within a specific environmental context, natural selection favors traits that give a reproductive advantage to the individuals who have them.) Therefore, behavior constitutes a phenotype. So, individuals whose behavioral phenotypes increase reproductive fitness will pass on their genes at a faster rate than those with less beneficial behavioral phenotypes. But this doesn't mean primatologists think that genes code for specific behaviors, such as a gene for aggression, another for cooperation, and so on. Studying complex behaviors from an evolutionary viewpoint doesn't imply a one gene–one behavior relationship, nor does it suggest that behaviors that are influenced by genes can't be modified through learning.

Much of the behavior of insects and other invertebrates is largely under genetic control. In other words, most of their behaviors aren't learned; they're innate. However, in many vertebrates, especially birds and mammals, the proportion of behavior that is due to learning is substantially increased, while the proportion under genetic control is reduced. This is especially true of primates; and in humans, who are so much a product of culture, most behavior is learned. But at the same time, we also know that in higher organisms, some behaviors are at least partly influenced by gene products such as hormones. For example, you're probably aware that elevated levels of testosterone increase aggression in many species. And you may also know that conditions like depression, schizophrenia, and bipolar disorder are caused by abnormal levels of certain chemicals produced by brain cells.

Behavior is a complex trait, and it's a product of *interactions between genetic and environmental factors.* Among species, there is considerable variation in the limits and potentials for learning and for behavioral **plasticity** or flexibility. In some species, the potentials are extremely broad; in others, they aren't. Ultimately, those limits and potentials are set by genetic factors that have been selected for throughout the evolutionary history of every species. That history, in turn, has been shaped by the ecological setting not only of living species *but also of their ancestors.*

A major goal of primatology is to determine how behaviors influence reproductive fitness and how ecological factors have shaped the evolution of these behaviors. While the actual mechanics of behavioral evolution aren't yet fully understood, new technologies and methodologies are beginning to answer numerous questions. For example, genetic analysis has recently been used to establish paternity in a few primate groups, and these results have helped support hypotheses about some behaviors (see p. 154). But, in general, an evolutionary approach to the study of behavior doesn't provide definitive answers to many research questions. Rather, it creates a valuable framework within which primatologists can analyze data to generate and test hypotheses concerning behavioral patterns.

Because primates are among the most social of animals, social behavior is a major topic in primate research. This broad subject includes *all* aspects of behavior that occur in social groupings—even some behaviors you may not think of as social, like feeding. To understand the function of one behavioral element, it's necessary to determine how that element is influenced by numerous interrelated factors. As an example, we'll discuss some of the more important variables that influence **social structure**.

SOME FACTORS THAT INFLUENCE SOCIAL STRUCTURE

Body Size   As a general rule, larger animals require fewer calories per unit of weight than smaller animals do, because they have a smaller ratio of surface area to mass than do smaller animals. Since body heat is lost at the surface, larger animals are better able to retain heat more efficiently, so they require less energy per unit of body weight.

Basal Metabolic Rate (BMR) and Diet   **Metabolism** is the rate at which the body uses energy to maintain all bodily functions. The BMR is the rate energy is used during a resting state in an external temperature that doesn't require cooling or heating. Since BMR is closely correlated with body size, smaller animals, in general, have a higher BMR than larger ones (Fig. 7–1). Consequently, smaller primates like galagos, tarsiers, marmosets, and tamarins need an energy-rich diet that is high in protein (insects), fats (nuts and seeds), and

plasticity   The capacity to change. In a behavioral context, the ability of animals to modify actions in response to differing circumstances.

social structure   The composition, size, and sex ratio of a group of animals. Social structures are partly the results of natural selection in specific habitats, and they guide individual interactions and social relationships.

metabolism   The chemical processes within cells that break down nutrients and release energy for the body to use. (When nutrients are broken down into their component parts, such as amino acids, energy is released and made available for the cell to use.)

FIGURE 7–1

This tiny dwarf lemur has a high BMR and requires an energy-rich diet of insects and other forms of animal protein.

Russ Mittermeier

carbohydrates (fruits and seeds). Some larger primates, which tend to have a lower BMR, can do well with less energy-rich foods such as leaves. For example, gorillas eat huge quantities of leaves, pith from bamboo stems, and other types of vegetation (Fig. 7–2). Although these foods may not be rich in energy, in large amounts they provide enough even for animals the size of gorillas.

Distribution of Resources   Different kinds of foods are distributed in various ways. Leaves can be abundant and dense and will therefore support large groups of animals. Other foods, such as insects, may be widely scattered, and animals that rely on them usually feed alone or perhaps in the company of one or two others.

Fruits and nuts, widely dispersed on trees and shrubs, occur in clumps. These can most efficiently be exploited by smaller groups of animals, so large groups frequently break up into smaller subunits while feeding. Some species that rely on foods distributed in small clumps tend to be protective of resources, especially if their feeding area is small enough to be defended. Some of these species live in small groups composed of male-female pairs (siamangs) or a female with one or two males (marmosets and tamarins) and dependent offspring.

Predation   Primates are vulnerable to many types of predators, including snakes, birds of prey, leopards, wild dogs, lions, and even other primates, including humans. Typically, where predation pressure is high, large communities are advantageous. These may be multimale-multifemale groups or congregations of one-male groups (see p. 146).

Relationships with Other, Nonpredatory Species   Many primate species associate with other primate and nonprimate species for various reasons, including predator avoidance. When they do share habitats with other species, they exploit somewhat different resources, and this helps reduce competition for resources.

Dispersal   Dispersal is another factor that influences social structure and relationships within groups. As is true of most mammals (and indeed, most vertebrates), members of one sex leave the group in which they were born (their *natal group*) about the time they become sexually mature. Male dispersal is the most common pattern in primates (ring-tailed lemurs, vervets, and macaques, to name a few). Female dispersal is seen in some colobus species, hamadryas baboons, chimpanzees (frequently), and mountain gorillas. Those individuals who leave usually find mates outside their natal group, and so dispersal is generally believed to decrease the likelihood of close inbreeding. Another consequence of dispersal is that individuals of either sex who remain in their natal group enjoy certain advantages because they're able to establish long-term bonds with relatives and other animals they've known their entire lives.

Life Histories   **Life history traits** are characteristics or developmental stages that typify members of a given species and that influence potential reproductive rates. Examples include length of gestation, length of time between pregnancies (interbirth interval), period of infant dependency and age at weaning, age at sexual maturity, and life expectancy.

Life history traits have important consequences for many aspects of social life and social structure, and they can be critical to species survival. Shorter life histories are advantageous to species that live in marginal or unpredictable habitats (Strier, 2003). Since these species mature early and have short interbirth intervals, reproduction can occur at a relatively fast rate, which helps to compensate for an environment that may not permit individual longevity. Conversely, species with extended life histories, such as gorillas, are well suited to stable environmental conditions, and their tendency to live longer permits them to invest more time and energy in fewer offspring.

FIGURE 7–2

This large male mountain gorilla does well on a diet of less energy-rich leaves and other plant materials.

life history traits   Also called life history strategies; characteristics and developmental stages that influence rates of reproduction.

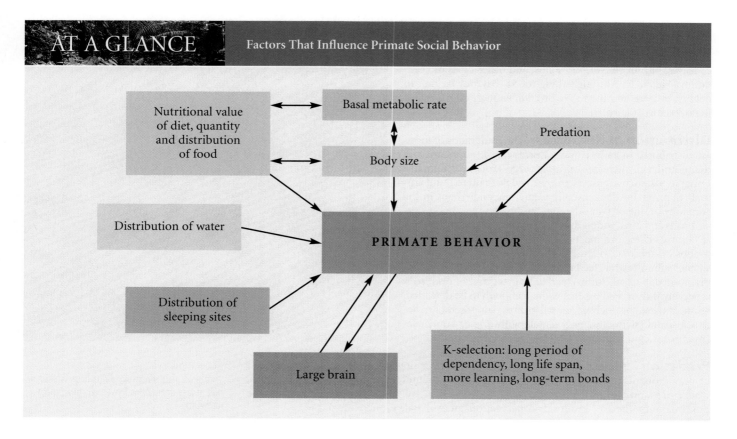

AT A GLANCE   Factors That Influence Primate Social Behavior

Distribution and Types of Sleeping Sites   Gorillas are the only nonhuman primates that sleep on the ground. Primate sleeping sites can be located in trees or on cliff faces, and their spacing can be related to social structure, predator avoidance, and how many sleeping sites are available.

Activity Patterns   As you know, most primates are diurnal, but several small-bodied prosimians and one New World monkey (the owl monkey) are nocturnal. Nocturnal species tend to forage for food alone or in groups of two or three, and many use concealment to avoid predators.

Human Activities   Virtually all nonhuman primate populations are now affected by human hunting and forest clearing (see p. 136). These activities severely disrupt and isolate groups, reduce numbers, reduce resource availability, and eventually can cause extinction.

Why Be Social?

Group living exposes animals to competition with other group members for resources, so why don't they live alone? After all, competition can lead to injury or even death, and it's costly in terms of energy expenditure. One widely accepted answer to this question is that the costs of competition are offset by the benefits of predator defense provided by associating with others. Groups composed of several adult males and females (multimale-multifemale groups) are advantageous in areas where predation pressure is high, particularly in mixed woodlands and on open savannas. Leopards are the most significant predator of terrestrial primates, and they also take a substantial number of arboreal monkeys (Fig. 7–3). Where members of prey species occur in larger groups, the chances of early predator detection (and thus, avoidance) are increased simply because there are more pairs of eyes looking about.

Savanna baboons have long been used as an example of these principles. They're found in semiarid grassland and broken woodland habitats throughout sub-Saharan Africa. To avoid nocturnal predators, savanna baboons sleep in trees, but during the day they spend a good deal of time on the ground foraging for food. If a predator appears, baboons flee back into the trees, but if they're some distance from safety, adult males (and sometimes females) may join forces to chase the intruder. The effectiveness of male baboons in this regard shouldn't be underestimated, since they've been known to kill domestic dogs and even to attack leopards and lions.

There is probably no single answer to the question of why primates live in groups. More than likely, predator avoidance is a major factor, but it's not the only one. Group living evolved as an adaptive response to a number of ecological variables, and it has served primates well for a very long time.

FIGURE 7–3

When a baboon strays too far from its troop, as this one has done, it's more likely to fall prey to predators. Leopards are the most serious non-human threat to terrestrial primates.

Primate Social Behavior

Because primates solve their major adaptive problems in a social context, we should expect them to display several behaviors that reinforce the integrity of the group. We describe the better-known of these behaviors in the sections that follow. Remember, all these behaviors have evolved as adaptive responses during more than 50 million years of primate evolution.

DOMINANCE

Many primate societies are organized into **dominance hierarchies**, which impose a certain degree of order by establishing parameters of individual behavior. Although aggression is frequently a means of increasing an individual's status, dominance usually serves to reduce the amount of actual physical violence. Not only are lower-ranking animals unlikely to attack or even threaten a higher-ranking one, but dominant animals are also frequently able to exert control simply by making a threatening gesture.

Individual rank or status can be measured by access to resources, including food items and mating partners. Dominant animals are given priority by others, and they usually don't give way in confrontations.

Many primatologists think that the primary benefit of dominance is the increased reproductive success of high-ranking animals. This may be true in general, but there's good evidence that lower-ranking males of some species also successfully mate. In addition, high-ranking females have greater access to food than subordinate females do, and since they obtain more energy for the production and care of offspring (Fedigan, 1983), the high-ranking females presumably have higher reproductive success.

Pusey and colleagues (1997) demonstrated that the offspring of high-ranking female chimpanzees at Gombe National Park in Tanzania, had significantly higher rates of infant survival. Their daughters also matured faster, which meant they had shorter interbirth intervals and consequently produced more offspring.

Social rank isn't permanent; that is, it changes throughout the lifetime of an individual. It's influenced by many factors, including sex, age, level of aggression, amount of time spent in the group, intelligence, perhaps motivation, and sometimes the mother's social position (particularly true of macaques).

In species organized into groups containing a number of females associated with one or several adult males, the males are generally dominant to females. Within such groups, males and females have separate hierarchies, although very high-ranking females can dominate the lowest-ranking males (particularly young males). But, there are exceptions to this pattern of

dominance hierarchies Systems of social organization in which individuals within a group are ranked relative to one another. Higher-ranking animals have greater access to preferred food items and mating partners than do lower-ranking individuals. Dominance hierarchies are sometimes called pecking orders.

FIGURE 7–4

An adolescent male savanna baboon threatens the photographer with a characteristic "yawn" that shows the canine teeth. Note also that the eyes are closed briefly to expose light, cream-colored eyelids. This has been termed the "eye-lid flash."

FIGURE 7–5

One young male savanna baboon mounts another as an expression of dominance.

communication Any act that conveys information, in the form of a message, to another individual. Frequently, the result of communication is a change in the recipient's behavior. Communication may not be deliberate, but may instead be the result of involuntary processes or a secondary consequence of an intentional action.

autonomic Pertaining to physiological responses not under voluntary control. An example in chimpanzees would be the erection of body hair during excitement. Blushing is a human example. Both responses convey information regarding emotional states, but neither is deliberate and communication isn't intended.

male dominance. In many lemur species, females are the dominant sex. And, in species that live in pairs (for example, indris and gibbons), males and females are codominant.

All primates *learn* their position in the hierarchy. From birth, an infant is carried by its mother, and it observes how she responds to every member of the group. Just as important, the infant sees how others react to her. Dominance and subordination are indicated by gestures and other behaviors, and some of these are universal throughout the primate order (including humans). Young primates also acquire social rank through play with age peers and, as they spend more time with play groups, their social interactions widen. Through competition and rough-and-tumble play, they learn the strengths and weaknesses of peers, and they carry this knowledge with them throughout their lives. Thus, young primates learn to negotiate their way through the complex web of social interactions that make up their daily lives.

COMMUNICATION

Communication is universal among animals and includes scents and unintentional, **autonomic** responses and behaviors that convey meaning. Such attributes as body posture convey information about an animal's emotional state. For example, a purposeful striding gait implies confidence. In addition, autonomic responses to threatening or novel stimuli, such as raised body hair (most species) or enhanced body odor (gorillas), indicate excitement.

Many intentional behaviors also serve as communication. In primates, these include a wide variety of gestures, facial expressions, and vocalizations, some of which we humans share. Among many primates, an intense stare signifies a mild threat—and indeed, we humans find prolonged eye contact with strangers very uncomfortable. (For this reason, people should avoid making eye contact with captive primates.) Other threat gestures are a quick yawn to expose canine teeth (baboons, macaques) (Fig. 7–4); bobbing back and forth in a crouched position (patas monkeys); and branch shaking (many monkey species). High-ranking baboons *mount* the hindquarters of subordinates to express dominance (Fig. 7–5). Mounting may also serve to defuse potentially tense situations by indicating something like, "It's okay, I accept your apology."

Other behaviors indicate submission, reassurance, or amicable intentions. Submission is indicated by a crouched position (most primates) or by presenting the hindquarters (baboons). Reassurance takes the form of touching, patting, hugging, and holding hands (Fig. 7–6). Grooming also serves in a number of situations to indicate submission or reassurance.

A wide variety of facial expressions indicating emotional state are seen in chimpanzees and, especially, in bonobos (Fig. 7–7). These include the well-known play face (also seen in several other primate and nonprimate species), associated with play behavior, and the fear grin (seen in *all* primates) to indicate fear and submission.

Primates also use a wide array of vocalizations for communication. Some vocalizations, such as the bark of a baboon that has just spotted a leopard, are unintentional startled reactions. Others, such as the chimpanzee food grunt, are heard only in specific contexts. Nevertheless, both serve the same function: to inform others, although not necessarily deliberately, of the possible presence of predators or food.

Primates (and other animals) also communicate through **displays**, which are more complicated, frequently elaborate combinations of behaviors. For example, the exaggerated courtship dances of many male birds, often enhanced by colorful plumage, are displays. Chest slapping and tearing of vegetation are common gorilla threat displays.

All nonhuman animals use various vocalizations, body postures, and, to some degree, facial expressions that transmit information. But, the array of communicative devices is much richer among nonhuman primates, even though they don't use language the way humans do. Communication is important, for it truly is what makes social living possible. Submissive gestures act to reduce aggression and make physical violence less likely. Likewise, friendly intentions and relationships are reinforced through physical contact and grooming. Indeed, we humans can most clearly see ourselves in other primate species by observing their instantly familiar use of nonverbal communication.

AGGRESSIVE INTERACTIONS

Within primate societies, there is an interplay between **affiliative** behaviors, which promote group cohesion, and aggressive behaviors, which can lead to group disruption. Conflict within a group frequently develops out of competition for resources, including mating partners and food items. Instead of actual attacks or fighting, most intragroup aggression occurs in the form of various signals and displays, frequently within the context of a dominance hierarchy. Primates thus resolve the majority of tense situations by using various submissive and appeasement behaviors.

Of course, conflict isn't always resolved peacefully, and it can have serious consequences. For example, high-ranking female macaques frequently intimidate, harass, and even attack lower-ranking females, in order to keep them away from food. Competition between males for mates frequently results in injury and even death. In species that have a distinct breeding season (e.g., squirrel monkeys), conflict between males is most common during that time. In species not restricted to a mating season, competition between males can be ongoing.

Between groups, aggression is used to protect resources or **territories**. Primate groups are associated with a *home range*, where they remain permanently. (Although individuals may leave their home range and join another community, the group itself remains in a particular area.) Within the home range is a portion called the **core area**, which contains the

FIGURE **7–6**
Adolescent savanna baboons holding hands.

displays Sequences of repetitive behaviors that serve to communicate emotional states. Nonhuman primate displays are most frequently associated with reproductive or aggressive behavior.

affiliative Pertaining to amicable associations between individuals. Affiliative behaviors, such as grooming, reinforce social bonds and promote group cohesion.

territories Portions of an individual's or group's home range that are actively defended against intrusion, especially by members of the same species.

core area The portion of a home range containing the highest concentration and most reliable supplies of food and water. The core area is usually defended.

FIGURE **7–7**
Chimpanzee facial expressions.

Relaxed | Relaxed with dropped lip | Horizontal pout face (distress) | Fear grin (fear/excitement) | Full play face

highest concentration of predictable resources, and it's where the group is most frequently found. Although parts of the home range may overlap the home ranges of other groups, core areas of adjacent groups don't overlap. The core area can also be said to be a group's territory, and it's the portion of the home range defended against intrusion. However, in some species, other areas of the home range may also be defended. Whatever area is defended is termed the *territory*.

Not all primates are territorial. In general, territoriality is associated with species whose ranges are small enough to be patrolled and protected (e.g., gibbons and vervets). And, you already know that in many species, group encounters are frequently nonaggressive.

But male chimpanzees are highly intolerant of unfamiliar chimpanzees, especially other males, and they fiercely defend their territories and resources. Therefore, chimpanzee intergroup interactions are almost always characterized by aggressive displays, chasing, and actual fighting.

Beginning in 1974, Jane Goodall and her colleagues witnessed at least five unprovoked and extremely brutal attacks by groups of chimpanzees on other chimpanzees. To explain these attacks, it's necessary to point out that by 1973, the original Gombe community had divided into two distinct groups, one located in the north and the other in the south of what had once been the original group's home range. In effect, the smaller offshoot group had denied the others access to part of their former home range.

By 1977, all seven males and one female of the splinter group were either known or suspected to have been killed. All observed incidents involved several animals, usually adult males, who brutally attacked lone individuals. Although it isn't possible to know exactly what motivated the attackers, it was clear that they intended to incapacitate their victims (Goodall, 1986).

A similar situation was also reported for a chimpanzee group in the Mahale Mountains south of Gombe. Over a 17-year period, all the males of a small community disappeared. Although no attacks were actually observed, there was circumstantial evidence that most of these males had met the same fate as the Gombe attack victims (Nishida et al., 1985, 1990).

Even though the precise motivation of chimpanzee intergroup aggression may never be fully explained, it appears that acquiring and protecting resources (including females) are involved (Nishida et al., 1985, 1990; Goodall, 1986; Manson and Wrangham, 1991; Nishida, 1991). By carefully examining shared aspects of human and chimpanzee social life, we can develop hypotheses regarding how intergroup conflict may have arisen in our own lineage. Early hominids and chimpanzees may have inherited from a common ancestor the predispositions that lead to similar patterns of strife between populations. It's not appropriate or possible to draw direct comparisons between chimpanzee conflict and human warfare, owing to later human elaborations of culture, use of symbols (for example, national flags), and language. But it's still important to speculate on the fundamental issues that may have led to the development of similar patterns in both species.

AFFILIATION AND ALTRUISM

As you've just seen, even though it can be destructive, a certain amount of aggression helps to maintain order within groups and to protect either individual or group resources. Fortunately, to minimize actual violence and to defuse potentially dangerous situations, there are many behaviors that reinforce bonds between individuals and enhance group stability.

Common affiliative behaviors include reconciliation, consolation, and simple amicable interactions between friends and relatives. These involve various forms of physical contact and, in fact, physical contact is one of the most important factors in primate development. It is crucial in promoting peaceful relationships in many primate social groups.

Grooming is one of the most important affiliative behaviors in many primate species, and it plays an important role in day-to-day life (Fig. 7–8). Because grooming involves using the fingers to pick through the fur of another individual (or one's own) to remove insects, dirt, and other materials, it serves hygienic functions. But it's also an immensely pleasurable activity that members of some species (especially chimpanzees) engage in for long periods of time.

Grooming occurs in a variety of contexts. Mothers groom infants. Males groom sexually receptive females. Subordinate animals groom dominant ones, sometimes to gain favor. Friends groom friends. In general, grooming is comforting. It restores peaceful relationships

grooming Picking through fur to remove dirt, parasites, and other materials. Social grooming is common among primates and reinforces social relationships.

(a)   (b)

(c)   (d)

between animals who have quarreled and provides reassurance during tense situations. In short, grooming reinforces social bonds and consequently helps to maintain and strengthen the structure of the group.

Conflict resolution through reconciliation is another important aspect of primate social behavior. Reconciliation takes many forms, including hugging, kissing, and grooming. Even uninvolved individuals may take part, either by grooming one or both participants or by forming their own grooming parties. In addition, bonobos are unique in their use of sex to promote group cohesion, restore peace after conflicts, and relieve tension within the group (de Waal, 1987, 1989).

Altruism, behavior that benefits another while involving some risk or sacrifice to the performer, is common in many primate species, and altruistic acts sometimes contain elements of what might be interpreted as compassion and cooperation. (However, using the term *compassion* to describe any nonhuman behavior is risky because we can't know the animals' true motivation.) The most fundamental of altruistic behaviors, the protection of dependent offspring, is ubiquitous among mammals and birds, and in the majority of species, most altruistic acts are confined to this context. However, among primates, recipients of altruistic acts may include individuals who aren't offspring and who may not even be closely related to the performer. Stelzner and Strier (1981) witnessed a female baboon chasing a hyena that was in pursuit of a young adult male baboon. This female's unsuccessful rescue

FIGURE 7–8

Grooming primates. (a) Patas monkeys; female grooming male. (b) Longtail macaques. (c) Savanna baboons. (d) Chimpanzees.

altruism   Behavior that benefits another individual but at some potential risk or cost to oneself.

reproductive strategies The complex of behavioral patterns that contributes to individual reproductive success. The behaviors need not be deliberate, and they often vary considerably between males and females.

K-selected Pertaining to an adaptive strategy whereby individuals produce relatively few offspring, in whom they invest increased parental care. Although only a few infants are born, chances of survival are increased for each one because of parental investments in time and energy. Examples of K-selected nonprimate species are birds and canids (e.g., wolves, coyotes, and dogs).

r-selected An adaptive strategy that emphasizes relatively large numbers of offspring and reduced parental care (compared to K-selected species). *K-selection* and *r-selection* are relative terms; for example, mice are r-selected compared to primates but K-selected compared to fish.

attempt was intriguing because not only was she too small to engage the hyena, but she was also unrelated to the victim. Chimpanzees routinely come to the aid of relatives and friends; female langurs join forces to protect infants from infanticidal males; and male baboons protect infants and cooperate to chase predators. In fact, the primate literature abounds with examples of altruistic acts, whereby individuals place themselves at some risk to protect others from attacks by conspecifics or predators.

Adoption of orphans is a form of altruism that has been reported for macaques and baboons, and it's common in chimpanzees. When chimpanzee youngsters are orphaned, they are almost always adopted, usually by older siblings who are solicitous and highly protective. Adoption is crucial to the survival of orphans, who would certainly not survive on their own. In fact, it's extremely rare for a chimpanzee orphan less than three years of age to survive even if it's adopted.

Reproduction and Reproductive Behaviors

In most primate species, sexual behavior is tied to the female's reproductive cycle, with females being receptive to males only when they're in estrus. Estrus is characterized by behavioral changes that indicate when a female is receptive. In Old World monkeys and apes that live in multimale groups, estrus is also accompanied by swelling and changes in color of the skin around the genital area. These changes serve as visual cues of a female's readiness to mate (Fig 7–9).

Permanent bonding between males and females isn't common among nonhuman primates. However, male and female savanna baboons sometimes form mating *consortships*. These temporary relationships last while the female is in estrus, and the two spend most of their time together, mating frequently. Mating consortships are also seen in chimpanzees and are particularly common in bonobos. In fact, a male and female bonobo may spend several weeks primarily in each other's company. During this time, they mate often, even when the female isn't in estrus.

Such a male-female bond may result in increased reproductive success for both sexes. For the male, there is the increased likelihood that he will be the father of any infant the female conceives. At the same time, the female potentially gains protection from predators or others of her group and perhaps assistance in caring for offspring she may already have.

FEMALE AND MALE REPRODUCTIVE STRATEGIES

Reproductive strategies, and especially how they differ between the sexes, have been a primary focus of primate research. The goal of these strategies is to produce and successfully rear to adulthood as many offspring as possible.

Primates are among the most **K-selected** of mammals. By this we mean that individuals produce only a few young, in whom they invest a tremendous amount of parental care. Contrast this pattern with **r-selected** species, where individuals produce large numbers of offspring but invest little or no energy in parental care. Good examples of r-selected species include insects, most fishes, and, among mammals, mice and rabbits.

When we consider the degree of care required by young, dependent primate offspring, it's clear that enormous investment by at least one parent is necessary and

FIGURE **7–9**
Estrous swelling of genital tissues in a female chimpanzee.

Lynn Kilgore

that in a majority of species, the mother carries most of the burden both before and after birth. Primates are totally helpless at birth. They develop slowly and are thus exposed to expanded learning opportunities within a *social* environment. This trend has been elaborated most dramatically in great apes and humans, especially in the latter. So, what we see in ourselves and our close primate kin is a strategy wherein a few "high-quality," slowly maturing offspring are produced through extraordinary investment by at least one parent, usually the mother.

Finding food and mates, avoiding predators, and caring for and protecting dependent young are difficult challenges for nonhuman primates. Moreover, in most species, males and females use different strategies to meet these challenges.

Female primates spend almost all of their adult lives pregnant, lactating, and/or caring for offspring, and the resulting metabolic demands are enormous. A pregnant or lactating female, although perhaps only half the size of her male counterpart, may require about the same number of calories per day. Given these physiological costs, and the fact that her reproductive potential is limited by lengthy intervals between births, a female's best strategy is to maximize the amount of resources available to her and her offspring. Indeed, as we just discussed, females of many primate species (gibbons, marmosets, and macaques, to name a few) are viciously competitive with other females and aggressively protect resources and territories. In other species, as we have seen, females distance themselves from others to avoid competition. Males, however, face a separate set of challenges. Having little investment in the rearing of offspring and the continuous production of sperm, it's to the male's advantage to secure as many mates and produce as many offspring as possible. And, to achieve this goal, males must compete with each other for females.

SEXUAL SELECTION

One outcome of different mating strategies is **sexual selection**, a phenomenon first described by Charles Darwin and perhaps most evident in many bird species. Sexual selection is a type of natural selection that operates on only one sex, usually males, whereby the selective agent is male competition for mates and, in some species, mate choice in females. The long-term effect of sexual selection is to increase the frequency of those traits that lead to greater success in acquiring mates.

Sexual selection in primates is most common in species in which mating is **polygynous** and male competition for females is prominent. In these species, sexual selection produces dimorphism with regard to a number of traits, most noticeably body size. As you have seen, the males of many primate species are considerably larger than females, and males also sometimes have larger canine teeth.

Conversely, in species that live in pairs (for example, gibbons) or where male competition is reduced, sexual dimorphism in canine teeth and body size is either reduced or nonexistent. For these reasons, the presence or absence of sexually dimorphic traits in a species can be a reasonably good indicator of mating structure.

INFANTICIDE AS A REPRODUCTIVE STRATEGY?

One way males may increase their chances of reproducing is by killing infants fathered by other males. This explanation was first offered in an early study of Hanuman langurs in India (Hrdy, 1977). Hanuman langurs (Fig. 7–10) typically live in groups composed of one adult male, several females, and their offspring. Other males without mates form "bachelor" groups that frequently forage within sight of the one-male associations. These peripheral males occasionally attack and defeat a reproductive male and drive him from his group. After such takeovers, some or all of the group's infants (fathered by the previous male) are sometimes killed by the new male.

Infanticide would appear to be counterproductive, especially for a species as a whole. However, individuals act to maximize their *own* reproductive success, no matter what the effect may be on the population or ultimately the species. And that's what the male langur may be doing, albeit unknowingly. While a female is producing milk and nursing an infant, she doesn't come into estrus, and therefore she isn't sexually available. But, when an infant dies, its mother resumes cycling and becomes sexually receptive. Consequently, an infanticidal new male avoids waiting two to three years for the infants to be weaned before he can mate

sexual selection   A type of natural selection that operates on only one sex within a species. It's the result of competition for mates, and it can lead to sexual dimorphism with regard to one or more traits.

polygynous   Referring to polygyny, a mating system whereby males have more than one mate.

FIGURE 7–10
Hanuman langurs.

Joe MacDonald/Animals Animals

with their mothers. What's more, he doesn't expend energy and put himself at risk defending infants who don't carry his genes.

Hanuman langurs aren't the only primates that practice infanticide. Infanticide has been observed (or surmised) in many species, such as redtail monkeys, red colobus, blue monkeys, savanna baboons, howlers, orangutans, gorillas, chimpanzees (Struhsaker and Leyland, 1987), and humans. In the majority of reported nonhuman primate examples, infanticide coincides with the transfer of a new male into a group or, as in chimpanzees, an encounter with an unfamiliar female and infant. (It should also be noted that infanticide occurs in numerous nonprimate species, including rodents, cats, and horses.)

Numerous objections to this explanation of infanticide have been raised. Alternative explanations have included competition for resources (Rudran, 1973), aberrant behaviors related to human-induced overcrowding (Curtin and Dohlinow, 1978), and inadvertent killing during aggressive episodes, where it wasn't clear that the infant was actually the target animal (Bartlett et al., 1993). Sussman and colleagues (1995), as well as others, have questioned the actual prevalence of infanticide, arguing that although it does occur, it's not particularly common. These authors have also suggested that if indeed male reproductive fitness is increased through the killing of infants, such increases are negligible. Yet others (Struhsaker and Leyland, 1987; Hrdy et al., 1995) maintain that the incidence and patterning of infanticide by males are not only significant, but consistent with the assumptions established by theories of behavioral evolution.

Henzi and Barrett (2003) report that when chacma baboon males migrate into a new group, they "deliberately single out females with young infants and hunt them down." However, reports such as this don't prove that infanticide increases a male's reproductive fitness. In order to do this, primatologists must demonstrate two crucial facts:

1. Infanticidal males *don't* kill their own offspring.
2. Once a male has killed an infant, he subsequently fathers another infant with the victim's mother.

Borries and colleagues (1999) collected DNA samples from the feces of infanticidal males and their victims in several groups of free-ranging Hanuman langurs specifically to find out if these males killed their own offspring. Their results showed that in all 16 cases where infant and male DNA was available, the males were not related to the infants they had either attacked or killed. Secondly, DNA analysis also showed that in four out of five cases where victim's mothers subsequently gave birth, their new infants were fathered by the infanticidal males. Although still more evidence is needed, this DNA evidence strongly suggests that infanticide may indeed give males an increased chance of fathering offspring.

Mothers, Fathers, and Infants

The basic social unit among all primates is the female and her infants (Fig. 7–11). Except in those species in which monogamy or **polyandry** occurs, males usually don't directly participate in the rearing of offspring. The mother-infant bond begins at birth. Although the exact nature of the bonding process isn't fully known, there appear to be predisposing factors that strongly attract the female to her infant, so long as she herself has had sufficiently normal experience with her own mother. This doesn't mean that primate mothers possess innate knowledge of how to care for an infant, and in fact they don't. Monkeys and apes raised in captivity without contact with their own mothers not only don't know how to care for a newborn infant, but they may also fear it and attack or even kill it. Thus, learning is critically important in establishing a mother's attraction to her infant.

In the 1950s, a series of experiments conducted by a psychologist named Harry Harlow showed that monkeys raised in isolation or with no physical contact with their mothers weren't capable of forming lasting affectional ties. None of the motherless males ever successfully copulated, and those females who were (somewhat artificially) impregnated either paid little attention to their infants or were aggressive toward them (Harlow and Harlow, 1961). The point is that monkeys reared in isolation were denied opportunities to *learn* the rules of social and maternal behavior. Moreover, and just as essential, they were denied the

polyandry A mating system wherein a female continuously associates with more than one male (usually two or three) with whom she mates. Among nonhuman primates, polyandry is seen only in marmosets and tamarins. It also occurs in a few human societies.

(a)   (b)   (c)

(d)   (e)

FIGURE 7–11

Primate mothers with young. (a) Mongoose lemur. (b) Chimpanzee. (c) Patas monkey. (d) Orangutan. (e) Sykes monkey.

all-important physical contact so necessary for normal primate psychological and emotional development.

The importance of a normal relationship with the mother is demonstrated by field studies as well. From birth, infant primates are able to cling to their mother's fur, and they're in more or less constant physical contact with her for several months. During this critical period, infants develop a closeness with their mothers that doesn't always end with weaning. It may even be maintained throughout life (especially among some Old World monkeys). In some species, presumed fathers also participate in infant care. Male siamangs are actively involved, and marmoset and tamarin infants are usually carried on the father's back and transferred to their mother only for nursing. Even in species where adult males aren't directly involved in infant care, they may take more than a casual interest in them, and this has been frequently noted in hamadryas and savanna baboons (Fig. 7–12). Also, during disputes, male baboons frequently intervene to protect youngsters. Buchan and colleagues (2003) used DNA analysis to show that males intervened significantly more often on behalf of their own offspring than for unrelated juveniles. Because disputes can lead to severe injury or death, Buchan and colleagues considered the male intervention to be an example of parental care.

This male savanna baboon with a youngster on his back is exhibiting infant care, but he may not be the father.

Primate Cultural Behavior

One important trait that makes primates attractive as models for behavior in early hominids may be called *cultural behavior.* Although many cultural anthropologists and others prefer to use the term *culture* to refer specifically to human activities, most biological anthropologists think it's appropriate to use the term in reference to nonhuman primates also (McGrew, 1992, 1998; de Waal, 1999; Whiten et al., 1999). In fact, the term *cultural primatology* is now being used more frequently.

Undeniably, most aspects of culture are uniquely human, and one must be cautious when interpreting nonhuman animal behavior. But again, since humans are products of the same evolutionary forces that have produced other species, we can be expected to exhibit some of the same *behavioral patterns,* particularly of other primates. However, because of increased brain size and learning capacities, humans express many characteristics to a far greater degree. We would argue that the *aptitude for culture* as a means of adapting to the natural environment is one such characteristic.

Among other things, cultural behavior is *learned;* it's passed from generation to generation not biologically, but through learning. Humans deliberately teach their young; but except for a few reports, it seems that free-ranging nonhuman primates don't. But at the same time, like young nonhuman primates, human children also acquire a tremendous amount of knowledge through observation rather than instruction (Fig. 7–13a). Nonhuman primate infants, by observing their mothers and others, learn about food items, appropriate behaviors, and how to use and modify objects to achieve certain ends (Fig. 7–13b). In turn, their own offspring will observe their activities. What emerges is a *cultural tradition* that may eventually come to typify an entire group or even a species.

The earliest reported example of cultural behavior in nonhuman primates concerned a study group of Japanese macaques that, in 1952, researchers began provisioning with sweet potatoes. The following year, a young female named Imo began washing her potatoes in a freshwater stream before eating them. Within three years, several monkeys were following her example, but they had switched from using the stream to washing their potatoes in the ocean nearby. (Maybe they just liked the salt.)

The researchers pointed out that dietary habits and food preferences are learned and that potato washing was an example of nonhuman culture. Because the practice arose as an innovative solution to a problem (removing dirt) and gradually spread through the troop until it became a tradition, it was seen as containing elements of human culture.

A study of orangutans in Borneo and Sumatra listed 19 behaviors that showed sufficient regional variation to be classed as "very likely cultural variants" (van Schaik et al., 2003). Four of these were differences in how nests were used or built. Other behaviors that varied included using branches to swat insects and pressing leaves or hands to the mouth to amplify sounds.

For years, primatologists have focused on how nonhuman primates use objects as tools, and there are many examples. Capuchins are small New World monkeys that exhibit a variety of tool using behaviors. In captivity, they use stones as hammers and anvils (Visalberghi, 1990), and free-ranging capuchins display a number of tool-using behaviors. They use leaves to get water from cavities in trees (Phillips, 1998); they smash objects against stones (Izawa and Mizuno, 1977); and recently they were observed digging for roots with stones (Moura and Lee, 2004).

In a very recent report, Breuer and colleagues (2005) described a female lowland gorilla using a tree branch as a walking stick as she waded through a pond. It also appeared that she was using the branch to gauge the water's depth. This report is significant since it's the first to document tool use in free-ranging gorillas.

Chimpanzees exhibit more elaborate types of tool use. They insert twigs and grass blades into termite mounds in a practice called "termite fishing." When termites grab the twig, the chimpanzee withdraws it and eats them. To some extent, chimpanzees also alter objects for later use even at another location. For example, a chimpanzee will carefully choose a piece of vine or a twig and modify it by removing leaves, and then—even before arriving at the termite mound—break off portions until it's the proper length for termite fishing.

All this preparation has several implications. First, the chimpanzees are involved in an activity that prepares them for a future (not immediate) task at a somewhat distant location, and this implies planning and forethought. Second, attention to the shape and size of the raw material indicates that chimpanzees have a preconceived idea of what the finished product needs to be in order to be useful. To produce even a simple tool, based on a concept, is an extremely complex behavior. Scientists previously believed that such behavior was the exclusive domain of humans, but now we question this assumption.

Chimpanzees also crumple and chew handfuls of leaves, which they dip into tree hollows where water accumulates. Then they suck the water from their newly made "leaf sponges." Chimpanzees also use leaves to wipe substances from body hair; they sometimes use twigs as toothpicks; they may use stones as weapons; and they drag or roll various objects, such as branches and stones, to enhance displays.

FIGURE 7–13
(a) This little girl is learning the basic skills of computer use by watching her older sister.
(b) A chimpanzee learns the art of termiting through intense observation.

Lynn Kilgore

(a)

Manoj Shah/The Image Bank

(b)

<figure>FIGURE 7–14</figure>
Chimpanzees in Bossou, Guinea, West Africa, use a pair of stones as hammer and anvil to crack oil-palm nuts.

Chimpanzees in several West African study groups use hammerstones along with platform stones to crack nuts and hard-shelled fruits (Boesch et al., 1994) (Fig. 7–14). However, they don't deliberately manufacture either of these tools.

One important finding is that chimpanzees show regional variation in both the types and methods of tool use. Only West African groups use stone hammers and platforms. And at central and eastern African sites, chimpanzees "fish" for termites with stems and sticks; but at some West African locations, they don't (McGrew, 1992).

Chimpanzees also show regional dietary preferences (Nishida et al., 1983; McGrew, 1992, 1998). For example, chimpanzees at many locations, including Gombe, eat oil palm fruits and nuts, but even though these foods are present in the Mahale Mountains, they aren't eaten by the chimpanzees there. Such regional patterns in tool use and food preferences that aren't related to availability are reminiscent of the cultural variations seen in humans.

Using sticks, twigs, and stones enhances the ability of chimpanzees to exploit resources. They learn these behaviors during infancy and childhood, partly through prolonged contact with the mother (see Fig. 7–14). Of course, exposure to other members of a social group provides additional learning opportunities. These statements also apply to early hominids. Sticks and unmodified stones don't remain to tell tales, but our early ancestors surely used these same objects as tools in much the same way chimpanzees do today.

Culture has become the environment in which modern humans live. Quite clearly, using sticks in termite fishing and hammerstones to crack nuts is hardly comparable to modern human technology. Even so, modern human technology had its beginnings in these very types of behaviors. But we can't take this to mean that nonhuman primates are "on their way" to becoming human. Remember, evolution isn't goal directed, and such a conclusion has no validity in discussions of evolutionary processes.

Language

One of the most significant events in human evolution was the development of language. We've already described several behaviors and autonomic responses that convey information in primates. But, although we emphasized the importance of communication to nonhuman primate social life, we also said that nonhuman primates don't use language in the way that humans do.

Traditionally, most linguists and behavioral psychologists have held that nonhuman communication consists of mostly involuntary vocalizations and actions that animals use to convey information solely about their emotional state (anger, fear, etc.). Nonhuman animals haven't been considered capable of communicating about external events, objects, or other animals, either in close proximity or removed in space or time. For example, when a startled baboon barks, other group members know only that it's startled. They don't know what prompted the bark, and this they can determine only by looking around. In general, then, it's been assumed that nonhuman animals, including primates, use a "closed system" of communication, where the use of vocalizations and other modalities doesn't include references to specific external phenomena.

For several years, the traditional views have been challenged (Steklis, 1985; King, 1994). We now know, for example, that vervet monkeys (Fig. 7–15) use specific vocalizations to refer to particular categories of predators, such as snakes, birds of prey, and leopards (Struhsaker, 1967; Seyfarth, Cheney, and Marler, 1980a, 1980b). When researchers made tape recordings of various vervet alarm calls and played them back within hearing distance of free-ranging vervets, they saw different responses to various calls. When the monkeys heard leopard-alarm

Tetsuro Matsuzawa

Lynn Kilgore

FIGURE 7–15
Group of free-ranging vervets.

calls, they climbed trees; eagle-alarm calls caused them to look toward the sky; and they responded to snake-alarm calls by looking around at nearby grass.

These responses demonstrate that vervets use distinct vocalizations to refer to specific components of the external environment. The calls aren't involuntary, and they don't refer solely to the individual's emotional state (alarm). Such findings dispel certain long-held misconceptions about nonhuman communication (at least for some species), but they also indicate certain limitations. Vervet communication is restricted to the present; as far as we know, no vervet can communicate about a predator it saw yesterday or one it might see in the future.

Other studies have shown that numerous nonhuman primates, including cottontop tamarins (Cleveland and Snowdon, 1982), Goeldi's monkeys (Masataka, 1983), red colobus (Struhsaker, 1975), and gibbons (Tenaza and Tilson, 1977), use distinct calls that have specific references. There's also evidence that many birds and some nonprimate mammals use specific predator alarm calls (Seyfarth, 1987).

In contrast, humans use *language,* a set of written and/or spoken symbols that refer to concepts, other people, objects, and so on. This set of symbols is said to be *arbitrary* because the symbol itself has no inherent relationship with whatever it stands for. For example, when the English word *flower* is written or spoken, it neither looks, sounds, smells, nor feels like the thing it represents. Moreover, humans can recombine linguistic symbols in an infinite number of ways to create new meanings, and we can use language to refer to events, places, objects, and people far removed in space and time. For these reasons, language is described as an "open system" of communication, based on the human ability to think symbolically.

Language, as distinct from other forms of communication, has always been considered a uniquely human achievement, setting humans apart from the rest of the animal kingdom. But work with captive apes has raised some doubts about certain aspects of this notion. Reports from psychologists, especially those who work with chimpanzees, leave little doubt that apes can learn to interpret visual signs and use them to communicate. The fact that apes can't speak has less to do with lack of intelligence than with differences in the anatomy of the vocal tract and *language-related structures in the brain.*

Because of unsuccessful attempts by others to teach young chimpanzees to speak, psychologists Beatrice and Allen Gardner designed a study to test language capabilities in chimpanzees by teaching an infant female named Washoe to use ASL (American Sign Language for the deaf). The project began in 1966, and in three years, Washoe acquired at least 132 signs. "She asked for goods and services, and she also asked questions about the world of objects and events around her" (Gardner et al., 1989, p. 6).

Years later, an infant chimpanzee named Loulis was placed in Washoe's care. Psychologist Roger Fouts and colleagues wanted to know if Loulis would acquire signing skills from Washoe and other chimpanzees in the study group. Within just eight days, Loulis began to imitate the signs of others. And, amazingly, Washoe deliberately *taught* Loulis some signs.

FIGURE 7–16

The bonobo Kanzi, as a youngster, using lexigrams to communicate with human observers.

Other ape species have been used in language studies, too. Dr. Francine Patterson, who taught ASL to Koko, a female lowland gorilla, reports that Koko uses more than 500 signs. Michael, an adult male gorilla who was also involved in the study until his death in 2000, had a considerable sign vocabulary, and the two gorillas regularly signed to each other.

In the late 1970s, a two-year-old male orangutan named Chantek began to use signs after one month of training. Eventually, he acquired approximately 140 signs, which he sometimes used in referring to objects (and people) that weren't present. Chantek also invented signs and recombined them in novel ways, and he appeared to understand that his signs were *representations* of items, actions, and people (Miles, 1990).

Questions have been raised about this type of experimental work. Do the apes really understand the signs they learn, or are they merely imitating their trainers? Do they learn that a symbol is a name for an object, or simply that using it will produce that object? Partly in an effort to address some of these questions and criticisms, Sue Savage-Rumbaugh taught two chimpanzees to use symbols to categorize *classes* of objects, such as "food" or "tool." She did so because in previous studies, apes had been taught symbols for *specific* items. But if the chimpanzees could classify things into groups, it would indicate that they can use symbols referentially. As it turned out, both chimpanzees were able to place unfamiliar items into broad categories, an accomplishment that added support to the argument that chimpanzees do indeed have the capacity to use at least some symbols referentially.

A major assumption during the early years of ape language studies was that unlike human children—who learn language through exposure, without being taught—young chimpanzees must be *taught* to use symbols. But because the young chimpanzee, Loulis, imitated gestures soon after being exposed to them, that assumption clearly wasn't true. It was also significant when Savage-Rumbaugh and her colleagues reported that a young male bonobo named Kanzi, was *spontaneously* acquiring and using symbols at the age of $2^1/_2$ years (Savage-Rumbaugh et al., 1986) (Fig. 7–16). And, Kanzi's younger half sister also began to use symbols spontaneously when she was only 11 months old. It's important to emphasize that both animals had been exposed to the use of lexigrams, or illustrated symbols that represent words, when they accompanied their mother to training sessions, but neither had received instruction and in fact they weren't even involved in these sessions.

Even though Kanzi and his sister showed a high degree of learning ability, it's still evident that apes don't acquire and use language in the same way humans do. And it appears that not all signing apes understand the referential relationship between symbol and object, person, or action. At any rate, we now have abundant evidence that humans aren't the only species capable of some degree of symbolic thought and complex communication.

The Primate Continuum

It's an unfortunate fact that humans generally view themselves as separate from the rest of the animal kingdom. This perspective is, in no small measure, due to a prevailing lack of knowledge about the behavior and abilities of other species. What's more, for humans these notions are continuously reinforced through exposure to advertising, movies, and television (Fig. 7–17).

For decades, behavioral psychology taught that animal behavior represents nothing more than a series of conditioned responses to specific stimuli. (This perspective is very convenient for people who exploit nonhuman animals, for whatever purposes, and want to remain free of guilt.) Fortunately, in recent years this attitude has been changing to reflect a growing awareness that humans, although in many ways unquestionably unique, are nevertheless part of a biological continuum. Indeed, we are also part of a behavioral continuum.

Where do humans fit, then, in this **biological continuum**? Are we at the top? The answer depends on the criteria used. We're certainly the most intelligent species, if we define intelligence in terms of problem-solving abilities and abstract thought. But if we take a closer look, we recognize that the differences between ourselves and our primate relatives, especially chimpanzees and bonobos, are primarily quantitative and not qualitative.

Although the human brain is absolutely and relatively larger, neurological processes are functionally the same. The necessity of close bonding with at least one parent and the need for physical contact are essentially the same. Developmental stages and dependence on learning are strikingly similar. Indeed, in the chimpanzees' capacity for cruelty and aggression combined with compassion, tenderness, and altruism, we can see a close parallel to the dichotomy between "evil" and "good" so long recognized in ourselves. The main difference between how chimpanzees and humans express these qualities (and therefore the dichotomy) is one of degree. Humans are much more adept at cruelty and compassion, and we can reflect on our behavior in ways that chimpanzees can't. Like the cat that plays with a mouse, chimpanzees don't seem to understand the suffering they inflict on other animals. But humans do. Likewise, even though an adult chimpanzee may sit next to a dying relative, it doesn't appear to feel intense grief to the extent a human normally does.

To arrive at any understanding of what it is to be human, it's important to recognize that many of our behaviors are elaborate extensions of those of our hominid ancestors and close primate relatives. The fact that so many of us prefer to bask in the warmth of the "sun belt" with literally millions of others reflects our heritage as social animals adapted to life in the tropics. And the sweet tooth that afflicts so many of us is a result of our earlier primate ancestor's predilection for high-energy sugar contained in sweet, ripe fruit. As we explore how

FIGURE 7–17

This unfortunate advertising display is a good example of how humans misunderstand and thus misrepresent our closest relatives.

biological continuum Refers to the fact that organisms are related through common ancestry and that behaviors and traits seen in one species are also seen in others to varying degrees. (When expressions of a phenomenon continuously grade into one another so that there are no discrete categories, they are said to exist on a continuum. Color is such a phenomenon.)

humans came to be and how we continue to adapt, it's critically important to recognize our primate heritage. In fact, this recognition is the key to understanding ourselves, and without it, most attempts to explain the complexities of human behavior will fail.

Summary

In this chapter, we've presented the major theoretical models for the evolution of behavior in primates. We've also discussed some of the evidence, including some reports that use genetic data to support these models. The subject of the evolution of behavior is extremely complex because it requires research into the interactions of dozens, if not hundreds, of ecological and physiological variables.

The fundamental principle of behavioral evolution is that aspects of behavior (including social behavior) are influenced by genetic factors. And because some behavioral elements are therefore inherited, natural selection can act on them in the same way it acts on physical and anatomical characteristics. We pointed out that in more primitive organisms, such as insects and most other invertebrates, the proportion of behavior that is directly influenced by genes is much greater than in mammals and birds.

Behavioral ecology is the discipline that examines behavior from the perspective of complex ecological relationships and the role of natural selection as it favors behaviors that increase reproductive fitness. This approach generates many models of behavioral evolution that can be applied to all species, including humans. Members of each species inherit a genome that is species-specific, and some part of that genome influences behaviors. But in more complex animals, the genome allows for greater degrees of behavioral flexibility and learning. And, in humans, who rely on cultural adaptations for survival, most behavior is learned.

Critical Thinking Questions

1. Apply some of the topics presented in this chapter to some nonprimate species that you are familiar with. Can you develop some hypotheses to explain the behavior of some domestic species? You might want to speculate on how behavior in domestic animals may differ from that of their wild ancestors. (Chapter 2 might help you here.)
2. Can you speculate on how the behavioral ecology of nonhuman primates may be helpful in explaining human behavior?
3. How might infanticide be seen as a reproductive strategy for males? If this concept were to be applied to human males, do you think some people would object? Why or why not? Do you object?

CHAPTER

8

Understanding
the Past:
Archaeological and
Paleoanthropological
Methods

FOCUS QUESTIONS

What are the central aspects of paleoanthropology in general? Of archaeology, in particular?

Why, from a biocultural perspective, do we want to learn about *both* the behavior and the anatomy of ancient hominids?

Go to the following CD-ROMs for interactive activities and exercises on topics covered in this chapter:

• Virtual Laboratories for Physical Anthropology CD-ROM, Third Edition

hominid Colloquial term for members of the family Hominidae, which includes all bipedal hominoids back to the divergence from African great apes.

Introduction

A portion of a pig's tusk, a small sample of volcanic sediment, a battered cobble, a primate's molar tooth: What do these seemingly unremarkable remains have in common, and more to the point, why are they of interest to paleoanthropologists and archaeologists? First of all, if they are all discovered at certain sites in Africa or in Eurasia, they may be quite ancient—indeed, perhaps millions of years old. Further, some of these materials actually inform scientists directly of accurate and precise dating of the finds—in this case, 2.2 million years old. Last, and most exciting, some of these finds may have been modified, used, and discarded by creatures who looked and behaved in some ways like us, but were, in other respects, very different. And what of that molar tooth? Is it a fossilized remnant of an ancient **hominid**? These are the kinds of questions asked by paleoanthropologists and archaeologists, and to answer them, these researchers travel to remote locales in the Old World.

How do we identify possible hominids from other types of animals, especially when all we have are fragmentary fossil remains from just a small portion of a skeleton? How do humans and our most distant ancestors compare with other animals? In the last three chapters, we've seen how humans are classified as primates, both structurally and behaviorally, and how our evolutionary history coincides with that of other mammals and, specifically, other primates. But we are a unique kind of primate, and our ancestors have been adapted to a particular lifestyle for several million years. Some primitive hominoid probably began this process close to 7 million years ago, but with better-preserved fossil discoveries, scientists now have more definitive evidence of hominids shortly after 5 mya.

The hominid nature of these remains is revealed by more than the structure of teeth and bones; we know that these animals are hominids also because of the way they behaved—emphasizing once again the biocultural nature of human evolution. Most of our understanding of these events and changes is the result of paleoanthropological, including most especially archaeological, research. In this chapter, we describe the basic concepts of these interrelated lines of investigation so you can approach the rest of the book with a solid grounding in the research methods upon which reconstruction of the human past is based. We'll begin with broader aspects of paleoanthropology, which, in addition to archaeology, examines early hominid behavior and ecology through study of fossil remains. This sets the stage for Chapters 9–12, in which we examine the fossil evidence of human ancestors and near relatives.

As part of paleoanthropology, some archaeologists specialize in studying the early phases of human biocultural development. This work certainly makes archaeology a major component of paleoanthropological research, but in this chapter we'll also cover a variety of research perspectives and methods that are practiced by *all* archaeologists (including those investigating later phases of prehistory as well as historical contexts). Our more specific focus on archaeology emphasizes it as a related body of methods to those used by other paleoanthropologists. But while archaeology explores similar questions about the human past, it does so primarily through examination of material remains. The importance of archaeological methods increases gradually throughout Chapters 9–12 and becomes the dominant source of information in Chapters 13–16. At the end of this chapter, you'll be able to appreciate the close partnership of paleoanthropology and archaeology in the study of the early human past by reading our discussion of the best-known early hominid site locality in the world: Olduvai Gorge in East Africa.

Definition of Hominid

So far, the earliest hominid traces that have been found date to the end of the Miocene, and they include primarily dental and cranial pieces. Indeed, of the numerous hominoid fossils from throughout the Miocene, primarily teeth and jaws have been preserved. But dental features alone do not describe the special features of hominids, and they're certainly not the most distinctive of the later stages of human evolution. Modern humans, as well as our most immediate hominid ancestors, are distinguished from the great apes by more obvious features than tooth and jaw dimensions. For example, various scientists have pointed to such distinctive hominid characteristics as bipedal locomotion, large brain size, and toolmaking behavior as being significant (at some stage) in defining what makes a hominid a hominid.

MOSAIC EVOLUTION

It's important to recognize that not all these characteristics developed simultaneously or at the same pace. In fact, over the last several million years of hominid evolution, quite a different pattern has been evident, in which each of the components (dentition, locomotion, brain size, and toolmaking) have developed at quite different rates. This pattern, in which physiological and behavioral systems evolve at different rates, is called **mosaic evolution**. As we first pointed out in Chapter 1 and will emphasize in this and the next chapter, the single most important defining characteristic for the full course of hominid evolution is bipedal locomotion. In the earliest stages of hominid emergence, skeletal evidence indicating bipedal locomotion is the only truly reliable indicator that these fossils were indeed hominids. But in later stages of hominid evolution, other features, especially those relating to brain development and behavior, become highly significant (Fig. 8–1).

WHAT'S IN A NAME?

Throughout this book, we refer to members of the human family as hominids (technical name for the family is Hominidae). This terminology has been widely used for decades, and the inherent evolutionary relationships it reflects are shown in Fig. 8–2a. However, as we mentioned in Chapter 6, this classification has some drawbacks, since it fails to recognize several basic evolutionary relationships among the great apes (most important, that chimpanzees and bonobos are more closely related to us and our bipedal predecessors than the other great apes are).

Owing to the inadequacies of the traditional classification, a revised one has been proposed (e.g., by Wood and Richmond, 2000). In this scheme (Fig. 8–2b), two further levels of classification have been added (subfamily and tribe) to allow finer-tuned and evolutionarily more accurate distinctions. Here, the term *hominid* refers to all great apes as well as to the human line ("us"). When referring to the human line (us) exclusively, the term now used is *hominin*, a distinction made at the taxonomic level of tribe.

If this terminology seems highly confusing, that's because, unfortunately, it is—so much so, in fact, that the revised classification still hasn't been very widely accepted.* Even so, it's important to recognize that the evolutionary relationships depicted (see Fig. 8–2b) are more accurate, and they're widely accepted by evolutionary biologists. Settling on what to label the various levels remains in flux. For purposes of clarity in this book, we'll continue to use the term *hominid* to refer to the lineage of bipedal hominoids since its divergence from our closest cousins (chimpanzees and bonobos). (If you should see the term *hominin* elsewhere, it's being used synonymously with our usage of *hominid*.)

mosaic evolution A pattern of evolution in which the rates of evolution in one functional system vary from those in other systems. For example, in hominid evolution, the dental system, locomotor system, and neurological system (especially the brain) all evolved at markedly different rates.

---

*For example, at major meetings of the world's largest professional association of physical anthropologists (The American Association of Physical Anthropologists) in 2003 and 2004, all the sessions dealing with human evolution were listed using the traditional classification (that is, hominid). In 2003, however, 50 percent of specific titles of presentations in these sessions used the revised term, *hominin*, while the other half used *hominid*. In 2004, most presentations reverted to the term *hominid*.

	Locomotion	Brain	Dentition	Toolmaking Behavior
(Modern *Homo sapiens*) 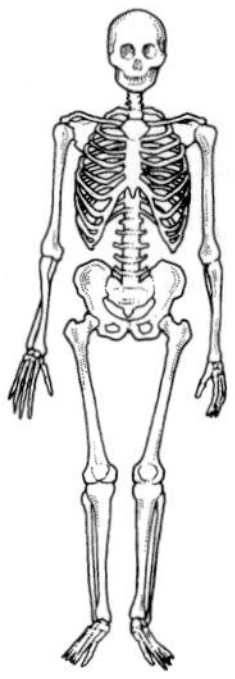	Bipedal: shortened pelvis; body size larger; legs longer; fingers and toes not as long	Greatly increased brain size—highly encephalized	Small incisors; canines further reduced; molar tooth enamel caps thick	Stone tools found after 2.5 mya; increasing trend of cultural dependency apparent in later hominids
(Early hominid) 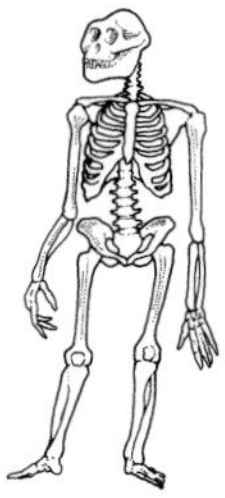	Bipedal: shortened pelvis; some differences from later hominids, showing smaller body size and long arms relative to legs; long fingers and toes; probably capable of considerable climbing	Larger than Miocene forms, but still only moderately encephalized; prior to 6 mya, no more encephalized than chimpanzees	Moderately large front teeth (incisors); canines somewhat reduced; molar tooth enamel caps very thick	In earliest stages unknown; no stone tool use prior to 2.5 mya; probably somewhat more oriented toward tool manufacture and use than chimpanzees
(Miocene, generalized hominoid) 	Quadrupedal: long pelvis; some forms capable of considerable arm swinging, suspensory locomotion	Small compared to hominids, but large compared to other primates; a fair degree of encephalization	Large front teeth (including canines); molar teeth variable, depending on species; some have thin enamel caps, others thick enamel caps	Unknown—no stone tools; probably had capabilities similar to chimpanzees

Time line markers: 0.5 mya, 1 mya, 2 mya, 3 mya, 4 mya, 20 mya

FIGURE 8–1

Mosaic evolution of hominid characteristics: a postulated time line.

Biocultural Evolution: The Human Capacity for Culture

One of the most distinctive behavioral features of humans is our extraordinary elaboration of and dependence on culture. Certainly other primates, and many other animals, for that matter, modify their environments. As we saw in Chapter 7, chimpanzees especially are known for such behaviors as using termite sticks, and some even carry rocks to use for crushing nuts. Because of such observations, we're on tenuous ground when it comes to drawing sharp lines between early hominid toolmaking behavior and that exhibited by other animals.

Another point to remember is that human culture, at least as it's defined in contemporary contexts, involves much more than toolmaking capacity. For humans, culture integrates an entire adaptive strategy involving cognitive, political, social, and economic components. The *material culture*, the tools humans use, is but a small portion of this cultural complex.

Nevertheless, when we examine the archaeological record of earlier hominids, what is available for study is almost exclusively limited to material culture, especially residues of stone

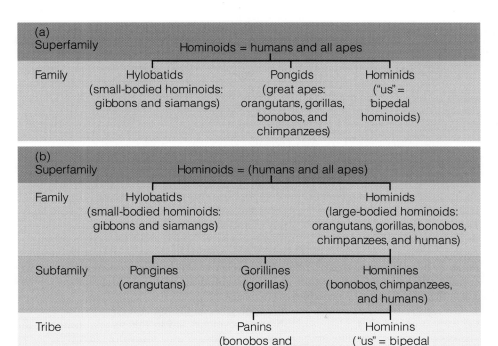

FIGURE 8–2
(a) Traditional classification of hominoids.
(b) Revised classification of hominoids. Note that two other levels of classification are added (subfamily and tribe) to show more precisely and more accurately evolutionary relationships among the apes and humans. In this classification, *hominin* is synonymous with the use of *hominid* in Figure 8–2a.

tool manufacture. So it's extremely difficult to learn anything about the earliest stages of hominid cultural development before the regular manufacture of stone tools. As you will see, this most crucial cultural development has been traced to approximately 2.5 mya (Semaw et al., 1997). Yet, hominids were undoubtedly using other kinds of tools (made of perishable materials) and displaying a whole array of other cultural behaviors long before then. However, without any "hard" evidence preserved in the archaeological record, our understanding of the early development of these nonmaterial cultural components remains elusive.

The fundamental basis for human cultural success relates directly to cognitive abilities. Again, we're not dealing with an absolute distinction, but a relative one. As you have already learned, other primates, as documented in chimpanzees and bonobos, have some of the language capabilities exhibited by humans. Even so, modern humans display these abilities in a complexity several orders of magnitude beyond that of any other animal. And only humans are so completely dependent on symbolic communication and its cultural by-products that contemporary *Homo sapiens* could not survive without them.

At this point you may be wondering, when did the unique combination of cognitive, social, and material cultural adaptations become prominent in human evolution? In answering that question, we must be careful to recognize the manifold nature of culture; we can't expect it to always contain the same elements across species (as when comparing ourselves to nonhuman primates) or through time (when trying to reconstruct ancient hominid behavior). Richard Potts (1993) has critiqued such overly simplistic perspectives and suggests instead a more dynamic approach, one that incorporates many subcomponents (including aspects of behavior, cognition, and social interaction).

We know that the earliest hominids almost certainly did not regularly manufacture stone tools (at least, none that have been found and identified as such). These earliest members of the hominid lineage, dating back to approximately 7–5 mya, could be referred to as **protohominids**. These protohominids may have carried objects such as naturally sharp stones or stone flakes, parts of carcasses, and pieces of wood around their home ranges. At the very least, we would expect them to have displayed these behaviors to at least the same degree as that exhibited in living chimpanzees.

As you'll soon see, by at least 5 mya and perhaps even by 7 mya, hominids had developed one crucial advantage: They were bipedal and could therefore much more easily carry all manner of objects from place to place.

protohominids The earliest members of the hominid lineage, as yet only poorly represented in the fossil record; thus, their structure and behavior are reconstructed largely hypothetically.

What we know for sure is that over a period of several million years, during the formative stages of hominid emergence, many components interacted, but not all of them developed simultaneously. As cognitive abilities developed, more efficient means of communication and learning resulted. Largely because of consequent neurological reorganization, more elaborate tools and social relationships also emerged. These, in turn, selected for greater intelligence, which in turn selected for further neural elaboration. Quite clearly, then, these mutual dynamic interactions are at the very heart of what we call hominid *biocultural* evolution.

Paleoanthropology

To adequately understand human evolution, we obviously need a broad base of information. It's the paleoanthropologist's task to recover and interpret all the clues left by early hominids. *Paleoanthropology* is defined as "the study of ancient humans." As such, it's a diverse **multidisciplinary** pursuit seeking to reconstruct every possible bit of information concerning the dating, structure, behavior, and ecology of our hominid ancestors. In the last few decades, the study of early humans has marshaled the specialized skills of many different kinds of scientists. Included in this growing and exciting adventure are geologists, archaeologists, physical anthropologists, and paleoecologists (Table 8–1).

Geologists, usually working with anthropologists, do the initial surveys to locate potential early hominid sites. Many sophisticated techniques aid in this search, including the analysis of aerial and satellite imagery. Paleontologists are usually involved in this early survey work, for they can help find fossil beds containing faunal remains. Where conditions are favorable for the preservation of bone from such species as pigs and elephants, hominid remains may also be preserved. In addition, paleontologists can (through comparison with known faunal sequences) give approximate age estimates of fossil sites without having to wait for the results of more time-consuming analyses.

Fossil beds likely to contain hominid finds are subjected to extensive field surveying. For some sites, generally those postdating 2.5 mya (roughly the age of the oldest identified human artifacts), archaeologists take over in the search for hominid material traces. We don't necessarily have to find remains of early hominids themselves to know that they consistently occupied a particular area. Such material clues as **artifacts** also inform us directly about early hominid activities. Modifying rocks according to a consistent plan, or simply carrying them around from one place to another (over fairly long distances in a manner not explicable by natural means—such as streams or glaciers) is characteristic of no other animal but a hominid. So, when we see such material evidence at a site, we know absolutely that hominids were present.

Because organic materials such as wooden and bone tools aren't usually preserved in the archaeological record of the oldest hominids, we have no solid evidence of the earliest stages

multidisciplinary Pertaining to research that involves mutual contributions and cooperation of experts from various scientific fields (i.e., disciplines).

artifacts Objects or materials made or modified for use by hominids. The earliest artifacts are usually made of stone or, occasionally, bone.

TABLE 8–1	Contributing Scientific Fields to Paleoanthropology	
Physical Sciences	**Biological Sciences**	**Social Sciences**

Geology
  Stratigraphy
  Petrology
  (rocks, minerals)
  Pedology (soils)
	Physical anthropology	Archaeology

	Ecology
	  Paleontology
	  (fossil animals)
	  Palynology
	  (fossil pollen)
		Ethnoarchaeology

		Cultural anthropology Ethnography
Geomorphology		Psychology
Geophysics	Primatology	
Chemistry		
Taphonomy		

of hominid cultural modifications. On the other hand, our ancestors at some point showed a veritable fascination with stones, because they provided not only easily accessible and transportable materials (to use as convenient objects for throwing or for holding down other objects, such as skins and windbreaks) but also the most durable and sharpest cutting edges available at that time. Luckily for us, stone is almost indestructible, and some early hominid sites are strewn with thousands of stone artifacts. The earliest artifact sites now documented are from the Gona and Bouri areas in northeastern Ethiopia, dating to 2.5 mya (Semaw et al., 1997; de Heinzelin et al., 1999). Other contenders for the "earliest" stone assemblage come from the adjacent Hadar and Middle Awash areas, immediately to the south in Ethiopia, dated 2.5–2 mya.

If an area is clearly demonstrated to be a hominid site, much more concentrated research will then begin. We should point out that a more mundane but very significant aspect of paleoanthropology not reflected in Table 8–1 is the financial one. Just the initial survey work in usually remote areas costs many thousands of dollars, and mounting a concentrated research project costs several hundred thousand dollars. For such work to go on, massive financial support is required from government agencies and private donations. A significant amount of a paleoanthropologist's efforts and time is necessarily devoted to writing grant proposals or speaking on the lecture circuit to raise the required funds for this work.

Once the financial hurdle has been cleared, a coordinated research project can begin. Usually headed by an archaeologist or physical anthropologist, the field crew continues to survey and map the target area in great detail. In addition, field crew members begin searching carefully for bones and artifacts eroding out of the soil, taking pollen and soil samples for ecological analysis, and carefully collecting rock samples for use in various dating techniques. If, in this early stage of exploration, members of the field crew find fossil hominid remains, they will feel very lucky indeed. The international press usually considers human fossils the most exciting kind of discovery, a situation that produces wide publicity and often ensures future financial support. More likely, the crew will accumulate much information on geological setting, ecological data (particularly faunal remains), and, with some luck, artifacts and other archaeological traces.

Although paleoanthropological fieldwork is typically a long and arduous process, the detailed analyses of collected samples and other data back in the laboratory are even more time-consuming. Archaeologists must clean, sort, label, and identify all artifacts, and paleontologists must do the same for all faunal remains. Knowing the kinds of animals represented—whether forest browsers, woodland species, or open-country forms—greatly helps in reconstructing the local *paleoecological* settings in which early hominids lived. Analyzing the fossil pollen collected from hominid sites by a palynologist further aids in developing a detailed environmental reconstruction. All these paleoecological analyses can assist in reconstructing the diet of early humans. Also, the **taphonomy** of the site must be worked out in order to understand its depositional history—that is, how the site formed over time, and if its present state is in a *primary* or *secondary* **context**.

In the concluding stages of interpretation, the paleoanthropologist draws together the following essentials:

1. *Dating*
      geological
      paleontological
      geophysical
2. *Paleoecology*
      paleontology
      palynology
      geomorphology
      taphonomy
3. *Archaeological traces of behavior*
4. *Anatomical evidence from hominid remains*

By analyzing all this information, scientists try to "flesh out" the kind of animal that may have been our direct ancestor, or at least a very close relative. Primatologists may assist here by showing the detailed relationships between the anatomical structure and behavior of humans and that of contemporary nonhuman primates (see Chapters 6 and 7). Cultural

taphonomy (from Greek *taphos*, meaning "dead") The study of how bones and other materials came to be buried in the earth and preserved as fossils. A taphonomist studies the processes of sedimentation, the action of streams, preservation properties of bone, and carnivore disturbance factors.

context The environmental setting where an archaeological trace is found. *Primary* context is the setting in which the archaeological trace was originally deposited. A *secondary* context is one to which it has been moved (e.g., by the action of a stream).

anthropologists may contribute ethnographic information concerning the varied nature of human behavior, particularly ecological adaptations of those contemporary hunter-gatherer groups exploiting roughly similar environmental settings as those reconstructed for a hominid site.

The end result of years of research by dozens of scientists will (we hope) produce a more complete and accurate understanding of human evolution—how we came to be the way we are. Both biological and cultural aspects of our ancestors contribute to this investigation, each process developing in relation to the other.

Archaeology

As we've noted in Chapter 1, archaeology is a body of methods designed to understand the human past through the examination and study of its material remains. Archaeologists use basically the same methods and techniques to research early hominid sites in the Old World as they do to study the prehistory of modern humans and their cultures. The big differences are, first, that the archaeological record holds much less material evidence of the lifeways of early hominids than of modern humans, and second, that the oldest archaeological data are difficult to interpret accurately because early hominids were physically and culturally quite different from modern humans. As we move closer in time to modern humans, the archaeological record becomes more extensive, more diverse, and more amenable to interpretation.

GOALS OF ARCHAEOLOGY

In its study of the human past, anthropological archaeology has at least four main goals, several of which play a role in virtually every research project. The first goal, a very basic one, is to reconstruct the chronicle of past human events as they were played out across space and through time. This goal is essentially that of providing order to the archaeological record, an order that implicitly answers the fundamental "when" and "where" questions. When did plant domestication arise in the Near East? What sustained contacts existed between the people of western Mexico and northern Peru in 800–400 B.C.? Does the distribution of hand axes (a type of stone tool discussed in Chapter 10) extend into Southeast Asia? Descriptive questions such as these, anchored as they are in time and space, are essential to the successful examination of more challenging questions about the human past.

Archaeology's second main goal is to reconstruct past human lifeways. Using clues from recovered artifacts, archaeological features, sites, and contexts, archaeologists try to understand how people actually created and used those cultural products to interact with each other and their surroundings. What was the function of these tools? How were people treated in death? What did their huts or shelters look like? Think of this area of research as the archaeological equivalent of the ethnographies of cultural anthropology.

Third, archaeologists want to *explain* how and why the past happened as it did (see Digging Deeper). Why didn't the economic dependence on food production take place until after the end of the last Ice Age? Are social inequalities inevitable correlates of the development of the state? Such questions are tough to answer because of their general nature and because the answers can sometimes require an understanding of world prehistory that exceeds the current state of the art.

Theoretical changes in archaeology over the past two decades also yielded what many researchers now regard as a fourth main goal, which can be loosely described as interpreting the cognitive and symbolic aspects of past cultures. This research complements the search for general explanations of past cultural patterns and explores questions that reflect archaeology's roots in the humanities. What can changing representational conventions of clothing in medieval Hindu art tell us about changes in the nature of kingship and the relations between kings? To what extent is the current scientific understanding of Russian prehistory biased by the values, beliefs, and social history of past generations of archaeologists? Such questions defy *general* explanation but are just as important to our understanding of the human past.

DIGGING DEEPER

Mechanisms of Cultural Variation and Change

We've stressed the idea that modern human beings are *biocultural* organisms, meaning that our biology and culture interact to influence the course of our evolution. One clear advantage of cultural behavior is that it allows people to respond quickly to stimuli, and it's also more versatile than biological evolution. Because people can so readily create new behaviors or easily modify old ones, the world's geographically dispersed societies display a wide range of cultural variation.

In attempting to explain cultural variability and to account for the nature of cultural change, some archaeologists (following the lead of evolutionary biologists) view cultural variation and change as resulting from cultural factors that are comparable in their effect to those evolutionary factors influencing population genetics (see Chapter 4). Thus, prehistorians consider that several mechanisms of cultural variation and change may have a role in determining the course of cultural development:

- *Cultural drift* describes the imperfect transmission of cultural information from generation to generation or over increasing distances. For example, minor *unintended* varia-tions inevitably creep into hand-painted designs on clay pots or filter into the wording of a sacred chant, so that over time distinctive cultural varieties may evolve out of the original version.

- *Invention and innovation* represent sources of *intentional* variation. The invention of a new cultural item, whether a device for trapping birds or a novel projectile point style, represents a significant departure from the status quo. An innovation, on the other hand, may simply improve on or provide a new use for an existing element of culture, such as adding a grip to a digging stick so that it won't slip from the hand.

- *Cultural selection* is the process by which new cultural traits are either generally accepted or rejected. For example, a social group may or may not adopt the new projectile point style, or they may make further innovations to improve its effectiveness. Obviously, cultural traits or objects that are advantageous and become popular tend to show up more often in the archaeological record.

- *Diffusion* describes the transmission of cultural objects or behaviors into new regions. People may carry cultural traits with them as they migrate or go off to war, or they may spread them through trade or other means of contact and communication.

ARCHAEOLOGICAL RESEARCH PROJECTS

Modern archaeology, like paleoanthropology, is a complex undertaking that often draws on the expertise of specialists from many fields. Field projects range in scale from relatively simple tasks that can be completed in a few days (Fig. 8–3) to major undertakings that may take decades to complete (Fig. 8–4). The justification for allocating resources to such research also varies greatly, from cultural resource management (CRM) projects intended to meet legal guidelines for conserving historical sites and monuments to public or private agency-sponsored projects designed to answer specific questions about the past.

Given a question or heritage management task to motivate research, and a geographically defined region where the project is to take place, archaeological field-work assumes a fairly common pattern. First, the archaeological resources of that region are identified and inventoried. Second, sites selected from the pool of all known sites in the region are subjected to careful examination, often using nonintrusive methods. Finally, some sites may be wholly or partially excavated.

FIGURE 8–3

Excavation of this "test pit" at a late prehistoric site in western Kentucky will enable archaeologists to assess the site's depositional history, its approximate age, how well-preserved it is, and the diversity and kind of remains preserved there. Researchers will compare this information with the results of similar test pits at other sites in the same region and use it in deciding which sites should be excavated more extensively.

Barry Lewis

Excavation of this large, deeply stratified archaeological site in western Illinois took years of sustained effort by large field crews and support
staff to complete. It yielded far greater contextual information than researchers would expect
to find in something like a test pit (Fig. 8–3).

Barry Lewis

site survey   The process of discovering
the location of archaeological sites; sometimes called site reconnaissance.

Michael L. Hargrave

FIGURE 8–5
Dr. Michael L. Hargrave conducts an electrical
resistance survey to locate archaeological features at a site in central Missouri. The survey
works by measuring the electrical resistance
between two electrodes inserted in the earth. By
systematically recording these measures across
an archaeological site, researchers can plot the
data to show soil disturbances such as ditches,
walls, roads, and similar features that show no
visible traces on the ground surface.

Modern archaeologists and other paleoanthropologists can (and do) turn to an extraordinary array of high-tech tools to help them discover the location of sites, including aerial
and satellite imagery and remote sensing technologies with such esoteric-sounding names as
ground-penetrating radar, side-scan sonar, proton magnetometers, and subbottom profilers,
to name only a few (Fig. 8–5). Even so, fieldworkers on foot who look for artifacts and other
telltale material evidence on the ground surface probably still discover most sites.

As they identify sites in the field, archaeologists record information about the local terrain; the kinds of artifacts and other cultural debris that may be present on the surface; the
area encompassed by this scatter of material, and other basic facts that become part of the
permanent record of that site. Later, back in the lab, analyses of these data often yield estimates of the approximate age of each site, what the prehistoric site inhabitants did there, how
long they used the site, and sometimes even where they may have come from and the rough
age and sex composition of the group (Fig. 8–6).

Information from this **site survey**, as it is often called, enables the project directors to make
informed decisions about excavating the sites. They'll choose sites that are most likely to yield
information necessary to solve the problem that motivated the research or, if it is a CRM project, to comply with relevant heritage management priorities, guidelines, and laws.

The popular stereotype of archaeology and archaeologists is that they spend most of their
time digging square holes in the ground. Although this kind of activity will always be archaeology's defining characteristic, the professional attitude toward excavation changed during
the twentieth century from a this-is-what-we-do attitude to a deep appreciation of the fact
that the archaeological record is a finite resource, much like oil and gas deposits. We can be
confident, for example, that all the 2,000-year-old sites that will ever exist were laid down
2,000 years ago. There aren't going to be any more of them, only fewer. And, since excavation
is obviously destructive, it's not like archaeologists do a site any favor by digging it up! Having
come to this realization in the second half of the twentieth century, archaeologists have since
tried to take a leadership role in promoting the adoption of national policies that conserve
the world's remaining archaeological resources for the maximum public and scientific benefit. In the long run this means, yes, that excavation will always be a distinctively archaeological
activity. Even so, such excavations should happen only in those situations where the data are
needed to answer specific nontrivial questions about the human past or to collect basic
archaeological information about sites that face imminent threat of destruction. Anything else
simply vandalizes our collective heritage.

Barry Lewis

FIGURE 8–6

By analyzing this collection of cultural debris from the surface of a prehistoric site in Southeast Missouri, the archaeologist can estimate the site age and the kinds of activities its inhabitants performed there. Other information about the site—including approximate site area, site preservation conditions, soil type, ground cover, and visible cultural features—was recorded when this surface collection was made.

Piecing Together the Past

Archaeology produces useful information only because we can reasonably assume that the organization and structure of the archaeological record reflects the behavior of humans in the past. Were this assumption to be false, archaeology would cease to exist. It's also undeniably true that it's easier to use archaeological data in examining some aspects of the past than others. Archaeologists, for example, seem to delight in telling us about what ancient people ate. They're typically far less prepared to tell us about such things as regional patterns of Neandertal ethnic identity in southwestern France, or the social meaning of tattooed faces among the late prehistoric Native American villagers of the American Southeast.

It's not because no one cares about these things. It's just that it's far easier to talk about the archaeology of food than about the archaeology of identity and body art. After all, the archaeological record really is "other people's garbage"; it only becomes something more than garbage when we attempt to use it to inform ourselves about the past. It's then that we must confront the possibility that what we wish to know may not be preserved in the archaeological record or be amenable to direct examination. If that's the case, then the researcher must explore ways to examine the phenomenon of interest indirectly. And if that doesn't work, the archaeologist smacks up against the state-of-the-art wall, something that exists in every field and beyond which the potentially knowable cannot yet be known until someone develops new technologies or theoretical approaches that make it possible.

ARTIFACTS, FEATURES, AND CONTEXTS

Four essential products—artifacts, **features**, **ecofacts**, and contexts—result from archaeological research. The relationships between these categories of remains are most often observed on *sites*, which are the locations of past human activity where archaeologists concentrate their research efforts.

features Products of human activity that are usually integral to a site and therefore not portable. Examples include fire hearths and house foundations.

ecofacts Natural materials that give environmental information about a site. Examples include plant and animal remains that were discarded as food waste, and pollen grains preserved in the soil.

FIGURE 8–7

The discovery of these sherds of decorated Native American pottery on the surface of a Mississippi Gulf Coast prehistoric site enables the archaeologist to estimate how old the site is and identify regional ties between the group who lived at this site and other parts of the Gulf Coast.

FIGURE 8–8

Burials, such as the remains of this cow that were exposed during the excavation of a nineteenth-century Illinois farm, are classic examples of archaeological features. They can be exposed and studied in the archaeological record but cannot be removed without taking them apart.

Artifacts are tangible objects; in fact, anything that was made or modified by people in the past qualifies as an artifact (Fig. 8–7). It might be a stone tool or a sherd (fragment) of broken pottery or even a tin can. Artifacts differ from archaeological features because they can be removed as a single entity from the archaeological record. You can't do that with *features*, such as a medieval Hindu temple, a mud-lined hearth or fireplace, or a human burial, because none of them can be taken from the archaeological record in one piece (Fig. 8–8). *Ecofacts* are natural materials that are used mostly to reconstruct the local environment of a site (Fig. 8–9). Ecofacts can be found as both artifacts and features.

Context describes the spatial and temporal associations existing in the archaeological record among and between artifacts and features (Fig. 8–10). What was the object's precise location, recorded from several coordinates so as to provide its three-dimensional position within the site? Was it associated somehow with any other artifact or feature? For example, was this projectile point recovered from deep within a trash pit, found on the floor of a hunter's shelter, or lodged between the ribs of a large animal? Can we be certain that this apparent association was really contemporaneous and not the result of natural processes of erosion or mixing (a key consideration of taphonomy; see p. 169)? You can appreciate that the context is just as important as the artifact itself in understanding the past. With only artifacts, archaeology can tell us relatively little about the past, but with artifacts and their context, the limitations of what we can potentially know about the past probably rest more with archaeologists than with the archaeological record.

FIGURE 8–9

Thousands of land snails like the ones resting on this Lincoln penny were collected from a 4,000-year-old campsite in Illinois. These snails lived on the site location before, during, and after it was used by Native Americans; by analyzing them, archaeologists can reconstruct how the local site environment changed during that time.

Barry Lewis

FIGURE 8–10

The large, dark wedge of soil is a partially excavated late prehistoric house in southeast Missouri. Preserved parts of the house wall are dotted along the upper edge of the feature in the upper half of the photo. The remains of this house provide archaeological context for the artifacts, ecofacts, and smaller features found within it.

ETHNOARCHAEOLOGY

In addition to site surveys and excavations, archaeologists sometimes seek to enhance their understanding and interpretations of the past by turning to **ethnoarchaeology**, which examines contemporary societies to gain insights into past human behavior (Fig. 8–11).

An ethnoarchaeologist personally conducts in-depth ethnographic research among a living group, such as the !Kung San in southern Africa (Yellen, 1980), Australian aborigines (Gould, 1977; Meehan, 1982), the Nunamiut peoples of the Alaskan Arctic (Binford, 1978), or urban America (see Digging Deeper, p. 176). Such studies yield detailed information about hunting or gathering, toolmaking, discard of debris, residence data, and the like. By being "on the scene" as modern people literally create a site, the ethnoarchaeologist can better appreciate the comparable processes that formed the archaeological record (at the same time often becoming painfully aware of how much potential evidence simply decays and disappears between the time a site is created and the time an archaeologist may excavate it thousands or millions of years later).

So, how does ethnoarchaeological information get applied in archaeological research? It gives archaeologists testable ideas about the interpretation of archaeological patterns, in much the same way that paleoanthropologists apply observation studies of modern living primates to their understanding of the behavior and biology of hominids known only from the fossil record. The researcher examines the modern information and asks the question, "If early hominids behaved like modern hunter-gatherer X or supermarket shopper Y or rodeo performer Z, what physical evidence and associations should I expect to find in the archaeological record if—and only if—this is true?" If the predicted evidence and associations are found, then the researcher reasons that the observed modern human behavior can't be excluded as a possible interpretation of comparable patterning in the archaeological record.

ethnoarchaeology Approach used by archaeologists to gain insights into the past by studying contemporary people.

Dr. Colin Betts, Luther College

FIGURE 8–11

To learn about the pottery-making technology of prehistoric Native Americans in Iowa, archaeologist Colin Betts apprenticed himself to Afro-Caribbean potters who use similar methods on the island of Nevis in the West Indies. Here he stacks freshly made clay vessels so they can be fired, which is the final step that turns them into usable pots.

DIGGING DEEPER

Reconstructing Cultural Behavior from Garbage

Most of what we find at archaeological sites represents the debris of earlier societies, the material that was discarded, lost, or simply abandoned. Archaeologists have always assumed that the study of refuse can reveal something about past cultural behavior. William L. Rathje, of the University of Arizona, put that assumption to the test when he began looking at garbage generated in modern-day Tucson and at landfills in other urban areas (Fig. 1). By demonstrating the archaeologist's ability to learn about our present culture through the study of modern refuse, he reinforces the claim that the past can be revealed through archaeology.

Over a three-year period, Rathje and his students sampled more than 1,000 households in Tucson and classified more than 70,000 items into some 200 categories of food and other household goods. Referring to census data as a control, the researchers correlated statistics on family size, income, and ethnicity with the representative garbage samples they had collected.

Results from the Tucson study revealed much about the society that produced, used, and finally discarded the materials. For example, evidence from garbage provided substantially different (and, no doubt, more accurate) information concerning alcohol consumption than people admitted to in questionnaire surveys. It also demonstrated that middle-class households account for a higher percentage of wasted food (nearly 10 percent of the food purchased) than either the poor or the wealthy. Since the garbage data have been carefully sampled and quantified, we get an accurate idea of exactly how many usable items are thrown away. Despite the standard image of Americans as "conspicuous consumers," the archaeologists found few usable household items in garbage bags or trash dumps (Fig. 2). Instead, recycling furniture

FIGURE 2
Professor Rathje (right) and his students screen material from the Fresh Kills landfill to search for small artifacts of modern American culture.

and appliances through yard sales and charities seems to be a common practice. Higher-income households do tend to replace items at a somewhat higher rate, thus replenishing the supply of goods entering the system.

This "archaeological" approach to modern garbage clarifies our understanding of contemporary cultural behavior and supports the notion that we can study the past in similar ways. Rathje's work with garbage demonstrates that archaeological methods work especially well in conjunction with historical documentation to reveal new information about more recent periods, up to and including modern times. His studies also serve as a sobering reminder of the environmental consequences of our behavior as consumers and refuse producers.

SOURCES:

"Once and Future Landfills," by William L. Rathje, *National Geographic* 179(5), 1991:116–134.
Rubbish! The Archaeology of Garbage, by William L. Rathje and Cullen Murphy (Tucson: University of Arizona Press, 2001).

FIGURE 1
A crew under the direction of archaeologist William L. Rathje employs a bucket auger to sample deep levels of the Fresh Kills landfill on Staten Island. New York City's solid waste accumulated here at the rate of 14,000 tons per day before the dump reached its capacity and was closed in 2001.

FIGURE 8–12

Archaeologist Richard Vanderhoek taught himself how to make and use spear technology like that found in the earliest Alaskan sites so he could better understand and interpret the lifeways of the first inhabitants of the New World.

FIGURE 8–13

Drawing upon archaeological research and tribal ingenuity, modern descendants of New England's aboriginal people construct a traditional-style round house, or wigwam, at Plimoth Plantation, Massachusetts. Saplings set into the ground, bent and lashed together, provide a framework for the house, which will be lined and covered with water-deflecting reed matting.

EXPERIMENTAL ARCHAEOLOGY

Yet another way to gain a closer understanding of our ancestors is by learning how they made their tools (Fig. 8–12), containers, houses (Fig. 8–13), and other artifacts and features and how they used and discarded them. After all, it's the artifactual traces of prehistoric tools of stone (and, to a lesser degree, of bone) that constitute our primary information about the earliest identified human behavior. As we mentioned earlier, stone is by far the most common residue of prehistoric cultural behavior, and tons of stone tool debris litter archaeological sites worldwide. For example, if you were taking a casual walk along the bottom of Olduvai Gorge in Tanzania, you'd likely be interrupted every few seconds by tripping over prehistoric tools!

But what do these artifacts tell us about our ancestors? Quite a lot. Let's say your excavation reveals a bunch of stone axe heads from the remains of an ancient campsite. If you were to make copies of these axe heads using appropriate technology, **haft** them on wooden shafts in ways that replicate the wear patterns found on the ancient axe heads, and use them for a few hours in a set of experiments (say, cutting down a tree with one axe, clearing brush with another, and so on), you'd end up with a much better understanding of how the ancient axes were made, used, and, very likely, why they tended to break in patterned ways. You would even be able to compare the wear patterns of modern stone axes used for different tasks with observable wear on the archaeological specimens and identify the tasks for which the ancient tools were used. It's precisely this logic that drives **experimental archaeology**, which, like ethnoarchaeology, uses observations of modern behavior as testable ideas about the interpretation of archaeological patterning.

Dating Methods

An essential consideration of archaeology and, more generally, paleoanthropology is to establish the age of artifacts, fossils, features, and sites. Only after placing discoveries firmly in time and space can researchers accurately interpret the relationships of archaeological materials and sites to each other and construct a valid and reliable picture of human evolution. Because of the fundamental importance of dating to every chapter that follows, in this section we provide a basic introduction to the kinds of dating methods and how they work. Table 8–2 summarizes the main characteristics of each method.

haft To equip a tool or implement with a handle or hilt.

experimental archaeology Research that attempts to replicate ancient technologies and construction procedures to test hypotheses about past activities.

TABLE 8–2   Summary of Dating Methods Described in This Chapter

Method	Basis	Limitations	Comments
Relative dating methods establish the relative order of events			
Stratigraphy	Principle of superpositioning of strata	Most robust relative dating method	Geological stratigraphy and archaeological stratigraphy are created by different processes and must be interpreted separately
Biostratigraphy	Estimates of consistent modifications in evolving lineages of animals; presence/absence of species	Requires very well-documented sequences and somewhere must be correlated with chronometric results (e.g., with K/Ar)	Best estimates in East Africa using pigs, monkeys, antelope, and rodents; has been important dating method in South Africa
Cross-dating	Shared similarities of material remains found in an undated context with remains from a context of known age	Weak when used by itself; best applied in conjunction with other dating methods	Widely applied in archaeological research, the logic of cross-dating is similar to that of biostratigraphy
Seriation	Orders artifacts from different sites or contexts into series based on presence/absence or frequencies of shared attributes	There's no way to know which end of a seriated sequence of artifacts is the oldest unless it is determined by stratigraphic or chronometric methods	Gradually being replaced in archaeological research by a quantitative method called correspondence analysis, which achieves the same end
Fluorine analysis	Estimates the relative age of bones from a given site based on fluorine content	Applicable only to bones found in the same location	The key to exposing the Piltdown hoax in the early 1950s
Chronometric methods give absolute measures of age, often scaled in calendar years			
Potassium-argon (K/Ar)	Regular radioactive decay of potassium isotope	Contamination can occur; usually requires corroboration from other independent methods	Can be used only on sediments that have been superheated (usually volcanic deposits)
Argon-argon (^{40}Ar/^{39}Ar)	Works similar to potassium-argon technique	Same as above	Same as above; often used to check the validity and reliability of potassium-argon results
Fission-track dating	Regular fission of uranium atoms, leaving microscopic tracks	Usually derived from volcanic deposits; estimates generally less accurate than for K/Ar	Very important corroboratory method in East Africa
Paleomagnetism	Regular shifts in earth's geomagnetic pole; evidence preserved in magnetically charged sediments	Requires precise excavation techniques; both major and minor reversals occur and can easily confuse interpretation	Important corroboratory method in East and South Africa
Radiocarbon dating	Measures the ^{14}C/^{12}C ratio in samples of organic materials	Applications limited to roughly the past 50,000 years	Most widely used chronometric dating method
Thermoluminescence (TL)	Measures the accumulated radiation dose since the last heating or sunlight exposure of an object	Yields the estimated age of the *last* heating event	Widely used for dating ceramics, hearths, and other artifacts and features that were subjected to extremes of heat
Electron spin resonance (ESR)	Measurement (counting) of accumulated trapped electrons	Age estimates can be biased by tooth enamel uptake of uranium; best applied in conjunction with other dating methods	Widely applied in paleoanthropology to date fossil tooth enamel
Uranium series dating	Radioactive decay of short-lived uranium isotopes	Can yield high-precision age estimates; main limitation is the potential range of datable materials	Used to date limestone formations (e.g., stalagmites) and ancient ostrich eggshells
Dendrochronology	Tree-ring dating	Direct archaeological applications limited to temperate regions for which a master chart exists for tree species that were used by humans in the past	Although very important for archaeological dating in some parts of the world (e.g., the American Southwest), its greatest general application is to calibrate radiocarbon age estimates, which greatly enhances their accuracy and precision

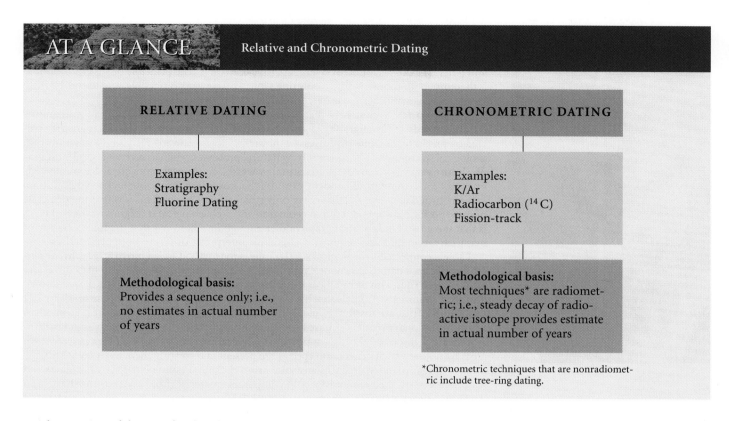

Relative and Chronometric Dating

RELATIVE DATING	CHRONOMETRIC DATING
Examples: Stratigraphy Fluorine Dating	Examples: K/Ar Radiocarbon (^{14}C) Fission-track
Methodological basis: Provides a sequence only; i.e., no estimates in actual number of years	**Methodological basis:** Most techniques* are radiometric; i.e., steady decay of radioactive isotope provides estimate in actual number of years

*Chronometric techniques that are nonradiometric include tree-ring dating.

The question of the age of archaeological and other paleoanthropological materials can be answered in two ways. First, we can say that the hominid that became fossil X lived before or after the hominid that became fossil Y. This is an example of *relative dating*, which establishes the relative order of events but does not scale the amount of time that separates them. Many questions can be answered by knowing only relative ages. Second, we can say that a particular village site is X number of years old. This is an example of *chronometric dating*, which establishes the age of events (and, obviously, their relative order too) according to some fixed time scale—often, as in this example, in calendar years. Chronometric dating is sometimes called *absolute dating* because the result is a measured quantity of time, not a relative order.

Both relative and chronometric dating are used daily in archaeological research. Because like most instruments, every dating method has its strengths and limitations, researchers often employ multiple methods to estimate the age of a given artifact or context. This helps to ensure that their interpretations are based on the most valid and reliable age estimates.

RELATIVE DATING

The oldest relative dating method is **stratigraphy**. A basic understanding of the nature of geological stratigraphy and the **principle of superpositioning** has been critical to the development of the scientific understanding of human evolution for at least the past 150 years. When you stand and look at the rock layers visible in the side of the Grand Canyon, the Rift Valley in East Africa, or even many interstate highway road cuts, there's nothing that cries out to you that the stuff on top must have been put there last, and that, therefore, the stuff on the bottom is older than the top. To make sense of it you must, like James Hutton, Charles Lyell, and other nineteenth-century geologists, understand the processes by which sedimentary strata form and how they change. Once you grasp these concepts, then it's obvious that every stratigraphic exposure is a time-ordered record that if systematically studied can inform you about the past (Fig. 8–14).

Conveniently, the layer upon layer of sedimentary rock and other earth strata that compose much of the earth's near-surface geological record also contains most of the fossil evidence of our earliest ancestors and relatives. And, even now, when so many chronometric

stratigraphy Study of the sequential layering of deposits.

principle of superpositioning In a stratigraphic sequence, the lower layers were deposited before the upper layers. Or, simply put, the stuff on top of a heap was put there last.

William Turnbaugh

FIGURE 8–14

Archaeological stratigraphy of a prehistoric Native American site along the Susquehanna River in Pennsylvania. Spanning 6,000 years of prehistory, the strata bearing numbered tags represent periods during which people occupied the site. The intervening layers are natural flood deposits laid down by river overflows.

stratum   (*pl.*, strata) A single layer of soil or rock; sometimes called a level.

biostratigraphy   A relative dating technique based on regular changes seen in evolving groups of animals as well as presence or absence of particular species.

index fossils   Fossil remains of known age, used to estimate the age of the geological stratum in which they are found. For example, extinct marine arthropods called trilobites can be used as an index fossil of Cambrian and Ordovician geological formations.

cross-dating   Relative dating method that estimates the age of artifacts and features based on their similarities with comparable materials from dated contexts.

dating methods exist, every researcher in the field knows that when he or she finds a fossil piece of an early hominid skull weathering out of an exposure in a geological **stratum**, then it must be more recent than skull fragments found in context in stratigraphic layers below it and older than fossils found in layers superimposed on it. The principle of superpositioning is therefore both robust, because only one sequence of events is possible, and useful, because this sequence establishes the order, or relative dating, of events.

It's appropriate to note here that geological stratigraphy and archaeological stratigraphy (in other words, the stratigraphy of an archaeological site) are not the same, nor are they created by precisely the same processes. As the archaeologist Edward Harris (1989) points out, geological stratigraphy is formed only by natural processes, whereas archaeological stratigraphy is formed by both cultural and natural processes. Geological strata are also typically sedimentary rocks that formed under water and that cover large areas, but archaeological strata are unconsolidated deposits that cover only small areas. The good news is that the principle of superpositioning applies both to geological and archaeological stratigraphy; the bad news is that these two kinds of stratigraphy differ enough in other ways that the interpretation of many early hominid sites requires stratigraphic interpretations from both perspectives.

Closely connected to geological stratigraphy is the method called **biostratigraphy**, or *faunal correlation*, a dating technique employed in the Lower Pleistocene deposits at Olduvai and other African sites. This technique is based on the regular evolutionary changes in well-known groups of mammals. Animals that have been widely used in biostratigraphic analysis in East and South Africa are fossil pigs, elephants, antelopes, rodents, and carnivores. From areas where evolutionary sequences have been dated by chronometric means (such as potassium-argon dating, discussed shortly), approximate ages can be extrapolated to other lesser-known areas by noting which genera and species are present and treating them as **index fossils**.

In a similar manner, archaeologists use **cross-dating** to estimate the age of artifacts and features based on their similarities with comparable materials from contexts that have been dated by other means. The reasoning is simple. Suppose that you'd excavated the remains of an ancient burned hut and found several rusted iron hoes of a distinctive design in one corner of the building. If you were to turn to the archaeological literature for that region and research the evidence for similar hoes, you might find that other excavated sites had yielded hoes of the same shape in contexts dated by chronometric techniques to between A.D. 1450 and 1600. By applying the logic of cross-dating, you could tentatively infer that the hoes—and perhaps more important, the hut in which the hoes were found—cannot be older than A.D. 1450. The weakness of such reasoning is its assumption that close material similarities are a reliable measure of contemporaneity of contexts; although it's often true, this assumption is false enough of the time to warrant caution. Consequently, cross-dating is best applied as one of several independent methods of estimating the age of a given context.

Archaeologists also exploit the tendency for many items of material culture to change in patterned ways over time in another relative dating method called **seriation**, which simply orders artifacts into series based on their similar attributes or the frequency of these attributes. The familiar Stone–Bronze–Iron Age sequence long recognized by prehistorians is a good example of seriation: Sites containing metal tools are generally more recent than those where only stone was used, and since bronze technology is known to have developed before iron making, sites containing bronze but no iron occupy an intermediate chronological position. Likewise, the presence of clay vessels of a specific form in a given site may allow researchers to place that site in a sequence relative to others containing only pots known to be of earlier or later styles. Using this approach, archaeologists working in the southwestern United States determined the correct sequence of ancient Pueblo Indian sites based on the presence or absence of pottery and a comparison of stylistic traits. Later, radiocarbon dating—a chronometric technique—confirmed this sequence. Unless we have some independent means of actually assigning chronometric dates to some or all of the artifacts in the series, we know only that certain types (and, by extension, the sites where they occur) are relatively older or younger than others.

Another method of relative dating is **fluorine analysis**, which can be applied only to bones (Oakley, 1963). Bones in the earth are exposed to the seepage of groundwater that often contains fluorine. The longer a bone lies in the earth, the more fluorine it will incorporate during the fossilization process. This means that bones deposited at the same time in the same location should contain the same amount of fluorine. The use of this technique by Kenneth Oakley of the British Museum in the early 1950s exposed the famous Piltdown (England) hoax by demonstrating that a human skull was considerably older than the jaw (ostensibly also human) found with it (Weiner, 1955). A discrepancy in fluorine content led Oakley and others to more closely examine the bones, and they found that the jaw was not that of a hominid at all, but of a young adult orangutan!

Unfortunately, fluorine is useful only with bones found at the same location. Because the amount of fluorine in groundwater is based on local conditions, it varies from place to place. Also, some groundwater may not contain any fluorine. For these reasons, comparing bones from different localities by fluorine analysis is impossible.

CHRONOMETRIC DATING

It's impossible to calculate the age in calendar years of a site's geological stratum, and the objects in it, by using only relative dating techniques. To estimate absolute measures of age, scientists have developed a variety of chronometric techniques based on the phenomenon of **radiometric decay**. The theory is quite simple: Radioactive isotopes are unstable; over time, these isotopes decay and form an isotopic variation of another element. Since the rate of decay is known, the radioactive material can be used to measure past time in the geological and archaeological records. By measuring the amount of decay in a particular sample, scientists can calculate the number of years it took for the given radioactive isotope to decay to produce the measured level. The result is an age estimate that can be converted to calendar years. As with relative dating methods, chronometric methods have strengths and limitations. Some can be used to date the immense geological age of the earth; others may be limited to artifacts less than 1,000 years old. (For more on these techniques, see Lambert, 1997; Taylor and Aitken, 1997.)

The most important chronometric technique used to date early hominids involves potassium-40 (^{40}K), which has a **half-life** of 1.25 billion years and produces argon-40 (^{40}Ar). Known as the K/Ar or **potassium-argon method**, this procedure has been extensively used by paleoanthropologists in dating materials in the 1- to 5-million-year range, especially in East Africa. In addition, a variant of this technique, the $^{40}Ar/^{39}Ar$ or **argon-argon method**, has recently been used to date a number of hominid localities. The $^{40}Ar/^{39}Ar$ method allows analysis of smaller samples (even single crystals), reduces experimental error, and is more precise than standard K/Ar dating. Consequently, it can be used to date a wide chronological range—indeed, the entire hominid record, even up to modern times. Recent applications have provided excellent dates for several early hominid sites in East Africa (discussed in Chapter 9) as well as somewhat later sites in Java (discussed in Chapter 10). In fact, the technique was recently used to date the famous Mt. Vesuvius eruption of A.D. 79 (which destroyed the city of Pompeii). Remarkably, the midrange date obtained by the $^{40}Ar/^{39}Ar$ method was A.D. 73, just six years from the known date (Renne et al., 1997)! Organic material, such as bone, cannot be measured by these techniques, but the rock matrix in which the bone is found can be. K/Ar was used to provide a minimum date for the deposit containing the *Zinjanthropus* cranium by dating a volcanic layer above the fossil.

Rocks that provide the best samples for K/Ar and $^{40}Ar/^{39}Ar$ are those heated to extremely high temperatures, such as that generated by volcanic activity. When the rock is in a molten state, argon, a gas, is driven off. As the rock cools and solidifies, potassium-40 continues to break down to argon, but now the gas is physically trapped in the cooled rock. To obtain the date of the rock, it is reheated and the escaping gas measured.

When dating relatively recent samples (from the perspective of a half-life of 1.25 billion years for K/Ar, *all* paleoanthropological material is relatively recent), the amount of radiogenic argon (the argon produced by decay of a potassium isotope) is going to be exceedingly small. Experimental errors in measurement can therefore occur as well as the thorny problem of distinguishing the atmospheric argon normally clinging to the outside of the sample from the radiogenic argon. In addition, the initial sample may have been contaminated, or argon leakage may have occurred while it lay buried. Due to these potential sources of error, K/Ar dating must be cross-checked using other independent methods.

Fission-track dating is one of the most important techniques for cross-checking K/Ar determinations. The key to fission-track dating is that uranium-238 (^{238}U) decays regularly by spontaneous fission. By counting the fraction of uranium atoms that have fissioned (shown as microscopic tracks caused by explosive fission of ^{238}U nuclei), we can determine the age of a mineral or natural glass sample (Fleischer and Hart, 1972). One of the earliest

seriation Relative dating method that orders artifacts into a temporal series based on their similar attributes or the frequency of these attributes.

fluorine analysis Relative dating method that measures and compares the amounts of fluorine that bones have absorbed from groundwater during burial.

radiometric decay A measure of the rate at which certain radioactive isotopes disintegrate.

half-life The time period in which one-half the amount of a radioactive isotope is converted chemically (into a daughter product). For example, after 1.25 billion years, half the ^{40}K remains; after 2.5 billion years, one-fourth remains.

potassium-argon (K/Ar) method Dating technique based on accumulation of argon-40 gas as a by-product of the radiometric decay of potassium-40 in volcanic materials; used especially for dating early hominid sites in East Africa.

argon-argon ($^{40}Ar/^{39}Ar$) method Working on a similar basis as the potassium-argon method, this approach uses the ratio of argon-40 to argon-39 for dating igneous and metamorphic rocks; it offers precision and temporal range advantages for dating some early hominid sites.

fission-track dating Dating technique based on the natural radiometric decay (fission) of uranium-238 atoms, which leaves traces in certain geological materials.

applications of this technique was on volcanic pumice from Olduvai, giving a date of 2.30 ± 0.28 mya—in good accord with K/Ar dates.

Another important means of cross-checking dates is called **paleomagnetism**. This technique is based on the constantly shifting nature of the earth's magnetic pole. Of course, the earth's magnetic pole is now oriented in a northerly direction, but it hasn't always been. In fact, the orientation and intensity of the geomagnetic field have undergone numerous documented changes in the last few million years. From our present point of view, we call a northern orientation "normal" and a southern one "reversed." Here are the major epochs (also called chrons) of recent geomagnetic time:

0.7 mya–present	Normal
2.6–0.7 mya	Reversed
3.4–2.6 mya	Normal
?–3.4 mya	Reversed

Paleomagnetic dating is accomplished by carefully taking samples of sediments that contain magnetically charged particles. Since these particles maintain the magnetic orientation they had when they were consolidated into rock (many thousands or millions of years ago), they function as a kind of fossil compass. Then the paleomagnetic sequence is compared against the K/Ar dates to check if they agree. Some complications may arise, for during an epoch, a relatively long period of time can occur when the geomagnetic orientation is the opposite of what is expected. For example, during the reversed epoch from 2.6 to 0.7 mya (the Matuyama epoch), there was an *event* lasting about 210,000 years when orientations were normal (Fig. 8–15). (Because this phenomenon was first conclusively demonstrated at Olduvai, it is appropriately called the *Olduvai event.*) Once these oscillations in the geomagnetic pole are worked out, though, the sequence of paleomagnetic orientations can provide a valuable cross-check for K/Ar and fission-track age determinations.

FIGURE 8–15

Paleomagnetic sequences correlated for some East African sites—Olduvai, East Turkana, and Omo (After Isaac, 1975).

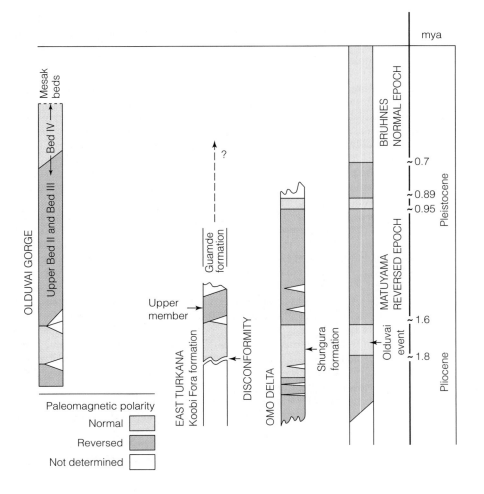

paleomagnetism   Dating method based on the earth's shifting magnetic pole.

The standard chronometric method for dating later prehistory is carbon-14 (^{14}C) dating, also known as **radiocarbon dating**. This technique has been used to date organic material ranging from less than 1,000 years old up to around 50,000 years old. The radiocarbon dating method is based on the following natural processes: cosmic radiation enters the earth's atmosphere as nuclear particles, some of which react with nitrogen to produce small quantities of an unstable isotope of carbon, ^{14}C. This radioactive ^{14}C diffuses through the atmosphere, mixing with ordinary carbon-12 (^{12}C). Combined with oxygen (O_2) in the form of carbon dioxide (CO_2), carbon is taken up by plants during photosynthesis. Herbivorous animals absorb it by feeding on plants, and carnivores absorb it by feeding on herbivores. So, ^{14}C and ^{12}C are found in all living forms at a ratio that reflects the atmospheric proportion. Once an organism dies, it absorbs no more ^{14}C, neither through photosynthesis nor in its diet. Without replacement, the ^{14}C atoms in the tissue continue decaying at a constant rate to nitrogen-14 (^{14}N) and a beta particle, while the ^{12}C remains unchanged. Thus, the ^{14}C/^{12}C ratio in the tissues of a dead plant or animal decreases steadily through time at a rate that can be precisely measured.

This method is limited primarily to dating organic materials that were once alive and part of the carbon cycle, but the constraint can be a somewhat loose one. For example, South African archaeologist Nikolaas van der Merwe (1969) successfully devised a technique to use radiocarbon dating for archaeological samples of iron alloy, a material that was obviously never alive itself but that does contain carbon from living things due to its manufacturing process. This alone is sufficient for it to be dated by the radiocarbon method.

Carbon-14 has a radiometric half-life of 5,730 years, meaning it takes 5,730 years for half the remaining ^{14}C to decay. Let's say that charred wood, the remains of a campfire, is found at an archaeological site and analyzed for its ^{14}C/^{12}C ratio. First, the sample is carefully collected to avoid contamination. It doesn't have to be a large sample, because even tiny quantities of carbon—just a few milligrams—can be analyzed. In the laboratory, radiation detectors measure the residual ^{14}C (Fig. 8–16). Suppose the findings show that only 25 percent of the original ^{14}C remains, as indicated by the ^{14}C/^{12}C ratio. Since we know that it takes 5,730 years for half the original number of ^{14}C atoms to become ^{14}N and another 5,730 years for half the remaining ^{14}C to decay, the sample must be about 11,460 years old. Half of the yet-remaining ^{14}C will disappear over the next 5,730 years (when the charcoal is 17,190 years old), leaving only 12.5 percent of the original amount. This process continues, and as you can estimate, there would be very little ^{14}C left after 40,000 years, when accurate measurement becomes difficult. Radiocarbon dates (and most other chronometric age determinations) are often reported as a mean age estimate and its associated standard error (1 standard deviation, by convention). So the age estimate of the campfire charcoal, as reported by the dating lab, might be expressed as 11,460 ± 200 radiocarbon years ago. Expressed in words, such an estimate states that the true age of the dated specimen will fall between 11,260 and 11,660 radiocarbon years ago about two times out of three, or roughly 68 percent of the time.

Some inorganic artifacts can be directly dated through the use of **thermoluminescence** (TL). Used especially for dating ceramics, but also applied to clay cooking hearths and even burned flint tools and hearthstones on later hominid sites (see p. 294), this method, too, relies on the principle of radiometric decay. Clays used in making pottery invariably contain trace amounts of radioactive elements, such as uranium or thorium. As the potter fires the ware (or a campfire burns on a hearth), the rapid heating releases displaced beta particles trapped within the clay. As the particles escape, they emit a dull glow known as thermoluminescence. After that, radioactive decay resumes within the fired clay or stone, again building up electrons at a steady rate. To determine the age of an archaeological sample, the researcher must heat the sample to 500°C and measure its thermoluminescence; from that, the date can be calculated. TL is routinely used to authenticate fine ceramic vessels prized by collectors and museums, and the technique has exposed many fake Greek and Maya vases displayed in prominent collections.

Like TL, two other techniques also used to date sites from the latter phases of hominid evolution (where neither K/Ar nor radiocarbon is possible), are uranium series dating and electron spin resonance (ESR) dating. Uranium series dating relies on radioactive

radiocarbon dating Method for determining the age of organic archaeological materials by measuring the decay of the radioactive isotope of carbon, ^{14}C; also known as ^{14}C dating.

thermoluminiscence (TL)
(ther-mo-loo-min-ess´-ence) Technique for dating certain archaeological materials, such as ceramics, that release stored energy of radioactive decay as light upon reheating.

FIGURE 8–16
Technician in a radiocarbon dating laboratory.

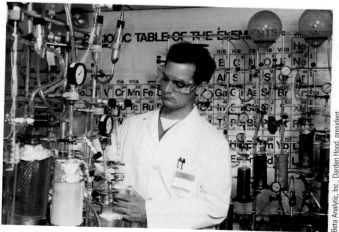

Beta Analytic, Inc., Darden Hood, president

William Turnbaugh

FIGURE 8–17

Doorway in White House Ruin, Canyon de Chelly, Arizona. Wooden beams and supports can be dated by dendrochronology. Archaeologists have removed a core sample from the left end of the lintel (on the left at the top of the door) for dating.

dendrochronology   Archaeological dating method based on the study of yearly growth rings in ancient wood.

decay of short-lived uranium isotopes, and ESR is similar to TL because it's based on measuring trapped electrons. However, while TL is used on heated materials such as clay or stone tools, ESR is used on dental enamel of animals. All three of these dating methods have been used to provide key dating controls for hominid sites discussed in Chapters 11 and 12.

An archaeologically important chronometric dating technique that does not involve radioactive elements is **dendrochronology**, or dating by tree rings. Its use is limited to contexts in temperate latitudes, where trees show pronounced seasonal growth rings and where ancient wood is commonly preserved. So far, the longest dendrochronological sequences have been developed in the arid American Southwest and the bogs of western Europe, especially Ireland and Germany.

Because tree rings represent seasonal growth layers, the amount of new wood added each year depends directly on rainfall and other factors. People have known for centuries, if not millennia, that the growth rings of an individual tree read like its biography. If we know when the tree was cut and then count from the outer rings inward toward the center, we can readily determine the year the tree began growing. The outstanding contribution of A. E. Douglass, an early twentieth-century astronomer, was to systematically exploit this idea; that is, if we can tell how old a tree is by counting its seasonal growth rings, then we should be able to take a tree of known age and match its growth-ring pattern with the patterns compiled from older and older trees of the same species. The limit on how old this "master chart" of growth rings can extend into the past depends entirely on the extent to which old tree trunks are preserved, because they provide data from which the chart can be built.

By cutting or drawing core samples from living trees, recently dead trees, and successively older wood (including archaeological sources such as ancient house posts or beams), archaeologists obtain overlapping life histories of many trees. When compared, these life histories form an extensive record of tree-ring growth through many centuries. Remember, the archaeologist is mostly interested in determining precisely when a tree *stopped* growing and became part of a cultural process such as construction or cooking. As a result, a tree used as a beam in a prehistoric Southwestern structure may be dated to the very year in which it was felled (Fig. 8–17), since the distinctive pattern of its growth should exactly match some segment of the tree-ring record compiled for the region. Archaeologists studying the ceiling beams in the traditional homes still occupied by the Acoma people in northern New Mexico were able to precisely date construction undertaken in the mid-seventeenth century (Robinson, 1990). Wood from the commonly used pinyon pines and the long-lived Douglas fir trees, sequoia redwoods, and bristlecone pines of the American West, as well as preserved oak logs from western European bogs, afford archaeologists continuous regional tree-ring records extending back thousands of years.

But there is yet another dimension to tree-ring dating. By radiocarbon dating wood taken from individual growth rings of known age, researchers have used dendrochronology to fine-tune ^{14}C technology, factoring in past fluctuations in the atmospheric reservoir of ^{14}C over the past 9,800 years (the period for which tree-ring dates are available). They then use this factor to recalibrate the raw dates obtained by standard ^{14}C analyses, thereby enabling archaeologists to convert radiocarbon age estimates into calendar year ages. Recently, by comparing ^{14}C dates obtained from coral reefs with dates on the same samples obtained using a uranium-thorium ($^{234}U/^{230}Th$) dating method, technicians have been able to adjust the radiocarbon calibration curve back to 23,700 years ago (Fiedel, 1999b).

In some areas, including Egypt and Central America, the recorded calendar systems of ancient civilizations have been cross-referenced to our own, resulting in direct dating of some sites and inferential or cross-dating of others shown to be contemporaneous with them by the presence of distinctive artifacts. For example, firmly dated artifacts originating in the Nile valley and traded into the Aegean allow us to assign dates to archaeological contexts of Bronze Age Greece. Obviously, this approach is of little use outside those regions having some connection with literate societies.

Since the advent of radiocarbon and other chronometric dating methods in the latter half of the twentieth century, the age of many archaeological and paleoanthropological finds has been precisely and accurately estimated. Although no other dating technique is as widely used as radiocarbon dating, each is an ingenious method with its own special applications. Still, as with any instrument, researchers must consider the strengths and limitations of each chronometric method, both when applying it in the field and when interpreting the lab results.

Paleoanthropology/Archaeology at Olduvai Gorge

We conclude this methodological introduction to paleoanthropology and archaeology with a case study from East Africa—Olduvai Gorge (Fig. 8–18), a locality that has yielded the finest quality and greatest abundance of anthropological information concerning the behavior of early hominids and an extraordinarily informative sequence of excavated **Lower Paleolithic** sites.

Olduvai Gorge was first brought to the world's attention in the early twentieth century, not by paleoanthropologists or archaeologists, but by Wilhelm Kattwinkel, a German butterfly collector, who found the ravine by falling into it. After Olduvai had so effectively caught his attention, Kattwinkel noticed as he scrambled out that it was an outstanding fossil bed. How's that for serendipity? In 1931, after reading about the paleontological promise of this locality, Louis Leakey visited Olduvai Gorge and realized its significance for studying early humans. From 1935, when she first worked there, until she retired in 1984, Mary Leakey (Fig. 8–19), Louis's wife, directed archaeological excavations at Olduvai. Together, Mary and Louis Leakey made Olduvai Gorge one of the most widely known place names in Africa. It was, you might say, one of the best mom-and-pop shops in twentieth-century paleoanthropology.

Located on the Serengeti Plain of northern Tanzania, Olduvai is a steep-sided valley resembling a miniature version of the Grand Canyon (Fig. 8–20). A massive ravine some 300 feet deep, Olduvai cuts for more than 25 miles across the grassy plateau of East Africa. The present semiarid climate of the Olduvai region is believed to be similar to what it has been for the last 2 million years. The surrounding countryside is a grassland savanna dotted with scrub bushes and acacia trees. Dry though it may be, this environment presently (as well as in the past) supports a vast number of mammals (such as zebra, wildebeest, and gazelle), representing an enormous supply of "meat on the hoof."

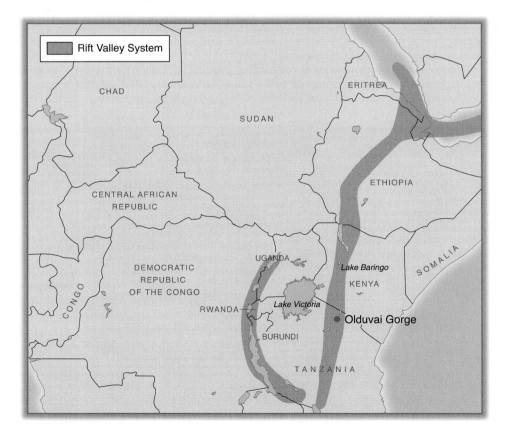

FIGURE 8–18
Olduvai Gorge and the Rift Valley System in East Africa.

Lower Paleolithic A unit of archaeological time that begins >2.5 mya with the earliest identified tools made by hominids and ends around 200,000 B.C.

FIGURE 8–19

Mary Leakey (1913–1996), a major figure in twentieth-century paleoanthropology, devoted most of her life to fieldwork in Olduvai Gorge, where she made many important discoveries, including the *Zinjanthropus* skull (Fig. 8–21) in 1959.

FIGURE 8–20

View of the main gorge at Olduvai. Note the clear sequence of geological beds. The discontinuity to the right is a major fault line.

Geographically, Olduvai is located on the eastern branch of the Great Rift Valley, which stretches for 4,000 miles down the east side of Africa (see Fig. 8–18). The geological processes associated with forming the Rift Valley make Olduvai (and many other East African regions) extremely important because they create an environment that favored the preservation of hominid remains and make it easier for paleoanthropologists and archaeologists to discover these remains. Here are the four most significant results of geological rifting:

1. Faulting, or earth movement, exposes geological strata that are normally hidden deep in the earth.
2. Active volcanic processes cause rapid sedimentation, which often yields excellent preservation of bone and artifacts that normally would be scattered by carnivore activity and erosion forces.
3. Strata formed by rapid sedimentation and, more important, the hominid fossils and archaeological sites preserved within them, can be dated by relative methods such as stratigraphy and cross-dating.
4. Volcanic activity provides a wealth of materials datable by chronometric methods.

As a result, Olduvai offers researchers superb preservation of ancient hominids, reconstructable environments in which these hominids lived, and sites containing the material remains of their existence in datable contexts, all of which are readily accessible. Such advantages cannot be ignored, and Olduvai continues to be the focus of considerable archaeological and other paleoanthropological research.

Over the decades of paleoanthropological fieldwork, partial remains of more than 40 fossilized hominids have been found at Olduvai. Many of these individuals are quite fragmentary, but a few are excellently preserved. Although the center of hominid discoveries has now shifted to other areas of East Africa, it was the initial discovery by Mary Leakey of the *Zinjanthropus* skull at Olduvai in July 1959 that focused the world's attention on this remarkably rich area (see Fig. 8–21 and Digging Deeper). "Zinj" is an excellent example of how financial support can result directly from hominid fossil discoveries. Prior to 1959, the Leakeys had worked sporadically at Olduvai on a financial shoestring, making marvelous paleontological and archaeological discoveries but never attracting the financial assistance they needed for large-scale excavations. However, following the discovery of Zinj, the National Geographic Society funded the Leakeys' research, and within a year, more than twice as much dirt had been excavated than during the previous 30 years!

Olduvai's greatest contribution to paleoanthropological research in the twentieth century was the establishment of an extremely well-documented and correlated *sequence* of archaeological, geological, paleontological, and hominid remains over the last 2 million years. At the

DIGGING DEEPER

Discovery of *Zinjanthropus*, July 17, 1959

That morning I woke with a headache and a slight fever. Reluctantly I agreed to spend the day in camp.

With one of us out of commission, it was even more vital for the other to continue the work, for our precious seven-week season was running out. So Mary departed for the diggings with Sally and Toots [two of their dalmatians] in the Land-Rover, and I settled back to a restless day off.

Some time later—perhaps I dozed off—I heard the Land-Rover coming up fast to camp. I had a momentary vision of Mary stung by one of our hundreds of resident scorpions or bitten by a snake that had slipped past the dogs.

The Land-Rover rattled to a stop, and I heard Mary's voice calling over and over: "I've got him! I've got him! I've got him!"

Still groggy from the headache, I couldn't make her out.

"Got what? Are you hurt?" I asked.

"Him, the man! Our man," Mary said. "The one we've been looking for (for 23 years). Come quick, I've found his teeth!"

Magically, the headache departed. I somehow fumbled into my work clothes while Mary waited.

As we bounced down the trail in the car, she described the dramatic moment of discovery. She had been searching the slope where I had found the first Oldowan tools in 1931, when suddenly her eye caught a piece of bone lodged in a rock slide. Instantly, she recognized it as part of a skull—almost certainly not that of an animal.

Her glance wandered higher, and there in the rock were two immense teeth, side by side. This time there was no question: They were undeniably human. Carefully, she marked the spot with a cairn of stones, rushed to the Land-Rover, and sped back to camp with the news.

The gorge trail ended half a mile from the site, and we left the car at a dead run. Mary led the way to the cairn, and we knelt to examine the treasure.

I saw at once that she was right. The teeth were premolars, and they had belonged to a human. I was sure they were larger than anything similar ever found, nearly twice the width of modern man's.

I turned to look at Mary, and we almost cried with sheer joy, each seized by that terrific emotion that comes rarely in life. After all our hoping and hardship and sacrifice, at last we had reached our goal—we had discovered the world's earliest known human.

SOURCE:

"Finding the World's Earliest Man," by L. S. B. Leakey, *National Geographic*, 118 (September 1960):431. Reprinted with permission of the publisher.

---

very foundation of all paleoanthropological research is a well-established geological context. At Olduvai, the geological and paleogeographical situation is now known in minute detail, having been the object of decades of painstaking fieldwork. It's been a great help that Olduvai is a geologist's delight, containing sediments in some places 350 feet thick, accumulated from lava flows (basalts), tuffs (windblown or waterborne fine deposits from nearby volcanoes), sandstones, claystones, and limestone conglomerates, all neatly stratified (see Fig. 8–20). A hominid site can therefore be accurately dated relative to other sites in the Olduvai Gorge by cross-correlating known stratigraphic marker beds.

Because the vertical cut of the Olduvai Gorge provides a ready cross section of 2 million years of earth history, sites can be excavated by digging "straight in" rather than first having to remove tons of overlying dirt (Fig. 8–22). In fact, sites are usually discovered in Olduvai Gorge by merely walking the stratigraphic exposures and observing what kinds of bones, stones, and so forth are eroding out, just as archaeologists often do when discovering sites in other parts of the world.

At the most general geological level, the stratigraphic sequence at Olduvai is broken down into four major beds (Beds I–IV), each containing hominid and other animal fossils and sites with artifacts and features that were created by early hominid cultural behavior. These contexts are reasonably well dated by both relative and chronometric methods. The fossilized remains of more than 150 species of animals, including fishes, turtles, crocodiles, pigs, giraffes, horses, and many birds, rodents, and antelopes, have been found throughout these Olduvai beds and provide much of the basis for reconstructing the environmental conditions that existed when the early hominid sites were deposited.

Beginning at the earliest identified hominid site (circa 1.85 mya), there is already a well-developed stone tool kit called *Oldowan* (after Olduvai), which includes many small flake tools (Leakey, 1971). The specific nature of the Oldowan tool industry is the object of continuing research, much of it focused on the function or use of these tools. Many of our insights about

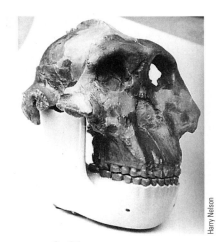

Harry Nelson

FIGURE 8–21

Zinjanthropus skull, discovered by Mary Leakey at Olduvai Gorge in 1959. The skull and reconstructed jaw depicted here are casts at the National Museums of Kenya, Nairobi. As we will see in Chapter 9, this fossil is now included as part of the genus *Australopithecus*.

FIGURE 8–22

FIGURE 8–22
Excavations in progress at Olduvai. This site, more than 1 million years old, was located when a hominid ulna (arm bone) was found eroding out of the side of the gorge.

Robert Jurmain

the tools come from the results of experimental archaeology projects in which researchers try to replicate the wear, breakage, and discard patterns of artifacts found in Olduvai sites.

In the mid-twentieth century, when archaeologists were just beginning to investigate the early hominid sites at Olduvai Gorge, Oldowan was described as primarily a "chopping tool industry" because it was thought that the large, broken cobbles found in these sites were heavy chopper-like implements—also called core tools by many archaeologists. Over the decades, as archaeologists excavated more Oldowan sites and compared the artifacts to similar implements made by researchers who were trying to recreate the same kinds of debris patterns found in Oldowan contexts, it became evident that such interpretations were not supported by the data. For example, Richard Potts (1991, 1993) of the Smithsonian Institution analyzed the frequency of attributes of Oldowan artifacts from Bed I at Olduvai and concluded that the so-called core tools were really not tools after all. He suggests instead that what early hominids were deliberately producing were flake tools, and the various stone nodule forms (discoids, polyhedrons, choppers, etc.) were simply "incidental stopping points in the process of removing flakes from cores" (Potts, 1993, p. 60).

Such a seemingly trivial change as deciding that one class of artifacts is not what we once thought it was can actually have important implications for how we look at early hominids as cultural animals. It certainly had that effect with the Oldowan. If Oldowan tool use emphasized cutting (the flake tools), not chopping (the so-called core tools), then what were they cutting? What kinds of use wear are present on the flake tools, and what kinds of cutting scars are present on the animal bones found in Oldowan sites? And what are the lumps of rock once thought to be core tools? Just broken bits of raw material, or something else entirely? Researchers have paid a fair amount of attention to such questions over the past couple of decades, and their results continue to change and enhance our understanding of how early hominids, as creatures that were still learning to be tool-using animals, exploited the landscapes in which they lived.

The recognition of flake tools as the key components of the Oldowan tool industry forces paleoanthropologists and archaeologists to reassess ideas about early human tool use, but a comparable impact may be felt from recent research on rocks that early humans may not have used at all! The Oldowan industry traditionally includes *manuports*—unmodified rocks of types that are not present in the geology of the immediate vicinity of the Oldowan sites where they are found. In other words, they're just rocks, and the only reasons for not treating them as such are that they are geologically out of place and that they are found in archaeological contexts believed to be the product of hominid behavior.

For decades, archaeologists have believed that the best explanation for the presence of manuports in Oldowan sites was that early hominids picked up the stones where they naturally occurred and carried them to the site where they were much later excavated. If that's true, such an otherwise irrelevant artifact depends for its significance entirely on the assumption that an early human moved it from point A to point B. So long as we can believe the evidence supports only this interpretation, these rocks are artifacts; once we cannot believe this evidence, they're just rocks.

Although they don't seem important, manuports became key elements in some interpretations of the ecological niche of early hominids as tool-using animals on the arid savannas of East Africa. For example, among the several kinds of Oldowan sites excavated in Olduvai Gorge are those originally identified as "multipurpose localities," or campsites, which were interpreted as general-purpose areas where hominids possibly ate, slept, and put the finishing touches on tools. Mary Leakey and the archaeologist Glynn Isaac (1976, pp. 27–28) were strong proponents of this interpretation, which carried with it the necessary implication that early hominids were **home-based foragers**. Lewis Binford's (1983) comparisons of bone assemblages from early hominid contexts at Olduvai and similar assemblages drawn from his ethnoarchaeological research in Alaska on modern human and animal behavior led him to a different conclusion. He argued that much of the accumulated bone refuse on Oldowan sites can be explained as the result of nonhominid (that is, predator) activities and that early hominids were little more than passive scavengers of big game kills. This stance opened the door to a continuing debate about whether early hominids were primarily hunters or scavengers (e.g., Domínguez-Rodrigo, 2002; Domínguez-Rodrigo and Pickering, 2003; O'Connell et al., 2002).

One of the alternative interpretations put forth in the hunter versus scavenger debate came from Richard Potts (1988, 1991), who claimed that these sites served as stockpiles or caches for raw materials, such as manuports, in anticipation of future use. Potts' argument is important, partly because other researchers picked up the idea and incorporated it into their own models of early hominid behavior and partly because the argument implies a particular set of behaviors as part of the way early hominids used landscapes and interacted with technology. De la Torre and Mora (2005) recently reanalyzed the Olduvai manuport collections and concluded that it's unlikely they are raw material caches in Potts' sense, because (1) they share few characteristics with objects that were modified by early hominids, and (2) natural geomorphological processes are sufficient to account for their presence in Olduvai sites. In other words, many, perhaps most, manuports have nothing to do with the behavior of early hominids.

Research will undoubtedly continue on Oldowan chopping tools as well as manuports, but their stories make good examples of how we learn about the human past. As in every scientific endeavor, archaeologists and other paleoanthropologists will never cease to question everything they may currently think is accurate, knowing full well that tomorrow, or the next day, or 10 years from now, someone will conduct the test, excavate the site, or simply ask a different question that opens the door to fresh understanding about how and why we made it from the African savannas to exploring other planets.

Summary

In this chapter, we've seen that in any meaningful study of human origins, the biocultural nature of human evolution requires us to examine both biological and cultural information. The multidisciplinary approach of paleoanthropology, including especially archaeology, brings together varied scientific specializations to reconstruct the anatomy, behavior, and environments of early hominids. Such a task centers on the knowledge, skills, and abilities of the archaeologist, geologist, paleontologist, paleoecologist, and physical anthropologist.

In a sense, our view of the past is something like what we see out of the small passenger window of a jet cruising high above the continent. On the ground far below us, we may see much evidence of human activity—in the net of roadways, plowed fields, towns, and other large constructions. But from our high altitude, we usually can't see the individuals who produced these patterns on the landscape. A cultural landscape without people does not tell the whole story. Still, by observing their handiwork, even at a distance, we can at least gain some insight into their society.

In paleoanthropology in general and archaeology in particular, it's *time* rather than space that separates us from those we study, and one of the main tasks of this chapter is to describe

home-based foragers Hominids that hunt, scavenge, or collect food and raw materials from the general locality where they habitually live and bring these materials back to some central or home-base site to be shared with other members of their co-residing group.

the varied ways in which researchers estimate past time. In this chapter, we've also seen that archaeologists and other paleoanthropologists apply a battery of research methods to discover, excavate, and evaluate sites, features, and artifacts associated with the development and dispersion of hominids to all regions of the globe. Essentially, all of these techniques are attempts to close the distance between ourselves and our predecessors, so that we might better understand their lives.

The chapter closes with a quick look at Olduvai Gorge in East Africa, one of the best-known early hominid localities in the world. By reviewing the history of research at Olduvai, we've seen how scientists apply many of the methods described in the first part of the chapter, the close collaboration of paleoanthropology and archaeology, and—recalling some of the lessons learned in Chapter 1—how gaining scientific understanding of the past is a continuing process of learning, integrating, and reassessing the empirical basis of our knowledge.

Critical Thinking Questions

1. How are early hominid sites found, and what kinds of specialists are involved in excavating and analyzing such sites?
2. Why are cultural remains so important in interpreting human evolution? What do you think is the most important thing you can learn from cultural remains, let's say, from a site that is 2 million years old? What is the most important thing you *can't* learn?
3. Compare relative dating and chronometric dating. Name one or two examples of each, and briefly explain the principles used in determining the dates.
4. What kinds of cultural information may not be represented by artifacts alone? How do archaeologists attempt to compensate for these shortcomings through approaches such as ethnoarchaeology and ethnographic analogy?

Reconstructing the Diets of Earlier Humans

What an animal eats and how it obtains its food are crucial aspects of its adaptation, and this is obviously also true for humans. For this reason physical anthropologists and archaeologists are keenly interested in reconstructing diets of earlier people from evidence found on archaeological sites. The archaeological record is an extraordinarily rich source of subsistence and diet information because it is, after all, nothing if not the garbage heaps of the past! For a long time, archaeologists based most inferences about past human diets on the direct evidence of identifiable bones and plant remains, which were collected by hand or painstakingly recovered from soil samples taken from site contexts. While such information continues to be important, new technologies and methods are fundamentally changing archaeological research on human diets and greatly enhancing our ability to reconstruct important aspects of past human diets. Many of these methods focus on microscopic, even molecular, data; and many even work in archaeological contexts where such things as animal bones, fish scales, nut shells, and seeds are not preserved.

Many new insights have come from a technique analyzing stable isotopes (variable forms of carbon and nitrogen atoms) that are found in bone, teeth, or, as we'll see, in other tissues as well. These isotopes reflect the food consumed, and their relative proportions can tell us interesting things about what earlier hominids were eating. For example, in an innovative study of early hominid remains from South Africa, Matt Sponheimer from the University of Colorado–Boulder and Julia Lee-Thorp from the University of Cape Town found that the teeth contain telltale isotopic signatures relating to diet (Sponheimer and Lee-Thorp, 1999). In particular, the proportions of stable carbon isotopes indicated that these early hominids either ate grass products (such as seeds) or the meat or marrow of animals that, in turn, had eaten grass products. In other words, their research suggests that some early hominids *might* well have derived a considerable portion of their diet from animal protein. Nevertheless, the proportion of early hominid diets contributed by meat or marrow is still controversial.

Among later hominids, the increased dietary importance of meat—and the hunting necessary to obtain it—is less arguable. For example, isotopic analysis of Neandertal bones reveals a diet dominated by animal protein (Bocherens et al., 1999). Even more recent populations are also being intensively investigated using similar isotopic analyses. A 10,000-year-old cemetery in Ukraine shows that Epipaleolithic hunter-gatherers in this part of eastern Europe still depended on freshwater resources for much of their food (Lille et al., 2003). What's more, analyses of stable isotopes also showed that children in the Ukrainian community were weaned fairly late, probably somewhere between 2 and 4 years of age.

The Ukrainian Epipaleolithic information is interesting and quite significant. As we discuss in later chapters, crucial popu-lation consequences of more sedentary habitation patterns are earlier weaning, shorter birth-spacing, and ultimately, increased population growth. For example, at Çatalhöyük, a 9,000-year-old large-scale village in Turkey (see Chapter 15), the weaning age was younger than 2 years (Fig. 1). An earlier weaning age is expected in farming populations like the people who lived at Çatalhöyük, compared to hunter-gatherers such as those who inhabited the Epipaleolithic Ukrainian site. This distinction can be seen even in more recent sites in South Africa, where hunter-gatherers 5,000–7,000 years ago still showed a delayed weaning age of between 2 and 4 years old (Clayton et al., 2006).

Archaeological applications of stable isotope research are not limited just to data gleaned from bones. Even pottery sherds from prehistoric sites are yielding new clues about ancient diets through the isotopic analysis of residues that were absorbed into the walls of cooking pots and storage vessels. For example, geochemists such as M. S. Copley and her colleagues (Copley et al., 2003; Copley et al., 2004) recently discovered the first direct evidence of prehistoric dairying in Britain more than 6,000 years ago through the isotopic analysis of fat residues extracted from hundreds of potsherds excavated in Neolithic, Bronze Age, and Iron Age sites. Their research also demonstrated that it's possible to distinguish dairy fat from carcass fat using isotopic analysis, a fact that may not seem all that interesting at first glance. Recall, however, that the isotopic data are being extracted from pottery sherds and that archaeologists can reconstruct the size, form, and other attributes of the vessels of which these sherds were once a part. Combine this information with the isotopic data, and it's possible to identify general characteristics of foods cooked in different types of vessels. Copley and colleagues (2004) show that in Iron Age Britain, big pots tend to have greater evidence of carcass fats (for example, having been used

Clark Larsen, © Çatalhöyük Archaeological Project

FIGURE 1

A burial of two infants found on a house floor during excavations at Çatalhöyük, Turkey.

Reconstructing the Diets of Earlier Humans CONTINUED

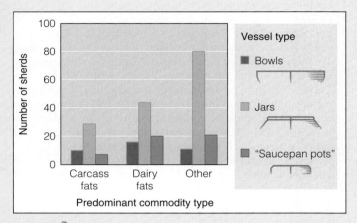

FIGURE 2

The analysis of different kinds of fats preserved in the walls of potsherds from Iron Age sites in Britain enables researchers to identify what kinds of foods were cooked in different types of vessels.

to cook meat), while dairy fats are more evident in smaller pots (Fig. 2).

Further inventive uses of isotopic analysis have been carried out on mummified remains, most notably the famous 5,200-year-old "Iceman" discovered in the Italian Alps (see p. 273 for more details). Here, however, it was his hair, not bone, that was analyzed. The isotopic results and the wear patterns on his teeth support the inference that he ate a mostly vegetarian diet, supplemented by smaller amounts of meat (Macko et al., 1999).

Molecular analysis of the Iceman's stomach and intestine contents also gives a detailed picture of his last meals. A group of Italian biologists, led by Franco Rollo of the Molecular Anthropology/Ancient DNA Laboratory of the University of Camerino, analyzed the Iceman's digestive tract and found that his last meal was red deer meat and possibly cereal grains, and that his preceding meal had been ibex meat, cereal grains, and other plant foods (Rollo et al., 2002). The researchers also were able to determine that his next-to-last meal was apparently consumed at a lower altitude than the 10,500-foot elevation locale where he died. This discovery is supported by other DNA studies of pollen found in his lungs, showing that he passed through a midaltitude coniferous (evergreen trees, such as pine and spruce) forest on the way to his death.

Fresh perspectives on the prehistoric human use of plant foods also come from the study of larger, but still invisible to the naked eye, plant *microfossils* recovered from archaeological sites. Among their several characteristics that make them extremely useful, plant microfossils, principally pollen, starch grains, and phytoliths (see Digging Deeper on pp. 344–345) preserve better than seeds, cereal grains, tubers, and other easily identified plant parts in the archaeological record. Consequently, they are both

relatively abundant and a ready check on other data sources. The study of phytoliths, for example, enabled archaeologists Emma Harvey and Dorian Fuller of the Institute of Archaeology of University College London to reconstruct patterns of prehistoric plant use in north-central India. Phytoliths are microscopic inorganic structures that are both taxonomically distinct and present in most plants. Harvey and Fuller's (2005) study examined phytoliths from a Neolithic site at which few seeds, cereal grains, and other plant remains such as stems and husks were found. From their analysis, they conclude that the site inhabitants grew rice and probably millet. Had they based their study only on plant remains visible to the naked eye, they could not have excluded the possibility that no crops were grown at this site!

SOURCES:

Bocherens, H., D. Billiou, and A. Patou-Mathias, et al. 1999. "Palaeoenvironmental and Palaeodietary Implications of Isotopic Biochemistry of Last Interglacial Neanderthal and Mammal Bones in Scaldina Cave (Belgium)." *Journal of Archaeological Science* 26:599–607.

Clayton, F., J. Sealy, and S. Pfieffer. 2006. "Weaning Age among Foragers at Matjes River Rock Shelter, South Africa from Stable Nitrogen and Carbon Isotope Analyses." *American Journal of Physical Anthropology* 129:311–317.

Copley, M. S., R. Berstan, S. N. Dudd, S. Aillaud, A. J. Mukherjee, V. Straker, S. Payne, and R. P. Evershed. 2004. "Processing of Milk Products in Pottery Vessels through British Prehistory." *Antiquity* 79:895–908.

Copley, M. S., R. Berstan, S. N. Dudd, G. Docherty, A. J. Mukherjee, V. Straker, S. Payne, and R. P. Evershed. 2003. "Direct Chemical Evidence for Widespread Dairying in Prehistoric Britain." *Proceedings of the National Academy of Sciences* 100:1524–1529.

Harvey, Emma L., and Dorian Q. Fuller. 2005. "Investigating Crop Processing Using Phytolith Analysis: The Example of Rice and Millets." *Journal of Archaeological Science* 32:739–752.

Lille, M., M. P. Richards, and K. Jacobs. 2003. "Stable Isotope Analysis of Twenty-One Individuals from the Epipalaeolithic Cemetery of Vasilyevka III, Dnieper Rapids Region, Ukraine." *Journal of Archaeological Science* 30:743–752.

Richards, M. P., J. A. Pearson, T. I. Molleson. 2003. "Palaeodietary Evidence from Neolithic Çatalhöyük, Turkey." *Journal of Archaeological Science* 30:67–76.

Rollo, Franco, Massimo Ubaldi, Lucca Ermini, and Isolina Marota. 2002. "Otzi's Last Meals: DNA Analysis of the Intestinal Content of the Neolithic Glacier Mummy from the Alps." *Proceedings of the National Academy of Sciences* 99:12594–12599.

Sponheimer, Matt, and Julia A. Lee-Thorp. 1999. "Isotopic Evidence for the Diet of an Early Hominid, *Australopithecus africanus*." *Science* 283:368–370.

PALEOANTHROPOLOGY/FOSSIL HOMINIDS

CHAPTER

9

Hominid Origins

FOCUS QUESTION

Who are the oldest members of the human family, and how do these early hominids compare with modern humans? With modern apes? How do they fit within a biological continuum?

Introduction

Our species today dominates our planet, as we use our brains and cultural inventions to invade every corner of the earth. Yet, 5 million years ago, our ancestors were little more than bipedal apes, confined to a few regions in Africa. What were these creatures like? When and how did they begin their evolutionary journey?

In Chapter 8, we discussed the techniques archaeologists use to locate and excavate sites as well as the multidisciplinary approaches used by paleoanthropologists to interpret discoveries. In this chapter, we turn first to the physical evidence of earlier primates and then to the hominid fossils themselves. The earliest fossils identifiable as hominids are all from Africa. During the early Pliocene—by 4 million years ago (mya)—the fossil discoveries become fairly abundant, and paleoanthropologists consider them unambiguously members of the hominid family. Indeed, the fossil evidence becomes more complete over the next several million years, encompassing the Pliocene and the first half of the Pleistocene epochs. Together, this time period is usually referred to as the **Plio-Pleistocene**.

Hominids, of course, evolved from earlier primates (dating from the Eocene to late Miocene), and we'll briefly review this prehominid fossil record to provide a better context for understanding the subsequent evolution of the human family. From new discoveries, the earliest hominids are now thought to date as far back as the end of the Miocene (7–5 mya). This fossil material is extremely exciting, because it extends the evidence of the human family back 2 million years into prehistory. What's more, these discoveries have all been made very recently—just in the last few years. As a result, detailed evaluations are still in process, and conclusions must remain tentative.

One thing is certain, however. The earliest members of the human family were confined to Africa. Only much later do their descendants disperse from the African continent to other areas of the Old World (this "out of Africa" saga will be the topic of the next chapter).

Early Primate Evolution

Long before bipedal hominids first evolved in Africa, more primitive primates had diverged from even more distant mammalian ancestors. The roots of the primate order go back to the beginnings of the placental mammal radiation, about 65 mya. So, the earliest primates were diverging from quite early primitive placental mammals. We've seen (in Chapter 6) that strictly defining living primates using clear-cut derived features isn't easy. The further back we go in the fossil record, the more primitive and, in many cases, the more generalized the fossil primates become. Such a situation makes classifying them all the more difficult.

In fact, we only have scarce traces of the earliest primates. Some anthropologists have suggested that recently discovered bits and pieces from North Africa *may* be those of a very small primitive primate. But until more evidence is found, we'll just have to wait and see.

Fortunately, a vast number of fossil primates from the Eocene (55–34 mya) have been discovered and now total more than 200 recognized species (see Fig. 5–4, p. 103, for a geological chart). Unlike the available Paleocene forms, those from the Eocene display distinctive primate features. Indeed, primatologist Elwyn Simons (1972, p. 124) called them "the first primates of modern aspect." These animals have been found primarily in sites in North America and Europe (which were then still connected). It's important to recall that the landmasses that con-

Go to the following CD-ROMs for interactive activities and exercises on topics covered in this chapter:

- Virtual Laboratories for Physical Anthropology CD-ROM, Third Edition
- Hominid Fossils: An Interactive Atlas CD-ROM, First Edition

Plio-Pleistocene   Pertaining to the Pliocene and first half of the Pleistocene, a time range of 5–1 mya. For this time period, numerous fossil hominids have been found in Africa.

nect continents, as well as the water boundaries that separate them, have obvious impacts on the geographical distribution of such terrestrially bound animals as primates (see p. 105).

Some interesting late Eocene forms have also been found in Asia, which was joined to Europe by the end of the Eocene epoch. Looking at the whole array of Eocene primates, it's certain that they were (1) primates, (2) widely distributed, and (3) mostly extinct by the end of the Eocene. What's less certain is how any of them might be related to the living primates. Some of these forms are probably ancestors of the *prosimians*—the lemurs and lorises.* Others are probably related to the tarsier. New evidence of Eocene *anthropoid* origins has also recently been discovered in several sites from North Africa, the Persian Gulf, and China. These newly discovered fossils demonstrate that anthropoid origins were well established by 35 mya.

Some new discoveries of very small primates from China are particularly interesting. Dating from the early Eocene (55–45 mya), some of these Chinese fossils are among the earliest definite primates yet known. They show three particularly interesting and somewhat surprising features. First, because of certain characteristics such as forward rotation of the eyes, they are thought to be on the evolutionary lineage leading to tarsiers and anthropoids (that is, haplorhines; see p. 124) and thus already distinct from the lemur-loris lineage (that is, strepsirhines). Second, a newly discovered cranium shows small eye sockets, suggesting that early primates may have been diurnal (Ni et al., 2004). (*Note:* Primate biologists had previously assumed that the earliest primates were nocturnal.) And third, these ancient Chinese haplorhine primates were all apparently extremely small, weighing less than 1 ounce (Gebo et al., 2000).

The Oligocene (34–23 mya) has yielded many additional fossil remains of several different species of early anthropoids. Most of these forms are *Old World anthropoids*, all discovered at a single locality in Egypt, the Fayum (Fig. 9–1). In addition, from North and South America, there are a few known bits relating only to the ancestry of New World monkeys. By the early Oligocene, continental drift had separated the New World (the Americas) from the Old World (Africa and Eurasia). Some of the earliest Fayum forms, nevertheless, *may* potentially be close to the ancestry of both Old and New World anthropoids. It's been suggested that late in the Eocene or very early in the Oligocene, the first anthropoids (primitive "monkeys") arose in Africa and later reached South America by "rafting," on drifting chunks of vegetation, over the water separating the two continents. What we call "monkey," then, may have a common Old World origin, but the ancestry of New and Old World varieties remains separate after about 35 mya. The closest evolutionary affinities that humans have after this time are with other Old World anthropoids, that is, with Old World monkeys and apes.

We can see evidence of the possible roots of anthropoid evolution in different forms from the Fayum; one is the genus *Apidium*. Well known at the Fayum, *Apidium* is represented by several dozen jaws or partial dentitions and more than 100 specimens from the limb and trunk skeleton. Because of its primitive dental arrangement, some paleontologists have suggested that *Apidium* may lie near or even before the evolutionary divergence of Old and New World anthropoids. Researchers have found so much fossil material of teeth and limb bones of *Apidium* that they can engage in some informed speculation regarding diet and locomotor behavior. They think that this small, squirrel-sized primate ate mostly fruits and some seeds and was most likely an arboreal quadruped, adept at leaping and springing (Table 9–1).

FIGURE **9–1**

Location of the Fayum, an Oligocene primate site in Egypt.

TABLE **9–1**	Inferred General Paleobiological Aspects of Oligocene Primates			
	Weight Range	**Substratum**	**Locomotion**	**Diet**
Apidium	750–1,600 g (2–3 lb)	Arboreal	Quadruped	Fruit, seeds
Aegyptopithecus	6,700 g (15 lb)	Arboreal	Quadruped	Fruit, some leaves?
Source: After Fleagle, 1999.				

---

*In strict classification terms, especially from a cladistic viewpoint, lemurs and lorises should be referred to as strepsirhines (see p. 124).

FIGURE 9-2
Major events in early primate evolution.

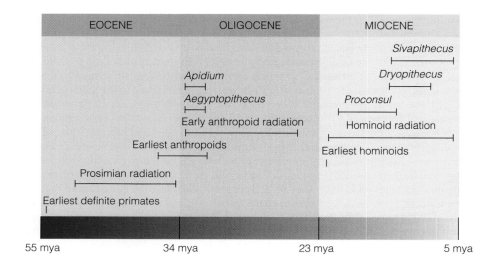

The other significant genus from the Fayum is *Aegyptopithecus*. This genus, also well known, is represented by several well-preserved crania and abundant jaws and teeth. The largest of the Fayum anthropoids, *Aegyptopithecus* is roughly the size of a modern howler monkey (13 to 20 pounds) (Fleagle, 1983), and it's thought to have been a short-limbed, slow-moving arboreal quadruped (see Table 9–1). *Aegyptopithecus* is important because, better than any other known form, it bridges the gap between the Eocene fossils and the succeeding Miocene hominoids.

But by any standard, *Aegyptopithecus* is a very primitive Old World anthropoid. It has a small brain and a long snout and shows no derived features of either Old World monkeys or hominoids. What this means is that it may be close to the ancestry of *both* major groups of living Old World anthropoids. Found in geological beds dating to 35–33 mya, *Aegyptopithecus* further suggests that the crucial evolutionary divergence of hominoids from other Old World anthropoids occurred *after* this time (Fig. 9–2).

Miocene Fossil Hominoids

During the approximately 18 million years of the Miocene (23–5 mya), a great deal of evolutionary activity took place. In Africa, Asia, and Europe, a diverse and highly successful group of hominoids emerged (Fig. 9–3). There certainly were many more forms of hominoids from the Miocene than are found today (now represented by the highly restricted groups of apes and one species of humans). In fact, the Miocene could be called "the golden age of hominoids." Many thousands of fossils have been found from dozens of sites scattered in East Africa, southwest Africa, southwest Asia, into western and southern Europe, and extending into southern Asia and China.

During the Miocene, significant transformations relating to climate and repositioning of landmasses took place. By 23 mya, *major* continental locations were quite similar to where they are today (except that North and South America were separate). The movements of South America and Australia further away from Antarctica had significantly altered ocean currents. Likewise, the continued movement of the South Asian plate into Asia produced the Himalayan Plateau. Both of these paleogeographical modifications affected the climate significantly, and the early Miocene was considerably warmer than the preceding Oligocene had been. What's more, by 16 mya, the Arabian Plate (which had been separate) "docked" with northeastern Africa. As a result, migrations of animals from Africa directly into southwest Asia (and in the other direction as well) became possible. Among the earliest transcontinental migrants (soon after 16 mya) were African hominoids, who colonized Asia and later Europe.

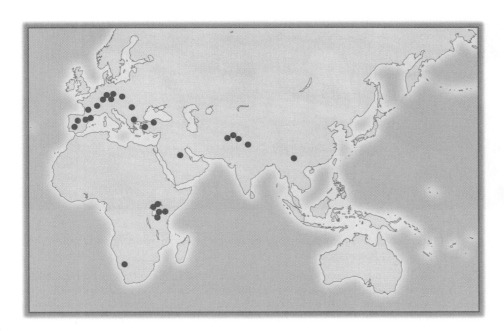

FIGURE 9–3
Miocene hominoid distribution, from fossils thus far discovered.

There's a problem with any attempt to simplify the complex evolutionary situation of Miocene hominoids. For example, for many years paleontologists tended to think of these fossil forms as either "apelike" or "humanlike" and used modern examples as models. But as we've just noted, very few hominoids remain; so we should avoid hastily generalizing from the living forms to the much more diverse fossil forms. If we do, we'll obscure the evolutionary uniqueness of these animals. We should also try not to expect all fossil forms to be directly or even particularly closely related to living species. In fact, we should expect the opposite; that is, most lines vanish without descendants.

Over the last three decades, the Miocene hominoid assemblage has been interpreted and reinterpreted. The more fossils we find, the more complicated the evolutionary picture becomes. The vast array of fossil forms has not yet been completely studied, so conclusions remain tenuous. Given this uncertainty, it's probably best, for now, to group Miocene hominoids geographically:

1. *African forms (23–14 mya)* Known especially from western Kenya, these include quite generalized, and in many ways primitive, hominoids. The best-known genus is *Proconsul* (Fig. 9–4). In addition to the well-known East African early Miocene hominoids, a more recent discovery (in 1992) from Namibia has further extended—by over 1,800 miles—the known range of African Miocene hominoids (Conroy et al., 1992).

2. *European forms (16–11 mya)* Known from widely scattered localities in France, Spain, Italy, Greece, Austria, Germany, and Hungary, most of these forms are quite derived. However, this is a varied and not well-understood group. The best-known forms are placed in the genus Dryopithecus; the Hungarian and Greek fossils are usually assigned to other genera. The Greek fossils are called *Ouranopithecus,* and remains have been dated to sites that are 9–10 million years of age. Evolutionary relationships are uncertain, but several researchers have suggested a link with the African ape/hominid group. New discoveries in 1999 and 2003 from sites in Germany and Turkey have yielded yet another hominoid genus (called *Griphopithecus*) and helped to bolster this hypothesis (Begun, 2003).

3. *Asian forms (16–7 mya)* The largest and most varied group of Miocene hominoids, these Asian fossils are geographically dispersed from Turkey through India and Pakistan and east to the highly prolific site Lufeng, in southern China. Most of these Asian fossil hominoids are *highly* derived. The best-known genus is *Sivapithecus* (known from Turkey and Pakistan). The Lufeng material (now totaling more than

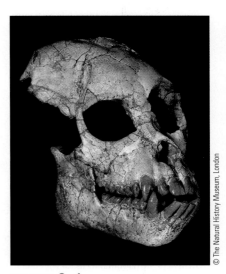

FIGURE 9–4
Proconsul africanus skull (from early Miocene deposits on Rusinga Island, Kenya).

© The Natural History Museum, London

David Pilbeam

FIGURE 9-5

Comparison of *Sivapithecus* cranium (center) with that of modern chimpanzee (left) and orangutan (right). The *Sivapithecus* fossil is specimen GSP 15000, from the Potwar Plateau, Pakistan, c. 8 mya.

1,000 specimens) is usually placed in a separate genus from *Sivapithecus* (and is referred to as *Lufengpithecus*).

There are four general points we know for certain about Miocene hominoid fossils: They are widespread geographically; they are numerous; they span a considerable portion of the Miocene, with *known* remains dated between 23 and 6 mya; and they are currently not well understood. However, we can reasonably draw the following conclusions:

1. These are hominoids—they're more closely related to the ape-human lineage than to Old World monkeys.
2. They are mostly **large-bodied hominoids**; that is, they're more similar to the lineages of orangutans, gorillas, chimpanzees, and humans than they are to smaller-bodied apes (gibbons).
3. Most of the Miocene forms thus far discovered are so derived that they're probably not ancestral to *any* living form.
4. One lineage that appears well established relates to *Sivapithecus* from Turkey and Pakistan. This form shows some highly derived facial features similar to the modern orangutan, suggesting a fairly close evolutionary link (Fig. 9-5).
5. Evidence of *definite* **hominids** from the Miocene has not yet been indisputably confirmed. But exciting new (and not fully studied) finds from Kenya, Ethiopia, and Chad (the latter dating as far back as 7 mya) strongly suggest that hominids diverged sometime in the later Miocene (see pp. 202–204 for further discussion). As we'll soon see, the most fundamental feature of the early hominids is the adaptation to bipedal locomotion.

large-bodied hominoids   Those hominoids including the great apes (orangutans, chimpanzees, gorillas) and hominids, as well as all ancestral forms back to the time of divergence from small-bodied hominoids (i.e., the gibbon lineage).

hominids   Colloquial term for members of the family Hominidae, which includes all bipedal hominoids back to the divergence from African great apes.

The Bipedal Adaptation

As we mentioned in Chapter 6, there's a general tendency in all primates for erect body posture. But of all living primates, efficient bipedalism as the primary form of locomotion is seen *only* in hominids. Functionally, the human mode of locomotion is most clearly shown in our striding gait, during which we alternately place weight on a single, fully extended hind limb. We've developed this specialized form of locomotion to a point where we use energy levels to nearly peak efficiency. That's not the case in nonhuman primates, who move bipedally with their hips and knees bent and maintain balance in a clumsy and inefficient way.

From a survey of our close primate relatives, it's apparent that even while still in the trees, our ancestors were adapted to a fair amount of upper-body erectness. Prosimians, monkeys, and apes all spend considerable time sitting erect while feeding, grooming, or sleeping. Presumably, our early ancestors also displayed similar behavior. We don't know what caused these forms to come to the ground and embark on the unique way of life that would eventually lead to humans; that part is still a mystery. Perhaps natural selection favored some Miocene hominoids coming occasionally to the ground to forage for food on the forest floor and forest fringe. In any case, once they were on the ground and away from the immediate safety offered by trees, bipedal locomotion could become a tremendous advantage.

First of all, bipedal locomotion freed the hands for carrying objects and for making and using tools. Such early cultural developments had an even more positive effect on speeding the development of yet more efficient bipedalism—once again emphasizing the dual role of biocultural evolution. In the bipedal stance, animals also have a wider view of the surrounding countryside, and in open terrain, early spotting of predators (particularly the large cats, such as lions, leopards, and saber-tooths) would be vital. We know that modern ground-living primates, such as savanna baboons and vervets, occasionally adopt this posture to "look around" when they're out in open country. It's also been hypothesized that a bipedal stance would have been more effective in cooling early hominids while out in the open. In bipeds, less of the body is exposed directly to the sun than it is in quadrupeds. More of the biped's body is farther from the ground, keeping it farther from the heat radiating from the ground surface. It may have been most adaptive for early hominids to favor such cooling mechanisms if they had adopted activity patterns exposing them in the open during midday. We can't really test this last supposition, but if hominids had ranged more freely at midday, they would have avoided competition from more nocturnal predators and scavengers (such as large cats and hyenas).

For another thing, bipedal walking is an efficient means of covering long distances, and when large game hunting came into play (several million years after the initial adaptation to ground living), further refinements in the locomotor complex may have been favored. It's hard to say exactly what initiated the process, but all these factors probably played a role in the adaptation of hominids to their special niche through a special form of locomotion.

Our mode of locomotion is indeed extraordinary, involving, as it does, a unique kind of activity in which "the body, step by step, teeters on the edge of catastrophe" (Napier, 1967, p. 56). The challenge is to maintain balance on the "stance" leg while the "swing" leg is off the ground. In fact, during normal walking, both feet are simultaneously on the ground only about 25 percent of the time, and as our speed of locomotion increases, that figure becomes even smaller.

Maintaining a stable center of balance in this complex form of locomotion calls for many drastic structural and functional changes in the basic primate quadrupedal pattern. Functionally, the foot must be altered to act as a stable support instead of a grasping limb. When we walk, we use our foot like a prop, landing on the heel and pushing off on the toes, particularly the big toe. In addition, our legs have become elongated to increase the length of our stride. An efficient bipedal adaptation required further remodeling of the lower limb to allow full extension of the knee and to keep the legs close together during walking, in this way maintaining the center of support directly under the body. Finally, we've undergone significant changes in the pelvis that stabilize our weight as it's transmitted from the upper body to the legs and that help us to further maintain balance.

These major structural changes are essential for bipedalism, and they're all seen in the earliest hominids from East and South Africa. (To date, no early hominid **postcranial** bones have been found in central Africa.) In the pelvis, the ilium (the upper bone of the pelvis, shaped like a blade) is shortened from top to bottom, permitting more stable weight support in the erect position by lowering the center of gravity (see Figs. 9–6 and 9–7). Also, the ilium is bent backward and downward, thus altering the position of the muscles that attach along the bone. Most important, these muscles increase in size and act to stabilize the hip. One of these muscles (the *gluteus maximus*) also becomes important as an extensor, pulling the thigh back during running, jumping, and climbing.

Other structural changes we see even in the earliest definitively hominid postcranial evidence further confirm the morphological pattern seen in the pelvis. For example, the vertebral column, known from beautifully preserved specimens from South and East Africa, shows the same forward curvature as in modern hominids, bringing the center of support forward. In addition, the lower limb is elongated and seems to be proportionately about as long as in

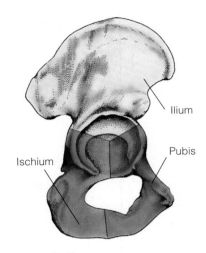

FIGURE 9–6

The human os coxae, composed of three bones (right side shown).

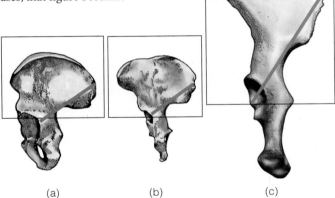

(a)   (b)   (c)

FIGURE 9–7

Ossa coxae. (a) *Homo sapiens.* (b) Early hominid (*Australopithecus*) from South Africa. (c) Great ape. Note especially the length and breadth of the iliac blade (boxed) and the line of weight transmission (shown in red).

postcranial   (*post* meaning "after") In a quadruped, referring to that portion of the body behind the head; in a biped, referring to all parts of the body *beneath* the head (i.e., the neck down).

modern humans. Fossil evidence of a knee fragment from South Africa and pieces from East Africa also shows that this joint could be fully extended, allowing the leg to straighten completely, as when a field-goal kicker follows through.

Fossil evidence of early hominid foot structure has come from two sites in South Africa. Especially important are some recently announced new fossils coming from the same individual as the mostly complete skeleton currently being excavated (see p. 212) (Clarke and Tobias, 1995). These foot specimens, consisting of four articulating elements from the ankle and big toe, indicate that the heel and longitudinal arch were both well adapted for a bipedal gait. However, paleoanthropologists Ron Clarke and Phillip Tobias also suggest that the large toe was *divergent* and thus unlike the hominid pattern. If the large toe really did have this (abducted) anatomical position, it most likely would have aided the foot in grasping. In turn, this grasping ability (as in other primates) would have enabled early hominids to more effectively exploit arboreal habitats. Finally, since anatomical remodeling is always limited by a set of complex functional compromises, a foot that's highly capable of grasping and climbing is

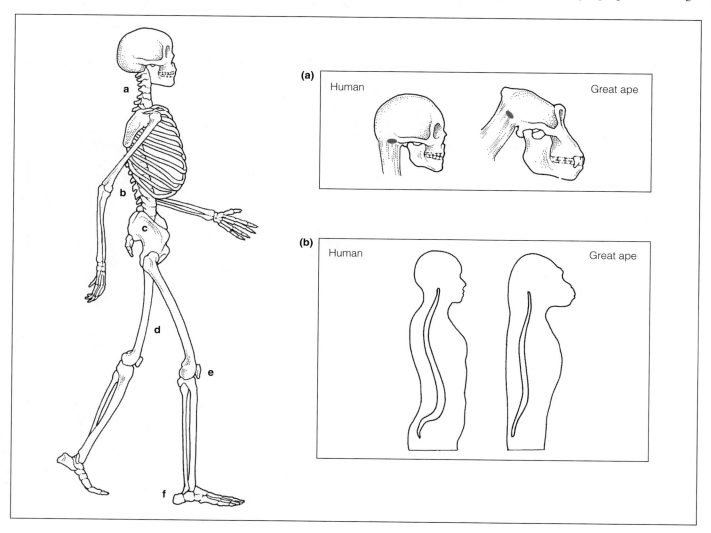

FIGURE 9–8

Major features of hominid bipedalism. During hominid evolution, several major structural features throughout the body have been reorganized (from that seen in other primates) to facilitate efficient bipedal locomotion. These are illustrated here, beginning with the head and progressing to the foot: (a) The *foramen magnum* (shown in red) is repositioned farther underneath the skull, so that the head is more or less balanced on the spine (and thus requires less robust neck muscles to hold the head upright). (b) The spine has two distinctive curves—a backward (thoracic) one and a forward (lumbar) one—that keep the trunk (and weight) centered above the pelvis. (c) The

less capable as a stable platform during bipedal locomotion. This is why some researchers think that early hominids may not have been quite as fully committed to bipedal locomotion as are later hominids.

From two sites in East Africa, where numerous fossilized elements have been recovered, we have even more evidence for evolutionary changes in the foot. As in the remains from South Africa, the East African fossils suggest a well-adapted bipedal gait. The arches are developed, but some differences in the ankle also imply that considerable flexibility was possible (again, perhaps indicating some continued adaptation to climbing). From this evidence, some researchers have recently concluded that many forms of early hominids spent a fair amount of time in the trees. Even so, to this point, *all* the early hominids that have been identified from Africa are thought by most investigators to have been quite well-adapted bipeds (despite the new evidence from South Africa, which will require further study), and most, if not all, early hominids probably displayed both **obligate bipedalism** and **habitual bipedalism**. For a review of the anatomical features associated with bipedal locomotion, see Figure 9–8.

obligate bipedalism Bipedalism as the *only* form of hominid terrestrial locomotion. Since major anatomical changes in the spine, pelvis, and lower limb are required for bipedal locomotion, once hominids adapted it, other forms of locomotion on the ground became impossible.

habitual bipedalism Bipedal locomotion as the form of locomotion shown by hominids most of the time.

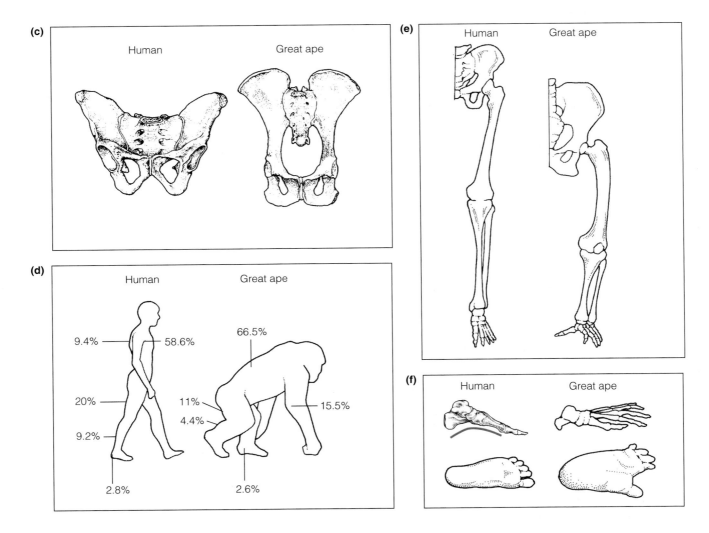

pelvis is shaped more in the form of a basin to support internal organs; moreover, the ossa coxae (specifically, iliac blades) are shorter and broader, thus stabilizing weight transmission. (d) Lower limbs are elongated, as shown by the proportional lengths of various body segments (e.g., in humans the thigh comprises 20 percent of body height, while in gorillas it comprises only 11 percent). (e) The femur is angled inward, keeping the legs more directly under the body; modified knee anatomy also permits full extension of this joint. (f) The big toe is enlarged and brought in line with the other toes; in addition, a distinctive longitudinal arch forms, helping absorb shock and adding propulsive spring.

Early Hominids from Africa

Over the last 80 years, a tremendous number of hominid fossils have been discovered in Africa. The first finds came from South Africa, but by the 1970s, more significant fossils were being found in East Africa (particularly along the Rift Valley in Ethiopia, Kenya, and Tanzania). This shift in the focus and significance of discovery resulted from many factors. The geological circumstances found in East Africa produce a clearer stratigraphic picture and better association of hominids with archaeological artifacts, and equally important, these materials are much more easily datable (using chronometric methods). In addition, fossils are generally easier to find in East Africa, although hominid fossils aren't easy to find anywhere. Erosion from wind, rain, and gravity expose fossils on the ground surface, where they can simply be picked up—assuming, of course, that you know exactly *where* to look. In South Africa, by contrast, the fossils are embedded in rock matrix, making precise archaeological recovery extraordinarily difficult. At any rate, excavations have continued at several South African sites. From this ongoing work, some new and highly productive locales have been explored, and as of this writing, perhaps the most intact early hominid skeleton ever discovered is being excavated at Sterkfontein Cave, just outside Johannesburg.

The saga of new and more intriguing African hominid discoveries is not yet completed—in fact, it hasn't even slowed. Just in 2002, perhaps the most remarkable discovery in the last 75 years was announced. What made this discovery (from Chad) so surprising was (1) its location (in central Africa, *not* in either South or East Africa), (2) its age (estimated at close to 7 mya, making it by far the earliest hominid found anywhere), and (3) its physical appearance (quite unexpected, and unlike anything discovered before; more on this in a minute).

So, if we accept the latest discoveries and provisional dating as accurate, hominid origins go back in Africa approximately 7 million years. Hominids, as far as current evidence indicates, stayed in Africa for the next 5 million years, first emigrating to other Old World locales 2 mya. It appears that for the first 70 percent of hominid history, our family was restricted to Africa.

EARLIEST TRACES: PRE-*AUSTRALOPITHECUS* FINDS

Being designated "the earliest hominid" draws worldwide media coverage, but it's a notoriously fickle title. When this textbook was first published in 1981, the earliest hominid was dated at between 3 and 4 mya. By the seventh edition (1999), based on some Ethiopian fossils, this had been pushed back to 4.4 mya. By 2000 (based on Kenyan material), the date was further extended to close to 6 mya. And in 2002, the startling find from Chad suggested that the current bearer of the "earliest" title is 7 million years old.

With this brief history, we don't intend to force unsuspecting students to memorize exactly what was found when. Our point is to illustrate how rapidly discoveries have taken place; in the last decade alone, the known span of hominid existence has almost doubled!

Central Africa   The most stunning of these new finds is also the oldest. The fossil, a nearly complete cranium, was discovered in 2001 at a site called Toros-Menalla in northern Chad (Brunet et al., 2002). Provisional dating using faunal correlation (biostratigraphy; see p. 180) suggests a date nearly 7 mya (Vignaud et al., 2002). Surprisingly, the very early suggested age of this fossil places it at almost 1 million years earlier than *any* of the other proposed early hominids (and nearly 3 million years earlier than the oldest well-established hominid discoveries).

The fossil's morphology is unusual, with a combination of characteristics unlike that found in other early hominids. The braincase is small, estimated at no larger than a modern chimpanzee's (preliminary estimate is in the range of 320 to 380 cm^3), but it is massively built, with huge browridges in front, a crest on top, and large muscle attachments in the rear (Fig. 9–9). Yet, combined with these apelike features is a smallish, vertical face containing front teeth very unlike an ape's. In fact, the lower face, being more tucked in under the brain vault (and not protruding, as in most other early hominids), is a *derived* feature more commonly expressed in much later hominids, especially members of genus *Homo*. Also, unlike the dentition seen in apes (and some early hominids), the upper canine is reduced and is worn down from the tip rather than being sheared along its side against the first lower premolar.

In recognition of this unique combination of characteristics, the lead researcher, Michael Brunet (of the University of Poitiers, in France), has placed the Toros-Menalla remains into a new genus and species of hominid, *Sahelanthropus tchadensis* (Sahel being the region of the southern Sahara in North Africa).

These new finds from Chad have forced researchers to immediately begin a significant reassessment of early hominid evolution. But two cautions about this process are in order. First, the dating is only approximate, because it's based on biostratigraphic correlation with sites in Kenya (1,500 miles to the east). Even so, the faunal sequences seem to be clearly bracketed by two very well-dated sequences in Kenya. Second, and perhaps more serious, is the hominid status of the Chad fossil. With its facial structure and dentition, it's hard to see how *Sahelanthropus* could be anything but a hominid. However, some researchers (Wolpoff et al., 2002) have questioned the evolutionary interpretation of *Sahelanthropus*, suggesting that this fossil may be that of an ape rather than a hominid. As we noted earlier, the best-defining anatomical characteristics of hominids relate to bipedal locomotion. Unfortunately, no postcranial elements have been recovered from Chad—at least not yet. So, we don't yet know the locomotor behavior of *Sahelanthropus*—and this raises even more fundamental questions: What if further finds show this form isn't bipedal? Should we still consider it a hominid? What, then, are the defining characteristics of our family?

East Africa   Two areas in East Africa, one in the Tugen Hills area near Lake Baringo in central Kenya and the other from the Middle Awash area of northeastern Ethiopia, have also quite recently yielded very early hominid remains. The earliest of these finds, dated provisionally by radiometric methods to about 6 mya, come from four localities in the Tugen Hills. They include mostly dental remains, but also some quite complete lower limb bones that researchers interpret as clearly indicating bipedal locomotion (Pickford and Senut, 2001; Senut et al., 2001; Galik et al., 2004). After a preliminary analysis of the fossils, the primary researchers (Brigitte Senut and Martin Pickford) have suggested placing these early hominids in a separate genus—*Orrorin*.

The last group of fossil hominids thought to date to the late Miocene comes from five localities in the Middle Awash, in the Afar Triangle of Ethiopia. Radiometric dating places the age of these fossils in the very late Miocene, 5.8–5.2 mya. The fossil remains themselves are mostly bits and pieces. Some of the dental remains resemble some later fossils from the Middle Awash (discussed shortly), and Yohannes Hailie-Selassie, the researcher who first found and described these earlier materials, has provisionally assigned them to a new species of the genus *Ardipithecus* (Haile-Selassie et al., 2004) (see At a Glance, p. 204). Some postcranial elements also have been preserved, most informatively a toe bone—a phalanx from the middle of the foot (see Appendix A, Fig. A–8). From clues in this bone, Hailie-Selassie concludes that this primate was a well-adapted biped (once again, the best supporting evidence of hominid status).

From later in the geological record in the Middle Awash region, along the banks of the Awash River, a very large and significant group of fossil hominids has been discovered at the **Aramis** site. Radiometric calibration firmly dates this site at about 4.4 mya.

Fossil remains from Aramis were excavated between 1992 and 1995 and include up to 50 different individuals (Wolpoff, 1999). This crucial and quite large fossil assortment includes several dental specimens as well as an upper arm bone (humerus) and some cranial fragments. Most exciting of all, in 1995, 40 percent of a skeleton was discovered; there are also reports of other partial skeletons from Aramis. But in all cases, the bones are encased in limestone matrix, so it's a long and tedious process to remove the fossils intact from the cement-like material surrounding them. In fact, as of this writing, the Aramis remains (including the skeletons) still haven't been fully described. Even so, details from initial reports strongly suggest that these remains are, in fact, very early hominids.

What makes the Aramis researchers conclude they've found early hominid fossils? First of all, in an Aramis partial cranium, the *foramen magnum* is positioned farther forward in the base of the skull than it is in quadrupeds (Fig. 9–10). Second, features of the humerus are different from those seen in quadrupeds, indicating that in locomotion the Aramis humerus wasn't used to support weight. From these two features, Tim White, of the University of California, Berkeley, and his colleagues conclude that the Aramis individuals were *bipedal*. What's more, their preliminary interpretation of the partial skeleton (while not yet fully cleaned and reported) also suggests obligate bipedalism (Wolpoff, 1999).

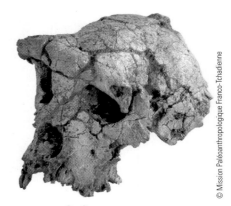

FIGURE **9–9**
A nearly complete cranium of *Sahelanthropus* from Chad, dating to 7 mya.

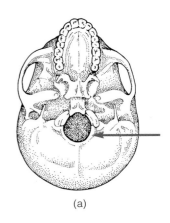

(a)

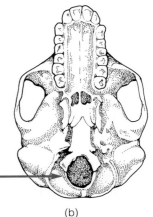

(b)

FIGURE **9–10**
Position of the *foramen magnum* in (a) a human and (b) a chimpanzee. Note the more forward position in the human cranium.

Aramis   (air´-ah-miss)

TABLE 9–2	Estimated Body Weights and Stature in Plio-Pleistocene Hominids				
	Body Weight		**Stature**		
	Male	Female	Male	Female	
A. afarensis	45 kg (99 lb)	29 kg (64 lb)	151 cm (59 in.)	105 cm (41 in.)	
A. africanus	41 kg (90 lb)	30 kg (65 lb)	138 cm (54 in.)	115 cm (45 in.)	
South African "robust"	40 kg (88 lb)	32 kg (70 lb)	132 cm (52 in.)	110 cm (43 in.)	
East African "robust"	49 kg (108 lb)	34 kg (75 lb)	137 cm (54 in.)	124 cm (49 in.)	
H. habilis	52 kg (114 lb)	32 kg (70 lb)	157 cm (62 in.)	125 cm (49 in.)	

Source: After McHenry, 1992.

In any case, these were clearly primitive hominids, displaying an array of characteristics quite distinct from other members of our family. These primitive characteristics include flattening of the cranial base and relatively thin enamel caps on the molar teeth. From measurements of the humerus head, Wolpoff (1999) estimates a body weight of 93 pounds; if this humerus comes from a male individual, this weight estimate is very similar to that hypothesized for other Plio-Pleistocene hominids (see Table 9–2).

Current conclusions—which will be either unambiguously confirmed or falsified as the skeleton is fully cleaned and studied—interpret the Aramis remains as among the earliest hominids yet known. These individuals were very primitive hominids, but they were apparently bipedal, although not necessarily in the same way that later hominids were.

Tim White and colleagues have argued (White et al., 1995) that the fossil hominids from Aramis are so primitive and so different from other early hominids that they should be assigned to a new genus—and, necessarily, a new species as well: *Ardipithecus ramidus.* Most especially, the thin enamel caps on the molars contrast dramatically with those of all other confirmed early hominids, whose enamel is quite thick. These other early hominid forms, all somewhat later than *Ardipithecus,* are placed in the genus **Australopithecus.** White and his associates have further suggested that, as the earliest and most primitive hominid yet discovered, *Ardipithecus* could be the root species for all later hominids. This view doesn't consider the recently discovered Tugen Hills finds, which are provisionally assigned to the new genus *Orrorin.* But it does encompass the earlier remains from the Middle Awash—which, at least for now, are also included within *Ardipithecus.*

Another intriguing aspect of all these late Miocene/early Pliocene locales—that is, Tugen Hills, early Middle Awash sites, and Aramis—relates to the ancient environments associated with the suggested earliest of hominids. Rather than the more open grassland savanna habitats that characterize most of the later hominid sites, the environments at these early locales are more heavily forested. At Aramis and these other ancient sites, we may be seeing the very beginnings of hominid divergence, very soon after the division from the African apes!

Australopithecus   An early hominid genus, known from the Plio-Pleistocene of Africa, characterized by bipedal locomotion, a relatively small brain, and large back teeth.

AT A GLANCE		Key Very Early Fossil Hominid Discoveries (pre-*Australopithecus;* prior to 4 mya)		
	Site	Dates (mya)	Hominids	
East Africa	Middle Awash (Ethiopia; five localities)	5.8–5.2	*Ardipithecus*	
	Aramis (Ethiopia)	4.4	*Ardipithecus ramidus*	
	Tugen Hills	~6.0	*Orrorin tugenensis*	
Central Africa	Toros-Menalla	~7.0	*Sahelanthropus tchadenis*	

Australopithecus from East Africa

The best-known, most widely distributed, and most diverse of the early African hominids are placed in the genus *Australopithecus*. These hominids have an established time range of over 3 million years, stretching back as early as 4.2 mya and not becoming extinct until apparently close to 1 mya—making them the longest-enduring hominid yet documented. These hominids also have been found in all the major geographical areas of Africa that have, to date, produced early hominid finds—namely, South Africa, central Africa (Chad), and East Africa. From all these areas combined, it seems there was considerable complexity in evolutionary diversity; in fact, up to eight species are recognized by many (but not all) authorities (see Appendix B for a complete listing and more discussion of early hominid fossil finds).

Before discussing this pivotal group of early hominids, we'd like to make one more point. Many researchers prefer to divide what we're including in one genus (*Australopithecus*) into two different genera (*Australopithecus* and **Paranthropus**). There is, in fact, a good evolutionary justification for splitting these diverse hominids into two genera. But to keep it simple—and following close to 50 years of general consensus—we'll group all these forms together in the single genus *Australopithecus*. In any case, all these hominids share many features in common:

1. They're all clearly bipedal (although not necessarily identical to *Homo* in this regard).
2. They all have relatively small brains (at least compared to *Homo*).
3. They all have large teeth, particularly the back teeth, with thick to very thick enamel on the molars.

In short, then, all these species of *Australopithecus* are relatively small-brained, big-toothed bipeds.

The earliest finds of *Australopithecus* have been located at two sites in northern Kenya, dating to about 4.2–3.9 mya. Like many of the other finds discussed in this chapter, these hominids were discovered quite recently (mostly in the mid-1990s). Among the fossils of these earliest **australopithecines** thus far discovered, a few postcranial pieces clearly indicate that locomotion was *bipedal*. There are, however, a few primitive features in the dentition, including a large canine and a **sectorial** lower first premolar (Fig. 9–11).

Since these particular fossils have initially been interpreted as more primitive than all the later members of the genus, Meave Leakey and associates have provisionally assigned them to a separate species of *Australopithecus* (see Appendix B). Further study and (with some luck) additional more complete remains will help decide whether such a distinction is warranted.

Slightly later and much more complete remains of *Australopithecus* have come from the sites of Hadar (in Ethiopia) and Laetoli (in Tanzania). Researchers have known much of this material for some time (since the mid-1970s), and they've thoroughly studied the fossils; in fact, some of them are quite famous. For example, the Lucy skeleton was discovered at Hadar in 1974, and the Laetoli footprints were first found in 1978.

Literally thousands of footprints have been found at Laetoli, representing more than 20 different kinds of animals (Pliocene elephants, horses, pigs, giraffes, antelopes, hyenas, and an abundance of hares). Several hominid footprints have also been found, including a trail more than 75 feet long made by at least two—and perhaps three—individuals (Leakey and Hay, 1979) (Fig. 9–12). Such discoveries of well-preserved hominid footprints are extremely important in furthering our understanding of human evolution. For the first time, we can make *definite* statements regarding the locomotor pattern and stature of early hominids. Analyses of these Pliocene footprints suggest a height of about 4 feet 9 inches for the larger individual and 4 feet 1 inch for the smaller individual.

Studies of these impression patterns clearly show that these hominids used bipedal locomotion (Day and Wickens, 1980). As we've emphasized, the development of bipedal locomotion is the most important defining characteristic of

Paranthropus (par´-an-throw´-puss) A genus of hominid characterized by very large back teeth and jaws. Frequently, this genus is combined into *Australopithecus*.

australopithecine (os-tra-loh-pith´-e-seen) The colloquial name for members of the genus *Australopithecus*. The term was first used as a subfamily designation, but it's now most commonly used informally.

sectorial Adapted for cutting or shearing; among primates, refers to the compressed (side-to-side) first lower premolar, which functions as a shearing surface with the upper canine.

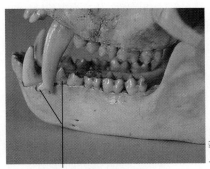

Sectorial lower first premolar

Lynn Kilgore

FIGURE 9–11
Left lateral view of the teeth of a male patas monkey. Note how the large upper canine shears against the elongated surface of the *sectorial* lower first premolar.

FIGURE 9–12
Hominid footprint from Laetoli, Tanzania. Note the deep impression of the heel and the large toe (arrow) in line (adducted) with the other toes.

Peter Jones

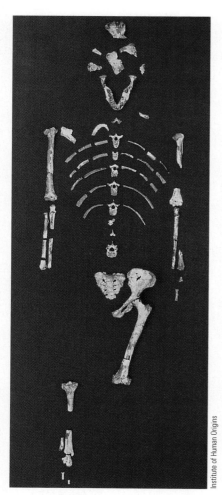

FIGURE 9–13

"Lucy," a partial hominid skeleton, discovered at Hadar in 1974. This individual is assigned to *Australopithecus afarensis*.

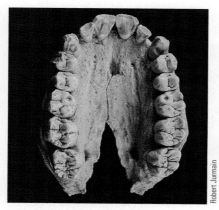

FIGURE 9–14

Jaw of *Australopithecus afarensis*. Maxilla, AL 200-1a, from Hadar, Ethiopia. (Note the parallel tooth rows and large canines.) (photograph of cast)

early hominid evolution. Some researchers, however, have concluded that these early hominids were not bipedal in quite the same way that modern humans are. From detailed comparisons with modern humans, scientists have estimated the Laetoli hominids' stride length, cadence, and speed of walking; they've concluded that these hominids got around in a slow-moving, "strolling" fashion with a rather short stride (Chateris et al., 1981).

One extraordinary discovery at Hadar is the Lucy skeleton (Fig. 9–13), found by Don Johanson eroding out of a hillside. This fossil is scientifically designated as Afar Locality (AL) 288-1, but is usually just called Lucy (after the Beatles song "Lucy in the Sky with Diamonds"). Representing almost 40 percent of a skeleton, this is one of the three most complete individuals from anywhere in the world for the entire period before about 100,000 years ago.*

Because the Laetoli area was covered periodically by ashfalls from nearby volcanic eruptions, accurate dating is possible and has provided dates of 3.7–3.5 mya. Dating from the Hadar region has not proved as straightforward, but more complete dating calibration using a variety of techniques has determined a range of 3.9–3.0 mya for the hominid discoveries from this area.

AUSTRALOPITHECUS AFARENSIS FROM LAETOLI AND HADAR

Several hundred specimens, representing a minimum of 60 individuals (and maybe as many as 100), have been excavated at Laetoli and Hadar. These materials currently represent the largest *well-studied* collection of early hominids, and they're among the most significant of the hominids discussed in this chapter. It's also been suggested that fragmentary specimens from other locales in East Africa are remains of the same species as that found at Laetoli and Hadar. Most scholars refer to this species as *Australopithecus afarensis*.

Without question, *A. afarensis* is more primitive than are any of the other later australopithecine fossils from South or East Africa (we'll discuss them later in this section. By *primitive*, we mean that *A. afarensis* is less evolved in any particular direction than are later-occurring hominid species. That is, *A. afarensis* shares more primitive features with other early homin*oids* and with living great apes than do later hominids, who display more derived characteristics.

For example, the teeth of *A. afarensis* are quite primitive. The canines are often large, pointed teeth. What's more, the lower first premolar is semisectorial—that is, it provides a shearing surface for the upper canine—and the tooth rows are parallel, even converging somewhat toward the back of the mouth (Fig. 9–14).

The cranial portions that are preserved also display several primitive hominoid characteristics, including a crest in the back as well as several primitive features of the cranial base. Cranial capacity estimates for *A. afarensis* show a mixed pattern when compared to later hominids. A provisional estimate for the one partially complete cranium—apparently a large individual—gives a figure of 500 cm³, but another, even more fragmentary cranium is apparently quite a bit smaller and has been estimated at about 375 cm³ (Holloway, 1983). So for some individuals (males?), *A. afarensis* is well within the range of other australopithecine species (see Digging Deeper), but others (females?) may have a significantly smaller cranial capacity. Currently, however, it's not possible to depict cranial size for *A. afarensis* in detail because this part of the skeleton is unfortunately too poorly represented. One thing is clear: *A. afarensis* had a small brain, probably averaging for the whole species not much over 420 cm³.

On the other hand, researchers have found a large assortment of postcranial pieces at Hadar. Initial impressions suggest that in comparison to lower limbs, the upper limbs are longer than in modern humans—a condition that's also seen in primitive hominoids. (But don't take this statement to mean that *A. afarensis* had arms that were longer than its legs.) The wrist, hand, and foot bones also show several differences from modern humans (Susman et al., 1985). From such excellent postcranial evidence, researchers can now confidently estimate height: *A. afarensis* was a short hominid. From her partial skeleton, Lucy is estimated to be only 3½ to 4 feet tall. However, Lucy—as demonstrated by her pelvis—was probably a

---

*The others are a specimen from Sterkfontein, in South Africa (see p. 212), and a *Homo erectus* skeleton from west of Lake Turkana, Kenya (p. 235). Also note that the crushed and embedded skeleton from Aramis may be nearly as complete as Lucy.

DIGGING DEEPER

Cranial Capacity

Cranial capacity is usually reported in cubic centimeters, and it's a measure of brain size, or volume. The brain itself, of course, does not fossilize. But the space once occupied by brain tissue (the inside of the cranial vault) is sometimes preserved, at least when researchers can recover fairly complete crania.

For purposes of comparison, it's easy to obtain cranial capacity estimates for contemporary species (including humans) from analyses of skeletonized specimens in museum collections. Based on studies like these, researchers have made the following estimates of cranial capacities for modern hominoids (Tobias, 1971, 1983):

	Range (cm^3)	Average (cm^3)
Human	1150–1750*	1325
Chimpanzee	285–500	395
Gorilla	340–752	506
Orangutan	276–540	411
Bonobo	—	350

These data for living hominoids can then be compared with those obtained from early hominids:

	Average (cm^3)
Sahelanthropus	~350
Orrorin	Not presently known
Ardipithecus	Not presently known
Australopithecus anamensis	Not presently known
Australopithecus afarensis	438
Later australopithecines	410–530
Early members of genus *Homo*	631

As you can see by comparing these tables, cranial capacity estimates for australopithecines fall within the range of most modern great apes, and gorillas actually average slightly more than *A. afarensis*. It's important to remember, though, that gorillas are very large animals, while australopithecines probably weighed on the order of 100 pounds (see Table 9–2, p. 204). Since brain size is partially correlated with body size, comparing such different-sized animals isn't meaningful. Compared to living chimpanzees, most of which are slightly larger than early hominids, and bonobos (which are somewhat smaller), australopithecines had *proportionately* about 10 percent bigger brains, and so we can say that these early hominids were more *encephalized*.

*The range of cranial capacity for modern humans is very large. In fact, it's even larger than the range shown here, which is the approximate cranial capacity for the *majority* of contemporary *H. sapiens*.

female, and there's evidence of larger individuals at Hadar and Laetoli as well. The most economical hypothesis explaining this variation is that *A. afarensis* was quite sexually dimorphic: The larger individuals are male, and the smaller ones, like Lucy, are female. Estimates of male stature can be approximated from the larger footprints at Laetoli, inferring a height of not quite 5 feet. If we accept this interpretation, *A. afarensis* was a very sexually dimorphic form indeed. In fact, for overall body size, this species may have been as dimorphic as *any* living primate—that is, as much as gorillas, orangutans, or baboons. A controversial recent study has suggested quite a different view, suggesting that *A. afarensis* was not very sexually dimorphic (Reno et al., 2003). However, this interpretation runs counter to most other paleoanthropological interpretations of early hominids and has not been widely supported (Ruff and McHenry, 2004).

In a majority of dental and cranial features, *A. afarensis* is clearly more primitive than later hominids. In fact, from the neck up, *A. afarensis* is so primitive that if we had no evidence from the limbs, we'd be hard-pressed to call it a hominid at all (although the back teeth are large and heavily enameled, unlike pongids, and the position of the foramen magnum indicates an upright posture).

What, then, makes *A. afarensis* a hominid? The answer is revealed by the way it moves about. From the abundant limb bones recovered from Hadar and those beautiful footprints from Laetoli, we know without a doubt that *A. afarensis* walked bipedally when on the ground. (Right now, we don't have nearly such good evidence concerning locomotion for *any* of the earlier hominid finds.) Whether Lucy and her contemporaries still spent considerable time in the trees, and just how efficiently they walked, have become topics of some controversy. Most researchers do agree that *A. afarensis* was an efficient habitual biped while on the ground. These hominids were also clearly *obligate* bipeds, which would have hampered their climbing abilities but would not necessarily have kept them out of the trees altogether. As one physical anthropologist has summed it up: "One could imagine these diminutive early hominids making maximum use of *both* terrestrial and arboreal resources in spite of their commitment to exclusive bipedalism when on the ground. The contention of a mixed arbo-real and terrestrial behavioral repertoire would make adaptive sense of the Hadar australo-pithecine forelimb, hand, and foot morphology without contradicting the evidence of the pelvis" (Wolpoff, 1983b, p. 451).

A CONTEMPORANEOUS NON-AUSTRALOPITHECINE FIND?

The pace of hominid discoveries in East Africa has increased dramatically in recent years, and many of these new discoveries have revealed a different combination of anatomical features from those recognized in remains discovered earlier. Among the most distinctive and intrigu-ing of these newer finds is a cranium unearthed in 1999 on the west side of Lake Turkana in northern Kenya (Leakey et al., 2001).

Dated to 3.5 mya, this fossil hominid is contemporaneous with *Australopithecus afaren-sis*. Yet, it shows a quite distinctive combination of facial and dental features (most especially, a flat lower face and fairly small molar teeth). In these respects, this newly discovered Kenyan hominid is different from *A. afarensis* and, in fact, from *all* known australopithecines. Because the skull has been severely distorted, it's hard to determine cranial capacity. But the best esti-mates suggest that the cranial capacity is similar to that of *Australopithecus* (in the range of 400–500 cm^3).

Because of its unusual anatomical features, Meave Leakey and her colleagues have pro-posed creating an entirely new hominid genus for this cranium. It remains to be seen whether further, more detailed analysis will support this designation. At the very least, this and all the other discoveries from recent years are forcing a major reassessment of the early stages of hominid evolution (see Appendix B listing for *Kenyanthropus*).

LATER EAST AFRICAN AUSTRALOPITHECINE FINDS

At several East African locales, researchers have recovered an assortment of fossil hominids, including many specimens of later members of the genus *Australopithecus*, from geological contexts with dates after 3 mya. Up to 10 different such sites are now known (in the time range of 3–1 mya), but here we'll concentrate on the three most significant ones: East Lake Turkana, West Lake Turkana (both in northern Kenya), and Olduvai Gorge (in northern Tanzania and discussed in Chapter 8).

Koobi Fora (East Lake Turkana)   Under the direction of Richard Leakey—and, for several years, the late Glynn Isaac—research in this vast arid area in northern Kenya has yielded the richest assemblage of Plio-Pleistocene hominids from the African continent. Current archaeological fieldwork is being supervised by Offer Bar Yosef, of Harvard University. The current total exceeds 150, probably representing at least 100 individuals, with most of these fossils dated to about 1.8 mya. Among this fine sample are several complete skulls, many jaws, and an assortment of postcranial bones. Also, except for Olduvai Gorge, sites on the east side of Lake **Turkana** have produced the most information about the behav-ior of early hominids.

West Turkana   Across the lake from the fossil beds just described are other deposits that have yielded very exciting discoveries. In 1984, on the west side of Lake Turkana, work-ers found a nearly complete skeleton of a 1.6-million-year-old *Homo erectus* adolescent (see Chapter 10), and the following year, they found a well-preserved 2.4-million-year-old skull. This find—called "the black skull"—is a most important discovery that has sparked a major reevaluation of Plio-Pleistocene hominid evolution (Fig. 9–15).

Olduvai Gorge   As we pointed out in Chapter 8, Olduvai is probably the most famous early hominid site in the world. This reputation is justly deserved, considering the wealth of paleoanthropological remains found at this remarkable site. While Olduvai was the first locality of an early hominid fossil find in East Africa, now other areas have yielded hundreds of additional finds. Still, among the 40 or so individuals excavated at Olduvai, there are some very significant individual fossils (for example, the "Zinj" cranium; see Fig. 8–21, p. 187).

FIGURE 9–15

The "black skull," WT 17000, discovered at West Lake Turkana in 1985. This specimen is provision-ally assigned to *Australopithecus aethiopicus*. It is called the "black skull" owing to the dark color from the fossilization (mineralization) process.

Turkana   (tur-kahn´-ah)

Olduvai   (ohl´-doo-vye)

Early *Homo*

Along with the australopithecine remains in East Africa, there's another largely contemporaneous hominid that is quite distinctive. In fact, as best documented by fossil discoveries from Olduvai and Koobi Fora, these materials have been assigned to the genus *Homo*—and thus are interpreted as different from all species assigned to *Australopithecus*.

The earliest appearance of genus *Homo* in East Africa may be as ancient as that of the robust australopithecines. (As we've said, the black skull from West Turkana has been dated to approximately 2.4 mya.) Discoveries in the 1990s from central Kenya and from the Hadar area of Ethiopia suggest that early *Homo* was present in East Africa by 2.4–2.3 mya.

Based on fragmentary remains found at Olduvai Gorge in the early 1960s, Louis Leakey first suggested the presence of a Plio-Pleistocene hominid with a significantly larger brain than that seen in *Australopithecus*. Leakey and his colleagues gave a new species designation to these fossil remains, naming them **Homo habilis**.

The *Homo habilis* material at Olduvai ranges in time from 1.85 mya for the earliest to about 1.6 mya for the latest. Because the fossil remains are so fragmented, interpretations have been difficult and much disputed. The most immediately obvious feature that distinguishes the *H. habilis* material from the australopithecines is cranial size. For all the measurable *H. habilis* skulls, the estimated average cranial capacity is 631 cm³, compared to 520 cm³ for all measurable robust australopithecines and 442 cm³ for the less-robust species (McHenry, 1988; see Digging Deeper on p. 207). So, *Homo habilis* shows an increase in cranial size of about 20 percent over the larger of the australopithecines and an even greater increase over some of the smaller-brained forms (from South Africa, discussed shortly). When first describing *H. habilis,* Leakey and his associates also pointed to differences from australopithecines in cranial shape and in tooth proportions (larger front teeth in comparison to back teeth, and narrower premolars).

Naming this fossil material as *Homo habilis* ("handy man") was meaningful from two perspectives. First of all, Leakey argued that members of this group were the early Olduvai toolmakers. Second, and most significantly, by calling this group *Homo,* Leakey was arguing for at least *two separate branches* of hominid evolution in the Plio-Pleistocene. Clearly, only one of those branches could be on the main branch eventually leading to *Homo sapiens*. By labeling this new group *Homo* rather than *Australopithecus,* Leakey was guessing that he had found our ancestors.

Because the initial evidence was so incomplete and fragmentary, most paleoanthropologists were reluctant to accept *H. habilis* as a valid species distinct from *all* australopithecines. Later discoveries, especially those from Lake Turkana, of better-preserved fossils have shed further light on early *Homo* in the Plio-Pleistocene. The most important of this additional material is a nearly complete cranium discovered at Koobi Fora (Fig. 9–16). With a cranial capacity of 775 cm³, this individual is well outside the known range for australopithecines and actually overlaps the lower boundary for *Homo erectus*. In addition, the shape of the skull vault is in many respects unlike that of australopithecines. However, the face is still quite robust (Walker, 1976), and the fragments of tooth crowns that are preserved indicate that this individual's back teeth were quite large.* Dating of the Koobi Fora early *Homo* material places it in the same time period with the Olduvai remains—that is, about 1.8–1.6 mya.

Based on evidence from Olduvai and Koobi Fora, we can reasonably propose that one or more species of early *Homo* were present in East Africa probably by 2.4 mya, developing in parallel with at least one line of australopithecines. These two hominid lines lived contemporaneously for a minimum of 1 million years, after which the australopithecine lineage apparently disappeared forever. At the same time, probably the early *Homo* line was evolving into one or more species of later *Homo*.

---

* In fact, some researchers have suggested that all these "early *Homo*" fossils are better classified as *Australopithecus* (Wood and Collard, 1999a).

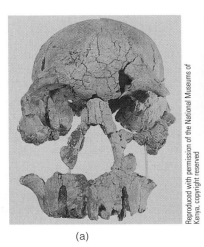

(a)

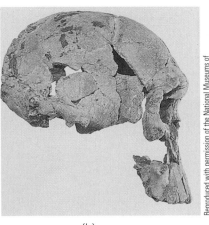

(b)

FIGURE **9–16**

A nearly complete early *Homo* cranium from East Lake Turkana (ER 1470), one of the most important single fossil hominid discoveries from East Africa. (a) frontal view (b) lateral view.

Homo habilis   (hab´-ih-liss) A species of early *Homo*, well known from East Africa but possibly also found in other regions.

South African Hominids

The earliest and most numerous early hominids have been found in Central and especially in East Africa. However, many fossils discovered in South Africa are also important, and lots of them were discovered several years before further finds came to light in other regions of Africa.

EARLIEST DISCOVERIES

Raymond Dart; photo by Alun Hughes

FIGURE 9–17
Raymond Dart, shown working in his laboratory.

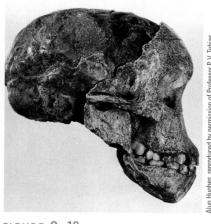

Alun Hughes, reproduced by permission of Professor P. V. Tobias

FIGURE 9–18
The Taung child, discovered in 1924. The endocast is in back, with the fossilized bone mandible and face in front.

endocast   A solid impression of the inside of the skull, often preserving details relating to the size and surface features of the brain.

The discipline of paleoanthropology was in its scientific infancy during the first quarter of the twentieth century. Most scientists believed the human family had likely originated in Asia, where fossil forms of a primitive kind of *Homo* had been found in Indonesia in the 1890s. Europe was also considered a center of hominid evolution, for spectacular discoveries there of premodern humans (including the famous Neandertals) and millions of stone tools had come to light, particularly in the early 1900s.

Not many scholars would have accepted this prediction made by Darwin:

> In each region of the world the living mammals are closely related to the extinct species of the same region. It is, therefore, probable that Africa was formally inhabited by extinct apes closely allied to the gorilla and chimpanzee, and as these two species are now man's nearest allies, it is somewhat more probable that our early progenitors lived on the African continent than elsewhere. (Darwin, *The Descent of Man*, 1871)

Of course, many more decades would pass before the East African discoveries came to light. But in the 1920s, in this atmosphere of preconceived biases, the discoveries of a young Australian-born anatomist jolted the foundations of the scientific community. Raymond Dart (Fig. 9–17) arrived in South Africa in 1923 at the age of 30 to take up a teaching position in Johannesburg. Fresh from his evolution-oriented training in England, Dart had developed a keen interest in human evolution. He was thus well prepared when startling new evidence began showing up at his very doorstep.

The first clue came in 1924, when Dart received a shipment of fossils from the commercial limeworks quarry at Taung (200 miles southwest of Johannesburg). He immediately recognized something that was quite unusual—a natural **endocast** of a higher primate. The endocast fit into another limestone block containing the fossilized front portion of the skull, face, and lower jaw (Fig. 9–18). However, these were difficult to see clearly, for the bone was hardened into a cemented limestone matrix. Dart patiently chiseled away for weeks, later describing the task:

> No diamond cutter ever worked more lovingly or with such care on a precious jewel—nor, I am sure, with such inadequate tools. But on the seventy-third day, December 23, the rock parted. I could view the face from the front, although the right side was still imbedded. . . . What emerged was a baby's face, an infant with a full set of milk teeth and its permanent molars just in the process of erupting. I doubt if there was any parent prouder of his offspring than I was of my Taung baby on that Christmas. (Dart, 1959, p. 10)

Judging by the formation and eruption of the teeth, the Taung child was probably about 3 to 4 years old. Interestingly, the development rate of this and many other Plio-Pleistocene hominids was more like that of apes than of modern *Homo* (Bromage and Dean, 1985). Dart's first impression that this form was a hominoid was confirmed when he could observe the face and teeth more clearly. But as it turned out, it took considerably more effort before Dart could see all of the teeth—he worked for 4 years to separate the upper and lower jaws.

But Dart was convinced long before he had an unimpeded view of the dentition that this discovery was a remarkable one, an early hominoid from South Africa. The question was, what kind of hominoid? Dart realized it was highly unlikely that this specimen could have been a forest ape, for South Africa has had a relatively dry climate for millions of years.

But if it wasn't an ape, then what was it? Features of this small child's skull and teeth held clues that Dart seized on almost immediately. The foramen magnum at the base of the skull (see Fig. 9–10) was farther forward in the Taung skull than in modern great apes, though not as much as in modern humans. From this fact Dart concluded that the head was balanced *above* the spine, indicating erect posture. In addition, the forehead did not recede as much as in apes, the milk canines were exceedingly small, and the newly erupted permanent molars were very large, broad teeth. In all these respects, the Taung fossil was fundamentally more similar to hominids than to apes. There was, however, a disturbing feature that confused many scientists for several years: The brain was quite small. More recent studies have estimated the Taung child's brain size at approximately 405 cm^3 (which translates to a full adult estimate of 440 cm^3), so it's not very large (for a hominid) when compared to the brain of modern great apes (see Digging Deeper, p. 207).

The estimated cranial capacity of the Taung fossil falls within the range of modern great apes, and gorillas actually average about 10 percent greater. But remember that gorillas are very large animals, while the Taung specimen comes from a population in which adults may have averaged less than 80 pounds. Since brain size is partially correlated with body size, it's not reasonable to compare such differently sized animals. A more meaningful comparison would be with the bonobo (*Pan paniscus*), whose body weight is similar. Bonobos have adult cranial capacities averaging 356 cm^3 for males and 329 cm^3 for females, and thus the Taung child—versus a *comparably sized* ape—displays a 25 percent increase in cranial capacity.

Dart saw that despite its relatively small brain size, the Taung fossil was no ape. Realizing the immense importance of his findings, Dart promptly reported them in the British scientific weekly *Nature* on February 7, 1925—a bold venture, since Dart, only 32, was presumptuously proposing an entirely new view of human evolution. Dart named the small-brained Taung child ***Australopithecus africanus*** (southern ape of Africa), and saw it as a kind of halfway "missing link" between modern apes and humans. This concept of a single "missing link" was a fallacious one, but Dart correctly emphasized the hominid-like features of the fossil.

Not all scientists were ready to accept such a theory, and from such an unlikely source. They received Dart's report with indifference, disbelief, and even caustic scorn. Dart realized that to support his claim, he needed more complete remains. The skeptical world would not accept the evidence of one partial immature individual, no matter how suggestive the clues. Most scientists in the 1920s regarded this little Taung child as an interesting but deviant kind of ape. Clearly, more fossil evidence was needed, particularly adult crania (since these would show more diagnostic features). Because he was not an experienced fossil hunter, Dart sought further assistance in the search for more australopithecines.

FURTHER DISCOVERIES OF SOUTH AFRICAN HOMINIDS

Soon after publishing his controversial theories, Dart found a strong ally in Robert Broom (Fig. 9–19). From two of Dart's students, Broom learned of another commercial limeworks site, called **Sterkfontein,** not far from Johannesburg (and now, counting the more recent discoveries, the most prolific of South African sites). There, as at Taung, the quarrying involved blasting out large sections with dynamite, leaving piles of debris that often contained fossilized remains. Broom asked the quarry manager to keep his eyes open for fossils, and when Broom returned to the site in August 1936, the manager asked, "Is this what you are looking for?" Indeed it was, for Broom held in his hand the endocast of an adult australopithecine— exactly what he had set out to find! Looking further over the scattered debris, Broom was able to find most of the rest of the skull of the same individual.

Such remarkable success, just a few months after beginning his search, was not the end of Broom's luck. His magical touch kept working for several more years. In the 1930s and 1940s Broom discovered two other hominid sites, including **Swartkrans,** the second most productive of all South African Plio-Pleistocene locales (it has since yielded hundreds of fossils). Many extremely important discoveries came from these additional sites, discoveries that would eventually swing the tide of intellectual thought to the views that Dart had expressed back in 1925.

Since the 1970s, more systematic exploration of the South African hominid sites has continued, and many important discoveries have been made. The most spectacular new find took place in 1997 at Sterkfontein, where Ron Clarke and his associates from the University of Witwatersrand found the remains of a virtually complete australopithecine skeleton (Fig. 9–20). Most of the remains are still embedded in the surrounding limestone matrix, and it may take years to remove, clean, and reconstruct them (Clarke, 1998).

FIGURE **9–19**
Robert Broom.

Australopithecus africanus
(os-tral-oh-pith´-kus af-ri-kan´-us)

Sterkfontein (sterk´-fon-tane)

Swartkrans (swart´-kranz)

FIGURE 9-20

Australopithecine skeleton embedded in lime-stone matrix at Sterkfontein. Much of the skeleton still is not visible. Clearly seen are the cranium (with articulated mandible) and part of an upper limb.

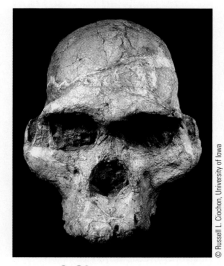

FIGURE 9-21

A gracile australopithecine cranium from Sterkfontein (Sts 5). Discovered in 1947, this specimen is the best-preserved gracile skull yet found in South Africa.

Dating of all the South African Plio-Pleistocene sites has proved most difficult; estimates for the Sterkfontein australopithecine skeleton are between 3.6 and 2.5 mya. Even though the remains haven't been fully excavated, this is still recognized as an unusual and highly significant find. Because such complete individuals are so rare in the hominid fossil record, this discovery has tremendous potential to shed more light on the precise nature of early hominid locomotion. For example, will the rest of the skeleton confirm what foot bones of the same individual have implied regarding arboreal climbing in this bipedal hominid (see p. 201)? Scientists also can obtain much more accurate information from such a completely preserved skeleton, including relative proportion of brain size to body size, better estimates of overall body size, and relative proportions of the limbs.

REVIEW OF HOMINIDS FROM SOUTH AFRICA

The Plio-Pleistocene hominid discoveries from South Africa are most significant. First, they were the initial hominid discoveries in Africa and helped point the way to later finds in East Africa. Second, morphology of the South African hominids shows broad similarities to the forms in East Africa, but with several distinctive features, which argues for separation at least at the species level. Finally, there's a large assemblage of hominid fossils from South Africa, and exciting discoveries are still being made (Fig. 9–21).

Further discoveries are also coming from entirely new sites. In the 1990s, the site known as Drimolen was found in South Africa, very near to Sterkfontein and Swartkrans (Keyser, 2000). So far the findings are only provisionally published, but we do know that close to 80 specimens have been recovered—including the most complete *Australopithecus* cranium found anywhere in Africa.

A truly remarkable collection of early hominids, the remains from South Africa come from nine different caves and, counting all isolated teeth as separate items, they total more than 1,000. The number of individuals is now more than 200. From an evolutionary viewpoint, the most meaningful remains are those of the pelvis, which now include portions of nine (see Fig. 9–7). Remains of the pelvis are so important because, better than any other area of the body, this structure reveals the unique requirements of a bipedal animal (as in modern humans *and* in our hominid forebears).

"Robust" Australopithecines   In addition to similar discoveries in East Africa, many robust australopithecines have been found in South Africa. Like their East African cousins, the South African robust forms also have small cranial capacities. (The only measurable specimen equals 530 cm³; the Drimolen cranium is smaller and might come from a female, but no cranial measurements have as yet been published.) Their faces are large and broad, and their premolars and molars are very large—although not as massive as those in East African forms. Owing to these differences in dental proportions, as well as to important differences in facial architecture (Rak, 1983), most researchers now agree that there is a species-level difference between the later East African robust variety and the South African group.

Despite these differences, all members of the robust lineage appear to be specialized for a diet made up of hard food items, such as seeds and nuts. For many years, paleoanthropologists (e.g., Robinson, 1972) had speculated that robust australopithecines ate a greater proportion of heavy vegetable foods than was the case in diets of other early hominids. Later research that included examining microscopic polishes and scratches on the teeth confirmed this view.

"Gracile" Australopithecines   Another variety of australopithecine—also small-brained, but not as large-toothed as the robust varieties—is known from Africa. While the robust lineage is represented in both East and South Africa, this other (gracile) australopithecine form is known only from the southern part of the continent. First named *A. africanus* by Dart for the single individual at Taung, this australopithecine is also found at other sites, especially Sterkfontein (Figs. 9–21 and 9–22).

Traditionally, scientists thought there was a significant variation in body size between the gracile and robust forms. But as mentioned earlier and shown in Table 9–2, there really isn't much difference in body size among the australopithecines. In fact, most of the differences between the robust and gracile forms are found in the face and dentition.

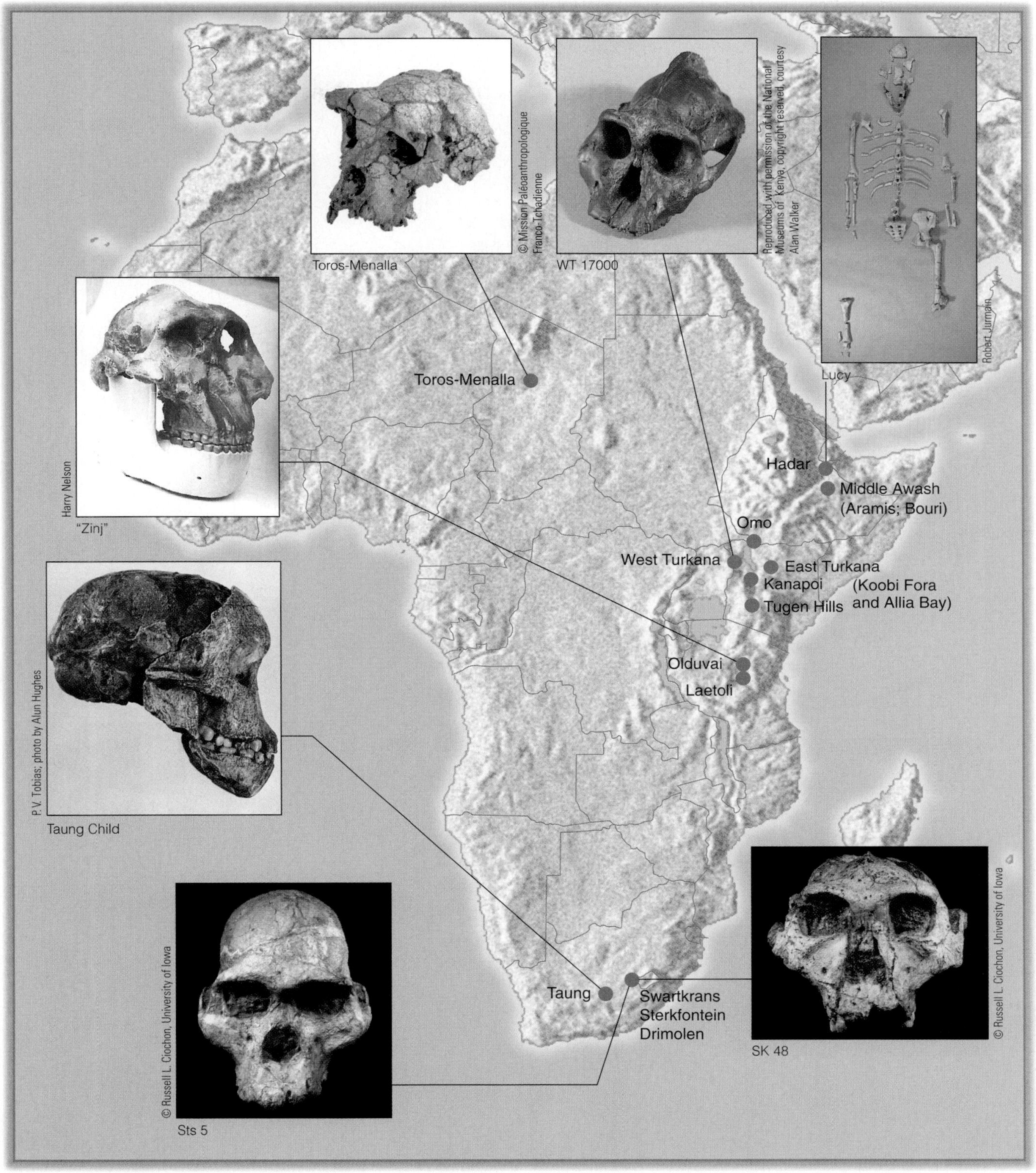

Toros-Menalla
© Mission Paléoanthropologique Franco-Tchadienne
WT 17000
Reproduced with permission of the National Museums of Kenya, copyright reserved, courtesy Alan Walker
Robert Jurmain
Lucy
Harry Nelson
"Zinj"
Toros-Menalla
Hadar
Middle Awash (Aramis; Bouri)
Omo
West Turkana
East Turkana (Koobi Fora and Allia Bay)
Kanapoi
Tugen Hills
Olduvai
Laetoli
P.V. Tobias; photo by Alun Hughes
Taung Child
Taung
Swartkrans
Sterkfontein
Drimolen
© Russell L. Ciochon, University of Iowa
SK 48
© Russell L. Ciochon, University of Iowa
Sts 5

FIGURE 9–22
Early hominid fossil finds and localities (pre-*Australopithecus* and *Australopithecus* discoveries).

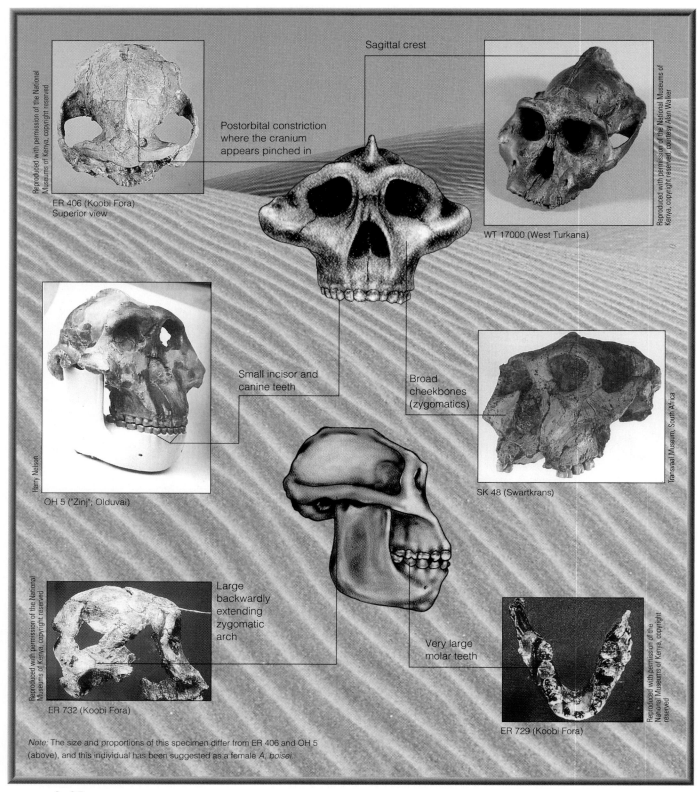

Sagittal crest

Postorbital constriction
where the cranium
appears pinched in

ER 406 (Koobi Fora)
Superior view

WT 17000 (West Turkana)

Small incisor and
canine teeth

Broad
cheekbones
(zygomatics)

OH 5 ("Zinj"; Olduvai)

SK 48 (Swartkrans)

Large
backwardly
extending
zygomatic
arch

Very large
molar teeth

ER 732 (Koobi Fora)

ER 729 (Koobi Fora)

Note: The size and proportions of this specimen differ from ER 406 and OH 5
(above), and this individual has been suggested as a female *A. boisei.*

FIGURE 9–23

Morphology and variation of robust australopithecines. (Note both the typical features and the range of variation
as shown in different specimens.)

The facial structure of the gracile australopithecines is more lightly built and somewhat dish-shaped compared to the more vertical configuration seen in robust specimens. But the most distinctive difference observed between gracile and robust australopithecines is in the dentition. Compared to modern humans, they both have relatively large teeth that are, however, definitely hominid in pattern. In fact, these early forms exhibit an exaggerated back-tooth grinding complex that is more pronounced than that seen in modern humans; so if anything, australopithecines are "hyperhominid" in their dentition. (In other words, they're dentally more *derived* than modern humans are.) In robust forms this trend is emphasized to an extreme degree, showing deep jaws and huge back teeth—particularly the molars—and leaving little room in the front of the mouth for the anterior teeth (incisors and canines). These differences in the relative proportions of the teeth and jaws best define a gracile, as compared to a robust, australopithecine (Fig. 9–23). In fact, most of the differences in skull shape we have discussed can be directly attributed to contrasting jaw function in the two forms. Both the sagittal crest and the broad vertical face of the robust form are related to the muscles and biomechanical requirements of the heavy back-tooth chewing adaptation seen in this animal.

Early *Homo* in South Africa   As in East Africa, early members of the genus *Homo* have also been found in South Africa, apparently living at the same time as australopithecines. At both Sterkfontein and Swartkrans, and perhaps Drimolen as well, fragmentary remains have been recognized as most likely belonging to *Homo*. In fact, Ron Clarke (1985) has shown that the key fossil of early *Homo* from Sterkfontein (Stw 53) is nearly identical to the OH 24 *Homo habilis* cranium from Olduvai.

However, a problem with both OH 24 and Stw 53 is that while most experts agree that the fossils belong to the genus *Homo,* they strongly disagree on whether they should be included in the species *habilis*. In the following sections, we'll discuss the relationships of the Plio-Pleistocene fossil hominids to one another and the difficulties of placing them in a particular genus and species. A time line for the Plio-Pleistocene hominids discussed in the text is shown in Figure 9–24.

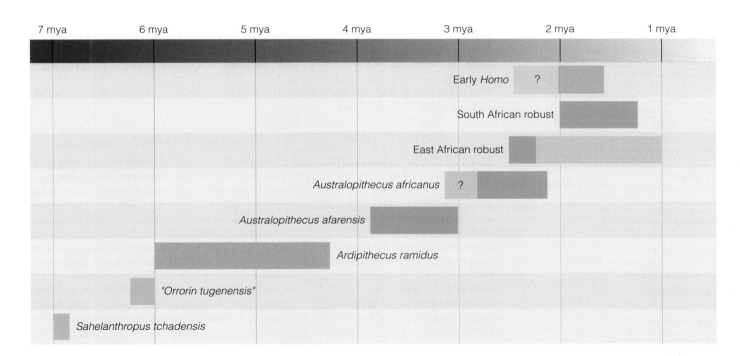

FIGURE 9–24

Time line of early hominids. Note that most dates are approximations. Question marks indicate those estimates that are most tentative.

Interpretations: What Does It All Mean?

By now you may have concluded that anthropologists are pretty much obsessed with finding small scraps buried in the ground and then assigning them confusing numbers and taxonomic labels that are impossible to remember. But it's important to realize that collecting all the basic fossil data we can find is the very foundation of human evolutionary research. Without fossils, our speculations would be completely hollow. Several large, ongoing paleoanthropological projects are now devoted to collecting additional data in attempting to answer some of the more perplexing questions about our evolutionary history.

The numbering of specimens, which may at times seem somewhat confusing, is an attempt to keep the designations neutral and to make the references to each individual fossil as clear as possible. The formal naming of finds as *Australopithecus*, *Homo habilis*, or *Homo erectus* should come much later, since it involves a lengthy series of complex interpretations. Assigning generic and specific names to fossil finds is more than just a convenience; when we attach a particular label, such as *A. africanus*, to a particular fossil, we should be fully aware of the biological implications of such an interpretation.

From the time that fossil sites are first located to the eventual interpretation of hominid evolutionary events, several steps are necessary. Ideally, they should follow a logical order, for if interpretations are made too hastily, they confuse important issues for many years. Here's a reasonable sequence:

1. Selecting and surveying sites
2. Excavating sites and recovering fossil hominids
3. Designating individual finds with specimen numbers for clear reference
4. Cleaning, preparing, studying, and describing fossils
5. Comparing with other fossil material—in chronological framework if possible
6. Comparing fossil variation with known ranges of variation in closely related groups of living primates and analyzing ancestral and derived characteristics
7. Assigning taxonomic names to fossil material

The task of interpretation is still not complete, for what we really want to know in the long run is what happened to the populations represented by the fossil remains. Indeed, in looking at the fossil hominid record, we're looking for our ancestors. In the process of eventually determining those populations that are our most likely antecedents, we may conclude that some hominids are on evolutionary side branches. If this conclusion is accurate, those hominids necessarily must have become extinct. It's both interesting and relevant to us as hominids to try to find out what influenced some earlier members of our family to continue evolving while others died out.

CONTINUING UNCERTAINTIES—TAXONOMIC ISSUES

As we've already mentioned, paleoanthropologists are concerned with making biological interpretations of variation found in the hominid fossil record. Most especially, researchers try to assign extinct forms to particular genera and species. We saw that for the diverse array of Miocene hominoids, the evolutionary picture is exceptionally complex. As new finds accumulate, there's continued uncertainty even about family assignment, to say nothing of genus and species!

For the very end of the Miocene and for the Plio-Pleistocene, the situation is much clearer. First, there's a larger fossil sample from a more restricted geographical area (South Africa, central Africa, and East Africa) and from a more concentrated time period (spanning about 6 million years, from 7 to 1 mya). Second, the specimens are more complete (for example, Lucy), and so we have good evidence for most parts of the body. For these reasons, there's considerable consensus on several basic aspects of evolutionary development during the Plio-Pleistocene. For materials prior to 4 mya, not all scholars are as yet convinced of clear hominid status. But for fossils dating later than 4 mya, researchers agree unanimously that these forms are hominids (members of the family Hominidae). And as support for this point, all these forms are seen as habitual, well-adapted bipeds, at least partly committed to a terrestrial niche. What's more, researchers generally agree as to genus-level assignments for most of the forms, although *Sahelanthropus*, *Orrorin*, and *Ardipithecus* have all been so recently named that they haven't been fully evaluated and accepted. (There's also some disagreement about how to group the robust australopithecines, as well as on the status of early *Homo.*)

As for species-level designations, there's very little consensus. In fact, as new fossils are discovered, the picture seems to get muddier. Once again, we're faced with a complex evolutionary process. In trying to deal with it, we impose varying degrees of simplicity. In so doing, we hope that the evolutionary processes will become clearer—not just for introductory students, but for professional paleoanthropologists and textbook authors too. Nevertheless, evolution is not a simple process, and disputes and disagreements are bound to arise, especially in making such fine-tuned interpretations as species-level designations.

We may find it's impossible to work out clear patterns of relationships among the early hominids. Despite our best attempts, the number and complexity of hominid groups (more technically called *taxa*), which seem to increase monthly, may frustrate all attempts at simplification.

One especially puzzling obstacle is sorting out the various combinations of anatomical characteristics, which we find especially complex in the earliest suggested members of the hominid family. For example, *Sahelanthropus* has a very primitive-looking braincase (especially in the back) combined with a fairly advanced hominid-looking face and canine teeth. Similarly, *Orrorin* combines what some claim are very chimpanzee-looking teeth with a highly efficient bipedal gait. Lastly, *Ardipithecus* combines some aspects of primitive-looking teeth with other components of a suggested bipedal gait. In addition, from preliminary conclusions by some researchers familiar with the *Ardipithecus* finds, its style of locomotion is thought to have been quite different from that seen in any other hominid—suggesting it might have been a very derived hominid and therefore unlikely to be the ancestor of later forms.

Fueled by all these admittedly confusing combinations of characteristics is some researchers' suspicion (e.g., Bernard Wood, 2002) that roughly similar characteristics (like some form of bipedality or reduction of the canine teeth) could have evolved more than once—that is, separately in different lineages of hominids (or possibly even in other hominoids closely related to hominids). This evolutionary process results from what we've called *homoplasy* (see p. 98). If, indeed, this inherently messy evolutionary factor was widespread among our late Miocene and Pliocene relatives, it may be almost impossible to determine which forms are related to others and which ones are more closely related to us. Worse yet, it may prove extremely tricky even to identify some of these forms as hominids at all.

PUTTING IT ALL TOGETHER

Despite all the difficulties, paleoanthropologists still want to understand the broad patterns of early hominid evolution. The interpretation of our paleontological past in terms of which fossils are related to other fossils, and how they might be related to modern humans, is usually shown in the form of a diagram, called a **phylogeny**. Such a diagram is a family tree of fossil evolution. (Note that strict practitioners of cladistics prefer to use cladograms; see p. 98). This kind of interpretation is the eventual goal of evolutionary studies, but it's the final goal, only after adequate data are available to understand what's going on.

Another, more basic way to handle these data is to divide the fossil material into subsets. This avoids (for the moment) what are still problematic phylogenetic relationships. This means, for the Plio-Pleistocene hominid material from Africa, that we can divide the data into three broad groupings:

Set I. Pre-*Australopithecus*/basal hominids (7.0–4.4 mya) The earliest (and most primitive) collection of remains that have been classified as hominids are those from Toros-Menalla, the Tugen Hills, and the Middle Awash, the latter area also including the site of Aramis. For now, these fossils have been assigned to three separate (and newly proposed) genera—*Sahelanthropus, Orrorin,* and *Ardipithecus*—so each of them is provisionally interpreted as being generically distinct from all the other early hominid forms (listed in sets II and III). Analysis at this point indicates that at least for the later Aramis fossils, these forms were likely bipedal, but with a primitive dentition. Brain size of *A. ramidus* is not yet known, but was almost certainly quite small.

phylogeny A schematic representation showing ancestor-descendant relationships, usually in a chronological framework.

Set II. *Australopithecus*

Subset A. Early primitive forms (4.2–3.0 mya) This grouping comprises one well-known species, *A. afarensis*, especially well-documented at Laetoli and Hadar. Slightly earlier, closely related forms (possibly representing a distinct second species) come from two other sites and are provisionally called *Australopithecus anamensis*. Best known from analysis of the *A. afarensis* material, the hominids in this set are characterized by a small brain, large teeth (front and back), and a bipedal gait (probably still allowing for considerable climbing).

Subset B. Later, more derived *Australopithecus* (2.5–1.4 mya; possibly as early as 3.5 mya) This group is composed of numerous species. (Most experts recognize at least three; some subdivide this material into five or more species.) Remains have come from several sites in both South and East Africa. All of these forms have very large back teeth and, compared to *A. afarensis*, do not show much brain enlargement (encephalization).

Set III. Early *Homo* (2.4–1.8 mya) The best-known specimens are from East Africa (East Turkana and Olduvai), but early remains of *Homo* have also been found in South Africa (Swartkrans and possibly Sterkfontein and Drimolen). This group is composed of possibly just one, but probably more than one, species. Early *Homo* is characterized (compared to *Australopithecus*) by greater encephalization, altered cranial shape, and smaller (especially molars) and narrower (especially premolars) teeth (see Appendix B for more details).

Although we've now accumulated a great amount of hominid fossil evidence, so much of the material has been discovered so recently that it's too soon to make any firm judgments concerning the route of human evolution. However, paleoanthropologists certainly aren't deterred from making their best guesses, and diverse hypotheses have abounded in recent years. The vast majority of the hundreds of recently discovered fossils from Africa are still in the descriptive and early analytical stages. At this time, constructing the phylogenies of human evolution can be compared to building a house with only a partial blueprint. We aren't even sure how many rooms there are! Until we've adequately studied the existing fossil evidence, to say nothing about possible new finds, we must view speculative hypotheses with a critical eye.

Adaptive Patterns of Early African Hominids

As you're aware by now, there are several different African hominid genera and certainly lots of species. This, in itself, is interesting. Speciation was occurring quite frequently among the various lineages of early hominids, more frequently, in fact, than among later hominids. What explains this pattern?

Evidence has been accumulating at a furious pace in the last decade, but it's still far from complete. We know that we'll never have anything approaching a complete record of early hominid evolution—so significant gaps will remain. After all, we can discover hominids only in those special environmental contexts where fossilization was likely. All the other potential habitats they might have exploited are now invisible to us.

Even so, patterns are emerging from the fascinating data we do have. First, it appears that early hominid species (pre-*Australopithecus*, australopithecines, and early *Homo*) all had restricted ranges, so it's likely that each hominid species exploited a relatively small area and could easily have become separated from other populations of its own species. Consequently, genetic drift (and to some extent, natural selection as well) could have led to rapid genetic divergence and eventual speciation.

Second, most of these species appear to be at least partially tied to arboreal habitats, although researchers disagree on this point regarding early *Homo* (see Wood and Collard, 1999b; Foley 2002). Besides, robust australopithecines were probably somewhat less arboreal than *Ardipithecus* or other forms of *Australopithecus*. These highly megadont hominids apparently concentrated on a diet of coarse, fibrous plant foods, such as roots. Exploiting such resources may have routinely taken these hominids farther away from the trees than would be the case for their dentally more gracile—and possibly more omnivorous—cousins.

Third, except for some early *Homo* individuals, there's very little in the way of an evolutionary trend of increased body size or of markedly greater encephalization. Beginning with *Sahelanthropus*, brain size was no more than that in chimpanzees—although when controlling for body size, this earliest of all known hominids may have had a proportionately larger brain than any living ape. Close to 6 million years later—that is, at the time of the last surviving australopithecine species—relative brain size increased by no more than 10 to 15 percent. It may be that, tied to this relative stasis in brain capacity, there's no absolute association of any of these hominids with patterned stone tool manufacture.

Although conclusions are becoming increasingly controversial, for the moment it seems that early *Homo* is a partial exception, showing both increased encephalization and numerous occurrences of likely association with stone tools—though at many of the sites, researchers *also* found australopithecine fossils.

Lastly, all of these early African hominids show an accelerated developmental pattern, similar to that seen in African apes and quite different from the *delayed* developmental pattern characteristic of *Homo sapiens*—and our immediate precursors. What's more, this apelike development is also seen in some early *Homo* individuals (Wood and Collard, 1999a). Rates of development can be accurately reconstructed by examining dental growth markers (Bromage and Dean, 1985), and these data perhaps provide a crucial window into understanding this early stage of hominid evolution.

These African hominid predecessors were rather small, able bipeds, but still closely tied to arboreal and climbing niches. They had fairly small brains and, compared to later *Homo*, matured rapidly. It would take a major evolutionary jump to push one of their descendants in a more human direction. For the next chapter in this more human saga, read on.

Summary

The earliest evidence of the evolutionary radiation of the primates dates to the Eocene, approximately 50 mya. These early primates are quite prosimian-like, but during the Oligocene, there was a broad adaptive radiation of early anthropoids. Throughout the Miocene, a wide array of hominoids evolved in the Old World. Most of these are large-bodied forms—that is, they're closely related to great apes and hominids. Although most of these hominoids went extinct by the late Miocene, it's likely that some of the fossils discovered are fairly closely related to ancestors of the great apes and early hominids. Newly discovered fossils now allow us to trace (at least provisionally) the beginnings of the hominid family to late Miocene locales in central and eastern Africa.

Questions about relationships are particularly nagging in regard to all the earliest suggested hominids (the pre-*Australopithecus* fossils, dated prior to 4 mya). In fact, at this point, with all this material so recently discovered and seemingly displaying highly complex patterns of hominid evolution, it's unwise to make anything but the most general of hypotheses.

The picture after 4 mya is somewhat clearer. It appears, for the moment, that we can still view *Australopithecus afarensis* as a good potential common ancestor of most—if not all—later hominids. The relationships among the later, more derived australopithecines aren't as clear, and it's not certain which of the earlier Pliocene fossils is most closely related to *Homo*. As a further study aid, Table 9–3 presents the early hominid materials we consider the most significant. For those keen to pursue a more detailed evaluation of the early hominids, see Appendix B.

Science is a journey of discovery, of seeking to find as many documented facts as possible. Science is also a search for clarity. The last few years of paleoanthropological research have immensely enriched our record of facts. The search for clarity continues. No doubt, more discoveries are on the horizon. We certainly live in interesting times.

Epoch	Site	Dates (mya)	Taxonomic Designation	Comments
TABLE 9–3			Chronological Summary of Most Significant Hominid Fossils Discussed in This Chapter	
Plio-Pleistocene	East Turkana (Koobi Fora) and Olduvai	1.8–1.0	Derived *Australopithecus* and early *Homo*	Highly derived *Australopithecus* and first relatively complete fossils of early *Homo*
	Taung and Sterkfontein	3.3–2.0?	*Australopithecus africanus*	Best-known early hominid from South Africa; many well-preserved fossils
	Hadar and Laetoli	3.7–3.0	*Australopithecus afarensis*	Earliest well-documented group of early hominids; potentially ancestral to later *Australopithecus* and early *Homo*
	Aramis	4.4	*Ardipithecus ramidus*	Earliest large sample of hominid fossils; not yet well described; likely shows very unusual mosaic of characteristics (some highly derived)
Miocene	Toros-Menalla	~7.0	*Sahelanthropus*	Earliest proposed hominid fossils; unusual mosaic of characteristics

Critical Thinking Questions

1. In what ways are the remains of *Sahelanthropus* and *Ardipithecus* primitive? How do we know that these forms are hominids? How sure are we?

2. Assume that you're in the laboratory, analyzing the "Lucy" *A. afarensis* skeleton. You also have complete skeletons from a chimpanzee and a modern human. (a) Which parts of the Lucy skeleton are more similar to the chimpanzee? Which are more similar to the human? (b) Which parts of the Lucy skeleton are *most informative*?

3. Discuss the first thing you would do if you found an early hominid fossil and were responsible for its formal description and publication. What would you include in your publication?

4. Discuss two current disputes regarding taxonomic issues concerning early hominids. Try to give support for alternative positions.

5. What is a phylogeny? Construct one for early hominids (7–1 mya). Make sure you can describe what conclusions your scheme makes. Also, try to defend it.

CHAPTER 10

The Earliest Dispersal of the Genus *Homo:* *Homo erectus* and Contemporaries

FOCUS QUESTION

Who were the first members of the human family to disperse out of Africa, and what were they like (behaviorally and anatomically)?

Introduction

Go to the following CD-ROMs for interactive activities and exercises on topics covered in this chapter:

- Hominid Fossils: An Interactive Atlas CD-ROM, First Edition

- Virtual Laboratories for Physical Anthropology CD-ROM, Third Edition

Sometime, close to 2 million years ago, something decisive took place in human evolution. As this chapter's title suggests, for the first time, hominids expanded widely out of Africa into other areas of the Old World.

All the early hominid fossils have been found *only* in Africa, suggesting that hominids may have been restricted to this continent for perhaps 5 million years. The later, more widely dispersed hominids were quite different both anatomically and behaviorally from their African ancestors. They were much larger, were more committed to a completely terrestrial habitat, used more elaborate stone tools, and may have eaten meat.

There's some variation among the different geographical groups of these highly successful hominids, and anthropologists are still debating how to classify them. Discoveries continue as well. In particular, new finds from Europe are forcing a major reevaluation of exactly which hominids were the first to leave Africa (Fig. 10–1).

In any case, after 2 million years ago (mya), there's less diversity in these hominids than we can see in their pre-*Australopithecus* and *Australopithecus* predecessors. So, there's universal agreement that the hominids found outside of Africa are all members of genus *Homo*. Taxonomic debates thus focus solely on how many species are represented. The species for which we have the most evidence is called *Homo erectus*. What's more, this is the one group that almost all paleoanthropologists distinguish. For these reasons, in this chapter we'll concentrate our discussion on *Homo erectus*. We will, however, also discuss alternative interpretations that call for splitting the fossil sample into more species.

A New Kind of Hominid

Discoveries of the fossils we now refer to as *H. erectus* began in the nineteenth century. Later in this chapter, we'll discuss in some detail the historical background of these earliest discoveries in Java and the somewhat later discoveries in China. From this work, as well as presumably related finds in Europe and North Africa, scientists suggested a variety of taxonomic names. The most significant of these earlier terms were *Pithecanthropus* (for fossils from Java) and *Sinanthropus* (for those from northern China).

It's important to realize that in the early years of paleoanthropology, taxonomic *splitting* (which this terminology reflects) was quite common. More systematic biological thinking came to the fore only after World War II and with the incorporation of the Modern Synthesis into paleontology (see p. 57). Most of the fossils that were given these varied names are now placed in the species *Homo erectus*—or at least they've all been lumped into one genus (*Homo*).

In the last few decades, discoveries from East Africa of firmly dated finds have established the clear presence of *Homo erectus* by 1.8 mya. Some researchers see several anatomical differences between these African representatives of an *erectus*-like hominid and their Asian cousins (hominids that almost everybody* refers to as *Homo erectus*). Thus, they place the African fossils into a separate species, one they call *Homo ergaster* (Andrews, 1984; Wood, 1991).

---

*At least one researcher (Wolpoff, 1999) refers to all the hominids discussed in this chapter as *Homo sapiens*.

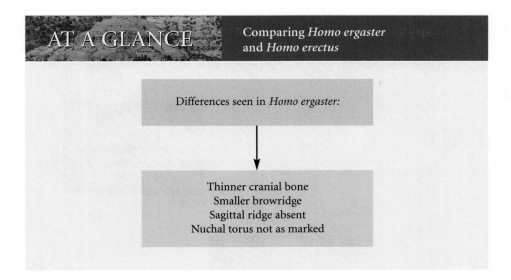

AT A GLANCE   Comparing *Homo ergaster* and *Homo erectus*

Differences seen in *Homo ergaster:*

Thinner cranial bone
Smaller browridge
Sagittal ridge absent
Nuchal torus not as marked

While there are some anatomical differences between the African specimens and those from Asia, it's clear that they're all *closely* related—either members of one species or of two closely related species. In the broad sense, we'll refer to these hominids as either *Homo erectus* or *Homo erectus/ergaster.* In a stricter sense, when referring to just the Asian fossils (and at least one find from Europe), we'll always call them *Homo erectus.*

All analyses have shown that *H. erectus/ergaster* represents a grade of evolution different from that of their more ancient African predecessors. A **grade** is an evolutionary grouping of organisms showing a similar adaptive pattern. Increase in body size and robustness, changes in limb proportions, and greater encephalization all indicate that these hominids were more like modern humans in their adaptive pattern than their African ancestors were.* We should point out that a grade only implies general adaptive aspects of a group of animals; it tells us nothing directly about shared ancestry (organisms that share common ancestry are said to be in the same **clade**). For example, orangutans and African great apes could be said to be in the same grade, but they are not in the same clade.

The hominids discussed in this chapter are not only members of a new and distinct grade of human evolution, they're also closely related to each other. Whether they all belong to the same clade is debatable. Even so, it's clear from these fossils that a major adaptive shift had taken place—one setting hominid evolution in a distinctly more human direction.

The Morphology of *Homo erectus*

We've mentioned that there's considerable variation in different regional populations of hominids broadly defined as *Homo erectus.* New discoveries are showing even more dramatic variation, suggesting that some of these hominids may not fit closely at all with this general adaptive pattern (more on this soon). For the moment, however, let's review what *most* of these fossils look like.

BRAIN SIZE

Homo erectus differs in several respects from both early *Homo* and *Homo sapiens.* The most obvious feature is cranial size, which of course is closely related to brain size. Early *Homo* had cranial capacities ranging from as small as 500 cm³ to as large as 800 cm³. *H. erectus,* on the other hand, shows considerable brain enlargement, with a cranial capacity of 750[†] to 1,250 cm³

grade   A grouping of organisms sharing a similar adaptive pattern. Grade isn't necessarily based on closeness of evolutionary relationship, but it does contrast organisms in a useful way (e.g., *Homo erectus* with *Homo sapiens*).

clade   A group of organisms sharing a common ancestor. The group includes the common ancestor and all descendants.

---

*We did note in Chapter 9 that early *Homo* is a partial exception, because it's transitional in some respects.
[†]Considerably smaller cranial capacities have been found in recently discovered fossils from Europe.

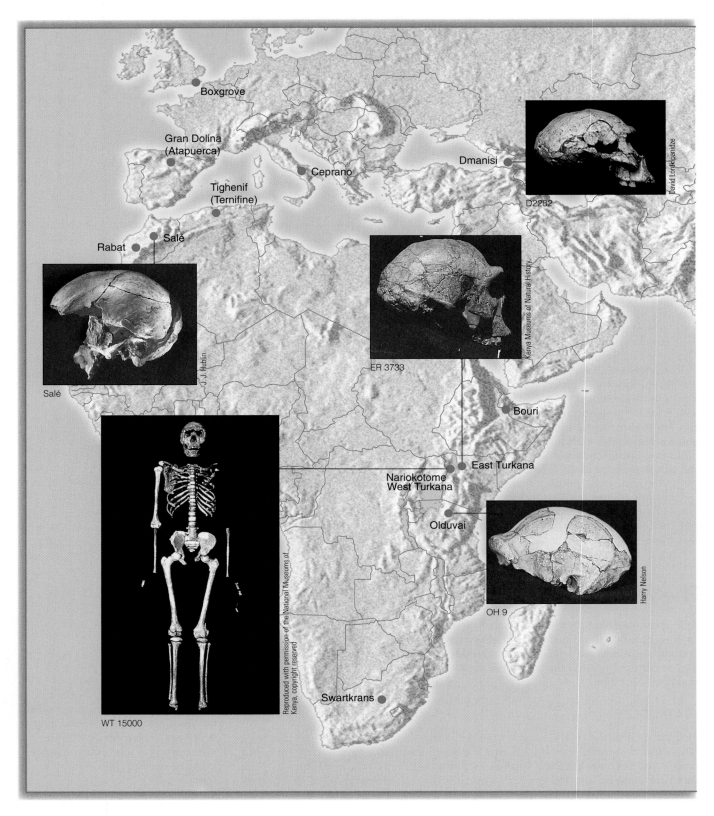

Boxgrove

Gran Dolina
(Atapuerca)

Ceprano

Tighenif
(Ternifine)

Dmanisi

David Lordkipanidze

D2282

Rabat   Salé

J. J. Hublin

Salé

Kenya Museums of Natural History

ER 3733

Bouri

Reproduced with permission of the National Museums of Kenya, copyright reserved

East Turkana

Nariokotome
West Turkana

Olduvai

Harry Nelson

OH 9

WT 15000

Swartkrans

FIGURE 10–1

Major *Homo erectus* sites and localities of other contemporaneous hominids.

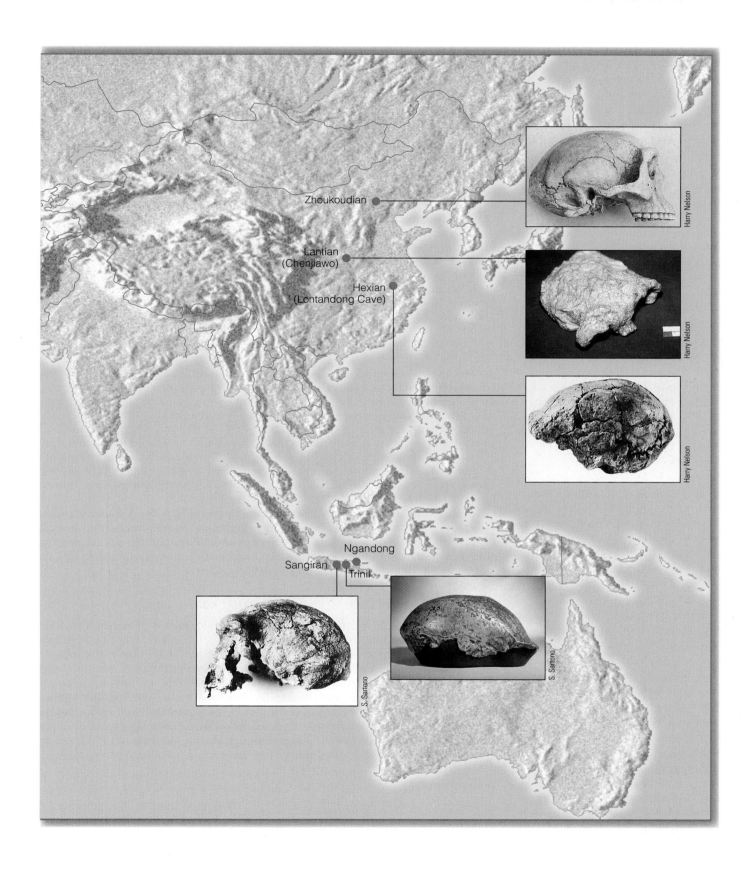

Zhoukoudian

Lantian
(Chenjiawo)

Hexian
(Lontandong Cave)

Ngandong

Sangiran

Trinil

Harry Nelson

Harry Nelson

Harry Nelson

S. Sartono

S. Sartono

(and a mean of approximately 900 cm^3). However, in making such comparisons, we must bear in mind two key questions: What is the comparative sample, and what were the overall body sizes of the species being compared?

As for the first question, you may recall that many anthropologists are now convinced that more than one species of early *Homo* existed in East Africa around 2 mya. If so, only one of them could have been the ancestor of *H. erectus.* (In fact, it's possible that neither species gave rise to *H. erectus,* and that, perhaps, we have yet to find direct evidence of the ancestral species.) Taking a more optimistic view that at least one of these fossil groups is a likely ancestor of later hominids, the question still remains—which one? If we choose the smaller-bodied sample of early *Homo* as our presumed ancestral group, then *H. erectus* shows as much as a 40 percent increase in cranial capacity. But, if the comparative sample is the larger-bodied group of early *Homo* (for example, skull 1470, from East Turkana), then *H. erectus* shows a 25 percent increase in cranial capacity.

As we've discussed, brain size is closely tied to overall body size. We've focused on the increase in *H. erectus* brain size, but *H. erectus* was also considerably larger overall than earlier members of the genus *Homo.* In fact, when we compare *H. erectus* with the larger-bodied early *Homo* sample, their *relative* brain size is about the same (Walker, 1991). What's more, when you compare the relative brain size of *H. erectus* with that of *H. sapiens,* you'll note that *H. erectus* was considerably less encephalized than later members of the genus *Homo* were.

BODY SIZE

As conclusively shown by the discovery of a nearly complete skeleton in 1984 from **Nariokotome** (on the west side of Lake Turkana in Kenya), we know that *H. erectus* was larger than earlier hominids. From this specimen and other less-complete ones, anthropologists estimate that some *Homo erectus* adults weighed well over 100 pounds, with an average adult height of about 5 feet 6 inches (McHenry, 1992; Ruff and Walker, 1993; Walker and Leakey, 1993). Another point to keep in mind is that *Homo erectus* was quite sexually dimorphic—at least as indicated by the East African specimens. So, for male adults, weight and height in some individuals may have been considerably greater than the average figures just mentioned. In fact, if the Nariokotome boy had survived, he probably would have grown to an adult height of over 6 feet (Walker, 1993).

Increased height and weight in *H. erectus* are also associated with a dramatic increase in robusticity. In fact, very heavy body build was to dominate hominid evolution not just during *H. erectus* times, but through the long transitional era of premodern forms as well. Only with the appearance of anatomically modern *H. sapiens* did a more gracile skeletal structure emerge, and it still characterizes most modern populations.

CRANIAL SHAPE

Homo erectus crania display a highly distinctive shape, partly because of increased brain size, but probably more correlated with significant body size (robusticity). The ramifications of this heavily built cranium are reflected in thick cranial bone (most notably in Asian specimens) and large browridges (supraorbital tori) in the front of the skull, and a projecting **nuchal torus** at the rear (Fig. 10–2).

The braincase is long and low, receding from the large browridges with little forehead development. Moreover, the cranium is wider at the base compared with earlier *and* later species of genus *Homo.* The maximum breadth is below the ear opening, giving the cranium a pentagonal shape (when viewed from behind). In contrast, the skulls of early *Homo* and *H. sapiens* have more vertical sides, and the maximum width is *above* the ear openings.

DENTITION

The dentition of *Homo erectus* is much like that of *Homo sapiens,* but the earlier species exhibits somewhat larger teeth. However, compared with early *Homo, H. erectus* does show some dental reduction.

Nariokotome
(nar´-ee-oh-koh´-tow-may)

nuchal torus (nuke´-ul, pertaining to the neck) A projection of bone in the back of the cranium where neck muscles attach; used to hold up the head.

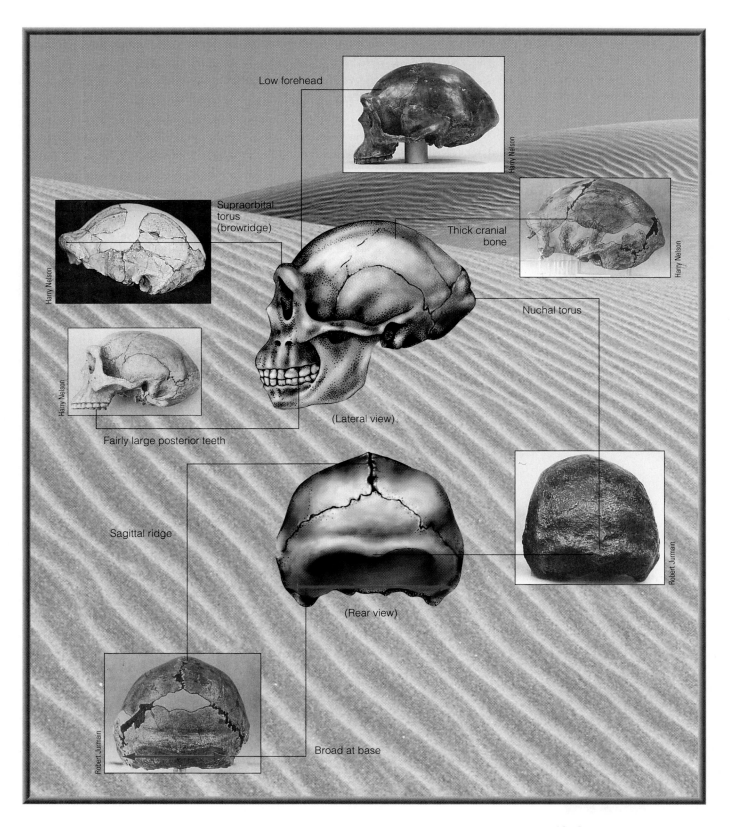

Low forehead

Supraorbital
torus
(browridge)

Thick cranial
bone

Nuchal torus

Fairly large posterior teeth

(Lateral view)

Sagittal ridge

(Rear view)

Broad at base

Harry Nelson

Harry Nelson

Harry Nelson

Harry Nelson

Robert Jurmain

Robert Jurmain

FIGURE **10–2**
Morphology and variation in *Homo erectus*.

Who Were the Earliest African Emigrants?

The fossils from East Africa imply that a new grade of human evolution appeared in Africa not long after 2 mya. So, we generally assume that the hominids who migrated to Asia and Europe were their immediate descendants. This conclusion makes good sense on at least three levels: geography, anatomy, and behavior. Geographically, Africa is where *all* the earlier hominids lived, so *H. erectus/ergaster* would probably have first appeared there (and East Africa especially would have been a likely place). What's more, these bigger, brainier hominids were now capable of traveling longer distances. Finally, their tool kit was more advanced, so they could exploit a wider range of resources.

So, consider the following reasonable hypothesis: *Homo erectus/ergaster* first evolved in East Africa close to 2 mya, and with its new physical and behavioral abilities, soon emigrated to other areas of the Old World. This hypothesis helps pull together several aspects of hominid evolution, and it's supported by much of the fossil evidence after 2 mya. But there are some problems with this tidy view, and recently discovered evidence seriously challenges it.

First, while 1.8 mya is a well-established date for the appearance of *H. erectus/ergaster* in East Africa, similar hominids also appear at just about the same time in Indonesia and soon afterward in eastern Europe (see Fig. 10–1). Radiometric dates of sediments on the island of Java have recently placed *H. erectus* (strictly defined) at sites 1.8 and 1.6 million years old. It's possible for our hypothesis to explain these hominids in Asia at this early date *if* we assume that *H. erectus* evolved in East Africa by 1.8 mya (or slightly earlier) and, in just a few thousand years, expanded rapidly to other regions.

Besides that, at an almost equally early date, hominids were also present in the Caucasus region of easternmost Europe. Newly discovered fossils from the **Dmanisi** site in the Republic of Georgia (see Fig. 10–1) have been radiometrically dated to 1.75 mya. Could this occurrence at yet another distant locality from the probable East African homeland still be accommodated within our hypothesis? Maybe—but we're beginning to stretch the limits of how quickly these hominids could have migrated.

THE DMANISI HOMINIDS

Even more problematic for our hypothesis is the physical appearance of the hominids from Dmanisi. They're quite different from all the other hominids discussed in this chapter. In fact, they may not even belong to the same grade of hominid evolution as all these other (*H. erectus*) hominids. These discoveries thus have dramatic implications.

The Dmanisi materials have been quite recently discovered, beginning in the early 1990s. The most informative specimens are four well-preserved crania; one cranium, discovered in 2001, is almost complete (Fig. 10–3). These remains are important because they're the best-preserved hominids of this age found anywhere *outside* of Africa. Additionally, they show a mixed pattern of characteristics, some quite unexpected (Vekua et al., 2002).

In some respects, the Dmanisi crania are similar to *H. erectus* (for example, the long, low braincase, wide base, and thickening along the sagittal midline; see especially Fig. 10–3b and compare with Fig. 10–2). In other characteristics, however, the Dmanisi individuals are dif-

Dmanisi (dim´-an-eese´-ee)

FIGURE 10–3

Dmanisi crania discovered in 1999 and 2001 and dated to 1.8–1.7 mya. (a) Specimen 2282. (b) Specimen 2280. (c) Specimen 2700.

(a)

David Lordkipanidze

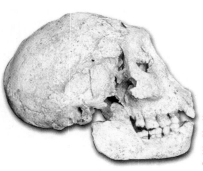

(b)

David Lordkipanidze

(c)

David Lordkipanidze

ferent from other hominid finds outside of Africa. In particular, the most complete specimen (specimen 2700; see Fig. 10–3c) has a less robust and thinner browridge, a projecting lower face, and a large upper canine. So at least from the front, this skull is more reminiscent of the smaller early *Homo* specimens from East Africa than of *Homo erectus*. And, this individual's cranial capacity is very small—estimated at only 600 cm^3, well within the range of early *Homo*. In fact, the three Dmanisi crania so far described have small cranial capacities—the other two were estimated at 650 cm^3 and 780 cm^3.

Probably the most remarkable discovery yet from Dmanisi is a fourth skull that researchers excavated in 2002 (and published in 2005). This nearly complete cranium is of an older adult male, and very surprisingly for such an ancient find, he has only one tooth remaining in his jaws. Because his jawbones show advanced resorption of bone, it seems that he went essentially toothless for some time (Fig. 10–4). David Lordkipanidze, who leads the excavations at Dmanisi, and colleagues have tentatively suggested this individual required a fair amount of assistance to survive during the Lower Pleistocene in such a challenging environment (Lordkipanidze et al., 2005). However, this contention requires more detailed investigation before it can be further confirmed.

Researchers have also recovered some stone tools at Dmanisi. The tools are similar to early ones from Africa, and they're quite different from the seemingly more advanced technology of the Acheulian industry broadly associated with *H. erectus* in much of the Old World (see p. 238).

Based on these recent, startling revelations from Dmanisi, we can ask several questions:

1. Was *Homo erectus* the first hominid to leave Africa—or was it an earlier form of *Homo?*
2. Did hominids require a large brain and sophisticated stone tool culture to disperse out of Africa?
3. Was the large, robust body build of *H. erectus* a necessary adaptation for the initial occupation of Eurasia?

Of course, since the Dmanisi discoveries are very new, it's important to view any conclusions as highly tentative. But in any case, the recent evidence raises important and exciting possibilities. It now seems likely that the first transcontinental hominid migrants were a form of early *Homo*, similar to the smaller East African species, *Homo habilis* (see p. 209). At best, and as the Dmanisi findings suggest, the first hominids to leave Africa were a very early form of *H. erectus*, apparently one much more primitive than any of the other specimens from Africa, Asia, or Europe discussed in this chapter. Certainly the smaller individuals from Dmanisi didn't have large brains (by *H. erectus* standards), nor did they have an advanced stone tool culture. Instead, their tools were very similar to the earliest ones from East and South Africa.

Several postcranial bones, from at least two individuals, have been recovered at Dmanisi. Although only provisionally published (Fischman, 2005), it appears that these hominids were not especially tall, with an estimated height of barely over 4^{1}/$_{2}$ ft. Certainly, they seem much smaller than the full *H. erectus/ergaster* from East Africa or from Asia. In both body and brain size, they look more similar to early *Homo*.

Because of these startling and still provisional observations, it appears that the Dmanisi hominids don't meet any of the criteria used to define the more human evolutionary grade of all the other *Homo erectus/ergaster* individuals. At the very least, we have to admit that our hypothesis isn't looking nearly as tidy as we might have hoped.

So it seems that researchers are facing the prospect of major reappraisals about the status of early *Homo* as well as what constitutes membership in the genus *Homo* itself. What's more, the core of our hypothesis, explaining those factors that initially "propelled" hominids out of Africa, may well be largely falsified. Some researchers have become quite skeptical, suggesting even that some hominids might have evolved first in Asia and later migrated *back* to Africa (Dennell and Roeboeks, 2005). But be aware that the hypothesis might still hold for a *second* migration, one that may have occurred shortly after the time of the Dmanisi inhabitants. All this evidence is so new, however, that it's too soon even to predict what further revisions may be required.

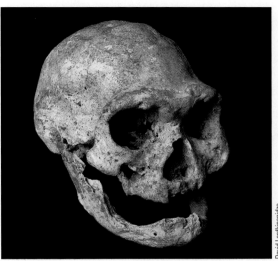

David Lordkipanidze

FIGURE 10–4

Most recently discovered cranium from Dmanisi, almost totally lacking in teeth (with both upper and lower jaws showing advanced bone resorption).

Historical Overview of *Homo erectus* Discoveries

Homo erectus, as broadly defined, is found widely distributed across three continents. But it's difficult to organize these materials in a clear chronological order (as we did for African hominids in Chapter 9). First, there's the problem of complexity. As already noted, the earliest members of the group all appear nearly simultaneously—at around 1.8 mya, in Africa, Asia, and Europe. And second, since we can't use radiometric dating for most of the later fossils, our knowledge of the chronological placement of many specimens is still quite sketchy.

The best way to proceed is to discuss these fossil hominids from a historical perspective—that is, in the order in which they were discovered. We believe that this approach is useful, because the discoveries cover a broad range of time—in fact, almost the entire history of paleoanthropology. Due to this relatively long history of scientific discovery, researchers have assessed the later finds in light of the earlier ones—so we can still understand them best in their historical context.

JAVA

Eugene Dubois (1858–1940), a Dutch anatomist (Fig. 10–5), was the first scientist to deliberately design a research plan that would take him from his anatomy lab to where fossil bones might be buried. Until that time, embryology and comparative anatomy were considered the proper methods of studying humans and their ancestry, and the research was done in the laboratory. Dubois changed all this. The publication of Darwin's *On the Origin of Species* in 1859 had ushered in a period of intellectual excitement. This stimulating intellectual climate surrounded the youthful Dubois when he left Holland for Sumatra in 1887 to search for, as he phrased it, "the missing link."

In October 1891, along the Solo River near the town of Trinil, his field crew unearthed a skullcap that was to become internationally famous. The following year, a human femur was recovered about 15 yards upstream in what Dubois claimed was the same level as the skullcap, and he assumed that the skullcap (with a cranial capacity of slightly over 900 cm³) and the femur belonged to the same individual.

After studying these discoveries for a few years, Dubois startled the world in 1894 with a paper titled "*Pithecanthropus erectus,* A Manlike Species of Transitional Anthropoid from Java." Dubois' views were harshly criticized, but eventually, there was general acceptance that he had been correct in identifying the skull as representing a previously undescribed species; that his estimates of cranial capacity were reasonably accurate; that *Pithecanthropus erectus,* or *H. erectus* as we call it today, is a close relative and perhaps an ancestor of *H. sapiens;* and that bipedalism preceded enlargement of the brain.

By 1930 the controversy had faded, especially in light of important new discoveries near Peking (Beijing), China, in the late 1920s (discussed shortly). Similarities between the Beijing skulls and Dubois' *Pithecanthropus* were obvious, and scientists pointed out that the Java form was not an "apeman," as Dubois contended, but instead was closely related to modern *Homo sapiens.* You might think that Dubois would welcome the finds from China and the support they provided for the human status of *Pithecanthropus,* but he didn't. In fact, he refused to recognize any connection between the Beijing and Java materials.

HOMO ERECTUS FROM JAVA

Six sites in eastern Java have yielded all the *H. erectus* fossil remains found to date on that island. The dating of these fossils has been hampered by the complex nature of Javanese geology, but it's been generally accepted that most of the fossils belong to the Middle **Pleistocene** and are less than 800,000 years old. But as we noted earlier, more precise chronometric dating estimates have suggested one find to be close to 1.8 million years old, and another fossil from a site called Sangiran may be approximately 1.6 million years old.

At Sangiran, where the remains of at least five individuals have been excavated, cranial capacities range from 813 cm³ to 1,059 cm³. Another site called Ngandong has yielded the remains of another 12 crania (Fig. 10–6), and these finds have surprisingly been dated to the

FIGURE 10–5

Eugene Dubois, discoverer of the first *H. erectus* fossil to be found.

FIGURE 10–6

Rear view of a Ngandong skull. Note that the cranial walls slope downward and outward (or upward and inward), with the widest breadth low on the cranium, giving it a pentagonal form.

Pleistocene   The epoch of the Cenozoic from 1.8 mya until 10,000 ya. Frequently referred to as the Ice Age, this epoch is associated with continental glaciations in northern latitudes.

Upper Pleistocene. Two specialized dating techniques, discussed in Chapter 8, have determined that animal bones found at the site—and presumably associated with the hominids—are only about 50,000 to 25,000 years old (Swisher et al., 1996). These dates are controversial, but further confirmation is now establishing a *very* late survival of *Homo erectus* in Java, long after the species had disappeared elsewhere. So, these individuals would be contemporary with *Homo sapiens*—which, by this time, had expanded widely throughout the Old World. As we'll also see in Chapter 12, even later—and very unusual—hominids have been found elsewhere, apparently evolving while isolated on another Indonesian island.

We can't say much about the *H. erectus* way of life in Java. Very few artifacts have been found, and those have come mainly from river terraces, not from primary sites: "On Java there is still not a single site where artifacts can be associated with *H. erectus*" (Bartstra, 1982, p. 319).

PEKING (BEIJING)

The story of Peking *H. erectus* is another saga filled with excitement, hard work, luck, and misfortune. Europeans had known for a long time that "dragon bones," used by the Chinese as medicine and aphrodisiacs, were actually ancient mammal bones. Scientists eventually located one of the sources of these bones near Beijing at a site called **Zhoukoudian**. Serious excavations were begun there in the 1920s under the direction of a young Chinese geologist named Pei Wenshong. In 1929 a fossil skull was discovered, and Pei brought the specimen to anatomist Davidson Black. The result was worth the labor. The skull turned out to be a juvenile's, and although it was thick, low, and relatively small, Black was sure it belonged to an early hominid. The response to this discovery, quite unlike that which greeted Dubois almost 40 years earlier, was enthusiastically favorable.

Franz Weidenreich (Fig. 10–7), a distinguished anatomist well known for his work on European fossil hominids, succeeded Black. After Japan invaded China in 1933, Weidenreich decided to move the fossils. He left China in 1941, taking plaster casts, photographs, and drawings of the material with him. After he left, the bones were packed, and arrangements were made for the U.S. Marine Corps in Beijing to take them to the United States. But the bones never reached the United States, and they've never been found. To this day, no one knows what happened to them.

FIGURE 10–7
Franz Weidenreich.

ZHOUKOUDIAN *HOMO ERECTUS*

The fossil remains of *H. erectus* discovered in the 1920s and 1930s, as well as some more recent excavations at Zhoukoudian (Fig. 10–8), are by far the largest collection of *H. erectus* material found anywhere. This excellent sample includes 14 skullcaps (Fig. 10–9), other cranial

FIGURE 10–8
Zhoukoudian Cave, a view of the original Locality 1 excavation as seen from Pigeon Hall looking toward the western wall of the excavation.

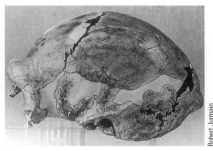

FIGURE 10–9
H. erectus (cast of specimen from Zhoukoudian). From this view, the supraorbital torus, low vault of the skull, and nuchal torus can clearly be seen.

Zhoukoudian (Zhoh´-koh-dee´-en)

pieces, and more than 100 isolated teeth, but only a scattering of postcranial elements (Jia and Huang, 1990). Various interpretations to account for this unusual pattern of preservation have been offered, ranging from ritualistic treatment or cannibalism by the hominids themselves to the more mundane suggestion that the *H. erectus* remains are simply the leftovers of the meals of giant hyenas (discussed shortly).

At any rate, the hominid remains belong to upward of 40 adults and children and together provide much evidence. Because of Weidenreich's meticulous work, the Zhoukoudian fossils have led to a good overall picture of Chinese *H. erectus*. Like the materials from Java, they have typical *H. erectus* features, including a supraorbital torus in front and a nuchal torus behind. Also, the skull has thick bones, a sagittal ridge, and a protruding face and, like the Javanese forms, is broadest near the bottom.

Cultural Remains   More than 100,000 artifacts have been recovered from this vast site, which was occupied intermittently for many thousands of years. Early on, tools are generally crude and shapeless, but they become more refined over time. Common tools at the site are choppers and chopping tools, but retouched flakes were fashioned into scrapers, points, burins, and awls (Fig. 10–10).

The way of life at Zhoukoudian has traditionally been described as that of hunter-gatherers who killed deer, horses, and other animals and gathered fruits, berries, and ostrich eggs. Fragments of charred ostrich eggshells and abundant deposits of hackberry seeds unearthed in the cave suggest that these hominids supplemented their diet of meat by gathering herbs, wild fruits, tubers, and eggs. Layers of what has long been thought to be ash in the cave (over 18 feet deep at one point) have been interpreted as indicating the use of fire by *H. erectus*; but as we'll see, researchers don't really know whether Beijing hominids could actually make fire.

More recently, several researchers have challenged this picture of Zhoukoudian life. Lewis Binford and colleagues (Binford and Ho, 1985; Binford and Stone, 1986a, 1986b) reject the description of Beijing *H. erectus* as hunters and argue that the evidence clearly points more accurately to scavenging. Using advanced archaeological techniques of analysis, Noel Boaz and colleagues have even questioned whether the *H. erectus* remains at Zhoukoudian represent evidence of hominid habitation of the cave. By comparing the types of bones, as well as the damage to the bones, with that seen in contemporary carnivore dens, Boaz and Ciochon (2001) have suggested that much of the material in the cave likely accumulated through the activities of a giant extinct hyena. In fact, they hypothesize that most of the *H. erectus* remains, too, are the food refuse of hyena meals.

Boaz and his colleagues do recognize that the tools in the cave, and possibly the cut marks on some of the animal bones, provide evidence of hominid activities at Zhoukoudian. They also recognize that more detailed analysis is required to test their hypotheses and to "determine the nature and scope" of the *H. erectus* presence at Zhoukoudian (see Digging Deeper).

Probably the most intriguing archaeological aspect of the presumed hominid behavior at Zhoukoudian has been the long-held assumption that *H. erectus* deliberately used fire inside the cave. Controlling fire was one of the major cultural breakthroughs of all prehistory. By providing warmth, a means of cooking, an aid to further modify tools, and so forth, controlled

FIGURE **10–10**

Chinese tools from Middle Pleistocene sites. (Adapted from Wu and Olsen, 1985.)

Quartzite chopper

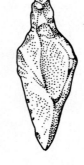

Flint point

Flint awl

Graver, or burin

Controllers of Fire

There's an important distinction between the *making* of fire and the *using* of fire captured from natural sources. Some very ancient methods that could have been used deliberately to make fire might have included striking hard rocks together or rubbing wood together to create sparks through friction. Without such technological innovations, earlier hominids would have been limited to obtaining and transporting fire from natural sources, such as lightning strikes and geothermal localities.

We may never collect enough archaeological evidence to make this distinction very precisely. But we can say that, *at minimum*, the consistent use of fire would have been a major technological breakthrough and could have had potentially marked influence on hominid biological evolution as well. For example, because of cooking, food items would have been softer; in turn, chewing stresses would have been reduced, possibly leading to selection for reduced size of the dentition.

It's possible that australopithecines took advantage of and used naturally occurring fire, but it's not always easy to interpret the evidence relating to the use of fire. At open-air sites, for example, remains suggesting an association between hominids and burning may be found. However, ashes may already have been blown away, and stones and bones blackened by fire could be the result of a natural brush fire, as could charcoal and baked earth. What's more, remains found on the surface of a site might be the result of a natural fire that occurred long after the hominids had left.

Here are some of the possible advantages that controlled use of fire may have provided to earlier hominids:

1. Warmth
2. Cooking meat and/or plant foods, thus breaking down fibers and, in the case of many plants, neutralizing toxins
3. Fire-hardening wood, such as the end of a spear
4. Causing the flaking of certain stone materials to be more predictable, thus aiding in the production of stone tools
5. Chasing competing predators (such as bears) from caves and keeping dangerous animals at bay
6. Providing illumination in caves and, more fundamentally, extending usable light into the night

This last implication of human control of fire may have profoundly affected human sleep cycles, as well as altering activity patterns, neurological functioning, and hormonal balance. In fact, recent experiments have suggested that humans today can still readily and comfortably adjust to "natural" light-dark cycles with periods of inactivity of up to 14 hours, thus simulating winter conditions *before* the systematic control of fire.

Because controlling fire is so important to humans, it would be useful to know who tamed the wild flames and when, where, and how they did it. With that knowledge, we could learn much more about our ancient ancestors' culture and evolution.

Archaeologists are not certain who the first fire makers were. Two of the earliest presumed examples of fire use come from Africa, and both have been suggested as indicating deliberate hominid pyrotechnics *prior* to 1 mya. At Chesowanja in southern Kenya, patches of burned clay dated at 1.4 mya were found in association with stone tools. John Gowlett and his colleague, Jack Harris, have suggested that the burned clay is the residue of ancient campfires. And in more recent excavations from upper levels at Swartkrans, in South Africa, C. K. Brain and Andrew Sillen have recovered many pieces of burnt bone, again in association with stone tools dated at 1.3–1 mya. (For a further discussion of Swartkrans, see pp. 211–212.) Both of these possible occurrences of hominid control of fire in Africa are thought to be associated with *Homo erectus*. However, neither of the early African contexts has yet to fully convince other experts.

True caves* may be a more probable source for finding human-made fire, because caves, except at the entrance, are damp, very dark, and impossible to inhabit without light. Also, by the time humans began to occupy caves, they may have invented a method of making fire. It's possible, of course, to carry a natural fire into a cave, which is another snag in determining whether the fire was deliberately made or natural.

Probably the most famous cave site is Zhoukoudian (discussed in this chapter), where both Chinese and Western archaeologists have been working for more than 70 years. Evidence of supposed fire is abundant, but this evidence—including charred animal bones, layers of ash, charcoal, and burned stone artifacts—has led to differing interpretations and recent reassessments by archaeologists (see discussion in text).

There appears to be evidence of fire at other open sites in China and several caves in Europe, provisionally dated to about 300,000 years ago. They have yielded evidence of fire possibly made by later hominids. But again, not all archaeologists are persuaded that humans were responsible.

Other prehistorians are sure that Neandertals (discussed in Chapter 11), who built hearths, were the first to make fire toward the end of the Middle Pleistocene (about 125,000 ya). A deliberately built hearth is probably the best evidence for human-controlled fire. Ancient hearths are usually built with stone cobbles, arranged in a circular or oval shape to contain the fire. The presence of numerous hearths at a site (like finding a box of matches near a fire) tends to serve as proof that humans probably started the fires. It's the absence of identifiable hearths that is so troublesome at the older sites and that immediately makes researchers doubt that hominids made—or even systematically used—the fire. It will take the development of carefully constructed interpretive techniques to overcome the difficulties of solving the case of the first significant controllers of fire.

---

*Swartkrans was not a cave during the time of hominid archaeological accumulation, but it's been shown to have been a natural fissure into which animals and other objects fell.

fire would have been a giant technological innovation. While some potential early African sites have yielded evidence that to some have suggested hominid control of fire, it's long been concluded that the first *definite* evidence of hominid fire use comes from Zhoukoudian.

Recent evidence has radically altered this assumption. Much more detailed excavations at Zhoukoudian were carried out in 1996 and 1997 by biologist Steve Weiner and colleagues. These researchers also carefully analyzed soil samples for distinctive chemical signatures that would show whether fire had occurred in the cave (Weiner et al., 1998). They found that burnt bone was only rarely found in association with tools. And in most cases, the burning appeared to have taken place *after* fossilization—that is, the bones were not cooked. In fact, it turns out that the "ash" layers mentioned earlier aren't actually ash, but naturally accumulated organic sediment. This last conclusion was derived from chemical testing that showed absolutely no sign of wood having been burnt inside the cave. Finally, the "hearths" that have figured so prominently in archaeological reconstructions of presumed fire control at this site are apparently not hearths at all. They are simply round depressions formed in the past by water.

Another provisional interpretation of the cave's geology suggests that the cave wasn't open to the outside like a habitation site, but was accessed only through a vertical shaft. This theory has led archaeologist Alison Brooks to remark, "It wouldn't have been a shelter, it would have been a trap" (quoted in Wuethrich, 1998). These serious doubts about control of fire, coupled with the suggestive evidence of bone accumulation by carnivores, have led anthropologists Noel Boaz and Russell Ciochon to conclude that "Zhoukoudian cave was neither hearth nor home" (Boaz and Ciochon, 2001).

OTHER CHINESE SITES

More work has been done at Zhoukoudian than at any other Chinese site. Even so, there are other hominid sites worth mentioning. Three of the more important ones, besides Zhoukoudian, are two in Lantian County (often simply referred to as Lantian) and another in Hexian County (usually referred to as the Hexian find).

At Lantian, an almost complete mandible containing several teeth was found in 1963. It's quite similar to those from Zhoukoudian but has been given an earlier date of about 650,000 years ago (ya). The following year, a partial cranium was discovered at a nearby Hexian locality. Provisionally dated to as much as 1.15 mya (Etler and Tianyuan, 1994), this may be the oldest Chinese *Homo erectus* fossil yet known.

But probably the most significant find was the 1980 Hexian discovery, during which researchers recovered the remains of several individuals. One of the specimens is a well-preserved cranium (with a cranial capacity of about 1,025 cm^3) lacking much of its base. Because this cranium has been dated at roughly 250,000 ya, it's not surprising that it displays several more derived features. The cranial constriction, for example, is not as pronounced as in earlier forms, and certain temporal and occipital characteristics are "best compared with the later forms of *H. erectus* at Zhoukoudian" (Wu and Dong, 1985, p. 87).

In 1993, Li Tianyuan and Dennis Etler reported that two relatively complete skulls were discovered in 1989 at a site in Yunxian County and dated to approximately 350,000 ya (Fig. 10–11). These crania are both quite a lot larger and more robust than those from Zhoukoudian. Unfortunately, both skulls are still covered with a hard matrix, and until they're

FIGURE **10–11**

(a) EV 9002 (Yunxian, China). The skull is in better shape than its companion, and its lateral view clearly displays features characteristic of *H. erectus*: flattened vault, receding forehead (frontal bone), angulated occiput, and supra-orbital torus. (b) EV 9001 (Yunxian). Unfortunately, the skull was crushed, but it preserves some facial structures absent in EV 9002.

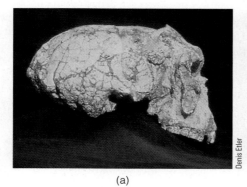

(a)

(b)

cleaned and reconstructed, it's too early to make accurate assessments. In any case, these Yunxian crania will ultimately provide considerable data to help clarify hominid evolution in China and possibly elsewhere in the Old World as well.

The Asian crania from both Java and China share many similar features, which may be explained by *H. erectus* migration from Java to China perhaps around 1 million years ago. African *H. erectus* forms are generally older than most Asian forms, and they're different from them in several ways.

EAST AFRICA

Olduvai   Back in 1960, Louis Leakey unearthed a fossil skull at Olduvai (OH 9) that he identified as *H. erectus*. Skull OH 9 from Upper Bed II is dated at 1.4 mya and preserves a massive cranium, but it's faceless except for a bit of nose below the supraorbital torus. Estimated at 1,067 cm^3, the cranial capacity of OH 9 is the largest of all the African *Homo erectus* specimens (defined in the broad sense; these specimens are also referred to as *H. ergaster*). The browridge is huge, the largest known for any hominid, but the walls of the braincase are thin. This latter characteristic is seen in most East African *H. erectus* specimens, and in this respect they differ from Asian *H. erectus*, in which cranial bones are thick. This and other differences have led some researchers to place East African specimens in a separate species.

East Turkana   Some 400 miles north of Olduvai Gorge, on the northern boundary of Kenya, is Lake Turkana. Explored by Richard Leakey and colleagues since 1969, the eastern shore of the lake has been a virtual gold mine for australopithecine, early *Homo*, and *H. erectus* fossil remains.

The most significant *H. erectus/ergaster* discovery from East Turkana is a nearly complete skull (Fig. 10–12) dated at 1.8 mya—that is, as early as the earliest *H. erectus* from Java. The cranial capacity is estimated at 848 cm^3, at the lower end of the range for *H. erectus*, but this isn't surprising considering its early date. It generally resembles Asian *H. erectus* in many features—but with some important differences, which we'll soon discuss. Not many tools have been found at *H. erectus* sites in East Turkana. Researchers have unearthed Oldowan flakes, cobbles, and core tools, and they know that the introduction of **Acheulian** tools about 1.4 mya replaced the Oldowan tradition.

West Turkana   In August 1984, Kamoya Kimeu, a member of Richard Leakey's team, enhanced his reputation as an outstanding fossil hunter when he discovered a small piece of skull on the west side of Lake Turkana. Leakey and his colleague, Alan Walker of Pennsylvania State University, excavated the site known as Nariokotome in the 1980s.

The dig was a resounding success and produced the most complete *H. erectus* skeleton ever found (Fig. 10–13). Known properly as WT 15000, the all but complete skeleton includes facial bones and most of the postcranial bones, making it a very unusual discovery for *H. erectus* (broadly defined) because these elements are scarce at other sites. The Nariokotome skeleton is quite ancient, dated chronometrically to about 1.6 mya. The skeleton is that of a boy about 12 years of age with an estimated height of about 5 feet 3 inches. Had he grown to maturity, it's estimated that his height would have been more than 6 feet—taller than *H. erectus* was previously thought to have been. The postcranial bones look quite similar, though not identical, to those of modern humans. The cranial capacity of WT 15000 is estimated at 880 cm^3; brain growth was nearly complete, and the boy's adult cranial capacity would have been approximately 909 cm^3 (Begun and Walker, 1993). See Digging Deeper on page 236.

Bouri   Two sites from Ethiopia have yielded *H. erectus* fossils, the most significant coming from the Bouri locale in the Middle Awash region. Numerous remains of earlier hominids have come from this area; see Chapter 9 and Appendix B. The recent discovery of a mostly complete cranium from Bouri is important because this individual (dated at approximately 1 mya) is more like Asian *H. erectus* than are most of the earlier East African remains we've discussed (Asfaw et al., 2002). Consequently, the suggestion by several researchers that East African fossils are a different species from (Asian) *Homo erectus* isn't supported by the morphology of the Bouri cranium.

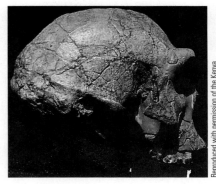

FIGURE 10–12
ER 3733, the most complete East Turkana *H. erectus* cranium.

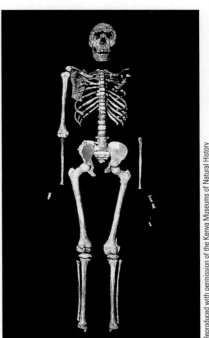

FIGURE 10–13
WT 15000 from Nariokotome, Kenya: the most complete *H. erectus* specimen yet found.

Acheulian   (ash´-oo-lay-en) Pertaining to a stone tool industry from the Lower and Middle Pleistocene; characterized by a large proportion of bifacial tools (flaked on both sides). Acheulian tool kits are very common in Africa, Southwest Asia, and western Europe, but they're thought to be less common elsewhere. Also spelled *Acheulean*.

The Nariokotome Skeleton

Discovering the spectacularly well-preserved skeleton from Nariokotome on the west side of Lake Turkana has given anthropologists considerable new insight into key anatomical features of *Homo erectus*. Since its recovery in 1984 and 1985, detailed studies have been undertaken, and the published results (Walker, 1993; Walker and Leakey, 1993) have allowed researchers to draw some initial conclusions. In addition, the extraordinary quality of the remains has also allowed anthropologists to speculate on some major behavioral traits of *H. erectus** in Africa—and, more generally, of the entire species.

The remains comprise an almost complete skeleton, lacking only most of the small bones of the hands and feet and the unfused ends of long bones. This degree of preservation is remarkable, and it makes this individual the most complete skeleton of *any* fossil hominid yet found from before about 100,000 ya (after that time, deliberate burial greatly improved preservation). This superior preservation may well have been aided by rapid sedimentation in what is thought to have been an ancient, shallow swamp. Once the individual died, his skeleton would have been quickly covered up, but even then some disturbance and breakage occurred—from chewing by catfish, but most especially from trampling by large animals wading in the swamp 1.6 mya.

As we've said, the individual was not fully grown when he died. His age (11 to 13 years; Walker, 1993) is determined by the stage of dental eruption—his permanent canines are not yet erupted—and by union of the ends of long bones. Also, as we have noted, this young *Homo erectus* male was quite tall (5 feet 3 inches), and using modern growth curve approximations, his adult height would have been over 6 feet if he'd lived to full maturity.

More than simply being tall, the body proportions of this boy's skeleton are intriguing. Reconstructions suggest that he had a linear build with long appendages, conforming to predictions of *Allen's rule* for inhabitants of hot climates (see Chapter 4). Further extrapolating from this observation, Alan Walker suggests that *H. erectus* must have had a high sweating capacity in order to dissipate heat in the modern human fashion. (See pp. 83–84 for a discussion of heat adaptation in humans.)

The boy's limb proportions suggest that mean annual temperature (90°F/30°C) in East Africa was quite warm 1.6 mya. Paleoecological reconstructions confirm this estimate of tropical conditions; they were much like the climate today in northern Kenya.

We can observe a final interesting feature in the pelvis of this adolescent skeleton. It's very narrow and is thus correlated with a narrow, bony birth canal. Walker (1993) again draws a behavioral inference from this anatomical feature. He estimates that a newborn with a cranial capacity no greater than a mere 200 cm³ could have passed through this pelvis. As we showed elsewhere, the adult cranial capacity estimate for this individual was slightly greater than 900 cm³—thus arguing for significant postnatal growth of the brain (exceeding 75 percent of its eventual size) and again mirroring the modern human pattern. Walker speculates that this slow neural expansion (compared to other primates) leads to delayed development of motor skills and thus a prolonged period of infant-child dependency (what Walker terms secondary altriciality). This conclusion, however, is not supported by more recently analyzed dental data, which show an accelerated, australopithecine-like, rate of maturation (Dean et al., 2001).

---

*H. erectus, broadly defined, and inclusive of *H. ergaster.*

SUMMARY OF EAST AFRICAN *HOMO ERECTUS/ERGASTER*

The *Homo erectus* remains from East Africa show several differences from the Javanese and Chinese fossils. Some African cranial specimens—particularly ER 3733, presumably a female, and WT 15000, presumably a male—aren't as strongly buttressed by supraorbital or nuchal tori, and their cranial bones aren't as thick. As we've noted, some researchers are so impressed by these differences, as well as others in the postcranial skeleton, that they're arguing for a *separate* species status for the African material, to distinguish it from the Asian samples. Bernard Wood, the leading proponent of this view, has suggested that the name *Homo ergaster* be used for the African remains and that *H. erectus* be reserved solely for the Asian material (Wood, 1991). In addition, the very early dates now postulated for the dispersal of *H. erectus* into Asia (Java) would argue for a more than 1-million-year separate history for Asian and African populations.

In any case, this species division has not been fully accepted, and the current consensus (and the one we prefer) is to continue referring to all these hominids as *Homo erectus* (Kramer, 1993; Conroy, 1997; Rightmire, 1998; Asfaw et al., 2002). So, as with some earlier hominids, we'll have to accommodate a considerable degree of intraspecific variation within this species. Wood has concluded, regarding variation within such a broadly defined *H. erectus* species, that "It is a species which manifestly embraces an unusually wide degree of variation in both the cranium and postcranial skeleton" (Wood, 1992a, p. 329).

NORTH AFRICA

North African remains, consisting almost entirely of mandibles (or mandible fragments) and a partial parietal bone, have been found at three sites in Algeria and Morocco. The three Algerian mandibles and the parietal fragment are quite robust and have been dated to about 700,000 ya. The Moroccan material isn't as robust and may be a bit younger, at 500,000 years. In addition, an interesting cranium was found north of the town of Salé, in Morocco. The walls of the skull vault are thick, and several other features resemble those of *H. erectus*. Some features alternatively suggest that the Salé fossil should be placed in a later species of *Homo*, but an estimated cranial capacity of about 900 cm³ throws doubt on that interpretation.

EUROPE

Because of the recent discoveries from Dmanisi (see p. 228), the time frame for the earliest hominid occupation of Europe is being dramatically pushed back. For several decades, researchers assumed that hominids didn't reach Europe until late in the Middle Pleistocene (after 400,000 ya) and were already identifiable as a form very similar to *Homo sapiens*. So, they concluded that *H. erectus* (and contemporaries) never got there. But, as the new discoveries are evaluated, these assumptions are being questioned, and radical revisions concerning hominid evolution in Europe are becoming necessary.

While not as old as the Dmanisi material, fossils from the Gran Dolina site in northern Spain are extending the antiquity of hominids in western Europe. (Gran Dolina is located in the very productive region called Atapuerca, where later hominid fossils have also been found.) The dating of Gran Dolina, based on specialized techniques discussed in Chapter 8 (see p. 183), is approximately 850,000–780,000 ya (Parés and Pérez-González, 1995; Falguéres et al., 1999). These early Spanish finds are thus *at least* 250,000 years older than any other hominid yet discovered in western Europe. Because all the remains so far identified are fragmentary, assigning these fossils to particular species poses something of a problem; but initial analysis suggests that these fossils aren't *H. erectus*. The facial remains are especially distinctive, and they look much more modern than does *H. erectus*. Spanish paleoanthropologists who have studied the Gran Dolina fossils have decided to place these hominids into another (separate) species, one they call *Homo antecessor* (Bermúdez de Castro et al., 1997; Arsuaga et al., 1999). However, it remains to be seen whether this newly proposed species will prove to be distinct from other species of *Homo* (see p. 267 for further discussion). Another potentially early western European hominid find comes from the 500,000-year-old Boxgrove site in southern England, where a hominid tibia (shinbone) was unearthed in 1994. Recently discovered archaeological evidence, also from southern England, shows that humans had occupied Britain as early as 700,000 years ago (Parfitt et al., 2005). This is the earliest evidence of hominids in northern Europe, and be aware that Britain was connected to the continent at this time.

Finally, the southern European discovery of a well-preserved cranium from the Ceprano site in central Italy may be the best evidence yet of *H. erectus* (strictly defined) in Europe (Ascenzi et al., 1996). Provisional dating of a partial cranium from this important site suggests a date between 800,000 and 900,000 ya. Phillip Rightmire (1998) has concluded that cranial morphology places this specimen quite close to *H. erectus*. Italian researchers have proposed other views. At first they agreed with Rightmire's interpretation (Ascenzi et al., 1996), but more recently they've suggested that the Ceprano cranium might belong to yet another (and separate) species (Manzi et al., 2001). This degree of splitting is quite extreme and isn't likely to be considered favorably by most paleoanthropologists.

After about 400,000 ya, the European fossil hominid record becomes increasingly abundant. More fossils mean more variation, so it's not surprising that interpretations regarding the proper taxonomic assessment of many of these remains have been debated, in some cases for decades. In recent years, several of these somewhat later "premodern" specimens have been considered either as early representatives of *Homo sapiens* or as a separate species, one immediately preceding *H. sapiens*. These enigmatic premodern humans are discussed in Chapter 11. A time line for the *H. erectus* discoveries discussed in this chapter as well as other finds of more uncertain status is shown in Figure 10–14.

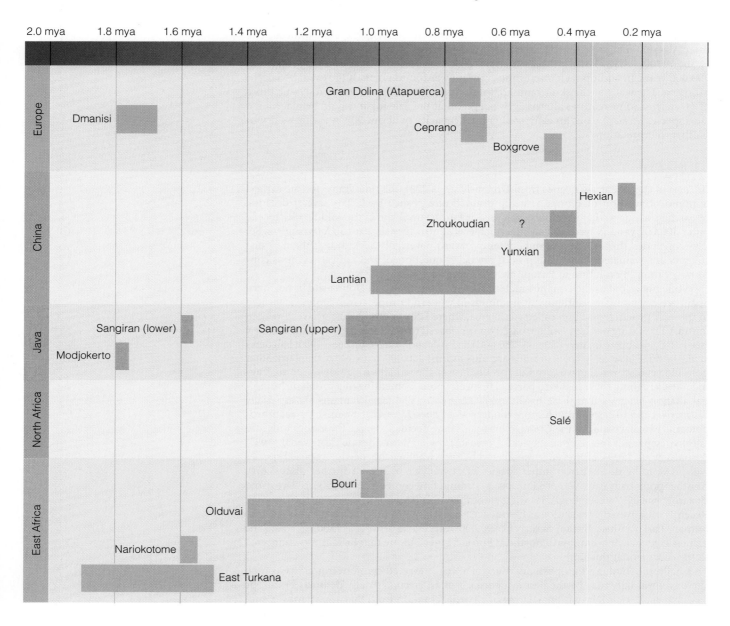

Note: Most dates are only imprecise estimates. However, the dates from East African sites are chronometri-cally determined and are thus much more secure. In addition, the early dates from Java are also radiometric and are gaining wide acceptance.

FIGURE **10–14**

Time line for *Homo erectus* discoveries and other contemporary hominids. Note that most dates are approximations.

Technological and Population Trends in *Homo erectus*

TECHNOLOGICAL TRENDS

Many researchers have noted the remarkable stability of the physical and cultural characteristics of *Homo erectus* populations, which seemed to change so little in the more than 1.5 million years of their existence. There is, however, dispute on this point. Some anthropologists (Rightmire, 1981) see almost no detectable changes in cranial dimensions over more than 1 million years of *H. erectus* evolution.* Others (e.g., Wolpoff, 1984), who use different methodologies to date and subdivide their samples, draw a different conclusion, because they see some significant long-term morphological trends. Accepting a moderate position, we can postulate that there were some changes: The brain of later *H. erectus* was somewhat larger, the nose more protrusive, and the body not as robust as in earlier populations. What's more, there were modifications in stone tool technology.

Expansion of the brain presumably enabled *H. erectus* to develop a more sophisticated tool kit than seen among earlier hominids. The important change in this kit was a core worked on both sides, called a *biface* (known widely as a hand axe or cleaver; Fig. 10–15). The biface had a flatter core than seen in the roundish, earlier Oldowan pebble tool. And, probably even more important, this *core* tool was obviously a target design, that is, the toolmaker's main goal. This greater focus and increased control enabled the stoneknapper to produce sharper, straighter edges, resulting in a more efficient implement. With only minor modification, this Acheulian stone tool became standardized as the basic *H. erectus* all-purpose tool for more than a million years. It served to cut, scrape, pound, and dig. This most useful tool has been found in Africa, parts of Asia, and later in Europe. It should also be noted that Acheulian tool kits also included several types of small tools (Fig. 10–16).

---

*This conclusion does not take into account the Dmanisi remains, but refers to more obvious and more derived *H. erectus* specimens.

FIGURE **10–15**
Acheulian biface ("hand axe"), a basic tool of the Acheulian tradition.

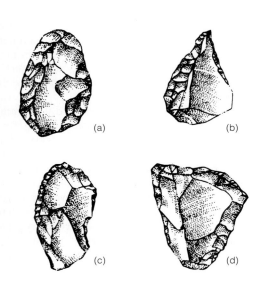

FIGURE **10–16**
Small tools of the Acheulian industry. (a) Side scraper. (b) Point. (c) End scraper. (d) Burin.

(a)

(b)

Robert Jurmain

Robert Jurmain

FIGURE 10–17

(a) A Middle Pleistocene butchering site at Olorgesailie, Kenya, excavated by Louis and Mary Leakey, who had the catwalk built for observers. (b) A close-up of the Acheulian tools, mainly hand axes, found at the site.

For many years, scientists thought that a cultural "divide" separated the Old World, with Acheulian technology found *only* in Africa, southwest Asia, and western Europe, but not elsewhere; in other words, they assumed it was absent in eastern Europe and most of Asia. However, recently reported excavations from more than 20 sites in southern China have forced reevaluation of this hypothesis (Yamei et al., 2000). As we've noted, the most distinctive tools of the Acheulian are bifaces, and they are the very tools thought lacking throughout most of the Pleistocene in eastern Europe and most of Asia. The new archaeological assemblages from southern China are securely dated at about 800,000 ya and contain numerous bifaces, very similar to contemporaneous Acheulian bifaces from Africa (see Figs. 10–15 and 10–17b). It now appears likely that cultural traditions relating to stone tool technology were largely equivalent over the *full* geographical range of *H. erectus* and its contemporaries.

While geographical distinctions are not so obvious, temporal changes in tool technology are evident. Early toolmakers used a stone hammer (simply an oval-shaped stone about the size of an egg or a bit larger) to remove flakes from the core, leaving deep scars that produced a sharp edge. Later, they used other materials, such as wood and bone, as soft hammers, and this gave them more control over flaking, ultimately yielding even sharper edges and a more symmetrical form.

Evidence of butchering is widespread at *H. erectus* sites, and in the past, such evidence has been cited in arguments for consistent hunting. For example, at the Olorgesailie site in Kenya (Fig. 10–17), dated at approximately 800,000 ya, thousands of Acheulian hand axes have been recovered in association with remains of large animals, including giant, now extinct baboons. However, the assumption of consistent hunting has been challenged, especially by archaeologists who argue that the evidence doesn't prove the hunting hypothesis. Instead, they suggest that *H. erectus* was primarily a scavenger, a hypothesis that also has not yet been proved conclusively. We thus discuss *H. erectus* as a potential hunter *and* scavenger. It's crucial to remember, too, that these hominids frequently *gathered* wild plant foods. Indeed, most of the calories they consumed probably came from such gathering activities.

Additionally, as we have seen, the mere *presence* of animal bones at archaeological sites doesn't prove that hominids were killing animals or even necessarily eating meat. In fact, as was the case in the earlier South African sites (discussed in Chapter 9), the hominid remains themselves may have been the meal refuse of large carnivores. So, in making interpretations of early hominid sites, we must consider a variety of alternatives. As archaeologist Richard Klein has concluded regarding Middle Pleistocene sites, the interpretations are far from clear: "In sum, the available data do not allow us to isolate the relative roles of humans, carnivores, and factors such as starvation, accidents, and stream action in creating bone assemblages. . . . Certainly, as presently understood, the sites do not tell us how successful or effective *Homo erectus* was at obtaining meat" (1989, p. 221).

POPULATION TRENDS

H. erectus is the first hominid for which we have definite evidence of *wide* geographical dispersion—that is, across more than one continent. Descendants of early *Homo* ancestors in Africa, the earliest migrants into Eurasia were similar in many ways to their early *Homo* forebears (although they may be seen as a primitive form of *H. erectus*). These initial migrants were possibly followed quite quickly by a second migration from Africa into Eurasia. By then, those hominids had attained the full physical and cultural capacities of *H. erectus*, and the populations dispersed far and wide in the Old World—far beyond the relatively narrow ranges of earlier hominids.

The life of hunter-scavengers—and, no doubt, *primarily* gatherers—was nomadic, and the woodland and savanna that covered the southern tier of Asia would have been an excellent environment for *H. erectus*, since it was similar to the econiche of their African ancestors. As the population grew, small groups budded off and moved on to find new locations. This process, repeated again and again, led *H. erectus* east—crossing to Java, where they arrived, it seems, as early as the most ancient known sites in East Africa itself. At about the same time, another migratory route took hominids to eastern Europe. This migration, however, might have involved a more primitive form of *Homo* and didn't meet with the wide success ultimately attained by *Homo erectus*.

Interpretations of *Homo erectus*: Continuing Uncertainties

Several aspects of the geographical, physical, and behavioral patterns shown by *H. erectus* (broadly defined) seem clear. But new discoveries and more in-depth analyses are making some of our simpler conclusions seem shaky. The fascinating fossil hominids discovered at Dmanisi are perhaps the most challenging piece of this puzzle.

The approach we've taken in this chapter and stated in our earlier hypothesis (see p. 228) suggests that *Homo erectus* was able to emigrate from Africa owing to more advanced culture and a more modern anatomy as compared to earlier African predecessors. Yet, the Dmanisi cranial remains show that these very early Europeans still had small brains, and in one case, the cranium looks more like early *Homo* than like *Homo erectus*. Besides, these hominids had only a very basic stone tool kit, one apparently no more advanced than very early African ones.

So it seems that part of our hypothesis is not fully accurate. At least some of the earliest emigrants from Africa didn't yet show the entire suite of *Homo erectus* physical and behavioral traits. How different the Dmanisi hominids are from the full *H. erectus* pattern remains to be seen, and the discovery of more complete postcranial remains will be most illuminating.

Going a step further, the four crania from Dmanisi are extremely variable; one of them, in fact, does look more like *Homo erectus*. It would be tempting to conclude that more than one type of hominid is represented here—but they're all found in the same geological context. The archaeologists who excavated the site are convinced that all the fossils are closely associated with each other. The simplest hypothesis is that they all are members of the *same* species. This degree of apparent intraspecific variation is biologically noteworthy, and it's influencing how paleoanthropologists interpret all of these fossil samples.

This growing awareness of the broad limits of intraspecific variation among some hominids brings us to our second consideration: Is *Homo ergaster* in Africa a separate species from *Homo erectus*, as strictly defined in Asia? While this interpretation has been increasingly popular in the last decade, it now seems to be losing steam. The finds from Dmanisi raise fundamental issues of interpretation. Among these four crania from one locality (see Fig. 10–4), we see more variation than between the African and Asian forms, which many researchers have interpreted as different species. Also, the new discovery from Bouri (Ethiopia) of a more *erectus*-looking cranium further weakens the separate-species interpretation of *Homo ergaster.*

The separate-species status of the early European fossils from Spain (Gran Dolina) is also not yet clearly established. We still don't have much good fossil evidence from this site; but an early date, prior to 750,000 ya, is well confirmed. Recall also that no other western European hominid fossils are known until at least 250,000 years later, and a seemingly almost contemporaneous find from Italy looks like *Homo erectus.* The more modern-looking face of the Gran Dolina hominid might be explained by a fairly early expansion, from Africa into Spain, of more modern-looking humans. Further complicating this interpretation, the best evidence comes from a young individual, estimated to have died at around 12 years of age. So, the "modern" facial morphology may simply reflect the immature developmental stage of this adolescent. In any case, whether these hominids ever dispersed elsewhere in Europe remains to be seen. However, later in the Pleistocene, their possible descendants are well established both in Africa and in Europe. These later premodern humans are the topic of the next chapter.

In conclusion, we return again to our hypothesis regarding the initial dispersal of genus *Homo.* It seems that more than one such dispersal occurred, soon after 2 mya. One, as represented by the Dmanisi fossils, involved a less-derived *Homo* than the full-blown *H. erectus* pattern. These hominids, nevertheless, quite remarkably migrated as far as eastern Europe; but current evidence doesn't indicate that this more primitive *Homo* species expanded much beyond that initial foothold.

As we've suggested, it may have been a second migration—deriving from early African *H. erectus*—that expanded so widely in the Old World. We have evidence of such an expansion of the full *H. erectus* physical and behavioral grade from sites in East Africa, North Africa, southeastern Asia, eastern Asia, and Europe.

When looking back at the evolution of *H. erectus,* we realize how significant this early human's achievements were. It was *H. erectus* who increased in body size with more efficient bipedalism; who embraced culture wholeheartedly as an adaptive strategy; whose brain was reshaped and increased in size to within the range of *H. sapiens;* who became a more efficient scavenger and likely hunter with a greater dependence on meat; and who apparently established more permanent living sites. In short, it was *H. erectus,* committed to a cultural way of life, who transformed hominid evolution to human evolution. As Richard Foley states, "The appearance and expansion of *H. erectus* represented a major change in adaptive strategy that influenced the subsequent process and pattern of human evolution" (1991, p. 425).

Summary

Homo erectus remains are found in geological contexts dating from about 1.8 million to at least 200,000 years ago—and probably much later—and spanning a period of more than 1.5 million years. While the nature and timing of migrations are uncertain, it's likely that *H. erectus* first appeared in East Africa and later migrated to other areas. This widespread and highly successful hominid defines a new and more modern grade of human evolution, but some more limited dispersal out of Africa by a more primitive species of *Homo* now seems likely.

Historically, the first finds were made by Dubois in Java, and later discoveries came from China and Africa. Differences from early *Homo* are notable in *H. erectus*' larger brain, taller stature, robust build, and changes in facial structure and cranial buttressing.

The long period of *H. erectus* existence was marked by a remarkably uniform technology over space and time. Even so, compared to earlier hominids, *H. erectus* and contemporaries introduced more sophisticated tools and probably ate novel and/or differently processed foods. By using these new tools and—at later sites—possibly fire as well, they were also able to move into different environments and successfully adapt to new conditions.

It's generally assumed that certain *H. erectus* populations evolved into later premodern humans, some of which, in turn, evolved into *Homo sapiens.* Evidence supporting such a series of transitions is seen in the Ngandong fossils (and others discussed in Chapter 11), which display both *H. erectus* and *H. sapiens* features. There are still many questions about *H. erectus*

TABLE 10–1 The Most Significant Hominid Fossils Discussed in This Chapter

	Site	Dates (ya)	Taxonomic Designation	Comments
Asia	Java (6 locales)	1,800,000–25,000	*Homo erectus*	First *H. erectus* discovery; most finds in disturbed river terrace contexts
	China (6 locales; most significant is Zhoukoudian)	400,000+–200,000?	*Homo erectus*	Up to 40 individuals at Zhoukoudian; also, many artifacts; Zhoukoudian, however, probably not primary living site
Europe	Ceprano	900,000–800,000	*Homo erectus*	One individual; well-preserved cranium; Similar to Asian *H. erectus*
	Gran Dolina (Atapuerca, Spain)	780,000?	Quite likely not *H. erectus*; referred to by discoverers as "Homo antecessor"	Remains quite incomplete; oldest W. European fossil hominid discovery
	Dmanisi (Republic of Georgia)	1,800,000–1,700,000	*Homo erectus/Homo ergaster* (very primitive example—or could be classified as early *Homo*)	Three well-preserved crania plus partial mandible; among oldest *H. erectus* found anywhere
Africa	Bouri (Ethiopia)	1,000,000	*Homo erectus*	Well-preserved cranium plus postcranial bones; morphology quite similar to Asian *H. erectus*
	Nariokotome (West Turkana, Kenya)	1,600,000	*Homo erectus*, also frequently referred to as *Homo ergaster*	Nearly complete adolescent skeleton, probably of a male; shows some differences from Asian *H. erectus*
	East Turkana (Kenya)	1,800,000	*Homo erectus*, also frequently referred to as *Homo ergaster*	Well-preserved cranium plus several other postcranial remains likely coming from same group; cranium likely of female; shows several differences from Asian *H. erectus*

behavior—for example, did they hunt? did they control fire?—and about their relationship to later hominids—was the mode of evolution gradual or rapid, and which *H. erectus* populations contributed genes? The search for answers continues.

In Table 10–1 you'll find a useful summary of the most significant hominid fossils discussed in this chapter.

Critical Thinking Questions

1. Why is the nearly complete skeleton from Nariokotome so important? What kinds of evidence does it provide?
2. Assume that you're in the laboratory and have the Nariokotome skeleton as well as a skeleton of a modern human. First, given a choice, what age and sex would you choose for the human skeleton, and why? Second, what similarities and differences do the two skeletons show?

3. What fundamental questions of interpretation do the fossil hominids from Dmanisi raise? Does this evidence completely overturn the hypothesis concerning *H. erectus* dispersal from Africa? Explain why or why not.

4. How has the interpretation of fire use by *Homo erectus* at Zhoukoudian been revised in recent years? What kinds of new evidence from this site have been used in this reevaluation, and what does that tell you about modern archaeological techniques and approaches? What kinds of archaeological evidence would convince you that *H. erectus* used fire?

5. You're interpreting the hominid fossils from three sites in East Africa (Nariokotome, Olduvai, and Bouri)—all considered possible members of *H. erectus*. What sorts of evidence would lead you to conclude that there was more than one species? What would convince you that there was just one species? Why do you think some paleo-anthropologists (splitters) would tend to see more than one species, while others (lumpers) would generally not? What kind of approach would you take, and why?

PALEOANTHROPOLOGY/FOSSIL HOMINIDS

CHAPTER
11

Premodern Humans

FOCUS QUESTION

Who were the immediate precursors to modern *Homo sapiens*, and how do they compare with modern humans?

Go to the following CD-ROMs for interactive activities and exercises on topics covered in this chapter:

- Hominid Fossils: An Interactive Atlas CD-ROM, First Edition

- Virtual Laboratories for Physical Anthropology CD-ROM, Third Edition

Introduction

What do you think of when you hear the term *Neandertal?* Most people think of imbecilic, bent-over brutes. Yet, Neandertals were quite advanced; they had brains at least as large as ours, and they showed many sophisticated cultural capabilities. What's more, they definitely weren't bent over, but fully erect (as hominids had been for millions of years previously). In fact, Neandertals and their immediate predecessors could easily be called human.

And that brings us to possibly the most basic of all questions: What does it mean to be human? The meaning of this term is highly varied, encompassing religious, philosophical, and biological considerations. As you know, physical anthropologists primarily concentrate on the biological aspects of the human organism. Living people are all members of one species, all showing a common anatomical pattern and similar behavioral potentials. We call hominids like us "fully modern humans," and in the next chapter we'll discuss the origin of forms that were essentially identical to living people.

When in our evolutionary past can we say that our predecessors were obviously human? Certainly, the further back we go in time, the less hominids look like contemporary *Homo sapiens*. This is, of course, exactly what we'd expect in an evolutionary sequence. As more proof, the hominid fossil record, which has become increasingly rich in recent years, now provides a detailed picture of this sequence.

We saw in Chapter 10 that *Homo erectus* took crucial steps in the human direction and defined a new grade of human evolution. In this chapter, we'll review those hominids who continued this journey. Both physically and behaviorally, they're much like modern humans; but they still show several significant differences. So, while most paleoanthropologists are comfortable referring to these hominids as "human," we need to qualify this recognition a bit in order to set them apart from fully modern people. And so, in this book, we'll refer to these fascinating immediate predecessors as premodern humans.

When, Where, and What

THE PLEISTOCENE

Middle Pleistocene The portion of the Pleistocene epoch beginning 780,000 ya and ending 125,000 ya.

Upper Pleistocene The portion of the Pleistocene epoch beginning 125,000 ya and ending approximately 10,000 ya.

glaciations Climatic intervals when continental ice sheets cover much of the northern continents. Glaciations are associated with colder temperatures in northern latitudes and more arid conditions in southern latitudes, most notably in Africa.

Most of the hominids discussed in this chapter lived during the **Middle Pleistocene**, a period beginning 780,000 years ago (ya) and ending 125,000 ya. In addition, some of the later premodern humans, especially the Neandertals, lived well into the **Upper Pleistocene** (125,000–10,000 ya).

The Pleistocene has been called the Ice Age because, as had occurred before in geological history, it was marked by periodic advances and retreats of massive continental glaciations. During the glacial interludes, temperatures were very cold and ice accumulated, since more snow fell each year than melted. We should mention that there were numerous advances and retreats of ice; in fact, during the Pleistocene, at least 15 major and 50 minor glacial advances have been documented in Europe (Tattersall et al., 1988).

It's important to remember that these **glaciations**, which enveloped huge swaths of Europe, Asia, and North America as well as Antarctica, were mostly confined to northern latitudes. As a result, hominids—all still restricted to the Old World—were severely affected as the climate, flora, and animal life shifted during these Pleistocene oscillations. For the

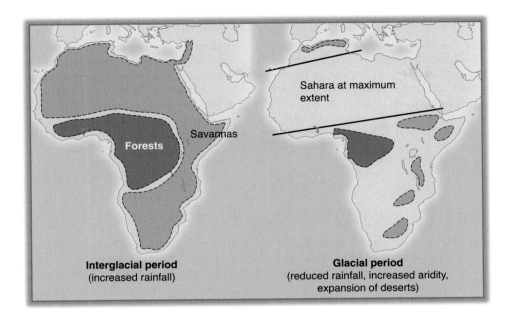

FIGURE **11–1**
Changing Pleistocene environments in Africa.

hominids living during this time, the most dramatic of these effects were in Europe and northern Asia—less so in southern Asia and in Africa.

To the south, climates also fluctuated, but most notably in Africa, the main effects were related to changing rainfall patterns. During glacial periods, the climate in Africa became more arid, while during **interglacials**, rainfall increased. The changing availability of food resources certainly affected hominids in Africa, but probably even more important, migration routes also swung back and forth. In North Africa during glacial periods (Fig. 11–1), the Sahara expanded and blocked migration in and out of sub-Saharan Africa (Lahr and Foley, 1998).

In Eurasia, as well, glacial advances greatly affected migration routes. As the ice sheets expanded, sea levels dropped, more northern areas became uninhabitable, and some key passages between areas became blocked by glaciers. For example, during glacial peaks, much of western Europe would have been cut off from the rest of Eurasia (Fig. 11–2).

During the warmer—and, in the south, wetter—interglacials, the ice sheets shrank, sea levels rose, and certain migration routes reopened (for example, from central into western Europe). Clearly, to understand Middle Pleistocene hominids, it's crucial to view them within their shifting Pleistocene world.

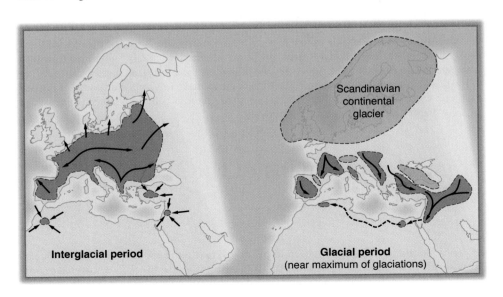

FIGURE **11–2**
Changing Pleistocene environments in Eurasia. Purple areas show regions of likely hominid occupation. Orange areas are major glaciers. Arrows indicate likely migration routes

interglacials Climatic intervals when continental ice sheets are retreating, eventually becoming much reduced in size. Interglacials in northern latitudes are associated with warmer temperatures, while in southern latitudes the climate becomes wetter.

DISPERSAL OF MIDDLE PLEISTOCENE HOMINIDS

Like their *Homo erectus* predecessors, later hominids were widely distributed in the Old World, with discoveries coming from three continents—Africa, Asia, and Europe. For the first time, in fact, it appears that Europe became more permanently and densely occupied; Middle Pleistocene hominids have been discovered widely from England, France, Spain, Germany, Italy, Hungary, and Greece. Africa, as well, probably continued as a central area of hominid occupation, and finds have come from North, East, and South Africa. Finally, Asia has yielded several important finds, most especially from China (see Fig. 11–4 on pp. 250–251). We should point out, though, that these Middle Pleistocene premodern humans didn't vastly extend the geographical range of *Homo erectus*, but largely replaced the earlier hominids in habitats previously exploited. One exception appears to be the more successful occupation of Europe, a region where earlier hominids have only sporadically been found.

MIDDLE PLEISTOCENE HOMINIDS: TERMINOLOGY

The premodern humans of the Middle Pleistocene (that is, after 780,000 ya) generally succeeded *H. erectus*. But in some areas, especially in Asia, there apparently was a long period of coexistence, lasting 300,000 years or longer—you'll recall the very late dates for the Javanese Ngandong *H. erectus* (see p. 231).

Earlier representatives of the premoderns retain several *H. erectus* characteristics. For example, the face is large, the brows are projected, the forehead is low, and in some cases the cranial vault is still thick. Even so, some of their other features show that they were more derived, in the human direction, than their predecessors were. Compared to *Homo erectus*, more modern features in premodern humans include increased brain size, a more rounded braincase (that is, maximum breadth is higher up on the sides), a more vertical nose, and a less-angled back of the skull (occipital). We should note that the maximum span of time encompassed by Middle Pleistocene premodern humans is at least 500,000 years. It's no surprise that over time, we can observe certain trends. The later representatives, for example, show more brain expansion and a less-angled occipital than do earlier forms.

So, we know that premodern humans were a diverse group dispersed over three continents. Deciding how to classify them has been in dispute for decades, and anthropologists still have disagreements. However, a growing consensus has recently emerged. Beginning perhaps as early as 850,000 ya and extending to about 200,000 ya, the fossils from Africa and Europe are placed within *Homo heidelbergensis*, named after a fossil found in Germany in 1907.

Until recently, many researchers regarded these fossils as early but more primitive members of *Homo sapiens*. In recognition of this somewhat transitional status, the fossils were called "archaic *Homo sapiens*," but most paleoanthropologists find this terminology unsatisfactory. For example, Phillip Rightmire concludes that "simply lumping diverse ancient groups with living populations obscures their differences" (1998, p. 226). In our own discussion, we recognize *H. heidelbergensis* in this transitional period. Keep in mind, however, that this species was probably an ancestor of both modern humans and Neandertals. It's debatable whether these Middle Pleistocene hominid samples actually represent a fully separate species in the *biological* sense, that is, following the biological species concept (see p. 100). Still, it's useful to give them a separate name to make this important stage of human evolution more easily identifiable. (We'll return to this issue later in the chapter, when we discuss the theoretical implications in more detail.)

Premodern Humans of the Middle Pleistocene

AFRICA

In Africa, premodern fossils have been found at several sites (Figs. 11–3 and 11–5). One of the best known is Broken Hill (Kabwe). At this site in Zambia, fieldworkers discovered a complete cranium, together with other cranial and postcranial elements belonging to several indi-

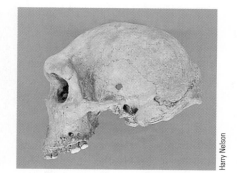

FIGURE 11–3

Broken Hill (Kabwe). Note the very heavy supraorbital torus.

Harry Nelson

viduals. In this and other African premodern specimens, we can see a mixture of older and more recent traits. Dating estimates of Broken Hill and most of the other premodern fossils from Africa have ranged throughout the Middle and Upper Pleistocene, but recent estimates have given dates for most of the sites in the range of 600,000–125,000 ya.

A total of eight other crania from South and East Africa also show a combination of retained ancestral with more derived (modern) characteristics, and they're all mentioned in the literature as being similar to Broken Hill. The most important of these African finds come from the sites of Florisbad and Elandsfontein in South Africa, Laetoli in Tanzania, and Bodo in Ethiopia (see Fig. 11–5 on pp. 250–251).

Bodo is the most significant of these other African fossils, because it's a nearly complete cranium that's been dated to quite early in the Middle Pleistocene (estimated at 600,000 ya). The Bodo cranium is also interesting because it shows a distinctive pattern of cut marks, similar to modifications seen in butchered animal bones. Researchers have thus hypothesized that the Bodo individual was defleshed by other hominids, but for what purpose is not clear. It may have been cannibalism; it may have been some other purpose. In any case, this is the earliest evidence of deliberate bone processing of hominids by hominids (White, 1986).

The general similarities in all these African premodern fossils indicate a close relationship between them, almost certainly representing a single species (most commonly referred to as *H. heidelbergensis*). These African premodern humans also are quite similar to those found in Europe.

EUROPE

More fossil hominids of Middle Pleistocene age have been found in Europe than in any other region. Maybe it's because more archaeologists have been searching longer in Europe than elsewhere. In any case, during the Middle Pleistocene, Europe was more widely and consistently occupied than it was earlier in human evolution.

The time range of European premoderns extends the full length of the Middle Pleistocene and beyond. At the earlier end, the Gran Dolina finds from northern Spain (discussed in Chapter 10; see p. 237) are definitely not *Homo erectus*. As proposed by Spanish researchers, they may be members of yet another hominid species. Conversely, they may represent the same *grade* of hominid discussed in this chapter—that is, a population of premodern humans. As noted in Chapter 10, the Gran Dolina hominids might represent the same species (*H. heidelbergensis*) as their later European successors (a view also proposed by Rightmire, 1998). If this interpretation should be further confirmed, Gran Dolina would represent the earliest well-dated occurrence of *H. heidelbergensis*, dating back as early as 850,000 ya.

More recent and more completely studied *H. heidelbergensis* fossils have been found throughout much of Europe. Examples of these finds come from Steinheim and Ehringsdorf (Germany), Swanscombe (England), Arago (France), and Atapuerca (Spain). Like their African counterparts, these European premoderns have retained *H. erectus* traits, but they're mixed with more derived ones—for example, increased cranial capacity, more rounded occiput, parietal expansion, and reduced tooth size (Fig. 11–4).

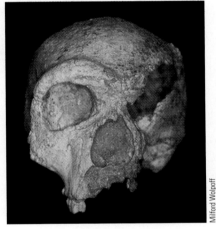

(a)

Milford Wolpoff

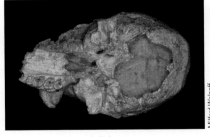

(b)

Milford Wolpoff

FIGURE 11–4

Cast of an archaic *Homo heidelbergensis* skull from Germany (Steinheim). (a) Frontal view showing damaged skull. (b) Basal view showing how the *foramen magnum* was enlarged, apparently for removal of the brain, perhaps for dietary or ritualistic purposes.

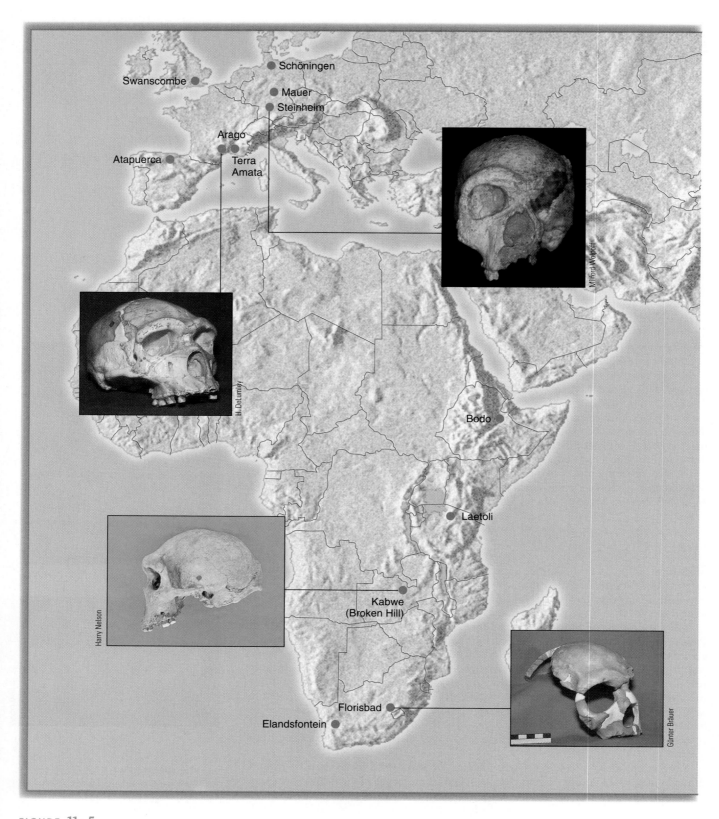

FIGURE 11–5
Fossil discoveries and archaeological localities of Middle Pleistocene premodern hominids.

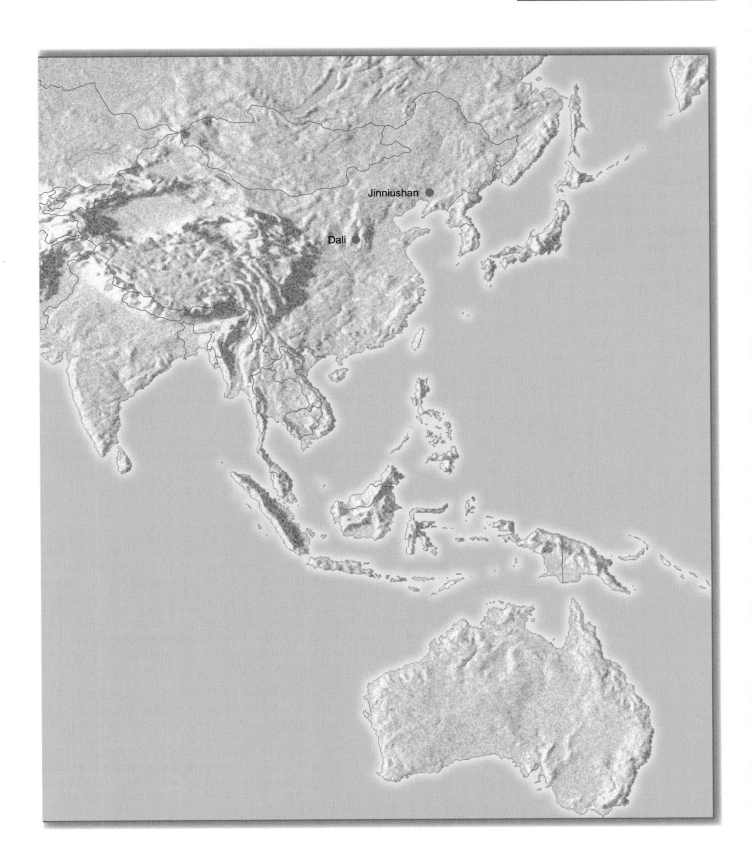

Site	Dates (ya)	Human Remains
Arago (Tautavel) (France)	400,000–300,000; date uncertain	Face; parietal perhaps from same person; many cranial fragments; up to 23 individuals represented
Atapuerca (Sima de los Huesos, northern Spain)	320,000–190,000, probably 300,000	Minimum of 28 individuals, including some nearly complete crania
Steinheim (Germany)	300,000–250,000; date uncertain	Nearly complete skull, lacking mandible
Swanscombe (England)	300,000–250,000; date uncertain	Occipital and parietals

AT A GLANCE — Key Middle Pleistocene Premodern Human (*H. heidelbergensis*) Fossils from Europe

The hominids from Atapuerca are especially interesting. These finds come from another cave in the same area as the Gran Dolina discoveries. Dated to approximately 350,000 ya, a total of at least 28 individuals have been recovered from a site called Sima de los Huesos, literally meaning "pile of bones." In fact, with more than 4,000 fossil fragments recovered, Sima de los Huesos contains more than 80 percent of all the Middle Pleistocene hominid remains from the whole world (Bermudez de Castro et al., 2004). Excavations continue at this remarkable site, where bones have somehow accumulated within a deep chamber inside a cave. From initial descriptions, paleoanthropologists interpret the hominid morphology as showing several indications of an early Neandertal-like pattern, with arching browridges, projecting midface, and other features (Rightmire, 1998).

ASIA

Like their contemporaries in Europe and Africa, Asian premodern specimens discovered in China also display both earlier and later characteristics. Chinese paleoanthropologists suggest that the more ancestral traits, such as a sagittal ridge (see p. 227) and flattened nasal bones, are shared with *H. erectus* fossils from Zhoukoudian. They also point out that some of these features can be found in modern *H. sapiens* in China today, indicating substantial genetic continuity. That is, some Chinese researchers have argued that anatomically, modern Chinese didn't evolve from *H. sapiens* in either Europe or Africa; instead, they evolved specifically in China from a separate *H. erectus* lineage. Whether such regional evolution occurred or whether anatomically modern migrants from Africa displaced local populations is the subject of a major ongoing debate in paleoanthropology. This important controversy will be the central focus of the next chapter.

Dali, the most complete skull of the late Middle or early Upper Pleistocene fossils in China, displays *H. erectus* and *H. sapiens* traits. It also has a relatively small cranial capacity (1,120 cm^3). Like Dali, several other Chinese specimens combine both earlier and later traits. In addition, a partial skeleton from Jinniushan, in northeast China, has been given a provisional date of 200,000 ya (Tiemel et al., 1994). The cranial capacity is fairly large (approximately 1,260 cm^3), and the walls of the braincase are thin. These are both modern features, and they're somewhat unexpected in an individual this ancient—if the dating estimate is indeed correct. How to classify these Chinese Middle Pleistocene hominids has been a subject of debate and controversy. Recently, though, a leading paleoanthropologist has concluded that they're regional variants of *Homo heidelbergensis* (Rightmire, 2004).

AT A GLANCE Key Middle Pleistocene Premodern Human
(*H. heidelbergensis*) Fossils from Asia

Site	Dates (ya)	Human Remains
Dali (China)	Late Middle Pleistocene (230,000–180,000)	Nearly complete skull
Jinniushan (China)	Late Middle Pleistocene (200,000)	Partial skeleton, including a cranium

A Review of Middle Pleistocene Evolution

Premodern human fossils from Africa and Europe resemble each other more than they do the hominids from Asia. The mix of some ancestral characteristics—retained from *Homo erectus* ancestors—with more derived features gives the African and European fossils a distinctive look; they're usually referred to as *H. heidelbergensis*.

The situation in Asia is not so tidy. To some researchers, the remains, especially those from Jinniushan, seem more modern than do contemporary fossils from either Europe or Africa. This observation explains why Chinese paleoanthropologists and some American colleagues conclude the Jinniushan remains are early members of *H. sapiens*. Other researchers (e.g., Rightmire, 1998, 2004) suggest that they represent a regional branch of *H. heidelbergensis*.

The Pleistocene world forced many small populations into geographical isolation. Most of these regional populations no doubt died out. Some, however, did evolve, and their descendants are likely a major part of the later hominid fossil record. In Africa, *H. heidelbergensis* is hypothesized to have evolved into modern *H. sapiens*. In Europe, *H. heidelbergensis* evolved into Neandertals. Meanwhile, the Chinese premodern populations may all have met with extinction. Right now, though, there's no consensus on the status or the likely fate of these enigmatic Asian Middle Pleistocene hominids (Fig. 11–6).

FIGURE 11–6
Time line of Middle Pleistocene hominids. Note that most dates are approximations. Question marks indicate those estimates that are most tentative.

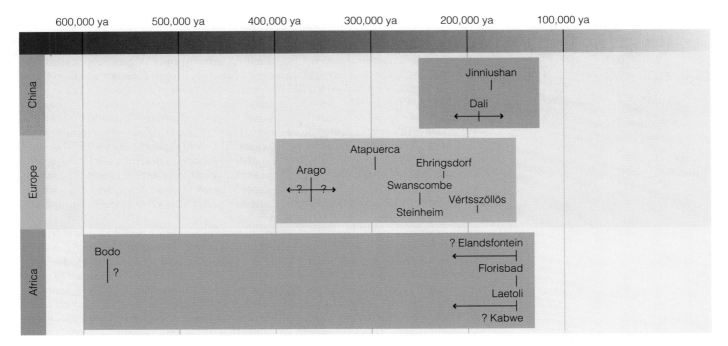

Nodule

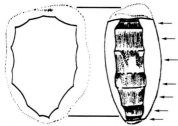

The nodule is chipped
on the perimeter.

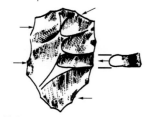

Flakes are radially
removed from top surface.

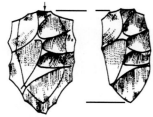

A final blow at one end
removes a large flake.

FIGURE 11–7
The Levallois technique.

Middle Pleistocene Culture

The Acheulian technology of *H. erectus* carried over into the Middle Pleistocene with relatively little change until near the end of the period, when it became slightly more sophisticated. Bone, a very useful tool material, was apparently practically unused during this time. Stone flake tools similar to those of the earlier era persisted, possibly in greater variety. Some of the later premodern humans in Africa and Europe invented a method—the Levallois technique (Fig. 11–7)—for controlling flake size and shape. Requiring several coordinated steps, this was no mean feat, and it suggests increased cognitive abilities in later premodern populations.

Interpreting the distribution of artifacts during the later Middle Pleistocene has generated considerable discussion among archaeologists. As we noted in Chapter 10, a general geographical distribution characterizes the Lower Pleistocene, with bifaces (mostly hand axes) found quite often at sites in Africa, only rarely at sites in most of Asia, and not at all among the rich assemblage at Zhoukoudian. Also, where hand axes proliferate, the stone tool industry is referred to as Acheulian, while at localities without hand axes, various other terms are used—for example, *chopper/chopping tool*, which is a misnomer since most of the tools are actually flakes.

Acheulian assemblages have been found at many African sites as well as numerous European ones—for example, Swanscombe in England and Arago in France. Even though there are broad geographical patterns in the distribution of what we call Acheulian, this shouldn't blind us to the considerable intraregional diversity in stone tool industries. Clearly, a variety of European sites do show a typical Acheulian complex, rich in bifacial hand axes and cleavers. But at other contemporaneous sites in Germany and Hungary, fieldworkers found a variety of small retouched flake tools and flaked pebbles of various sizes, but no hand axes.

So it seems that different stone tool industries coexisted in some areas for long periods. Various explanations (Villa, 1983) have been offered to account for this apparent diversity: (1) The tool industries were produced by different peoples—that is, different cultures, possibly hominids that also were biologically different; (2) the tool industries represent different types of activities carried out at separate locales; (3) the presence (or absence) of specific tool types—bifaces—represents the availability (or unavailability) of appropriate local stone resources.

Premodern human populations continued to live both in caves and in open-air sites, but they may have increased their use of caves. Did these hominids control fire? Klein (1999), in interpreting archaeological evidence from France, Germany, and Hungary, suggests that they did. What's more, Chinese archaeologists insist that many Middle Pleistocene sites in China contain evidence of human-controlled fire. Still, not everyone is convinced.

We know that Middle Pleistocene hominids built temporary structures, because researchers have found concentrations of bones, stones, and artifacts at several sites. We also have evidence that they exploited many different food sources, such as fruits, vegetables, fish, seeds, nuts, and bird eggs, each in its own season. They also exploited marine life. The most detailed reconstruction of Middle Pleistocene life in Europe comes from Terra Amata, a site in what is now the city of Nice, in southern France (de Lumley and de Lumley, 1973; Villa, 1983). This site provides fascinating evidence relating to short-term, seasonal visits by hominid groups, who built flimsy shelters, gathered plants, ate food from the ocean, and possibly hunted medium- to large-sized mammals.

The hunting capabilities of premodern humans, as for earlier hominids, are still being disputed. So far, the evidence doesn't clearly establish widely practiced advanced abilities. In earlier professional discussions (as well as in earlier editions of our texts), archaeological evidence from Terra Amata and Torralba and Ambrona (in Spain) was used to argue for advanced hunting skills. However, reconstruction of these sites by Richard Klein and others has now cast doubt on those conclusions. Once again, we see that applying scientific rigor—which is simply good critical thinking—makes us question previously held assumptions. Sometimes we have to conclude that other less dramatic (and less romantic) explanations fit the evidence as well as or better than those based on our preliminary and more imaginative scenarios.

A recent and exceptional find is once again challenging some assumptions about hunting capabilities of premodern humans in Europe. In 1995, from the site of Schöningen in Germany, researchers discovered three remarkably well-preserved wooden spears (Thieme, 1997). As we've noted before, fragile organic remains, such as wood, can rarely be preserved more than a few hundred years; yet these beautifully crafted implements are provisionally dated to 400,000–380,000 ya. Beyond this surprisingly ancient date, the spears are intriguing for several other reasons. First, they're all large (about 6 feet long), very finely made of hard spruce wood, and expertly balanced. Each spear would have required considerable planning, time, and skill to manufacture. Additionally, the weapons were most likely used as throwing spears, presumably to hunt large animals. Also interesting in this context, the bones of numerous horses were recovered at Schöningen. Archaeologist Hartmut Thieme has thus concluded that "the spears strongly suggest that systematic hunting, involving foresight, planning and the use of appropriate technology, was part of the behavioural repertoire of premodern hominids" (1997, p. 807). These extraordinary spears from Schöningen make a strong case that at least some Middle Pleistocene populations had advanced hunting skills.

As documented by the fossil remains as well as artifactual evidence from archaeological sites, the long period of transitional hominids in Europe was to continue well into the Upper Pleistocene (after 125,000 ya). But here, with the appearance and expansion of the Neandertals, the evolution of premodern humans was to take a unique turn.

Neandertals: Premodern Humans of the Upper Pleistocene

Since their discovery more than a century ago, the Neandertals have haunted the minds and foiled the best-laid theories of paleoanthropologists. They fit into the general scheme of human evolution, and yet they are misfits. Classified either as *H. sapiens* or a sister species, they are like us and yet different. It's not easy to put them in their place. Many anthropologists classify Neandertals as *H. sapiens*, but they're included as a subspecies, *Homo sapiens neanderthalensis**—the subspecies for anatomically modern *H. sapiens* is designated as *Homo sapiens sapiens*. However, not all experts agree with this interpretation.

Neandertal fossil remains have been found at dates approaching 130,000 ya, but in the following discussion of Neandertals, we'll focus on those populations that lived especially during the last major glaciation, which began about 75,000 ya and ended about 10,000 ya (Fig. 11–8, p. 256). We should also note that the evolutionary roots of Neandertals apparently reach quite far back in western Europe, as evidenced by the 300,000-year-old remains from Sima de los Huesos, Atapuerca, in northern Spain. The majority of fossils have been found in Europe, where they've been most studied. Our description of Neandertals is based primarily on those specimens, usually called *classic* Neandertals, from western Europe. Not all Neandertals—including others from eastern Europe and western Asia and those from the interglacial period just before the last glacial one—exactly fit our description of the classic morphology. They tend to be less robust, possibly because the climate in which they lived was not as cold as in western Europe during the last glaciation.

One striking feature of Neandertals is brain size, which in these hominids actually was larger than that of *H. sapiens* today. The average for contemporary *H. sapiens* is between 1,300 and 1,400 cm^3, while for Neandertals it was 1,520 cm^3. The larger size may be associated with the metabolic efficiency of a larger brain in cold weather. The Inuit (Eskimo), also living in very cold areas, have a larger average brain size than most other modern human populations do. We should also point out that the larger brain size in both premodern and contemporary human populations adapted to *cold* climates is partially correlated with larger body size, which has also evolved among these groups (see Chapter 4).

---

*Thal, meaning "valley," is the old spelling; but due to rules of taxonomic naming, this spelling is retained in the formal species designation (although the *h* was *never* pronounced). The modern spelling, *tal*, is now used this way in Germany; we follow contemporary usage in the text with the spelling *Neandertal*.

FIGURE 11-8

Correlation of Pleistocene subdivisions with archaeological industries and hominids. Note that the geological divisions are separate and different from the archaeological stages (e.g., Upper Pleistocene is *not* synonymous with Upper Paleolithic).

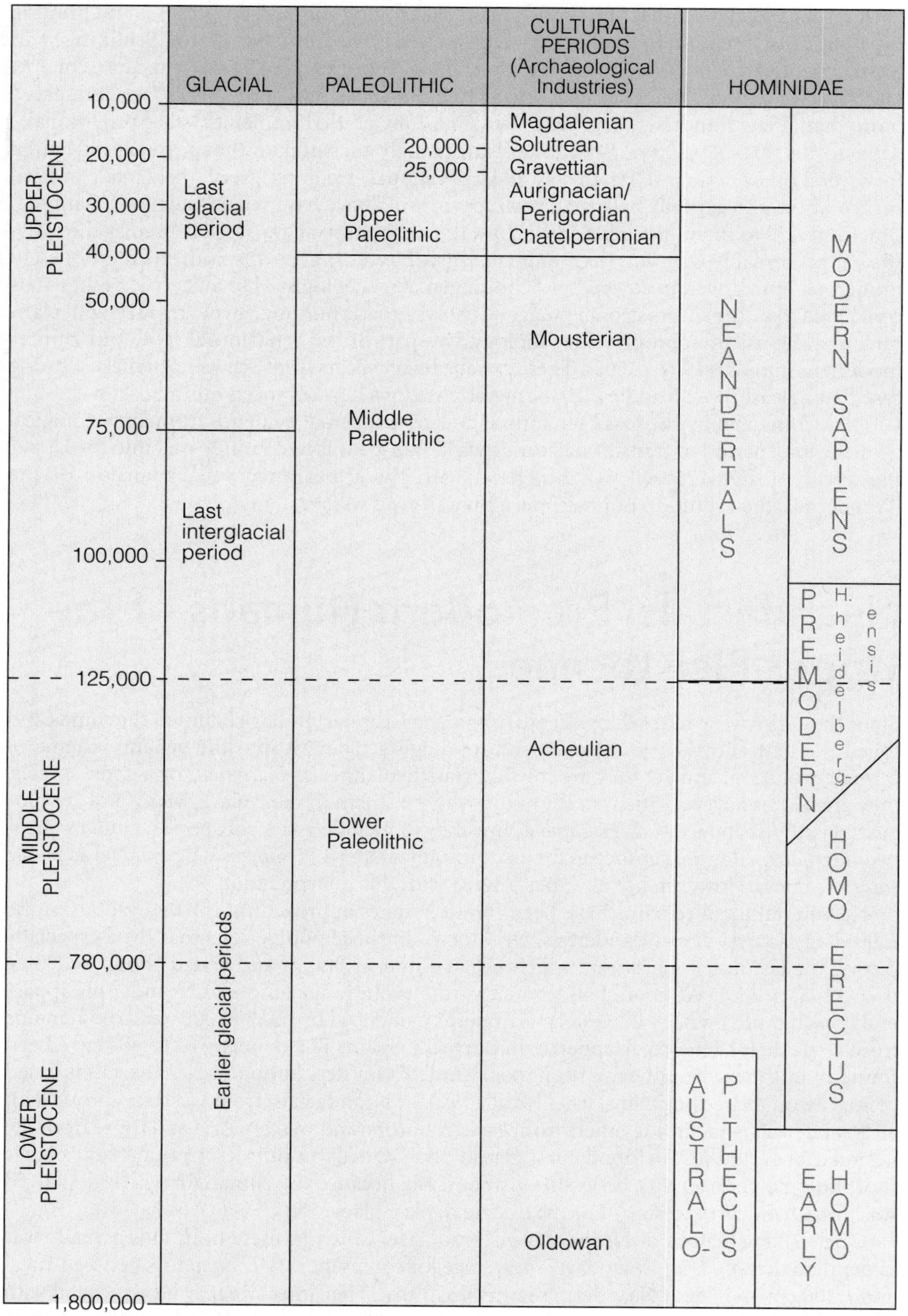

		GLACIAL	PALEOLITHIC	CULTURAL PERIODS (Archaeological Industries)	HOMINIDAE
UPPER PLEISTOCENE	10,000				MODERN SAPIENS
	20,000	Last glacial period		20,000 – Magdalenian Solutrean	
	30,000		Upper Paleolithic	25,000 – Gravettian Aurignacian/ Perigordian Chatelperronian	
	40,000				
	50,000			Mousterian	NEANDERTALS
	75,000		Middle Paleolithic		
	100,000	Last interglacial period			
	- - 125,000				PREMODERN H. heidelberg-ensis
MIDDLE PLEISTOCENE		Earlier glacial periods	Lower Paleolithic	Acheulian	HOMO ERECTUS
	- - 780,000				
LOWER PLEISTOCENE				Oldowan	AUSTRALO-PITHECUS / EARLY HOMO
	1,800,000				

The classic Neandertal cranium is large, long, low, and bulging at the sides. Viewed from the side, the occipital bone is somewhat bun shaped, but the marked occipital angle typical of many *H. erectus* crania is absent. The forehead rises more vertically than that of *H. erectus*, and the browridges arch over the orbits instead of forming a straight bar (Fig. 11–9).

Compared with anatomically modern humans, the Neandertal face stands out. It projects almost as if it were pulled forward. This feature can be seen by comparing the distance of the nose and teeth from the eye orbits with that of modern *H. sapiens*. Postcranially, Neandertals were very robust, barrel-chested, and powerfully muscled. This robust skeletal structure, in fact, dominates hominid evolution from *H. erectus* through all premodern forms. Still, the

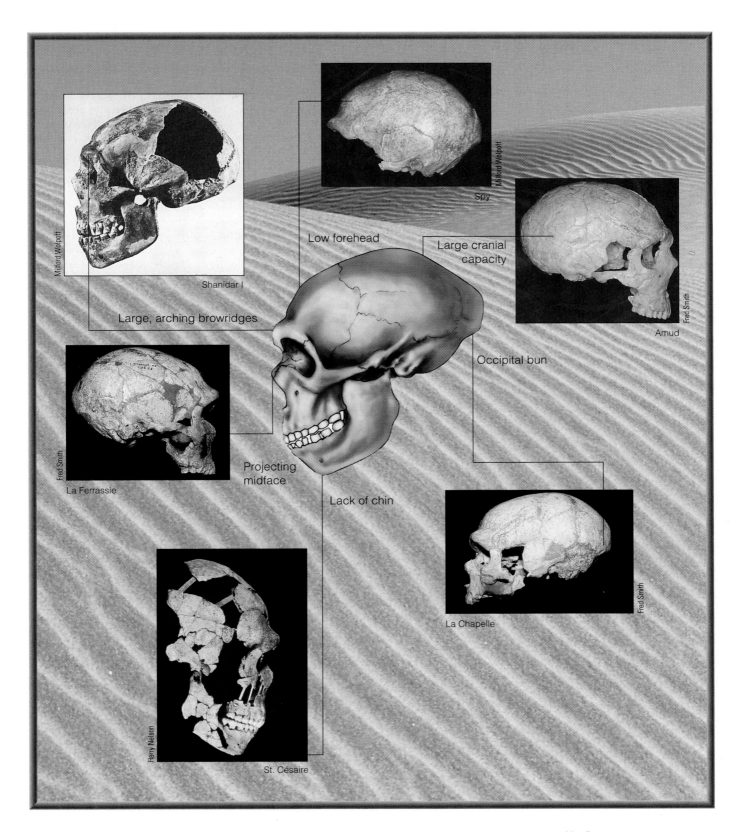

FIGURE 11–9
Morphology and variation in Neandertal crania.

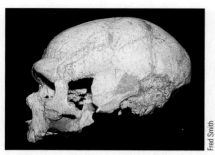

FIGURE 11-10
La Chapelle-aux-Saints. Note the occipital bun, projecting face, and low vault.

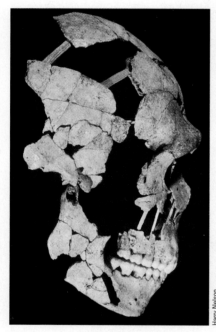

FIGURE 11-11
St. Césaire, among the "last" Neandertals.

flexed   The position of the body in a bent orientation, with arms and legs drawn up to the chest.

Upper Paleolithic   A cultural period usually associated with modern humans, but also found with some Neandertals, and distinguished by technological innovation in various stone tool industries. Best known from western Europe; similar industries are also known from central and eastern Europe and Africa.

Neandertals appear particularly robust, with shorter limbs than seen in most modern *H. sapiens* populations. Both the facial anatomy and the robust postcranial structure of Neandertals have been interpreted by Erik Trinkaus, of Washington University in St. Louis, as adaptations to rigorous living in a cold climate.

For about 100,000 years, Neandertals lived in Europe and western Asia (see Fig. 11–14 on pp. 260–261),and their coming and going have raised more questions and controversies than for any other hominid group. As we've noted, Neandertal forebears date back to the later premodern populations of the Middle Pleistocene. But these were transitional forms, and it's not until the Upper Pleistocene that Neandertals become fully recognizable.

FRANCE AND SPAIN

One of the most important Neandertal discoveries was made in 1908 at La Chapelle-aux-Saints in southwestern France. A nearly complete skeleton was found buried in a shallow grave in a **flexed** position. Several fragments of nonhuman long bones had been placed over the head, and over them, a bison leg. Around the body were flint tools and broken animal bones.

The skeleton was turned over for study to a well-known French paleontologist, Marcellin Boule, who depicted the La Chapelle Neandertal as a brutish, bent-kneed, not fully erect biped. Because of this exaggerated interpretation, some scholars, and certainly the general public, concluded that all Neandertals were highly primitive creatures.

Why did Boule draw these conclusions from the La Chapelle skeleton? Today, we think he misjudged the Neandertal posture because this adult male skeleton had osteoarthritis of the spine. Also, and probably more important, Boule and his contemporaries found it difficult to fully accept as a human ancestor an individual who appeared in any way to depart from the modern pattern.

The skull of this male, who was possibly at least 40 years of age when he died, is very large, with a cranial capacity of 1,620 cm³. As is typical for western European classic forms, the vault is low and long; the supraorbital ridges are immense, with the typical Neandertal arched shape; the forehead is low and retreating; and the face is long and projecting. The back of the skull is protuberant and bun shaped (Figs. 11–9 and 11–10).

The La Chapelle skeleton isn't a typical Neandertal, but an unusually robust male who "evidently represents an extreme in the Neandertal range of variation" (Brace et al., 1979, p. 117). Unfortunately, this skeleton, which Boule claimed didn't even walk completely erect, was widely accepted as "Mr. Neandertal." But not all Neandertal individuals express the suite of classic Neandertal traits to the degree seen in this one.

Another Neandertal site excavated recently in southern France has revealed further fascinating details about Neandertal behavior. From the 100,000- to 120,000-year-old Moula-Guercy Cave site, Alban Defleur, Tim White, and colleagues have analyzed 78 broken skeletal fragments from probably six individuals (Defleur et al., 1999). The intriguing aspect of these remains concerns *how* they were broken. Detailed analysis of cut marks, pits, scars, and other features clearly suggests that these individuals were *processed*—that is, they "were defleshed and disarticulated. After this, the marrow cavity was exposed by a hammer-on-anvil technique" (Defleur et al., 1999, p. 131). What's more, the nonhuman bones at this site, especially the deer remains, were processed in an identical way. In other words, the Moula-Guercy Neandertals provide the best-documented evidence thus far of Neandertal *cannibalism.*

Some of the most recent of the western European Neandertals come from St. Césaire in southwestern France and are dated at about 35,000 ya (Fig. 11–11). The bones were recovered from a bed including discarded chipped blades, hand axes, and other stone tools of an **Upper Paleolithic** tool industry associated with Neandertals. There's another late site in central Europe, where radiocarbon dating has indicated that the most recent Neandertal remains at Vindija, in Croatia (discussed shortly), are about 32,000 to 33,000 years old (Smith et al., 1999).

An even more recent site in Portugal has been interpreted as showing hybridization between Neandertals and modern *Homo sapiens.* We'll discuss this intriguing suggestion in more detail in Chapter 12.

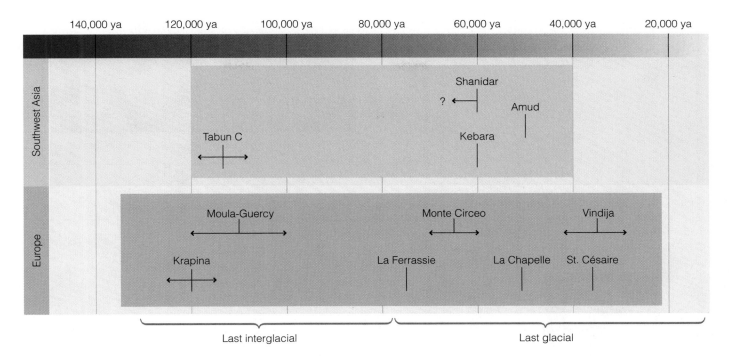

FIGURE 11–12
Time line for Neandertal fossil discoveries.

The St. Césaire and Vindija sites are important for several reasons. Anatomically modern humans were living in central and western Europe by about 35,000 ya or a bit earlier. So, it's possible that Neandertals and modern *H. sapiens* were living quite close to each other for several thousand years (Fig. 11–12). How did these two groups interact? Evidence from a number of French sites indicates that Neandertals borrowed technological methods and tools (such as blades) from the anatomically modern populations and thereby modified their own tools, creating a new industry, the **Chatelperronian**.

CENTRAL EUROPE

There are quite a few other European classic Neandertals, including significant finds in central Europe (see Fig. 11–14 on pp. 260–261). At Krapina, Croatia, researchers have recovered an abundance of bones—1,000 fragments representing up to 70 individuals—and 1,000 stone tools or flakes (Trinkaus and Shipman, 1992). Krapina is an old site, possibly the earliest showing the full classic Neandertal morphology, dating back to the beginning of the Upper Pleistocene (estimated at 130,000–110,000 ya). And, despite the relatively early date, the characteristic Neandertal features of the Krapina specimens, although less robust, are similar to the western European finds (Fig. 11–13). Krapina is also important as an intentional burial site—one of the oldest on record.

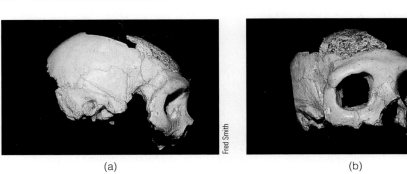

(a)   (b)

FIGURE 11–13
Krapina C. (a) Lateral view showing characteristic Neandertal traits. (b) Three-quarters view.

Chatelperronian   Pertaining to an Upper Paleolithic industry found in France and Spain, containing blade tools and associated with Neandertals.

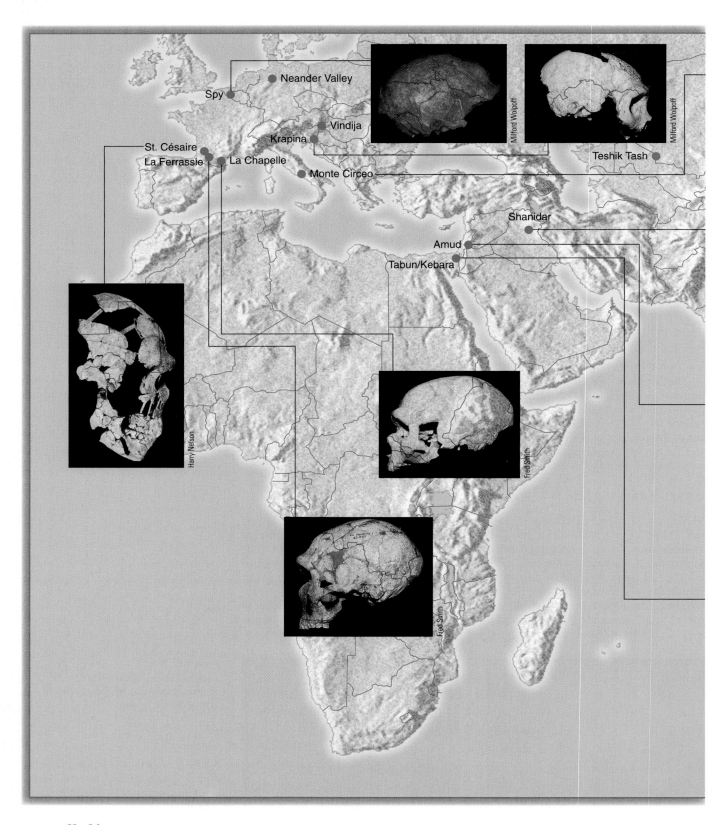

FIGURE 11–14
Fossil discoveries of Neandertals.

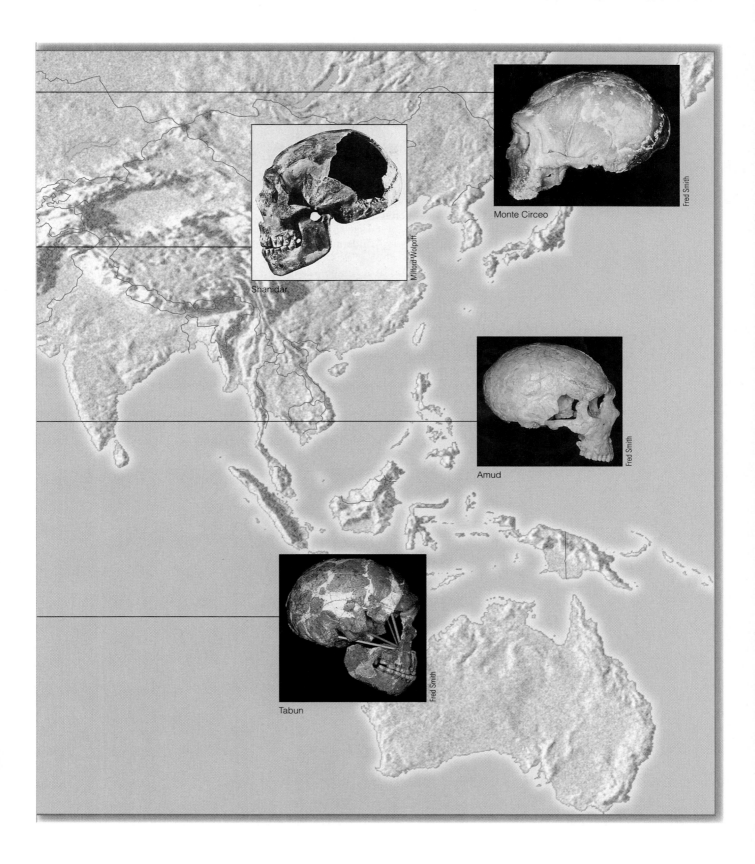

Shanidar

Milford-Wolpoff

Monte Circeo

Fred Smith

Amud

Fred Smith

Tabun

Fred Smith

About 30 miles from Krapina, Neandertal fossils have also been discovered at Vindija. The site is an excellent source of faunal, cultural, and hominid materials stratified in *sequence* throughout much of the Upper Pleistocene. Neandertal fossils consisting of some 35 specimens are dated between about 42,000 and 32,000 ya. (The latter date would be the best verified of the more recent Neandertal discoveries; Higham et al., 2006.) Even though some of their features approach the morphology of early modern south-central European *H. sapiens*, the overall pattern is definitely Neandertal. Even so, these modified Neandertal features, such as smaller browridges and slight chin development, have led some researchers to suggest a possible evolutionary trend toward modern *H. sapiens*.

WESTERN ASIA

Israel   In addition to European Neandertals, many important discoveries have been made in southwest Asia. Several specimens from Israel display some modern features and are less robust than the classic Neandertals of Europe, but again, the overall pattern is Neandertal. The best known of these discoveries is from Tabun—short for Mugharet-et-Tabun, meaning "cave of the oven"—at Mt. Carmel, a short drive south from Haifa (Fig. 11–15). Tabun, excavated in the early 1930s, yielded a female skeleton, recently dated by thermoluminescence (TL) at about 120,000–110,000 ya. If this dating is accurate, Neandertals at Tabun were generally contemporary with early modern *H. sapiens* found in nearby caves. (TL dating is discussed on p. 183.)

A more recent Neandertal burial, a male discovered in 1983, comes from Kebara, a neighboring cave of Tabun at Mt. Carmel. A partial skeleton, dated to 60,000 ya, contains the most complete Neandertal pelvis so far recovered. Also recovered at Kebara is a hyoid—a small bone located in the throat, and the first ever found from a Neandertal; this bone is especially important because of its usefulness in reconstructing language capabilities.*

Iraq   A most remarkable site is Shanidar, in the Zagros Mountains of northeastern Iraq, where fieldworkers found partial skeletons of nine individuals, four of them deliberately buried. Among these individuals is a particularly interesting one called Shanidar 1. This is a

FIGURE 11–15
Excavation of the Tabun Cave, Mt. Carmel, Israel.

---

*The Kebara hyoid is identical to that of modern humans, suggesting that Neandertals did not differ from *H. sapiens sapiens* in this key element.

skeleton of a male who lived to be approximately 30 to 45 years old, a considerable age for a prehistoric human (Fig. 11–16). His height is estimated at 5 feet 7 inches, and his cranial capacity is 1,600 cm³. This individual shows several fascinating features:

> There had been a crushing blow to the left side of the head, fracturing the eye socket, displacing the left eye, and probably causing blindness on that side. He also sustained a massive blow to the right side of the body that so badly damaged the right arm that it became withered and useless; the bones of the shoulder blade, collar bone, and upper arm are much smaller and thinner than those on the left. The right lower arm and hand are missing, probably not because of poor preservation . . . but because they either atrophied and dropped off or because they were amputated. (Trinkaus and Shipman, 1992, p. 340)

Besides these injuries, the man had further trauma to both legs, and he probably limped. It's hard to imagine how he could have performed day-to-day activities. Both Ralph Solecki, who supervised the work at Shanidar Cave, and Erik Trinkaus, who has studied the Shanidar remains, believe that to survive, Shanidar 1 must have been helped by others: "A one-armed, partially blind, crippled man could have made no pretense of hunting or gathering his own food. That he survived for years after his trauma was a testament to Neandertal compassion and humanity" (Trinkaus and Shipman, 1992, p. 341).

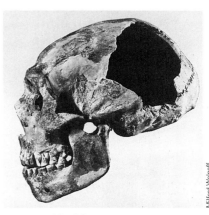

FIGURE 11–16

Shanidar 1. Does he represent Neandertal compassion for the disabled?

CENTRAL ASIA

About 1,600 miles east of Shanidar in Uzbekistan, inside a cave at Teshik-Tash, researchers found what may be the easternmost Neandertal discovery. Actually, new analyses suggest that the Teshik-Tash skeleton may be that of a modern human, which means it's not a Neandertal (Glantz et al., 2004). The skeleton is that of a nine-year-old boy who appears to have been deliberately buried. It was reported that five pairs of wild goat horns surrounded him, suggesting a burial ritual or perhaps a religious cult, but owing to inadequate published documentation of the excavation, this interpretation has been seriously questioned. The Teshik-Tash individual, like some specimens from Croatia and southwest Asia, also shows a mixture of Neandertal traits (heavy browridges and occipital bun) and modern traits (high vault and definite signs of a chin).

The Teshik-Tash site may be the easternmost location for Neandertals. Based on the assumed evidence that Teshik-Tash is a Neandertal, geographical distribution of the Neandertals extended from France eastward, possibly extending to central Asia—a distance of about 4,000 miles.

AT A GLANCE — Key Neandertal Fossil Discoveries

Site	Dates (ya)	Human Remains
Vindija (Croatia)	42,000–28,000	35 specimens; almost entirely cranial fragments
La Chapelle (France)	50,000	Nearly complete adult male skeleton
Shanidar (Iraq)	70,000–60,000	9 individuals (partial skeletons)
Tabun (Israel)	110,000 date uncertain	2 (perhaps 3) individuals, including almost complete skeleton of adult female
Krapina (Croatia)	125,000–120,000	Up to 40 individuals, but very fragmentary

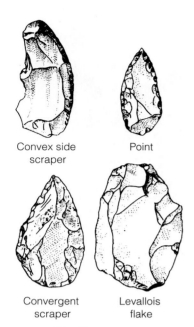

Convex side
scraper

Point

Convergent
scraper

Levallois
flake

FIGURE 11–17
Mousterian tools. (After Bordes.)

Culture of Neandertals

Anthropologists almost always associate Neandertals, who lived in the cultural period known as the Middle Paleolithic, with the **Mousterian** industry—although they don't always associate the Mousterian industry with Neandertals. Early in the last glacial period, Mousterian culture extended across Europe and North Africa into the former Soviet Union, Israel, Iran, and as far east as Uzbekistan and possibly even China. Also, in sub-Saharan Africa, the contemporaneous Middle Stone Age industry is broadly similar to the Mousterian.

TECHNOLOGY

Neandertals improved on previous prepared-core techniques—that is, the Levallois—by inventing a new variation. They trimmed a flint nodule around the edges to form a disk-shaped core. Each time they struck the edge, they produced a flake, and they kept at it until the core became too small and was discarded. In this way, they produced more flakes per core than their predecessors did. They then reworked the flakes into various forms including scrapers, points, and knives (Fig. 11–17).

Neandertal craftspeople elaborated and diversified traditional methods, and there's some indication that they developed specialized tools for skinning and preparing meat, hunting, woodworking, and hafting. But in strong contrast to the next cultural period, the Upper Paleolithic, there's almost no evidence that they used bone tools. Still, Neandertals advanced their technology well beyond that of earlier hominids. It's quite possible that their technological advances helped provide a basis for the remarkable changes of the Upper Paleolithic, which we'll discuss in the next chapter.

SUBSISTENCE

We know, from the abundant remains of animal bones at their sites, that Neandertals were successful hunters. But while it's clear that Neandertals could hunt large mammals, they may not have been as efficient at this task as were Upper Paleolithic hunters. For example, it wasn't until the beginning of the Upper Paleolithic that the spear-thrower, or atlatl, came into use (see p. 290). Soon after that, the bow and arrow greatly increased efficiency (and safety) in hunting large mammals. Because they had no long-distance weaponry and were mostly limited to thrusting spears, Neandertals may have been more prone to serious injury—a hypothesis supported by paleoanthropologists Thomas Berger and Erik Trinkaus. Berger and Trinkaus (1995) analyzed the pattern of trauma, particularly fractures, in Neandertals and compared it with that seen in contemporary human samples. Interestingly, the pattern in Neandertals, especially the relatively high proportion of head and neck injuries, was most similar to that seen in contemporary rodeo performers. Berger and Trinkaus concluded that "The similarity to the rodeo distribution suggests frequent close encounters with large ungulates unkindly disposed to the humans involved" (Berger and Trinkaus, 1995, p. 841).

We know much more about European Middle Paleolithic culture than any earlier period, because it's been studied longer and by more scholars. Recently, however, Africa has been a target not only of physical anthropologists but also of archaeologists, who have added considerably to our knowledge of African Pleistocene hominid history. In many cases, the technology and assumed cultural adaptations in Africa were similar to those in Europe and southwest Asia. We'll see in the next chapter that the African technological achievements also kept pace with, or even preceded, those in western Europe.

SYMBOLIC BEHAVIOR

There are a variety of hypotheses concerning the speech capacities of Neandertals, and many of these views are contradictory. Some researchers argue that Neandertals were incapable of human speech, but the prevailing consensus has been that they *were* capable of articulate speech, maybe even fully competent in the range of sounds produced by modern humans. However, recent genetic evidence may call for a reassessment of just when fully human language first emerged (Enard et al., 2002). In humans today, mutations in a particular gene (locus) are known to produce serious language impairments. From an evolutionary per-

Mousterian Pertaining to the stone tool industry associated with Neandertals and some modern *H. sapiens* groups. Also called Middle Paleolithic. This industry is characterized by a larger proportion of flake tools than found in Acheulian tool kits.

spective, what's perhaps most significant concerns the greater variability seen in the alleles at this locus in modern humans as compared to other primates. One explanation for this increased variation is intensified selection acting on human populations, perhaps quite recently—and thus potentially after the evolutionary divergence of the Neandertals.

But even if we conclude that Neandertals *could* speak, it doesn't necessarily mean their abilities were at the level of modern *Homo sapiens*. Today, paleoanthropologists are quite interested in the apparently sudden expansion of modern *H. sapiens* (discussed in Chapter 12), and they've proposed various explanations for this group's rapid success. Also, as we attempt to explain how and why *H. sapiens sapiens* expanded its geographical range, we're left with the problem of explaining what happened to the Neandertals. In making these types of interpretations, a growing number of paleoanthropologists suggest that *behavioral* differences are the key. Further confirmation of a recent evolutionary shift, resulting from the mutation of a crucial gene that influences language capacity, will help support this view.

Researchers believe that Upper Paleolithic *H. sapiens* had some significant behavioral advantages over Neandertals and other premodern humans. Was it some kind of new and expanded ability to symbolize, communicate, organize social activities, elaborate technology, obtain a wider range of food resources, or care for the sick or injured—or, was it some other factor? Compared with *H. sapiens sapiens*, were the Neandertals limited by neurological differences that may have contributed to their demise?

The direct anatomical evidence derived from Neandertal fossils isn't much help in answering these questions. Ralph Holloway (1985) has maintained that Neandertal brains—at least as far as the fossil evidence suggests—aren't significantly different from those of modern *H. sapiens*. What's more, Neandertal vocal tracts and other morphological features, compared with our own, don't appear to have seriously limited them.

Most of the reservations about advanced cognitive abilities in Neandertals are based on archaeological data. Interpretation of Neandertal sites, when compared with succeeding Upper Paleolithic sites—especially those documented in western Europe—have led to several intriguing contrasts, as shown in Table 11–1.

TABLE 11–1 Cultural Contrasts* Between Neandertals and Upper Paleolithic Modern Humans	
Neandertals	**Upper Paleolithic Modern Humans**
Tool Technology Numerous flake tools; few, however, apparently for highly specialized functions; use of bone, antler, or ivory very rare; relatively few tools with more than one or two parts	Many more varieties of stone tools; many apparently for specialized functions; frequent use of bone, antler, and ivory; many more tools comprised of two or more component parts
Hunting Efficiency and Weapons No long-distance hunting weapons; close-proximity weapons used (thus, more likelihood of injury)	Use of spear-thrower and bow and arrow; wider range of social contacts, perhaps permitting larger, more organized hunting parties (including game drives)
Stone Material Transport Stone materials transported only short distances—just "a few kilometers" (Klein, 1989)	Stone tool raw materials transported over much longer distances, implying wider social networks and perhaps trade
Art Artwork uncommon; usually small; probably mostly of a personal nature; some items perhaps misinterpreted as "art"; others may be intrusive from overlying Upper Paleolithic contexts; cave art absent	Artwork much more common, including transportable objects as well as elaborate cave art; well executed, using a variety of materials and techniques; stylistic sophistication
Burial Deliberate burial at several sites; graves unelaborated; graves frequently lack artifacts	Burials much more complex, frequently including both tools and remains of animals

*The contrasts are more apparent in some areas (particularly western Europe) than others (eastern Europe, Near East). Elsewhere (Africa, eastern Asia), where there were no Neandertals, the cultural situation is quite different. Even in western Europe, the cultural transformations were not necessarily abrupt, but may have developed more gradually from Mousterian to Upper Paleolithic times. For example, Straus (1995) argues that many of the Upper Paleolithic features were not consistently manifested until after 20,000 ya.

Due to this type of behavioral and anatomical evidence, Neandertals in recent years have increasingly been viewed as an evolutionary dead end. Right now, we can't say whether their disappearance and ultimate replacement by anatomically modern Upper Paleolithic peoples—with their presumably "superior" culture—was the result of cultural differences alone, or whether it was also influenced by biological variation.

BURIALS

Anthropologists have known for some time that Neandertals deliberately buried their dead. Undeniably, the spectacular discoveries at La Chapelle, Shanidar, and elsewhere were the direct results of ancient burial, which permits much more complete preservation. Such deliberate burial treatment goes back at least 90,000 years at Tabun. And, from a much older site, some form of consistent "disposal" of the dead—not necessarily belowground burial—is evidenced at Atapuerca, Spain, where at least 28 individuals comprising more than 700 fossilized elements were found in a cave at the end of a deep vertical shaft. From the nature of the site and the accumulation of hominid remains, Spanish researchers are convinced that the site demonstrates some form of human activity involving deliberate disposal of the dead (Arsuaga et al., 1997).

The provisional 300,000-year-old age for Atapuerca suggests that Neandertals—more precisely, their immediate precursors—were, by the Middle Pleistocene, handling their dead in special ways. Such behavior was previously thought to have emerged only much later, in the Upper Pleistocene. And, as far as current data indicate, this practice is seen in western European contexts well before it appears in Africa or in eastern Asia. For example, in the premodern sites at Kabwe and Florisbad (discussed earlier), deliberate disposal of the dead is not documented. Nor is it seen in African early modern sites—for example, the Klasies River Mouth, dated at 120,000–100,000 ya (see p. 280).

Yet, in later contexts (after 35,000 ya), where anatomically modern *H. sapiens* (*H. sapiens sapiens*) remains are found in clear burial contexts, their treatment is considerably more complex than in Neandertal burials. In these later (Upper Paleolithic) sites, grave goods, including bone and stone tools as well as animal bones, are found more consistently and in greater concentrations. Because many Neandertal sites were excavated in the nineteenth or early twentieth century, before more rigorous archaeological methods had been developed, many of these supposed burials are now in question. Still, the evidence seems quite clear that deliberate burial was practiced not only at La Chapelle, La Ferrassie (eight graves), Tabun, Amud, Kebara, Shanidar, and Teshik-Tash but also at several other localities, especially in France. In many cases, the *position* of the body was deliberately modified and placed in the grave in a flexed posture (see p. 258). This flexed position has been found in 16 of the 20 best-documented Neandertal burial contexts (Klein, 1999).

Finally, the placement of supposed grave goods in burials, including stone tools, animal bones (such as cave bear), and even arrangements of flowers, together with stone slabs on top of the burials, have all been postulated as further evidence of Neandertal symbolic behavior. Unfortunately, in many instances, again due to poorly documented excavation, these statements are questionable. Placement of stone tools, for example, is occasionally seen, but it apparently wasn't done consistently. In those 33 Neandertal burials for which we have adequate data, only 14 show definite association of stone tools and/or animal bones with the deceased (Klein, 1989). It's not until the next cultural period, the Upper Paleolithic, that we see a major behavioral shift, as demonstrated in more elaborate burials and development of art.

Genetic Evidence

With the revolutionary advances in molecular biology (discussed in Chapter 3), fascinating new avenues of research have become possible in the study of earlier hominids. It's becoming fairly commonplace to extract, amplify, and sequence ancient DNA from contexts spanning the last 10,000 years or so. For example, researchers have analyzed DNA from the 5,000-year-old "Iceman" found in the Italian Alps.

It's much harder to find usable DNA in even more ancient remains. Because they're mineralized, the organic components, usually including the DNA, have been destroyed. Still, in the past few years, very exciting results have been announced about DNA found in eight different Neandertal fossils dated between 32,000 and 50,000 ya. These fossils come from sites in France (including La Chapelle), Germany (from the original Neander Valley locality), Belgium, Croatia, and Russia (Krings et al., 1997, 2000; Ovchinnikov et al., 2000; Schmitz et al., 2002; Serre et al., 2004).

The technique used in studying the Neandertal fossils involves extracting mitochondrial DNA (mtDNA), amplifying it through polymerase chain reaction, or PCR (see p. 56), and sequencing nucleotides in parts of the molecule. Results from the Neandertal specimens show that these individuals are genetically more different from contemporary *Homo sapiens* populations than modern human populations are from each other—in fact, about three times as much. Consequently, Krings and colleagues (1997) have hypothesized that the Neandertal lineage separated from that of our modern *H. sapiens* ancestors sometime between 690,000 and 550,000 ya.

But this intriguing hypothesis hasn't been fully confirmed, and it's most certainly not accepted by all paleoanthropologists. It's still not clear how rapidly mtDNA evolves, nor is it obvious how genetically different from us we should expect 40,000-year-old relatives to be. In other words, right now, we can't exclude the possibility of evolutionary relationships on the basis of available genetic evidence. Even so, such data probably offer the best hope of ultimately untangling the place of Neandertals in human evolution and perhaps even of understanding something of their fate.

Trends in Human Evolution: Understanding Premodern Humans

As you can see, the Middle Pleistocene hominids are a very diverse group, broadly dispersed through time and space. There is considerable variation among them, and it's not easy to get a clear evolutionary picture. Because we know that regional populations were small and frequently isolated, many of them probably died out and left no descendants. So it's a mistake to see an "ancestor" in every fossil find.

Still, as a group, these Middle Pleistocene premoderns do reveal some general trends. In many ways, for example, it seems they were *transitional* between the hominid grade that came before them (*H. erectus*) and the one that followed them (*H. sapiens sapiens*). It's not a stretch to say that all the Middle Pleistocene premoderns derived from *H. erectus* forebears and that some of them, in turn, were probably ancestors of the earliest fully modern humans.

Paleoanthropologists are certainly concerned with such broad generalities as these, but they also want to focus on meaningful anatomical, environmental, and behavioral details as well as underlying processes. So they consider the regional variability displayed by particular fossil samples as significant—but just *how* significant is up for debate. In addition, increasingly sophisticated theoretical approaches are being used to better understand the processes that shaped the evolution of later *Homo*, at both macroevolutionary and microevolutionary levels.

Scientists, like all humans, assign names or labels to phenomena, a point we addressed in discussing classification in Chapter 5. Paleoanthropologists are certainly no exception. Yet, working from a common evolutionary foundation, paleoanthropologists still come to different conclusions about the most appropriate way to interpret the Middle/Upper Pleistocene hominids. Consequently, a variety of species names have been proposed in recent years.

At the extreme lumping end of the spectrum, only one species is recognized for all the premodern fossils. They are called *Homo sapiens* and are thus further lumped with modern humans, although they're partly distinguished by such terminology as "archaic *H. sapiens*" (see Fig. 11–18a).

At the other end of the spectrum, paleontological splitters have identified at least three species, all distinct from *H. sapiens*. Two of these, *H. heidelbergensis* and *H. neanderthalensis*, were discussed earlier; and a third species, called *Homo helmei*, has recently been proposed

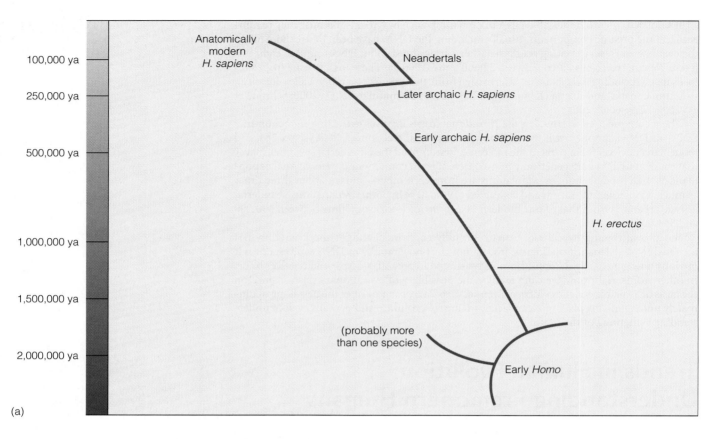

(a)

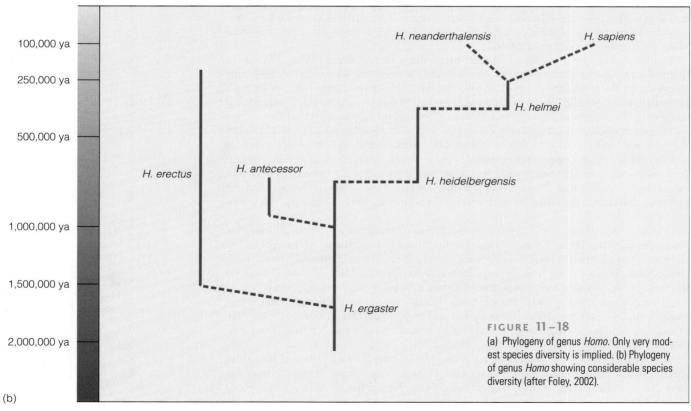

(b)

FIGURE 11–18

(a) Phylogeny of genus *Homo*. Only very modest species diversity is implied. (b) Phylogeny of genus *Homo* showing considerable species diversity (after Foley, 2002).

DIGGING DEEPER

Are They Human?

At the beginning of this chapter we posed the question, What does it mean to be human? Applying this term to our extinct hominid predecessors is somewhat tricky. Various prior hominid species share with contemporary *Homo sapiens* a mosaic of physical features. For example, they're all bipedal, most (but not all) have fairly small canine teeth, some are completely terrestrial, and some are moderately encephalized (while others are much more so). Thus, the *physical* characteristics that define humanity appear at different times during hominid evolution.

Even more tenuous are the *behavioral* characteristics frequently identified as signifying human status. The most significant of these proposed behavioral traits include major dependence on culture, innovation, cooperation in acquiring food, full language, and elaboration of symbolic representations in art and body adornment. Once again, the characteristics become apparent at different stages of hominid evolution. But distinguishing when and how these behavioral characteristics became established in our ancestors is even more problematic than analyzing anatomical traits. While the archaeological record provides considerable information regarding stone tool technology, it's mostly silent on other aspects of material culture. The social organization and language capabilities of earlier hominids are as yet almost completely invisible.

From the available evidence, we can conclude that *H. erectus* took significant steps in the human direction—well beyond that of earlier hominids. *H. erectus* vastly expanded hominid geographical ranges, achieved the full body size and limb proportions of later hominids, had increased encephalization, and became considerably more culturally dependent.

H. heidelbergensis (in the Middle Pleistocene) and, to an even greater degree, Neandertals (in the Upper Pleistocene), maintained several of these characteristics—such as body size and proportions—while also showing further evolution in the human direction. Most particularly, relative brain size increased further,

expanding on average about 22 percent beyond that of *H. erectus* (Fig. 1); notice, however, that the largest jump in proportional brain size occurs very late in hominid evolution—only with the appearance of fully modern humans.

In addition to brain enlargement, cranial shape also was remodeled in *H. heidelbergensis* and Neandertals, producing a more globular shape of the vault as well as suggesting further neurological reorganization. Stone tool technology also became more sophisticated during the Middle Pleistocene, with the manufacture of tools requiring a more complicated series of steps. Also, for the first time, fire was definitely controlled and widely used; caves were routinely occupied; hominid ranges were successfully expanded throughout much of Europe as well as into northern Asia (that is, colder habitats were more fully exploited); structures were built; and more systematic hunting took place.

Some premoderns also were like modern humans in another significant way. Analysis of teeth from a Neandertal shows that these hominids had the same *delayed maturation* found in modern *H. sapiens* (Dean et al., 2001). We don't yet have similar data for earlier *H. heidelbergensis* individuals, but it's possible that they, too, showed this distinctively human pattern of development.

Did these Middle and Upper Pleistocene hominids have the full language capabilities and other symbolic and social skills of living peoples? It's impossible to answer this question completely, given the types of fossil and archaeological evidence available. Yet, it does seem probable that neither *H. heidelbergensis* nor the Neandertals had this entire array of *fully* human attributes. That's why we call them premodern humans.

So, to rephrase our initial question, Were these hominids human? We could answer conditionally: They *were* human—at least, mostly so.

---

*There are no direct current data for body size in *Sahelanthropus*. Body size is estimated from tooth size in comparison with *A. afarensis*. Data abstracted from McHenry, 1992; Wood and Collard, 1999; Brunet, 2002; and Carroll, 2003.

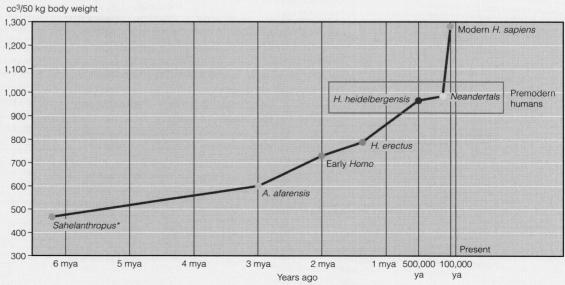

FIGURE 1
Relative brain size in hominids. The scale shows brain size as cc³ per 50 kg of body weight. Premodern humans have a more than 20% increase in relative brain size compared to *H. erectus,* but modern humans show another 30% expansion beyond that in premodern humans.

(Foley and Lahr, 1997; Lahr and Foley, 1998). It's been suggested that this last group is a possible African ancestor of *both* modern humans and Neandertals, but one that appears fairly late in the Middle Pleistocene (300,000–250,000 ya) and so comes largely after *H. heidelbergensis*. This more complex evolutionary interpretation is shown in Figure 11–18b.

We addressed similar differences of interpretation in Chapters 9 and 10, and we know that disparities like these can be frustrating to students who are new to paleoanthropology. The proliferation of new names is confusing, and it might seem that experts in the field are endlessly arguing about what to call the fossils.

Fortunately, it's not quite that bad. There's actually more agreement than you might think. No one doubts that all these hominids are closely related to each other as well as to modern humans. And everyone agrees that only some of the fossil samples represent populations that left descendants. Where paleoanthropologists disagree is when they start discussing which hominids are the most likely to be closely related to later hominids. The grouping of hominids into evolutionary clusters (clades) and assigning of different names to them is a reflection of differing interpretations—and, more fundamentally, of somewhat differing philosophies.

But we shouldn't emphasize these naming and classification debates too much. Most paleoanthropologists recognize that a great deal of these disagreements result from simple, practical considerations. Even the most enthusiastic splitters acknowledge that the fossil "species" are not true species as defined by the biological species concept (see p. 100). For example, the scheme shown in Figure 11–18b reflects the views of Robert Foley, who readily admits: "It is unlikely they are all biological species. . . . These are probably a mixture of real biological species and evolving lineages of subspecies. In other words, they could potentially have interbred, but owing to allopatry (that is, geographical separation) were unlikely to have had the opportunity" (Foley, 2002, p. 33).

Even so, Foley, along with an increasing number of other professionals, distinguishes these different fossil samples with species names to highlight their distinct position in hominid evolution. That is, these hominid groups are more loosely defined as a type of paleospecies (see p. 102) rather than as fully biological species. Giving distinct hominid samples a separate (species) name makes them more easily identifiable to other researchers and makes various cladistic hypotheses more explicit—and, equally important, more directly testable. Eminent paleoanthropologist F. Clark Howell of the University of California, Berkeley also recognizes these advantages, but he is less emphatic about species designations. Howell recommends the term *paleo-deme* for referring to either a species or subspecies classification (Howell, 1999).

The hominids that best illustrate these issues are the Neandertals. Fortunately, they are also the best known, represented by dozens of well-preserved individuals. With all this evidence, researchers can systematically test and evaluate many of the differing hypotheses.

Are Neandertals very closely related to modern *H. sapiens*? Certainly. Are they physically and behaviorally distinct from both ancient and fully modern humans? Yes. Does this mean Neandertals are a fully separate biological species from modern humans and therefore theoretically incapable of fertilely interbreeding with modern people? Probably not. Finally, then, should Neandertals be considered a separate species from, or a subspecies of, *H. sapiens*? For most purposes, it doesn't matter, since the distinction at some point is arbitrary. Speciation is, after all, a *dynamic* process. Fossil groups like the Neandertals represent just one point in this process (Fig. 11–19).

We can view Neandertals as a distinctive side branch of later hominid evolution. Similar to the situation among contemporary baboons—comparing savanna to hamadryas—we could say that Neandertals were an incipient species. Given enough time and enough isolation, they likely would have separated completely from their modern human contemporaries. But as fossil, archaeological, and genetic data are making increasingly clear, Neandertals never got that far. Their fate, in a sense, was decided for them as more successful competitors expanded into Neandertal habitats. These highly successful hominids were fully modern humans, and in the next chapter we'll focus on their story.

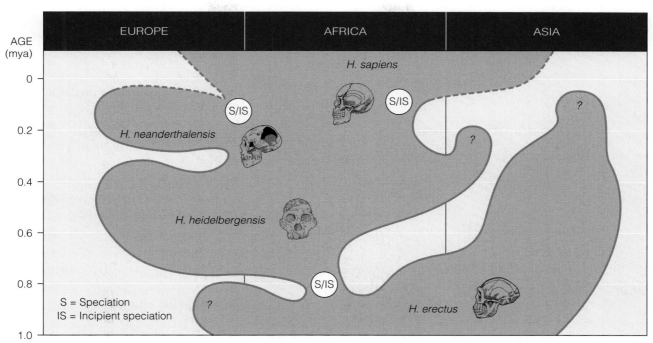

AGE (mya)

| EUROPE | AFRICA | ASIA |

S = Speciation
IS = Incipient speciation

H. neanderthalensis

H. sapiens

H. heidelbergensis

H. erectus

S/IS

S = Speciation
IS = Incipient speciation

FIGURE 11-19
Possible evolutionary relationships of Middle and Upper Pleistocene hominids.

Summary

The Middle Pleistocene (780,000–125,000 ya) was a period of transition in human evolution. Fossil hominids from this period show similarities both with their predecessors (*H. erectus*) and with their successors (*H. sapiens*). They've also been found in many areas of the Old World, in Africa, Asia, and Europe—in the latter case, being the first truly successful occupants of that continent. Because these transitional hominids are more derived—and advanced in the human direction—than *H. erectus*, we can refer to them as premodern humans. With this terminology, we also recognize that these hominids display several significant anatomical and behavioral differences from modern humans.

Although there's some dispute about the best way to formally classify the majority of Middle Pleistocene hominids, most paleoanthropologists now prefer to call them *H. heidelbergensis*. Similarities between the African and European Middle Pleistocene hominid samples suggest that they all can be reasonably seen as part of this same species. The contemporaneous Asian fossils, however, don't fit as neatly into this model, and conclusions regarding these premodern humans remain less definite.

Some of the later *H. heidelbergensis* populations in Europe likely evolved into Neandertals. Abundant Neandertal fossil and archaeological evidence has been collected from the Upper Pleistocene time span of Neandertal existence, about 130,000–29,000 ya. But unlike their Middle Pleistocene (*H. heidelbergensis*) predecessors, Neandertals are more geographically restricted; they're found only in Europe and southwest Asia. Various lines of evidence—anatomical, archaeological, and genetic—also suggest that they were isolated and distinct from other hominids.

These observations have led to a growing consensus among paleoanthropologists that the Neandertals were largely a side branch of later hominid evolution. Still, there remain significant differences in theoretical approaches regarding how to best deal with the Neandertals; that is, should they be considered as a separate species or as a subspecies of *H. sapiens*? We suggest that the best way to view the Neandertals is within a dynamic process of speciation. Neandertals can thus be interpreted as an incipient species—one in the process of splitting from early *H. sapiens* populations.

Site	Dates (ya)	Taxonomic Designation	Comments
La Chapelle	50,000	Neandertal (*Homo neanderthalensis, Homo sapiens neanderthalensis*)	Historically most important site in France in description of Neandertal morphology
Tabun	110,000	Neandertal (*Homo neanderthalensis, Homo sapiens neanderthalensis*)	Important early Neandertal site; shows clear presence of Neandertals in Near East
Atapuerca (Sima de los Huesos)	320,000–190,000	*Homo heidelbergensis*	Large sample; earliest evidence in Europe of Neandertal morphology; evidence of disposal of the dead
Steinheim	300,000–250,000?	*Homo heidelbergensis*	Transitional-looking fossil
Jinniushan	200,000?	*Homo heidelbergensis* Early *Homo sapiens,* as termed by the Chinese	Possibly oldest example of *H. sapiens* in China, but status uncertain
Kabwe (Broken Hill)	130,000+?	*Homo heidelbergensis*	Transitional-looking fossil; similar to Bodo
Bodo	600,000	*Homo heidelbergensis*	Earliest evidence of *H. heidelbergensis* in Africa and perhaps anywhere

TABLE 11–2 The Most Significant Premodern Human Fossil Discoveries Discussed in This Chapter

In Table 11–2 you'll find a useful summary of the most significant premodern human fossils discussed in this chapter.

Critical Thinking Questions

1. Why are the Middle Pleistocene hominids called premodern humans? In what ways are they human?
2. What is the general popular conception of Neandertals? Do you agree with this view? (Cite both anatomical and archaeological evidence to support your conclusion.)
3. Compare the skeleton of a Neandertal with that of a modern human. In which ways are they most alike? In which ways are they most different?
4. What evidence suggests that Neandertals deliberately buried their dead? Do you think the fact that they buried their dead is important? Why? How would you interpret this behavior (remembering that Neandertals were not identical to us)?
5. How are species defined, both for living animals and for extinct ones? Use the Neandertals to illustrate the problems encountered in distinguishing species among extinct hominids. Contrast specifically the interpretation of Neandertals as a distinct species with the interpretation of Neandertals as a subspecies of *H. sapiens*.

Ancient DNA

An exciting and potentially highly informative new direction of research has focused on extracting and analyzing DNA samples from ancient remains. Some of these finds, most notably insect tissue embedded in amber (fossilized tree resin), can be extremely ancient. Some of the insect DNA derived from these sources is upward of 120 million years old; and these discoveries, first reported back in 1992, were the inspiration for Michael Crichton's *Jurassic Park.*

Amber provides a very unusual and favorable environment for long-term preservation of small organisms—a situation, unfortunately, that doesn't apply to larger organisms such as vertebrates. Even so, following the introduction of PCR technology, it became possible to look for *very* small amounts of DNA that just might still linger in ancient human remains.

In 1986, researchers reported results of sequenced brain DNA obtained from mummified remains found in a Florida bog dated at 7,000–8,000 ya (Doran et al., 1986). The famous "Iceman" mummy discovered in the Alps in 1991 also yielded widely publicized DNA information about his population origins, which were shown to be near where he died (Fig. 1).

Another intriguing line of evidence comes from mitochondrial DNA (mtDNA) analysis of early European farmers at a 7,500-year-old site in Germany (Haak et al., 2005). As we'll discuss in Chapter 14, food production developed in the Middle East well before it appeared in Europe. The most interesting aspects of these new data concern, first, how farming spread initially to Europe, and second, who are the ancestors of contemporary Europeans. Right now, the new molecular information doesn't fully answer these questions, and it conflicts with some prior data from the Y chromosome. Still, this kind of information is very exciting and opens vast new opportunities for understanding ancient population migrations.

In all of these examples, no nuclear DNA was identified, so researchers used the more plentiful mitochondrial DNA. Their successes gave hope that even more ancient remains containing preserved human DNA could be analyzed.

And indeed, in 1997 Matthias Krings and associates from the University of Munich and the Max Planck Institute of Evolutionary Anthropology (see p. 139) made a startling breakthrough (Krings et al., 1997). They successfully extracted, amplified, and sequenced DNA from a Neandertal skeleton. As discussed in this chapter (p. 267), seven other Neandertals (ranging in date from 50,000 to 32,000 y.a.) have since yielded enough mtDNA for analysis.

As we've noted, the place of Neandertals in human evolution has been and continues to be a topic of fascination and contention. This is why the Neandertal DNA evidence is so important. What's more, comparing Neandertal DNA patterns with those of early modern humans would be extremely illuminating. Certainly, some of the early *H. sapiens* skeletons from Europe and elsewhere (many of which we discuss in the next

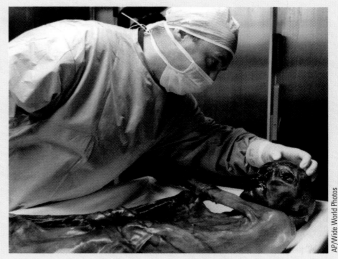

AP/Wide World Photos

FIGURE 1
Iceman.

chapter) are still likely to contain some DNA. And—as we'll see in the next chapter—in just the last three years, nine early modern *H. sapiens* individuals have had their DNA sequenced (Caramelli et al., 2003; Serre, et al, 2004; Kuklikov et al., 2004).

These new finds, all coming from Europe or westernmost Asia and extending from France in the west to Russia in the east, support the view that Neandertal DNA is quite distinct from living people *as well as* from the first modern *H. sapiens* finds in Europe. Questions, however, remain concerning possible contamination of the ancient samples. With PCR, even the tiniest amounts of extraneous DNA—even a single molecule—can be replicated millions of times; so, there's always a chance of contamination from handling by excavators or lab investigators. In fact, one researcher has estimated that there's more DNA in the few skin cells shed by researchers in the lab than there is in most fossils! So, even with the best attempts at contamination control, inadvertent contamination can never be ruled out.

What this means is that *any* ancient human shown to be a very close genetic match to living people falls under immediate suspicion. The DNA of an early modern *sapiens* (from Italy) was essentially identical to that of living people—thus increasing such scrutiny even further. In fact, the eminent molecular biologist Svante Pääbo, who is a director at the Max Planck Institute for Evolutionary Anthropology, has concluded that "Cro-Magnon (early modern) DNA is so similar to modern human DNA that there is no way to say whether what has been seen is real" (Pääbo, quoted in Abbott, 2003, p. 468).

Similar difficulties have surrounded the analysis of a potentially older early modern human from the Lake Mungo site in Australia (see Chapter 12, p. 286, for further discussion). In

Ancient DNA CONTINUED

addition to possible recent contamination, there are potential problems caused by mutant mtDNA insertions into nuclear DNA (forming "pseudogenes"). Any molecular analysis using mtDNA may actually be getting readings from these altered/inserted genes rather than from "real" mtDNA.

Analysis of nuclear DNA from ancient specimens would help alleviate some of these difficulties, although as yet no nuclear DNA has been obtained from any hominid older than a few thousand years. Even so, positive results may be forthcoming. Nuclear DNA has recently been sequenced from remains of a 27,000-year-old Siberian Mammoth (Poinar et al, 2005) as well as of cave bears from two sites in Austria dated between 45,000 and 40,000 ya (Noonan et al., 2005). Notably, as well, new molecular approaches were used in both of these studies. The international team working on the mammoth DNA used a powerful new genome sequencer and were able to identify a staggering 13 million mammoth base pairs—normally, the best that can be expected from nuclear DNA is a mere few hundred bases. While the new technology has tremendous potential, we need to recognize that the mammoth DNA came from an animal sealed in permafrost, which yields unusually good preservation. The cave-bear bones were not buried in permafrost, and for these remains the researchers isolated ancient DNA by using a new direct cloning procedure rather than PCR. Certainly, these new approaches and successes in sequencing ancient nuclear DNA from other mammals give us hope that we'll soon get similar information for equally ancient hominids. In fact, the Mezmaiskaya Neandertal has been reported to retain so much mtDNA that further testing might just come up with usable amounts of nuclear DNA as well.

SOURCES:

Abbott, Alison. 2003. "Anthropologists Cast Doubt on Human DNA Evidence." *Nature* (News) 423:468.

Caramelli, David, Carles Lalueza-Fox, and Cristano Vernesi et al. 2003. "Evidence for a Genetic Discontinuity between Neandertals and 24,000-Year-Old Anatomically Modern Europeans." *Proceedings of the National Academy of Sciences* 100:6593–6597.

Doran, G. H., D. N. Dickel, and W. E. Ballinger Jr. et al. 1986. "Anatomical, Cellular, and Molecular Analysis of 8,000-Yr-Old Human Brain Tissue from the Windover Archaeological Site." *Nature* 323:803–806.

Haak, Wolfgang, Peter Forster, and Barbara Bramanti et al. 2005. "Ancient DNA from the First European Farmers in 7500-Year-Old Neolithic Sites." *Science* 310:1016–1018.

Noonan, James P., Michael Hofreiter, and Doug Smith et al. 2005. "Genomic Sequencing of Pleistocene Cave Bears." *Science* 309:597–600.

Krings, M., A. Stone, and R. W. Schmitz et al. 1997. "Neandertal DNA Sequences and the Origin of Modern Humans." *Cell* 90:19–30.

Kulikov, Eugene E., Audrey B. Poltaraus, and Irina A. Lebedeva. 2004. "DNA Analysis of Sunghir Remains." Poster Presentation, European Paleopathology Association Meetings, Durham, U.K., August 2004.

Poinar, Hendrik N., Carsten Schwarz, and Ji Qi et al. 2005. "Metagenomics to Paleogenomics: Large-Scale Sequencing of Mammoth DNA." *Science Express*, December 20, 2005. www.scienceexpress.org/20 December 2005/

Serre, David, Andre Langaney, and Marie Chech et al. 2004. "No Evidence of Neandertal DNA Contribution to Modern Humans." *PloS Biology* 2:313–317.

PALEOANTHROPOLOGY/FOSSIL HOMINIDS

CHAPTER

12

The Origin and Dispersal of Modern Humans

FOCUS QUESTION

Is it possible to determine when and where modern people first appeared?

Go to the following CD-ROMs for interactive activities and exercises on topics covered in this chapter:

- Virtual Laboratories for Physical Anthropology CD-ROM, Third Edition

- Hominid Fossils: An Interactive Atlas CD-ROM, First Edition

Introduction

Sometime, probably close to 150,000 years ago (ya), the first modern *Homo sapiens* evolved in Africa. Within 100,000 years or so, their descendants had spread across most of the Old World, even expanding as far as Australia (and somewhat later to the Americas).

Who were they, and why were these early modern people so successful? And what was the fate of the other hominids, such as the Neandertals, who were already long established in areas outside Africa? Did they evolve as well, leaving descendants among some living human populations? Or were they completely swept aside and replaced by African emigrants?

In this chapter, we'll discuss the origin and dispersal of modern *H. sapiens*. All contemporary populations—more than 6 billion living humans—are placed in the subspecies *Homo sapiens sapiens*. Most paleoanthropologists agree that several fossil forms, dating back as far as 100,000 years ago (ya), should also be included in the same subspecies.

In addition, some recently discovered fossils from Africa also are clearly *H. sapiens*, but they show some (minor) differences from living people and could thus be described as near-modern. Still, we can think of these early African humans as well as their somewhat later relatives as "us."

These first modern humans, who evolved by 150,000 ya, are probably descendants of some of the premodern humans we discussed in Chapter 11. In particular, African populations of *H. heidelbergensis* are the most likely ancestors of the earliest modern *H. sapiens*. The evolutionary events that took place as modern humans made the transition from more ancient premodern forms and then dispersed throughout most of the Old World were relatively rapid, and they raise several basic questions:

1. When (approximately) did modern humans first appear?
2. Where did the transition take place? Did it occur in just one region or in several?
3. What was the pace of evolutionary change? How quickly did the transition occur?
4. How did the dispersal of modern humans to other areas of the Old World (outside their area of origin) take place?

These questions concerning the origins and early dispersal of modern *Homo sapiens* continue to fuel much controversy among paleoanthropologists. And it's no wonder, for members of early *Homo sapiens* are our *direct* ancestors, which makes them close relatives of all contemporary humans. They were much like us skeletally, genetically, and (most likely) behaviorally, too. In fact, it's the various hypotheses regarding the behaviors and abilities of our most immediate predecessors that have most fired the imaginations of scientists and laypeople alike. In every major respect, these are the first hominids that we can confidently refer to as fully human.

In this chapter, we'll also discuss archaeological evidence from the Upper Paleolithic (see p. 259). This evidence will give us a better understanding of the technological and social developments during the period when modern humans arose and quickly came to dominate the planet.

The evolutionary story of *Homo sapiens sapiens* is really the biological autobiography of all of us. It's a story that still has many unanswered questions; but several theories can help us organize the diverse information that's now available.

Approaches to Understanding Modern Human Origins

In attempting to organize and explain modern human origins, paleoanthropologists have developed two major theories: the complete replacement model and the regional continuity model. These two views are quite distinct, and in some ways they're completely opposed to each other. What's more, the popular press has further contributed to a wide and incorrect perception of irreconcilable argument on these points by "opposing" scientists. But in fact there's a third theory, which we call the partial replacement model, that's a compromise hypothesis incorporating some aspects of the two major theories. Because so much of our contemporary view of modern human origins is influenced by the debates linked to these differing theories, let's start by briefly reviewing each one. Then we'll turn to the fossil evidence itself to see what it can contribute to answering the four questions we have posed.

THE COMPLETE REPLACEMENT MODEL: RECENT AFRICAN EVOLUTION

The complete replacement model was developed by British paleoanthropologists Christopher Stringer and Peter Andrews (1988). It's based on the origin of modern humans in Africa and later replacement of populations in Europe and Asia (Fig. 12–1). This theory proposes that anatomically modern populations arose in Africa within the last 200,000 years and then migrated from Africa, *completely replacing* populations in Europe and Asia. This model doesn't account for any transition from premodern forms to modern *H. sapiens* anywhere in the world except Africa. A critical deduction of the Stringer and Andrews theory is that anatomically modern humans appeared as the result of a biological speciation event. So in this view, migrating African modern *H. sapiens* could not have interbred with local non-African populations, because the African modern humans were a *biologically* different species. Taxonomically, all of the premodern populations outside Africa would, in this view, be classified as belonging to different species of *Homo*. For example, the Neandertals would be classified as *H. neanderthalensis* (see p. 270 for further discussion). This speciation explanation fits nicely with, and in fact helps explain, *complete* replacement, but Stringer has more recently stated that he isn't dogmatic on this issue. He does suggest that even though there may have been potential for interbreeding, apparently very little actually took place.

Interpretations of the latter phases of human evolution have recently been greatly extended by newly available genetic techniques. Advances in molecular biology have revolutionized the biological sciences, including physical anthropology, and have recently been applied to the question of modern human origins. Using numerous contemporary human populations as a data source, geneticists have precisely determined and compared a wide variety of DNA sequences. The theoretical basis of this approach assumes that at least some of the genetic patterning seen today can act as a kind of window on the past. In particular, the genetic patterns observed today between geographically widely dispersed humans are thought to partly reflect migrations occurring in the late Pleistocene. This hypothesis can be further tested as various types of contemporary population genetic patterning are better documented.

To get a clearer picture of these genetic patterns, geneticists have studied both nuclear and mitochondrial DNA (see p. 55). They consider Y chromosome and mitochondrial DNA patterns particularly informative, since neither is significantly recombined during sexual reproduction. As a result, mitochondrial inheritance follows a strictly maternal pattern (inherited through females), while the Y chromosome follows a paternal pattern (transmitted only from father to son).

As these new data have accumulated, consistent relationships are emerging, especially in showing that indigenous African populations have far greater diversity than do populations from elsewhere in the world. The consistency of the results is highly significant, because it strongly supports an African origin for modern humans and some mode of replacement elsewhere.

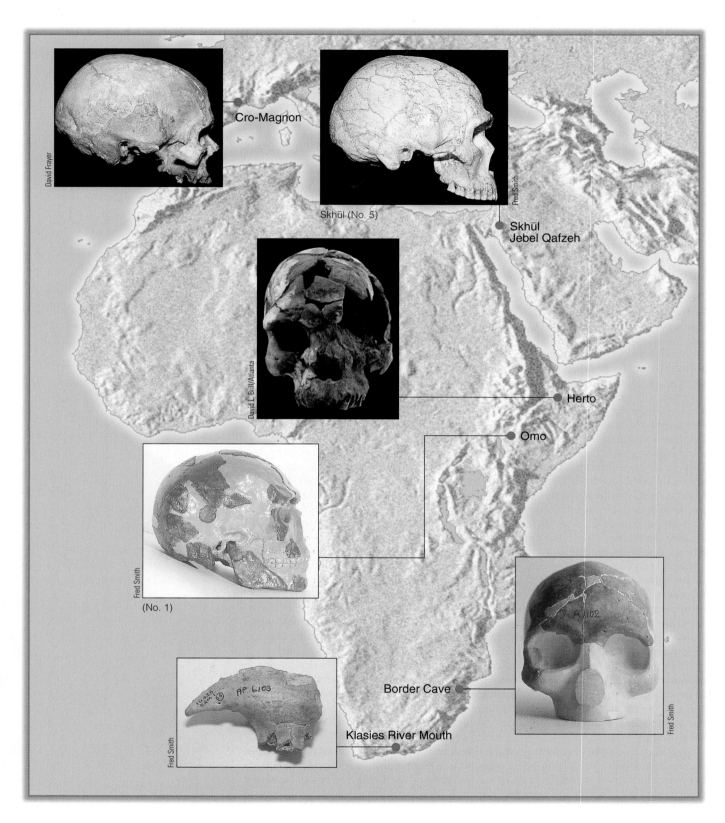

FIGURE 12–1

Anatomically modern humans in Europe, the Near East, and Africa.

Certainly, most molecular data come from contemporary species, since DNA is not *usually* preserved in long-dead individuals. Even so, exceptions do occur, and these cases open another genetic window—one that can directly illuminate the past. As discussed in Chapter 11 (see p. 267), Neandertal DNA has been recovered from eight Neandertal fossils.

In addition, nine ancient anatomically modern skeletons from sites in Italy, France, the Czech Republic, and Russia have recently had their mtDNA sequenced (Caramelli et al., 2003; Kulikov et al., 2004; Serre et al., 2004). The results show mtDNA sequence patterns very similar to the patterns seen in living humans—and thus significantly different from the mtDNA patterns found in the eight Neandertals so far analyzed.

If these results are further confirmed, they provide strong *direct* evidence of a genetic discontinuity between Neandertals and these early fully modern humans. In other words, these data suggest that no—or very little—interbreeding took place between Neandertals and anatomically modern humans.

But there's a potentially serious problem with these latest DNA results from the early modern skeletons. The mtDNA sequences are so similar to those of modern humans that they could, in fact, be the result of contamination—that is, the amplified and sequenced DNA could belong to some person who recently handled the fossil. Even though the molecular biologists who did this research took many experimental precautions, following standard practices used by other laboratories, there's currently no way to rule out such contamination. Still, the results do fit with an emerging overall agreement on the likely distinctions between Neandertals and modern humans.

PARTIAL REPLACEMENT MODELS

Various alternative perspectives also suggest that modern humans originated in Africa and then, when their population increased, expanded out of Africa into other areas of the Old World. But unlike those who subscribe to the complete replacement hypothesis, the supporters of these partial replacement models claim that some interbreeding occurred between emigrating Africans and resident premodern populations elsewhere. So, partial replacement assumes that *no* speciation event occurred, and all these hominids should be considered members of *H. sapiens*. Günter Bräuer, of the University of Hamburg, suggests that very little interbreeding occurred—a view supported recently by John Relethford (2001) in what he describes as "mostly out of Africa." Fred Smith, of Loyola University, also favors an African origin of modern humans, but his "assimilation" model hypothesizes that in some regions more interbreeding took place (Smith, 2002; Smith et al., 2005).

THE REGIONAL CONTINUITY MODEL: MULTIREGIONAL EVOLUTION

The regional continuity model is most closely associated with paleoanthropologist Milford Wolpoff, of the University of Michigan, and his associates (Wolpoff et al., 1994, 2001). They suggest that local populations—not all, of course—in Europe, Asia, and Africa continued their indigenous evolutionary development from premodern Middle Pleistocene forms to anatomically modern humans. But if that's true, then we have to ask how so many different local populations around the globe happened to evolve with such similar morphology. In other words, how could anatomically modern humans arise separately in different continents and end up so much alike, both physically and genetically? The multiregional model answers this question by (1) denying that the earliest modern *H. sapiens* populations originated *exclusively* in Africa, challenging the notion of complete replacement; and (2) asserting that some gene flow (migration) between premodern populations was extremely likely, which means that modern humans can't be considered a separate species from premodern hominids.

Through gene flow and natural selection, according to the multiregional hypothesis, local populations would *not* have evolved totally independently from one another, and such mixing would have "prevented speciation between the regional lineages and thus maintained human beings as a *single*, although obviously *polytypic* (see p. 72), species throughout the Pleistocene" (Smith et al., 1989).

Advocates of the multiregional model aren't dogmatic about the degree of regional continuity. They recognize that a likely strong influence of African migrants existed throughout the world—and is still detectable today. Agreeing with Smith's assimilation model, this modified multiregionalism suggests that only perhaps minimal gene continuity existed in several regions (for example, western Europe) and that most modern genes are the result of large African migrations and/or more incremental gene flow (Relethford, 2001; Wolpoff et al., 2001).

SEEING THE BIG PICTURE

Looking beyond the arguments concerning modern human origins—which the popular media often overstates and overdramatizes—most paleoanthropologists now recognize an emerging consensus view. In fact, new evidence from fossils and especially from molecular comparisons is providing even more clarity. Data from sequenced ancient DNA, various patterns of contemporary human DNA, and the newest fossil finds from Ethiopia all suggest that a "strong" multiregional model is extremely unlikely. Supporters of this more extreme form of multiregionalism claim that modern human populations in Asia and Europe evolved *mostly* from local premodern ancestors—with only minor influence coming from African population expansion. But with the breadth and consistency of the latest research, for practical purposes, this strong version of multiregionalism is falsified.

Also, as various investigators integrate these new data, views are beginning to converge even further. Several researchers suggest an out-of-Africa model that leads to virtually complete replacement elsewhere. At the moment, this complete replacement rendition can't be falsified. Still, even devoted advocates of this strong replacement version recognize that *some* interbreeding was possible—although they believe it was very minor. We can conclude, then, that during the latter Pleistocene, one or more major migrations from Africa fueled the worldwide dispersal of modern humans. However, the African migrants might well have interbred with resident populations outside Africa. In a sense, it's all the same, whether we see this process either as very minimal mulitregional continuity or as not quite complete replacement.

The Earliest Discoveries of Modern Humans

AFRICA

In Africa, several early fossil finds have been interpreted as fully anatomically modern forms (see Fig. 12–1). These specimens come from the Klasies River Mouth on the south coast (which could be the earliest find), Border Cave slightly to the north, and Omo Kibish 1 in southern Ethiopia. Using relatively new techniques, paleoanthropologists have dated all three sites to about 120,000–80,000 ya. The original geological context at Border Cave is uncertain, and the fossils may be younger than those at the other two sites. For several years, some paleoanthropologists have considered these fossils the earliest known anatomically modern humans. Problems with dating, context, and differing interpretations of the evidence have led other paleoanthropologists to question whether the *earliest* modern forms (Fig. 12–2) really did evolve in Africa. Other modern *H. sapiens* individuals, possibly older than these African fossils, have been found in the Near East.

Herto   The announcement in June 2003 of well-preserved *and* well-dated *H. sapiens* fossils from Ethiopia has now gone a long way toward filling gaps in the later Pleistocene African fossil record. As a result, these fossils are helping to resolve key issues regarding modern human origins. Tim White of the University of California, Berkeley, and his colleagues have been working for over a decade in the Middle Awash area of Ethiopia. They've discovered a remarkable array of early fossil hominids (*Ardipithecus* and *Australopithecus garhi*) as well as somewhat later forms (*H. erectus*). From this same area in the Middle Awash—in the Herto member of the Bouri formation—highly significant new discoveries came to light in 1997. For simplicity, these new hominids are referred to as the Herto remains.

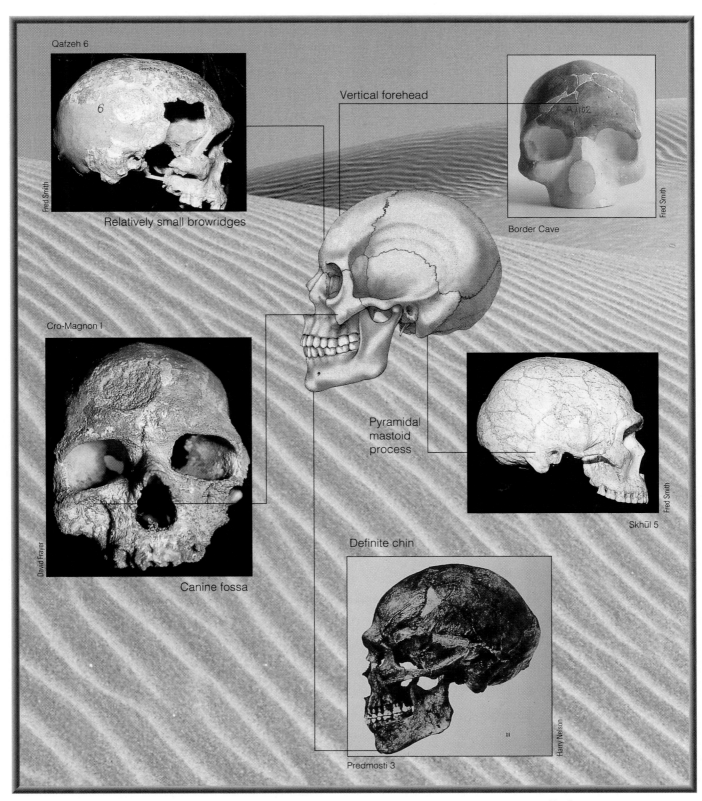

Qafzeh 6

Relatively small browridges

Vertical forehead

Border Cave

Cro-Magnon 1

Pyramidal
mastoid
process

Skhūl 5

Canine fossa

Definite chin

Predmosti 3

FIGURE 12–2
Morphology and variation in early specimens of
modern *Homo sapiens*.

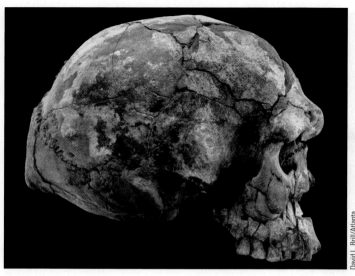

David L. Brill/Atlanta

FIGURE 12–3

Herto cranium from Ethiopia, dated 160,000–154,000 y.a. This is the best-preserved early modern *H. sapiens* cranium yet found.

These exciting new Herto fossils include a mostly complete adult cranium, a fairly complete (but heavily reconstructed) child's cranium, and another adult incomplete cranium as well as a few other cranial fragments. Following lengthy reconstruction and detailed comparative studies, White and colleagues were prepared to announce their findings in 2003.

What they found caused quite a sensation among paleoanthropologists, and it was reported in the popular press as well. First, well-controlled radiometric dating (^{40}Ar/^{39}Ar) securely places the remains at between 160,000 and 154,000 ya, making these the best-dated hominid fossils from this time period from anywhere in the world. Second, the preservation and morphology of the remains leave little doubt about their relationship to modern humans. The mostly complete adult cranium (Fig. 12–3) is very large, with an extremely long cranial vault. The cranial capacity is 1,450 cm³, well within the range of contemporary *H. sapiens* populations. The skull is also in some respects heavily built, with a large, arching browridge in front and a large, projecting occipital protuberance in back. The face does not project, in stark contrast to Eurasian Neandertals.

The overall impression is that this individual—as well as the child, aged six to seven years, and the incomplete adult cranium—are clearly *Homo sapiens*. White and his team performed comprehensive statistical studies, comparing these fossils with other early *H. sapiens* remains as well as with a large series (over 3,000 crania) from modern populations. They concluded that while not identical to modern people, the Herto fossils are near-modern. To distinguish these individuals from fully modern humans (*H. sapiens sapiens*), the researchers have placed them in a newly defined subspecies: *Homo sapiens idaltu*. The word *idaltu*, from the Afar language, means "elder" (White et al., 2003).

Further analysis has shown that the morphological patterning of the crania doesn't specifically match that of *any* contemporary group of modern humans. What can we then conclude? First, we can say that these new finds strongly support an African origin of modern humans. The Herto fossils are the right age, and they come from the right place. Besides that, they look much like what we might have predicted. These new Herto finds are the most conclusive fossil evidence yet supporting an African origin of modern humans. They're thus compatible with an array of genetic data indicating some form of replacement model for human origins.

AT A GLANCE	Key Early Modern *Homo sapiens* Discoveries from Africa and the Near East	
Site	**Dates (ya)**	**Human Remains**
Qafzeh (Israel)	110,000	Minimum of 20 individuals (*H. sapiens sapiens*)
Skhūl (Israel)	115,000	Minimum of 10 individuals (*H. sapiens sapiens*)
Klasies River Mouth (South Africa)	120,000?	Several individuals; highly fragmentary (*H. sapiens sapiens*)
Herto (Ethiopia)	160,000–154,000	Dental and cranial remains of 4 individuals (*H. sapiens idaltu*)

Harry Nelson

FIGURE **12–4**
Mt. Carmel, studded with caves, was home to *H. sapiens sapiens* at Skhūl (and to Neandertals at Tabun and Kebara).

THE NEAR EAST

In Israel, researchers found early modern *H. sapiens* fossils, including the remains of at least 10 individuals, in the Skhūl Cave at Mt. Carmel (Figs. 12–4 and 12–5a), very near the Neandertal site of Tabun. Also from Israel, the Qafzeh Cave has yielded the remains of at least 20 individuals (Fig. 12–5b). Although their overall configuration is definitely modern, some specimens show certain premodern (that is, Neandertal) features. Skhūl has been dated to about 115,000 ya, and Qafzeh has been placed at around 100,000 ya (Bar-Yosef, 1993, 1994); the chronology of these fossils is shown in Figure 12–6.

Such early dates for modern specimens pose some problems for those advocating local replacement, also known as the multiregional model. How early do the premodern

FIGURE **12–5**
(a) Skhūl 5. (b) Qafzeh 6. These specimens from Israel are thought to be representatives of early modern *Homo sapiens*. The vault height, forehead, and lack of facial projection are modern traits.

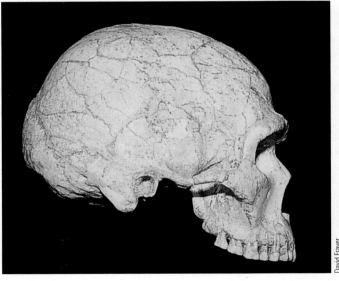
(a)

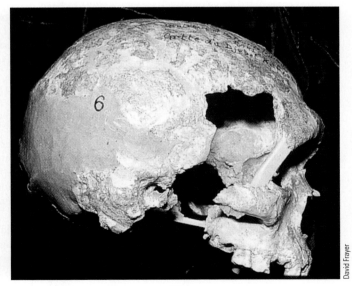
(b)

David Frayer

283

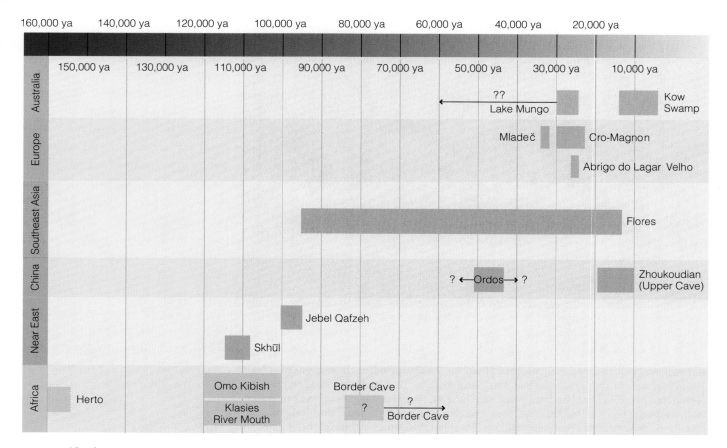

FIGURE 12–6

Time line of modern *Homo sapiens* and *Homo floresiensis* discoveries. Note that most dates are approximations. Question marks indicate those estimates that are most tentative.

human populations—that is, Neandertals—appear in the Near East? A recent chronometric calibration for the Tabun Cave suggests a date as early as 120,000 ya. So, Neandertals may *slightly* precede modern forms in the Near East, but there seems to be considerable overlap in the timing of occupation by these different humans. And, as you'll recall, the modern site at Mt. Carmel (Skhūl) is very near the Neandertal site at Tabun. Clearly, the dynamics of *Homo sapiens* evolution in the Near East are highly complex (Shea, 1998), and no simple model may adequately explain later hominid evolution.

CENTRAL EUROPE

Central Europe has been a source of many fossil finds, including numerous fairly early anatomically modern *H. sapiens*. At several sites, it appears that some fossils display both Neandertal and modern features, which supports some form of regional continuity in going from Neandertal to modern. Such genetic continuity from earlier (Neandertal) to later (modern *H. sapiens*) populations was perhaps the case at Vindija in Croatia, where typical Neandertals were found in earlier contexts (see p. 262).

Smith (1984) offers another example of local continuity from Mladeč, in the Czech Republic. Among the earlier European modern *H. sapiens* fossils, dated to about 33,000 ya, the Mladeč crania display a great deal of variation, probably in part due to sexual dimorphism. Although each of the crania (except for one of the females) displays a prominent supraorbital torus, it's reduced from the typical Neandertal pattern. Even though there's some suggestion of continuity from Neandertals to modern humans, Smith is confident that, given certain anatomical features, the Mlade? remains are best classified as *H. sapiens sapiens*.

WESTERN EUROPE

For several reasons, one of which is probably serendipity, western Europe and its fossils have received the most attention. Over the last 150 years, many of the scholars interested in this kind of research happened to live in western Europe, and the southern region of France happened to be a fossil treasure trove. Also, early on, discovering and learning about human ancestors caught the curiosity and pride of the local population.

Because of this scholarly interest, beginning back in the nineteenth century, a great deal of data accumulated, and little reliable comparative information was available from elsewhere in the world. As a result, theories of human evolution were based almost exclusively on the western European material. It's only been in recent years, with growing evidence from other areas of the world and with the application of new dating techniques, that recent human evolutionary dynamics are being seriously considered from a worldwide perspective.

Western Europe has yielded many anatomically modern human fossils, possibly going back 35,000 years or more, but by far the best-known sample of western European *H. sapiens* is from the **Cro-Magnon** site. Remains of eight individuals were discovered in 1868 inside a rock shelter in the village of Les Eyzies, in southern France.

The Cro-Magnon materials are associated with an **Aurignacian** tool assemblage, an Upper Paleolithic industry. Dated at 30,000 ya, these individuals represent the earliest of France's anatomically modern humans. The so-called Old Man (Cro-Magnon I) became the original model for what was once termed the Cro-Magnon, or Upper Paleolithic, "race" of Europe (Fig. 12–7). Actually, of course, there's no such valid biological category, and Cro-Magnon I is not typical of Upper Paleolithic western Europeans—and not even all that similar to the other two male skulls found at the site.

The question of whether continuous local evolution produced anatomically modern groups directly from Neandertals in some regions of Eurasia is far from settled. From central Europe, some variation indicates a combination of both Neandertal and modern characteristics and may suggest gene flow between the two different *H. sapiens* groups. However, tracing such relatively minor genetic changes—considering the ever-present problems of dating, lack of fossils, and fragmented fossil finds—has proved extremely difficult.

However, a newly discovered child's skeleton from Portugal provides some of the best evidence yet of possible hybridization between Neandertals and anatomically modern *H. sapiens*. This important new discovery from the Abrigo do Lagar Velho site was excavated in late 1998 and is dated to 24,500 ya—that's at least 5,000 years *later* than the last clearly Neandertal find. Associated with an Upper Paleolithic industry, and buried with red ocher and pierced shell, is a fairly complete skeleton of a four-year-old child (Duarte et al., 1999). Cidália Duarte, Erik Trinkaus, and colleagues, who have studied the remains, found a highly mixed set of anatomical features. Many characteristics, especially of the teeth, lower jaw, and pelvis, were

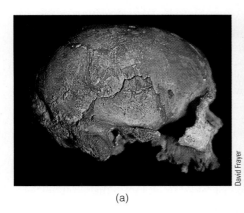

(a)

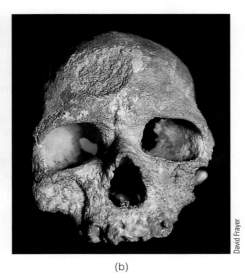

David Frayer

(b)

FIGURE 12–7

Cro-Magnon I (France). In this specimen, modern traits are quite clear. (a) Lateral view. (b) Frontal view.

Cro-Magnon (crow-man´-yon)

Aurignacian Pertaining to an Upper Paleolithic stone tool industry in Europe beginning at about 40,000 ya.

like those seen in anatomically modern humans. Yet, several other features including lack of chin, limb proportions, and muscle insertions were more similar to Neandertals. The authors thus conclude that "The presence of such admixture suggests the hypothesis of variable admixture between early modern humans dispersing into Europe and local Neandertal populations" (Duarte et al., 1999, p. 7608). And they suggest that this new evidence provides strong support for the partial replacement model while seriously weakening the complete replacement model. Of course, the evidence from one child's skeleton—while intriguing—is certainly not going to convince everyone.

ASIA

There are six early anatomically modern human localities in China, the most significant of which are Upper Cave at Zhoukoudian and Ordos in Mongolia. The fossils from these sites are all fully modern, and most are considered to be of quite late Upper Pleistocene age. Upper Cave at Zhoukoudian has been dated to between 18,000 and 10,000 ya. The Ordos find (see Fig. 12–6) may be the oldest anatomically modern material from China, possibly dating to 50,000 ya or more (Etler, personal communication).

In addition, the Jinniushan skeleton discussed in Chapter 11 (see p. 253) has been suggested by some researchers (Tiemel et al., 1994) as hinting at modern features in China as early as 200,000 ya. If this date—as early as that proposed for direct antecedents of modern *H. sapiens* in Africa—should prove accurate, it would cast doubt on the complete replacement model. In fact, taking a position quite contrary to the complete replacement model and more in support of regional continuity, many Chinese paleoanthropologists see a continuous evolution first from Chinese *H. erectus* to premodern forms and finally to anatomically modern humans. This view is supported by Wolpoff, who mentions that materials from Upper Cave at Zhoukoudian "have a number of features that are characteristically regional" and that these features "are definitely not African" (1989, p. 83).*

In addition to the well-known finds from China, anatomically modern remains have also been discovered in southern Asia. At Batadomba Iena, in southern Sri Lanka, modern *Homo sapiens* finds have been dated to 25,500 ya (Kennedy and Deraniyagala, 1989).

AUSTRALIA

During glacial times, the Indonesian islands were joined to the Asian mainland, but Australia was not. It's likely that by 50,000 ya, Sahul—the area including New Guinea and Australia—was inhabited by modern humans. Bamboo rafts may have been the means of crossing the sea between islands, which would not have been a simple exercise. It's not known just where the future Australians came from, but Borneo, Java, and New Guinea have all been suggested.

Human occupation of Australia appears to have occurred quite early, with some archaeological sites dating to 55,000 ya. There's some controversy about dating of the earliest Australian human remains, which are all modern *H. sapiens*. The earliest finds so far discovered have come from Lake Mungo in southeastern Australia. In agreement with archaeological context and radiocarbon dates, the hominids from this site have been dated at approximately 30,000–25,000 ya. Newly determined age estimates, using electron spin resonance (ESR) and uranium series dating (see Chapter 8), have dramatically extended the suggested time depth to about 60,000 ya (Thorne et al., 1999). The lack of correlation of these more ancient age estimates with other data, however, has some researchers seriously concerned (Gillespie and Roberts, 2000).

The recovery and sequencing of mitochondrial DNA from these prehistoric Australians is as intriguing—and controversial—as the early dating estimates (Adcock et al., 2001). Although the primary researchers are confident that these samples are authentically ancient, the nagging possibility of contamination can't be entirely ruled out. Indeed, other researchers remain unconvinced that the mtDNA from Lake Mungo is ancient at all (Cooper et al., 2001). Obviously, because of the uncertainties, we'll need further corroboration for both the dating and DNA findings before passing judgment.

---

*Wolpoff's statement supports his multiregional hypothesis. His reference to Africa is a criticism of the complete replacement hypothesis.

AT A GLANCE	Key Early Modern *Homo sapiens* Discoveries from Europe, Asia, and Australia	
Site	**Dates (ya)**	**Human Remains***
Abrigo do Lagar Velho (Portugal)	24,500	Four-year-old child's skeleton
Cro-Magnon (France)	30,000	8 individuals
Ordos (Mongolia, China)	50,000	1 individual
Kow Swamp (Australia)	14,000–9,000	Large sample (more than 40 individuals), including adults, juveniles, and infants
Lake Mungo (Australia)	?60,000–30,000	3 individuals, one a cremation

*Note: All fossils are classified as *H. sapiens sapiens*.

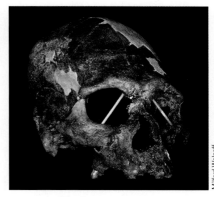

Milford Wolpoff

FIGURE **12–8**

Kow Swamp (Australia). Note the considerable robusticity in this relatively late Australian *Homo sapiens sapiens* cranium.

Unlike the more gracile early Australian forms from Lake Mungo are the Kow Swamp people, who are thought to have lived between about 14,000 and 9,000 ya (Figs. 12–8 and 12–9). These fossils display certain archaic traits—such as receding foreheads, heavy supraorbital tori, and thick bones—that are difficult to explain since these features contrast with the postcranial anatomy, which matches that of recent native Australians.

Something New and Different

As we've seen, by 25,000 years ago, modern humans had dispersed to all major areas of the Old World, and they would soon journey to the New World as well. But at about the same time, there were still remnant populations of earlier hominids surviving in a few remote and isolated corners. We mentioned in Chapter 9 that populations of *Homo erectus* in Java managed to survive on this island long after their cousins had disappeared from other areas, for example, China and East Africa. What's more, even though they persisted well into the Upper Pleistocene, physically these Javanese hominids were still very similar to other *H. erectus* (see p. 230).

But it seems that other populations branched off from some of these remnant Indonesian *H. erectus* groups and either intentionally or accidentally found their way to other, smaller islands to the east. There, under even more extreme isolation pressures, they evolved in an astonishing direction. In late 2004, the world awoke to the startling announcement that an extremely small-bodied, small-brained hominid had been discovered on the island of Flores, east of Java (see Fig. 12–9). The remains consist of an incomplete skeleton of an adult female, as well as additional pieces from six other individuals. The female skeleton is remarkable in several ways (Fig. 12–10). First, she stood barely 3 feet tall—as short as the smallest australopithecine—and her brain, estimated at a mere 380 cm^3, was no larger than that of a chimpanzee (Brown et al., 2004). And possibly most startling of all, these extraordinary hominids were still living on Flores just 13,000 years ago (Morwood et al., 2004)!

Where did they come from? As we said, their predecessors were probably *H. erectus* populations like those found on Java. How they got to Flores—some 400 miles away, partly over open ocean—is a mystery. There are several connecting islands, and to get between them, these hominids may have drifted across on rafts; but there's no way to be sure of this.

How did they get to be so physically different from all other known hominids? Here we're a little more certain of the answer. Isolated island populations can quite rapidly diverge from their relatives elsewhere—as we noted in Chapter 2 when discussing the famous Galápagos finches observed by Darwin. Among such isolated animals, natural selection frequently favors reduced body size. For example, populations of dwarf elephants are found on islands

FIGURE **12–9**
Anatomically modern *Homo sapiens* and *Homo floresiensis* (Asia and Australia).

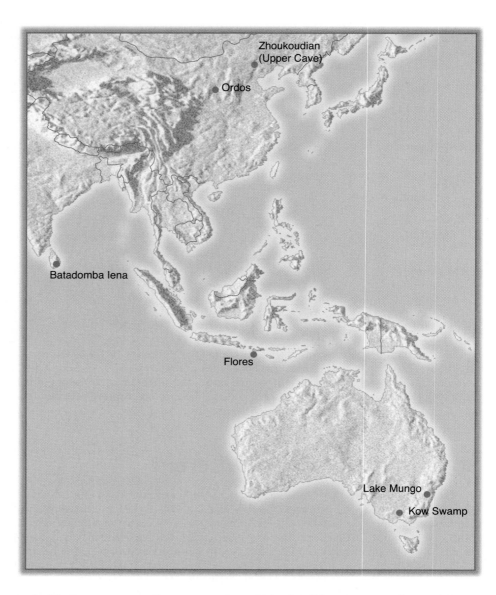

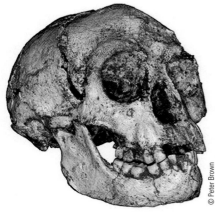

FIGURE **12–10**
Cranium of adult female *Homo floresiensis* from Flores, Indonesia, dated 18,000 ya.

in the Mediterranean as well as on some channel islands off the coast of southern California. And perhaps most interesting of all, dwarf elephants *also* evolved on Flores; they were found in the same beds with the little hominids. The evolutionary mechanism thought to explain such dwarfing in both the elephants and the hominids is an adaptation to a reduced amount of resources, leading through selection to smaller body size.

Other than short stature, what did the Flores hominids look like? In their cranial shape, thickness of cranial bone, and dentition, they most resemble *Homo erectus*. Still, they have some derived features that also set them apart from all other hominids. For that reason, researchers have placed them in a separate species, *Homo floresiensis*.

What became of the Flores hominids, and could some still be out there somewhere? They were extremely divergent and probably specialized as well. Not long after 13,000 ya, modern humans reached Flores, and it seems their arrival spelled doom for *H. floresiensis*. They seem to have perished quickly, leaving no descendants. It's very unlikely that not much later than 10,000 years ago, anything like these strange hominids survived anywhere. Currently, with more than 6 billion modern humans inhabiting every corner of the planet, all of us devouring resources as we go, the likelihood of finding *any* living "archaic" hominid—whether it be yeti, Bigfoot, or an *H. floresiensis* hominid—is extraordinarily slight.

Technology and Art in the Upper Paleolithic

EUROPE

The cultural period known as the Upper Paleolithic began in western Europe approximately 40,000 years ago (Fig. 12–11). Upper Paleolithic cultures are usually divided into five different industries, based on stone tool technologies: (1) Chatelperronian, (2) Aurignacian, (3) Gravettian, (4) Solutrean, and (5) Magdalenian. Major environmental shifts were also apparent during this period. During the last glacial period, about 30,000 ya, a warming trend lasting several thousand years partially melted the glacial ice. The result was that much of Eurasia was covered by tundra and steppe, a vast area of treeless country dotted with lakes and marshes. In many areas in the north, permafrost prevented the growth of trees but permitted the growth, in the short summers, of flowering plants, mosses, and other kinds of vegetation. This vegetation served as an enormous pasture for herbivorous animals, large and small, and carnivorous animals fed off the herbivores. It was a hunter's paradise, with millions of animals dispersed across expanses of tundra and grassland, from Spain through Europe and into the Russian steppes.

Large herds of reindeer roamed the tundra and steppes, along with mammoths, bison, horses, and a host of smaller animals that served as a bountiful source of food. In addition, humans exploited fish and fowl systematically for the first time, especially along the southern tier of Europe. It was a time of relative abundance, and ultimately Upper Paleolithic people spread out over Europe, living in caves and open-air camps and building large shelters. Far more elaborate burials are also found, most spectacularly at the 24,000-year-old Sungir site near Moscow (Fig. 12–12), where grave goods included a bed of red ocher, thousands of ivory beads, long spears made of straightened mammoth tusks, ivory engravings, and jewelry (Formicola and Buzhilova, 2004). During this period, either western Europe or perhaps portions of Africa achieved the highest population density in human history up to that time.

Humans and other animals in the midlatitudes of Eurasia had to cope with shifts in climatic conditions, some of them quite rapid. For example, at 20,000 ya another climatic "pulse" caused the weather to become noticeably colder in Europe and Asia as the continental glaciations reached their maximum extent for this entire glacial period, which is called the Würm in Eurasia.

As a variety of organisms attempted to adapt to these changing conditions, *Homo sapiens* had a major advantage: the elaboration of an increasingly sophisticated technology, and most likely other components of culture as well. In fact, probably one of the greatest challenges facing numerous late Pleistocene mammals was the ever more dangerously equipped humans—a trend that has continued to modern times.

The Upper Paleolithic was an age of technological innovation that can be compared to the past few hundred years in our recent history of amazing technological change after centuries of relative inertia. Anatomically modern humans of the Upper Paleolithic not only invented new and specialized tools (Fig. 12–13), but as we have seen, also greatly increased

GLACIAL	UPPER PALEOLITHIC (beginnings)	CULTURAL PERIODS
W Ü R M	17,000 –	Magdalenian
	21,000 –	Solutrean
	27,000 –	Gravettian
	40,000 –	Aurignacian Chatelperronian
Middle Paleolithic		Mousterian

FIGURE **12–11**

Cultural periods of the European Upper Paleolithic and their approximate beginning dates.

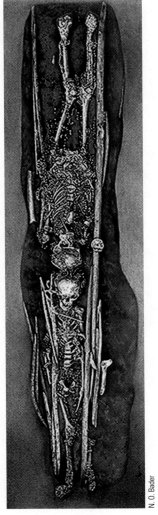

N. O. Bader

FIGURE **12–12**

Skeleton of two teenagers, a male and a female, from Sungir, Russia. Dated 24,000 ya, this is the richest find of any Upper Paleolithic grave.

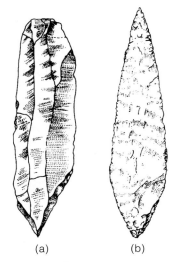

(a)   (b)

FIGURE **12–13**

(a) Burin. A very common Upper Paleolithic tool. (b) Solutrean blade. This is the best-known work of the Solutrean tradition. Solutrean stonework is considered the most highly developed of any Upper Paleolithic industry.

DIGGING DEEPER

Maybe, You Can Take It with You

The practice of deliberately burying the dead is an important and distinctive aspect of later human biocultural evolution. We saw in Chapter 11 that Neandertals buried their dead at a number of sites; but we also noted that the assortment of grave goods found in Neandertal burials was pretty sparse (see p. 266).

Something remarkable happened with the appearance and dispersal of modern humans. Suddenly—at least in archaeological terms—graves became much more elaborate. And, it wasn't just that many more items were placed with the deceased, it was also the kinds of objects. Neandertal graves sometimes contain a few stone tools and some unmodified animal bones, such as cave bear. But fully modern humans seem to have had more specialized and far more intensive cultural capacities. For example, from 40,000 years ago at Twilight Cave in Kenya, researchers have found 600 fragments of carefully drilled ostrich shell beads (Klein and Edgar, 2002). These beads are not directly associated with a human burial, but they do show us an intensification of craft specialization and possibly a much greater interest in personal adornment.

A locale where such elaborate grave goods (including beads) have been found in association with Upper Paleolithic modern human burials is the famous Cro-Magnon site in southwestern France. Likewise, numerous elaborate grave goods were found with human burials at Grimaldi in Italy.

No doubt the richest Upper Paleolithic burials are those at Sungir in Russia. Parts of several individuals have been recovered there, dating to about 24,000 ya. However, three individuals were found in direct association with thousands of ivory beads and other elaborate grave goods. Two of the individuals, a girl and boy aged 9–10 and 12–13, were buried together head to head in a spectacular grave (see Fig. 12–12). The more than 10,000 beads exca-

vated here likely once were woven into clothing, a task that would have been extraordinarily time-consuming. The two individuals were placed directly on a bed of red ocher, and with them were two magnificent spears made of straightened mammoth tusks—one of which is more than 6 $\frac{1}{2}$ ft. (240 cm) long! Plus, there were hundreds of drilled fox canine teeth, pierced antlers, and ivory carvings of animals, as well as ivory pins and pendants (Formicola and Buzhilova, 2004).

Producing all of these items that were so carefully placed with these two young individuals took thousands of hours of labor. Indeed, one estimate suggests that it took 10,000 hours just to make the beads (Klein and Edgar, 2002). What were the Magdalenian people who went to all this trouble thinking? The double burial is certainly the most extravagant of any from the Upper Paleolithic, but another at Sungir is almost as remarkable. Here, the body of an adult male—perhaps about 40 years old when he died—was also found with thousands of beads, and he too was carefully laid out on a bed of red ocher.

Sungir is likely a somewhat extraordinary exception; still, far more elaborate graves are often found associated with early modern humans than was ever the case in earlier cultures. At Sungir, and to a lesser extent at other sites, it took hundreds or even thousands of hours to produce the varied and intricate objects.

The individuals who were buried with these valuable goods must have been seen as special. Did they have unique talents, were they leaders or children of leaders, or did they have some special religious or ritual standing? For sure, this evidence is the earliest we have from human history revealing highly defined social status. Thousands of years later, the graves of the Egyptian pharaohs express the same thing—as do the elaborate monuments seen in most contemporary cemeteries. The Magdalenians and other Upper Paleolithic cultures were indeed much like us. They too may have tried to defy death and "take it with them!"

the use of—and probably experimented with—new materials, such as bone, ivory, and antler.

Solutrean tools are good examples of Upper Paleolithic skill and perhaps aesthetic appreciation as well (see Fig. 12–13b). In this lithic (stone) tradition, stoneknapping developed to the finest degree ever known. Using specialized flaking techniques, the artist/technicians made beautiful parallel-flaked lance heads, expertly flaked on both surfaces. The lance points are so delicate that they can be considered works of art that quite possibly never served, nor were they intended to serve, a utilitarian purpose.

The last stage of the Upper Paleolithic, known as the **Magdalenian**, saw even more advances in technology. The spear-thrower, or *atlatl*, was a wooden or bone hooked rod that acted to extend the hunter's arm, thus enhancing the force and distance of a spear throw (Fig. 12–14). For catching salmon and other fish, the barbed harpoon is a clever example of the craftsperson's skill. There's also evidence that the bow and arrow may have been used for the first time during this period. The introduction of much more efficient manufacturing methods, such as the punch blade technique (Fig. 12–15), provided an abundance of standardized stone blades. These could be fashioned into **burins** (see Fig. 12–13a) for working wood, bone,

Magdalenian   Pertaining to the final phase of the Upper Paleolithic stone tool industry in Europe.

burins   Small, chisel-like tools with a pointed end; thought to have been used to engrave bone, antler, ivory, or wood.

(a) A large core is selected and the top portion is removed by use of a hammerstone.

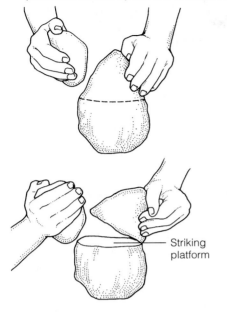

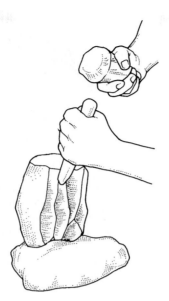

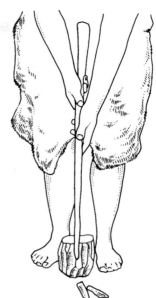

Striking platform

(b) The objective is to create a flat surface called a striking platform.

(c) Next, the core is struck by use of a hammer and punch (made of bone or antler) to remove the long narrow flakes (called blades).

(d) Or the blades can be removed by pressure flaking.

(e) The result is the production of highly consistent sharp blades, which can be used, as is, as knives; or they can be further modified (retouched) to make a variety of other tools (such as burins, scrapers, and awls).

and antler; borers for drilling holes in skins, bones, and shells; and knives with serrated or notched edges for scraping wooden shafts into a variety of tools.

By producing many more specialized tools, Upper Paleolithic peoples probably made more resources available to them and may also have had an impact on the biology of these populations. Emphasizing a biocultural interpretation, C. Loring Brace of the University of Michigan has suggested that with more efficient tools used for food processing, anatomically modern *H. sapiens* would not have required the large front teeth (incisors) seen in earlier populations.

In addition to their reputation as hunters, western Europeans of the Upper Paleolithic are even better known for their symbolic representation, or what has commonly been called art. Given uncertainties concerning what actually should be called "art," archaeologist Margaret Conkey of the University of California, Berkeley, refers to Upper Paleolithic cave paintings, sculptures, engravings, and so forth as "visual and material imagery" (Conkey, 1987, p. 423). We'll continue using the term *art* to describe many of these prehistoric representations, but you should recognize that we do so mainly as a cultural convention—and perhaps a limiting one.

FIGURE **12–14**
The punch blade technique.

FIGURE **12–15**
Spear-thrower (atlatl). Note the carving.

FIGURE 12–16
Magdalenian bone artifact. Note the realistic animal engraving on this object, the precise function of which is unknown.

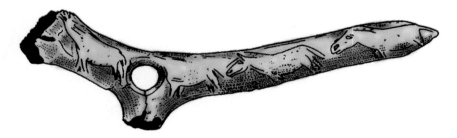

It's also important to remember that there is an extremely wide geographical distribution of symbolic images, best known from many parts of Europe, but now also well documented from Siberia, North Africa, South Africa, and Australia. Given a 25,000-year time depth of what we call Paleolithic art, and its nearly worldwide distribution, we can indeed observe marked variability in expression.

In addition to cave art, there are many examples of small sculptures excavated from sites in western, central, and eastern Europe. Beyond these quite well-known figurines, there are numerous other examples of what's frequently called portable art, including elaborate engravings on tools and tool handles (Fig. 12–16). Such symbolism can be found in many parts of Europe and was already well established early in the Aurignacian—by 33,000 ya. Innovations in symbolic representations also benefited from, and probably further stimulated, technological advances. New methods of mixing pigments and applying them were important in rendering painted or drawn images. Bone and ivory carving and engraving were made easier with the use of special stone tools (see Fig. 12–13). At two sites in the Czech Republic, Dolni Vestonice and Predmosti (both dated at 27,000 ya), small animal figures were fashioned from fired clay. This is the first documented use of ceramic technology anywhere, and in fact it precedes later pottery invention by more than 15,000 years.

Female figurines, popularly known as Venuses, were sculpted not only in western Europe, but in central and eastern Europe and Siberia as well. Some of these figures were realistically carved, and the faces appear to be modeled after actual women (Fig. 12–17). Other figurines may seem grotesque, with sexual characteristics exaggerated possibly for fertility or other ritual purposes (Fig. 12–18).

But it wasn't until the final phases of the Upper Paleolithic, particularly during the Magdalenian, that European prehistoric art reached its climax. Cave art is now known from more than 150 separate sites, the vast majority from southwestern France and northern Spain. Apparently, in other areas the rendering of such images did not take place in deep caves. Peoples

FIGURE 12–17
Venus of Brassempouy. Upper Paleolithic artists were capable of portraying human realism (shown here) as well as symbolism (depicted in Fig. 12–18). (a) Frontal view. (b) Lateral view.

in central Europe, China, Africa, and elsewhere certainly may have painted or carved representations on rock faces in the open, but these images long since would have eroded. So, we're fortunate that the people of at least one of the many sophisticated cultures of the Upper Paleolithic chose to journey belowground to create their artwork, preserving it not just for their immediate descendants, but for us as well. The most spectacular and most famous of the cave art sites are Lascaux and Grotte Chauvet in France and Altamira in Spain (Fig. 12–19).

In Lascaux Cave, immense wild bulls dominate what is called the Great Hall of Bulls; and horses, deer, and other animals drawn with remarkable skill adorn the walls in black, red, and yellow. Equally impressive, at Altamira the walls and ceiling of an immense cave are filled with superb portrayals of bison in red and black. The "artist" even took advantage of bulges in the walls to create a sense of relief in the paintings. The cave is a treasure of beautiful art whose meaning has never been satisfactorily explained. It could have been religious or magical, a form of visual communication, or simply art for the sake of beauty.

Yet another spectacular example of cave art from western Europe was discovered in 1994 at Grotte Chauvet in southeastern France. Preserved inside the cave, unseen for perhaps 30,000 years, are a multitude of images, including dots, stenciled human handprints, and, most dramatically, hundreds of animal representations (Fig. 12–19). Radiocarbon dating has placed the paintings during the Aurignacian, more than 30,000 ya, making Grotte Chauvet considerably earlier than the Magdalenian sites of Lascaux and Altamira.

AFRICA

Early accomplishments in rock art, possibly as early as in Europe, are seen in southern Africa (Namibia), where a site containing such art is dated between 28,000 and 19,000 ya. In addition, evidence of portable personal adornment is seen as early as 38,000 ya in the form of beads fashioned from ostrich eggshells.

In terms of stone tool technology, microliths (thumbnail-sized stone flakes hafted to make knives, saws, etc.) and blades characterize Late Stone Age* African industries. In central Africa there was also considerable use of bone and antler, some of it possibly quite early. Recent excavations in the Katanda area of the eastern portion of the Democratic Republic of the Congo (Fig. 12–20) have shown remarkable development of bone craftwork. In fact, preliminary reports by Alison Brooks of George Washington University and John Yellen of the National Science Foundation have demonstrated that these technological achievements rival those of the more renowned European Upper Paleolithic (Yellen et al., 1995).

The most important artifacts discovered in the Katanda area are a dozen intricately made bone tools excavated from three sites. These tools, made from the bones of large mammals,

Jim Cartier/Photo Researchers

FIGURE 12–18
Venus of Willendorf, Austria. (*Note:* This figure is among the most exaggerated and should be compared with Fig. 12–17.)

FIGURE 12–19
Cave art from Grotte Chauvet, France. (a) Bear. (b) Aurochs and rhinoceros.

Jean Clottes/Document elaborated with the support of the French Ministry of Culture and Communication, Regional Direction for Cultural Affairs, Rhône-Alpes, Regional Department of Archaeology.

(a)

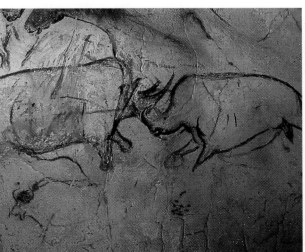

Jean-Marie Chauvet/Document elaborated with the support of the French Ministry of Culture and Communication, Regional Direction for Cultural Affairs, Rhône-Alpes, Regional Department of Archaeology.

(b)

*The Late Stone Age in Africa is equivalent to the Upper Paleolithic in Eurasia.

FIGURE **12–20**
Upper Paleolithic archaeological sites. (Katanda, in the Democratic Republic of the Congo, may be considerably older than the European sites, perhaps dating to the Middle Stone Age.)

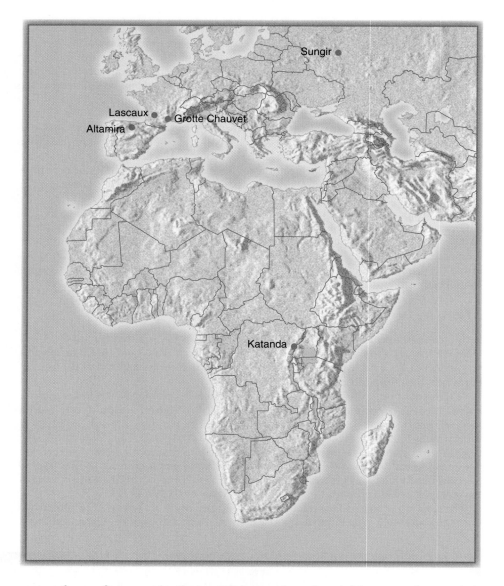

apparently were first ground to flatten and sharpen them. Some of them were then precisely pressure-flaked to produce a row of barbs. In form, these tools are similar to what have been called harpoons from the later Upper Paleolithic of Europe (Magdalenian, about 15,000 ya).

The dating of the Katanda sites is crucial for drawing useful comparisons with the European Upper Paleolithic. Unfortunately, the bone used for the tools was unsuitable for radiocarbon dating (it may have been too old and beyond the range of this technique). As a result, the other techniques now used for this time range—thermoluminescence (TL), electron spin resonance (ESR), and uranium series dating (see Table 8–2, p. 178)—were all applied. The results proved consistent, indicating dates between 180,000 and 75,000 ya.*

However, there are still some problems in clearly associating the bone implements with the materials that have supplied the chronometric age estimates. In fact, Richard Klein, a coauthor of one of the initial reports (Brooks et al., 1995), doesn't accept the suggested great antiquity for these finds; he believes they may be much younger. Even so, if the early age estimates should hold up, once again we'll look *first* to Africa as the crucial source area for human origins—not just for biological aspects, but for cultural aspects.

———————
*If these dates are proven accurate, Katanda would actually be earlier than Late Stone Age and thus be considered Middle Stone Age.

Summary of Upper Paleolithic Culture

In looking back at the Upper Paleolithic, we can see it as the culmination of 2 million years of cultural development. Change proceeded incredibly slowly for most of the Pleistocene; but as cultural traditions and materials accumulated, and the brain—and, we assume, intelligence—expanded and reorganized, the rate of change quickened.

Cultural evolution continued with the appearance of early premodern humans and moved a bit faster with later premoderns. Neandertals in Eurasia and their contemporaries elsewhere added deliberate burials, technological innovations, and much more.

Building on existing cultures, late Pleistocene populations attained sophisticated cultural and material heights in a seemingly short—by previous standards—burst of exciting activity. In Europe and central Africa particularly, there seem to have been dramatic cultural innovations, among them big game hunting with powerful new weapons such as harpoons, spear-throwers, and possibly the bow and arrow. Other innovations included body ornaments, needles, "tailored" clothing, and burials with elaborate grave goods—a practice that may indicate some sort of status hierarchy.

This dynamic age was doomed, or so it seems, by the climatic changes of about 10,000 ya. As the temperature slowly rose and the glaciers retreated, animal and plant species were seriously affected, and in turn these changes affected humans. As traditional prey animals were depleted or disappeared altogether, humans had to seek other means of obtaining food.

Grinding hard seeds or roots became important, and as humans grew more familiar with propagating plants, they began to domesticate both plants and animals. Human dependence on domestication became critical, and with it came permanent settlements, new technology, and more complex social organization. This continuing story of human biocultural evolution will be the topic of the remainder of this text.

Summary

For the past decade, and there's no end in sight, researchers have fiercely debated the date and location of the origin of anatomically modern human beings. One hypothesis (complete replacement) claims that anatomically modern forms first evolved in Africa more than 100,000 ya and then, migrating out of Africa, completely replaced premodern *H. sapiens* in the rest of the world. Another school (regional continuity) takes a completely opposite view and maintains that in various geographical regions of the world, local groups of premodern *H. sapiens* evolved directly to anatomically modern humans. A third hypothesis (partial replacement) takes a somewhat middle position, suggesting an African origin but also accepting some later hybridization outside of Africa.

Recent research coming from several sources is beginning to clarify the origins of modern humans. Molecular evidence, as well as the dramatic new fossil finds from Herto in Ethiopia, suggests that a multiregional origin of modern humans is unlikely. Sometime, soon after 150,000 ya, complete replacement of all hominids outside Africa may have occurred when migrating Africans displaced the populations in other regions. However, such absolutely *complete* replacement will be very difficult to prove, and it's not really what we'd expect. More than likely, at least some interbreeding probably did take place. Still, it's looking more and more like there wasn't much intermixing of populations.

Archaeological evidence of early modern humans also paints a fascinating picture of our most immediate ancestors. The Upper Paleolithic was an age of extraordinary innovation and achievement in technology and art. Many new and complex tools were introduced, and their production indicates fine skill in working wood, bone, and antler. Cave art in France and Spain displays the masterful ability of Upper Paleolithic painters, and beautiful sculptures have been found at many European sites. Sophisticated symbolic representations have also been found in Africa and elsewhere. Upper Paleolithic *Homo sapiens* displayed amazing development in a relatively short period of time. The culture produced during this period led the way to still newer and more complex cultural techniques and methods.

In Table 12–1 you'll find a useful summary of the most significant fossil discoveries discussed in this chapter.

TABLE 12-1	Most Significant Modern *Homo sapiens* and *Homo floresiensis* Discoveries Discussed in This Chapter			
Site	**Dates (ya)**	**Human Remains**	**Comments**	
Flores (Indonesia)	95,000–13,000*	Incomplete skeleton; pieces of 6 other individuals	Dwarfed species (*H. floresiensis*); very divergent, very small body size and brain size; almost certainly an evolutionary dead end	
Abrigo do Lagar Velho (Portugal)	24,500	Four-year-old child's skeleton	Possible evidence of hybridization between Neandertals and modern *H. sapiens*	
Cro-Magnon (France)	30,000	8 individuals	Famous site of early modern *H. sapiens*, but there are dozens of other sites in Europe and elsewhere	
Lake Mungo (Australia)	?60,000–30,000	3 individuals	Early dating estimate is surprising; if confirmed, would be earlier than established evidence in Europe or East Asia	
Qafzeh (Israel)	110,000	Minimum of 20 individuals	Quite early site; shows considerable variation	
Skhūl (Israel)	115,000	Minimum of 10 individuals	Earliest well-dated modern *H. sapiens* outside of Africa; also perhaps contemporaneous with neighboring Tabun Neandertal site	
Herto (Ethiopia)	160,000–154,000	3 individuals and other fragments	Earliest well-dated modern humans; placed in separate subspecies (*H. sapiens idaltu*); location (in Africa) is notable	

*The full estimated time range for all seven individuals. The partial skeleton is dated to approximately 18,000 ya.

Critical Thinking Questions

1. What anatomical characteristics define *modern* as compared to *premodern* humans? Assume that you're analyzing an incomplete skeleton that may be early modern *H. sapiens*. Which portions of the skeleton would be most informative, and why?

2. Go through the chapter and list all the forms of evidence that you think support the complete replacement model. Now, do the same for the regional continuity model. What evidence do you find most convincing, and why?

3. Why are the fossils recently discovered from Herto so important? How does this evidence influence your conclusions in question 2?

4. What archaeological evidence shows that modern human behavior during the Upper Paleolithic was significantly different from that of earlier hominids? Do you think that early modern *H. sapiens* populations were behaviorally superior to the Neandertals? Be careful to define what you mean by *superior*.

5. Why do you think some Upper Paleolithic people painted in caves? Why don't we find such evidence of cave painting from a wider geographical area?

ARCHAEOLOGY

CHAPTER 13

Early Holocene Hunters and Gatherers

FOCUS QUESTIONS

Where did first inhabitants of the New World come from?

What major cultural changes accompanied the end of the last Ice Age in the Americas and Old World?

Introduction

During the summer of 1996, two men found a human skull and other bones along the muddy shore of the Columbia River near Kennewick, Washington. They reported the discovery to the police and coroner, who in turn asked James Chatters, a forensic anthropologist and archaeologist, to examine the remains and provide an initial assessment. The results suggested that they were probably dealing with a Caucasian male in his mid-40s, but one who looked thousands of years old. When a CAT scan also showed a large stone spear point embedded in the man's hip, Chatters and others understandably wondered just how old this skeleton was (Chatters, 2001). Bone samples sent for radiocarbon dating returned an early **Holocene** age estimate of roughly 9,300 years ago (ya).* Instead of explaining this man's past, the analyses just added to the mystery. Who was this guy?

"Kennewick Man," as he was soon called, became the center of an extraordinary controversy, one that was more legal than scientific; it took nine years and more than $8,500,000 of taxpayers' money to sort out the case in federal courts (Dalton, 2005). It involved a swarm of attorneys, the U.S. Army Corps of Engineers, the U.S. Department of the Interior, several Native American tribal groups, a handful of internationally known anthropologists, a Polynesian chief, and federal judges, decisions, and appeals. Several important legal questions were ultimately at issue, not the least of which was the right of the American public to information about the distant past. At stake on the scientific side of the picture was what could be learned from the physical remains of a person who lived during the early days of the human presence in North America, when there were few people spread over this huge continent. So few human skeletons (currently less than 10 individuals) are known in North America from this period that each new one, like Kennewick Man, is a major discovery that potentially opens a fresh window on the prehistory of the continent.

As we noted in Chapter 12, men, women, and children made the first human footprints in New World mud sometime between 30,000 and 13,500 years ago. With those first steps, they expanded the potential range of our species by more than 16 million square miles, spanning two continents and countless islands, or roughly 30 percent of the earth's land surface. It was a big deal, comparable in scope and significance to the dispersal of the first hominids out of Africa during the Lower Paleolithic.

In this chapter we'll consider the story of these first New World inhabitants and also begin to look at the major cultural developments of roughly the past 10,000 years, during which world cultural changes increased at a dramatic rate (Fig. 13–1). Following the end of the last Ice Age, the world's modest human population of perhaps a few tens of millions sustained itself by collecting food from the natural environment, living in small groups, constructing humble shelters, and making use of effective but simple equipment crafted from basic natural materials. Some 600 generations later, there are more than 6 billion of us, nearly all of whom regularly consume foods derived from a select inventory of domesticated plants and

Holocene The geological epoch during which we now live. The Holocene follows the Pleistocene epoch and began roughly 11,000–10,000 years ago.

---

*Dates cited in the early American prehistory sections of this chapter have been adjusted to reflect calendar years before the present.

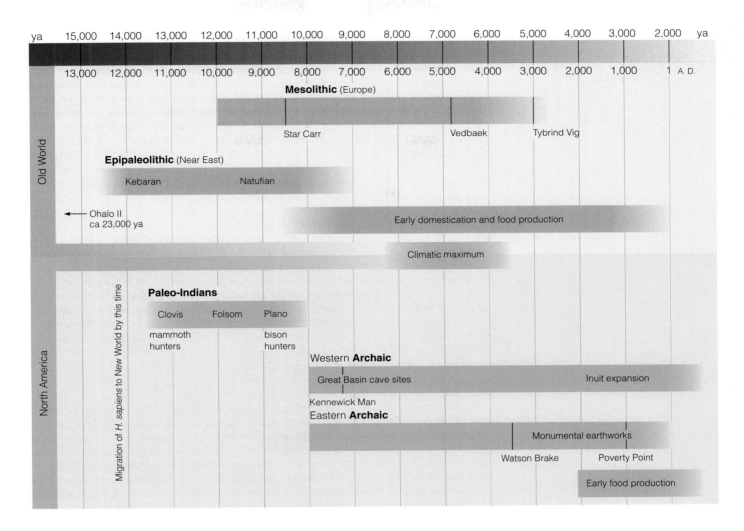

FIGURE 13–1
Time line for Chapter 13.

animals. The world's surface has been transformed to accommodate our farms and cities and other cultural landscapes. Most of the earth's natural resources, including even deeply buried ores, fossil fuels, and radioactive elements, are routinely processed into consumer products and industrial or military devices of remarkable ingenuity. Humankind has plumbed the deepest seas, explored the solar system, and decimated ecosystems worldwide. And along the way we have learned to write poetry, college textbooks, blogs, and that vein of music you hear only in elevators.

It's important to recall that these changes are not primarily the result of human physical evolution, which has played a decreasing role in human changes during the short span since the last Ice Age (see Chapters 4 and 5). Rather, the most radical developments affecting the human condition continue to be the consequences of our uniquely human *biocultural evolution*, for the most part stimulated by cultural innovations and the inescapable effects of our ever-growing population.

In this chapter, we examine the archaeological and biological clues relating to the origins of the first Americans and review the evidence indicating not only when they first arrived but also what cultural adjustments they made in their new homeland. We'll then explore how lifeways changed for many human groups both in the New and Old Worlds after the end of the last Ice Age, as the glaciers retreated, average sea levels rose, plant and animal communities migrated—and even such seemingly permanent entities as rivers and lakes became transformed in a postglacial world.

Entering the New World

Major archaeological problems, such as the entry of the first humans into the New World, inevitably attract a lot of research interest, if not also a little contentious debate. When did the first humans arrive in the Americas? Where did they come from? How did they get here? How did they make a living after they arrived? We want firm answers to these questions, but, as with all research that centers on "first" events, finding the answers is never easy. Consider, for example, the crucial question of *when* the first humans arrived in the New World. Strictly speaking, to answer it you need to identify the locality—somewhere in the 16 million square miles of two continents—where the oldest material evidence of the presence of humans is preserved in well-dated archaeological contexts. It's as though you're trying to find a particular sand grain that may or may not be on a beach. Once you understand the difficulty of finding "the" answer, it's easy to see why the question is likely to remain with us for a while.

When people arrived is necessarily tied up with *where* they came from because the two, taken together, tell us where to search for these first New World immigrants in the archaeological record. There's general consensus that the late Pleistocene marked something of a watershed in human prehistory. Glacial periods had waxed and waned for millions of years while humans evolved from ancestral primates. This activity meant little to our remote ancestors because continental glaciation primarily affected the higher latitudes, and early hominids ranged the tropics, where relatively few effects of such climatic changes reached them. But by late Pleistocene times, during the Upper Paleolithic of Europe and the Later Stone Age of Africa, modern humans had long ago pushed well into the temperate latitudes and even into regions just exposed by glacial meltwaters (see Chapter 12). These humans were capable of adapting culturally to changing natural and social environments and could do so at a pace that would have been unthinkable to their Lower Paleolithic ancestors. It was members of these human groups who were the first New World immigrants.

Archaeologists depend on geographical, biological, cultural, and linguistic evidence to trace the earliest Americans back to their Old World origins and construct today's answers to the when and where questions. Right now, there are three major competing hypotheses to explain the route of entry of humans into the New World: by way of the Bering land bridge that connected Asia and North America several times during the late Pleistocene (Fig. 13–2); along the coast of the northern Pacific Rim (Fig. 13–3); and by following the ice edge across the northern Atlantic from western Europe (Fig. 13–4). Although more than one scenario could be true, they're not equally likely. Let's consider the evidence for each in turn.

FIGURE **13–2**

The earliest inhabitants of North America may have entered the continent during the late Pleistocene epoch by way of the Bering land bridge, which was exposed during periods of maximum glaciation. These groups may have passed southward into what is now the United States by following the "ice-free corridor" that periodically emerged between the Cordilleran and Laurentian ice sheets in western Canada.

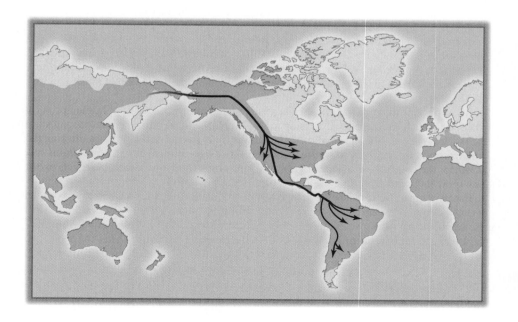

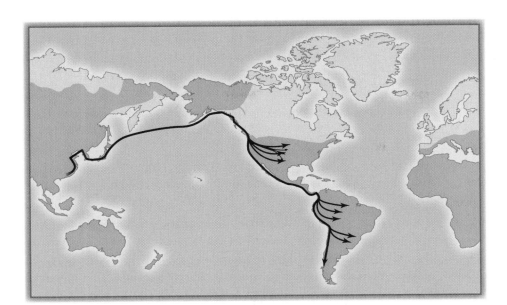

FIGURE **13-3**
The "Pacific coastal route" hypothesis asserts that the earliest immigrants into the Americas may have traveled by boat along the islands and environmental refugia that dotted the Pacific coast during the late Pleistocene.

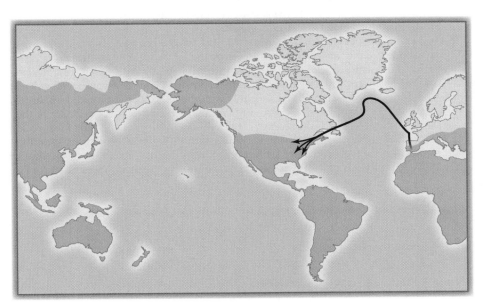

FIGURE **13-4**
The "North Atlantic Ice-Edge Corridor" hypothesis argues that the earliest arrivals in the New World may have come not from Asia, but from the Solutrean culture of western Europe, which was technologically similar to the Clovis Paleo-Indian culture in North America. These groups would have traveled north up the coast of Europe and across to North America by following the edge of the ice sheet that stretched between the two continents in late Pleistocene times.

BERING LAND BRIDGE

As long ago as the late sixteenth century, José de Acosta, a Jesuit priest with extensive experience in Mexico and Andean South America, examined the geographical and other information available to him and argued that humans must have entered the New World from Asia (Acosta, 2002). Until recently, few practicing archaeologists questioned this interpretation of events.

A lot of evidence favors this idea. First, there's the basic geography of the situation. If you cast around for a feasible, low-tech way to get people into the Americas, a quick check of a world map will draw your eyes to the Bering Strait, where northeastern Asia and northwestern North America are separated by only 50 miles of ocean (see Fig 13–2). An equally quick visit to the geology section of your local library will also reveal that there were several long intervals during the Pleistocene when lowered sea levels actually exposed the floor of the shallow Bering Sea, creating a wide "land bridge" (West and West, 1996). The land bridge formed during periods of maximum glaciation, when the volume of water locked up in glacial ice

AT A GLANCE   Important Northeastern Asia Sites and Regions

Site	Dates (ya)	Comments
Yana RHS (Russia)	30,000	Earliest evidence of late Pleistocene hunters beyond the Artic Circle in northern Siberia; stone tools and horn and ivory spear foreshafts similar to that found much later on North American Paleo-Indian sites
Berelekh (Russia)	c. 14,000–13,000	Archaeological evidence of Arctic human adaptations
Bering Land Bridge (Russia & USA)	c. 75,000–45,000 and 25,000–11,000	Also called "Beringia"; a Pleistocene land bridge that formed between northeastern Aisa and northwestern North America during periods of maximum glaciation

sheets reduced worldwide sea levels by 300 to 400 feet.* During the Last Glacial Maximum (28,000–15,000 ya), **Beringia**, as it is known, comprised a broad plain up to 1,300 miles wide from north to south (see Fig. 13–2). Ironically, the cold, dry arctic climate kept Beringia relatively ice-free. The primary plant cover of this low-lying windswept area included mostly mosses and lichens, but patches or *refugia* of boreal trees and shrubs also managed to preserve a toehold in the region (Brubaker et al., 2005).

Beringia's dry steppes and **tundra** supported herds of grazing animals and could just as easily have supported human hunters who preyed on them. The region was, after all, an extension of the familiar landscape of northern Asia. Archaeology confirms that during the later phases of the Pleistocene, Upper Paleolithic hunters pursuing large herbivores with efficient stone- and bone-tipped weapons, and probably with the aid of domesticated dogs, drifted into the farthest reaches of Eurasia (Soffer and Praslov, 1993). The earliest evidence of their presence in northern Siberia is the recently reported Yana RHS site in the Yana River region (Fig. 13–5), where archaeologists have found rhinoceros horn and mammoth ivory spear foreshafts as well as stone tools and other artifacts in contexts dated to about 30,000 ya (Pitulko et al., 2004). Yana RHS is at least twice as old as the western Beringia site of Berelekh (see

FIGURE 13–5
Late Pleistocene sites in Siberia and Beringia mentioned in the text.

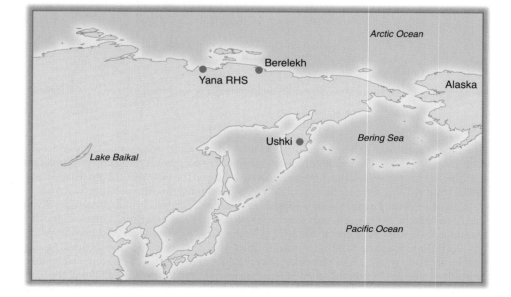

Beringia (bare-in´-jya) The dry-land connection between Asia and America that existed periodically during the Pleistocene epoch.

tundra Treeless plains characterized by permafrost conditions that support the growth of shallow-rooted vegetation such as grasses and mosses.

*To put these glaciers in perspective, visualize a mile-high ice sheet where Chicago is now—not a film of ice on your car's windshield in the winter.

Fig. 13–5), the next oldest candidate for a possible Arctic Circle campsite, and it demonstrates that at a very early date, people were successfully adapted to high-latitude conditions similar to what hunters would have encountered in crossing Beringia. Culturally and geographically, these Asian hunters were capable of becoming the first Americans.

Geologists have determined that except for short spans, the Bering passage was dry land between about 25,000 and 11,000 ya and for other extended periods even before then (especially between 75,000 and 45,000 ya). If the first humans entered the New World by traveling on foot across Beringia, they probably made their trips during the later episode. As yet, there's no generally accepted evidence of humans in the Americas before that time.

After entering Alaska by way of Beringia, early immigrants would not have had easy access to the rest of the Americas. Major glaciers to the southeast of Beringia blocked the further movement of both game and people throughout most of the Pleistocene Epoch. The **Cordilleran** ice mass covered the mountains of western Canada and southern Alaska, and the **Laurentian** glacier, centered on Hudson Bay, spread a vast ice sheet across much of eastern and central Canada and the northeastern United States (see Fig. 13–2). Around 20,000 ya, these glaciers coalesced into one massive flow. Toward the close of the Pleistocene, the edges of the Cordilleran and Laurentian glaciers finally separated, allowing animals and, in principle, their hunters to gain entry to the south through an "ice-free corridor" along the eastern flank of the Canadian Rockies. Some researchers maintain that the ice-free corridor was passable as early as 15,000 ya (Holmes, 1996), which would be consistent with generally accepted early sites in North America below the glaciers. Others point to the geographical pattern of radiocarbon age estimates from western North America that indicate humans could not have traveled down this ice-free corridor much before 11,000 ya (Arnold, 2002). If that's true, the corridor couldn't be considered a major pathway for the entry of the earliest humans into the Americas south of the glaciers.

Cordilleran (cor-dee-yair´-an) Pleistocene ice sheet originating in mountains of western North America.

Laurentian (lah-ren´-shun) Pleistocene ice sheet centered in the Hudson Bay region and extending across much of eastern Canada and the northern United States.

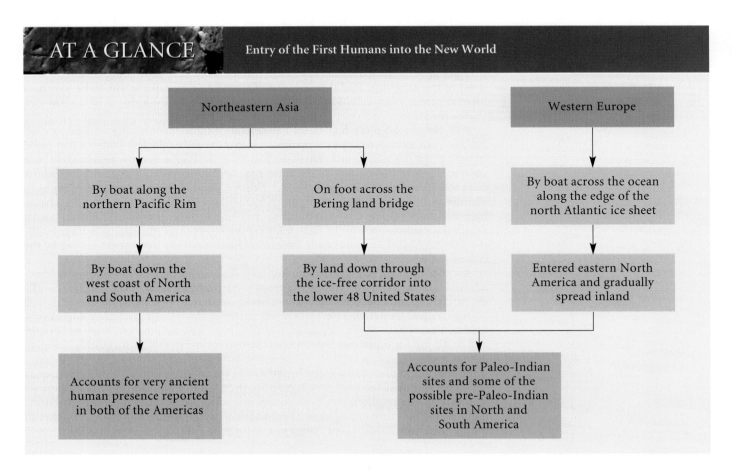

AT A GLANCE — Entry of the First Humans into the New World

Northeastern Asia → Western Europe

- **Northeastern Asia**
  - By boat along the northern Pacific Rim
    - By boat down the west coast of North and South America
      - Accounts for very ancient human presence reported in both of the Americas
  - On foot across the Bering land bridge
    - By land down through the ice-free corridor into the lower 48 United States
- **Western Europe**
  - By boat across the ocean along the edge of the north Atlantic ice sheet
    - Entered eastern North America and gradually spread inland

Accounts for Paleo-Indian sites and some of the possible pre-Paleo-Indian sites in North and South America

To sum things up, the Bering land bridge model for the entry of people into the New World rests on several key notions. First, the technologically simplest way to get from the Old World to the New World was on foot. Second, lots of other animals arrived by this route during the Pleistocene, so, archaeologists reason, it was feasible for people to do the same. Third, as we discuss in a later section, the skeletal, mtDNA, and linguistic evidence clearly favor an Asian origin for Native Americans. The main problem with the Bering land bridge explanation is that the age estimates for the earliest humans in North and, especially, South America are hard to reconcile with the age estimates for the most favorable intervals during which humans could have crossed Beringia and then passed down the ice-free corridor.

PACIFIC COASTAL ROUTE

The second scenario also envisions the earliest New World inhabitants coming from Asia. But it has them moving along the coast, where climatic conditions were generally not as harsh as those of the interior, and where they could simply go around the North American glaciers. Looking again at the northern Pacific Rim between Asia and North America (see Fig. 13–3), we can see that, given canoes, rafts, or other form of water transport, it was geographically possible for humans to enter the New World by traveling along the coast. Unlike the Bering land bridge, this route would have been less dependent on the waxing or waning of glaciers. In principle, therefore, humans traveling by this route could have arrived in the New World tens of thousands of years ago (Dixon, 1999; Erlandson, 2002).

But why should we assume that the late Pleistocene inhabitants of East Asia had water transport capable of making this trip? Here sound archaeological evidence comes to our rescue. As discussed in Chapter 12, humans colonized Australia sometime before 40,000 ya, and it could only be reached by water. So, the technology necessary to carry humans successfully along the Pacific Coast—but not, apparently, across the Pacific Ocean—from Asia to the New World must have existed before the first people began to settle in the Americas.

Many archaeologists find the possibility that people used a coastal route to enter the New World an attractive idea, partly because it avoids the time constraints on the availability of the Bering land bridge and ice-free corridor, and partly because migrants traveling by boat along the northern Pacific coast need not have abandoned their boats once they got around the glaciers. They could just as easily have kept going down the west coast of the Americas. Had they done so, it would help to explain why there may be a lot of apparently very early South America sites, but few in the interior of North America (Kelly, 2003).

Still, the coastal route hypothesis has several possible shortcomings. An often cited problem, one even noted by its proponents, is that the archaeological evidence that could be used to test this assumption rests at the bottom of the Pacific Ocean—having likely been covered, if not destroyed, by rising sea levels as the glaciers melted. Fortunately, coastlines react locally, not globally, to such changes. Paleogeographical researchers are beginning to identify specific parts of the modern coasts and offshore islands of Canada that would have been exposed land where human migrants may have traveled (Hetherington et al., 2003). So, the door is now open to the archaeological site surveys and excavations in these localities that might just demonstrate if the earliest humans in the New World arrived by the coastal route.

Another problem is that currently we have little archaeological evidence of marine-adapted human populations along the coast of northeastern Asia—from which the earliest immigrants into the New World would have been drawn—until *after* the end of the last Ice Age. If immigrants to the New World had arrived by this route, most archaeologists with firsthand experience in the region feel that they must have had the necessary technology and Arctic marine experience that enabled them to survive in this harsh, quickly changing environment.

Finally, the Pacific coastal route hypothesis as yet doesn't account for the discrepancy between the earliest-reported sites in both South and North America. Working from a set of reasonable assumptions about the coastal migrants, their demographic characteristics, lifeways, and how they moved along the coastline, a computer simulation of the migration process along the Pacific Coast "failed to demonstrate that coastal migration alone could have produced the observed archaeological record" (Surovell, 2003). While a simulation never *proves* anything by itself, Surovell's research does suggest that if the earliest people entered the New World by the coastal route, we still have much to learn about how and why it happened.

So to sum things up, the Pacific coastal route was feasible in principle. Considering the generally milder climate and rich resources of the coast relative to the interior, the presence of natural refugia, and the apparent technological capabilities of late Pleistocene Asian populations, the earliest migrants could have pulled it off. Factoring the Bering land bridge and the glaciers out of the equation also removes the temporal bottlenecks on migration that haunt the land bridge hypothesis. These are definitely marks in its favor. The main problems are first, if the earliest people came by this route, then much—but fortunately not all—of the archaeological evidence is in the muck on the floor of the Pacific. And, as with the land bridge hypothesis, the Pacific coastal route hypothesis doesn't necessarily enable archaeologists to explain the earliest reported South American sites. At any rate, it's still a testable hypothesis for explaining how the first inhabitants of the New World arrived.

NORTH ATLANTIC ICE-EDGE CORRIDOR

The main concern of the third and final scenario in our lineup of possible migration hypotheses is to explain the origins of the **Clovis** culture (13,500–13,000 ya), which many archaeologists continue to view as the remains of the earliest and most widespread inhabitants of North America. Although Clovis itself is reasonably well known, archaeologists have yet to find any clear antecedents for the sophisticated Clovis technology in the Upper Paleolithic sites of Siberia. Given the lack of Asian precursors for Clovis and the problems of getting the earliest inhabitants across the Bering land bridge and south of the Canadian glaciers before the oldest Clovis sites were being deposited, Bradley and Stanford (2004) suggest that it's time to look elsewhere. Rather than continuing to focus on the possible Asia–North America link, they argue that we should be trying to identify the most similar technology that could be ancestral to Clovis and then exploring how it may have reached the shores of North America.

According to Bradley and Stanford's "North Atlantic Ice-Edge Corridor" hypothesis, the Upper Paleolithic *Solutrean* culture of southwestern France and northern Spain is technologically very similar to Clovis, and old enough to be its original source. The technological similarities are so close, they argue, that if a Solutrean site were found in Siberia, it would immediately answer the question of Clovis origins. Since that hasn't happened after decades of fieldwork, they argue that Solutrean peoples may have entered North America by following the edge of the North Atlantic sea-ice bridge that linked Europe and North America during the Last Glacial Maximum (see Fig. 13–4). Eventually, having traversed the southwestern edge of the glacial ice to eastern North America, these groups dispersed inland, became North America's earliest human inhabitants, and laid the foundation for the distinctive stone, bone, and ivory tool assemblages that archaeologists call Clovis.

To sum up the case for the Solutrean-Clovis connection, the two strengths of the hypothesis are that first, it clearly identifies a very similar technology that is older than Clovis, and second, it describes a process by which people who made and used this technology could have crossed the Atlantic and entered North America. The idea also has many shortcomings, not the least of which is that—as Lawrence Straus, a Solutrean specialist, points out—the Solutrean ended about 5,000 years, or roughly 250 generations, before the earliest-dated Clovis material in North America. This is not a tiny glitch that can be easily overcome, and the Solutrean-to-Clovis case looks doubtful at best. In the long run, the main contribution of the North Atlantic Ice-Edge Corridor hypothesis may well be that it encourages archaeologists to break away from the centuries-long obsession with the Bering Strait and Asia and consider other possible routes by which the earliest inhabitants arrived in the Americas. To the extent that Bradley and Stanford are successful in doing this, the results will benefit the scientific understanding of the human colonization of both North and South America.

Clovis   Phase of North American prehistory, 13,500–13,000 ya in the West, during which short-fluted projectile points were used in hunting mammoths.

The Earliest Americans

We'll now leave behind the questions of how the first people arrived in North America and explore some ideas about who they were.

BIOLOGICAL AND GENETIC EVIDENCE

Biological data bearing directly on the earliest people to reach the New World are frustratingly scarce. Well-documented skeletons are especially rare. The physical remains of fewer than two dozen North American individuals appear to date much before 9,500 ya, by which time humans had certainly been present in the New World for millennia. The tremendous information value of well-preserved and documented early skeletons is *the* reason that archaeologists just spent nine years in federal courts contesting what they believed to be the government's well-intentioned but misguided decision to turn over the remains of Kennewick Man to Native American tribal groups for reburial before they could be studied (see Digging Deeper).

The rare early finds provide valuable insights on ancient life and death. What little we currently know about Kennewick Man (Fig. 13–6), for example, is that he suffered multiple violent trauma and other health problems during his 40–50 years of life. His most intriguing injury is an old wound in his pelvis that had healed around a still-embedded stone spear

FIGURE **13–6**

Location of some early New World sites. The dates for many of these sites are still disputed as archaeologists grapple with mounting evidence that the earliest evidence of humans in the New World is older than the 13,000–13,500 ya Paleo-Indian Clovis culture of North America.

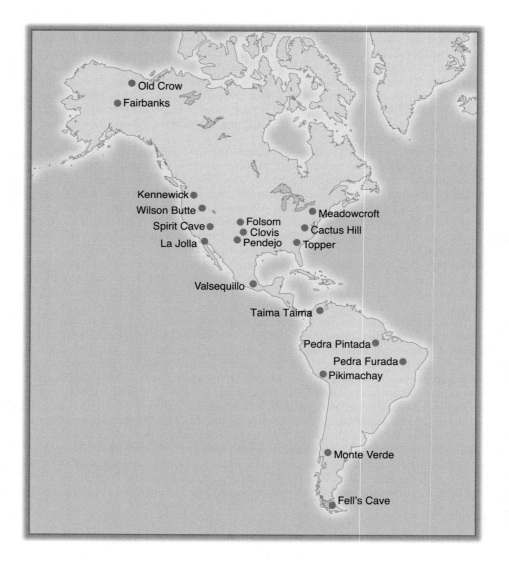

DIGGING DEEPER

Kennewick Man— Put Yourself in His Place

After a long but physically hard life, with more than your fair share of trouble, you end up dead on the river bank. Some 9,000 years later, your remains erode out of the river bank and are found by a couple of men who mistake you for a forensic case. Your surviving bones are whisked off to the lab, where a quick inspection shows you're not a forensic case and no one is certain who you are. There are more examinations, odd bits of you are pulverized so your birth date can be ballparked within a few hundred years, and still more of your parts are subjected to a CAT scan. From this, the one thing that emerges with certainty is that you died quite a long time ago.

Soon you're the object of a custody battle. The scientists want you because you represent a moment in the earliest prehistory of North America, about which there's little hard information and not much chance of there ever being much. Native American groups want you because your remains were found in their traditional homeland, and it's their duty to treat you as an ancestor according to their beliefs and rituals. The Corps of Engineers and the Department of the Interior want you because your remains were found in a navigable waterway, which means they're legally responsible for you. There's even a Polynesian chief who claims you because he thinks you're one of his ancestors.

The struggle for your remains pivots around a recently enacted federal law, called the Native American Graves Protection and Repatriation Act (P.L. 101–601), also known as NAGPRA. This law contains provisions restricting acquisition and ownership of Native American skeletal and artifactual materials by public institutions and, under some circumstances, by others. It also mandates the return, or repatriation, of Native American physical remains to lineal descendants, along with funerary artifacts and other objects that hold cultural, ceremonial, or religious significance.

But there's a peculiarity about every new law—to understand what it really means, you have to see how the courts interpret it when applying it to real cases. Your custody battle becomes contentious because it's an important, precedent-setting case regarding the interpretation of NAGPRA. It's part of a larger and as yet unresolved debate in the United States over several issues: Whose claim on the past—and, particularly, the objects of the past—is truly legitimate? Does any ethnically, religiously, or politically defined group have an *exclusive* right of possession or access to cultural materials? If so, under what circumstances, and how far back into the past does this right extend?

Your remains are locked up for years in yet another lab as attorneys for both sides in the legal conflict fight it out in U.S. District Court. The presiding judge in the case hands down his decision in August 2002, and the appeals process drags out the case for nearly another three years. Finally, in early summer 2005, the court battle is over (Dalton, 2005). The court decision grants permission for scientists to study your remains. Beyond that, the decision clarifies the limits of NAGPRA and, when placed in larger context, effectively affirms that the public has the right to certain scientific information about the past. However, the full impact of the court decision on other questions about ownership of the past will probably not be apparent for several years, as other court cases draw on what was learned in this one. Many of the stakeholders in your case are understandably disappointed by the court's decision, but they can take pride in knowing that they did their duty according to their convictions and responsibilities.

It'll be years before the world knows what the scientific analysis reveals about your life some 9,000 years ago. For now, here's what they say: "He was a relatively tall fellow of medium build with a big nose and, for his time, a fairly advanced age. He had a stiff neck that squeaked and a left arm perhaps weakened by an injury in his youth. As he breathed, some of his ribs were sucked in and pushed out, and any exertion that caused him to inhale deeply caused a dull, tearing pain around the old scars. It hurt to lift his right leg, and an old spear wound would ache from time to time. He oozed pus and fluids from an opening near his waist, which to top it all off, probably made him smell bad. His was a hard life indeed" (Chatters, 2001, p. 147).

We'll never know if you were a saint, a murderous letch, or just an ordinary man trying to get by. The amazing fact is simply that you're here. Even in death you're the ultimate survivor, and your life's greatest achievement will be the story written on your bones. It's your unique legacy to the modern world—and one well worth having.

SOURCES:

Ancient Encounters: Kennewick Man and the First Americans, by James C. Chatters (New York: Simon & Schuster, 2001).

Implementing the Native American Graves Protection and Repatriation Act: Resource Report (Washington, DC: American Association of Museums, 2000).

Kennewick Man Virtual Interpretive Center <http://www.kennewick-man.com/>; contains links to the relevant legal documents and news stories.

"Native American Graves Protection and Repatriation Act," Public Law 101–601, November 16, 1990 (Washington, DC: U.S. Government Printing Office, 1990).

No Bone Unturned: The Adventures of a Top Smithsonian Forensic Scientist and the Legal Battle for America's Oldest Skeletons, by Jeff Benedict (New York: HarperCollins, 2003).

Skull Wars: Kennewick Man, Archeology, and the Battle for Native American Identity, by David Hurst Thomas (New York: Basic Books, 2000).

FIGURE 13-7
Reconstruction of the facial features of Kennewick Man (right), based on a cast of the skull (left) found by two young men in the Columbia River, Washington, in 1996. The reconstruction was the collaborative effort of Tom McClelland (holding the skull) and James Chatters.

point. To this we can add the largely healed effects of massive blunt trauma to the chest, a depressed skull fracture, and a fracture of the left arm. He also had an infected head injury and a fractured shoulder blade (scapula), neither of which shows the effects of healing, as well as osteoarthritis (Chatters, 2004). What's more, the list is probably incomplete because it was compiled from a preliminary examination of the remains. But by any measure, this man had a pretty hard life. Just how hard it was will become evident in a couple of years, after researchers complete the scientific analysis of his remains.

Anthropologists are also analyzing other cases, all from the American West. The 12,800-year-old partial skeleton of a young woman, discovered in a cave above the Snake River near Buhl, Idaho, revealed signs of interrupted growth in both her long bones and in her teeth; this evidence suggests that the woman experienced some metabolic stress in childhood, possibly because of disease or seasonal food shortages (Green et al., 1998). At Spirit Cave, Nevada, researchers discovered the partially desiccated body of a man, wrapped in fine matting, who was in his early 40s when he died some 10,600 years ago; his skeleton exhibited a fractured skull and tooth abscesses as well as signs of back problems (Winslow and Wedding, 1997). Near Grimes Point rock-shelter, another Nevada site, researchers found a teenager from about the same period who died of his wounds after being stabbed in the chest with an obsidian blade that left slash marks and stone flakes embedded in one of his ribs (Owsley and Jantz, 2000).

Physical anthropologists who made the preliminary studies of Kennewick Man, the Spirit Cave mummy, and other early specimens announced surprising interpretations based on this modest sample. Statistical analyses comparing a series of standard cranial measurements—including those that define overall skull size and proportion, shape of nasal opening, face width, and distance between the eyes—place the earliest-known American remains outside the normal range of variation observed in modern Native American populations (Owsley and Jantz, 2000). The more derived craniofacial morphological traits seen in most modern Asian and Native American populations appear to be absent in this early population. Instead, the archaeological examples display relatively small, narrow faces combined with long skulls. In living populations today, physical anthropologists note these generalized (nonderived) traits among the Ainu of Japan and some Pacific Islanders and Australians. Crania that more closely resemble those of modern Native Americans became prevalent only after about 7,000 ya (Owsley and Jantz, 2000; Steele, 2000).

There are, of course, no uniform biological "types" of human beings in the sense once assumed by traditional classifiers of race (see Chapter 5). Generalities regarding human variation must, considering the nature of genetic recombination and the effects of environment and nutrition, be taken simply as that—generalities. Still, the lack of distinctive Native American physical markers on the oldest skeletal specimens has stimulated research on how the early population of the Americas, as represented by these individuals, may be related to contemporary populations.

Neves and colleagues (2004) compared the cranial morphology of nine individuals dated to around 10,200 ya from central Brazil. The researchers concluded that these individuals represent one of possibly several populations that participated in the peopling of the Americas from Asia. The researchers argue that the differences between the cranial morphology of these individuals and that of modern Native American populations are consistent with those seen in morphological comparisons elsewhere in the Americas (e.g., Brace et al., 2001; Owsley and Jantz, 2000). Similar differences also exist between late Pleistocene and recent populations in Asia, and the modern typical morphological pattern of Asia is likely a recent development that may have followed the adoption of agriculture (Jantz and Owsley, 2001).

Studies like these are a great help in placing recent finds such as Kennewick Man into context. When the facial reconstruction of Kennewick Man (Fig. 13–7) was completed in 1997, more than a few people wondered why it looked more like the British actor Patrick Stewart of *Star Trek* fame than the popular stereotype of Native Americans (think of the man's profile on the old U.S. buffalo nickel). Quite a lot was read into that reconstruction, but all it really showed was what researchers like Neves, Jantz, Owsley, and others already know: We don't have much data to work from, but what we do have shows similar morphological variation in Asia and the Americas among late Pleistocene–early Holocene skeletons. The data support Steele and Powell's (1999) conclusions that there seems to have been more than one prehistoric migration from Asia into the New World. The argument has intuitive appeal. After all, why would the supply of immigrants dry up after the first humans arrived in the New World?

If you were to seek the answer in the entire span of the human presence in the New World, it would be evident that the flow of people to the New World has roughly kept pace with the development of technology to bring them here throughout prehistory and down to the present. In this view, at least, the peopling of the New World can best be viewed as a continuing process, not as a one-time event.

Several other sources of biological data offer evidence bearing on Native American origins. In comparing specific details of dental morphology for many Asian and Native American populations, physical anthropologist Christy Turner recognized that a so-named Sinodont (literally, "Chinese tooth") pattern is found widely among New World native peoples, but in the Old World it's common to only one area of northern China (Turner, 1987). A high incidence of shovel-shaped incisors, distinctive roots on molar teeth, and a score of other dental diagnostics characterize the Sinodont groups, including nearly all Native Americans. In Turner's view, Chinese now living in Mongolia, who share these traits, are related to those people who first entered the New World thousands of years ago. More than 20,000 years ago, he postulates, these populations had started out somewhere in Southeast Asia.

It's widely acknowledged that contemporary Asian and Native American populations share many superficial physical similarities—for example, the texture, color, and distribution of head and body hair (see Chapter 4 for a discussion of the limited utility of such phenotypic characteristics). But they also display distinctive variations that set them apart from other populations. The distribution pattern of ABO blood types (antigens) among living Native Americans is one example. Modern Native Americans in North and South America exhibit unusually high frequencies of the type O allele (80 to 100 percent), along with a near absence of several other blood group antigens more commonly found in other populations (see Chapter 4).

This unique suite of specific traits shared by modern Native Americans surely reflects the limited variability of a small founding gene pool. (For a discussion of the founder effect, an example of genetic drift, see p. 59.) Recent analyses of mitochondrial DNA among contemporary Native American populations have led genetic researchers to suggest that just four or five maternal lineages contributed to the early peopling of the Americas (Schurr et al., 1990; Schurr, 2000). However, different interpretations based on these findings have been offered. Some geneticists surmise that the present distribution pattern of mtDNA derived from these maternal lineages is consistent with the hypothesis that the New World's original inhabitants derived from a single northeastern Asian population of small size (Merriwether et al., 1995). Others, however, see in the same data a dramatically different scenario, wherein the earliest immigrants from south-central Siberia entered the Americas by way of the coastal route sometime between 20,000 and 14,000 ya; a second wave of Siberian immigrants arrived later, possibly by the Bering land bridge; and more groups, this time from Beringia, entered North America following the Last Glacial Maximum (Schurr, 2004; Schurr and Sherry, 2004).

CULTURAL TRACES OF THE EARLIEST AMERICANS

Much of the cultural evidence documenting the presence of the earliest Americans is no less controversial than that gained from analyses of the skeletal data. Significantly, the recent mtDNA research that concludes there were three separate migratory "pulses" also finds support in the linguistic evidence. Linguists study relationships among modern Native American languages to calculate how much they've diverged, or "drifted" (linguistic, not genetic, in this case), from a common ancestral tongue (Greenberg, 1987; Ruhlen, 1994). Assuming a "normal" rate of drift, linguists then calculate the time needed to account for the observed differences. According to these reconstructions, the founding population of most of the living aboriginal groups of the New World arrived sometime after 18,000 ya. Perhaps by 9,000 ya, hunters who became ancestral to the **Athabaskan**-speaking peoples of central Alaska, the Northwest Coast, and the Canadian interior made their appearance. Finally, about 6,000 ya, according to linguists, Asian sea mammal hunters occupied the Arctic coasts and islands, establishing the distinctive Inuit/Eskimo and Aleut cultural traditions.

From the cultural data, archaeologists agree almost unanimously that Native Americans originated in Asia, yet they have varying opinions about when people first arrived in the New World and the routes by which they traveled (Meltzer, 1993b; Dillehay, 2000). Most of the controversy focuses on the span between 30,000 and 13,500 ya. The earlier date represents the time by which modern people first began to appear in those parts of Asia closest to North

Athabaskan Largest Native American language family in North America; includes more than 35 languages spoken in western North America.

America—for example, the Yana RHS site in Siberia (see p. 302). By the later date, verified sites associated with **Paleo-Indians** had been established in many parts of the Western Hemisphere.

Like the biological anthropologists, archaeologists have a tough time reaching consensus on answers to such basic questions as "What are the material remains of the earliest inhabitants of the New World?" "When did they arrive?" and "Where did they come from?" That robust answers are not forthcoming isn't for want of research; it is simply the case that the evidence is sparsely scattered over millions of square miles and is not necessarily very distinctive. As the biological anthropologists and archaeologists have learned, answering these questions takes decades of hard work—and more than a little luck.

What kind of archaeological evidence can we point to that *has* survived from this early period of American prehistory? The answer depends largely on how one evaluates the "evidence." For example, isolated artifacts, including stone choppers and large flake tools of simple form, are at times recovered from exposed ground surfaces and other undatable contexts in the Americas. They are sometimes proposed as evidence of a period predating the use of bifacial projectile points, which were common in North America by 13,500 ya. If typologically primitive-looking finds cannot be securely dated, most (but not all) archaeologists regard them with justifiable caution. The appearance of great age or crude condition may be misleading and is all but impossible to verify without corroborating evidence. To be properly evaluated, an artifact must be unquestionably the product of human handiwork and must have been recovered from a geologically sealed and undisturbed context that can be dated reliably.

Sounds pretty straightforward, right? The reality of the situation is not necessarily that easy. Take, for example, the projectile points. Alan Bryan and Ruth Gruhn (2003) point out that North American archaeologists' obsession with bifacially flaked stone points may ultimately do more harm than good to research, because we have no basis for believing that such tools were a consistent part of prehistoric assemblages everywhere in the Americas. They note, for example, that bifacially flaked projectile points are far less common in Central and South America than they are in the continental United States and southern Canada. In fact, in some parts of lowland South America, Native American groups never did use bifacially worked stone tool technology (Bryan and Gruhn, 2003, p. 175). The implication is obvious. The criteria that work for identifying the earliest Americans in one part of the two continents may not apply to other parts.

Most difficult to assess are some atypical sites that have been carefully excavated by researchers who sincerely believe that their work offers proof of great human antiquity in the New World. Currently, several sites fall into this disputed category (see Fig. 13–6). Pedra Furada is a rock-shelter in northeastern Brazil where excavators found what they claim to be simple stone tools in association with charcoal hearths dating back 40,000 years (Guidon et al., 1996). Others who have examined these materials remain convinced that natural, rather than cultural, factors account for them (Lynch, 1990; Meltzer et al., 1994). The dating of this and other sites in the same general region also continue to be reexamined. Additional radiocarbon age estimates—using the new ABOX-SC (acid-base-wet oxidation followed by stepped

Paleo-Indians (*paleo*, meaning "ancient") In the Americas, early hunter-gatherers, from about 14,000 to 8,000 ya.

AT A GLANCE		Important Pre–Paleo-Indian Sites in the New World
Site	**Dates (ya)**	**Comments**
Pedra Furada (Brazil)	?50,000– ?40,000	One of several South American sites for which great antiquity is claimed
Pendejo Cave (New Mexico)	37,000–12,000	North American site for which great antiquity is claimed; as with Pedra Furada in Brazil, the evidence continues to be carefully evaluated but, as yet, not widely accepted by other researchers
Meadowcroft (Pennsylvania)	19,000–14,000	North American site that is increasingly accepted as a valid example of the pre-Clovis presence of humans in North America
Monte Verde (Chile)	14,800	Pre-Clovis campsite in southern South America; the evidence is still hotly debated

combustion) procedure—on samples from hearths in the lowest levels of Pedra Furada recently yielded dates in excess of 50,000 ya (Santos et al., 2003). However, fresh radiocarbon dates on Pedra Furada pigments and rock paintings, both of which are thought by their excavators to be nearly 30,000 years old, yielded estimates of only 2,000–3,500 ya (Rowe and Steelman, 2003). So, it could be the oldest site in South America—or it could be so recent as to be irrelevant. Pedra Furada joins several other Central and South American locations that in recent decades have been proposed as extremely early cultural sites (Lynch, 1990; Parfit, 2000). Archaeologists have been uncertain how to evaluate most of them because the associated cultural materials are so typologically diverse and their contexts are frequently secondary, or mixed, geological deposits.

The United States, too, has its share of sites that defy easy explanation. At Pendejo Cave in southern New Mexico, excavators have discovered 16 friction skin prints impressed on fire-hardened clay nodules in three stratigraphic zones dated from 37,000 to 12,000 ya (Chrisman et al., 1996, 2003). Clear impressions of ridge patterns and even of sweat pores, visible under magnification, seem to confirm the palm prints and fingerprints as primate, and most likely human; but their origin and significance remain uncertain (Dincauze, 1997; Shaffer and Baker, 1997). Possible cultural materials from the same levels include charred wood, crude stone tools, and the toe bone of an extinct horse with what may be an embedded bone tool possibly used to extract marrow (MacNeish and Libby, 2003). Far to the east, at the Cactus Hill site along the Nottoway River in southern Virginia and at the Topper site in Allendale County, South Carolina, archaeologists have retrieved unusual assemblages of stone cores, flakes, and tools from strata lying well beneath more typical Paleo-Indian components (Dixon, 1999). The unusually early radiocarbon dates (15,000–18,000 ya) associated with these materials are consistent with their stratigraphic position (e.g., Wagner and McAvoy, 2004), but the evidence will require cautious review before these sites are generally accepted.

The scientific method is not a democratic process; we can't simply dismiss (or side with) unpopular positions without assessing the evidence as it is presented. The method is, however, a skeptical one; and the burden of proof to substantiate claims of great antiquity falls upon those who make them. Each allegation requires critical evaluation, a process that the general public sometimes perceives as unnecessarily conservative or obstructive. Information regarding dating results, archaeological contexts, and whether or not materials are of cultural origin must all be scrutinized and accepted before intense debate can resolve into consensus.

This evaluation process may take years. Consider, for example, the case of the Meadowcroft rock-shelter, near Pittsburgh, Pennsylvania. In a meticulous excavation over 25 years ago, archaeologists explored a deeply stratified site containing cultural levels dated between 19,000 and 14,000 ya by standard radiocarbon methods (Adovasio et al., 1990). Stratum IIa, from which the earliest dates derive, contained several prismatic blades, a retouched flake, a biface, and a knifelike implement (Fig. 13–8). None of the tools from this deep stratum are particularly distinctive, so it's hard to assess technological relationships with other known assemblages. Despite lingering concern over the possibility that fossil carbon from nearby coal seams may have contaminated the carbon-dated samples, more archaeologists are coming to accept the Meadowcroft evidence because of the excavators' careful documentation and the coherence of the dated strata with one another.

Excavations at Monte Verde in southern Chile revealed another remarkable site of apparent pre–Paleo-Indian age (Dillehay, 1989, 1997). Here, remnants of the wooden foundations of a dozen rectangular huts were arranged back to back in a parallel row. The structures measured between 10 and 15 feet on a side, and animal hides may have covered their sapling frameworks. Apart from the main cluster, a separate wishbone-shaped building contained stone tools and animal bones (Fig. 13–9). Numerous spheroids (possibly sling

FIGURE **13–8**
Knifelike implement from Stratum IIa at the Meadowcroft rock-shelter in Pennsylvania.

FIGURE **13–9**
The semicircular ridge of soil at lower right in the photograph marks the remains of a 14,800-year-old hut at Monte Verde, Chile. Mastodon bones, hide, and flesh were preserved in association with this feature, along with 26 species of medicinal plants.

Tom Dillehay

stones), flaked stone points, perforating tools, a wooden lance, digging sticks, mortars, and fire pits comprised the cultural equipment. Mastodon bones represented at least seven individuals, and remains of some 100 species of nuts, fruits, berries, wild tubers, and firewood testify to the major role of plants in subsistence activities at this site.

Monte Verde's excavator, Tom Dillehay, concludes that "the form and arrangement of the architecture and activity areas . . . reveal technological sophistication and a social and economic organization much more complex than previously suspected for a late Pleistocene culture of the New World" (Dillehay, 1989, p. 2). And that startling complexity is one reason Monte Verde's early dates—about 14,800 years old, with a few features possibly much older—have been hotly debated. In 1997, a "jury" of archaeological specialists reviewed the findings one more time and agreed that the excavator's claims for Monte Verde had been substantiated. The broader implications for American prehistory are not yet fully apparent, though Monte Verde's South American location clearly hints at an early entry of people into the New World. The site becomes the first in the New World to be recognized by the archaeological "establishment" as older than 13,500 years, but not everyone accepts the evidence as it has been presented (Meltzer et al., 1997; Fiedel, 1999a). As recently as 2004, Stuart Fiedel described Monte Verde as "an incongruously early (ca. 12,300 14C B.P. [before present]) regional anomaly, [with] the peculiar congeries of broken gravel, gomphothere bones, vegetation, and a half-dozen indisputable but Archaic-looking and inadequately provenienced artifacts" (2004, p. 95). This is not a move toward consensus.

Paleo-Indians in the Americas

Archaeological evidence of the presence of humans in the Americas becomes relatively common after about 13,500 ya—that is, during the final centuries of the Pleistocene. Indeed, more than a few well-respected and experienced archaeologists continue to view these sites as the earliest evidence for the entry of people below the Canadian glacial ice mass into North America. During the Paleo-Indian period, evidence for a lifeway of mobile hunting and gathering comes from widely scattered locations, including a great many sites in the western United States (Fig. 13–10). The distinctive **fluted point** is the period's hallmark artifact. Each face of a fluted point typically displays a groove (or "flute") resulting from the removal of a long channel flake, possibly to make it easier to use a special hafting technique for mounting the point on a shaft (Fig. 13–11). Other typical Paleo-Indian artifacts include a variety of stone cutting and scraping tools and, less commonly, preserved bone rods and points (Gramly, 1992).

While the general Paleo-Indian tool kit from North American probably would have been familiar to Upper Paleolithic groups in Siberia, no clear technological predecessors of fluted points have yet been identified in Asia. As you may recall, this was one of the main motivations for Bradley and Stanford's (2004) decision to look elsewhere for the entry of people into North America, a search that culminated with their argument for a northern Atlantic crossing from western Europe. It's entirely possible that fluted point technology is an American invention and there are no ancestral forms to find elsewhere, whether it be in Spain, Siberia, or Mongolia. Sites such as Yana RHS in Siberia demonstrate that Upper Paleolithic hunter-gatherers, like Paleo-Indians, made bifacially worked stone tools and tipped their spears with projectile points—but not *fluted* projectile points. These Siberian hunters set projectile points in bone or ivory foreshafts and were living in the general region of Beringia more than 15,000 years before the earliest evidence of Paleo-Indian camps appears in the New World. Bifacial points and knives are also part of the Nenana complex sites of central Alaska and the lower levels of Ushki Lake in Siberia's Kamchatka peninsula. All of these sites are currently believed to date to around 13,000–13,400 ya (Goebel et al., 2003), which is too late for their inhabitants to have been the ancestors of the people who developed Paleo-Indian fluted point technology, but the sites do demonstrate that generally similar tool industries *were* moving into the New World at an early date.

fluted point A biface or projectile point having had long, thin flakes removed from each face to prepare the base for hafting, or attachment to a shaft.

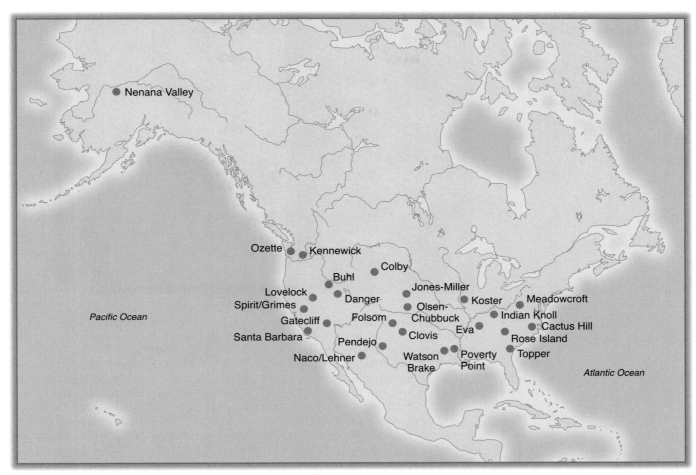

FIGURE 13–10
North American Paleo-Indian and Archaic sites.

PALEO-INDIAN LIFEWAYS

Most archaeologists think Paleo-Indians showed great uniformity in weaponry, hunting behavior, and early site contexts across the American continents. This apparent homogeneity is explained as the result of a fairly rapid spread of people throughout the New World, beginning about 13,500 ya. Hunters wielding spears tipped with fishtail-shaped, fluted points reached even the farthest extremes of South America and were already active around Fell's Cave in Patagonia (see Fig. 13–6) by some 11,000 ya. The wide distribution of the specialized fluted point sites implies that Paleo-Indians quickly made cultural adjustments as they dispersed through the varied environments of the New World during the terminal Pleistocene and early Holocene.

The main shortcoming of these interpretations is the assumption that the fluted point technology was a consistent part of prehistoric assemblages across the Americas and that people everywhere were using the technology to do the same things. As Bryan and Gruhn (2003) point out, there are certainly parts of the Americas in which these assumptions aren't warranted. To the extent that this is true, the uniformity of Paleo-Indian toolkits may often be more the creation of archaeologists than of the archaeology.

The same appears to be true of the long-held view of Paleo-Indians as specialized hunters of Pleistocene **megafauna**—animals over 100 pounds, including the mammoth, mastodon,

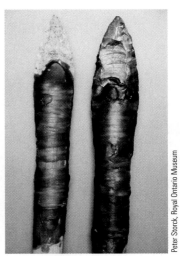

FIGURE 13–11
Clovis fluted points in simulated mountings.

megafauna Literally, "large animals," those weighing over 100 pounds.

FIGURE 13-12
Molar teeth of mastodon (left) and mammoth (right). Mastodons browsed on evergreen branches; mammoths grazed on low vegetation. Paleo-Indian hunters may have contributed to their extinction.

giant bison, horse, camel, and ground sloth (Fig. 13–12). Of the sites associated with Paleo-Indians, the most impressive are undoubtedly the places where ancient hunters actually killed and butchered such megafauna as mammoth and giant bison (Figs. 13–13 and 13–14). At many of these kill sites, knives, scrapers, and finely flaked and fluted projectile points are directly associated with the animal bones, all of which are convincing evidence that the megafauna were human prey. Even so, as Cannon and Meltzer (2004) recently discovered in a review of the faunal remains, taphonomy, excavation procedures, and archaeological features of 62 excavated early Paleo-Indian sites in the United States, the data "provide little support for the idea that all, or even any, Early Paleo-Indian hunter-gatherers were megafaunal specialists" (Cannon and Meltzer, 2004, p. 1955). The kinds of game they hunted and other foodstuffs they collected varied with the environmental diversity of the continent, which, when you think about it, isn't that surprising. So, in the end, yes, Paleo-Indian hunters killed megafauna, but was it an everyday event? Should we view the fortunate hunter as a rugged Terminator-like man who gnaws another notch in his trusty spear and then strides off into the sunset looking for the rest of the herd? Probably not.

FIGURE 13-13
The largest American woolly mammoths were over 13 feet high at the shoulder, with long, downward-curving tusks.

FIGURE 13-14
Giant Pleistocene long-horned bison were hunted by Paleo-Indians.

(a)　　　　　　(b)　　　　　　(c)　　　　　　(d)

FIGURE **13–15**

North American Paleo-Indian projectile points. (a) Clovis. (b) Folsom. (c) Plano. (d) Dalton (length 2.4 inches).

North American archaeologists have identified a sequence of Paleo-Indian cultures in the western Plains and Southwest based on changing tool technology, chronology, and the biggest game species thought to be typical of each period. The centuries between about 13,500 and 13,000 ya were the time of hunters who employed Clovis-type fluted points (Fig. 13–15a; also see Fig. 13–11). On at least 20 western sites, including Colby in Wyoming and Naco and Lehner in southern Arizona, their spear tips lie embedded in mammoth remains (Fig. 13–16). Similar points from northern Alaska retain residues that have been biochemically identified as mammoth red blood cells and hemoglobin crystals (Loy and Dixon, 1998). Meat—but not all of it from mammoths—was certainly a major component in the diet of these early Americans. Isotopic analysis of Buhl Woman's (see p. 308) bone collagen indicates that her diet was largely game and fish, much of it probably preserved by sun-drying or smoking. The heavy wear on her teeth suggests that she regularly ingested grit in her food, probably the residue of grinding stones used to pulverize the dried meat (Green et al., 1998).

Fluted projectile points are also found throughout eastern North America. In fact, more fluted projectile points are found in the East than in the West, yet more kill sites associated with late Pleistocene megafauna are found in the West than in the East. Here too the evidence indicates a varied Paleo-Indian diet; they were also eating caribou, deer, and smaller game (Cannon and Meltzer, 2004). Early Paleo-Indian sites in New Hampshire, Massachusetts, and New York appear to be the remains of caribou-hunting camps (Cannon and Meltzer, 2004, p. 1971). A mixed subsistence of smaller game, fish, and gathered plants supplied Paleo-Indians at a site in eastern Pennsylvania (McNett, 1985). In Florida, another site also yielded a bison skull that has what looks like part of a Paleo-Indian projectile point embedded in it. The age of this specimen, however, is uncertain (Mihlbachler et al., 2000). Acquiring such resources surely involved the use of a variety of equipment made from perishable materials, such as nets and baskets, but only the stone spear tips survive on most Paleo-Indian sites.

Excavations along the lower Amazon in northern Brazil provide further evidence for other kinds of Paleo-Indian food-getting practices (Roosevelt et al., 1996). Carbonized seeds, nuts, and faunal remains at Pedra Pintada Cave in the Amazon basin indicate a broad-based food-collecting, fishing, and small-game-hunting way of life in the tropical rain forest around 12,000 ya. In other sites along the Pacific slope of the

FIGURE **13–16**

Partially articulated remains of three mammoths, one of several bone piles that probably represent Paleo-Indian meat caches at the Colby site in Wyoming.

AT A GLANCE — Important Paleo-Indian Sites in the New World

Site	Dates (ya)	Comments
Colby (Wyoming) and **Naco/Lehner** (Arizona)	13,500–13,000	Paleo-Indian sites where tools and other artifacts are found associated with the remains of mammoths
Pedra Pintada Cave (Brazil)	c. 12,000	Early site with evidence of a broad spectrum hunter-gatherer way of life in the tropical rain forest
Olsen-Chubbuck (Colorado)	9,400	Bison kill site, created when a herd was stampeded across a narrow gully in eastern Colorado
Kennewick (Washington)	9,300	One of the few early North American human skeletons; object of a 9-year court battle to decide if scientists would be permitted to study his remains

Andes, mastodons, horses, sloths, deer, camelids, and smaller animals were consumed, along with tuberous roots (Lynch, 1983).

During later Paleo-Indian times on the Great Plains of North America, the Clovis fluted spear points gave way around 12,500 ya to another fluted point style that archaeologists call **Folsom** (see Fig. 13–15b). Smaller and thinner than Clovis points, but with a proportionally larger central flute, Folsom points are associated exclusively with the bones of the now-extinct giant long-horned bison (see Fig. 13–14).

In turn, Folsom points soon gave way to a long sequence of new point forms—a variety of unfluted but slender and finely parallel-flaked projectile points collectively called **Plano** (see Fig. 13–15c), which came into general use throughout the West even as modern-day *Bison bison* was supplanting its larger Pleistocene relatives. At some Great Plains sites, like Olsen-Chubbuck and Jones-Miller in Colorado, an effective technique of bison hunting was for hunters to stampede the animals into dry streambeds or over cliffs and then quickly dispatch those that survived the fall (Wheat, 1972; Frison, 1978). Remember, the horse had not yet been reintroduced onto the Plains (the Spanish brought them in the sixteenth century), so these early bison hunters were strictly pedestrians.

Again, there was regional variation, not only in how different groups of hunter-gatherers made a living in the diverse environments of North America but also in their technology. The temporal pattern of changing point styles found in the western United States does not hold in the East, where later Paleo-Indians employed other types of projectile points, such as the **Dalton** variety (see Fig. 13–15d). Poor bone preservation generally leaves us with little direct information about these groups' hunting techniques or favored prey in this region, though deer probably extended their range at the expense of caribou as oak forests expanded over much of the eastern United States.

Folsom Phase of southern Great Plains prehistory, around 12,500 ya, during which long-fluted projectile points were used for bison hunting.

Plano Great Plains bison-hunting culture of 11,000–9,000 ya, which employed narrow, unfluted points.

Dalton Late or transitional Paleo-Indian projectile point type that dates between 10,000 and 8,000 ya in the eastern United States.

AT A GLANCE — North American Paleo-Indian Cultures

Site	Dates (ya)	Comments
Clovis	13,500–13,000	Earliest universally acknowledged Late Pleistocene hunter-gatherers who occupied much of North America below the glacial ice masses of the northern latitudes; used distinctive fluted spear or dart projectile points
Folsom	c. 12,500	Late Pleistocene hunter-gatherers who hunted now-extinct giant long-horned bison in the American Southwest
Plano	11,000–9,000	Hunter-gatherers of the Great Plains; their unfluted spear or dart points are associated only with modern fauna

PLEISTOCENE EXTINCTIONS

Circumstantial evidence like that found mainly in the American West, where bones of the large herbivores are more often preserved in undeniable association with the weapons used to kill them, leads some researchers to blame Paleo-Indian hunters for the extinction of North American Pleistocene megafauna. Archaeologist Paul S. Martin (1967, 1982, 1999), who viewed Clovis sites as evidence of the first people in North America, argued for decades that overhunting by this newly arrived and rapidly expanding human population caused the swift extermination, around 13,000 ya, of these animals throughout the New World. He pointed out that over half of the large mammal species found in the Americas when humans first arrived were gone within just a few centuries, especially those whose habits and habitats would have made them most vulnerable to the hunters. Martin recognized a comparable extinction event with the peopling of Australia tens of thousands of years earlier, when most of that continent's native fauna died off. African and Eurasian species were less affected, he argued, due to the long coexistence of humans and their prey and the prey's conditioning to human hunting behaviors.

Clovis hunter-gatherers certainly hunted Pleistocene megafauna. As we noted earlier, archaeologists have excavated several sites where such game was killed and butchered. But, evidence that these animals were Paleo-Indian prey doesn't also prove that humans hunted them to extinction. The problem is complex, for several reasons. First, it has yet to be convincingly demonstrated that Paleo-Indian hunter-gatherers anywhere focused most of their food-getting effort on Pleistocene megafauna (Meltzer, 1993a; Cannon and Meltzer, 2004). What we're finding instead is that Paleo-Indian groups hunted and collected a range of animals and plants, the mix of which varied regionally.

Second, species extinction is a natural process, and it's no less common than the emergence of new species. It happens for various reasons and, at least until modern times, these reasons seldom had anything to do with human agency. Yes, many North American megafauna species went extinct toward the end of the Pleistocene. But, if you look at the North American geological record, you'll find that many species also became extinct in the Pliocene, Miocene, and so on. Our point is that the geological record provides abundant evidence that natural processes are sufficient to account for species extinctions in the absence of humans. The presence of Paleo-Indian hunters may also be sufficient, but it hasn't yet been convincingly demonstrated that these hunters are *necessary* to explain Pleistocene extinctions.

One possible exception appears to be the extinction of proboscideans—mammoths, mastodons, elephants, and their relatives. Surovell et al. (2005) took a long-term view of the problem and examined the global archaeological record of human exploitation of proboscideans in 41 sites that span roughly the past 1.8 million years. They conclude that local extinctions of proboscideans on five continents correlate well with the global colonization patterns of humans, not climatic changes or other natural factors. This finding suggests that we can't entirely dismiss the possibility that humans played an important role in the late Pleistocene extinctions of some species.

The end of the Pleistocene marked an interval of profound climatic and geographical changes (for example, the creation of the Great Lakes) in North America and elsewhere. Geoarchaeologists also recognize that late Pleistocene extinctions and the expansion of Paleo-Indian hunters coincided with a time of widespread drought that was immediately followed by rapidly plunging temperatures. The latter climatic event, called the **Younger Dryas**, returned to near-glacial conditions and persisted for 1,500 years, from 13,000 to 11,500 ya (Fiedel, 1999b). Some archaeologists suggest that humans took advantage of the vulnerability of animals drawn to shrinking water holes during the Younger Dryas before further climate changes finished the job (Haynes, 1993, 1999).

The degree of human involvement in these New World extinctions will continue to be a hotly debated issue in American archaeology. Grayson and Meltzer (2002, 2003, 2004) maintain that no archaeological evidence supports the idea that humans caused the mass extinction of Pleistocene megafauna in North America. They further argue that Paul S. Martin's original hypothesis has been altered into something that is no longer testable and that persists partly because it feeds contemporary political views concerning human effects on the environment. Others take issue with such views, both directly (e.g., Fiedel and Haynes, 2003) and indirectly (Barnosky et al., 2004), and argue for a possible human role.

Younger Dryas A stadial between roughly 13,500 and 11,500 ya; the climate of higher latitudes became colder and drier but did not mark a full return to glacial conditions.

Early Holocene Hunter-Gatherers

Across North America and Eurasia, gradual warming conditions during the transition from the late Pleistocene to the mid-Holocene had profound ecological effects that extended well beyond the waning glaciers. Much of the Northern Hemisphere experienced radical environmental change, leaving only the polar regions and Greenland with permanent ice caps. Climatic fluctuations, the redistribution or even extinction of many plant and animal species, and the reshaping of coastlines as glacial meltwaters flowed to the sea, all affected many of the world's human inhabitants. When we examine the archaeological record, we can see that people devised new technologies and economic patterns to adjust to their changing world.

ENVIRONMENTAL CHANGES

In the Old World, much as in the Americas, major changes in climate, landscapes, plants, and animals accompanied the end of the Pleistocene ice age. Dramatically higher temperatures—for example, an increase of average July temperature by perhaps 20°F—rapidly melted the glaciers. As they receded to higher latitudes, these great ice sheets left behind thick mantles of silt, mud, rocks, and boulders in **till plains**. Rivers and streams cut fresh channels and deposited new terraces with the ebb and flow of meltwater runoff. Tons upon tons of fine silt were lifted by winds across the newly exposed plains and redeposited as *loess*. In North America, the Great Lakes gradually formed as the glaciers retreated. Eventually, by 5,000 ya, sea levels had risen as much as 400 feet in some parts of the world, drowning the broad coastal plains and flooding into inlets to shape the continental margins we recognize today. By then, overflow from the rising Mediterranean had spilled into a low-lying basin to create the Black Sea, and the North and Baltic seas finally separated England and Scandinavia from the rest of Europe.

As deglaciation proceeded, the major biotic zones expanded northward, so that areas once covered by ice were clothed successively in tundra, grassland, fir and spruce forests, pine, and then mixed deciduous forests (Delcourt and Delcourt, 1991). Likewise, animals that thrived in temperate environments displaced their arctic counterparts. Grazers like the musk ox and caribou, or reindeer, which had ranged over open tundra or grasslands, gave way to browsing species, such as moose and white-tailed deer, which fed on leaves and the tender twigs of forest plants. Meanwhile, the annual mean summer temperatures continued to climb toward the local **climatic maximum**, attained between 8,000 and 6,000 ya in many areas. By then, July temperatures averaged as much as 5°F higher than at present. Lakes that had formed during the Ice Age as a result of increased precipitation in nonglaciated areas of the American West, southwest Asia (the Near East), and Africa now evaporated under more arid conditions, bringing great ecological changes to those regions, too.

These geoclimatic transformations most directly affected the temperate latitudes, including northern and central Europe and the northern parts of America. They were sufficient to alter conditions of life for plants and animals by creating new niches for some species and pushing others toward extinction. We can't measure precisely how these shifting natural conditions may have affected human populations, although they surely did.

CULTURAL ADJUSTMENTS

Environmental readjustments were the natural consequences of climatic change. Although many such changes happened at rates that were slow enough that they passed largely unnoticed by individuals, much depended on the terrain where the changes occurred. For example, on the low-lying coast of Denmark, where sea level rose 1.5–2.0 inches per year during the early Holocene, "during his lifetime many a Stone Age man must have seen his childhood home swallowed up by the sea" (Fischer, 1995, p. 380). The environmental impacts were cumulative, and in time the redistribution of living plant and animal species, plus variations in local topography, drainage, and exposure, resulted in a mosaic of new habitats, some of which invited human exploitation and settlement.

Cultures in both hemispheres kept pace with these changes by adjusting their ways of coping with local conditions. Distinctive climatic and cultural circumstances prevailed in different

till plain   Stones, boulders, mud, sand, and silt deposited by glaciers as they melt; a ground moraine.

climatic maximum   Episode of higher average annual temperatures that affected much of the globe for several millennia after the end of the last ice age; also known as the *altithermal* in the western United States or *hypsithermal* in the East.

Mesolithic   (*meso*, meaning "middle," and *lith*, meaning "stone") Middle Stone Age; period of hunter-gatherers, especially in northwestern Europe.

Epipaleolithic   (*epi*, meaning "after") Term used primarily in reference to the Near East, designating the time of Middle Stone Age foragers and collectors.

regions. Recognizing this variability,* archaeologists have devised specific terms to designate the early and middle Holocene cultures that turned to intensive hunting, fishing, and gathering lifeways in response to post-Pleistocene conditions. The term **Mesolithic** (literally, "middle stone") describes primarily the cultures of Europe. **Epipaleolithic** ("after old stone") pertains to similar cultural changes in the Near East and eastern Mediterranean, many of which began during the Late Pleistocene. New World archaeologists broadly apply the term **Archaic** ("ancient") to post-Pleistocene hunter-gatherers.

Holocene hunter-gatherers in temperate latitudes extracted their livelihood from a range of local resources by hunting, fishing, and gathering. The relative economic importance of each of these subsistence activities varied from region to region, and even from season to season within a given area. In some places, the focus on different food sources, particularly more plants, fish, shellfish, birds, and smaller mammals, corresponded to a lesser emphasis on hunting big game. What accounts for this shift? First, many former prey animals were by then extinct or—like the reindeer—locally unobtainable, having followed their receding habitat north with the waning ice sheets. Additionally, one way to accommodate both the environmental changes and human population growth was to broaden the definition of *food* by exploiting more species.

New habitats and prey species presented both challenges and opportunities. Among the important archaeological reflections of the cultural adjustments to the changing natural and social environments of the postglacial world were new tools and ways of making tools that can be found in the sites of these periods. Important raw materials for tools and other implements included stone, bone, antler, and leather, as well as bark and other plant materials (Clark, 1967; Bordaz, 1970). With the spread of forests, ground stone axes, adzes, and other tools became important items in tool kits (Fig. 13–17). Wood tended to replace animal bones, tallow, and herbivore dung as the primary fuel and served well for house posts, spear shafts, bowls, and countless smaller items. Wooden dugout canoes and skin-covered boats aided in navigating streams and crossing larger bodies of water. Hunter-gatherers caught large quantities of fish in nets, woven basketry traps, and brushwood or stone fish dams designed to block the mouths of small tidal streams. With the aid of axes and containers, the people extracted the honey of wild bees from hollow trees (Fig. 13–18).

Hunter-Gatherer Lifeways
Under the general category of *hunting and gathering*, researchers recognize a range of subsistence strategies used by early Holocene people as well as their more recent counterparts (Kelly, 1995).

These strategies often varied with the relative mobility of such groups. At one end of the spectrum are **foragers**, who tend to live in small groups that move camp frequently as valued food resources come into season across their home range. Viewed archaeologically, forager campsites often show little investment in substantial shelters, storage facilities, and other features that reflect a long-term commitment to that site. At the other end are **collectors**, who are typically less mobile, staying in some camps for long periods and drawing on a wide range of locally available plant and animal foods that they bring back to camp for consumption. Collector campsites tend to show evidence of long-term occupation, including **middens**, storage facilities, cemeteries, and mounds. As Conneller (2004, p. 920) simply puts it, "foragers can

FIGURE 13–17
European Mesolithic ground stone axe (lower left) in its antler sleeve (upper right), which is shaped to fit into the socket of a missing wooden haft or handle.

FIGURE 13–18
A Mesolithic forager uses a basket or bag to collect honey from a nest of wild bees in this ancient painting on a rock-shelter wall in southeastern Spain.

Archaic North American archaeological period that follows the end of the last Ice Age and traditionally ends with the beginning of the use of ceramics; equivalent to the Mesolithic in the Old World.

hunter-gatherers People who make their living by hunting, fishing, and gathering their food, and not by producing it.

foragers Hunter-gatherers who live in small groups that move camp frequently to take advantage of fresh resources as they come into season; few resources stored in anticipation of future use.

collectors Hunter-gatherers who tend to stay in one place for a long time; task groups may range far afield to hunt and collect food and other resources that are brought back to camp and shared among its inhabitants; valued food resources commonly stored in anticipation of future use.

middens Archaeological sites or features within sites formed largely by the accumulation of domestic waste.

---

*. . . and acknowledging regional differences in the history of archaeologists' reconstruction of the past . . .

be characterised as people moving to resources, while collectors move resources to people." Most hunter-gatherers lived somewhere between these extremes and emphasized more of one or the other foraging approaches as the changing natural and social conditions warranted.

Considering the environmental complexity of the temperate regions in the Holocene, including a diverse array of potentially exploitable plants and animals, the food-getting methods that worked well in one region were not always effective in another. Holocene hunter-gatherers invented specialized equipment to help them take advantage of local resources, and we can reasonably assume they approached cultural solutions to such problems with detailed practical knowledge and understanding of the local environment and its assets.

In foraging, anyone—young or old, male or female—might contribute to the general food supply by taking up whatever resources are at hand. But this isn't the same as saying that foragers might eat whatever comes to hand. Human food-getting is selective, whether it's based on what you encounter in the forest that day or find on sale in the local supermarket. Preferred foods are usually those that are most readily available, easily collected and processed, tasty, and nutritious. So, while the twentieth-century San people of the Kalahari Desert in southwestern Africa regarded about 80 local plants as edible, they relied mostly on about a dozen of them as primary foods (A. Smith et al., 2000). They used the rest of the foods less often, but knew they could eat them when times were tough. Like the first President Bush, you may feel the same way about broccoli.

Particularly in regions with only minor seasonal fluctuations in wild food supplies, foraging held prospects for good returns. Jochim (1976, 1998) estimated that foraging activities could maintain a stable population density of about one person per 4 square miles in some regions. More territory might be required to sustain people in less-favorable situations or where continuing environmental fluctuations influenced the composition and predictability of animal and plant communities or the stability of estuaries and coastlines.

In areas where dramatic seasonal variations in rainfall or temperature affected resource availability, day-to-day foraging might not always yield a stable diet. Human population density and equilibrium could be maintained only if the group adopted an alternative strategy. Familiarity with their environment enabled people to predict when specific resources should reach peak productivity or desirability. By making well-informed decisions, hunters and gatherers scheduled their movements so they would arrive on the scene at the optimum time for obtaining a particularly important food. **Seasonality and resource scheduling** are familiar issues for most, if not all, foragers.

Compared with foragers, food collectors relied much more on a few seasonally abundant resources, and their camps often show evidence of specialized processing and storage technologies that allowed them to balance out fluctuations and remain longer in one place. For example, migratory fish might be split and cured; and nuts or seeds could be parched and stored away in baskets or bags until needed.

Case Studies of Early Holocene Cultures

Now that we've looked at some general hunting and gathering strategies, we can get down to specifics. In this section we'll consider how the foragers and collectors from various regions found food and adjusted to changes in their environment.

ARCHAIC HUNTER-GATHERERS OF NORTH AMERICA

With the retreat of the North American glacial ice sheets, the environments, plants, animals, and people of the temperate and boreal latitudes changed significantly. *Archaic* hunter-gatherers exploited new options in their much-altered environments, which no longer included megafauna (see Fig. 13–10). In eastern North America, dense forests of edible nut-bearing trees spread across the midcontinent and offered rich resources that attracted humans and other animals alike. Along the coasts, rising sea levels submerged tens of thousands of square miles of low-lying coastlines, creating rich new estuarine and marine environments that Archaic people exploited with a broad array of gear, including fishing equipment, dugout boats, traps, weirs, and nets. The main killing weapon used by these hunter-gatherers

seasonality and resource scheduling Technique of hunter-gatherers to maximize subsistence by relocating in accord with the availability of key resources at specific times and places throughout the year.

was the spear and spear thrower or *atlatl* (see p. 290); the earliest archaeological evidence of the bow and arrow dates to 1,500–1,800 ya in much of the continental United States.

In many parts of North America, hunter-gatherer lifeways were more the collector than the forager type common among their Paleo-Indian ancestors. These collectors scheduled subsistence activities to coincide with the annual availability of particularly productive resources at specific locations within their territories. They lived in smaller and more circumscribed territories and acquired, through exchange with neighbors or more distant groups, whatever might be lacking locally. Especially in temperate regions, efficient exploitation of edible nuts, deer, fish, shellfish, and other forest and riverine products was enhanced by new tools, storage techniques, and regional exchange networks. The density of sites and their average size and permanence increased in many localities. Toward the end of the Archaic period, the archaeological remains of some sites exhibit signs of more complex sociopolitical organization, religious ceremonialism, and economic interdependence than had ever existed before.

Archaic Cultures of Western North America
Arid rock-shelters in the **Great Basin**, a harsh expanse between the Rocky Mountains and the Sierra Nevadas, preserve material evidence of desert Archaic lifeways (D'Azevedo, 1986). Hunting weapons, milling stones, twined and coiled basketry, nets, mats, feather robe fragments, fiber sandals and hide moccasins, bone tools, and even gaming pieces are sealed in deeply stratified sites, such as Gatecliff Shelter and Lovelock Cave in Nevada and Danger Cave in Utah, and illuminate nearly 10 millennia of hunting and gathering (Fig. 13–19). **Coprolites** (desiccated human feces) occasionally found in these deposits contain seeds, insect exoskeletons, and often the tiny scales and bones of fish, rodents, and amphibians, all of which provide direct evidence of diet and health (Reinhard and Bryant, 1992). Freshwater and brackish marshes were focal points for many subsistence activities—sources of fish, migratory fowl, plant foods, and raw materials during half the year—but upland resources such as pine nuts and game were important, too. Larger animals might be taken occasionally, though smaller prey such as jackrabbits and ducks and the seasonal medley of seed-bearing plants afforded these foragers their most reliable diet. Success in this environment was a direct measure of cultural flexibility (Fig. 13–20).

Prehistoric societies throughout California's varied environments likewise sustained themselves without agriculture. Rich oak forests fed much of the region's human and animal population. Hunter-gatherers routinely ranged across several productive resource zones, from seacoast to interior valleys. Typical California societies, such as the Chumash of the Santa Barbara coast and Channel Islands, obtained substantial harvests of acorns and deer in the fall, supplemented by migratory fish, small game, and plants throughout the year (Glassow, 1996). Collected wild resources sustained permanent villages of up to 1,000 inhabitants. The

FIGURE **13–19**
Danger Cave, Utah, the archaeological deposit of which spans much of the past 10,000 years.

FIGURE **13–20**
The arid Great Basin of the American West supported hunter-gatherer cultures for thousands of years.

Great Basin   Rugged, dry plateau between the mountains of California and Utah, comprising Nevada, western Utah, and southern Oregon and Idaho.

coprolites   Preserved fecal material, which can be studied for what the contents reveal about diet and health.

AT A GLANCE   Important Archaic Sites in the New World

Site	Dates (ya)	Comments
Danger Cave (Utah)	c. 10,000–historic	Deeply stratified site that contains rich evidence of desert Archaic lifeways
Koster (Illinois)	9,000–4,000	Stratified sequence of Archaic campsites that document the changing lifeways of people who lived on the edge of the Illinois River Valley throughout most of the Archaic period
Poverty Point (Louisiana)	3,500	A large series of earthworks that covers nearly one square mile; the most elaborate example of planned communities that were built in the Southeast in late Archaic times

Chumash were the latest descendants of a long sequence of southern California hunter-gatherers that archaeologists have traced back more than 8,000 years (Moratto, 1984). As environmental fluctuations and population changes necessitated adjustments among coastal and terrestrial resources, Archaic Californians at times ate more fish and shellfish, then more sea mammals or deer, and later more acorns and smaller animal species.

Archaeological and cultural anthropological studies along the northwestern coast of the United States and Canada have delineated other impressive nonfarming societies whose economies also centered around collecting rich and diverse sea and forest resources. Inhabitants of this region caught, dried, and stored salmon as the fish passed upriver from the sea to spawn each spring or fall. Berries and wild game such as bear and deer were locally plentiful; oily candlefish, halibut, and whales could be captured with the aid of nets, traps, large seaworthy canoes, and other well-crafted gear. Excavations at Ozette, on Washington's Olympic Peninsula, revealed a prosperous Nootka whaling community buried in a mud slide 250 years ago (Samuels, 1991).

By historical times along the northwestern coast, clan-based lineages resided in permanent coastal communities of sturdy plank-built cedar houses, guarded by carved cedar **totem** poles proclaiming their owners' genealogical heritage. They vied with one another for social status by staging elaborate public functions (now generally known as the **potlatch**) in which quantities of smoked salmon, fish or whale oil, dried berries, cedar-bark blankets, and other valuables were bestowed upon guests (Jonaitas, 1988). There are archaeological signs that these practices may be quite ancient, with substantial houses, status artifacts, and evidence of warfare dating back some 2,500 years (Ames and Maschner, 1999). While a successful potlatch earned prestige for the hosts and incurred obligations to be repaid in the future, it also served larger purposes. By fostering a network of mutual reciprocity that created both sociopolitical and economic alliances, this ritualized redistribution system ensured a wider availability of the region's dispersed resources. As a result, highly organized sedentary communities prospered without relying on domesticated crops.

Farther to the north, western Arctic Archaic bands pursued coastal sea mammals or combined inland caribou hunting with fishing; however, their diet included virtually no plant foods (McGhee, 1996). Beginning about 2,500 ya, Thule (Inuit/Eskimo) hunters expanded eastward across the Arctic with the aid of a highly specialized tool kit that included effective toggling harpoons for securing sea mammals; blubber lamps for light, cooking, and warmth; and sledges and *kayaks* (skin boats) for transportation on frozen land or sea.

totem An animal or being associated with a kin-group and used for social identification; also, a carved pole representing these beings.

potlatch Ceremonial feasting and gift-giving event among Northwest Coast Indians.

Archaic Cultures of Eastern North America
Locally varied environments across eastern North America supported a range of Archaic cultures after about 10,000 ya. A general warming and drying trend lasting several thousand years promoted deciduous forest growth as far north as the Great Lakes. Archaic societies exploited the temperate oak-hickory forests of the Midwest and the oak-chestnut forests and rivers of the Northeast and Appalachians. Nuts of many kinds were an important staple for these forest groups. Acorn, chestnut, black walnut, butternut, hickory, and beechnut represent plentiful foods that are

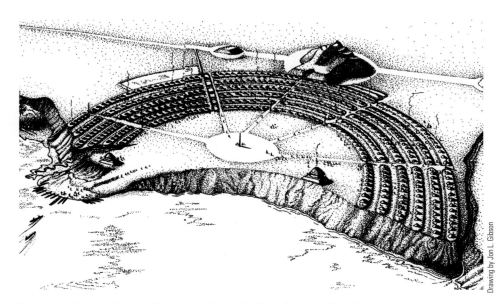

Drawing by Jon L. Gibson

FIGURE 13–21
The Late Archaic Poverty Point site in northeastern Louisiana.

both nutritious and palatable, rich in fats and oils, and above all easily stored. Some nuts were prepared by parching or roasting, others by crushing and boiling into soups; leaching in hot water neutralized the toxic tannic acids found in acorns. Whitetail deer and black bear provided meat, hides for clothing, and bone and antler for toolmaking. Other important food items included migratory fowl, wild turkey, fish, turtles, and small mammals such as raccoons, as well as berries and seeds.

In New England, some coastal Archaic groups from Massachusetts to Labrador used canoes to hunt sea mammals and swordfish with bone-bladed harpoons in summer, then relied on caribou and salmon the rest of the year (Snow, 1980). North of the St. Lawrence river, other Archaic bands dispersed widely through the sparse boreal forests, hunting caribou or moose, fishing, and trapping.

In the Midwest around the Great Lakes, seasonally mobile collectors employed an extensive array of equipment to fish, hunt, and gather. The productive valleys of the midcontinent, where a nexus of great rivers join the Mississippi, supported a riverine focus. Favored sites in this region attained substantial size and were occupied for many generations, some—such as Eva and Rose Island, in Tennessee, and Koster, in southern Illinois—for thousands of years. Trade networks moved valued raw materials and finished goods hundreds, and in some cases thousands, of miles—tools of soft native copper from northern Minnesota and Wisconsin have been found in Archaic sites as far away as Georgia and Mississippi, and marine shells from the Gulf Coast have been uncovered in western Great Lakes sites.

Eastern Archaic groups at times reinforced their claims to homelands by laying out cemeteries for their dead or by erecting earthwork mounds. These activities imply an emerging social differentiation within some of the preagricultural Archaic societies as well as a degree of **sedentism**. Archaeologists studying more than 1,000 Archaic burials at Indian Knoll, Kentucky (Webb, 1974), found possible status indicators reflected in the distribution of grave goods. Though two-thirds of the graves contained no offerings at all, certain females and children had been given disproportionate shares; only a few males were buried with tools and weapons (Rothschild, 1979).

Archaic people in the Lower Mississippi Valley began raising monumental earthworks beginning as early as 5,500 ya. Mound building required communal effort and planning. Near Monroe, Louisiana, Watson Brake is a roughly oval embankment enclosing a space averaging 750 feet across and capped by about a dozen individual mounds up to 24 feet in height (Saunders et al., 1997). Not far to the east, Poverty Point's elaborate 3,500-year-old complex of six concentric semicircular ridges is flanked by a large platform mound on its west side (Fig. 13–21), plus several nearby mounds, and covers a full square mile (Gibson, 2001). That hunter-gatherers chose to invest their energies in creating these planned earthworks with public spaces and dozens of other impressive structures suggests highly developed Archaic social organization and ritualism, though their precise meaning remains unclear.

sedentism To reside in a single location for most or all of the year; to become sedentary.

MESOLITHIC OF NORTHERN EUROPE

As in North America, people colonized Europe's northern reaches as the glacial ice retreated (Jochim, 1998). Rising waters began to reclaim low-lying coastlines, flooding the North and Baltic Seas and the English Channel and burying Paleolithic and Mesolithic sites in the process (Fischer, 1995). On land, temperate plant and animal species succeeded their Ice Age counterparts. Across northwestern Europe, as grasses and then forests invaded the open landscape, red deer, elk, and **aurochs** replaced the reindeer, horse, and bison of Pleistocene times. Human hunters, armed with efficient weapons, accommodated themselves to the relatively low **carrying capacity** of the northern regions (where plant foods, at least, were seasonally scarce) by eating more meat.

Star Carr, near the North Sea coast in east-central England (Fig. 13–22), provides clues to the early ecology and foraging economy practiced by northern Mesolithic peoples some 10,500 ya. Periodically over several centuries, this lakeshore site served as a temporary hunting camp, where the people regularly pursued aurochs, deer, elk, and wild pigs (Clark, 1972, 1979). Because deer grow and shed their antlers annually on a species-specific cycle, the discovery of deer skulls with antlers in different development stages indicated that Mesolithic hunters visited Star Carr throughout the year, though they used it much more in spring and summer (Mellars and Dark, 1999).

Again, as in the New World, Mesolithic hunter-gatherers modified the environment for their own purposes. At Star Carr, people used stone axes and adzes to fell birch trees with which they built platforms and trackways over the marshy ground. In spring, they burned off the reeds along the lake margin to open the view and probably also to induce new growth that would attract game. Hunters employed long wooden or bone arrows, knives, and spear points tipped by *microliths*—small flint blades of geometric shape—set into slots along the shaft and held in place by resin. Another extremely effective weapon, the bow was used in Europe even before the end of the last Ice Age—that is, considerably earlier than in the New World. Domesticated dogs probably aided in the hunt at Star Carr, as well. Barbed bone and antler spear points, butchering implements, and stone *burin* blades (see p. 290) for working antler were common artifacts.

Along the coasts of northern Europe, the British Isles, and even the Mediterranean, Mesolithic groups came to rely on coastal resources (Smith, 1998). Their favored site locations, sometimes marked by great shell middens, offered a combination of land and sea resources that encouraged year-round residence based on food collecting. By about 6,800 ya, the area around Vedbaek, near Copenhagen, Denmark, was more or less permanently occupied. More than 60 species representing diverse habitats between the forest and the coast appeared on the Mesolithic menu at this site (Price and Petersen, 1987). The impressive size of some middens—the countless shells of oysters, mussels, periwinkles, and scallops piled along the shore—should not disguise the fact that one red deer carcass may represent the caloric equivalent of 50,000 oysters (Bailey, 1975). Still, for at least some Mesolithic foragers, shellfish provided a readily available alternative source of protein, probably exploited primarily in the spring when their normal fare of fish, sea mammals, and birds was in shortest supply (Erlandson, 1988). This supplement could have encouraged people to remain longer in one location.

aurochs   European wild oxen, ancestral to domesticated cattle.

carrying capacity   In an environment, this is the maximum population of a specific organism that can be maintained at a steady state.

FIGURE **13–22**
Mesolithic sites of northern Europe mentioned in the text.

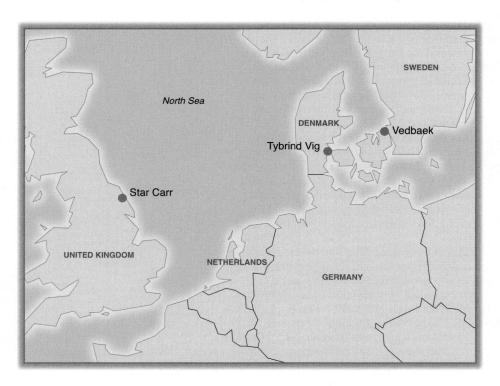

AT A GLANCE   Important Mesolithic and Epipaleolithic Sites in the Old World

Site	Dates (ya)	Comments
Star Carr (England)	10,500	Mesolithic campsite excavated by Grahame Clark; greatly influenced how archaeologists still view the Mesolithic in Europe
Tybrind Vig (Denmark)	c. 7,500–6,000	Mesolithic village submerged by rising sea levels off the coast of Denmark; excellent preservation of organic remains including such things as dugout canoes, paddles, fishing gear, and fabric
Ohalo II (Israel)	23,000	Kebaran or pre-Kebaran campsite; extraordinary preservation of huts, living floors, grass bedding, and plant remains, especially of small-grained grass seeds, which appear to have been a staple food
Abu Hureya (Syria)	13,000–7,800	Natufian and Neolithic site; the Natufian occupation was a sedentary hunter-gatherer village whose members, unlike their predecessors at Ohalo II, harvested mostly wild cereal grasses

Since many of these coastal sites were later covered by rising sea level, they can sometimes show extraordinary preservation of organic remains. For example, underwater excavations at Tybrind Vig, a late Mesolithic site that lies in 6–9 feet of water about 270 yards off the coast of Denmark, have recovered several dugout canoes and paddles, fishing line, fishhooks, and even pieces of fabric, along with plant and animal remains and several human burials (Malm, 1995).

EPIPALEOLITHIC OF THE NEAR EAST

Star Carr and other sites of northwestern Europe represent one end of a spectrum of early Holocene lifeways in the Old World. In those regions, plant foods were scarce for much of each year, and hunter-gatherers often relied mostly on hunting or fishing. Farther south, in central and southern Europe and the Near East—regions that were never covered by ice sheets, even during maximum glacial periods—late Pleistocene and early Holocene environmental and cultural changes proceeded along different lines. People in these regions tended to rely more heavily on wild plant resources, supplemented by animal protein. These distinctions in climate and culture justify the use of the separate term *Epipaleolithic* to distinguish late Pleistocene and early Holocene cultural changes of the Near East and adjacent parts of southwest Asia (Fig. 13–23) from their contemporaries in northern Europe. For the most part, Epipaleolithic subsistence strategies resulted merely in more efficient hunting and gathering. But in some locations, food-collecting strategies were already taking people quite perceptibly toward an entirely new way of making a living—the development of food production (see Chapter 14).

For the moment, let's consider the transition of hunter-gatherers from small-scale, mobile groups to what were essentially permanent communities in the Levant region, in what is today Israel and Lebanon. A late Pleistocene foraging culture known to archaeologists as the **Kebaran** occupied this region for millennia. Our understanding of Kebaran subsistence has until recently

Kebaran Late Pleistocene hunter-gatherers of the eastern Mediterranean region and Levant.

FIGURE 13–23
Epipaleolithic sites in the Levant region of the Near East.

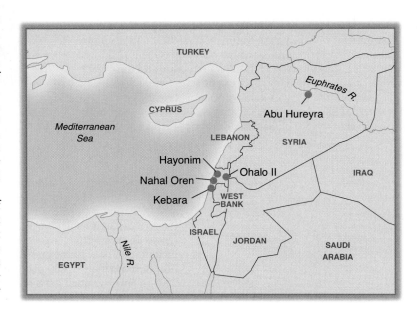

325

A Remarkable New Window on the Epipaleolithic

Discoveries of richly furnished Egyptian tombs, Upper Paleolithic art caves, and other visually spectacular ancient remains always grab a lot of media attention. Such finds succeed in bringing the past to life for many people, and they've sowed the seeds of more than one career in archaeology. But many truly important archaeological finds have so little "face appeal" that they get little more than a yawn from the mass media, even when they have the potential to change our understanding of parts of the human past.

Ohalo II, a 23,000-year-old campsite on the edge of the Sea of Galilee in Israel, is a case in point. It has qualities that make it an extraordinarily important archaeological site, but at the same time, it's about as visually engaging as a mud flat.

Its importance ultimately derives from three archaeological qualities: age, preservation, and context. Ohalo II is old, offering researchers a valuable new look at a moment of Near Eastern prehistory for which they've had almost no data. It's also remarkably well preserved, having been buried at the bottom of the sea for tens of thousands of years. And its archaeological context is such that it appears to be an entire community placed at a location that was not used before or after its time, so there are few uncertainties in interpreting what ancient remains are or are not associated with it. To archaeologists, finding all these qualities at one site is priceless because it means that, like Kennewick Man (see Digging Deeper on p. 307), Ohalo II has beaten the odds and offers a glimpse of past life we did not expect to have the good fortune to find.

Hunter-gatherers occupied the Ohalo II location during the Epipaleolithic (roughly 20,000–10,300 B.P.), a period of Near Eastern prehistory that's approximately equivalent to the Mesolithic in western Europe. Until Ohalo II was discovered, archaeologists assumed that Epipaleolithic hunter-gatherers were frequently on the move and that settled communities did not arise until later—during the Natufian, an archaeological culture that preceded the beginning of the Neolithic. Ohalo II showed that a basic continuity in community structure and the organization of household living space can be traced more than 10,000 years farther into the past than we once believed.

After the site was first exposed in 1989 by a deep drop in the water level of the Sea of Galilee, excavations revealed a cluster of six oval brush huts (Fig. 1), now claimed to be the oldest archaeological evidence of such dwellings (Nadel, 2004). The huts were small, with a median floor area of roughly 30 square feet, and their floors were set in shallow basins dug down 8–12 inches below ground surface. A rough frame of wooden poles set over this shallow basin was covered by branches, leaves, and grasses to form the hut walls. Evidence of the use and reuse of the huts and their house basins, along with seasonal clues provided by the analysis of the extraordinarily rich collection of organic remains from this site, demonstrated the surprising fact that Ohalo II wasn't merely a short-term campsite but was occupied throughout the year.

The hut data alone would have been enough to place Ohalo II on the map of very important archaeological discoveries, but the extraordinary preservation conditions at this site also led to other major surprises about Epipaleolithic life—some of which bear on the origins of agriculture in the Near East!

Because the hut floors were set in shallow basins, the interior living spaces of most huts were preserved and could be studied by archaeologists. These examinations revealed bunches of cut grass that had been arranged against the hut walls—the world's oldest evidence of bedding (Nadel et al., 2004). In Hut 1 (Fig. 2), the bedding was placed around an interior hearth and opposite

FIGURE 1

Ohalo II Hut 1 before excavation. The oval outline of the burned hut shows clearly in the soil.

Dr. Daniel Nadel, Director of Project, Zinman Institute of Archaeology, University of Haifa, Mt. Carmel, Israel

been based mostly on the analysis of faunal remains and tools used in plant food processing, because the direct evidence of plant remains was rarely found in excavations. Ohalo II, a very early Kebaran or pre-Kebaran (23,000 ya) site in the Sea of Galilee, recently demonstrated that archaeologists still have much to learn about late Pleistocene plant use in the Levant. The Ohalo II excavations (see Digging Deeper) revealed a camp comprised of several huts, including some with the grass bedding still intact, hearths, tools, and an outstanding collection of more than 90,000 plant remains, representing 142 genera and species (Weiss et al., 2004a). Small-grained grass seeds, including brome, foxtail, and alkali grass, were gathered for consumption as staple foods (Weiss et al., 2004b), as were seeds of wild cereals such as

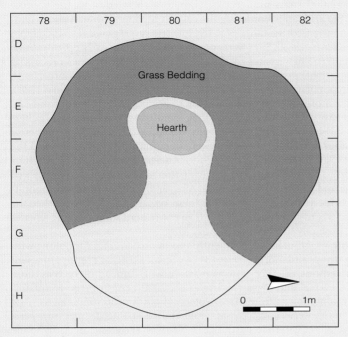

FIGURE 2

Floor area of brush hut showing the arrangement of grass bedding inside the hut wall around the central hearth.

"Stone Age hut in Israel yields world's oldest evidence of bedding," PNAS, 101(17):p. 6823. Copyright 2004 National Academy of Sciences, U.S.A. Reprinted with permission.

The outstanding preservation at Ohalo II is reflected in the food remains, too. The excavations recovered thousands of well-preserved faunal remains, from the analysis of which archaeologists infer that the site was occupied year-round (Nadel et al., 2004). The most common animal remains are small fishes, but the inhabitants of Ohalo II also hunted many kinds of mammals, especially gazelles, and more than 80 species of birds, notably ducks and other waterfowl.

The most spectacular discovery, however, has proved to be the more than 90,000 specimens of charred seeds and fruit that have been studied from these excavations. These remains provide strong evidence that local hunter-gatherers depended on the seeds of small-grained wild grasses as staple foods more than 10,000 years earlier than was, until recently, believed possible (Weiss et al., 2004a, 2004b). The discovery changes how archaeologists look at the Epipaleolithic. It also provides the first significant body of data necessary to test Kent Flannery's (1973) hypothesis that the domestication of cereal grasses and the beginnings of true agriculture developed through a gradual expansion or broadening of the staple resources used by hunter-gatherers to include items that took more work to process and were formerly of little value as food. This "broad spectrum revolution" (see Chapter 14, p. 337), Flannery argued, set the stage for the beginnings of agriculture. As Ohalo II proves, he may be right.

SOURCES:

"The Broad Spectrum Revisited: Evidence from Plant Remains," by Ehud Weiss, Wilma Wetterstrom, Dani Nadel, and Ofer Bar-Yosef, *Proceedings of the National Academy of Science* 101(26), 2004:9551–9555.

"The Ohalo II Brush Huts and the Dwelling Structures of the Natufian and PPNA Sites in the Jordan Valley," by Dani Nadel, *Archaeology, Ethnology and Anthropology of Eurasia* 1(13), 2004:34–48.

"Small-Grained Wild Grasses as Staple Food at the 23,000-Year-Old Site of Ohalo II, Israel," by Ehud Weiss, Mordechai E. Kislev, Orit Simchoni, and Dani Nadel, *Economic Botany* 58(supplement), 2004:S125–S134.

"Stone Age Hut in Israel Yields World's Oldest Evidence of Bedding," by Dani Nadel, Ehud Weiss, Orit Simchoni, Alexander Tsatskin, Avinoam Danin, and Mordechai Kislev, *Proceedings of the National Academy of Sciences* 101(17), 2004:6821–6826.

to what appears to have been the hut's entrance. Unlike the one in Hut 1, most other hearths were found outside the huts and were surrounded by food-processing and toolmaking debris (Nadel, 2004).

The Ohalo II structures share many similarities with Early Neolithic huts in the same general region. From such similarities as average size and the presence of only one living space and one entrance in each hut, archaeologists infer that the basic organization of family dwelling space was pretty stable for more than 10,000 years, during a time when technology and economic activities changed greatly (Nadel, 2004).

barley and wheat. Analysis of starch grains from a grinding slab found in one of the huts revealed that the small-grained grasses and the wild cereal grasses were processed for consumption (Piperno et al., 2004). The Ohalo II remains demonstrate that early Kebaran groups in the Levant were collector-type hunter-gatherers as early as the Last Glacial Maximum, if not before, and that the beginnings of the development of agriculture can be traced at least to Epipaleolithic times.

Viewed generally, many Kebaran groups adopted a strategy of **transhumance**, a specific seasonality and scheduling technique by which people divided their activities between resource zones at different elevations. We know from later Kebaran sites that they harvested

transhumance Seasonal migration from one resource zone to another, especially between highlands and lowlands.

FIGURE 13–24
Reconstruction of a Natufian gazelle-horn reaping knife with inset flint blades.

Natufian   Collector-type hunter-gatherers who established sedentary settlements in parts of the Near East after 12,000 ya.

dental caries   Erosions in teeth caused by decay; cavities.

seeds of wild cereal grasses in the lowlands from fall through springtime (Henry, 1989). In summer, they made extended forays into the sparsely wooded uplands to hunt and to gather nuts. Gazelles and fallow deer were the primary sources of meat, with smaller game becoming more common than deer in site assemblages toward the end of the Epipaleolithic (Bar-Oz, 2004), possibly as deer became scarce.

Between 11,000 and 12,000 ya, a moderating climate associated with the waning Pleistocene took effect in the arid lands bordering the eastern Mediterranean. As both temperatures and precipitation increased, the range of native lowland cereal grasses expanded into the higher forested zones (Henry, 1989). Sites were more permanent than early Epipaleolithic camps such as Ohalo II, and the newer sites contain house remains, heavy seed-processing equipment and other nonportable items, art objects, and cemeteries; they're also larger, with a five- or tenfold increase in population, accompanied by signs of social ranking (Henry, 1989).

Because the sites of these more sedentary collectors are so dramatically different from earlier camps, archaeologists gave their culture a new label, identifying it as **Natufian** (Belfer-Cohen, 1991). Natufian subsistence depended heavily on nuts, the seeds of wild cereal grasses—but not the small-grained grass seeds that were so common at Ohalo II—and the gazelle, a kind of antelope (Bar-Yosef, 1987; Henry, 1989). Ancient gazelle-hunting practices are revealed through a study of tooth eruption and wear patterns on animal teeth recovered from Natufian sites (Legge and Rowley-Conwy, 1987). After analyzing a nonselective population structure of newborns, yearlings, and adults, these researchers suggested that the dominant hunting method was to surround or ambush an entire herd soon after the females gave birth to their young, probably in late April or early May.

Gazelle horn sickles with inset flint blades frequently appear on Natufian sites, along with an abundance of grinding stones and mortars (Fig. 13–24). Small clusters of semipermanent pit houses with stone foundations, often in close association with cemeteries, such as those excavated at several sites in Israel and Syria (Moore et al., 2000), confirm the Natufians' reliance on local species without moving from place to place. These finds, as well as an increase in human **dental caries** (tooth decay), *hypoplasias* (interrupted enamel formation), periodontal disease, and an overall reduction in tooth size in Natufian skeletons, all testify to the fact that starchy cereal grains figured prominently in this group's diet (P. Smith et al., 1984).

Viewed across the span of the Epipaleolithic, hunter-gatherer groups took a more active role in manipulating the landscape to enhance the productivity or yield of favored species. Whether intentionally or not, they may have created forest clearings or eliminated competing animals or "weed" plants; or, as their camps expanded into fresh regions, they might have introduced wild food species into new habitats. At times, as among the Natufians in the Near East, these intensive exploitation patterns greatly altered the overall relationship between people and their environment, promoting further changes in their society as well as in the resources on which they depended. So, we see larger populations drawn to certain prime areas, where intergroup competition would be inevitable and where selection pressures on resources could become significant. In some cases, the changes brought about by collector-type hunter-gatherers were actually a prelude to food production, which we'll focus on in the next chapter.

Summary

By the early to middle Holocene, modern humans had expanded into all the inhabitable regions of the globe. Current evidence suggests that people initially arrived in the New World between 13,500 and 30,000 ya. Learning where they came from and how they entered the New World is an active area of research that continues to be hotly debated, but at least for now, the evidence most strongly supports some combination of entry from northeastern Asia by way of the Bering land bridge or the Pacific coastal route.

The scarce skeletal evidence that survives from the earliest era of New World prehistory shows considerable morphological diversity, and it has encouraged much speculation about Native American origins. Even so, available cultural and biological traces clearly link the first Americans with their Asian roots. The similarities of material culture between the earliest sites in the Americas and northeastern Asia are more general than archaeologists would like, but Siberian sites such as Yana RHS do offer encouraging evidence that researchers are on the right track. There isn't perfect consensus on these interpretations, and some archaeologists have suggested the possibility that during late Pleistocene times, people entered the New World by following the ice edge across the northern Atlantic from western Europe.

By about 12,000 ya, after the end of the Pleistocene ice age, significant climatic changes altered the weather, seasonal variations, average temperatures, topography, sea levels, and animal and plant communities across much of the Northern Hemisphere, including North America and Eurasia. The general warming trend across temperate latitudes promoted the expansion of grasslands and the reforestation of formerly glaciated areas. At the same time, many megafauna species became extinct, particularly in North America, where human hunters may have contributed to their demise.

Early Holocene foragers in Europe, the Near East, and North America adapted readily to the ongoing environmental changes. Generalized food-getting economies promoted long-term cultural stability for many hunter-gatherers, such as the Mesolithic hunters of Star Carr and the Archaic peoples of California, the Great Basin, and the eastern American woodlands, who exploited their environments' varied resources at relatively low levels of intensity. Especially in regions with great seasonal resource fluctuations, experiencing intensely dry or cold months, people tended to concentrate on a few more productive species, which they collected in quantity and stored. Long-term, and in some cases permanent, settlements became part of hunter-gatherer lifeways in many regions.

As sites like Ohalo II demonstrate, some food-collecting communities experienced economic changes, as long ago as the Last Glacial Maximum, that led to the use of a wide range of plants and animals as food. Such changes fostered the development of food production in some regions. Since we are looking back in time at these events, it's tempting, but misleading, to view them as a conscious step toward the invention of agriculture. Yet there's virtually no reason to think that Early Holocene foragers had the slightest inkling about how the eventual domestication of plants and animals would also fundamentally change humans.

We've organized the remaining chapters of this text around two primary cultural developments associated with humans in the later Holocene epoch: first, the process of food production, and second, the rise of civilizations. Much of what we associate with modern humanity is linked to these central driving forces.

In Table 13–1 on p. 330, you'll find a useful summary of the most important archaeological sites discussed in this chapter.

Critical Thinking Questions

1. What are the specific biological and cultural clues that point to an Asian ancestry for the *earliest* American populations? How convincing do you find the evidence?
2. What are some of the significant environmental changes associated with the end of the Pleistocene? Which of these changes would have most affected humans? Do you see parallels with climate changes today?
3. Is there enough archaeological evidence to prove that Paleo-Indians were primarily responsible for the extinction of Pleistocene animals? Discuss.
4. Contrast Middle Stone Age adaptations of northern Europe, as represented at Star Carr and Vedbaek, with those of the Near East, as represented by the Kebarans and Natufians in the Levant.
5. What are the differences between forager and collector types of hunter-gatherers? What are some of the economic and biocultural implications of each of these subsistence strategies?

TABLE 13–1		The Most Significant Archaeological Sites Discussed in This Chapter	
Location	**Site**	**Dates (ya)**	**Comments**
North America	**Poverty Point** (Louisiana)	3,500	A large series of earthworks that covers nearly one square mile; the most elaborate example of planned communities that were built in the Southeast in late Archaic times
	Koster (Illinois)	9,000–4,000	Stratified sequence of Archaic campsites that document the changing lifeways of people who lived on the edge of the Illinois River Valley throughout most of the Archaic period
	Kennewick (Washington)	9,300	One of the few early North American human skeletons; object of a 9-year court battle to decide if scientists would be permitted to study his remains
	Danger Cave (Utah)	~10,000–historic	Deeply stratified site that contains rich evidence of desert Archaic lifeways
	Meadowcroft (Pennsylvania)	19,000–14,000	North American site that is increasingly accepted as a valid example of the pre-Clovis presence of humans in North America
	Pendejo Cave (New Mexico)	37,000–12,000	North American site for which great antiquity is claimed; as with Pedra Furada in Brazil, the evidence continues to be carefully evaluated but, as yet, not widely accepted by other researchers
South America	**Monte Verde** (Chile)	14,800	Pre-Clovis campsite in southern South America; the evidence is still hotly debated
	Pedra Furada (Brazil)	?50,000–?40,000	One of several South American sites for which great antiquity is claimed
Old World	**Star Carr** (England)	10,500	Mesolithic campsite excavated by Grahame Clark; greatly influenced how archaeologists still view the Mesolithic in Europe
	Abu Hureya (Syria)	13,000–7,800	Natufian and Neolithic site; the Natufian occupation was a sedentary hunter-gatherer village whose members, unlike their predecessors at Ohalo II, harvested mostly wild cereal grasses
	Ohalo II (Israel)	23,000	Kebaran or pre-Kebaran campsite; extraordinary preservation of huts, living floors, grass bedding, and plant remains, especially of small-grained grass seeds, which appear to have been a staple food
	Yana RHS (Russia)	30,000	Earliest evidence of late Pleistocene hunters beyond the Arctic Circle in northern Siberia; stone tools and horn and ivory spear foreshafts similar to those found much later on North American Paleo-Indian sites

ARCHAEOLOGY

CHAPTER

14

Food Production

FOCUS QUESTIONS

What caused the beginnings of farming and herding in prehistory?

In what ways did farming and herding develop differently in the Old and New Worlds?

Introduction

By the end of the last Ice Age, humans were living in most of the world's inhabitable places. They achieved a global distribution without becoming multiple species in the process, which isn't the way things usually happen in nature. Having gotten this far in the book, if you suspect that they were able to do this because they were biocultural organisms, then you're right. More than anything else, the biocultural approach to survival is what gives humans such extraordinary adaptive flexibility. Without it, humans might still be restricted to the tropical and subtropical regions of the Old World.

For many parts of the world, the archaeological record provides abundant evidence that the rate of change in human lifeways accelerated markedly during the past 10,000 years or so. Throughout this long period, human cultural activity accounted for more and more of the observed change. By making cultural choices and devising new cultural solutions to age-old problems, human groups succeeded in mitigating some of the processes that operate in the natural world (for example, starvation due to seasonal food shortages, low average life expectancy), and either turned them to our advantage or at least tried to minimize their negative effects. However, humans also discovered that part of the cost of such cultural solutions were consequences that interacted with and affected the natural world and human biology as well. Some of the consequences were fantastically good; some weren't.

Two of the most profound and far-reaching developments of later prehistory are the shift from hunting and gathering to food production and the emergence of the early civilizations. We'll examine the origins of the first civilizations at length in Chapters 15 and 16. This chapter deals with plant and animal domestication and the associated spread of farming, both of them integral to the emergence of large-scale, complex societies. We'll start by examining competing explanations of the origins of food production. The review gives you a sense of the diverse perspectives from which researchers investigate how and why something like farming happened after the end of the last Ice Age. From there, we discuss the archaeological evidence for the development of food production in several regions around the world (Fig. 14–1). Finally, we'll wrap things up by reviewing some of the most important biocultural consequences of this fundamental change in lifeways, to which our species and the world continue to adjust.

The Neolithic Revolution

The change from hunting and gathering to agriculture is often called the **Neolithic Revolution**, a name coined decades ago by archaeologist V. Gordon Childe (1951) to acknowledge the fundamental changes brought about by the beginnings of food production. While hunter-gatherers collected whatever foods nature made available, farmers employed nature to produce only those crops and animals that humans selected for their own exclusive purposes.

Beyond domestication and farming, **Neolithic** activities stimulated other far-reaching consequences, including new settlement patterns, new technologies, and significant biocultural effects. The emergence of food production eventually transformed most human societies either directly or indirectly and, in the process, brought about dramatic changes in the natural realm as well. The world has been a very different place since humans began developing agriculture.

Neolithic Revolution Childe's term for the far-reaching consequences of food production.

Neolithic (*neo*, meaning "new," and *lith*, meaning "stone") New Stone Age; period of farmers.

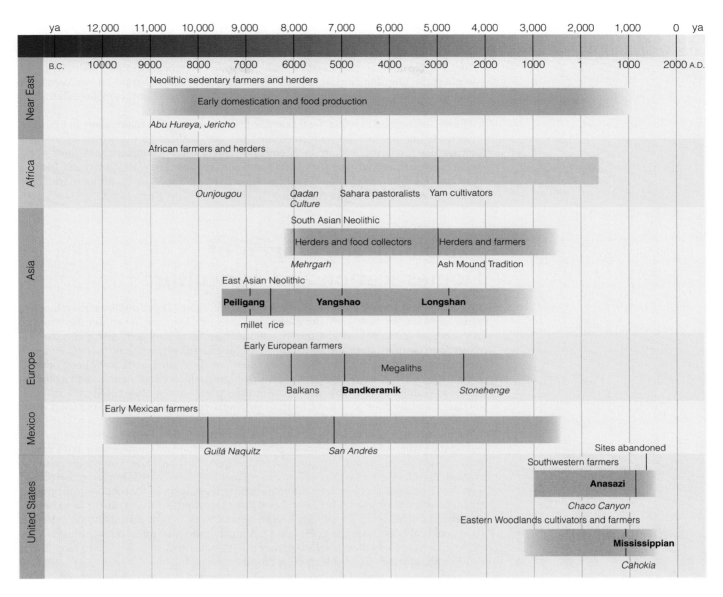

ya	12,000	11,000	10,000	9,000	8,000	7,000	6,000	5,000	4,000	3,000	2,000	1,000	0 ya
B.C.	10000	9000	8000	7000	6000	5000	4000	3000	2000	1000	1	1000	2000 A.D.

Near East
Neolithic sedentary farmers and herders
Early domestication and food production
Abu Hureya, Jericho

Africa
African farmers and herders
Ounjougou   *Qadan Culture*   Sahara pastoralists   Yam cultivators

Asia
South Asian Neolithic
Herders and food collectors   Herders and farmers
Mehrgarh   Ash Mound Tradition
East Asian Neolithic
Peiligang   **Yangshao**   **Longshan**
millet rice

Europe
Early European farmers
Megaliths
Balkans   **Bandkeramik**   *Stonehenge*

Mexico
Early Mexican farmers
Guilá Naquitz   *San Andrés*

United States
Sites abandoned
Southwestern farmers
Anasazi
Chaco Canyon
Eastern Woodlands cultivators and farmers
Mississippian
Cahokia

FIGURE **14–1**
Time line for Chapter 14.

Childe recognized that maintaining fields and herds demanded a long-term commitment from early farmers. Obliged to stay in one area to oversee their crops, Neolithic people became more or less settled, or *sedentary*. As storable harvests gradually supported larger and more permanent communities, towns and cities developed in a few areas. Within these larger settlements, fewer people were directly involved in food production, allowing for cultural tasks to be redefined. For example, **craft specialization** fostered many of the technological advances of the Neolithic. Such activities as cloth weaving, pottery production, and metallurgy are multistage processes that can be accomplished most efficiently when skilled specialists work cooperatively.

Decades after Childe's original study, archaeologists still accept his general characterization of the Neolithic Revolution, but later research enables us to refine some of the specifics. For example, we now recognize that sedentism actually *preceded* farming in certain locations where permanent settlements were sustained solely by gathering and hunting or fishing. In Chapter 13, we noted that the Chumash of southern California and the Natufian hunter-gatherers of the Near East, among others, established sizable villages. It's now also widely accepted that sedentism could often *stimulate* food production, rather than the other way around.

craft specialization Economic system that allows individuals to devote full time to certain occupations.

We also now realize that Neolithic lifeways evolved independently in separate areas of the world. Archaeologists see most regional Neolithic developments as the culmination of local cultural sequences rather than the result of **diffusion**, or spreading, from a single Near Eastern center. The Neolithic is still viewed as revolutionary in its cumulative impact on human lives, but not in the amount of time it took for these cultural changes to happen. As we learn more about the Neolithic, it's increasingly evident that this period represents complex, often inter-related biocultural changes that played out over thousands of years.

In the following discussion, we'll examine the beginnings of domestication and farming by considering evidence drawn from around the world. Although the process everywhere shared many similarities and produced equally dramatic consequences, archaeologists work-ing in the Americas rarely apply the term *Neolithic* to studies of New World farmers. Instead, they use regional terminology, such as *Formative* or *Preclassic* in Mesoamerica and *Mississippian* in eastern North America.

Explaining the Origins of Domestication and Agriculture

Archaeologists have always felt compelled to identify "firsts." When did the earliest humans arrive in Australia? Where are the oldest sites in South America? When did the bow and arrow arrive in the Midwest? Concerns about these firsts also dominate archaeological research on domestication and agriculture and will undoubtedly continue to do so. But we'll never know when or where the first person intentionally planted seeds in the hope of mak-ing a crop, and we'll never track down the first person who hitched an animal to a plough, or got an animal comfortable enough with their presence that they could milk it. What researchers really hope to achieve by their emphasis on firsts is to understand what made these changes happen.

In research on the origins of agriculture, we know that ancient hunter-gatherers who lived before the earliest identified archaeological evidence of food production were both intelli-gent and observant enough to figure out what happens to seeds after you put them in the ground. In fact, we have every reason to believe that Upper Paleolithic hunter-gatherers had a wealth of practical everyday knowledge and understanding about the natural world around them. So, when we search for the earliest evidence of agriculture in a region, the most impor-tant goal is not being able to say, "Ah, here's where we draw the line on our chronology chart of agricultural beginnings" (e.g., Fig. 14–1). A much more fundamental motivation is sim-ply to understand *why* these people became farmers. Why then? Why there? What conditions brought about these changes? Why these crops?

From the perspective of the modern world, we may find it hard to accept that earlier peo-ples didn't generally aspire to be farmers and that many no doubt avoided the opportunity for as long as possible. But the archaeological record and history alike are filled with exam-ples demonstrating that what we might now view as the self-evident benefits of food pro-duction have seldom been seen in the same light by hunter-gatherers. In recent centuries, many of the remaining hunter-gatherers on every continent resisted, sometimes successfully, the efforts of societies based on food production to convert them into peaceful, tax-paying farmers, voters, and consumers of mass-produced goods. Such attitudes call into question the inevitability of agriculture in biocultural evolution. Did it become the predominant economic basis of human communities because it offered so many obvious advantages? Because it offered the fewest disadvantages? Or because there just weren't a lot of alternatives?

Ironically, although farming didn't get started in a big way until later, it was the hunter-gatherers of the Archaic, Mesolithic, and Epipaleolithic periods who actually initiated the crit-ical processes and even developed many of the innovations we usually credit to the Neolithic. Essentially, the lifestyles of some hunter-gatherers anticipated many of the developments we associate with agriculture. Neolithic farmers were mostly the *recipients* of the domesticated species and agricultural ways from their predecessors.

diffusion   The idea that widely distrib-uted cultural traits originated in a single cen-ter and were spread from one group to another through contact or exchange.

DEFINING AGRICULTURE AND DOMESTICATION

To avoid confusion later on, it's useful to consider the difference between **domestication** and **agriculture**. These terms are often found together in discussions of the beginnings of food production, but they mean different things (Rindos, 1984).

Domestication is an *evolutionary process*. When we say that a certain plant or animal is domesticated, we mean that there's interdependency between this organism and humans, such that part of its life history depends on human intervention. To achieve and maintain this relationship requires the *genetic* transformation of a wild species by selective breeding or other ways of interfering, intentionally or not, with a species' natural life processes.

Agriculture differs from domestication because it's a *cultural activity*, not an evolutionary process. It involves the propagation and exploitation of domesticated plants and animals by humans. Agriculture in its broad sense includes all the activities associated with both farming and animal herding. Although domestication and agriculture are commonly grouped together in archaeological discussions of Neolithic lifeways, domestication isn't inevitably associated with an economic emphasis on food production. Plant and animal domestication can take place for purposes other than to improve the utility of a given organism as human food. For example, some cultures have raised birds and animals solely for ritual offerings or ornamental use. Native Americans of Mexico and the American Southwest reared colorful Macaw parrots for their bright plumage, and Peruvian natives herded alpaca camelids primarily for their wool. Many domesticated medicinal herbs, attractive flowers, and fibrous plants have also served nonfood uses.

True agriculture, on the other hand, would be unthinkable without domesticated plants and animals. Domestication makes agriculture possible, especially since humans manipulated life history strategies of other organisms to maximize particular qualities, such as yield per unit area, growth rate to maturity, ease of processing, seed color, average seed size, flavor, and so forth. The cultural activity we call agriculture ensures that the plants and animals with these desirable qualities are predictably available as human food and raw materials. One useful way to view this fundamental change in the relationships between humans and other animals and plants is as **symbiosis**, a mutually beneficial association between members of different species (Rindos, 1984).

In the next two sections, we'll give a brief but important overview of some of the major competing explanations for the beginnings of agriculture. Although most of these approaches address the problem of explaining the development of farming in the Near East, their authors tend to view them as generally applicable to the explanation of agricultural origins everywhere. The Near East dominates the discussion, mostly because it has received the lion's share of research on this problem over the past century, not because it was some sort of primal hearth for the development of agriculture. Also, as you review these sections, bear in mind that the central questions at issue are open areas of research. Right now, there's no single approach that can claim it is both sufficient and necessary to explain all known cases.

Loosely following Verhoeven (2004), we present our overview of approaches in two groups, those that primarily invoke natural or environmental factors to explain the development of agriculture and those largely based on cultural (including cognitive) factors.

ENVIRONMENTAL APPROACHES

Most approaches to explain the origins of domesticated plants and animals and the beginnings of agriculture identify one or more natural mechanisms, such as climate change or human population growth, that may have promoted the biocultural changes documented in the late Pleistocene and early Holocene archaeological record of many parts of the world. The reasoning behind such hypotheses is that if some change limits a society's ability to feed its numbers, the society typically has several options. The least disruption of everyday life can be achieved by reducing its population, by extending its territory, by making more intensive use of its environment, or by some mix of these options. Farming, of course, represents a more

domestication A state of interdependence between humans and selected plant or animal species. Intense selection activity induces permanent genetic change, enhancing a species' value to humans.

agriculture Cultural activities associated with planting, herding, and processing domesticated species; farming.

symbiosis (*syn*, meaning "together," and *bios*, meaning "life") Mutually advantageous association of two different organisms; also known as *mutualism*.

FIGURE **14–2**

Through a symbiotic relationship with humans, domesticated plants such as lettuce and tomatoes have even spread to Antarctica. There, they are grown by hydroponic farming techniques without the benefits of soil or sunlight in New Zealand's Scott Base greenhouse, which consists of two 20-foot shipping containers in which the staff grows vegetables, herbs, and flowers.

intensive use of the environment. Through their efforts, farmers attempt to increase the land's *carrying capacity* by harnessing more of its energy for the production of crops or animals that will feed people (Fig. 14–2).

In their most extreme form, environmental approaches smack of *environmental determinism,* or the notion that certain cultural effects or outcomes can be predicted from—or are determined by—a combination of purely environmental causes. For example, V. Gordon Childe himself conjectured that climate changes at the end of the last Ice Age increased Europe's rainfall while making southwestern Asia and North Africa much more arid (Childe, 1928, 1934). Humans, animals, and vegetation in the drought areas concentrated into shrinking zones around a few permanent water sources. At these **oases,** Childe hypothesized, the interaction between humans and certain plants and animals resulted in domestication of some species, including wheat, barley, sheep, and goats, which people then began to use to their advantage. The eventual result was the spread of sedentary village communities across the Near East.

Hypotheses based on any form of determinism tend to be relatively straightforward, which is both their strength and their weakness. Because they hold so many factors constant, it's easy to see how such approaches should work and why certain important outcomes should arise. The main drawback of such ideas is that their focus is typically too general to explain a given case because they omit the key contextual factors that are unique to a real event. In environmental approaches, such factors are often history and culture. What people are already familiar with and what they and their ancestors did in the past often, if not always, play a big role in their decisions. So, for example, a desert region might simultaneously sustain opportunistic hunter-gatherers, nomadic pastoralists, farmers using special deep-planting procedures, or even lawn-mowing suburbanites willing to pay for piped-in water, not because these groups are unaware of the possibilities posed by alternative ways of living, but because they are living their traditional ways of life and they prefer them.

To return to what has come to be called Childe's oasis theory, its simplicity quickly enabled archaeologist Robert Braidwood to demonstrate that the predicted outcomes didn't exist in the archaeological record (see p. 339 for details). Pollen and sediment profiles now confirm that at least some of the climatic changes hypothesized by Childe did occur in parts of the Near East prior to Neolithic times, and so they may have had a role in fostering new relationships between humans and other species in this marginal environment (Henry, 1989; Wright, 1993). Even so, both the causes and the apparent effects were complex. In places like the Near East, climate change that resulted in diminished or redistributed resource abundances didn't directly force people into farming (Munro, 2004), though it may have limited their choices so that farming became one of the more reasonable options. On the other hand, the arid conditions familiar to us today in some parts of the Near East may be as much a *result* as a cause of Neolithic activities in the region. That is, the ecologically disruptive activities of farmers and herd animals during the Neolithic period may have contributed to the destructive process of **desertification**. Their plowed fields exposed soil to wind erosion and evaporation, while the irrigation demands of their crops lowered the water table. And overgrazing herbivores rapidly reduced the vegetation that holds moisture and binds soil, thus destroying the fragile margin between grassland and desert.

One large group of environmental hypotheses that, unlike Childe's, continues to be examined by researchers looks to increased competition for resources. Whether the competition results from natural increases in population density or from climatic changes such as rising sea levels, increased rainfall, lower average seasonal temperatures, and the like, they're seen as major factors that encouraged the domestication of plants and animals and, ultimately, the beginnings of agriculture (e.g., Boserup, 1965; Binford, 1968; Flannery, 1973; Cohen, 1977). These explanations share the view that agriculture developed in societies where competition

oases   (*sing.,* oasis) Permanent springs or water holes in an arid region.

desertification   Any process resulting in the formation or growth of deserts.

for the resources necessary to sustain life favored increasing the diversity of staple foods in the diet. For one reason or another, population control or territorial expansion may not have been feasible or desirable choices in these societies. For example, competition may have arisen from decreased human mortality rates rather than increased fertility, or possibly even been driven by the increasing proportion of people living to an old age. The important point is that people faced a "prehistoric food crisis" (Cohen, 1977) unlike most modern cases because it was a chronic problem that worsened over decades and showed no sign of ever getting any better. Concentrated in a restricted territory or faced with the dwindling reliability of once-favored resources, such hunter-gatherers might take up **horticulture** or herding to enhance the productivity or distribution of one or more particularly useful species. It was this economic commitment that eventually led to the emergence of true farmers.

Binford's (1968) "packing model" develops one such hypothesis involving **demographic** stresses. As modern climatic conditions became established in the early Holocene, people lived throughout every prime habitat in the temperate regions of Eurasia. Foraging areas became confined as territories filled, leading to increased competition for resources and a more varied diet. Forced to make more intensive use of smaller segments of habitat, hunter-gatherers applied their Mesolithic technology to a broader range of species, including smaller animals and plants. A few of these resources proved more reliable, easier to catch or process, tastier, or even faster to reproduce than others, so they soon received greater attention. Archaeological evidence of such changes can be found on many Mesolithic/Epipaleolithic sites in the form of sickles, baskets and other containers, grinding slabs, and other processing tools.

As local populations continued to grow and other groups tried to expand their territory, their only choice would be to move into the marginal habitats of their territory, which lay at the edges of the optimal, resource-rich areas (Binford, 1968). Because population stress would again quickly reach critical levels in these marginal environments where resources were already sparse, it was here that domesticated plants were first developed. To feed itself, the expanding population might have tried to expand the native ranges of some of the resources they knew from their homeland by sowing seeds of the wild plants. Over time, this activity resulted in domestication of those species and fundamental changes in the relationship between them and the people who by then depended on them.

Aspects of Binford's approach appealed to many archaeologists, who agreed that some of the world's most important domesticates originally held a low status in the diet as wild foods. Many were small, hard seeds that were once seldom used except as secondary or emergency foods. Ethnographic research had also shown that, given their choice, hunter-gatherers everywhere prefer to eat fruit and meat (Yudkin, 1969). Still, grains and roots became increasingly important in the Mesolithic/Epipaleolithic diet—supplemented wherever possible by available animal or fish protein—and not only when the more desirable foods were in short supply. An interpretation based on increased competition for resources offered a testable explanation for why this happened.

Although he took issue with certain aspects of Binford's approach, Flannery (1973) agreed with the basic thesis because it explained why the earliest archaeological evidence of plant domestication should be found in what would have been marginal environments. Flannery described the increasing breadth of the Epipaleolithic diet as a "broad spectrum revolution" in which hunter-gatherers turned to many kinds of food resources in order to make up local shortfalls. Especially in marginal environments, this activity promoted the development of domesticates and, ultimately, the origins of true agriculture.

Henry (1989) also built on somewhat similar ground because he assumed climatic change was an important factor motivating the development of domestication and agriculture, specifically in the Levant. In Henry's view, the colder and dryer climate of the Younger Dryas (13,000–11,500 ya) created relatively resource-rich regions of the Levant that attracted human hunter-gatherers. As the climate shifted again at the end of the Younger Dryas, descendants of these populations experienced essentially the same stresses envisioned in other environmental approaches. The primary cause of these stresses, in Henry's view, was not so much the climatic changes after the Younger Dryas as it was the flexibility of human populations—living in what had been resource-rich regions during the Younger Dryas—in dealing with the changes. The outcomes, however, would be the same.

In short, environmental approaches are based on forces external to humans as the active ingredients in the development of agriculture. In these hypotheses, human agency is primarily reactive. Something in the environment changes, and it makes life increasingly hard

horticulture Farming method in which only hand tools are used; typical of most early Neolithic societies.

demographic Pertaining to the size or rate of increase of human populations.

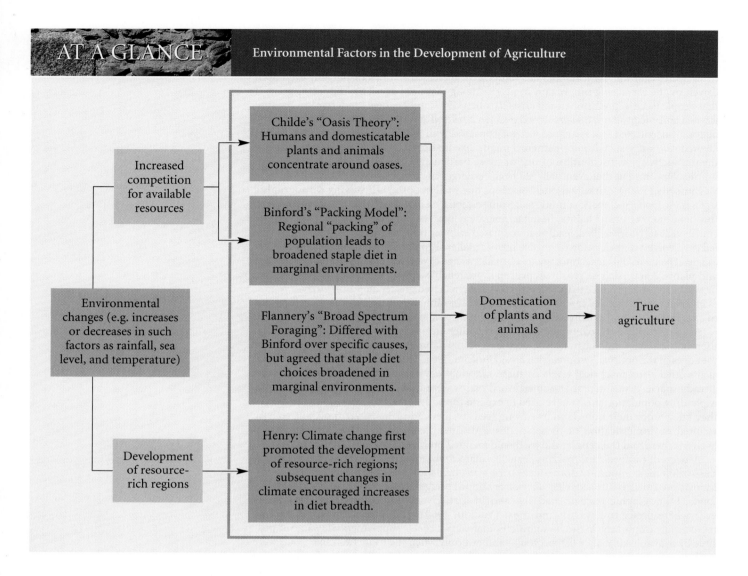

AT A GLANCE   Environmental Factors in the Development of Agriculture

for hunter-gatherers. They can react culturally to these changed circumstances in various ways, which include incorporating a wider range of less-preferred foods in their staple diet and colonizing marginal environments. At some point they take up the alternative of applying cultural means to increase the production of one or more food species. So basically, these approaches envision the development of agriculture more as something that humans backed into from a lack of better alternatives rather than something they enthusiastically embraced.

CULTURAL APPROACHES

Not everyone agrees that the roots of domestication and agriculture are to be explained by the operation of external environmental factors, all of which, by design, place human culture and agency in a passive role. Instead, some archaeologists contend, social and ideological factors, such as enhancing group or individual status through competitive feasting, tribute payments, or offerings to the deities (Price, 1995), may have pushed societies to come up with more food than could be readily obtained on a regular basis from natural sources. The reasoning behind these hypotheses is that human agency and culture alone may be sufficient and necessary to explain many of the fundamental changes documented in the archaeological record.

As you may suspect from your reading of the previous section, these approaches are also not immune to extreme positions. Just as we can identify some environmental approaches as teetering on the brink of determinism, we can find some cultural and cognitive approaches that seek to emphasize the role of human culture to the near, or certain, exclusion of non-cultural factors. In these approaches, such natural phenomena as climatic changes are either irrelevant to the explanation of cultural outcomes or were consciously exploited by people to further cultural objectives, so they weren't merely phenomena to which people reacted.

Robert Braidwood's (Braidwood and Howe, 1960) "nuclear zone" or "hilly flanks" hypothesis is a good mid-twentieth-century example to start with in looking at cultural approaches. Braidwood built on V. Gordon Childe's earlier work (see p. 336) and pointed out that subsequent research didn't find evidence of the environmental changes on which Childe based his oasis theory. What's more, the wild ancestors of common domesticated plants and animals in the Near East were in the foothills of the mountains, not around the oases, which is where they should be if Childe's oasis theory is correct. Without a clear environmental trigger or cause for the origins of domestication and agriculture, Braidwood and Howe (1960) reasoned that domestication and, ultimately, agriculture came about as early Holocene hunter-gatherers gradually became familiar with local plant and animal resources and grew increasingly inclined to the notion of domestication. In other words, domestication and agriculture happened when "culture was ready." But Braidwood never adequately addressed the compelling questions that such an argument stimulates: Why was culture "ready"? Why then and not, say, 30,000 years ago? Or 100,000 years ago? Or never?

In his examination of the beginnings of agriculture in Europe, Ian Hodder (1990) took a more evenhanded approach than Braidwood. Building on the symbolic meaning assigned to houses and household activities, Hodder developed an argument in which the process of domestication and the activities of agriculture were properly viewed as the human "transformation of nature into culture, with an expansion of cultural control and a domination of nature" (Verhoeven, 2004, p. 210). He identified both social and natural factors as possible pressures in bringing about the transition from foraging to agriculture at the end of the Pleistocene. The strength of Hodder's approach rests in his assignment of considerable weight both to human agency and culture as well as to the widely accepted effects of environmental factors.

Recently, Jacques Cauvin (2000) offered an ambitious interpretation of the Neolithic Revolution, which he views as a "revolution of symbols," not a revolution of economic arrangements. He feels there's not enough evidence to support such approaches as Binford's packing model, but he does see value in Braidwood's argument that domestication and agriculture didn't happen until culture was ready to receive it. To Cauvin, the Neolithic represents a fundamental transformation of worldviews that took place before the emergence of agricultural economies in the Near East. The primary symbols are the Goddess and the Bull, which represent the cultural creation of the divine and a fundamental symbolic transformation of the pre-Neolithic world. Cauvin's claim that the birth of the gods created a sense of self and, in turn, promoted the development of human agency and agriculture (Cauvin, 2000, p. 209) is reflected in his book's title, *The Birth of the Gods and the Origins of Agriculture.* Even though Cauvin asserts that domestication was the product of both cultural and natural factors, he devotes considerable attention to arguing against the possible role played by natural and some cultural factors, which, as Hodder (2001, p. 109) notes, leaves him "backed into the corner of arguing for a causal and chronological primacy for the psycho-cultural." Regrettably, Cauvin doesn't devote enough attention to explaining why these symbols were created, what caused them, and why they became particularly powerful during the Neolithic. As one archaeologist remarked (Rollefson, 2001, p. 102), in Cauvin's treatment they remain as mysterious and unexplained as the Black Monolith in Stanley Kubrick's film *2001: A Space Odyssey.*

So, to sum things up, cultural approaches to explain the origins of domestication and agriculture assume an active role for human agency and tend to discount, if not deny completely, the importance of natural or environmental factors. In these approaches, cultural changes such as a transformation of the human relationship with the divine, or of the conceptualization of self, can be enough in some cases to account for the changes we see in the archaeological record. The main drawback with these hypotheses is that sometimes it's not immediately clear why such transformations would occur. Such answers as Braidwood's "when culture was ready" were unacceptable even in 1960, and they're no less so now. These approaches envision the development of agriculture as something humans achieved through cultural means, and not necessarily from a lack of alternatives.

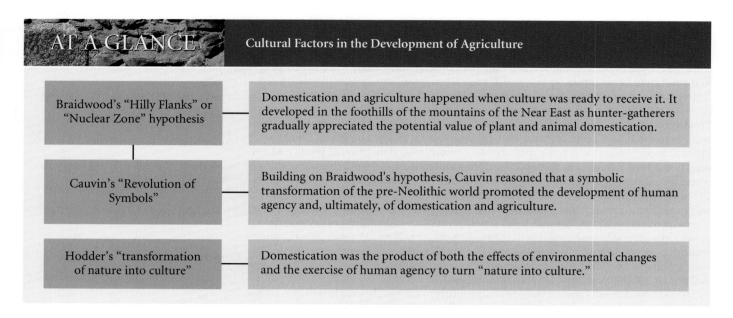

Braidwood's "Hilly Flanks" or "Nuclear Zone" hypothesis	Domestication and agriculture happened when culture was ready to receive it. It developed in the foothills of the mountains of the Near East as hunter-gatherers gradually appreciated the potential value of plant and animal domestication.
Cauvin's "Revolution of Symbols"	Building on Braidwood's hypothesis, Cauvin reasoned that a symbolic transformation of the pre-Neolithic world promoted the development of human agency and, ultimately, of domestication and agriculture.
Hodder's "transformation of nature into culture"	Domestication was the product of both the effects of environmental changes and the exercise of human agency to turn "nature into culture."

FROM COLLECTING TO CULTIVATING

If today we had to choose an explanation for the origins of domestication and agriculture (and we *must* at least indicate a preference, since this is an introductory college textbook), we would adopt one of the moderate environmental approaches as the most robust (that is, explains the most real cases). Most such approaches do consider cultural factors, but they assign the greatest weight to the forces of nature. For us, that's their greatest appeal. They don't require researchers to assume that, just because we're biocultural animals, humans are somehow exempt from natural factors that affect all living things. Disasters such as the devastating Southeast Asian tsunami of December 2004 and Hurricane Katrina in August 2005 are eloquent testimony that, for all our human posturing to the contrary, nature often has the final word.

Ultimately, we have no reason to believe that the origins of domestication and agriculture can be explained *only* by natural forces or *only* by cultural factors. These are complex problems for which there may even be multiple valid explanations. It could easily be the case that something like Verhoeven's (2004) holistic approach, which seeks explanations for these problems in the interaction of both natural and cultural forces, will prove to be the most productive route to follow.

So, working within our admitted preference for environmental approaches, let's now consider why and how hunter-gatherers became farmers in a real example drawn from the Near East. As Epipaleolithic gatherers in the Levant region harvested natural stands of wild cereal grasses such as wheat or barley, their movements would cause many of the ripened seed heads to shatter spontaneously, with considerable loss of grain. Each time someone used a gazelle-horn sickle to cut through a stalk, some of the seeds would fall to the ground. This normal process of seed dispersal is a function of the **rachis**, a short connector linking each seed to the primary stalk (Fig. 14–3). While the embryonic seed develops, the rachis serves as an umbilical that conveys the nutrients to be stored and later used by the germinating seed. Once the seed reaches its full development on the stalk, the rachis normally becomes dry and brittle, enabling the seed to break away easily.

Even without human interference, wild cereal grasses tended to be particularly susceptible to natural genetic modification (much more so than, say, nut-bearing trees), since the plants grew together in dense patches, were highly polytypic, and were quick to reproduce. In fact, a stand of wild grasses was like an enormous genetic laboratory. The normal range of genetic variability among the grasses included some plants with slightly larger seeds and others with tougher or more flexible rachis segments, meaning that their seed heads would be slightly less prone to shattering. As people worked through the stands, seeds from these genetic variants would end up in the gathering baskets slightly more often. Later, as the gatherers carried their baskets to camp, stored or processed the grain, or moved from place to place, a disproportionate number of the seeds they dropped, defecated, or perhaps even scat-

Schiemann, Elisabeth (1948). *Weizen, Roggen, Gerste: Systematik, Geschichte, und Verwendung.* Gustav Fischer, Jena.

FIGURE 14–3

In seedheads of wild cereal grasses, individual grains are linked together by a flexible jointed stem, or rachis, as they develop. At maturity, the rachis breaks apart and the seeds scatter. In domesticated forms, the rachis remains supple, keeping the seedhead intact until harvested. A, ear of wild einkorn wheat (1:1); B, grains of wild einkorn wheat (3:1).

rachis   The short stem by which an individual seed attaches to the main stalk of a plant as it develops.

tered purposely in likely growing areas would carry the flexible-rachis allele. (The same thing happened with the larger seeds preferred by the collectors.) As these genetic variants became isolated from the general wild population, each subsequent harvest advanced the "selection" process in favor of the same desirable traits.

So, human manipulation became an evolutionary force in modifying the species, a process Darwin labeled unconscious selection. People didn't have to be aware of genetic principles to act as effective agents of evolution. And where desirable traits could be readily discerned—larger grain size, plumper seedheads, earlier maturity, and so forth—human choice would even more predictably and consistently favor the preferred characteristics. The result within just a few seasons might be a significant shift in allele frequencies—that is, evolution—resulting from classic Darwinian selection processes, in this case the result of long-term pressure by gatherers, who consistently selected for those traits that improved the plant's productivity and quality (Rindos, 1984).

Of course, the rate of divergent evolution away from the wild ancestral forms of a plant (or animal) species accelerates as people continue to exercise control by selecting for genetically based characteristics they find desirable. With the cereal grasses such as barley and wheat, the human-influenced varieties typically came to average more grains per seedhead than their wild relatives had. The rachis became less brittle in domesticated forms, making it easier for people to harvest the grain with less loss because the seed head no longer shattered to disperse its own seed. At the same time, individual seed coats or husks (glumes) became less tough, making them easier for humans to process or digest. Many of these changes obviously would have been harmful to the plant under natural conditions. Frequently, a consequence of domestication is that the plant species becomes dependent on humans to disperse its seeds. After all, symbiosis is a mutual, two-way relationship.

Whenever favorable plant traits developed, hunter-gatherers could be expected to respond to these improvements by quickly adjusting their collecting behavior to take the greatest advantage, in turn stimulating further genetic changes in the subject plants and eventually producing a **cultigen**, or domesticate, under human control. Again, these unconscious, or artificial (as opposed to *natural*, in Darwin's terminology) selection pressures constitute an evolutionary force in their own right. As continuous selection and isolation from other plants of the same species continued to favor desirable genetic variants, the steps to full domestication would have been small ones.

Likewise, the distances that separated hunter-gatherers from early farmers were also small ones. It's usually impossible to determine archaeologically when harvesting activities may have expanded to include the deliberate scattering of selected wild seeds in new environments or the elimination of competing plants by "weeding" or even burning over a forest clearing. As they intensified their focus on wheat and barley in the Near East—or on species such as maize or runner beans in Mexico—hunter-gatherers finally abandoned the rhythm of their traditional food-collecting schedules and further committed themselves to increasing the productivity of these plants through cultivation.

Archaeological Evidence for Domestication and Agriculture

It could be argued that agriculture is the most far-reaching "invention" our species can claim. Nothing else has so profoundly affected other species. The accumulated archaeological evidence reveals that humans *independently* domesticated local species and developed agriculture in several geographically separate regions relatively soon after the Ice Age ended (see Digging Deeper on p. 342). Through recent applications of molecular genetics research and other methodological advances in archaeology, it's also clear that more independent instances of prehistoric domestication are likely to be identified, some locations currently identified as possible independent centers of domestication may be deleted from the list, and some plants and animals were probably domesticated multiple times in various places (Armelagos and Harper, 2005).

In examining independent centers of domestication around the world, it's important to realize that the domestication of a local species or two would not necessarily trigger the enormous biocultural consequences we usually associate with the Neolithic period in the Near

cultigen   A plant that is wholly dependent on humans; a domesticate.

DIGGING DEEPER

What's to Eat?

Origin and Approximate Dates of Domestication for Selected Plants and Animals

Asia

Banana *(Musa)*, 2,000 ya
Chicken *(Gallus)*, 8,000 ya
Millet *(Setaria)*, 9,000 ya
Orange *(Citrus)*, 2,000 ya
Peach *(Prunus)*, 6,000 ya
Rice *(Oryza)*, 7,000 ya
Soybean *(Glycine)*, 3,000 ya

Southwest Asia/Near East

Apple *(Malus)*, 3,000 ya
Barley *(Hordeum)*, 10,500 ya
Cattle *(Bos)*, 9,000 ya
Chickpea *(Cicer)*, 8,000 ya
Date *(Phoenix)*, 4,500 ya
Goat *(Capra)*, 10,500 ya
Horse *(Equus)*, 6,000 ya
Lentil *(Lens)*, 10,000 ya
Pea *(Pisum)*, 8,500 ya
Pig *(Sus)*, 9,500 ya
Pistachio *(Pistacea)*, ?
Sheep *(Ovis)*, 10,000 ya
Wheat *(Triticum)*, 10,500 ya

Mediterranean

Asparagus *(Asparagus)*, 2,200 ya
Broccoli *(Broccoli)*, 1,900 ya
Cabbage *(Brassica)*, 2,000 ya
Grape *(Vitus)*, 6,000 ya
Lettuce *(Lactuca)*, 6,500 ya
Olive *(Olea)*, 5,000 ya
Pear *(Pyrus)*, 2,500 ya
Rabbit *(Oryctolagus)*, 3,000 ya

Africa

Coffee *(Coffea)*, ?
Millet *(Pennisetum)*, 4,000 ya
Muskmelon *(Cucumis)*, 5,000 ya
Sorghum *(Sorghum)*, 4,500 ya
Watermelon *(Citrullus)*, 4,000 ya
Yam *(Dioscorea)*, ?

North America

Goosefoot *(Chenopodium)*, 3,000 ya
Gourd *(Cucurbita)*, 5,000 ya
Marsh elder *(Iva)*, 3,000 ya
Sunflower *(Helianthus)*, 3,000 ya

Mexico/Central America

Amaranth *(Amaranthus)*, 6,000 ya
Avocado *(Persea)*, 2,500 ya
Cacao *(Theobroma)*, 1,500 ya
Chili pepper *(Capsicum)*, 5,500 ya
Common bean *(Phaseolus)*, 7,000 ya
Maize *(Zea mays)*, 4,500 ya
Squash *(Cucurbita)*, 7,500 ya
Tomato *(Lycopersicon)*, ?
Turkey *(Agriocharis)*, 2,300 ya

South America

Cashew *(Anacardium)*, ?
Chili pepper *(Capsicum)*, 4,500 y.a.
Coca *(Erythroxylon)*, ?
Guinea pig *(Cavia)*, 4,000 ya
Lima bean *(Phaseolus)*, 7,000 ya

Llama *(Lama)*, 7,000 ya
Manioc *(Manihot)*, 4,200 ya
Muscovy duck *(Cairina)*, 3,000 ya
Papaya *(Carica)*, ?
Peanut *(Arachis)*, 4,000 ya
Pineapple *(Ananas)*, ?
Potato *(Solanum)*, 4,000 ya
Quinoa *(Chenopodium)*, 3,500 ya
Sweet potato *(Ipomoea)*, 4,500 ya
Tobacco *(Nicotiana)*, ?

SOURCES:

Crops and Man, 2nd ed., by Jack R. Harlan (Madison, WI: American Society of Agronomy/Crop Science Society of America, 1992).

Cultural Atlas of Mesopotamia and the Ancient Near East, by Michael Roaf (New York: Facts on File, 1996).

Historical Geography of Crop Plants: A Selected Roster, by Jonathan D. Sauer (Boca Raton, FL: CRC Press, 1994).

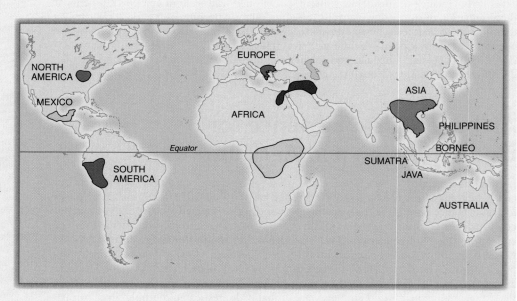

East. In fact, most altered species retained only local significance. For example, in the Eastern Woodlands of the United States, hunter-gatherers domesticated several small-seeded species very early; still, the wild forest products obtained by hunting and gathering retained their primary importance until relatively late prehistoric times, when true farming developed in the East. The prehistoric yam cultivators of sub-Saharan Africa serve as a similar example.

In most regions, agriculture didn't develop fully until people were exploiting a mosaic of plants—and sometimes animals, too—from different locations, brought together in various combinations to meet such cultural requirements as nutrition, palatability, hardiness, yield, processing ease, and storage. In the Near East this threshold was reached around 11,000 years ago (ya), when an agricultural complex consisting of wheat, barley, sheep, and goats was widely and rapidly adopted.

PLANTS

In most areas where agriculture emerged, early farmers relied on local plant species whose wild relatives grew close by. Old World cereal grasses, including barley and some wheat varieties, were native throughout the Near East and perhaps into southeastern Europe (Dennell, 1983). Wild varieties of these plants still flourish today over parts of this range. Therefore, barley or wheat domestication could have occurred anywhere in this region, possibly more than once. The same is true for maize and beans in Mexico. So, as we noted earlier, domestication and agriculture were "invented" independently in different regions around the world.

As we have emphasized, it's best to explain these separate but parallel processes from a cultural and ecological perspective. We've already seen that certain kinds of wild plants were more likely than others to become domesticated. Many of these species tend to grow in regions where a very long dry season follows a short wet period (Harlan, 1992). After the last Ice Age, around 10,000 ya, these conditions existed around the Mediterranean basin and the hilly areas of the Near East and in the dry forests and savanna grasslands of portions of sub-Saharan Africa, India, southern California, southern Mexico, and eastern and western South America.

Most scientific understanding of ancient human plant use has come from the **archaeobotanical** study of preserved seeds, fruits, nutshell fragments, and other plant **macrofossils** like those shown in Figure 14–4 (Pearsall, 2000). It isn't easy to preserve seeds, tubers, leaves, and other delicate organic materials for thousands of years. Archaeologists recover some macrofossils from depositional environments that are always dry, wet, or frozen, because all of these conditions slow down or halt the process of decomposition. Most, however, are preserved because the way they were harvested, threshed, processed for consumption, or discarded brought them into contact with enough fire to char them, but not enough heat to reduce them to ash. Once charred, macrofossils preserve well in many kinds of archaeological sites and can often be classified to genus, if not to species.

Macrofossils offer direct evidence for important archaeological research such as reconstructing hunter-gatherer plant use patterns, identifying farming area locations, and determining the precise nature of harvested crops. They also provide insights of other kinds. The presence of perennial and biennial weed seeds in an ancient agricultural context may suggest that each year's farming activities only minimally disturbed the soil; the seed planter may have used a digging stick, hoe, or simple scratch plow. If, on the other hand, seeds of annual weeds predominate, the farmer may have used a moldboard plow—one that turns over the soil as it cuts through.

Right now, the best archaeological data on the shift toward food production come from sites located in arid regions of both hemispheres, where ancient organic remains are best preserved. Were the first steps toward farming really taken in such seemingly marginal agricultural situations, or are dry areas just better environments for preservation? Many researchers are still convinced that most of our significant food plants originated in the dry temperate environments and that they were probably domesticated there, too. But not all archaeobotanists agree; some argue instead that early domesticated forms may have been introduced from other, more humid environments, where preservation is poor and research has been limited.

archaeobotany The analysis and interpretation of the remains of ancient plants recovered from the archaeological record.

macrofossil Plant parts such as seeds, nutshells, and stems, preserved in the archaeological record and large enough to be clearly visible to the naked eye.

FIGURE **14–4**

Plant remains from a pit feature in an Illinois archaeological site. Clockwise from top are pieces of charred wood, nutshell fragments, and seeds.

Barry Lewis

DIGGING DEEPER

Learning about Dead Plants: The Primary Data Are Getting Smaller

The major shortcomings of macrofossil-based interpretations of past human plant use are due to potential data biases. Considering that most seeds, nutshells, and other plant macrofossils are preserved because they were charred before entering the archaeological record (see Fig. 14–4 for examples), we can assume that such interpretations are biased in favor of those plants and plant parts that were most likely to come into contact with fire and most likely to have a morphology that would sustain being charred. For example, it's pretty easy to char a bean, but you'll be disappointed if you try the same thing with a leaf of lettuce. At any rate, because these conditions could undoubtedly be met only sometimes in prehistory, archaeologists are understandably concerned about the validity and reliability of many reconstructions of human plant use.

Fortunately, there's a fix at hand. It takes the form of exciting new data sources that also provide cross-checks on the validity of macrofossil research. Over the past couple of decades, archaeobotanists have devoted considerable research to the interpretive value of a wide range of *microfossils*, such as pollen, phytoliths, and starch grains (Bryant, 2003). These remains tend to preserve readily in many archaeological contexts, they can be classified as to the kind of plant they represent, and they can be archaeologically present even in sites where macrofossils were destroyed or never deposited.

Pollen grains (Fig. 1) have been a valuable source of environmental and subsistence data for decades. Their strengths are that they're abundant (as any hay fever sufferer can tell you); the grains are taxonomically distinctive and often can be classified to genus, if not to species; the outer shell of each grain is tough; and the rain of wind-borne pollen from seed-producing plants continues before, during, and after humans occupy a particular archaeological site. The main shortcoming of pollen grains is that they tend to preserve poorly in many kinds of open sites, depending on soil acidity, moisture, drainage, and weathering.

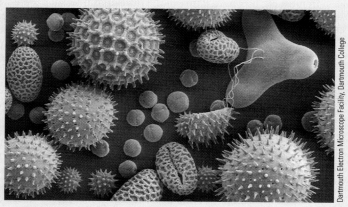

FIGURE 1

Example pollen grains from common flowering plants. The spiked ball in the lower left of the photograph is roughly 75 microns, or three-thousandths of an inch, in diameter.

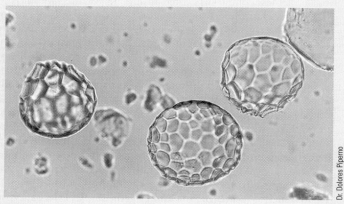

FIGURE 2

Squash *(Cucurbita ficifolia)* phytoliths. The large one in the lower center of the photo measures about 120 microns across.

---

microfossil Small to microscopic plant remains, most falling in a range of 10–100 microns, or roughly the size of individual grains of wheat flour in the bag from your grocer's shelf.

pollen Microscopic grains containing the male gametes of seed-producing plants.

phytoliths (*phyto*, meaning "plant," and *lith*, meaning "stone") Microscopic silica structures formed in the cells of many plants.

Plant **microfossils**, such as **pollen** and **phytoliths** (see Digging Deeper), are another important data source. They often survive even where macrofossils don't—for example, in residues on the cutting edges of ancient stone tools, inside pottery containers, and among other debris in refuse pits (Piperno, 1988; Traverse, 1988). Likewise, starch grains, fats, and amino acids may remain on the surfaces of scrapers, bowls, smoking pipes, kettles, and the like. No wonder archaeologists are becoming reluctant to clean artifacts just removed from the ground!

Studies of such microbotanical traces in Panama and elsewhere south of Mexico are beginning to change our perception of New World domestication (Piperno and Pearsall, 1998). The research reveals that root crops like **manioc** (*Manihot* sp.) and other tubers were important in the diet of early tropical farmers well before seed crops like maize arrived on the scene.

Phytoliths (Fig. 2) are less familiar, but potentially even more valuable than many macrofossils. They're microscopic, inorganic structures that form in many seed-producing plants as well as other plants. Like pollen, phytoliths are taxonomically distinctive. They even vary according to where they form in the plant, so phytoliths from leaves can be distinguished from those that formed in the stems and seeds of the same plant. Importantly, they don't suffer from the same preservation biases that macrofossils do. Are the plant remains at your site unidentifiable, reduced to a powdery ash, or simply not preserved? Not a problem. Chances are that the phytoliths from these plants are not only present in the archaeological deposit but also recoverable and identifiable.

Starch grains (Fig. 3) differ greatly from pollen and phytoliths because of their subcellular nature; that is, they form in all plant parts and are particularly abundant in such economically important portions as seeds and tubers (Coil et al., 2003). But, like pollen and phytoliths, starch grains can be taxonomically classified, currently mostly to family or genus. A good example of the archaeological application of starch grain analysis is the recent examination of the surface of a grinding stone found on the floor of one of the 23,000-year-old huts at Ohalo II in Israel (see Digging Deeper on pp. 326–327). This study, which was based on carefully sampled residues from cracks and pits in the working surface of the grinding stone, enabled archaeobotanists to identify that it was a specialized implement used to grind wild cereal grasses, including barley (Piperno et al., 2004).

Microfossil analyses complement and greatly extend the valuable insights that archaeobotanists have achieved through the study of macrofossils. Along with the growing field of *archaeogenetics*, which applies the methods of molecular genetics to archaeological problems, and improvements in radiocarbon dating, which can yield accurate age estimates from samples as small as 100 micrograms—that's one ten-thousandth of a gram, or roughly $1/5$ the weight of a grain of rice (Armelagos and Harper, 2005)—microfossil analyses promise many significant new advances in our understanding of the prehistory of the human use of plants and the beginnings of agriculture.

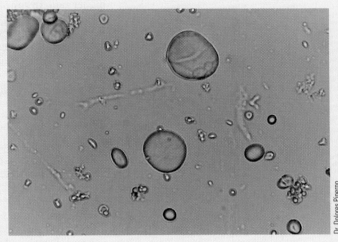

FIGURE 3
Wild emmer wheat (*Triticum dicoccoides*) starch grains, which show distinctive crater-like surface impressions. The largest starch grain (top center) is about 30 microns in diameter.

SOURCES:

"Genomics at the Origins of Agriculture, Part One," by George J. Armelagos and Kristin N. Harper, *Evolutionary Anthropology* 14 (2005):68–77.

"Invisible Clues to New World Plant Domestication," by Vaughn M. Bryant, *Science* 299 (2003):1029–1030.

"Laboratory Goals and Consideration for Multiple Microfossil Extraction in Archaeology," by James Coil, Alejandra Korstanje, Steven Archer, and Christine A. Hastorf, *Journal of Archaeological Science* 30 (2003):991–1008.

Phytolith Analysis: An Archaeological and Geological Perspective, by Dolores R. Piperno (San Diego, CA: Academic Press, 1988).

"Processing of Wild Cereal Grains in the Upper Paleolithic Revealed by Starch Grain Analysis," by Dolores R. Piperno, Ehud Weiss, Irene Holst, and Dani Nadel, *Nature* 430 (2004):670–673.

(Manioc is also known as cassava; if you've ever had tapioca pudding, then you've eaten manioc.) These studies also indicate that primitive varieties of maize, and probably beans as well, were introduced here long before they reached highland areas like Mexico's dry **Tehuacán Valley**, where researchers most commonly encounter macrofossil remains.

As we saw in Chapter 9, some plant species leave biochemical traces in those who consume them. Because the plants of temperate and tropical regions evolved with slightly different processes for photosynthesis, their chemical compositions vary in the ratio of carbon-13 to carbon-12. This distinctive chemical profile gets passed along the food chain, and the bones of the human skeleton may provide evidence of dietary change. For example, their lower ^{13}C levels reveal that females at Grasshopper Pueblo, in east-central Arizona, consumed mostly the local plants they gathered, while their male relatives at first enjoyed more

manioc Cassava, a starchy edible root crop of the tropics.

Tehuacán Valley (tay-wah-kahn´)
A dry highland region on the boundary of the states of Puebla and Oaxaca in southern Mexico.

maize, a plant higher in ^{13}C. Later, maize became a staple in everyone's diet at Grasshopper, resulting in equivalent carbon isotopes in males and females (Ezzo, 1993).

Other biochemical analyses, using different isotopes (see p. 191), have been devised to assess overall diet—not necessarily just the domesticated portions—from individual skeletons. (One drawback of performing these tests is that they destroy part of the specimen.) A higher ratio of nitrogen-15 to nitrogen-14 (^{15}N/^{14}N), for instance, corresponds to a greater seafood component (Schoeninger et al., 1983); and a higher strontium-to-calcium (Sr/Ca) ratio reflects the larger contribution of plant foods versus meat in the diet (Schoeninger, 1981). Other chemicals taken up by bones may inform us about ancient lifeways. For example, lead is a trace element found in unusually high concentration in Romans who drank wine stored in lead containers. The interplay among culture and diet and biology is, of course, a prime example of biocultural evolution. But to put it more simply, "You are what you eat."

ANIMALS

To some extent, the process of animal domestication differed from plant domestication, and it probably varied even from one faunal species to another. For example, the dog was one of the first domesticated animals; mtDNA evidence suggests an origin between 40,000 and 15,000 ya (Savolainen, 2002), and dogs may even have accompanied late Ice Age hunter-gatherers (Olsen, 1985). The dog's relationship with humans was different (and it still is) from that of most subsequently domesticated animals. Often valued less for its meat or hide, a dog's primary role was most likely as a ferocious hunting weapon under at least a bit of human control and direction. As people domesticated other animals, they changed the dog's behavior even more for service as a herder and later, in the Arctic and among the Native Americans of the Great Plains, as an occasional transporter of possessions. But the burial of a puppy with a Natufian person who died some 12,000 ya in the Near East suggests that dogs may have earned a role as pets very early (Davis and Valla, 1978).

Most other domesticated animals were maintained solely for their meat at first. Richard J. Harrison's (1985) insightful analysis of faunal collections from Neolithic sites in Spain and Portugal concluded that meat remained the primary product up until about 4,000 ya, when subsequent changes in herd composition (age and sex ratios), slaughter patterns, and popularity of certain breeds all point to new uses for some livestock. Oxen pulled plows, horses carried people and things, cattle and goats contributed milk products, and sheep were raised for wool. Animal waste became fertilizer in agricultural areas. Leather, horn, and bone—and even social status for the animals' owners—were other valued by-products. (In much the same way, recent East African cattle herders appreciate their animals as much more than packages of beefsteak, for a sizable herd testifies to a man's standing and may be used to fulfill social obligations such as bridewealth payments.)

Of course, animals are more mobile than plants, and most of them are no less mobile than the early people pursuing them. So it's unlikely that hunters could have promoted useful genetic changes in wild animals just by trying to restrict their movements or by selective hunting alone. Possibly, by simultaneously destroying wild predators and reducing the number of competing herbivores, humans became surrogate protectors of the herds, though this arrangement would not have had the genetic impact of actual domestication.

Animals such as gazelle or reindeer might be managed to a degree in the wild state, possibly by establishing a "rapport" with the herds and encouraging them to graze in cleared areas in the winter or by restricting hunting activities to a few quick raids, during which the herd might be selectively harvested or thinned. Culling out all nonbreeding males, for example, wouldn't limit the potential for herd expansion, and it wouldn't have much effect on the population genetics. Epipaleolithic Natufians in the Near East were once thought to have managed wild gazelle in this way (Legge, 1972); but reexamination of the faunal remains casts these peoples' gazelle hunting in a very different light, implying the use of large-scale surrounds or ambush techniques to nonselectively kill entire herds at once (Legge and Rowley-Conwy, 1987). This drastic approach would suppress the animal population for years. Obviously, true domestication, involving further genetic changes, must have been reached by other steps.

Since domestication is a process, not an event, it's nearly impossible to say precisely when a plant or animal species has been domesticated. The process involves much more than an indication of "tameness" in the presence of humans. More significant are the changes in allele frequencies that result from selective breeding and isolation from wild relatives. People may have started with young animals spared by hunters for that purpose or, in the case of large and dangerous species such as the ancestral aurochs cattle, with individuals that were exceptionally docile or small (Fagan, 1993). Maintained in captivity, these animals could be selectively bred for desirable traits such as more meat, fat, wool, or strength. (Captive animals that weren't suitable for breeding represented meat on the hoof—a convenient method of storing food against spoilage or future want.) Once early farmers were consistently selecting breeding stock according to some criteria and succeeding in perpetuating those characteristics through subsequent generations, then domestication—that is, evolution—clearly had occurred.

Overall, not many wild mammal species were ever domesticated. Those most amenable to domestication are animals that form hierarchical herds, are not likely to flee when frightened, and are not strongly territorial (Diamond, 1989). In other words, animals that will tolerate and transfer their allegiance to human surrogates make the best potential domesticates. Several large Eurasian mammals met these specifications, so that cultures of Asia, Europe, and Africa came to rely on sheep and goats, pigs, cattle, and horses (listed here in approximately their order of domestication) as well as water buffalo, camels, reindeer, and a few other regionally significant species (see Digging Deeper on p. 342).

Even fewer New World herd animals were capable of being domesticated. Aside from two South American camelids—the llama and the alpaca—no large American mammal was brought fully under human control (Fig. 14–5). Dogs had probably accompanied the first people into the New World. None of these animals were suitable for transporting or pulling heavy loads—llamas balk at carrying more than about 100 pounds, and Plains Indian dogs dragged only small bundles—so the people of the New World continued to bear their own burdens, till their fields by hand, and hunt and fight on foot until the introduction of the Old World's livestock in the 1500s.

Archaeological evidence of nonhuman animal domestication is subtle and difficult to assess from the bones themselves (Fig. 14–6). For most species, no significant increase in body size occurred, and early domesticated cattle, sheep, and goats are actually smaller than their

William Turnbaugh

FIGURE 14–5
Peoples of highland South America bred the llama primarily as a source of wool and, to a limited extent, to transport loads.

Barry Lewis

FIGURE 14–6
A typical collection of faunal remains from an excavation level in an Illinois archaeological site.

wild relatives. Comparisons of the bones of wild and domestic members of the same species disclose only relatively minor differences in skeletal form (Herre, 1969). For example, the bony horn cores of domestic goats display a somewhat flattened cross section when compared with their wild antecedents, and domesticated pigs exhibit a shortening of the upper jaw (maxilla) in relation to the lower jaw (mandible).

Archaeozoologists also examine changes in prehistoric herd demography to document domestication. The population curve for animals randomly hunted from a wild herd tends to reflect a normal distribution that approximates the overall age and sex ratio of the herd. On the other hand, a notable increase in the number of skeletal elements of, say, young adult rams found in kitchen refuse may indicate that humans were selecting those particular animals for slaughter while reserving most females and lambs for breeding purposes (Bokonyi, 1969). Such indicators are seldom definitive, however, unless very large samples of faunal remains confirm domestication.

Old World Farmers

As we've noted, independent invention accounts best for the diversity of domesticates and the distinctiveness of Neolithic lifeways in the Far East, Southeast Asia, India, sub-Saharan Africa, the Near East, and the Americas. What's more, we now recognize that many wild species, such as wheat and sheep, probably occupied more extensive natural ranges in the early Holocene and may in fact have undergone local domestication more than a few times (Armelagos and Harper, 2005).

But we can't entirely discount the *diffusion*, or spread, of Neolithic lifeways from place to place. As we'll see, in at least some areas—southeastern Europe, for example—colonizing farmers appear to have brought their domesticates and their culture with them as they migrated into new territories in search of suitable farmland. Neolithic practices also spread through secondary contact as people on the margins of established farming societies acquired certain tools, seeds, and ideas and passed them along to cultures still further removed. Seeds and animals often must have become commodities in prehistoric exchange networks, just like the Spanish horses obtained by Native Americans did in the sixteenth century. Maybe marriage partners from other groups introduced their in-laws to the new ways. It's important to bear in mind that each archaeological event is unique in its own way. "One-size-fits-all" explanations are rarely adequate, even if the results are the same—in this case, the expansion of Neolithic lifeways.

With that point in mind, let's consider a sampling of Neolithic societies from around the world to get some idea of the variations on this common theme.

THE NEAR EAST

Neolithic lifeways and their consequences appeared throughout the Near East and adjacent areas, but not necessarily because farming was a superior way of life. As we saw in Chapter 13, Epipaleolithic foraging cultures such as Kebaran and Natufian apparently took the first steps, though perhaps inadvertently, toward agriculture in the Near East (Fig. 14–7). As discussed in Chapter 13, the extraordinary preservation of plant remains at Ohalo II, an early Epipaleolithic campsite in northern Israel, shows that small-grained grass and wild cereal seeds were important in hunter-gatherer diets in the Levant by 23,000 ya (see p. 326; Piperno et al., 2004; Weiss et al., 2004a, 2004b). The diverse staple diet of these early Epipaleolithic hunter-gatherers also offers important support for Flannery's (1973) conception of a broad spectrum revolution, which should precede the development of domestication and agriculture.

Between 11,500 and 11,000 ya, at the site of Abu Hureyra in the upper Euphrates of Syria, hunter-gatherers consumed more than 250 plant species, only a few of which were staple foods (Moore et al., 2000, p. 397). With the beginning of the cooler and dryer conditions of the Younger Dryas, many of these species vanish from the Abu Hureyra archaeological record, to be replaced by increased frequencies of weed seeds and the earliest evidence of domesticated rye, specimens of which date to roughly 11,200–10,600 ya (Moore et al., 2000).

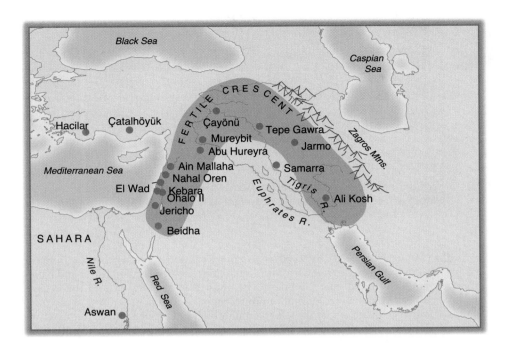

FIGURE 14–7
Early Neolithic sites of the Fertile Crescent.

These changes point to two important inferences: first, environmental conditions were sufficient to account for these shifts in Abu Hureyra's subsistence economy, and second, at least part of the economy of this settlement was based on the cultivation of domesticated plants (rye, in this case) by around 11,000 ya.

A similar story was played out at Kebara and El Wad, which are in Israel to the southwest of Abu Hureyra, where stone-bladed sickles aided in harvesting the ancestral varieties of wheat and barley by 10,000 ya (Henry, 1989). This technique, more efficient than plucking seeds by hand, netted greater yields during a short harvest period. The process of genetic selection that we've considered as the basis for plant domestication must have been well under way by this time. That we don't yet know the whole story about the selective forces acting on these species is evident from recent field research that demonstrated there is no reason Epipaleolithic hunter-gatherers couldn't also have harvested fallen grain. Kislev and colleagues (2004) collected spikelets of wild barley and wild wheat that had fallen to the ground at stands chosen from three areas of Israel and found that such harvesting methods would have yielded a reliable summer food supply. The Natufians adopted farming to augment food supplies for their rapidly growing population at a time when natural subsistence resources were again in decline. The warming trends that first had created optimal conditions for upland cereal and nut crops continued for several more centuries, leaving much of the Levant parched (Henry, 1989). Natufians then abandoned many upland sites, retreating to the lower stream valleys. There, in an effort to duplicate the once-productive natural environments of the highlands, some groups established new stands of cereal grasses by dispersing seeds in favorable areas along the streams near their villages (Bar-Yosef, 1998). It seems that, at least in this case, the stresses associated with a destabilized population/resource balance stimulated the agricultural response.

These food collectors and earliest farmers established the first permanent sedentary communities in the Near East. Drawn by an ever-flowing spring in an otherwise arid region, settlers at the site of Jericho (or Tell es-Sultan), in the West Bank, and at other Natufian sites in Israel built their round stone or mud-brick houses some 11,500 ya. Though they were made of more substantial materials, in form these structures closely resembled the temporary huts of the region's earlier hunters and gatherers. Numerous grinding stones and clay-lined pits testify to the significance of cereal grains (Moore, 1985; Bar-Yosef, 1987).

Foraging for the seeds of wild cereals, fruits, nuts, and the meat of wild game long remained an important, but slowly declining, component of the diet. At Abu Hureyra villagers were cultivating wheat, rye, and lentils by 9,800 ya, but wild plant food staples were still a part

AT A GLANCE   Important Near Eastern Sites and Regions

Site	Dates (ya)	Comments
Abu Hureya (Syria)	11,500–11,000	Hunter-gatherer settlement in which the economy was supplemented by domesticated plants, especially rye
Kebara & El Wad (Israel)	c. 10,000	Sites where hunter-gatherers supplemented their diet by harvesting the wild ancestral varieties of wheat and barley
Jericho (West Bank)	<11,000–3,500	Early permanent and sedentary community in the Levant that began in Natufian times and was occupied throughout the Neolithic

of the diet (Moore et al., 2000). By 9,000 ya, sedentary villagers across a broad arc from the Red Sea to western Iran—also known as the Fertile Crescent—engaged in wheat and barley agriculture and sheep and goat herding. As demonstrated at many sites in this region, Neolithic families lived in adjacent multiroom rectangular houses, in contrast to the compounds of individual small, round shelters commonly built by Epipaleolithic collectors as well as the early Jericho settlers. Flannery (1972) believes that this change in residence pattern signals a shift toward more economically and socially cohesive communities. Comprised of extended-family and multifamily groups, these villagers differed radically in outlook and actions from their predecessors. These were the beginnings of the region's later urbanism, which we'll look at in the next chapter.

AFRICA

Tracing Africa's Neolithic past is challenging, considering the continent's vast size, its varied climates and vegetation zones, and the extent to which many of its regions are still archaeologically unknown. What's more, because many tropical foods lack woody stems or durable seeds, they're poorly represented at archaeological sites; evidence of agriculture based on these kinds of products awaits more intensive microbotanical studies. Arid sections of North Africa have yielded some direct evidence of farming and herding.

Northern Africa   Archaeologists working in the Nile Valley have found sickles and milling stones relating to early wild-grain-harvesting activities (Wendorf and Schild, 1989). The so-called Qadan culture, whose sites are found near present-day Aswan, probably typified the Epipaleolithic food collectors who occupied the valley around 8,000 ya (Hoffman, 1991). Qadan people employed spears or nets for taking large Nile perch and catfish. Along the riverbanks they hunted wildfowl and gathered wild produce, processing starchy aquatic tubers on their milling stones. They also stalked the adjacent grasslands for gazelle and other game and may have begun the process of domesticating wild cattle (Wendorf and Schild, 1994). Considering the wealth of naturally occurring resources along the Nile, this foraging and collecting way of life might have continued indefinitely. So why did farming develop there at all?

Geologists and paleoecologists recognize that shifting rainfall patterns have affected North Africa since the late Pleistocene. Long-term cycles brought increased precipitation, which broadened the Nile and its valley and gave the river a predictable seasonal rhythm. Rains falling on its tropical headwaters, thousands of miles to the south, caused the river to overflow its downstream channels by late summer, flooding the low-lying basins of northern Egypt for about three months of the year. Although desiccation followed, the flood-deposited silt grew lush with wild grasses through the following season. Periodically, however, extended drought episodes intervened to narrow the river's life-giving flow.

The expansive area west of the Nile, known today as the Sahara, was particularly susceptible to these fluctuations. The Sahara was a fragile environment, always marginal for humans. Down to 11,000 ya, this arid region was uninviting even to hunter-gatherers. Then, a period of increased rainfall created shallow lakes and streams that nurtured the grasslands, attracting game animals and humans. Around 7,000 ya, people in the Sahara devised a strategy of nomadic pastoralism, allowing their herds of sheep, goats, and possibly cattle to act as ecological intermediaries by converting tough grasses into meat and by-products useful to humans (Wendorf and Schild, 1994). Soon after, around 6,000 ya, further deterioration of the region's climate—and possibly overgrazing—forced the herders and their animals to seek greener pastures closer to the river (Williams, 1984; Harlan, 1992; A. Smith, 1992).

As drought parched the adjacent areas, the narrowing Nile Valley attracted more settlers. Wild resources were then insufficient to feed the growing sedentary population, and even the local domesticates that had been casually cultivated on the floodplain gave way to more productive cereals—the domesticated wheat and barley that had been brought under human control elsewhere by people like the Natufians.

Farmers gradually made the river's rhythm their own. Communities of reed-mat or mud-brick houses appeared across the Nile delta and along its banks. Basket-lined storage pits or granaries, milling stones, and sickles indicate a heavy reliance on grain. Pottery vessels of river clay, linen woven from flax fibers, flint tools, and occasional hammered copper items were produced locally. These ordinary Neolithic beginnings laid the foundation for the remarkable Egyptian civilization, which we'll explore in Chapter 15.

Outside the Nile Valley, cattle herding took priority over farming in much of East Africa, where conditions were generally not suitable for cultivation.

Sub-Saharan Africa In West Africa along the southern edge of the Sahara, where little is currently known about the early Holocene human presence, the pattern appears similar to that described for the Sahara. At **Ounjougou**, in the Dogon Plateau region of central Mali, erosional gullies cut through a long sequence of Pleistocene and early Holocene sites, some of which were recently excavated (Huysecom, 2004). Hunter-gatherers appear to have been in the region from the earliest Holocene, around 12,000–11,000 ya. By 10,000–9,000 ya, such groups were harvesting wild cereal grasses and making and using ceramics.

The limited evidence available from archaeology and linguistic studies hints that hunters and gatherers in several other parts of Africa also experimented with local **cultivars**. For example, mobile foragers and semisedentary fishers of tropical Africa practiced yam horticulture in clearings and along riverbanks by at least 5,000 ya (Clark, 1976; Ehret, 1984). With digging sticks, they pried out the starchy wild yam tubers and carried them away for cooking. As an added bonus, the people discovered that if they pressed the leafy tops or cuttings of the largest roots into the soil at the edge of the camp clearing, the yams would regenerate into an informal garden.

In these tropical regions, the standard Near Eastern cereals tended to rot. So African farmers developed comparable domesticates from local cereal grasses, including local varieties of **millet** and **sorghum** (Fig. 14–8), which they successfully grew along the edges of the rain forest and the savanna grasslands (Sauer, 1994).

More dramatic shifts in sub-Saharan subsistence followed the introduction and spread of different Neolithic crops. Tropical plants from Southeast Asia reached Africa when

FIGURE 14–8
A stand of sorghum, which, along with rice and millet, is an important starch grain crop in many parts of Africa and Asia.

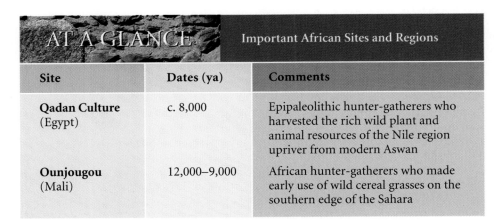

Site	Dates (ya)	Comments
Qadan Culture (Egypt)	c. 8,000	Epipaleolithic hunter-gatherers who harvested the rich wild plant and animal resources of the Nile region upriver from modern Aswan
Ounjougou (Mali)	12,000–9,000	African hunter-gatherers who made early use of wild cereal grasses on the southern edge of the Sahara

Ounjougou African hunter-gatherers who made early use of wild cereal grasses on the southern edge of the Sahara between 12,000 and 9,000 ya.

cultivars Wild plants fostered by human efforts to make them more productive.

millet Small-grained cereal grass native to Asia and Africa.

sorghum Cereal grass; some subspecies are grown for food grains, others for their sweet, juicy stalk.

351

FIGURE **14-9**
Bantu expansion in sub-Saharan Africa.

Polynesian voyagers crossed the Indian Ocean to Madagascar about 2,000 ya (Murdock, 1959; Harlan, 1992). These new products spread quickly to the interior, where people throughout the rain forest zone adopted bananas, **taro**, and Asian yams. Bantu-speaking peoples, native to west-central Africa, relied on these productive new crops to support their rapid expansion through central and southern Africa (Phillipson, 1984). Driving herds of domestic goats and cattle and acquiring the technology of ironworking as they moved southeastward through central Africa (Van Noten and Raymaekers, 1987), the Bantu easily overwhelmed most hunting and gathering groups. The conventional view is that, with iron tools and weapons, they carved out gardens and maintained large semipermanent villages, and today, their numerous descendants live in eastern, southern, and southwestern Africa (Fig. 14–9). There's at least some evidence that food-producing methods spread into parts of southern Africa before the Bantu. The bones of domesticated sheep found in Later Stone Age sites in South Africa may not be the result of the spread of pastoralists, as once widely believed, but the remains of the camps of Bushmen, whom Karim Sadr (2003) describes as "hunters-with-sheep."

ASIA

Several centers of domestication in southern and eastern Asia gave rise to separate Neolithic traditions based on the propagation of productive local plant and animal species. The exploitation of these resources spread widely and in turn heralded further economic and social changes associated with the rise of early civilizations in these regions (see Chapter 15).

South Asia   Excavations at Mehrgarh in central Pakistan have illuminated Neolithic beginnings on the Indian subcontinent (Jarrige and Meadow, 1980; Allchin and Allchin, 1982). Located at the edge of a high plain west of the broad Indus Valley (Fig. 14–10), the site's lower levels, dating between 8,000 and 6,000 ya, reveal the trend toward dietary specialization that accompanied the domestication of local plant and animal species. Early on, the people harvested both wild and domesticated varieties of barley and wheat, among other native plants. Mehrgarh's archaeological deposits also include bones of many local herbivores: water buffalo, gazelle, swamp deer, goats, sheep, pigs, cattle, and even elephants. By 6,000 ya, the cultivated cereals prevailed, along with just three animal species—domestic sheep, goats, and cattle. Researchers believe that this early Neolithic phase at Mehrgarh represents a transition from seminomadic herding to a more sedentary existence

FIGURE **14-10**
Early Farming in Asia.

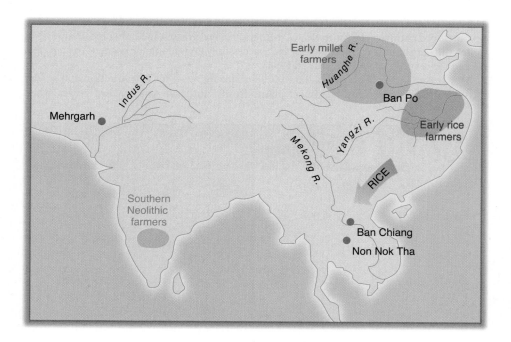

taro   Species of tropical plant with an edible starchy root.

that became the basis for later urban development in the Indus Valley. Other planned settlements boasting multiroom mud-brick dwellings and granaries soon appeared in the region, supported by a productive agriculture and bustling trade in copper, turquoise, shells, and cotton.

Archaeologists know much less about the origins of agriculture in South India. Recent archaeobotanical analyses of samples taken from Southern Neolithic or Ash Mound Tradition sites in Karnataka and Andhra Pradesh suggest that the earliest agriculture in these regions dates between 5,000 and 4,000 ya and was based on several native domesticated species, principally two lentils (horsegram and mung bean) and two species of millet (browntop millet and bristly foxtail grass), along with nonnative crops including wheat and barley (Fuller et al., 2004). The high frequencies of native domesticates in these samples lend support to Vavilov's (1992) identification of India as a possible independent center of domestication.

China Far to the east, village farmers of the Peiligang culture in northern China's central Yellow River basin were already cultivating local varieties of millet by perhaps 9,000 ya (Chang, 1986; Barnes, 1992). River terrace deposits of deep **loess** soil ensured large yields and undoubtedly contributed to the growth of populous settlements during this and the next Yangshao farming period around 2,000 years later (7,000 ya). Millet was a staple of both humans and their domesticated animals, which included pigs, chickens, and dogs; foraging continued to provide wild plants, fish, and animals. Wines and other fermented beverages, which have a long history in Chinese ceremonies, ritual feasting, and everyday life, were made from millet, rice, fruit, and other plant products as much as 9,000 ya (McGovern, 2004). At the site of Ban Po, more than 100 pit houses centered on a plaza and its communal house (see Fig. 14–10). Cemeteries and pottery kilns typically were located near the residential parts of Yangshao villages. Jade carving, painted ceramics of tripod form, silkworm cultivation, and elite burials anticipated some of the hallmarks of the later Neolithic, or Longshan, period beginning 4,700 ya.

In warmer and wetter central and southern China, rice agriculture supported substantial permanent villages, especially along the Yangtze River. Researchers now believe that food collectors were gathering this productive grain in southern China more than 11,000 ya and that cultivators were growing it in the Yangtze delta by 8,500 ya (Normille, 1997; Crawford and Shen, 1998). Farmers introduced rice into Southeast Asia over the next several thousand years, bringing settled village life and domesticated cattle, pigs, and dogs to locations such as Ban Chiang and Non Nok Tha. High yields and the varied conditions under which rice could be grown made it the basis for sustained population growth in many parts of this region (Higham and Lu, 1998; Kharakwal et al., 2004).

loess (luss) Fine-grained soil composed of glacially pulverized rock, deposited by the wind.

AT A GLANCE	Important Asian Sites and Regions	
Site	**Dates (ya)**	**Comments**
Mehrgarh (Pakistan)	8,000–6,000	Early Neolithic community in South Asia that depended on domesticated plants and animals; represents a transition from seminomadic herding to sedentary villages and towns
Southern Neolithic, or Ash Mound (India)	5,000–4,000	Early evidence of South Indian agriculture based on native crops of lentils and millet, plus introduced domesticates such as wheat and barley
Peiligang Culture (China)	c. 9,000	Early Yellow River basin farmers who cultivated local millet varieties
Ban Po (or Banpo) (China)	c. 7,000–6,000	Yangshao period (Neolithic) site near Xi'an, northern China; extensive excavations have exposed about 100 houses that formed a sedentary community

EUROPE

Farmers in southeastern Europe already were tilling the Balkan Peninsula by about 9,000 ya at such sites as Argissa and Franchthi Cave, which are in Greece (Fig. 14–11; Perlès, 2001). Researchers continue to debate whether the spread of farming into southeastern Europe was caused by the movement of people, ideas, or some combination of the two (Colledge et al., 2004). The current consensus, as far as we can speak of one, suggests that the earliest farming cultures of Europe were products of both the spread of farmers and cultural diffusion from the Near East. This view accounts for the seemingly sudden appearance of fully domesticated sheep, goats, wheat, and barley in southeastern Europe, along with a host of specific Near Eastern cultural traits, including structured settlements, burial practices, clay figurines, painted pottery, and specific flaked stone forms (Tringham, 1971). Cultivated cereals and domesticated animals were in use from Turkey to Iraq several millennia earlier than in Europe, and compact clusters of houses were typical features of Near Eastern agricultural communities long before similar settlements showed up in southeastern Europe alongside the other traits associated with early farming. In short, many southeastern European cultural elements can be interpreted as extensions of Near Eastern Neolithic culture.

Neolithic lifeways transformed other parts of Europe somewhat later than in the Balkans, and the source of these changes has also generated debate. Beginning around 7,000 ya, farming village sites littered with linear-decorated pottery, or **Bandkeramik** (Fig. 14–12), appeared across central and (still later) northern regions of the continent (Bogucki, 1988). Bandkeramik culture farmers sought deep, well-drained **alluvial** and loess soils located along the Danube, the Rhine, and their tributaries. There they cultivated cereals and legumes, raised cattle and pigs, and collected wild hazelnuts (Whittle, 1985; Howell, 1987). Their settlements consisted of sturdy timber-framed structures averaging 100 feet long, with some up to 150 feet. These longhouses sheltered extended families and possibly served as barns for storing harvested crops or for harboring animals. Wooden fences barred livestock from planted fields during the growing season and then, following the harvest, confined them in the field so that their manure could restore soil nutrients. The fertility of loess soils could be maintained for relatively long periods with simple manuring and crop rotation, and fixed-plot farming on rich alluvium could sustain permanent settlements for up to 500 years (Whittle, 1985; Howell, 1987).

In Britain, archaeologists have tried to view Neolithic ideology and subsistence as somewhat independent phenomena and explain the transition to agriculture in largely ideologi-

FIGURE 14–11
Early Neolithic Sites of Europe.

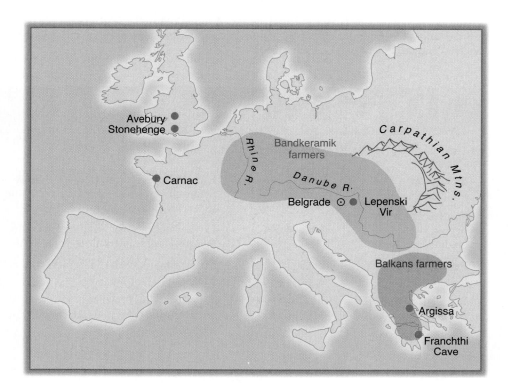

Bandkeramik   Literally, "lined pottery"; refers to a Neolithic ceramic ware widely encountered in central Europe and to the culture that produced it.

alluvial   Deposited by streams, usually during flood stages.

AT A GLANCE	Important European Sites and Regions	
Site	**Dates (ya)**	**Comments**
Argissa and **Franchthi Cave** (Greece)	9,000	Early Neolithic farming settlements in Greece
Bandkeramik Culture (central Europe)	c. 7,000	Archaeological culture that contains the earliest Neolithic farming communities in central Europe

FIGURE **14–12**
Bandkeramik vessel from Motzenstein, near Wattendorf, Germany.

cal terms (e.g., Thomas, 1988; Edmonds, 1999). In this view, the fundamental shift in the subsistence economy from foraging to food production *followed* rather than preceded the kinds of ideological changes that archaeologists see reflected in Neolithic material culture and monuments. If supported by data, this argument would have considerable implications for our general understanding of the Neolithic, because it would explain the development of the British Neolithic as resulting more from cultural than natural factors. Regrettably, data for the Mesolithic-Neolithic transition in Britain, Ireland, and southern Scandinavia support the possibly less-surprising inference that, while the transition to the Neolithic was rapid and probably traumatic, it was not primarily driven by ideological changes (Rowley-Conwy, 2004).

New World Farmers

While Old World Neolithic cultures generally relied on agricultural practices that linked domesticated cereal grasses together with herd animals, the farmers of the Americas focused almost exclusively on plant resources. Most of these plants had very limited ranges, but one important cereal grass—maize, or corn—came to dominate prehistoric Native American agriculture nearly everywhere it could be grown (Fig. 14–13).

Cereal grasses suitable for domestication were abundant on several continents, but the people of the Old World brought more of those species under control. Except for maize, whose wild ancestor may at first have been used in a different way, human cultural behavior in the New World did not induce the same genetic transformations in American grasses as it had in the Old World.

NEW WORLD DOMESTICATES

Considered together, the products of New World farmers make up a remarkable catalog of familiar plants. Besides maize, the list includes important staple foods like white potatoes, sweet potatoes, yams, manioc, many varieties of beans, peanuts, sunflowers, and **quinoa** (*Chenopodium* sp.). Nearly as important, but not staples, are domesticated vegetables and fruits including sweet peppers, chili peppers, tomatoes, squashes, and pumpkins, along with pineapples, papayas, avocados, guavas, and passion fruit. Vanilla and chocolate came from American tree beans. Tobacco, coca, and peyote were major stimulants, and a host of other American plant domesticates had medicinal, utilitarian, or ornamental uses long before the arrival of the Europeans. The principal New World domesticates were developed in several locations in Mexico and in South America, but the use of a few of these plants eventually spread well beyond those regional centers of domestication.

Aside from the dog, which probably accompanied the first humans into the New World, domesticated animals had a relatively minor role in the Americas, as we noted earlier (see p. 347). The llama and alpaca, long-haired relatives of the camel found in highland South America, were the only large domesticated species (Kent, 1987). Other domesticates—the guinea pig (raised for its meat, not as a pet) and Muscovy duck in western South America, turkeys in Mexico—were small in size and not very important beyond their localized distribution areas.

FIGURE **14–13**
A sample of modern maize diversity. Maize benefits from a very large gene pool, which was by no means ignored by early Native American farmers.

quinoa (keen-wah´) Seed-bearing member of the genus *Chenopodium*, cultivated by early Peruvians.

MEXICO

Of the more than 100 plant species fully domesticated by Native Americans, maize (a grass), beans (legumes), and squashes (cucurbits) ultimately attained the widest prehistoric significance for food purposes. Ancient use of this important set of crops has been documented in the states of **Oaxaca** and **Tamaulipas**, and especially in the Tehuacán Valley of Puebla, southeast of Mexico City. In the 1960s, archaeologist Richard MacNeish led an exemplary interdisciplinary study in this arid highland valley, where archaeology, botany, and paleo-ecology shed light on early phases of New World agriculture (Byers, 1967; MacNeish et al., 1972; MacNeish 1978).

The Tehuacán archaeological sites are especially important not because they could be a center of New World plant domestication, but because MacNeish's research yielded an excellent stratigraphic record of early human settlements in this dry valley. The early maize cobs and kernels excavated from Tehuacán sites represent an intermediate variety of maize that had developed elsewhere. In fact, the Tehuacán sites lie somewhat beyond the natural range of the variety of wild grass, **teosinte** (*Zea* sp.), that most archaeobotanists consider ancestral to maize (Beadle, 1980; Benz and Iltis, 1990; Piperno and Pearsall, 1998). Maize probably originated somewhere in the humid lowlands of southern or western Mexico. For example, researchers who analyzed soil cores pulled from the site of San Andrés, in the Gulf Coast state of Tabasco, recovered maize pollen dated to 7,100 ya (Pope et al., 2001) in contexts that suggest farmers were cultivating fields in the lowland rain forest more than a millennium before the earliest evidence of maize in the Mexican highlands.

Teosinte, which bears a few hard seed kernels on tiny "spikelets" growing from its multiple stalks, was probably just one of many wild plants that attracted local food collectors. Its young, green seeds were sweet and edible, as were the tender stems; mature seeds could either be ground or "popped" with heat and eaten. To promote teosinte, people may have scattered its seeds, transplanted young stalks to favorable locations, or reduced competition from other less-desirable plants by burning or weeding. Doing so may have inadvertently altered the genetic makeup of the plants by allowing them to cross-pollinate with other varieties.

DNA studies suggest that very few genetic loci control the features that distinguish teosinte from domestic maize (Doebley, 1994). Mutation of teosinte produced a variant having softer, naked kernels arranged around a spike or cob and encased in a single papery husk. Further artificial (human-induced) selection favored these heritable genetic changes, which became "fixed" when people carried the new varieties beyond teosinte's natural range, possibly to Tehuacán. So, in this way, New World farmers produced the first in a series of domesticated forms of maize, a cultigen having much larger, more numerous, and more easily collected and processed kernels; the plant also became dependent on human assistance for detaching and dispersing its seeds. Today's many varieties of maize make it one of the world's primary staples (see Fig. 14–13).

Other plants were coming under cultivation in southern Mexico around the same time, including several kinds of beans, squashes, gourds, chili peppers, avocados, and cactus fruit (Flannery, 1986; Smith, 1997). At least some of these plants also originated in the lowlands at some earlier time and at a considerable distance from their first recognized use at Tehuacán (Piperno and Pearsall, 1998). For example, domesticated seeds of pumpkin-like squashes excavated at Guilá Naquitz cave in Oaxaca proved to be nearly 10,000 years old.

Modern nutritionists recognize that maize and beans contain complementary amino acids that, when eaten together, form a "complete" protein that can be synthesized effectively by the body, thereby reducing the nutritional need for meat. Eating only one or the other type of seed doesn't have this beneficial effect. In any case, these two American plants, in tandem, became more nutritionally important than others and may have encouraged some groups to take further steps toward full agriculture.

How quickly did people in places like Tehuacán come to rely on food production? Based on the archaeobotanical fragments preserved in the excavated caves, MacNeish concluded (1964, 1967) that even with the availability of domesticated maize, beans, and other plants, agricultural products only gradually came to contribute even one-third of the diet. By getting involved in horticulture, these food collectors at first probably reaped no significant increases in *productivity*. Still, they may have benefited from greater *predictability* by using the stored seeds or dried flesh of domesticates as nutrition sources in leaner times (Wills, 1989).

Oaxaca   (wah-ha´-kah) A southern Mexican state bordering the Pacific Ocean.

Tamaulipas   (tah-mah-leep´-ahs) A Mexican state located on the Gulf Coast south of Texas.

teosinte   (taeo-sin´-tae) A native grass of southern Mexico, believed to be ancestral to maize.

AT A GLANCE   Important Mexican and South American Sites and Regions

Site	Dates (ya)	Comments
Tehuacán Valley (Mexico)	12,000–historic times	Valley in the state of Puebla, Mexico, that was the focus of a major 1960s archaeological field investigation of the origins of agriculture; project results include an excellent stratigraphic sequence of excavated early sites
San Andrés (Mexico)	7,100	Soil cores extracted from this site yielded maize pollen, which suggests that lowland farmers were cultivating fields in the rain forest more than 1,000 years before maize evidence is known from the highlands of Mexico
Guilá Naquitz (Mexico)	10,200–9,200	Small cave in Oaxaca occupied by 4–6 persons; early dated contexts for pumpkin-like squashes and maize cobs
Guitarrero Cave (Peru)	11,500–10,700?	Early evidence of cultivated plants in Andean South America
Paloma (Peru)	7,900–5,000	Coastal preceramic village mostly dependent on marine resources; planting some crops, such as bottle gourds, squashes, and beans

The tiny maize cobs from Tehuacán, recently submitted to an improved ^{14}C technique, yield dates of only 4,700–4,500 ya, much later than the 7,000 years at first indicated by standard carbon dating (Fritz, 1994). Currently, the oldest-known maize cobs date to about 6,250 ya and are from Guilá Naquitz Cave in Oaxaca.

SOUTH AMERICA

Research into the history of domestication and agriculture in South America is in progress, with several major issues at question. First, what were the relative roles of marine resources and agricultural products throughout prehistory on the continent's west coast? Second, to what extent did Mexican crops, particularly maize, contribute to South American agriculture? Finally, what was the nature of Amazonian agriculture in eastern South America?

Sites in southwestern Ecuador have yielded cucurbit (squash and gourd) phytoliths that date to 12,000–10,000 ya. Their large size suggests they're from domesticated plants; if this is true, it means that the beginnings of food production in lowland South America began about the same time, if not earlier, than in Mesoamerica (Piperno and Stothert, 2003).

Sediment cores and other geomorphological evidence indicate that the periodic climatic phenomenon known as **El Niño** became established between about 7,000 and 5,000 ya in the Pacific (Sandweiss et al., 1996). El Niño events are triggered when a persistent trough of atmospheric low pressure forces warm equatorial waters southward along South America's west coast, partially displacing the northward flow of deep cold currents. El Niño typically disrupts the maritime food chain and dramatically disturbs precipitation patterns over land, bringing excess rainfall and flooding to some areas, drought to others. El Niño returns every four years or so, on average, and some episodes are more severe or last longer than others.

Early farming in coastal Peru seems somewhat related to the El Niño pattern (Piperno and Pearsall, 1998). At Paloma (Chilca), a short distance south of present-day Lima, summer fishing expeditions had extended into year-round reliance on large and small fish species, shellfish, sea mammals, turtles, and sea birds. Midden contents, analyses of coprolites, and high strontium levels in human skeletons confirm the nearly exclusive role of sea resources by 5,000 ya (Moseley, 1992). Then the fishers began experimenting with nonlocal plant crops, they used bottle gourds for carrying water and ate a few kinds of squashes and beans. By about 4,500 ya, they had taken up small-scale horticulture in nearby river valleys, growing cotton for nets and cloth and, significantly, adding at least 10 more edible plants to supplement their predominantly seafood diet. While they would maintain their basic maritime focus for centuries to come, coastal Peruvians may have decided that a greater variety of foods would help to minimize the periodic shortfalls in sea resources that they could expect with most El Niño events every few years.

El Niño Periodic climatic instability, related to temporary warming of Pacific Ocean waters, which may influence storm patterns and precipitation for several years.

FIGURE 14–14
Early farming in the Americas.

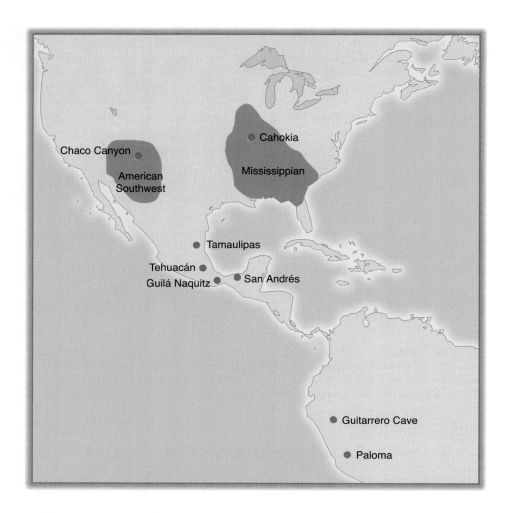

The intercontinental dispersal or exchange of American cultigens is a topic of active archaeobotanical research and debate (Smith, 1995; Piperno and Pearsall, 1998). Maize may have reached coastal South America not long after being domesticated in southern Mexico (Fig. 14–14). Preserved botanical elements, maize motifs on pottery, and even the impression of a kernel on a vessel, as well as an increase in grinding stones and human dental caries, attest to the early presence of maize in this region. Maize eventually became a significant food source for all the native cultures of western South America. Sixteenth-century Spanish chroniclers noted that many different varieties of maize accommodated Peru's demanding climatic and topographical diversity from sea level to 6,500 ft, with potatoes taking over at higher elevations. Each of these varieties, developed through careful selection and hybridization, probably derived from a common ancestral form of Mexican maize.

Plant cultivation had gotten under way in a few highland areas of South America before 8,500 ya. Nonfood species useful for fiber, containers, tool shafts, bedding, and medicines were tended even more often than edible plants around Guitarrero Cave in the Andes Mountains (Lynch, 1980). Native tree fruits, broad lima beans, small-seeded quinoa, and several starchy tubers were among the local food crops grown there (Lynch, 1980, 1983). One of these ancient root crops was the white potato, and when eventually adopted into Old World agriculture and cuisine, it became today's familiar baked potato, Dutch *frites met*, and Indian *alu masala*.

Other native South American cultigens were developed in the tropical forests on the eastern slopes of the Andes or in the humid Amazon basin to the east. Roots of manioc shrubs and sweet potatoes became the dietary staples in the eastern lowlands, supplying abundant carbohydrate energy, but little else. Peanuts added some protein and fats to the starchy diet, but fish and insects remained essential food resources for most of the natives of Amazonia, since their small gardens alone generally couldn't sustain them entirely.

SOUTHWESTERN UNITED STATES

Maize, beans, and squash seeds up to 3,000 years old are preserved on several Archaic sites in the southwestern United States (Simmons, 1986; Tagg, 1996). Introduced to the region possibly much earlier by farmers expanding northward in search of suitable planting areas, these domesticates came under increasing selection pressure as societies ever farther from the southern Mexican source area adopted them. Climatic conditions associated with higher latitudes and elevations shortened the growing season for these Mexican imports and thus slowed or limited agricultural expansion in some regions.

The maize-beans-squash complex gradually gained precedence over hunting and gathering in the American Southwest. Between 2,300 and 1,300 ya, reliance on these domesticated products promoted increased population density and overall cultural elaboration, resulting in the emergence of several distinctive prehistoric cultural traditions in the Southwest (Fig. 14–15). Archaeologists distinguish each of these regional traditions based on such features as pottery styles, architecture, religious ideas, and sociopolitical organization (Plog, 1997).

The **Hohokam** of southern Arizona were growing both food and cotton by 1,500 ya and possibly much earlier, irrigating their gardens through an extensive system of hand-dug channels that conveyed water from the Gila River or its tributaries. By around 1,000 ya, architecture and artifacts on large Hohokam sites, such as Las Colinas and Snaketown, near Phoenix, reveal links to Mexican centers of domestication and culture. They include ball courts and platform mounds as well as copper bells, parrot feathers, and other Mesoamerican products (Haury, 1976). The Hohokam crafted human figurines and shell and turquoise ornaments in sufficient quantities for trade (Crown, 1991). The Casas Grandes district of northern Chihuahua, Mexico, may have served as a major exchange corridor between Mesoamerica and the Southwest (DiPeso, 1974). But whether the Hohokam maintained direct contact with

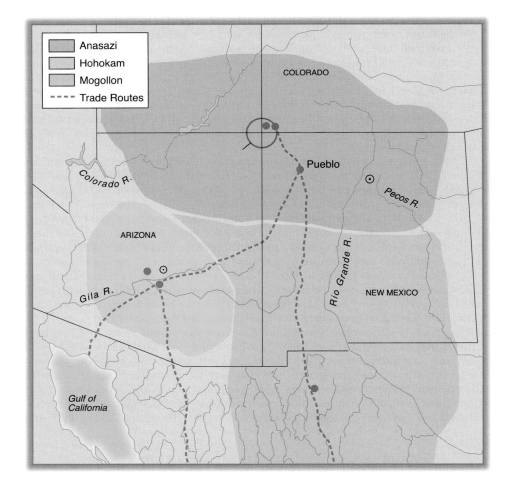

FIGURE 14–15
Village farming cultures of the American Southwest, showing trade routes (red) and sites mentioned in the text.

Hohokam (ho-ho-kahm´) Prehistoric farming culture of southern Arizona.

U.S. National Park Service

FIGURE 14–16
Pueblo Bonito is the largest prehistoric structure in Chaco Canyon National Historic Park, New Mexico. Its 650 rooms cover nearly two acres.

William Turnbaugh

FIGURE 14–17
Ruins of Anasazi rooms and kivas at Pueblo Bonito, Chaco Canyon, New Mexico.

Mogollon (mo-go-yohn´) Prehistoric village culture of northern Mexico and southern Arizona/New Mexico.

Anasazi (an-ah-saw´-zee) Ancient culture of the southwestern United States, associated with preserved cliff dwellings and masonry pueblo sites.

pueblos Spanish for "town," referring to multiroom residence structures built by village farmers in the American Southwest; also refers collectively to the several cultures that built and lived in such villages.

kivas Underground chambers or rooms used for gatherings and ceremonies by pueblo dwellers.

trace-element analysis A chemical technique for measuring the incidence of microminerals, or trace elements, in rocks; applied by archaeologists to identify the source areas of rocks used as raw materials by humans.

Mexican civilizations or simply participated in the diffusion of ideas and products passed along trade routes is a matter for debate.

The **Mogollon**, whose prehistoric culture straddled southern New Mexico and Arizona, lived in pit houses until about A.D. 1000. Around that time, they began constructing above-ground room blocks and—in imitation of their northern neighbors—creating boldly painted black-on-white pottery. Archaeological traces of the Mogollon faded a century or more before Europeans arrived in the mid-1500s, possibly as its people drifted southward into Mexico.

In the Four Corners region to the north, prehistoric farmers known to archaeologists as the **Anasazi** built impressive prehistoric masonry villages and towns, called **pueblos**, beginning around A.D. 900. With their scale, picturesque settings, and excellent preservation, some Anasazi sites—including Chaco Canyon, New Mexico, and the so-called cliff dwellings of Mesa Verde, Colorado—are among the most famous archaeological locations in the United States. Anasazi towns consisted of multiroom, multistory residential and storage structures and usually included underground ceremonial chambers, called **kivas**. Their compact sites were situated with good access to the limited agricultural lands and scarce water supply of this high and arid region.

Chaco Canyon, with a dozen large pueblos, served as a trade and religious center connected by nearly 1,000 miles of radiating foot roads to as many as 80 far-flung villages (Judge, 1984; Wicklein, 1994). Pueblo Bonito (Figs. 14–16 and 14–17), the primary town of Chaco Canyon, was a multistory, D-shaped building of some 600 rooms, built in stages between A.D. 900 and 1125. Its sandstone walls incorporated some 200,000 wooden beams and rafters carried from distant mountains, making Pueblo Bonito the largest building in America until the first modern skyscrapers were built just a century ago. Its many rooms could have held 2,000 people or more, but it seems they were used only intermittently, perhaps as temporary quarters, as workshops, or for storage (Sebastian, 1992; Wicklein, 1994). Huge kivas accommodated participants and observers at major ceremonies. **Trace-element analysis** indicates that turquoise mined in the vicinity of present-day Santa Fe was cut into beads and carvings at Chaco Canyon before being sent on toward Mexico (Harbottle and Weigand, 1992).

The rise of the Chaco town sites and related villages was probably stimulated by a brief period of increased rainfall and sustained by social factors such as political or religious ideology, trade, and internal strife. A growing body of evidence also points to Chaco-era warfare and terrorism among the Anasazi, extending even to cannibalism. Christy Turner (of Arizona State University) and others recognize patterns of cut marks, deliberate breakage, burning, and "pot polish"* on victims' bones from dozens of sites where people met a violent death and may have been cooked and eaten (White, 1992; Turner and Turner, 1999). And

---

*Angular surfaces of bones (presumably attached to meat) cooked in an earthenware pot can develop a polish from abrading against the wall of the vessel (Turner and Turner, 1999); hence the term "pot polish."

William Turnbaugh

FIGURE 14–18

Cliff Palace was the largest of the pueblos built by Anasazi farmers living at Mesa Verde, Colorado, about 800 ya.

recent biochemical analyses of residues in cooking vessels and a human coprolite recovered from a feature in a destroyed house at Cowboy Wash, Colorado, identified traces of human myoglobin from heart or muscle tissue (Marlar and Marlar, 2000), which could only have entered the digestive system by consuming human flesh. In accounting for the violence, different researchers have cited starvation, ritual executions, or the actions of a Mexican warrior cult (Kantner, 1999). Beginning in the mid-1100s, these disturbing activities declined as the people abandoned Chaco and, eventually, most of the region's other large pueblos.

By then, shifting precipitation patterns associated with a general warming period were leaving marginal zones of the Southwest, especially the Colorado Plateau, without adequate rainfall to grow maize (Cordell, 1998). As the drought worsened through the late 1200s, Anasazi townspeople persisted in a few places like Mesa Verde (Fig. 14–18), where they built

AT A GLANCE   Important North American Sites and Regions

Site	Dates (ya)	Comments
Las Colinas and **Snaketown** (Arizona)	1,000	Hohokam sites in the American Southwest that show ties to Mexican centers of domestication and culture
Chaco Canyon (New Mexico)	1,150–750	Region that contains several important Anasazi sites, many of which are characterized by monumental public and ceremonial architecture; now part of the Chaco Culture National Historical Park
Pueblo Bonito (New Mexico)	1050–825	This multistory building comprised approximately 600 rooms and was the primary town of Chaco Canyon
Cowboy Wash (Colorado)	c. 800	Recent excavations at this small village in the Four Corners region revealed possible evidence of cannibalism in human coprolites (preserved feces).
Mesa Verde (Colorado)	1,400–700	Anasazi sites, most widely known for their well-preserved "cliff dwellings"; forms Mesa Verde National Park
Cahokia (Illinois)	1,200–600	Large Mississippian town in the American Bottom region of west-central Illinois; Monks Mound is the largest prehistoric earthwork in the United States and Canada

their communities into easily defended niches in the steep cliffs and tilled their fields on the canyon rim by day. By A.D. 1300, even Mesa Verde stood empty; the Anasazi of the Four Corners had dispersed toward the south and southeast to become the people known today as Hopi, Zuni, and the Rio Grande Puebloans.

EASTERN NORTH AMERICA

In eastern North America, aboriginal peoples were developing an independent center of domestication and cultivation. Small gourds, apparently native to the region and not derived from Mesoamerican species, were widely cultivated by Archaic hunter-gatherers more than 5,000 ya, probably for use as containers and fishing-net floats rather than food (Fritz, 1999). Several other local plants—marsh elder or sumpweed, sunflower, and goosefoot (*Chenopodium* sp.)—are associated with ancient campsites and shell heaps along major river floodplains, where about 3,000 ya people maintained "incidental gardens" of plants selected to complement rather than replace foraging activities (Smith, 1985, 1989, 1995). In the next millennium, several more native species were added to the inventory: knotweed, maygrass, and little barley. Stone agricultural hoes began to appear on sites in the Illinois River Valley at about the same time (Odell, 1998).

It wasn't easy to harvest and process these weedy, small-seeded species, so they probably weren't much more than supplements to a diet of wild foods. Still, the river valleys of the Southeast and the Midwest as well as the rich forests covering much of the Northeast clearly supported large, successful communities even without maize agriculture. For example, the widespread practice of mound building and associated death and burial rituals began long before any reliance on maize. As we've seen, Late Archaic hunter-gatherers constructed mounds that, like those at Poverty Point, Louisiana (see Chapter 13), were considerably more than mere stacks of dirt.

Elaborate rituals centering on earthmound architecture and burial mounds were found throughout much of the midcontinent during the Middle Woodland period (ca. 2200–1600 ya). Middle Woodland **Hopewell** villagers participated in exchanges of ritual goods and ideological concepts, as shown in their elaborate burials and grave offerings (Fig. 14–19). It seems that not all the burial mounds were used in the same way. Some mounds cover the remains of individuals whose treatment in death suggests that they were prominent members of their communities; others cover the remains of more egalitarian facilities used for ritually processing the dead and may have been open to all members of a lineage or community.

It's not until after 1,200 ya in the Southeast and around 800 ya in the Northeast that we begin to see archaeological evidence of a widespread economic commitment to agriculture,

FIGURE 14–19

Cross section and floor of a 2,000-year-old Hopewell burial mound in Ohio. Cremated human bones and offerings deposited in a mica-lined burial chamber were covered with several layers of earth.

Hopewell   A Middle Woodland archaeological culture centered in the Midwest, but influencing a much wider region through trade and shared bodies of ritual.

possibly brought about by new varieties of maize and the introduction of domesticated beans (Smith, 1992; Hart and Scarry, 1999). Even then, wild nuts, seeds, fish, and game were staples in the diets of many groups. In the broad river valleys of the Southeast, maize farming was the economic mainstay of **Mississippian** chiefdoms (Fig. 14–20). Mississippian elites relied on elaborate rituals and displays of valued symbols to enhance their privileged positions. Populations and ceremonial centers throughout the region were linked by exchanges of symbolic copper, shell, pottery, and stone items, as well as a common focus on the construction of towns centered on impressive earthen-mound groups that flanked public spaces or plazas (Lewis and Stout, 1998; Emerson and Lewis, 2000). Most buildings that flanked the plazas were erected on substructure or platform mounds. Some of these buildings were dwellings; others were **charnel houses** and other community structures. The houses and workplaces of the town's rank and file clustered around these mound-and-plaza complexes.

The Mississippian site of Cahokia, located below the junction of the Missouri and Mississippi rivers near St. Louis, once boasted some 120 mounds (Milner, 1998; Pauketat and Wright, 2004). The primary earthwork was Monks Mound (Fig. 14–21), as long as three football fields and as high as a six-story building—the largest prehistoric structure north of Mexico. Cahokia's homes and garden plots spread over 6 square miles beyond the log stockade that enclosed the central mounds and elite living area (Fig. 14–22). Fields of maize, squash, and pumpkins extending along the river floodplain provided the harvest sheltered in many storage pits and granaries (Iseminger, 1996).

Among other New World societies, farming hadn't gained much importance even by the time Europeans were arriving with their own ways of life and their Old World domesticates (Brown, 1994). In fact, throughout much of the far West, the far North, and most of South America, hunting, fishing, and gathering were still the principal ways of making a living (Fig. 14–23). These lifeways persisted in part because the more productive American domesticates, those native to warm temperate zones, couldn't be introduced and maintained in other geographical settings without sustained effort. Even so, it wasn't always a question of whether farming was possible; it was often a matter of choice. Maize was far from an ideal crop, even where it could be grown most readily. Old World domesticated cereal grasses, including wheat, barley, oats, rye, millet, and rice, grew in dense stands that farmers could harvest readily with a sickle and clean by threshing and winnowing. Maize, the primary New World cereal grass, required more space per plant and more moisture during its long growing season, and it was much harder to harvest and process by hand.

FIGURE 14–20
Flint hoe blade used by Mississippian farmers.

FIGURE 14–21
Monks Mound at Cahokia Mounds State Historic Site, near Collinsville, Illinois. Built in late prehistoric times, it is about 1,000 feet long and 100 feet high.

Mississippian Late prehistoric chiefdoms of the southeastern United States and southern Midwest between roughly 1,100 and 300 ya.

charnel house A building that holds the bones or bodies of the dead.

FIGURE **14–22**

Reconstructed Mississippian village huts at Angel Mounds State Historic Site, near Evansville, Indiana.

Barry Lewis

Julian H. Steward, ed. *Handbook of South American Indians*, Vol. 1, plate 36. Washington, DC: U.S. Government Printing Office.

FIGURE **14–23**

Yahgan hunter of Cape Horn, South America, late nineteenth century.

What's more, these agricultural products could seldom beat the nutritional value of a mixed diet obtained through foraging. Maize itself is deficient in lysine (an amino acid) and niacin and contains a chemical that may promote iron-deficiency anemia. Similarly, in the Amazon basin in South America, the peoples who domesticated manioc, sweet potatoes, and other starchy root crops before 1,500 ya found that these foods supplied bulk and carbohydrates, but little protein—a deficiency the people of the Amazon overcame by continuing to rely on hunting, fishing, and gathering.

Biocultural Consequences of Food Production

Domestication and agriculture were the driving forces of the Neolithic Revolution, but we've seen that the impact of Neolithic lifeways went far beyond subsistence. Looking back, we can see that humans have reaped tremendous benefits and paid significant costs for the spread of food production; opinions differ regarding which is greater. One writer bluntly refers to agriculture as "the worst mistake in the history of the human race" (Diamond, 1987). Another, an ecologist who obviously looks at the evidence from a very different perspective, calls it the "most momentous event in the history of life" (Colinvaux, 1979). In the following sections we'll examine some of the reasoning behind such statements.

POPULATION DENSITY AND PERMANENT SETTLEMENTS

Some researchers theorize that population growth initiated the agricultural response; others see it happening the other way around. But there's no question that population size and density both tended to increase as farming activities produced larger and more predictable yields. People clustered into permanent villages and towns surrounded by fields and pastures. Sedentary living permitted closer birth spacing, since mothers no longer carried infants from site to site, and the availability of soft cereals for infant food allowed for earlier weaning. Potentially, therefore, a woman might bear more children. It's not surprising that even very early Neolithic settlements—such as Jericho, in the Jordan River valley, and Çatalhöyük, in Turkey—quickly reached considerable size. Today's world population, sustained largely by the

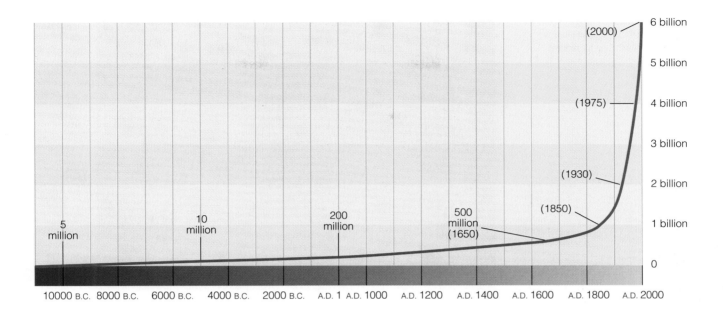

10000 B.C. 8000 B.C. 6000 B.C. 4000 B.C. 2000 B.C. A.D. 1 A.D. 1000 A.D. 1200 A.D. 1400 A.D. 1600 A.D. 1800 A.D. 2000

same set of Neolithic domesticates, has attained 6 billion people and shows no signs of slowing (Fig. 14–24). Such an extraordinary growth in human population would have been impossible without agriculture.

FIGURE **14–24**
World population growth.

TECHNOLOGIES

Changes in material culture accompanied food production and the development of permanent settlements. For example, farmers everywhere soon replaced most of their basketry and skin containers with bulkier but more versatile ceramic vessels. Their pottery (Fig. 14–25) made simmering and boiling more practical, more easily converting grains into digestible foods. They used looms to weave cloth from the wool and plant fibers that replaced wild animal skins; still, where durability was required, as in grinding slabs and axeheads, stone persisted for a time as the material of choice.

The traditional view is that, as harvests increased, some food-producing communities could support and in turn benefit from nonfarmers who engaged in specialized crafts, exchanging the products of their skill for food grown by others. So, for example, the use of copper in the Near East expanded once people could devote the necessary effort to refining and processing the ore into various metal implements and ornaments. While we've learned that it's quite a bit more complicated than that, it's still true that specialization encouraged a proliferation of new inventions that simply wouldn't have been sustainable in communities based solely on hunting and gathering.

FIGURE **14–25**
Prehistoric decorated pottery vessel from Arizona.

Museum of Primitive Art and Culture, Peace Dale, RI, photo by William Turnbaugh

ECONOMIC AND SOCIAL RELATIONS

Now and then, whether intentionally, by chance, or through coercion, farmers had surpluses in the form of stored grain or herds of animals at the end of the year. They could use these products to level out shortages in following seasons. Often, excess production served as a kind of capital, or wealth, that fostered new socioeconomic transactions. Thus, in Mesopotamia, barter and exchange flourished, as did credit, or lending against future productivity. (A need for accurate accounts inspired early writing here in the form of symbols pressed into clay tablets.)

As agricultural techniques and resulting harvests continued to improve, additional segments of the population were relieved of the obligation of producing food and came to fill specialized roles as priests, merchants, crafters, administrators, and the like. A social and economic hierarchy of productive peasants, nonfarming specialists of many kinds, and a tiny but dominant elite emerged in a few Neolithic state societies, or civilizations.

FIGURE 14-26
The Inka terraces, in Peru, required intensive effort to modify mountain land for farming.

Katherine Pomonis

ENVIRONMENTAL CHANGES

Unlike hunter-gatherers, who extracted their livelihood from the available natural resources, Neolithic farmers altered the environment by substituting their own domesticated plants and animals for native species. We aren't implying that all hunter-gatherers had been conservationists; but their numbers were few, their tools simple, and their needs relatively modest. On the other hand, Neolithic plowing, terracing, cutting of forests, draining of wetlands, and animal grazing contributed to severe soil erosion and the decline of many natural species (Fig. 14–26). At the same time, many of these practices encouraged the growth of weeds and created fresh habitats for crop-damaging insect pests and malaria-bearing mosquitoes.

Intensive agriculture depletes soil nutrients, especially potassium. In the lower Tigris-Euphrates Valley, high levels of soluble salts carried by irrigation waters slowly poisoned the fields once farmed by Ubaidians and Sumerians. In North Africa, Neolithic herders allowed their animals to overgraze the fragile Sahara grasslands, furthering the development of the world's largest desert. These early farming practices left many areas so damaged that they remained unproductive for thousands of years until they could begin to be reclaimed with the aid of modern technology. Unfortunately, comparable processes—such as burning forests for grazing lands—continue at an accelerated pace today.

ENVIRONMENTAL DIVERSITY

Some hunter-gatherers selected from hundreds of wild species for food and other purposes as they moved from camp to camp throughout the year. The strategy of most Neolithic societies was different, because they emphasized only a small number of domesticated crops and animal species. Through selective breeding practices, people tried to enhance the traits they valued—thicker wool or body fat, greater milk production, more and larger seeds, and so forth—while strictly limiting random variability. These experiments resulted in genetically similar strains.

Today, the earth's human population still relies primarily on the seeds of just a half-dozen grasses (wheat, barley, oats, rice, millet, maize), several root crops (potatoes, yams, manioc), and a few domesticated fowl and mammals (in addition to fish) for sustenance. Because of their relative genetic similarity, these species are highly susceptible to disease, drought, and pests. Agricultural scientists are trying to prevent potential disaster by reestablishing some genetic diversity in these plants and animals through the controlled introduction of heterogeneous (usually "wild") strains. A few farmers have realized the benefits of multicropping—interspersing different kinds of crops in a single agricultural plot. Combining grains, root crops, fruit trees, herbs, and plants used for fiber or tools mimics the natural species diversity and reduces soil depletion and insect infestation.

SCIENCE AND RELIGION

Prescribed rites, sanctions, and shrines ensured bountiful harvests and other supernatural blessings for Neolithic farmers. Hunter-gatherers certainly did not ignore the supernatural realm, but because of differences in population size and organization, farmers tended to make more impressive, permanent monuments to their beliefs and sometimes gave practitioners the opportunity to engage full-time in religious specialties. In some cultures, sciences such as astronomy, mathematics, and metallurgy developed early because they had diverse ritual and practical applications.

CULTURAL COMPETITION AND CHANGE

Neolithic societies were often on a collision course with their nonfarming neighbors. Expanding agriculturalists displaced hunter-gatherers or even eradicated them altogether because of direct competition for suitable land or due to habitat changes brought on by farming activities. Some food producers involved their nonfarming neighbors in exchange networks, trading surplus products of agriculture, animal husbandry, or new technology for raw materials, wild produce, and even slaves (Gregg, 1988). In time, farmers came to prevail almost everywhere, except in those marginal areas where agriculture or herding was impractical. And even those regions came under siege as modern food-producing and industrialized societies competed for land and other resources in the diminished domains left to hunter-gatherers. Today, few groups survive primarily by hunting and gathering. For others, fishing remains a viable option to farming.

HEALTH CONSEQUENCES

As with other biocultural aspects relating to the development of food production, the effects on human health were a mixed bag of benefits and costs. Working closely with archaeologists, physical anthropologists who study human skeletal remains have been particularly interested in evaluating how patterns of health and disease changed among early agriculturalists as compared to hunter-gatherers. These researchers who specialize in the closely related subfields of paleopathology and bioarchaeology (see Chapter 1, pp. 8–9, 13) have had much to say about this topic (Cohen and Armelagos, 1984; Cohen, 1989; Larsen, 1995; 1997).

It's easy to see why. First, as early agricultural groups became more sedentary and larger in size, they buried their dead in increasingly larger cemeteries than was generally the case for hunter-gatherers. Paleopathologists thus have many more skeletons from agricultural populations to study than they have for the vast majority of hunter-gatherer groups; and with more skeletons to analyze, they obviously have more opportunity to find some individuals with evidence of disease. Secondly, as population density increased among early food producers and people lived more permanently in one place, *infectious disease* became a much more serious factor (see Chapter 4, pp. 87–92).

As you know, infectious diseases can cause epidemics, some small, some catastrophic—for example, the Black Death of the Middle Ages or the influenza epidemic in 1918. They can potentially kill thousands or even millions of people. Because hunter-gatherer populations generally were small and not sedentary, the "reservoir" of human hosts for infectious pathogens (that is, viruses or bacteria) wasn't sufficient to sustain itself in such groups long-term.

Bioarchaeologists also use other skeletal indicators of health, including stature, tooth enamel defects, and bone changes resulting from anemia. Using these health indicators, numerous studies both in the Old World (Cohen and Armelagos, 1984) and the New World (Larsen, 1995; Steckel and Rose, 2002) have shown quite consistent results—that is, with the development of agriculture, health quality for most people declined. It's important to note, however, that a significant health decline didn't occur in all people in any given population nor, on average, in all populations. Still, the *general* trend of declining health has become a major focus of skeletal research in recent years.

Even with greater exposure to disease pathogens, along with other health risks associated with living in denser populations, the health picture for early (and later) farmers wasn't entirely bleak. After all, it's human success (that is, more people) that has also helped infectious pathogens to be more successful. Plus, the lives of hunter-gatherers weren't easy or disease-free by any means. Hunter-gatherers suffered periodic food shortages, traumatic injuries, and certainly some infectious diseases (even if there were no major epidemics). Most notably in new mothers following childbirth, bacterial infections took a heavy toll, and many females died. Likewise, after an injury, such as a cut or a broken bone that penetrated the skin, bacterial infections also killed many people. And, since they were frequently on the move, severely injured or ill members of hunter-gatherer groups didn't have a chance to rest while they healed. Possibly most devastating of all in terms of health impact, hunter-gatherer groups suffered from high infant mortality. It's fair to point out, though, that until quite recently infant mortality was high in all human populations, and it's still high in several parts of the world today. In fact, infant mortality probably wasn't much different for early food producers than it was for hunter-gatherers (Acsadi and Nemeskeri, 1970).

If many new mothers and infants died so often *both* before and after the agricultural transition, then how is it that population size grew among early food producers? The answer is simple: With more predictable food sources, women could wean their children earlier and reduce the amount of time between births. A woman could thus bear more offspring, and this fact alone meant that overall, more children survived to adulthood. For most of hominid history, our ancestors' reproductive capacity wasn't much different from that of our ape cousins. A woman who gave birth every three or four years was probably typical of hominids up to just a few thousand years ago. With food production and the ability to stay in one place, human populations began to expand—a trend that continues today in most of the world.

If it seems paradoxical that average health was declining among food producers at the same time that populations were expanding, that's because it is. As one researcher has commented, "Yet, although humans became physically worse-off in marked respects, they also became more numerous. The agricultural age made possible far denser populations, but less healthy ones than ever before. Historians, anthropologists, and others concerned with this apparent paradox are still exploring its implications in detail" (Curtin, 2002:606).

As we mentioned earlier, probably the greatest new challenge faced by sedentary food producers came from increased risk of infectious disease. One major contributor to heightened disease exposure came from close proximity of humans to domestic animals. Many pathogens—including viruses, bacteria, and intestinal parasites—can be transferred from nonhuman animals to humans. Diseases that can be transmitted to humans by other vertebrates, particularly mammals and birds, are called **zoonoses**. For example, influenza can be transmitted to humans by pigs or poultry.

Early farmers who grew crops and tended herds in ancient Mesopotamia, China, the Indus Valley, and elsewhere in the Old World (but not to the same degree in the New World, where animal domestication was little practiced) faced numerous dangerous health challenges. We noted in Chapter 3 how human cultural modifications with slash-and-burn agriculture produced a more conducive environment for the spread of malaria. Another major human disease likely stimulated by the activities of food producers is tuberculosis.

The origin of tuberculosis in humans isn't completely understood, but we do know that several wild animals harbor a form of the disease; it's seen in bison, moose, elk, deer, and domestic cattle. The tuberculosis variant called *bovine tuberculosis* can be transmitted from the animal host to a human through ingestion of infected meat or milk. Clearly, with the domestication of cattle—which, as we've shown, occurred in the Middle East by 8,000 ya—humans had much greater exposure to bovine tuberculosis, and their exposure increased even more with the development of dairying (Sherratt, 1981). In its later stages, tuberculosis can produce distinctive skeletal changes, especially of the spine (see photo, p. 9). The earliest evidence of such skeletal involvement comes from Italy and is dated to nearly 7,500 ya (Roberts and Buikstra, 2003).

Tuberculosis in humans has evolved over the last six millennia; in fact, today most infected humans carry a related variety of *pulmonary tuberculosis* that can spread from person to person. The relationship of bovine tuberculosis to pulmonary tuberculosis isn't clearly understood, but the pulmonary form may have evolved from the bovine one. What's more, this transformation seems to have occurred only *after* humans became agriculturalists.

Several other significant human diseases are associated with sedentism and increasing population size and density. Measles, for example, has been shown to require a very large population pool—in the thousands—to sustain itself long-term (Cohen, 1989). So, measles can be viewed as a condition that became prevalent only with the emergence of larger urban centers, making it a "disease of civilization." Likewise, cholera is most commonly found in urban contexts, where large numbers of people share a common (and contaminated) water source.

zoonoses (*sing.,* zoonosis) Diseases that can be transmitted to humans from other vertebrates.

LOOKING AT THE BIG PICTURE

In this chapter we've reviewed what may be the most important cultural and ecological transition the human species ever experienced. In those areas where food production was adopted, the ramifications were immediate and transformed human subsistence, technology, society, habitation patterns, relationship with other species, and much more. Eventually, the entire inhabitable portion of the world became involved, and the effects have been momentous. In fact, there's basically nothing recognizable in our cultural world today that would exist without the transformation to food production just a few thousand years ago. Keep in mind that in the larger picture of human prehistory—and even more so, considering the immense span of hominid evolution—this is but a flicker of time.

Some people, even some professional scientists, claim the costs of these changes outweigh the benefits. We've discussed some of the costs, especially relating to overall health, that took a toll on many early farmers. Still, the conclusion that the negatives outweigh the positives is highly debatable and, even more basically, this contention is pointless. There's no going back; the world we live in would be impossible without the remarkable contributions first made possible by the adoption of agriculture. For one thing, without efficient and widespread food production, most of us wouldn't be here at all. The useable part of the planet that could provide resources for hunter-gatherers might be able to sustain a population of 100 million people. But, that's less than 2 percent of the current world's population. What then of the more than 6 billion other human beings? Then too there would be no cities, no art, no educational institutions, no writing, no books—meaning, of course, no textbooks either. Also think of all the further innovations from the last few centuries, from which other extraordinary benefits have come, including for most populations a doubling of average life span, mass transportation, entertainment, diverse and easily obtainable foods, clothing, shelter, and so on.

There's no productive point in taking extreme views regarding what costs our ancestors paid to produce the modern world we have inherited. It would seem a more useful goal to engage in discussing where we choose to go. While the benefits we've been provided are undeniable, our species' remarkable success now is at a point where many people think that continuing down the same road will prove unsustainable.

Summary

In this chapter we've examined the record of plant and animal domestication and the origin of early agricultural societies. Archaeological site excavations, along with refined dating methods and the analytical techniques of archaeobotany and archaeozoology, have yielded a wealth of comparative data on Neolithic cultures in several regions of the globe. Even so, the answers to ultimate questions about how and why domestication and agriculture developed remain elusive.

The invention and widespread adoption of agriculture occurred within the past 12,000 years, during the early to mid-Holocene. This so-called Neolithic Revolution represents a major force in human biocultural evolution. As a species, our biology and our cultural behavior are inextricably linked. For example, many of the cultural activities associated with agriculture have actually stimulated further biological changes, such as the spread of the sickle-cell allele as an adaptive response to malaria, a disease harbored in tropical environments disturbed by farmers (see p. 78).

With the ability to produce food and support larger populations, the pace of human affairs has quickened dramatically in the social, political, and economic realms as well. One consequence of relying on agriculture was a society's basic need for large tracts of productive cropland and adequate water supplies. Maintaining access to these essential resources was critical to a farming culture's survival. Certainly, the primary functions of any Neolithic society, large or small, were securing land and water and supporting the vital agricultural process itself.

In a few areas of the world, the emergence of large-scale, complex societies followed quickly on the heels of the Neolithic Revolution. In the next two chapters we'll consider the development and course of some early civilizations founded on Neolithic food-producing economies in the Old World and in the Americas.

In Table 14–1 you'll find a useful summary of the most important archaeological sites discussed in this chapter.

TABLE 14-1		The Most Significant Archaeological Sites Discussed in This Chapter	
Location	**Site**	**Dates (ya)**	**Comments**
Old World	**Mehrgarh** (Pakistan)	8,000–6,000	Early Neolithic community in South Asia that depended on domesticated plants and animals; represents a transition from seminomadic herding to sedentary villages and towns
	Jericho (West Bank)	<11,000– 3,500	Early permanent and sedentary community in the Levant that began in Natufian times and was occupied throughout the Neolithic
New World	**Las Colinas** and **Snaketown** (Arizona)	1,000	Hohokam sites in the American Southwest that show ties to Mexican centers of domestications and culture
	Chaco Canyon (New Mexico)	1,150–750	Region that contains several important Anasazi sites, many of them characterized by monumental public and ceremonial architecture; now part of the Chaco Culture National Historical Park
	Cahokia (Illinois)	1,200–600	Large Mississippian town in the American Bottom region of west-central Illinois; Monks Mound is the largest prehistoric earthwork in the United States and Canada
	Mesa Verde (Colorado)	1,400–700	Anasazi sites, most widely known for their well-preserved "cliff dwellings"; forms Mesa Verde National Park
	San Andrés (Mexico)	7,100	Soil cores extracted from this site yielded maize pollen, which suggests that lowland farmers were cultivating fields in the rain forest more than 1,000 years before maize evidence is known from the highlands of Mexico
	Paloma (Peru)	7,900–5,000	Coastal preceramic village mostly dependent on marine resources; planting of some crops, such as bottle gourds, squashes, and beans
	Guilá Naquitz (Mexico)	10,200–9,200	Small cave in Oaxaca occupied by 4–6 persons; early dated contexts for pumpkin-like squashes and maize cobs
	Guitarrero Cave (Peru)	11,500–10,700?	Early evidence of cultivated plants in Andean South America
	Tehuacán Valley (Mexico)	12,000–historic times	Valley in the state of Puebla, Mexico, that was the focus of a major 1960s archaeological field investigation of the origins of agriculture; project results include an excellent stratigraphic sequence of excavated early sites

Critical Thinking Questions

1. What are the most important differences between the environmental and cultural approaches to explaining why farming began? Your essay should include mention of the basic assumptions, strengths, and weaknesses of each approach.
2. Based on your reading of this chapter as well as other materials outside of class, what are the three most important consequences, both good and bad, of the shift from foraging to food production for our species? Why are these consequences important? Compare your list with that of your classmates, and discuss the differences.
3. What kinds of evidence from the archaeological record do researchers use as indicators or measures of the extent of plant or animal domestication?

Geomatics: Analyzing Spatial Patterns of the Past

Our biocultural past happened in specific places and times. For researchers to identify and interpret the physical and material evidence of biocultural evolution, they also must first arrange this evidence in the time and space framework in which it occurred. Until recently, this was surprisingly hard to do.

In the section on relative and absolute dating in Chapter 8 (see pp. 177–184), we discussed some of the problems and technological solutions of measuring past time in the archaeological record. Measuring space can be nearly as knotty a problem as that of estimating past time. Although many important spatial data from the archaeological and paleoanthropological record are measured with tape, compass, calipers, and the like, the questions that researchers ask often outstrip the capabilities of such instruments and demand methods capable of simultaneously considering the effects of scores, if not hundreds, of spatial variables. Such questions may draw on data from many disciplines and include such variables as location, elevation, slope, aspect (the direction a slope faces), surface relief, drainage, soil type, ancient ground cover, modern land use, seasonal precipitation patterns, and seasonal wind patterns, to name only a few.

Throughout much of the nineteenth and twentieth centuries, archaeologists and paleoanthropologists had plenty of complex questions that required spatial answers, but they lacked the means to answer all but the simplest ones. For example, they plotted archaeological finds on maps to identify regional patterns of their presence or absence (Fig. 1), and they constructed distribution maps to show how common certain site types are in a region. The drawbacks of these efforts were that first, such maps took a lot of effort to make by hand, and second, they could seldom address more than just a few types of relevant evidence.

Things changed late in the twentieth century, initially with the development of cheap computing power in the 1970s and 1980s, followed by major advances in all aspects of computer performance and capabilities. Although computer software generally lags behind technological developments in hardware, one area that has grown rapidly is software for analyzing spatial data. This "geographic information systems," or GIS, software is specifically designed to analyze spatial problems (DeMers, 2005).

By the mid-1990s, GIS software was widely used in research and industry. Its capabilities continue to be enhanced both by technological advances and by the unstoppable flood of Internet-accessible spatial data. Many fields (including archaeology and physical anthropology) now identify GIS as a key element in the set of dynamic visualization tools for the analysis of spatial data (Knowles, 2002; Wheatley and Gillings, 2002). The emerging field of *geomatics* integrates GIS, global positioning satellite (GPS) technology, computer-assisted design (CAD), remote sensing, data visualization, surveying, 3-D modeling, and other technologies into a new discipline that embraces the science and technology of spatially referenced information.

For an example of the application of geomatics to archaeological research, let's examine how it helps researchers find important, but extraordinarily short-lived sites in glacial environments.

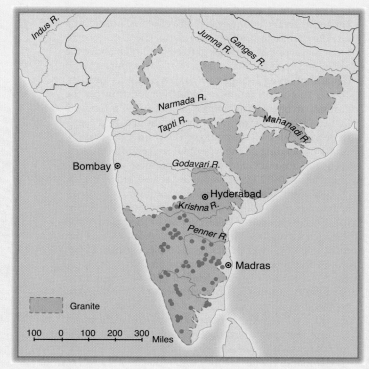

FIGURE 1

A mid-twentieth century archaeological thematic map showing the distribution of megalithic (literally "large stone") burial cists in relation to the presence of granite outcrops in South India.

Early India and Pakistan by Mortimer Wheeler. Copyright © 1959 by Frederick A. Praeger. Reproduced by permission of Greenwood Publishing Group, Inc., Westport, CT.

E. James Dixon and his colleagues at the University of Colorado at Boulder study the archaeology of glaciers and small ice patches, the melting of which has accelerated in recent years due to global warming. Every summer exposes a fresh crop of ancient organic remains such as bows, arrows, bark and wooden containers, human bodies—for example, the Iceman found in the Italian Alps (see Cutting Edge Research on pp. 273–274—clothing, tools, feces, fur, feathers, and so on. The good news is that all of these remains have been preserved for centuries, if not millennia, in the ice. The bad news is that many finds tend to be exceptionally delicate and may decompose or simply get blown away soon after being exposed to the air, wind, and temperature extremes. If they are to study these remains, then archaeologists must be in the right place at the right time. Working in the Wrangell–St. Elias National Park and Preserve of southeastern Alaska, Dixon and his colleagues (2005) constructed a GIS model to ensure that they're always working in the right place. The GIS model predicts where the researchers should focus their field searches for glacial and ice patch organic remains each summer (Fig. 2). And, since the results of each season's fieldwork are used to further refine the GIS model's accuracy, its research value increases over time.

Geomatics: Analyzing Spatial Patterns of the Past

The utility of the glacial and ice patch GIS model is enhanced greatly by the availability of global positioning satellite (GPS) technology and data. The U.S. government maintains 24 satellites in fixed orbit high above the earth, and each satellite continuously transmits a radio signal containing a set pattern of data about its location. To use this information to identify a location on the ground, archaeologists employ handheld GPS receivers that can interpret these radio signals and record the spatial coordinates of the receiver (Garmin Corporation, 2000). Depending on the type of GPS receiver technology used, the accuracy and precision of these coordinates range from 10–12 feet down to less than 1 inch.

GPS technology has become a common part of the archaeologist's tool kit, both for recording locations in the field, as Dixon and his colleagues do in their glacier and ice patch surveys, and to map archaeological sites and features. In the Peruvian Andes, for example, a team of Italian and Peruvian archaeologists depend on GPS to compensate for the relatively poor detail of national maps, most of which are printed at too small a scale (1:100,000) to be archaeologically useful and are often outdated (Capra et al., 2002). GPS enables these researchers to map the major cultural features of archaeological sites, as well as the mountainous terrain upon which they were constructed (Fig. 3).

Geomatics is in its infancy, and its capabilities will continue to grow. It has already demonstrated its worth in archaeological and physical anthropological research as *the* solution to many long-standing concerns about how to analyze multivariate spatial data. It's one area of research in which the future of the past looks very bright indeed.

FIGURE 2

GIS predictive model for glacial and ice patch archaeological site locations in the Wrangell–St. Elias National Park and Preserve, Alaska. Regions depicted in reddish colors are more likely to yield sites than those represented by blues. Purple dots mark GPS points recorded by field surveyors.

From James E. Dixon et al. *American Antiquity*, 70(1), p. 136.

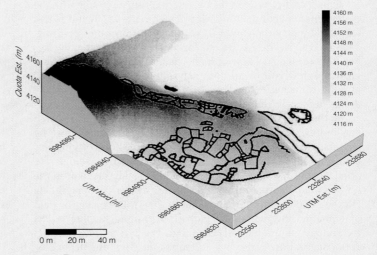

FIGURE 3

The use of GPS technology in the Peruvian Andes enabled archaeologists to construct a digital model of the local terrain, on which they could drape a measured plan of the site of Huacramarca for interpretation.

From A. Capra et al. 2002. *Journal of Cultural Heritage* 3, p. 96.

SOURCES:

Capra, Alessandro, Stefano Gandolfi, Laura Laurencich, Francesco Mancini, Alberto Minelli, Carolina, Orsini, and Aurelio Rodríguez. 2002. "Multidisciplinary Approach for Archeological Survey: Exploring GPS Method in Landscape Archeology Studies." *Journal of Cultural Heritage* 3:93–99.

DeMers, Michael N. 2005. *Fundamentals of Geographic Information Systems.* 3rd ed. Hoboken, NJ: Wiley.

Dixon, E. James, William F. Manley, and Craig M. Lee. 2005. The Emerging Archaeology of Glaciers and Ice Patches: Examples from Alaska's Wrangell–St. Elias National Park and Preserve. *American Antiquity* 70:129–143.

Garmin Corporation. 2000. *GPS Guide for Beginners.* Olathe, KS: Garmin International (http://www.garmin.com/manuals/GPS GuideforBeginners_Manual.pdf).

Knowles, Anne Kelly. 2002. *Past Time, Past Place: GIS for History.* Redlands, CA: ESRI Press.

Wheatley, David, and Mark Gillings. 2002. *Spatial Technology and Archaeology: The Archaeological Applications of GIS.* New York: Taylor & Francis.

CHAPTER

15

The First
Civilizations

FOCUS QUESTIONS
Why did the earliest civilizations develop?

What roles did cities play in these developments? Were cities essential to the emergence of all early civilizations?

Introduction

The ruins of the city of Vijayanagara lie strewn along the banks of the Tungabhadra River in South India (Fig. 15–1). As you walk south from the river, you're seldom out of sight of broken granite pillars and the shattered foundations of palaces, temples, and courtyards in fertile valleys surrounded by hills that look like great jumbles of boulders. Founded in the early fourteenth century and destroyed about two centuries later, Vijayanagara had a fairly short life as cities go, but by all accounts, it was an extraordinary place (Gollings et al., 1991). With a sixteenth-century population estimated at 500,000 (or about two and a half times the estimated population of London in 1600), the city covered roughly 10.5 square miles. It was the capital of a state and the centerpiece of an empire that included other states, both large and small, across South India. Following the defeat of its armies in A.D. 1565, Vijayanagara was destroyed, its buildings burned, blown apart, or pulled down with the aid of elephants; its citizens were scattered, its riches looted. The remnants of the empire limped along for another century or so with a new capital city at Penukonda in modern Andhra Pradesh, but never recovered their former strength (Stein, 1994).

The Vijayanagara ruins are now a UNESCO World Heritage site. Where once there were picturesque buildings, crowded markets, busy city streets, royal pageantry, and the scent of roses, there are now tour buses, shepherds, security guards, thornbushes, and the occasional leopard that snatches puppies for late-night snacks. Vijayanagara lives mostly in stories told to small children in villages across the South about such rulers as Krishnadevaraya and their dynasties, their might, and the great events they caused.

Vijayanagara exemplifies three interrelated concepts that are central to this and the next chapter—cities, states, and civilizations, the earliest instances of which can be identified in the archaeological record after the emergence of true agriculture thousands of years ago. Their appearance in the archaeological record marked a striking change in the scale and complex-

FIGURE 15–1

Ruins of royal buildings in the urban core of the late medieval city of Vijayanagara, Karnataka, India.

Barry Lewis

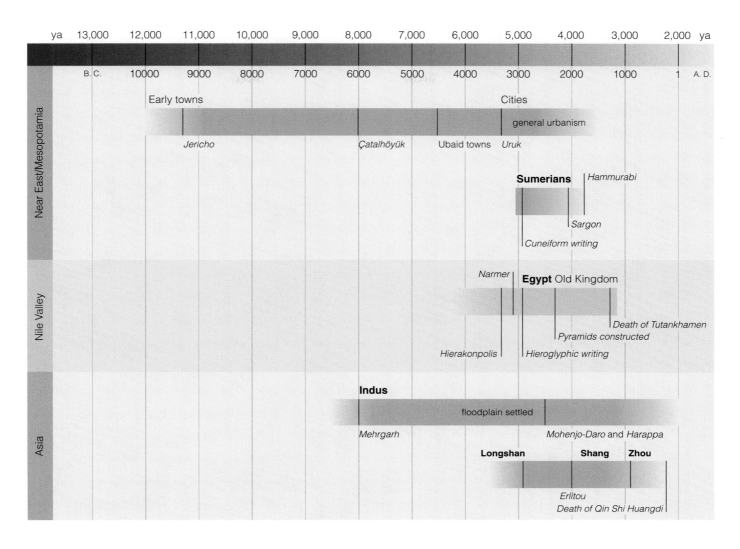

FIGURE 15–2
Time line for Chapter 15.

ity of societies, the effects of which were comparable to the dramatic changes initiated by Neolithic food production.

The appearance of the first cities and states and the civilizations of which they were a part marked the beginning of history in many parts of the world and laid the foundation for the modern era. By about 5,500 years ago (ya), several agricultural societies in both the Old and New Worlds were transforming themselves into states and civilizations (Fig. 15–2). In this chapter we examine the significance that archaeologists attach to these terms and survey some of the primary Old World examples of early civilizations (Fig. 15–3). New World civilizations are examined in Chapter 16.

Civilizations in Perspective

The term **civilization** is not, as many people think, just another word for *culture* or *society*, nor is it the same thing as a *city* or a *state*. In this section we'll focus on clarifying our use of the terms *city*, *state*, and *civilization* before putting them to use in discussing some examples.

CITIES

Most of us tend to take **cities** for granted. It just seems natural that they exist, they're big, and they're the social, political, and economic centers we often turn to. We even treat some cities,

civilization The larger social order that includes states related by language, traditions, history, economic ties, and other shared cultural aspects.

cities A city is an urban center that both supports and is supported by a hinterland of lesser communities.

375

FIGURE 15–3
Location of Old World civilizations discussed in
the text.

Shang
Civilization

National Geographic Society

Barry Lewis

such as London, Paris, and New York, as icons for entire civilizations. Six or seven thousand years ago, the complete absence of cities also seemed just as natural to our ancestors. Most settled communities were small hamlets, villages, or towns, and that's the way communities had been for thousands of years.

Cities, when they developed in prehistory, were often at the center of ancient states. Commonly, one or more prominent cities dominated smaller, dependent towns and villages in a region that also supported tiny farming hamlets. Cities are also characterized by social complexity, formal (nonkin) organization, and the concentration of specialized, nonagricultural roles (Redman, 1978). The city is the nucleus where production, trade, religion, and administrative activities converge (Cowgill, 2004). These central places usually proclaimed their own importance in prehistory by erecting prominent structures for ceremonial or other civic purposes.

The roots of cities or urbanism are currently best known archaeologically in the Near East, where settled communities existed in some regions before the beginning of the Neolithic and true agriculture (Fig. 15–4). In Chapter 14, for example, we saw that Natufians or their contemporaries in the lower Jordan River Valley had established a permanent community of dome-shaped dwellings at Jericho centuries before its residents became fully reliant on farming (Kenyon, 1981). Although it never attained the size or status of a true city, early Jericho anticipated some of the characteristics of later urban centers, including evidence of social complexity. Before 10,000 ya, Jericho traders also participated in the regional exchange of such commodities as salt, sulfur, shells, obsidian, and turquoise. Some of these products ended up as offerings in the graves of individuals buried at Jericho. More impressive were Jericho's remarkable construction features, clearly the products of organized communal effort. A massive stone wall 6 feet thick, incorporating a 28-foot stone tower with interior stairs, enclosed the settlement of several hundred modest houses. A deep trench, cut into the bedrock beyond

FIGURE 15–4
Sites associated with early civilizations in Mesopotamia and the Nile Valley.

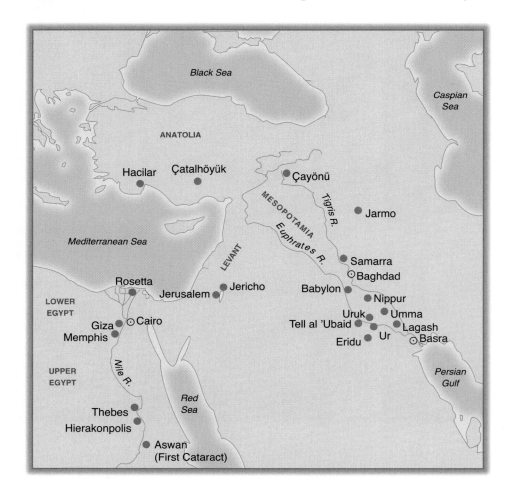

the wall, afforded even greater security, but against whom or what is uncertain. Viewed initially as fortifications against unknown human enemies, Jericho's wall and ditch may have been intended instead to divert mud flows brought on by severe erosion due to deforestation and poor farming practices in the vicinity (Bar-Yosef, 1986). The tower could have functioned either for defense or as a community shrine.

A 32-acre site in south-central Turkey, **Çatalhöyük** was both larger and somewhat later than Jericho (Hodder, 1996; Balter 2005). Çatalhöyük served as a trade and religious center some 9,000 ya, during early Neolithic times. Its densely packed houses of timber and mud brick had only rooftop entrances; their painted plaster interiors included living and storage space, sleeping platforms, and hearths. The community's several thousand inhabitants farmed outside its walls or engaged in craft production within. Some residents exploited nearby sources of obsidian or volcanic glass to make beads, mirrors, and blades to be exported in exchange for raw materials and finished goods. The wealth that this trade generated may have supported religious activities in the numerous elaborately decorated shrines uncovered in the excavated portion of the site. Many of these shrines held representations of cattle, then only recently domesticated, as focal points for the worshipers.

Jericho and Çatalhöyük may be somewhat exceptional because specialized trade or religious activities promoted their early development into relatively large and complex Neolithic communities. Even so, they were not truly cities, nor did they pertain to any larger cultural entity that could be described as a state. They simply surpassed in size and sophistication such contemporary settlements as Jarmo (Iraq), **Çayönü** (Turkey), and **Hacilar** (Turkey), which remained modest villages. Despite their size and local prominence, they did not evolve into real urban centers of the kind associated with most ancient civilizations.

The earliest true city yet discovered is Uruk, in southern Iraq. Associated with the Sumerian civilization of the southern Tigris-Euphrates Valley, Uruk boasts remnants of massive mud-brick temples and residential areas that housed tens of thousands of people after 5,500 ya. Several other contemporary sites in northern Iraq and Syria, not yet excavated, indicate that urbanism was getting under way throughout that region in the late fourth millennium B.C. (about 5,200 ya).

In time, many of these early towns and urban centers of the Near East, including Uruk, and even Jericho and Çatalhöyük, became **tells**. Tells are mounds of archaeological rubble, consisting of layers of mud brick, ash, stone, and other accumulated debris from successive settlements on the same spot (Fig. 15–5). Some of these features attained the size of small hills and are still prominent landmarks; others, such as Old Jerusalem, are still occupied. As you might expect, the older components of these sites generally lie closer to the base of the tell, nearer the original ground surface (recall the principle of superpositioning from Chapter 8). But neat layer-cake strata are the exception, since most tells accumulated sporadically as the people erected or demolished individual buildings or sections (Fig. 15–6). In most other areas of the world, where people usually occupied more dispersed settlements, tells did not form.

Andrews University/Institute of Archaeology, Berrien Springs, MI

FIGURE **15–5**
Tell Hesban in Jordan forms a hill of habitation and building debris that rises many feet above the surrounding countryside.

Çatalhöyük (chaetal´-hae-yook´) A large early Neolithic site in southern Turkey; the name is Turkish for "forked mound."

Çayönü (chayu´-noo)

Hacilar (ha-ji-lar´)

tells Mounds of accumulated rubble representing the site of an ancient city. A tell differs in both scale and content from a *midden.*

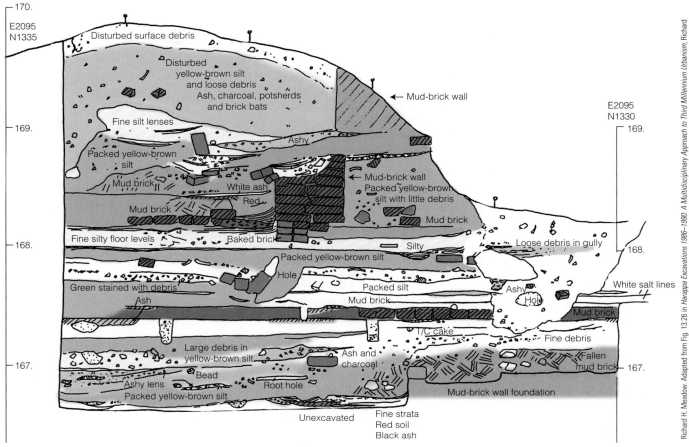

E2095
N1335

170.

Disturbed surface debris

Disturbed
yellow-brown silt
and loose debris
Ash, charcoal, potsherds
and brick bats

←— Mud-brick wall

Fine silt lenses

169.

Ashy

Packed yellow-brown
silt

Mud brick

White ash

←— Mud-brick wall
Packed yellow-brown
silt with little debris

E2095
N1330

169.

Red

Mud brick

Mud brick

Fine silty floor levels

Baked brick

Silty

Loose debris in gully

168.

168.

Packed yellow-brown silt

Hole

Packed silt

Green stained with debris

Mud brick

Ashy

White salt lines

Hole

Ash

T/C cake

Mud brick

167.

Large debris in
yellow-brown silt

Ash and
charcoal

Fine debris

Fallen
mud brick

167.

Bead

Root hole

Ashy lens

Packed yellow-brown silt

Mud-brick wall foundation

Unexcavated

Fine strata
Red soil
Black ash

Richard H. Meadow. Adapted from Fig. 13.26 in *Harappa Excavations 1986–1990: A Multidisciplinary Approach to Third Millennium Urbanism*, Richard H. Meadow (ed.). *Monographs in World Archaeology*, No. 3., p. 220. Madison, WI: Prehistory Press, 1991.

FIGURE 15–6

Cross section through a tell at Harappa, Pakistan.

STATES

If you were to examine the anthropological literature of the past century, you'd find many different perspectives on the concept of the *state*, some of which had considerable impact on archaeological research. Morton Fried (1967),* for example, described the evolution of political society as one that in its simplest form is "egalitarian." As the name implies, there's no social differentiation in egalitarian societies; leadership is informal, and "the best idea leads." Examples are most Paleolithic hunter-gatherer bands. *Ranked* societies are more complicated, particularly because some forms of social differentiation are present; a few people are "chiefs," but most are "Indians." These socially differentiated statuses and roles can be inherited, but there are no true social classes. Examples include Neolithic farming villages in the Near East and late prehistoric Mississippian chiefdoms in eastern North America. In *stratified* societies, we see significant differentiation, and true social classes do exist. An example is the Natchez, an early historic period Native American group of west-central Mississippi, whose society was rigidly hierarchical by comparison with Mississippian societies, which it resembled in other ways. Finally, in the *state* we find social classes, as well as the concept of citizenship, true administrative bureaucracies, the monopoly of the use of force, and the other types of governing and administrative institutions that are typical of the states in which most of us live today.

The main interpretive drawback of such typologies is that they promote a progressive or evolutionary view of past political institutions—even where there's little empirical evidence to suggest that such a view is warranted, except at a high level of abstraction, such as the gen-

---

*Another developmental typology of political complexity commonly applied by archaeologists in the late twentieth century is that of Elman Service (1962). The criticisms that we level against Fried apply equally to Service.

eral tendency for cultural change to become more complex over time.* In Fried's typology, for example, ranked societies followed egalitarian societies and preceded stratified societies, and so on. Through frequent application in research, the built-in sequence of cultural evolutionary "stages" represented by such schemes can begin to seem both real and discoverable in the empirical world. Even so, through archaeological research on such important questions as "How do we explain the rise of the first states?" we often discover that the changes identifiable in the archaeological record don't match these typologies very closely. Instead, researchers find that it's also useful to examine cultural differences, whether viewed through time or across space, as well as the similarities implied by such typologies in understanding the development of the earliest states (Trigger, 2003, p. 42). The result is still an evolutionary picture of the development of cities, states, and civilizations, but one that examines such changes within a web of possibilities rather than as the outcome of a succession of stages.

For our purposes, we take the *state* to mean a governmental center that persists by politically controlling a territory, and "by acting through a generalized structure of authority, making certain decisions in disputes between members of different groups, maintaining the central symbols of society, and undertaking the defense and expansion of the society" (Yoffee, 2005, p. 17). Examples include most modern nations.

With the emergence of the earliest states in antiquity, you also tend to see archaeological evidence of other important changes, among them **social stratification**, typically in the form of true social classes (recalling Fried, 1967). This is so consistent a feature of states that, in his recent comparative analysis of early civilizations, archaeologist Bruce Trigger (2003) describes them categorically as "class-based" societies. In ancient states, most people worked the land, while a smaller number performed essential specialized tasks of craft production, military service, trade, and religion. At the top of this social heap were a few elite individuals who closely controlled access to goods and services produced by others, information, the means of force, and symbols of valued status; these individuals also made most essential decisions that affected the working of society—usually with the proclaimed sanction of gods and the assistance of a bureaucracy of lesser officials. Such decisions covered many critical functions, including the capacity to create and enforce laws, levy and collect taxes, store and redistribute food and other basic goods, and defend or expand the state's boundaries.

The development of true social classes implies another important aspect of states: Their main social institutions are commonly organized on the basis of criteria other than that of kinship. This doesn't mean that families and kinship cease to be important at every level of society, from the greatest of rulers to the person who hauls out the garbage at the end of the day. Kin relations continue to be important on the individual level. What changes is that some of the roles and duties that were once handled by your kin are now decided by the state. For example, states tend to appropriate the right to decide which acts of murder committed by its citizens will be punished as crimes and which will be rewarded with medals and marching bands. They also may take over the authority to pass judgment on local civil disputes, such as village squabbles over property boundaries, contract breaches, and the like. In non-states, such as the kinds of communities we described in Chapter 14, these decisions were usually decided in kin-centered institutions such as families and lineages.

CIVILIZATIONS

For their part, civilizations comprise "the larger social order and set of shared values in which states are culturally embedded" (Yoffee, 2005, p. 17). This means we can speak of a medieval South Indian civilization that encompassed the Vijayanagara state—including other states, both large and small, that acknowledged its rule—as well as of neighboring states, such as the Gajapatis along the northern Bay of Bengal, who saw themselves mostly as competitors and equals.

One important quality to bear in mind as we begin our examination of the earliest cities, states, and civilizations is that they show considerable diversity. Unlike what archaeologists

---

*But as Norman Yoffee (2005) points out, not everything about the change from villages to cities and states necessarily involved increasing complexity. Some aspects of these changes actually became simplified with the beginning of the earliest states.

social stratification Class structure or hierarchy, usually based on political, economic, or social standing.

believed half a century ago, there's no simple trajectory we can trace in the archaeological record that leads inevitably from villages to cities and to states. For example, the Vijayanagara empire (roughly A.D. 1300–1650) appears to have been less unified but more urban than the Egyptian civilization during the Old Kingdom (2920–2134 B.C.) period. To understand why, you must consider differences of culture, technology, history, external relations, and even terrain, because they all played important roles as shown in the archaeological records of these two regions.

Why Did Civilizations Form?

Archaeological understanding of the development of the earliest civilizations (where the term is taken to include both states and civilizations as defined earlier) has increased considerably over the past century, especially during the past 50 years. Among the many things archaeologists have learned from this research is that answers to such questions as "Why did civilizations form?" tend to become more complex as our excavations teach us more about the past.

A half century ago, V. Gordon Childe specified the traits that he believed contributed to the evolution of early civilizations. His long list reflects his view of civilization as an outgrowth of increasing productivity, social complexity, and economic advantage (Childe, 1951, 1957). The use of writing, mathematics, animal-powered traction, wheeled carts, plows, irrigation, sailing boats, standard units of weight and measure, metallurgy, surplus production, and craft specialization, Childe argued, all had a stimulating effect and were themselves products of changes initiated by earlier Neolithic activities. But Childe's catalog of inventions and new social institutions failed to capture the central reality that a civilization is more than the sum of its parts.

What's more, it was evident even in the 1950s that Childe's trait list was not universally applicable. Although it characterized the Near Eastern civilizations that he was most familiar with, parts of it didn't fit New World societies such as the Maya and Inka.* These were clearly civilizations, even though they didn't use sailing boats, animal traction, wheeled carts, and so on.

Prehistorians tried to refine Childe's approach by singling out just the basic qualities shared by *all* civilizations. Harvard anthropologist Clyde Kluckhohn proposed that civilizations are societies having (1) permanent towns with at least 5,000 residents, (2) record keeping, and (3) monumental ceremonial architecture (Kraeling and Adams, 1960). Notice that each of these criteria is an outward indicator of a society's underlying complexity. So, if a culture is able to maintain thousands of people in a permanent town, then surely it's exercising some form of governance or administrative control based on something other than kinship—possibly through the redistribution of goods and services. Record keeping (usually writing) manifests a need to maintain accurate accounts, ranging from inventories, economic reports, and tax tallies to law codes, histories, and literature. Large-scale construction activities for temples, pyramids, and other ceremonial architecture represent a society's surplus production capabilities, since such projects may not contribute to immediate and basic needs, like food, in the direct way that digging an irrigation canal would. A culture that can afford the luxury of monumental structures demonstrates that it has attained a measure of success in supplying the needs of its population and in maintaining some control over it.

Still, descriptive approaches such as those of Childe and Kluckhohn remain inadequate because such lists ultimately fail to account for *why* and *how* the earliest civilizations emerged. The search for answers to such questions continues to be one of the most important objectives of archaeological research on complex societies. Let's now consider several recent competing explanations with emphasis on Near Eastern civilizations, which offer the advantage of being among the most studied of the world's earliest civilizations.

---

*Both *Inka* and *Inca* are accepted spellings; we've used *Inka* for the sake of consistency with other terms in the Quechua language spoken by the descendants of the native peoples of Peru.

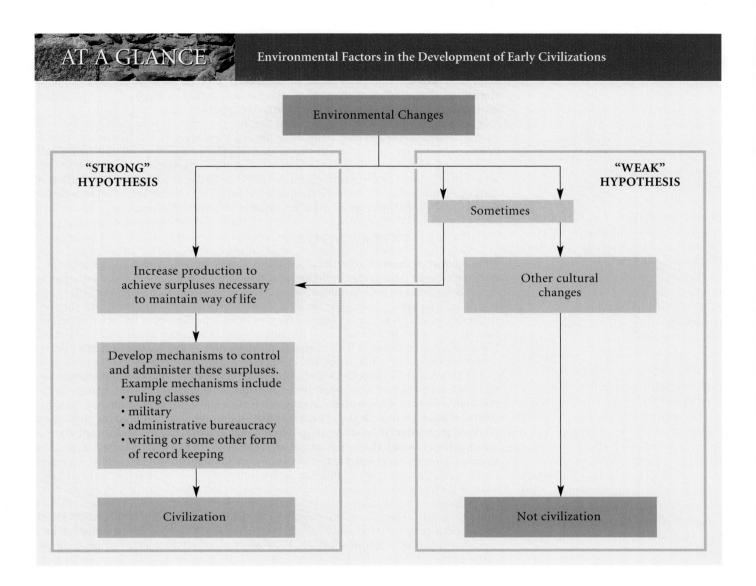

AT A GLANCE　　Environmental Factors in the Development of Early Civilizations

Environmental Changes

"STRONG" HYPOTHESIS

"WEAK" HYPOTHESIS

Sometimes

Increase production to achieve surpluses necessary to maintain way of life

Other cultural changes

Develop mechanisms to control and administer these surpluses. Example mechanisms include
• ruling classes
• military
• administrative bureaucracy
• writing or some other form of record keeping

Civilization

Not civilization

ENVIRONMENTAL EXPLANATIONS

Although at first glance it may seem unlikely that the rise of civilizations could be the product of purely natural causes, and independent of the actions of humans, researchers have weighed the merits of these and many other possible factors over the past century. Theories that account for the origins of civilization tend to take a position between the extremes of environmental determinism, in which people, culture, and everything else obey natural laws, and cultural determinism, the cultural relativist position that maintains human behavior can be explained only in cultural and historical terms (Trigger, 2003, pp. 653–655).

Let's look briefly at an example of a strong environmental hypothesis. Arie Issar, a geologist, and his colleague Mattanyah Zohar, an archaeologist, argue that the fluctuating availability of water resources with major climatic changes was a key factor in the development of civilization in the Near East (Issar and Zohar, 2004). Based on their time series analyses of isotopes from lake sediments and cave stalagmites, these researchers identify several major periods between 5,000 and 6,000 ya during which the Near East was drier than present and periods during which it was colder than present. When correlated with major cultural changes documented in the archaeological record of the region, climatic conditions, they argue, are sufficient to account both for production surpluses and for the concentration of the control of these surpluses in the hands of ruling classes. This control gradually became more successful as administrative institutions and such inventions as writing developed in Mesopotamian society. Interregional commerce, the military, administrative bureaucracies, and local ruling dynasties, they argue, emerged because of the changes fostered by optimal climatic conditions. Climatic changes may also account for the catastrophic flood legends that are indigenous to the region (Issar and Zohar, 2004, pp. 112–113).

Elsewhere, however, research has shown that the possible causal relationships between environmental factors and early civilizations are much less likely, In fact, in a recent international conference on the relationship between climatic change and early civilizations, the participants agreed on one main point: "Climatic change for each civilization or community can act as a driving force, or a supporting player, or merely as background noise" (Catto and Catto, 2004). In other words, environmental explanations generally and climatic change in particular can't, by themselves, explain the rise and fall of *all* early civilizations.

CULTURAL EXPLANATIONS

If environmental theories sometimes leave little room for human culture and agency to play important causal roles in the development of civilization, some cultural explanations go to the other extreme and deny that the environment plays much of a role. According to the views of cultural relativists, culture plays the significant role in shaping human behavior, not non-cultural factors, such as climate, population growth, and the like. From this perspective, culture cannot merely be reduced to the category of human reactions to the whims of nature, but is a force to be reckoned with in explaining major prehistoric changes such as the development of the earliest cities, states, and civilizations.

For example, the archaeologist Kwang-chih Chang argued that the rise of the earliest civilizations in China may have owed more to the differential access by some groups to the means of communication within Chinese society than to the means of production (Chang, 2000). In short, Chang (2000, p. 2) asserted that "the wealth that produced the civilization was itself the product of concentrated political power, and the acquisition of that power was accomplished through the accumulation of wealth. The key to this circular working of the ancient Chinese society was the monopoly of high **shamanism**, which enabled the rulers to gain critical access to divine and ancestral wisdom, the basis of their political authority. Most of the markers of the ancient civilization were in fact related centrally to this shamanism." Chang's hypothesis is particularly interesting because it depends on cultural factors alone as the active ingredients in developing early Chinese civilization. He pointedly denies the importance of technological advances and increasing control of the means of production, factors that are often mentioned as key aspects in general theories of the development of the early civilizations.

Although it's contested by many specialists on Chinese civilization, Chang's hypothesis has an interesting twist because he also argues that the central importance of controlling the means of communication was true for all early civilizations except Mesopotamia in the Near East (Chang, 2000, pp. 7–10). It was only in Mesopotamia, Chang reasons, that controlling the means of production was a key factor in developing the region's earliest civilizations. This difference, he conjectures, led to the creation of states that were fundamentally different from those of China and greatly influenced the development of much of Western civilization.

In his recent monumental worldwide comparative analysis of early civilizations, Bruce Trigger (2003) identifies several important uniformities that cast doubt on civilization theories that adopt extreme positions, whether they're in the direction of cultural relativism or environmental forces. To take only a few sociopolitical examples, Trigger found no evidence of Chang's control of the means of communication; but in the cases he examined, he did encounter relatively uniform conceptions of kingship, class systems, support of the upper classes through the controlled use of force, and control of the means of production (Trigger, 2003, pp. 272–273, 663). Trigger also found that only two types of political organization and two types of general administrative institutions are present in early civilizations. What's striking about these and the many other cultural similarities he identifies is that it's not the sort of picture you would expect to see if human culture was

shamanism Traditional practices that mediate between the world of humans and the world of spirits.

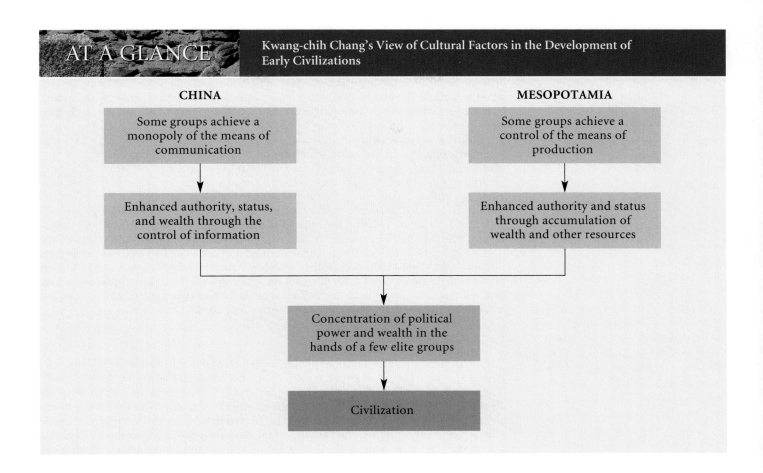

AT A GLANCE   Kwang-chih Chang's View of Cultural Factors in the Development of Early Civilizations

CHINA

Some groups achieve a monopoly of the means of communication

↓

Enhanced authority, status, and wealth through the control of information

MESOPOTAMIA

Some groups achieve a control of the means of production

↓

Enhanced authority and status through accumulation of wealth and other resources

Concentration of political power and wealth in the hands of a few elite groups

↓

Civilization

unconstrained by noncultural forces. If culture were a free agent, so to speak, we could expect to see considerable diversity in these and other institutions across early civilizations as they respond to local cultural traditions and history. Similarly, these cultural uniformities can't be easily explained by the action of general environmental factors, because the cases Trigger examines are environmentally diverse, ranging from tropical rain forest settings to near desert conditions.

If culture and natural factors such as climate don't fully explain the rise of the earliest civilizations, what is the answer? Trigger (2003, pp. 272–274) proposes an essentially functional argument based on information theory. At its root is the observation that the transition from villages to cities and states is fundamentally one of increasing societal complexity, driven by economic or political forces. With the increased complexity of the organization of society, there must also be comparable increases in the institutions that manage this complexity. To put it another way, you can't manage a Fortune 500 multinational corporation from a small storefront in a suburban strip mall. What's missing from that picture is the massive organizational infrastructure necessary to keep a major corporation running on a daily basis, much less to keep it profitable. To Trigger, a state faces the same basic problem. The growth of the earliest cities and states also required the creation of new decision-making institutions and the distribution of power and authority. This is effectively what's seen archaeologically with increased material evidence for the emergence of social classes, ruling elites, administrative bureaucracies, settlement hierarchies, and the like. But Trigger's most important point may be that, for all the ways in which early civilizations differed around the world— and there were many—"for societies to grow more complex they may have to evolve specific forms of organization." And as Trigger also observed, humans found only a limited number of ways to do this.

Old World Civilizations

So seemingly familiar are the ancient Near Eastern civilizations—Egypt and Mesopotamia—that we instinctively use them as a standard in measuring all others. Still, it's inappropriate to do so, for as Bruce Trigger (2003) stresses, it's essential to understand both the differences and the similarities between early civilizations if we are to explain how and why such entities developed.

The following survey of ancient civilizations is neither a random selection nor a truly representative one. For the most part, we'll focus on the premier civilizations to emerge in several major geographical regions of the Old World (we discuss New World states and civilizations in Chapter 16). The archaeological remains of these specific cultures have captured the general public's imagination and attracted scholars' attention for many decades. Each civilization left tantalizing traces of itself in the archaeological record, ranging from still-indecipherable written texts to the ruins of structures their architects intended to be everlasting. The information amassed by numerous research expeditions to the valleys of the Tigris-Euphrates, Nile, Indus, and Huang He has become the familiar fare of schoolrooms and travelogues, specifically because they're truly remarkable and deserve our attention. Each civilization devised ways of grappling with the challenges presented by entirely new social, political, and economic circumstances. Their legacies have survived for millennia, and we can often still recognize them within the framework of our modern civilizations.

MESOPOTAMIA

During the centuries after 8,000 ya, pioneering farmers settled the vast alluvial plains bordering the lower Tigris and Euphrates Rivers, an area called **Mesopotamia** (see Fig. 15–4). These agriculturists shared the heritage of such early Neolithic communities as Jarmo in the Zagros foothills to the east and Çayönü at the edge of the Anatolian plateau (Nissen, 1988). In fact, they were probably direct descendants of Samarran farmers, who had practiced small-scale irrigation agriculture along the edges of the central Tigris Valley and obtained painted pottery and obsidian through trade with upland communities. Now advancing onto the southern plains, possibly in search of vacant or more productive lands, these **Ubaid** farmers (as archaeologists call them) encountered great flood-prone streams bound only by immense mud flats and marshes.

The annual floods in this region began soon after the spring planting season, when young crops were particularly vulnerable. These seasonal overflows deposited rich layers of alluvium, and fifth-millennium B.C. sites have been found buried at depths of up to 16 feet below the modern ground surface (Crawford, 2004). When the waters receded, a long, dry summer followed. At first, farmers cultivated only the well-drained slopes above the river. But eventually they began the arduous task of redirecting the river's flow, even cutting through its banks to channel floodwater onto low-lying fields. Irrigation unlocked the fertility of the deep, stone-free silt that had accumulated on the floodplain for millennia. Barley was the Ubaidians' primary grain, but wheat and millet grew well too, along with the date palm and vegetable crops. Their animals included pigs and several kinds of sheep. Domesticated donkeys and oxen performed heavy tasks. The abundant harvests, supplemented by fish and game, more than kept pace with the rapidly growing floodplain communities.

By around 6,500 ya, Ubaid villagers were beginning to prosper in the southernmost Tigris-Euphrates valley (Lamberg-Karlovsky and Sabloff, 1995). A degree of cultural uniformity marked their settlements. Each of their more populous towns, such as Nippur, Eridu, and Uruk in the southern valley (see Fig. 15–4), centered around a platform-based temple; even the smaller communities had central shrines. Perhaps to obtain the resources lacking in their new homeland, Ubaidians stayed in touch with distant peoples through trade in decorated pottery, obsidian, ornamental stones, copper, and possibly grain. Archaeologists use chemical analyses of distinctive trace elements in raw materials and artifacts to track these exchanges throughout the region, from the Persian Gulf to the eastern Mediterranean (Roaf, 1996).

Important changes ushered in the late Ubaid period, around 5,500 ya. The population of certain communities rapidly swelled into the thousands as people from outlying districts massed together. Expanding irrigation systems in the lower Tigris-Euphrates valley produced more food for the concentrated populace. Altering the riverine environment on this scale by

Mesopotamia   (*meso*, meaning "middle," and *potamos*, meaning "river") Land between the Tigris and Euphrates Rivers, mostly included in modern-day Iraq.

Ubaid   (oo-bide´) Early formative culture of Mesopotamia, 7,500–6,200 ya; predecessor to Sumerian civilization.

digging drainage and irrigation channels was a daunting enterprise, one that the people could accomplish only with organized communal effort, including a great deal of cooperation and direction. The activity transformed not only the landscape but undoubtedly the nature of the agricultural societies themselves.

What might these concentrated populations mean to us? Certainly, we're witnessing the birth of the first true cities. But what stimulated their development? It's possible that intensified economic—or even military—rivalries in the region forced populations to come together for protection (Adams, 1981). Or maybe there was a more peaceful genesis, with urbanism an outgrowth of increased agricultural productivity and efficiency, in turn fostering sociocultural changes (social stratification, craft specialization, commerce, etc.) within the urban setting. Whatever the reason, these trends were occurring simultaneously at various settlements along the lower Tigris-Euphrates valley as people flocked to the developing cities. These cities seem to have provided the social environments needed for the earliest Mesopotamian states to emerge (Yoffee, 2005).

Sumerians Over several centuries, Uruk's population expanded to possibly as many as 20,000 people. Today, the ruins of Uruk's mud-brick buildings cover nearly 1 square mile in southern Mesopotamia, 150 miles southeast of modern Baghdad (Nissen, 2001). The most ancient portions of Uruk reveal some features of the earliest city. Two massive temple complexes, built in stages and dedicated to the sun and to the goddess of love, probably served as focal points of political, religious, economic, and cultural activities. Inscribed clay tablets associated with these structures record that the temples distributed food and controlled nearby croplands. Growing social and religious complexity (including the rise of powerful kings and priests) kept pace with the city's physical growth.

The developments associated with Uruk and the other urban centers were an immediate prelude and stimulus to a new order in southern Mesopotamia around 5,000 ya. The inscribed tablets, teeming populations, and large-scale religious structures indicate that the essential elements of civilization had come together. Uruk ushered in the period of the first complex urban civilization, usually identified with a people called the Sumerians.

The region known as Sumer encompassed about a dozen largely autonomous political units, called **city-states**, in the southernmost Tigris-Euphrates valley. About the same number of Akkadian city-states hugged the river to the north, near present-day Baghdad. The Sumerians and their neighbors shared the world's first modern society between 4,900 and 4,350 ya. Each Sumerian city-state incorporated a major population center—Ur, Lagash, Umma, Nippur, Eridu, and Uruk are examples—as well as some smaller satellite communities and, of course, a great deal of irrigated cropland. These city-states were controlled by hereditary kings, who often fought for dominance with their counterparts in neighboring cities.

The Sumerians had an urbanized and technologically accomplished culture, economically dependent on large-scale irrigation agriculture and specialized craft production (Kramer, 1963; Roaf, 1996). They were among the first to refine metals such as gold, silver, and copper and to make bronze alloys. Sophisticated architecture incorporated the true arch and the dome. Other practical innovations included the use of wheeled carts, draft animals, the plow, and sailing boats. Skilled crafters produced fine jewelry and textiles, while artists created

city-states An urban center and its supporting territory that forms an autonomous sociopolitical unit. Farmers and other food producers tended to live in the urban center and work their fields on the outskirts of the city.

AT A GLANCE   Important Near Eastern Sites and Regions

Site	Dates (ya)	Comments
Çatalhöyük (Turkey)	c. 9,000	A large Neolithic village with 5,000–8,000 inhabitants in south-central Turkey
Uruk (Iraq)	c. 5,500–1,800	Earliest true city; associated with the Sumerian civilization of the southern Tigris-Euphrates Valley
Ur (Iraq)	c. 4,600–2,500	City in southern Iraq; its cemetery of >1,800 graves includes 16 "royal" tombs

sculpture and music. Sumerian merchants and administrators relied on written records and a counting system based on multiples of 6, which they also applied to measuring time and devising calendars. (Buying a dozen doughnuts, counting minutes in our 24-hour day, and measuring degrees in a circle are modern reminders of ancient Sumerian numeration.) Their system of law became a basis for later legal codes, and Sumerian contributions to literature included many of the traditions subsequently reflected in the Old Testament.

The influence of these cities reached beyond Mesopotamia through exchange and possibly even colonization. Excavations in northern Iraq, Turkey, and the Nile Valley have revealed connections with Uruk through trade in prestige goods such as pottery, carved ivory, and lapis (Roaf, 1996). These valued products furnished the tombs of Sumerian elites in a society where social differentiation was becoming more pronounced.

Among the prerogatives of elite members of society was the right to burial in a lavish tomb. Sir Leonard Woolley's excavations of the 4,500-year-old "royal" tombs at Ur in the 1920s revealed that King Abargi and Queen Puabi were each accompanied in death by rich offerings—ceremonial vessels, tools, musical instruments, and even chariots complete with their animals and, apparently, also their human attendants—arranged within the burial pits (Woolley, 1929). Woolley interpreted other human remains found in association with these elite individuals as the men and women of their court, who were bedecked with precious jewelry, drugged, and then sealed into the tombs.

Mesopotamian citizens constructed brick walls around their city perimeters for security. The heart of each urban center was its sacred district, dominated by a grand temple and flanked by noble houses. In addition to a patron deity associated with each city, a pantheon of major and minor divinities received homage. Chief among them was Enlil, the air god. Like most Mesopotamian gods, Enlil exhibited remarkably human characteristics, taking a fatherly concern for mortals and their daily affairs but also meting out punishment and misfortune. Some cities, like Ur, regularly augmented their shrines and eventually created an impressive artificial mountain called a **ziggurat** (Fig. 15–7). Rising from an elevated platform roughly the size of a football field, these stepped temples were solidly built of millions of molded and baked mud bricks.

Outside the ceremonial district, narrow unpaved alleyways twisted through crowded residential precincts. Much like city dwellers everywhere, Sumerians endured social problems and pollution in their urban environment. The size and location of individual homes correlated with family wealth and position. Contemporary written accounts indicate that the populace comprised three general classes: nobility, commoners, and slaves. Some slaves were formerly free citizens who had fallen on hard times and sold themselves into bondage; others were captives taken in conflicts with neighboring city-states. Some of the

FIGURE **15–7**

Reconstructed lower stage of the late Sumerian ziggurat at Ur, Iraq.

National Geographic Society

ziggurat   Late Sumerian mud-brick temple-pyramid.

commoners specialized in craft or merchant activities, but many were farmers with fields and herds just beyond the surrounding walls. The houses of all but the nobility were generally one story, with several rooms opening onto a central courtyard. Wall and floor coverings brightened the interiors, which were furnished with wooden tables, chairs, and beds and an assortment of household equipment for cooking and storage.

From our perspective, their writing system was perhaps the Sumerians' most significant invention (see Digging Deeper on pp. 390–391), enabling us to discover more about them than their other artifacts and monuments could ever reveal. Literacy was a hard-won accomplishment. By about 5,000 ya, the original pictographic form of Sumerian writing was evolving into a more flexible writing system using hundreds of standardized signs. Highly trained scribes formed the characteristic wedge-shaped, or **cuneiform**, script by pressing a reed stylus onto damp clay pads; these tablets were then baked to preserve them (Fig. 15–8). Ninety percent of early Sumerian writing concerned economic, legal, and administrative matters; like us, the Sumerians belonged to a complex and bureaucratic society. Later scribes recorded more historical and literary works, including several epic accounts featuring the adventures of **Gilgamesh**, an early Uruk king and culture hero reputed to have performed many amazing deeds in the face of overwhelming odds.

The loose conglomeration of Mesopotamian city-states faced hard times after around 4,500 ya. At least part of the problem may have been their long dependence on irrigation agriculture, which was slowly destroying the fertility of their fields because the irrigation water deposited soluble mineral salts on the soil. Other researchers (e.g., Powell, 1985) question the hard evidence on which these inferences are based, and this area needs more research. Another part of the problem was that this early civilization spent much of its energy in fruitless internal competition. Clustered together in an area about the size of Vermont, the city-states of Sumer and neighboring Akkad, to the north, vied with one another for supremacy in commerce, prestige, and religion.

Finally, around 2334 B.C., a minor Akkadian official assumed the name Sargon of Agade and led armies from the north to victory in the Sumerian lands and united what had been a collection of city-states into a **territorial state**. Military expansion led to economic, political, and linguistic dominance over a broad area. Under Sargon, his sons, and grandsons, the Akkadian state endured only a century before dissolving. But once it began, the unification process continued on and off for many centuries in Mesopotamia—next under the kings of Ur, and later (about 3,800 ya) under **Hammurabi** of Babylon, who was famed for his "eye for an eye" law code, among other accomplishments. Soon after the reign of Hammurabi, the ancient lands were incorporated into the realm of the Assyrians until 2,600 ya, when a new Babylonian empire reclaimed dominance under King **Nebuchadnezzar**.

EGYPT

The pyramids of Egypt remain unrivaled as the ancient world's most imposing monuments. They have adorned the banks of the Nile for so long that they seem timeless. Even so, as we saw in Chapter 14, Egyptian culture was rooted in the Nile Valley long before the pyramids.

Archaeological evidence of these most ancient Nile cultures is rarely preserved in the unstable river floodplain (Trigger et al., 1983; Hays, 1984). Still, excavations reveal that the early farmers grew Near Eastern varieties of wheat and barley as well as raising sheep and goats first domesticated in the same region. Neolithic villages lined the great river's banks by 6,000 ya. Even at this early stage, settlements in the section of the valley known as Upper Egypt—just north of Aswan, the "First Cataract" of ancient times—contrasted somewhat with those in the delta region, called Lower Egypt, close to the river's mouth. Archaeologists recognize a Mesopotamian influence at work among the Upper Egypt villagers, possibly introduced through direct contact or by way of Palestinian traders (Hoffman, 1991). Mineral resources, especially gold, apparently drew outsiders to the region.

Around 5,300 years ago, increasing political and social cohesion brought some of these Upper Egypt settlements together as local chiefdoms. Walls protected the towns of Naqada and Hierakonpolis, and well-stocked stone and brick tombs were a final emblem of the social differentiation enjoyed by principal individuals (Wenke, 1990). Pottery making and trading became specialized economic enterprises (Fig. 15–9). Continuing contact with Mesopotamian cultures may have stimulated these developments, although researchers don't yet have evidence of comparable Egyptian influence in the other direction.

FIGURE 15–8
This small Sumerian clay tablet (actual size) is a 4,000-year-old tax receipt with cuneiform impressions on both sides.

cuneiform (*cuneus*, meaning "wedge") Wedge-shaped writing of ancient Mesopotamia.

Gilgamesh Semilegendary king and culture hero of early Uruk; reputed to have had many marvelous adventures.

territorial state A form of state political organization with multiple administrative centers and one or more capitals. The cities tend to house the elite and administrative classes, and food producers usually lived and worked in the surrounding hinterland.

Hammurabi (ham-oo-rah´-bee) Early Babylonian king, ca. 1800–1750 B.C.

Nebuchadnezzar (neh-boo-kud-neh´-zer) Late Babylonian king, ca. 605–562 B.C.

Who Invented Writing?

Who invented the first writing? Like many questions of its type in archaeology, this one is not easily answered. Some might argue that the paintings our Cro-Magnon relatives applied to cave walls in western Europe during the Upper Paleolithic between about 28,000 and 13,000 ya should be counted as writing (see Chapter 12). After all, Harvard University researcher Alexander Marshack and others have demonstrated that much of the cave art, as well as many small sculptural carvings and engraved bones and stones from the same period, surely were more than mere decorations. They were subject to manipulation and reworking and may have served in some symbolic way as reminders of significant or periodic events, including those associated with the annual progression of the seasons. However, a lack of standardized repetitive elements combined into meaningful patterns probably disqualifies this type of artwork as true writing. The magnificent and skillful renderings of Ice Age animals and other subjects may have conveyed significant meaning and possibly even information to their late Stone Age viewers, but they probably were not "read" in the way that we understand writing. Still, the distinctions tend to blur.

A more likely candidate for the world's earliest writing (or at least the source of its inspiration) may be the counting tokens of ancient Mesopotamia. Denise Schmandt-Besserat of the University of Texas, Austin, noted that small fired-clay objects were common on many Neolithic sites in the upper valley of the Tigris-Euphrates and the nearby Zagros Mountains. Represented in an array of geometric shapes—disks, spheres, triangles, rectangles, and others—these enigmatic objects, about the size of a fingernail, had long

puzzled archaeologists. They've been described as children's playthings, ornaments, or "ritual objects." Schmandt-Besserat was struck by their wide distribution and persistent appearance on sites in the Fertile Crescent over thousands of years; the earliest tokens dated to 10,000 ya, and great quantities came from Jarmo and nearby Zagros Neolithic sites after about 8,500 ya. She recognized that comparable clay geometrics had been used much later as counting tokens for tallying sheep, grain, and other products. Each distinctive shape represented a specific kind of agricultural or craft product. At Nuzi, a 3,500-year-old site in Iraq, the tokens were found in conjunction with other types of Sumerian accounting records, which seemed to verify their purpose.

The most surprising and convincing connection between the tokens and early writing is that many of the token shapes subsequently were carried over onto the earliest Sumerian pictographic tablets, including those found at Uruk, as signs representing numerals, sheep, cow, dog, bread, wool, and so on. Essentially, Schmandt-Besserat suggests a translation of three-dimensional tokens into a two-dimensional script during the period of Sumerian development (later Ubaid and Uruk times, 5,500–5,100 ya) because of an increased need for efficient records and the availability of numerous new products. Where loose clay tokens representing a transaction once had been strung together or stored in a hollow clay container, now the diverse token shapes became individual symbols that could be recorded conveniently on wet clay tablets and baked for preservation.

These earliest accounting tablets were primarily pictographic, but before about 5,000 ya, additional abstract signs were being devised to represent both concepts (ideograms) and sounds or syl-

In any event, during the next few centuries, this part of the Nile Valley transformed rapidly into a strong territorial state. Historical tradition and textual evidence, including the Narmer Palette, a relief-carved stone plaque from Hierakonpolis, record that one of Upper Egypt's early chiefs took the name Narmer and seized other communities of that region, successfully exerting his control over the delta villages in the north as well. This unification of Upper and Lower Egypt under Narmer, the traditional beginning of the First Dynasty of Egyptian civilization, dates to around 5,000 ya (3000 B.C.). The merger of Nile Valley societies under one king marked an important milestone in the development of ancient Egypt by creating the world's first nation-state.

After the first unification period, a 425-year span known as Old Kingdom times (4,575–4,150 ya) represented the first full flowering of Nile Valley civilization. Most of the estimated population of 1–3 million people lived in the far south (Trigger, 2003). The ruler, or **pharaoh**, was the supreme power of the society. Under his direction, Egypt became a wonder of the ancient world and a source of endless fascination for millennia to follow.

Brooklyn Museum

FIGURE 15–9

The design on this pot from Adaima, a Predynastic period center near Hierakonpolis, shows a boat and its passengers; the vessel is about 7 inches tall.

lables, resulting in a more comprehensive form of true writing. Eventually, the Sumerians' cuneiform ("wedge-shaped") writing included hundreds of different signs, many somewhat comparable to a letter in an alphabet, while others represented individual words (logograms).

Some authorities believe that the earliest Egyptian writing was the result of **stimulus diffusion** from Mesopotamia. Others argue that the stimulus went in the other direction, from Egypt to Mesopotamia. As with other kinds of archaeological "Who was first?" questions (recall the first inhabitants in the New World problem that we dealt with in the beginning of Chapter 13), the definitive answer may continue to elude us. Regardless, the Egyptians developed their own unique script, and the two systems of writing are so different that what may have moved between Egypt and Mesopotamia was simply the notion that it's possible to express language as graphical elements. The famous hieroglyphics ("sacred carvings") of ancient Egypt retain a deceptively simple pictographic look, but they're really both more syllabic and ideographic than they appear at first glance.

Writing in northern China already was in use by 3,000 ya, during the time of the late Shang civilization. A highly developed script of ideographic characters was inscribed on bone or bronze as well as on less-durable materials, such as wood, bamboo, and silk. The etched marks found on pottery vessels of the Dawenkou archaeological culture, which dates to roughly 4,500–4,000 ya in Shandong province, may mark an early stage in the development of writing.

Very few of the New World's aboriginal cultures employed writing. Sacred texts and calendars figure prominently only in sev-eral civilizations of Mesoamerica, particularly the Zapotec, Maya, and Aztec. After about 2,500 ya, calendrical notations in the form of hieroglyphic symbols representing both numerals and day names were carved onto stone monuments in southern Mexico. Within a few centuries, the Maya had developed their writing to include other ideograms and logograms, as well as signs standing for syllables and special emblem glyphs designating individual communities—some 800 different glyphs in all. With this advanced system, which is called logosyllabic, they recorded political and historical events and paid homage to their gods and kings.

And the rest, as they say, is history.

SOURCES:

"Babylonian Beginnings: The Origin of the Cuneiform Writing System in Comparative Perspective," by Jerrold S. Cooper, pp. 71–99 in *The First Writing: Script Invention as History and Process*, ed. Stephen D. Houston (Cambridge, UK: Cambridge University Press, 2004).

Before Writing, by Denise Schmandt-Besserat (Austin, TX: University of Texas Press, 1992).

Breaking the Maya Code, by Michael D. Coe (New York: Thames and Hudson, 1992).

The Roots of Civilization, rev. ed., by Alexander Marshack (Mount Kisco, NY: Moyer Bell, 1991).

"Writing Systems: A Case Study in Cultural Evolution," by Bruce Trigger, pp. 39–68 in *The First Writing* (Cambridge University Press, 2004).

Egyptians soon adopted a complex pictographic script called **hieroglyphics**, a writing system that is Egyptian in form but possibly Mesopotamian in inspiration. The earliest inscriptions are associated exclusively with the Egyptian royal court, as are other high-status products, such as cylinder seals, certain types of pottery, and specific artistic motifs and architectural techniques that also seem to be derived from beyond the Nile Valley. Advanced methods of copper working came into use as well, including ore refining and alloying, casting, and hammering techniques. Some of these processes likewise were invented elsewhere. An important by-product of copper metallurgy was **faience**, an Egyptian innovation produced by fusing powdered quartz, soda ash, and copper ore in a kiln. The blue-green glassy substance, molded into beads or statuettes, became a popular trade item throughout the region (Friedman, 1998).

Early pharaohs were godlike kings who ruled with divine authority through a bureaucracy of priests and public officials assigned to provinces throughout the kingdom. The pharaoh's power depended to a large degree on his assumed control over the annual Nile flood (Butzer, 1984), and throughout the course of Egypt's long history, pharaonic fortunes tended to fluctuate with the river's flow. Most Old Kingdom pharaohs maintained their royal courts at Memphis, about 15 miles south of present-day Cairo. In contrast to Mesopotamia, few urban centers emerged in the ancient Nile Valley, and even the capital was of modest size. Egypt remained almost entirely an agrarian and rural culture, the vast majority of its citizenry comprising farmers and a few tradespersons engaged in their timeless routines (Aldred, 1998). Only in the immediate vicinity of Memphis and the sacred mortuary complexes along the Nile's west bank was Egypt's grandeur clearly evident.

pharaoh   Title of the king or ruler of ancient Egypt.

stimulus diffusion   In the interaction of two societies, the knowledge of a cultural trait or feature in one society can stimulate the invention of a similar trait or feature in the other.

hieroglyphics   (*hiero*, meaning "sacred," and *glyphein*, meaning "carving") The picture-writing of ancient Egypt.

faience   (fay-ahnz´) Glassy material, usually of blue-green color, shaped into beads, amulets, and figurines by ancient Egyptians.

AT A GLANCE   Important Egyptian Sites and Regions

Site	Dates (ya)	Comments
Hierakonpolis	c. 5,300	Early Nile Valley urban center located about 45 miles to the south of Thebes; associated with the development of the unification of Egypt as one polity; home to the Narmer Palette
Memphis	c. 5,100–3,300	Old Kingdom capital city located about 10 miles south of Cairo; abandoned after A.D. 641
Giza	c. 4,500	Old Kingdom pyramid complex and Great Sphinx; located just to the southwest of Cairo
Valley of the Kings	c. 3,500–3,000	Desert valley near Thebes (modern Luxor) where more than 50 New Kingdom subterranean tombs of Pharaohs (including Tutankhamen) and other elites were found
KV5	c. 3,300–3,200	Tomb complex in the Valley of the Kings; used by Rameses II for his many sons
Rosetta	A.D. 1799	Small city near the mouth of the Nile where the Rosetta Stone was found

The familiar Old Kingdom pyramids on the Nile's west bank at Giza evolved out of a tradition of royal tomb building that began at Hierakonpolis. In that early community, brick-lined burial pits were dug with adjoining chambers to stock the offerings for a deceased king's afterlife, and these rooms were then capped with a low, rectangular brick tomb (Lehner, 1997). The scale of these structures increased as successive rulers outdid their predecessors. The monumental pyramids are the best example of the pharaoh's absolute authority over the people and resources of his domain (Fig. 15–10). In a sense, these constructions were immense public works projects that helped to solidify the power of the state while also glorifying the memory of individual rulers. Contrary to popular view, they weren't built by slave labor, but

FIGURE 15–10
Egyptian Old Kingdom pyramid and Sphinx at Giza.

© Corbis

by thousands of Egyptian farmers, put to work during the several months each year when the Nile floodwaters covered their fields.

In all, some 25 pyramids honored the Old Kingdom's elite (Lehner, 1997). The first stepped pyramids of stone were raised after 2630 B.C. (4,630 ya), and little more than a century later, the imposing tombs of Khufu and Khafra, Fourth Dynasty rulers, were among the last built in true pyramid form. Khufu's Great Pyramid is 765 feet square at its base and 479 feet in height, with 2.3 million massive limestone blocks required in its construction. Although Khafra's tomb is about 20 percent smaller, he compensated by having a nearby rock outcrop carved with the likeness of his face on the body of a lion, today called the Great Sphinx (Hawass and Lehner, 1994). Pyramid building ceased soon after, during a time of political decentralization and greater local control over such practical programs as state irrigation works.

The Old Kingdom pyramids represented a remarkable engineering triumph and an enormous cultural achievement that has inspired the civilizations that followed. Bear in mind that the stark structures we see along the Nile today were adjoined by extensive complexes of connecting causeways, shrines, altars, and storerooms filled with statuary and furnishings and ornamented with colorful friezes and carved stonework. The pyramids' slanting sides signified pathways to the sacred Sun. Worshipers flocked to them, paying reverence to the memory of the dead kings. The mortuary cult of the pharaohs absorbed a large share of the work and wealth of Egyptian society.

Later kings contented themselves with being buried in smaller, but still lavishly furnished tombs in a cramped desert valley below a natural pyramid-shaped mountain near Thebes (see Digging Deeper on p. 394). Discovered in the 1920s, the treasure-choked burial chamber of the young pharaoh **Tutankhamen**, who died more than 3,300 ya (about 1323 B.C.) during New Kingdom times, is convincing evidence that dead royalty were not neglected even after the era of pyramids had passed (Carter and Mace, 1923). Near the same location, in 1995, archaeologist Kent Weeks discovered another impressive New Kingdom tomb. Although looted long ago, rock-cut chambers prepared for many of the sons of Ramesses II ("the Great") formed a vast underground mausoleum containing more than 130 rooms. The tomb, now called KV5, currently is being systematically explored and conserved (Weeks, 2001).

Much of what we know of ancient Egypt's religion and rulers is due to the translation of countless hieroglyphic inscriptions (Fig. 15–11). In 1799 at Rosetta, a small Nile delta town, French soldiers discovered a 2.5-by-2.5-foot stone bearing an identical decree engraved in three scripts, including Greek and hieroglyphics. By working from these scripts, the brilliant

FIGURE **15–11**
Hieroglyphic inscriptions document this scene of a royal Egyptian hunting marsh birds from a papyrus boat.

Tutankhamen (toot-en-cahm´-en) Egyptian pharaoh of the New Kingdom period, who died at age 19 in 1323 B.C.; informally known today as King Tut.

393

DIGGING DEEPER

Mummies and the Archaeology of the Human Body

Most people are both attracted and repelled by mummies. Unlike skeletons, which are hard to imagine as living beings with hopes, passions, and dreams of a better tomorrow, with mummies it's disturbingly easy to be reminded that we're in the presence of a real person. When the preserved human body in front of you still wears the clothes that he or she died in, and has eyelids, lips, fingernails, hair, tattoos, and healed scars, the thousands of years separating the two of you melt away. Many of us are left feeling that we want to know their story, not in the clinical sense of analyzing yet another preserved specimen, but as a person. We want to ask, what was your world like? What were the circumstances of your death? Were you a ruler or merely a spear-carrying extra on life's movie set? All this and more begs to be explored and answered. Fortunately, thanks to modern technology, researchers are tackling these and many other questions about mummies—often with extraordinary results.

Although mummies are most commonly associated with ancient Egypt, exceptionally dry, cold, or wet conditions have allowed human bodies to be preserved in many parts of the world. Corpses buried thousands of years ago in China's Tarim Basin, in the Atacama Desert of western South America, and within dry rock-shelters in the American Southwest are often in surprisingly good condition. Natural freeze-drying accounts for the remarkable preservation of children placed as sacrifices atop high peaks in the Peruvian Andes centuries ago. The frozen Siberian tundra entombs 2,400-year-old corpses of Scythian chieftains. A melting Alpine glacier frees the body, clothes, and gear of the "Ice Man," a middle-aged man who died 5,300 years ago. Fully submerged in acidic, anaerobic (that is, lacking oxygen) wetlands for two millennia, victims of ritual sacrifice or execution in northwestern Europe come to light still wearing the cords that strangled them around their necks.

The ways that living people treat mummies have changed greatly over the past couple of hundred years. In the nineteenth century, archaeologists and curiosity seekers alike tended to view them as objects that could be bought and sold or placed in public displays like any other artifact from the past. In Egypt, where mummies were particularly abundant for both environmental and historical rea-

sons, the use of mummies reached bizarre extremes, with accounts of them even being exported to be ground up and recycled as a medicinal drug called, appropriately enough, mummy powder, and to serve as the base pigment for the oil paint color called mummy brown! By the late twentieth century researchers widely appreciated that, due to the preservation of soft tissues and organs of the body, mummies provide a unique biomedical and cultural window on the human past (Aufderheide, 2003; Pringle, 2001).

Mummy studies now range widely across many fields, from straightforward archaeological studies, to paleodemography and paleonutrition, and to medical studies of everything from the respiratory health of past peoples to prostate problems and the diversity of intestinal parasites. The recent examination of an Egyptian mummy (Fig. 1) curated by the Spurlock Museum at the University of Illinois provides a good example of modern mummy studies. In this project, which was conducted by the Program on Ancient Technologies and Archaeological Materials, the mummy was examined by a large team of anthropologists, chemists, physicians, and researchers from veterinary medicine, classics, textile science, and the National Center for Supercomputing Applications (Wisseman, 2001). The methods applied were all nondestructive, and each examination was designed to treat the human remains with respect. The results of this study provide a wealth of information about the small child still hidden from our eyes by mummy wrappings, including the child's relative physical condition in its 5–7 years of life, embalming methods, and even two facial reconstructions based on CAT scans (Fig. 2) that suggest the child was of mixed ancestry.

SOURCES

Mummies, Disease, and Ancient Cultures, 2nd ed., by Aidan Cockburn, Eve Cockburn, and Theodore A. Reyman (Cambridge, UK: Cambridge University Press, 1998).

The Mummy Congress: Science, Obsession, and the Everlasting Dead, by Heather Pringle (New York: Hyperion, 2001).

The Scientific Study of Mummies, by Arthur C. Aufderheide (Cambridge, UK: Cambridge University Press, 2003).

The Virtual Mummy, by Sarah U. Wisseman (Urbana: University of Illinois Press, 2003).

The Spurlock Museum, University of Illinois at Urbana–Champaign. Accession number 1989.06.001

FIGURE 1

Egyptian mummy of a small child, still preserved in its wrappings; dates to about A.D. 50–150.

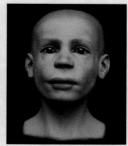

The Spurlock Museum, University of Illinois at Urbana–Champaign. Accession number P0094

FIGURE 2

Facial reconstruction of the child whose remains are preserved within the mummy wrappings.

French linguist Jean-François Champollion was able to decipher the mysterious and complex writing after 20 years of effort (Fig. 15–12).

Egyptian hieroglyphics are a combination of signs that represent ideas with others indicating sounds. Because hieroglyphics were used primarily in formal contexts by members of the elite classes and bureaucrats (much like Latin in more recent times), their translation tells us much about pharaohs and their concerns, revealing less about the commonplace events and people of the era. In fact, archaeologists can read disappointingly little about daily life in Egypt's Old Kingdom period outside the major administrative and mortuary centers, where tomb scenes occasionally portray peasants at work in their fields or winnowing or grinding grain. Happily, later periods of Egyptian society are more fully documented (Montet, 1981; Casson, 2001).

Although nothing surpassed the original glory of the Old Kingdom period, Egypt proved remarkably resilient through the centuries, surviving foreign invaders such as the Hyksos and Hittites of southwest Asia, as well as frequent episodes of internal misrule and rebellion. Its pharaohs enjoyed periods of resurgence and revival until, in a state of decline and defeated by the Persians (about 2,500 ya), Egypt fell into the Greek sphere under Alexander the Great and eventually came under the rule of Rome.

INDUS

As the first great pyramids rose beside the Nile, a collection of urban settlements that dotted a broad floodplain far to the east was forming into the Harappan, or Indus, civilization (Fig. 15–13). For seven centuries, beginning about 4,600 ya (2600–1900 B.C.), the banks of the Indus River and its tributaries in present-day Pakistan and India supported at least five primary urban centers with populations each numbering in the tens of thousands (Kenoyer, 1998; Possehl, 1999, 2002). Many hundreds of smaller farming villages were socially and economically, if not politically, linked to these central places.

The people of the Indus were relative newcomers to the valley. As we saw in Chapter 14, their ancestors cultivated the higher valley margins to the west at sites like Mehrgarh by 8,000 ya. Farming and herding, along with regional trade, had sustained village life from an early period in these uplands (Jarrige and Meadow, 1980). Around 5,300 ya, farmers began to populate the Indus floodplain itself, possibly seeking more productive cropland or better access to potential trade routes for valued copper, shell, and colorful stones. Occupying slight natural rises on the flat landscape at places like Kot Diji, they laid out fields for their vegetables, cereals, and cotton on the deep alluvium. As the new settlements grew, farmers cooperated in water management projects intended to provide irrigation for croplands and to reduce the effects of floods. They diverted part of the river's flow through irrigation sluices into their fields and constructed massive retaining walls or elevated platforms to repel its silty waters from their homes. Their work gained them a tentative control over the flood-prone stream.

Some of these settlements prospered and rapidly reached impressive size. By 4,600 ya, several large urban centers hugged the river. Why had people accustomed to living in small farming communities congregated into these cities? Possibly, an increased threat of flooding along the river—brought on by extensive deforestation and other poor farming practices—simply forced people to come together in building and maintaining more levees and irrigation canals. An alternative hypothesis proposes that trade was the "integrative force" behind Indus urbanization (Possehl, 1990). A few entrepreneurs may have fostered exchange between the valley settlements and the uplands, promoting resource development, craft specialization, and product distribution to stimulate and reap the economic benefits. As commerce began to pay off, other changes, including urbanism and social stratification, transformed Indus society even more. Once they had reached a critical mass, the cities continued to attract craftspeople, shopkeepers, and foreign traders.

As busy centers of craft production and trade, the cities prospered along the great river. Workshops in different neighborhoods turned out large quantities of wheel-thrown pottery, millions of burnt bricks, cut and polished stone beads and stamp seals, molded figurines, and work in copper, tin, silver, gold, and other metals. Merchants' scales used standardized stone cubes of precise weight to facilitate exchange transactions. The Indus itself became a commercial highway for boats loaded with goods moving up and down the river or destined for

British Museum

FIGURE 15–12

Rosetta Stone, which was the key to reading Egyptian hieroglyphics because it recorded the same long inscription in hieroglyphs, demotic (an ordinary local script), and Greek. If you could read at least one of these scripts, then you could use it as a key to decipher the other two.

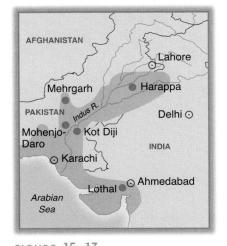

FIGURE 15–13

Location of the Indus civilization in Pakistan and India.

FIGURE **15–14**
Excavated base of an outdoor baking oven from the Indus site of Lothal in India.

Susan Johnston

Persian Gulf ports. Carts, too, carried the colorfully dyed cotton cloth, pottery, shell, and precious metal goods over land to Mesopotamia. For a while, a distant Harappan trade outpost was established near Sumerian Ur.

So far, archaeologists have carried out extensive excavations at only several of the major cities and a few of the smaller contemporary agricultural and pastoral villages (Fig. 15–14). The largest Indus sites excavated so far are **Mohenjo-Daro** and **Harappa**, which flourished between about 4,600 and 3,900 ya in present-day Pakistan. Raised on massive brick terraces above the river's flow, these cities were carefully planned, using grids of approximately 1,300 by 650 feet for the residential blocks. Although these large sites certainly reveal social complexity and a certain degree of central control, the Indus valley civilization lacks grand picturesque ruins of the type found in Egypt and Sumer. You won't find sumptuous palaces or monumental religious structures here. Their absence may suggest a basic feature of Harappan society, whose people were less focused on glorifying their individual rulers. Richard H. Meadow, who has been excavating at Harappa since 1987, describes this civilization as "an elaborate middle-class society" (Edwards, 2000, p. 116). Gregory L. Possehl (2002), another archaeologist with decades of Indus civilization research experience, draws a similar conclusion and describes it as a socioculturally complex civilization that lacks evidence of the state form of political organization. Possehl (2002, pp. 5–6, 56–57) argues that the criteria by which the state is archaeologically identified—a hierarchy of social classes, kingship, state bureaucracies and the monopolization of power, state religions, and so forth—aren't readily identifiable in the archaeological remains of the Indus civilization. This difference—that of a highly successful, complex society based on a form of political organization other than the state—sets the Indus civilization apart and makes it clear that we still have a lot to learn about this extraordinary development in South Asian prehistory.

Both Mohenjo-Daro and Harappa encompassed a public district and several residential areas (Fig. 15–15). Mohenjo-Daro's "great bath" lies near what has been interpreted as that city's government center—a complex that also included elite residences and a large assembly hall, all of which were set on massive mud-brick and burnt-brick platforms. Water was ideologically important to Indus peoples (Possehl, 2002), and they may have used features like the great bath for ritual cleansing as a part of worship. Nearly 700 brick-lined wells have been recorded by archaeologists at Mohenjo-Daro, and similar features are found at other Indus sites.

Not far from the great bath was a large, imposing building of uncertain function that some have interpreted as a granary, or grain storage facility. A building of this type was also found at Harappa. But, as at Mohenjo-Daro, there's still no direct evidence to confirm its tentative identification as a granary. In other sections of both cities, homes range from modest brick-walled dwellings that bordered unpaved streets and alleys to spacious multistoried houses

Mohenjo-Daro (mo-henjo-dar´-o) An early Indus Valley city in south-central Pakistan.

Harappa (ha-rap´-pa) A fortified city in the Indus Valley of northeastern Pakistan.

FIGURE 15–15
An excavated section of Mohenjo-Daro, Pakistan.

National Geographic Society

with interior courtyards. What has been proclaimed as the world's first efficient sewer system carried waste away from these densely packed dwellings, many of them equipped with indoor toilets and baths.

What might this culture have to say for itself? Unfortunately, the writing system, consisting of brief pictographic notations commonly found on seal stones and pottery, remains undeciphered (Parpola, 1994; Possehl, 1996).

The Indus civilization's decline seems to have been as rapid as its ascent. After little more than half a millennium, its major sites were virtually abandoned, although hundreds of smaller towns and villages outlasted them. Without written records or any archaeological evidence for invasion or revolution, we can only guess what caused its demise. Did competing trade routes bypass the Indus? Did the irrigation system fail, or did the river shift in its channel, either flooding the fields or leaving them parched? Was the society simply unable to maintain its urban centers? Floodwaters were a frequent threat; Mohenjo-Daro had been rebuilt perhaps 10 times before being given up to the Indus tide. All we know for sure is that in the end, the river that spawned the principal urban centers gradually reclaimed the surrounding fields and eventually the city sites themselves.

AT A GLANCE — Important Asian Sites and Regions

Site	Dates (ya)	Comments
Mohenjo-Daro (Pakistan)	c. 4,600–3,900	Most extensively excavated Indus civilization city, located in the Indus Valley of south-central Pakistan
Harappa (Pakistan)	c. 4,600–3,900	Indus civilization city in northeastern Pakistan
Erlitou (China)	c. 4,000	Elaborate site associated with the earliest phase of civilization in northern China
Shixianggou (China)	3,600–3,046	Capital city of the early Shang dynasty
Zhengzhou (China)	3,600–3,046	Early Shang capital city near the modern city of the same name
Shi Huangdi Tomb (China)	2,200	Tomb of the first emperor of China; his mausoleum at Mount Li, near the modern city of Xian, includes an entire terracotta army

NORTHERN CHINA

As we saw in Chapter 14 (see p. 353), the deep roots of China's early civilization were nurtured in the loess uplands and stark alluvial plains bordering the great rivers of the north. Specialized production and exchange of valued ritual goods came to characterize the prosperous farming societies along the central and lower Huang He (Yellow River) Valley and brought about increased contact and conflict among them. This phase of regional development and interaction continued during the later Neolithic, or Longshan, period beginning about 4,800 ya and culminated in the formation of a distinctive Chinese culture that emphasized social ranking and ritualism accompanied by persistent warfare (Chang, 1986).

In this Longshan period, the circulation of luxury products contributed to the concentration of wealth and the emergence of social hierarchies. Elite consumers supported craft specialties including fine wheel-thrown pottery, jade carving, and a developing metal industry based on copper and (later) bronze production. Status differences are reflected in the range of burial treatments—from unusually lavish to mostly austere—given to individuals in the large Longshan cemeteries. Walled towns, which were up to 1 mile in circumference, dominated the region's villages and hamlets (Yan, 1999). Some of the town walls were made of stamped earth, compacted to the hardness of cement, more than 20 feet high and 30 feet thick. These enormous constructions obviously required a large supervised labor force. Numerous arrowheads testify to the prevalence of warfare, but no clear explanations of these developments are yet possible.

Possibly because of the differential access by some individuals and groups to the means of communication within Chinese society (as Chang suggests; see p. 384), their success in organizing and controlling communal agricultural efforts, or conceivably more directly through violence and coercion, local leaders who emerged in northern China over the next few centuries commanded the allegiance of ever-larger regions. The rising nobility played an increasingly prominent role in the next era of Chinese civilization.

Many Chinese archaeologists believe that Erlitou (Fig. 15–16), in Henan province, confirms the existence of the legendary **Xia** dynasty, proclaimed in myth as the dawn of Chinese civilization (Chang, 1980, 1986). The site displays evidence of increasing social complexity around 4,000 ya. It's here, for the first time, that walled palaces set onto stamped earth foundations literally raised members of the royal household above all others. Valuable stone carvings and bronze and ceramic vessels figured in elaborate court ceremonies and rituals. Royal burials contrasted sharply with those of commoners, who were sometimes disposed of in rubbish pits.

Shang   The following Shang dynasty, beginning in the eighteenth century B.C. (3,600 ya), attained a level of sophistication in material culture, architecture, art styles, and writing that only a highly structured society could achieve. Enduring for some six centuries, Shang is generally acknowledged as China's first civilization. While the large population of peasant farmers lived and labored as they always had, an elite and powerful ruling class, supported by slaves, specialized crafters, scribes, and other functionaries, topped the rigid social hierarchy. Unlike the Indus civilization, the Shang territorial state covered multiple cities and a large territory of roughly 8,900 square miles.

The power and actions of Shang rulers were sometimes directed through the rite of **divination**, or prophecy. This practice was one of the original purposes for which writing was used in ancient China. Divination was performed by first inscribing a question on a specially prepared bone, such as the shoulder blade of an ox or deer, or on turtle shells. Applying heat to the thin bones made them crack, and then the answer to the question could be "read" from the patterns formed by the cracks. Divination was a vital activity to the Shang, and thousands of the marked bones survive as a unique historical archive offering insights to early Chinese politics and society (Fitzgerald, 1978).

Many scholars identify the two capital cities of the initial Shang period as Shixianggou and Zhengzhou, both of which are in Henan Province (Maisels 1999). At Zhengzhou, archaeologists revealed portions of a large walled precinct encompassing the residences of nobles and rulers as well as their temples and other ceremonial structures. Within sight of the high enclosure, extending in all directions for more than a mile, were clustered homes and specialized production areas including several bronze foundries, pottery kilns, and bone workshops.

FIGURE **15–16**
Centers of early civilization in Northern China.

Xia   (shah) Semilegendary kingdom or dynasty of early China.

Shang   The Shang or Yin dynasty was the first historic civilization in northern China.

Divination   Foretelling the future.

National Geographic Society

FIGURE **15–17**
Bronze ritual vessel of the Shang dynasty.

Paul G. Richmond

FIGURE **15–18**
Some of the 8,000 clay soldiers from the tomb complex of Shi Huangdi, the first emperor of China.

Shang artisans created remarkable bronze work, particularly elaborate cauldrons cast in sectional molds (Fig. 15–17). Decorated with stylized animal motifs and worshipful inscriptions, the massive metal vessels were designed to hold ritual offerings of wine and food dedicated to ancestors and deities. They also served as prominent funerary items in the royal tombs, about a dozen of which were in the vicinity of the later Shang capital at Anyang (Chang, 1986). Digging each of these grave pits and its four ramped entryways probably kept about 1,000 laborers occupied for a week. In addition to the bronzes, lavish offerings of carved jade, horse-drawn chariots, and scores of human sacrificial victims accompanied the rulers in death. In much later times, as in the tomb of Qin emperor **Shi Huangdi** (died 2,200 ya) at Xian, life-size clay sculptures of warriors and horses sometimes substituted for their living counterparts (Fig. 15–18).

It seems that the Shang kingdom was only one of several contentious feudal states in northern China. Despite their political competition, all shared a common culture, one that served as a foundation for most future developments in China. After the eclipse of the Shang state, successive **Zhou** rulers (1122–221 B.C.) adopted and extended the social and cultural innovations introduced by their Shang predecessors. Much of China remained apportioned among competitive warlords until the Qin and Han dynasties (221 B.C.–A.D. 220), when this huge region was at last politically unified into a cohesive Chinese empire. Consolidated by Shi Huangdi, and protected from the outer world behind his 3,000-mile Great Wall (Fig. 15–19), China in later times maintained many of the cultural traditions linking it to an ancient past.

Sue Lewis

FIGURE **15–19**
Section of the Great Wall, erected by Shi Huangdi.

Summary

The pace of cultural change and elaboration accelerated during the mid-Holocene. It's noteworthy that the emergence of early civilizations came directly after the people achieved sustainable food production in several regions. The primary civilizations of the Old World thrived particularly well on the alluvial plains of several major rivers. The earliest, the Sumerian civilization, emerged as a collection of city-states in the valley of the Tigris-Euphrates after 5,500 ya. A unified Egyptian state was formed around 5,000 ya along the banks

Qin Shi Huangdi   (chin-shee-huang-dee) First emperor of a unified China.

Zhou   (chew) Chinese dynasty that followed Shang and ruled between 1122 and 221 B.C.

TABLE 15–1	The Most Significant Archaeological Sites Discussed in This Chapter	
Site	**Dates (ya)**	**Comments**
Vijayanagara (India)	664–435	Capital city of the Vijayanagara empire, which ruled much of South India; located in north-central Karnataka
Çatalhöyük (Turkey)	ca. 9,000	A large Neolithic village with 5,000–8,000 inhabitants in south-central Turkey
Uruk (Iraq)	ca. 5,500–1,800	Earliest true city; associated with the Sumerian civilization of the southern Tigris-Euphrates Valley
Ur (Iraq)	ca. 4,600–2,500	City in southern Iraq; its cemetery of >1,800 graves includes 16 "royal" tombs
Memphis (Egypt)	ca. 5,100–3,300	Old Kingdom capital city located about 10 miles south of Cairo; abandoned after A.D. 641
Giza (Egypt)	ca. 4,500	Old Kingdom pyramid complex and Great Sphinx; located just to the southwest of Cairo
Mohenjo-Daro (Pakistan)	ca. 4,600–3,900	Most extensively excavated Indus civilization city; located in the Indus Valley of south-central Pakistan
Harappa (Pakistan)	ca. 4,600–3,900	Indus civilization city in northeastern Pakistan
Erlitou (China)	ca. 4,000	Elaborate site associated with the earliest phase of civilization in northern China
Shixianggou, Zhengzhou (China)	3,600–3,046	Early Shang capital cities

of the Nile, and the impressive cultural and architectural achievements of the Old Kingdom began several centuries later. Far to the east, urban commercial centers of the Harappan civilization dominated the Indus Valley by about 4,600 ya, and the Shang was one of a series of strongly hierarchical societies to emerge from the advanced Neolithic farming cultures on the Huang He floodplain of northern China by 3,600 ya.

In Table 15–1 you'll find a useful summary of the most important archaeological sites discussed in this chapter.

Critical Thinking Questions

1. List some of the essential differences between the lifeways of ancient village farmers and the residents of early urban communities. What are the social, economic, and political implications of city life?
2. Suggest why river valleys were the primary setting for so many early Old World civilizations.
3. Why is writing so closely associated with the rise of civilizations?

CHAPTER 16

New World Civilizations

FOCUS QUESTIONS

Why did the first civilizations develop independently in the Old and New Worlds?

How can the similarities and differences between Old and New World civilizations best be explained?

Introduction

The **Maya** city of Palenque (Fig. 16–1) sits on the edge of the Chiapas highlands in southern Mexico (Fig. 16–2). Although parts of it have been excavated and reconstructed by archaeologists, tropical rain forests still mask most of the site. Palenque's exposed buildings and spaces are extremely picturesque, framed as they are by rain forest-draped hills and richly decorated with stuccoed figures and moldings and bas-reliefs executed in a delicately fluid style. It was not a big city, having perhaps no more than about 6,000 inhabitants at its height around A.D. 800, but Maya cities were typically quite different from the **nucleated settlements** of the Near East or China that we examined in Chapter 15. Regardless of its size or pattern of urban design, Palenque's rulers could trace their pedigree over scores of generations as part of the greater web of cities, towns, and villages that formed Maya civilization. During this same era, England was mostly small villages periodically raided by Vikings, the Chinese were inventing gunpowder, the Holy Roman Empire had yet to happen, and the Old and New Worlds wouldn't know about each other's existence for another 700 years.

The history of ancient America's most highly advanced cultures (Fig. 16–3) was closely intertwined with the progress of New World agriculture. In many of the regions where early farming prevailed in the Americas, the combination of maize, beans, and plants such as squash came to substitute for diets rich in animal protein. In time, these primary domesticates nourished large populations and formed the economic basis for social and political elaboration, culminating in the development of states and civilizations in several New World areas.

Superficially, we can say that early New World cities, states, and civilizations are broadly comparable to those of the Old World. All shared some basic similarities: state economies

FIGURE **16–1**
The Palace at the Maya site of Palenque, Mexico.

Maya Prehistoric Mesoamerican culture consisting of regional kingdoms and known for its art and architectural accomplishments.

Nucleated settlement A city or village in which houses, administrative facilities, public areas, storehouses, and the like are clumped or clustered close together.

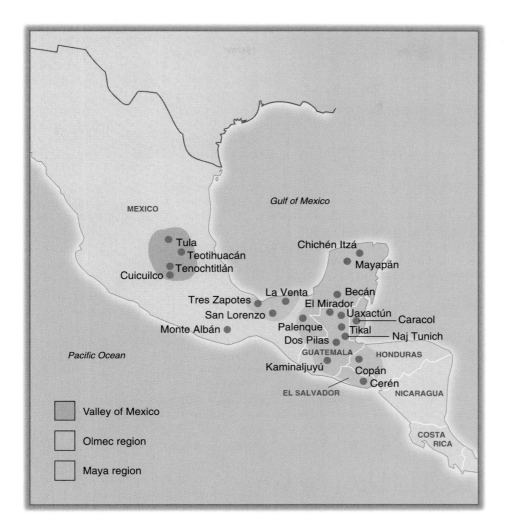

FIGURE 16-2
Mesoamerican archaeological sites mentioned in the text.

based on agriculture and long-distance trade; powerful leaders and social stratification; human labor invested in large-scale constructions; public art styles; state religions; record keeping; and the prominent role of warfare. Still, there are significant points of contrast as well. For example, domesticated animals played only a small part in New World agriculture; the technological role of metal was limited; and the wheel had no important function, nor did watercraft. We shouldn't view these cultural differences as deficiencies, but as resulting from different historical traditions, resources, and geography.

Lowland Mesoamerica

Beginning around 4,000 years ago (ya) and continuing over the next several centuries, more productive varieties of maize and better storage techniques encouraged people in parts of **Mesoamerica** to settle close to their fields. One archaeological marker for this shift to more sedentary settlements is an abundance of pottery fragments, or *sherds*. While mobile foragers found little use for heavy, fragile clay containers, farmers preferred pottery for cooking and storage. They could use pots for carrying water and other products, and they could place ceramic vessels directly over heat for as long as needed to convert starchy grains into a more digestible food. So, the distribution of pottery reflects the spread of village farming in Mesoamerica and elsewhere.

Mesoamerica (*meso*, meaning "middle") Geographical and cultural region from central Mexico to northwestern Costa Rica; formerly called "Middle America" in the archaeological literature.

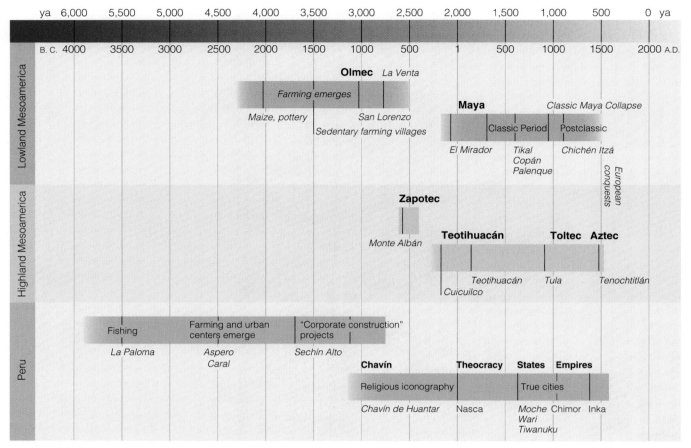

| ya | 6,000 | 5,500 | 5,000 | 4,500 | 4,000 | 3,500 | 3,000 | 2,500 | 2,000 | 1,500 | 1,000 | 500 | 0 ya |

| B.C. 4000 | 3500 | 3000 | 2500 | 2000 | 1500 | 1000 | 500 | 1 | 500 | 1000 | 1500 | 2000 A.D. |

Lowland Mesoamerica

Olmec *La Venta*

Farming emerges

Maize, pottery   *San Lorenzo*

Sedentary farming villages

Maya   *Classic Maya Collapse*

Classic Period   Postclassic

El Mirador   *Tikal*   *Chichén Itzá*
                Copán
                Palenque

European conquests

Highland Mesoamerica

Zapotec

Monte Albán

Teotihuacán   **Toltec** **Aztec**

Teotihuacán   *Tula*   *Tenochtitlán*
Cuicuilco

Peru

Fishing   *Farming and urban centers emerge*   *"Corporate construction" projects*

La Paloma   *Aspero*   *Sechín Alto*
                 Caral

Chavín   **Theocracy** **States** **Empires**

Religious iconography   *True cities*

Chavín de Huantar   *Nasca*   *Moche* *Chimor* *Inka*
                                    Wari
                                    Tiwanuku

FIGURE 16–3
Time line for Chapter 16.

Olmec   Prehistoric chiefdoms in the Gulf Coast lowlands of Veracruz and Tabasco, Mexico, with a highly developed art style and social complexity; flourished from 3,200 to 2,400 ya.

polity, polities   The political organization of a society or group.

OLMEC: CHIEFDOM OR STATE?

By roughly 3,500 ya, farming villages dotted the lowlands of Mesoamerica. Local chiefdoms arose, and their archaeological hallmarks included prominent house sites, status or ritual objects, and other signs of social differentiation, especially in burial offerings. For many years, archaeologists have been particularly interested in one of these groups, known as the **Olmec**, which achieved prominence in the river valleys, forests, and swamps of the southern Gulf Coast of Mexico between about 3,200 and 2,400 ya (Fig. 16–4).

The political organization of the Olmec is controversial, and there's no consensus in sight. Richard Diehl (2004) and Michael Coe (Diehl and Coe, 1996), who have both worked extensively on Olmec sites, identify Olmec as "America's first civilization" and one that exerted considerable influence on later Mesoamerican cultures. Other archaeologists (e.g., Flannery and Marcus, 2000; Spencer and Redmond, 2004) conclude that Olmec **polities** weren't states, but chiefdoms—what Fried (1967) would call a "ranked society"—and that they do not represent an early civilization. What's more, Spencer and Redmond (2004) argue that the most convincing archaeological evidence for the emergence of the earliest Mesoamerican state can be found not in the lowlands, but at the large Zapotec center of Monte Albán in the highlands of Oaxaca around 2,300 ya.

From an archaeological standpoint, it's probably more important to determine how extensively the Olmec affected contemporary societies in other parts of Mesoamerica than it is to decide in which sociopolitical pigeonhole their society belongs. Diehl and Coe, for example, believe that the Olmec anticipated, and may have inspired, important features that characterized subsequent Mesoamerican civilizations. Other archaeologists, including David Grove (1989, 1996), who has devoted much of his career to research on early Mesoamerican civilizations, rejects such arguments and feels that they were simply part of a web of chiefdoms and early states that interacted across Mesoamerica. Flannery and

Teotihuacán

Aztec

Monte Albán

Olmec

Maya

Chimu

Inka

William Turnbaugh

Mark A. Gutchen

Mark A. Gutchen

Mark A. Gutchen

William Turnbaugh

Wendell C. Bennett, "The Archaeology of the Central Andes," in Julian H. Steward, ed., *Handbook of South American Indians*, Vol. 2, plate 51. Washington, DC: Government Printing Office, 1947.

Carol Howell

FIGURE 16–4
Location of ancient American civilizations discussed in the text.

FIGURE **16–5**
Olmec figure, carved from jade.

FIGURE **16–6**
Monumental Olmec head excavated at La Venta, Mexico.

Marcus (2000) make a strong case to refute Diehl and Coe's (1996) supporting evidence point by point, arguing that there's little basis to view the Olmec as a Mesoamerican "mother culture."

The two best-known Olmec sites are San Lorenzo and La Venta (see Fig. 16–4), which Diehl (2004) identifies as the region's first cities. At both sites, people extensively modified the natural landscapes—without the aid of domestic animals or machinery—to convert them into proper settings for impressive constructions and sculptures of ritual significance (Coe, 1994; Diehl, 2004). Earthen-mound alignments enclose the wide courtyards, plazas, and artificial ponds at San Lorenzo. A 100-foot-high cone-shaped earthen pyramid dominates La Venta. Within and nearby the sites themselves, there are hundreds of smaller earthen platform mounds that once supported homes and workshops.

In addition to building ceremonial architecture, the Olmec produced remarkable monumental sculptures and smaller, well-crafted carvings of jade and other attractive stones (Fig. 16–5). **Anthropomorphic** forms predominate, including some figurines and bas-reliefs that combine the features of humans with those of felines, probably jaguars. Olmec art and iconography are fascinating but poorly understood. Who or what did these anthropomorphic beings represent? Equally intriguing are the colossal Olmec heads, each of which seems to be an individualized portrait of a ruler in helmet-like headgear, carved from massive boulders of basalt weighing up to 20 tons. Archaeologists estimate that the sustained effort of 1,000-member crews were needed to drag and raft the boulders from the distant source area, some 60 miles from the site (Lowe, 1989). Nine of these huge likenesses have been found at San Lorenzo itself (Fig. 16–6).

Curiously, the Olmec intentionally buried caches of beads, as well as carved figurines and implements made from their highly valued jade. One pit offering at La Venta consisted of 460 green stone blocks, arranged into a giant mosaic design and then buried at a depth of more than 20 feet. Another held an assemblage of small jade figures set into place so that they all seem to be confronting one individual. Then, still in position, the group was buried (Fig. 16–7).

The latest Olmec controversy concerns the origins of writing in Mesoamerica. Recent excavations at the site of San Andrés in the coastal state of Tabasco revealed a cylinder seal and other artifacts bearing **glyphs**, all found in contexts dated to 2,650 ya (Pohl et al., 2002). Mary

anthropomorphic   (*anthro*, meaning "man," and *morph*, meaning "shape") Having or being given humanlike characteristics.

glyph   A carved or incised symbolic figure.

Pohl and her colleagues interpret the iconography of these artifacts as elements of an Olmec writing system that contributed to the development of Mesoamerican writing. While they agree that these new finds are important, other archaeologists argue that the discoveries aren't enough evidence to justify saying that these were elements of a fully developed system of writing (Stokstad, 2004).

To sum things up, the Olmec represent a fascinating early development of complex society in the lowlands of the Mexican Gulf Coast, and archaeologists have considerably more good questions than firm answers about them. The view supported by the most evidence is that the Olmec chiefdoms of southern Veracruz and Tabasco were similar in many respects to their neighbors in the highlands to the south and west and to those throughout central Mexico. The archaeological evidence may or may not eventually live up to Diehl's claim that they were America's first civilization, but no one can deny the attraction that these unusual early communities and their extraordinary art and architecture hold for modern archaeologists and the public.

Philip Drucker, Robert Squier, Excavations at La Venta, Tabasco, 1955." Smithsonian Institution, Bureau of American Ethnology Bulletin 170, plate 20. Washington, DC: Government Printing Office, 1969.

FIGURE 16–7
Buried cache of small Olmec jade figurines found at La Venta, Mexico.

AT A GLANCE   Important Lowland Mesoamerica Sites and Regions

Site	Dates (ya)	Comments
Palenque (Mexico)	c. 1,300–1,100	Classic Maya center located on the edge of the Gulf Coast lowlands in Chiapas
San Lorenzo (Mexico)	3,150–2,900	Olmec civic-ceremonial center in southern Veracruz
La Venta (Mexico)	c. 2,800–2,400	Large Olmec civic-ceremonial center in the coastal lowlands of Tabasco
San Andrés (Mexico)	2,650	Olmec site near La Venta that recently yielded a cylinder seal with early evidence of writing in the Gulf Coast Lowlands; San Andrés also cited in Chapter 14 for the discovery of ancient maize pollen in a soil core pulled from pre-Olmec contexts
Uaxactún (Guatemala)	1,500–1,000	Maya center that flourished during the Classic period in the Petén of Guatemala
Cerén (El Salvador)	c. 1,400	Maya village buried by the eruption of a volcano; provides a Pompeii-like snapshot of Classic period Maya life
Copán (Honduras)	c. 1,600–1,200	Major Maya city in western Honduras with an estimated population of around 27,000 at its peak
Naj Tunich (Guatemala)	c. 1,750–1,450	A sacred cave in the Petén region that has furnished invaluable new information about Maya art, writing, and religious life
Tikal (Guatemala)	c. 2,200–1,100	Major Maya center in the Petén of northern Guatemala

CLASSIC MAYA

Another of the emerging Mesoamerican societies was the Classic Maya,* with whom we began this chapter at the city of Palenque. Analysis of pollen profiles obtained from swamps in the lowlands of eastern Mesoamerica indicates that the people who were directly ancestral to the Maya began practicing slash-and-burn maize farming in the lowlands between 4,000 and 3,000 ya (Piperno and Pearsall, 1998). Fire assisted in opening forest clearings and reducing the vegetation to soluble ash, which served as crop fertilizer. Some of the areas the farmers occupied, notably the scrublands of Yucatán and the Petén jungles farther south, couldn't support a growing population that relied solely on shifting, slash-and-burn plots. There, the farmers resorted to more labor-intensive agricultural techniques, set up redistribution networks among their growing communities, and established trade connections with more distant societies. They cleared more and larger forest tracts to bring more land under cultivation, and, in low places, they dredged organic swamp muck to create ridged planting fields. In their fields, they planted maize, beans, and squash along with root crops such as manioc.

As we noted earlier, some suggest that Classic period Maya civilization originated in part with the Olmec, whose art, architecture, and rituals are reflected in some early Maya sites. Others suggest that Maya civilization resulted from an internal reorganization of Maya society itself; or that it reflects the regional impact of the developing states of central Mexico (more on this in the next section); or, more generally, that it came from the competitive interaction between contemporary Mesoamerican chiefdoms, which ultimately resulted in some of them becoming true states and civilizations. Right now, the third explanation appears to be the most likely (Flannery and Marcus, 2000; Braswell, 2003).

By roughly 2,100 ya, the elements of Maya civilization were coming together. Crucial materials that were lacking in most of the Maya lowlands, especially suitable stone for making tools and milling slabs, were exchanged for commodities such as salt or the feathers of colorful jungle birds, both of which the highland groups desired. Control of trade routes or strategic waterways may have promoted the growth of the Late Preclassic† center at El Mirador, where archaeologists have found the earliest evidence of Maya palaces, and following that at **Uaxactún** and **Tikal**, all of which are in northern Guatemala (see Fig. 16–4).

At these sites and others, Maya society came to be dominated increasingly by an elite social class (Fig. 16–8). A host of Maya kings, each claiming descent through royal lineages

FIGURE **16–8**
Maya nobles depicted on carved stones set in an inner courtyard of the Palace, Palenque, Mexico.

Barry Lewis

Uaxactún  (wash-akh-toon´) Maya urban center in Guatemala.

Tikal (tee-kal´) Principal Maya city in Guatemala.

---

*The word *Classic* refers here to the archaeological period of the same name, which was between roughly A.D. 200 and 900.
†The Late Preclassic is a Mesoamerican archaeological period that dates roughly from 300 B.C. to A.D. 200.

FIGURE 16-9
The Temple of the Inscriptions at Palenque, Mexico, served as the tomb of the important Maya ruler Pacal, who died in A.D. 683.

Barry Lewis

back to the gods themselves, held sway over independent city-states, centered on elaborate ceremonial precincts. Under the patronage of these kings, writing, fine arts, and architecture flourished in the Maya lowlands, as did chronic warfare among rival kingdoms (Sharer, 1996; Coe, 1999). Lisa Lucero (2003) argues that successful Maya rulers acquired and maintained their political power by skillfully manipulating domestic rituals, which in turn promoted political cohesion.

The Maya are best known for their impressive Classic period urban centers, with Tikal, Copán (Honduras), and Palenque (Mexico), among them (Fig. 16–9). Such sites served as regional capitals allied with smaller local centers in their respective areas (Marcus, 1993). Archaeologists historically have devoted much of their attention to these spectacular places. But the importance of these urban centers is gradually being put into perspective as archaeological research focuses on the entire range of Classic Maya lifeways.

Extraordinary discoveries, such as the buried Maya community at Cerén, El Salvador, give us detailed glimpses of village life (Sheets, 2002, 2006). Cerén—once a hamlet of mud-walled, thatched huts—lay entombed for 1,400 years beneath 18 feet of ash from the eruption of a nearby volcano. The inhabitants fled their homes, which were quickly buried by the volcanic ash. Remarkable traces of Maya peasant life survived, including a plentiful harvest of maize, beans, squash, tomatoes, and chilies stored in baskets and pots, arranged as if they had just been gathered from nearby garden plots.

Estimates of overall population during the Classic period range widely, but Rice and Culbert (1990) judge that many regions supported a population density of roughly 466 persons per square mile. The local density of population varied with the suitability of land for agricultural development, whether by slash-and-burn or intensive farming methods such as raised or ridged fields in swampy zones, hillside terracing, irrigation and drainage, fertilization, and multiple cropping (Flannery, 1982), all of which the Maya used extensively. In addition, the Maya systematically hunted, fished, and collected wild plant foods.

These combined resources sustained the substantial Maya population, part of it clustered around some 200 towns and cities. Rural centers, having just one or two carved **stelae** (inscribed stone pillars) or a modest shrine maintained by nearby farmers, were secondary to regional centers, which were themselves under the domain of one of the city-states (such as Copán or Tikal) at the top of the hierarchy. The largest settlements were the focus of sociopolitical activity, religious ceremonies, and commerce (Lucero, 1999). They served essentially as capitals of regional Maya city-states, despite their somewhat dispersed populace. Including the ruling elite and their retainers, crafters, other specialists, and farmers, some 27,000 people were attached to the important city of Copán (Webster et al., 2000), although

stelae (sing., stela) (stee´-lee) Upright posts or stones, often bearing inscriptions.

FIGURE **16–10**

One of several temple pyramids and numerous stelae at the Maya ceremonial center of Tikal, in Guatemala.

two-thirds of them actually resided in farming compounds scattered through the Copán Valley, within walking distance of Copán.

Formal, large-scale architecture dominated the largest cities. Tikal, with over 50,000 residents, boasted more than 3,000 structures in its core precinct alone. Most impressive were the stepped, limestone-sided pyramids capped with crested temples (Fig. 16–10). Facing across the broad stuccoed plazas were multiroom palaces (presumably elite residences), generally a ritual ball court or two (Fig. 16–11), and always elaborately carved stelae (Figs. 16–12 and 16–13). Other features might include graded causeways leading into the complex masonry reservoirs for storing crucial runoff from tropical cloudbursts. The Maya preferred to paint their structures in bold colors, so the overall effect must have been stunning.

Scholars have made significant progress in deciphering the complex inscriptions on Maya stelae, temples, and other monuments (Houston et. al., 2001). Calendrical notations on the sculptures provide a precise chronology of major events in lowland Mesoamerica (see Digging Deeper on p. 412). For example, when the Maya calendar system is correlated with ours, the beginning of the Classic period can be set in the year A.D. 199 (Freidel, et al., 1993). Many stelae proclaim the ancestry and noble deeds of actual Maya rulers, while others record significant historical occasions (Schele and Miller, 1986). These inscriptions offer

FIGURE **16–11**

The ball court at Monte Albán, one of several types built by nearly all the major cultures of Mesoamerica.

FIGURE **16–12**
This elaborately carved Maya stela at Copán, Honduras, depicts King 18 Rabbit in ceremonial regalia.

FIGURE **16–13**
Maya hieroglyphs on a stela at Copán record the date and purpose of its dedication.

FIGURE **16–14**
This Classic Maya cylindrical jar with bird motif and glyphs was used in ceremonies.

direct insights to Classic Maya sociopolitical organization, including the uneasy and frequently embattled relationships among leading ceremonial centers and their rival aristocracies (Schele and Freidel, 1990; Coe, 1992).

Religion was a key component of Maya society, just as it was in all early civilizations. Maya architecture and art were dedicated to the veneration of divine kings and the worship of perhaps hundreds of major and minor deities (Fig. 16–14). Maya nobility included a priestly caste who carefully observed the sun, moon, and planet Venus; predicted the rains; prescribed the rituals; and performed the sacrifices. Most of the priestly lore and learning faithfully recorded in the Maya **codices**, or books, was lost when the Spanish burned the ancient texts during the conquest. But a number of sacred caves, like **Naj Tunich** in Guatemala, preserve some forgotten aspects of Maya religion. Within these dusky chambers, archaeologists have come upon Classic period offerings, paintings that graphically depict ritual intercourse and self-mutilation, and the remains of young sacrificial victims (Brady and Stone, 1986).

codices (*sing.*, codex)Illustrated books.

Naj Tunich (nah toon´-eesh) Maya sacred cave in Guatemala.

411

DIGGING DEEPER

How to Count and Measure Time—The Maya Way

The Maya devised a number system intended primarily to record the passage of time. They reckoned time by referring to an intricate calendar with three distinct components. Their *long-count chronology* recorded the number of individual days that had passed since the beginning of the Maya universe (on August 11, 3114 B.C., by our calendar); so, for example, January 15 in A.D. 2003 is 1,868,735 days since the Maya zero date. This continuing sequence served as the formal measure of Maya chronology that was recorded on their monuments and stelae. Next, a 260-day *Sacred Round* counted 13 months, each 20 days long, with each month-day combination holding religious significance. Finally, a *secular calendar* of 360 days—18 months of 20 days each—approximated the solar year, with a 5-day adjustment period added at the end. Every 52 years, or exactly 18,980 days, the Maya cycle of time began anew with the synchronization of both the secular and sacred calendars.

The Maya represented the numbers 1 through 19 by a simple bar-and-dot notation, in which a dot equaled 1 and a bar had a value of 5. Notice that the Maya used the 0, a device not invented in Europe until the Middle Ages. They expressed numbers larger than 19 as multiples of 20. The value of the number was determined by its position in a vertical column, in much the same way that the value of our numbers is indicated by their position rela-

tive to a decimal point. So, numbers in the first (lowest) position were multiplied by 1; those in the next higher position, by 20; in the third, by 360 (that is, 20 × 18—the number of days in the month multiplied by the number of months in the secular calendar); in the fourth, by 7,200 (20 × 360—the number of days in the month multiplied by the number of days in the secular year); in the fifth, by 144,000 (20 × 7,200); and so on.

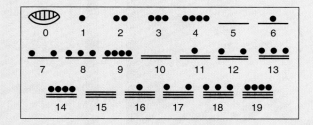

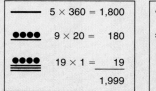

The number for 1,999

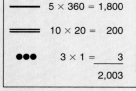

The number for 2,003

Classic Maya Collapse   The rise and fall of Maya city-states continued for centuries. And, now that Maya writing has been deciphered, we've learned a great deal about the historical events that figured in the changing fortunes of Maya kings. For example, the city of Tikal, one of the largest Maya cities, fell on hard times for more than a century after A.D. 562, when it was defeated by Caracol, a smaller city-state in modern-day Belize. Later, during A.D. 738, Copán's vigorous king, 18 Rabbit (see Fig. 16–12), lost his life at the hands of a neighboring ruler. These events reflect a common pattern of intrigue and competition between neighboring polities. Things came to a head around A.D. 900. Maya artisans no longer turned out their distinctive decorated ceramics, nor did they carve and erect inscribed stelae. The construction of palaces, temples, and other major works ceased altogether, and nearly all major sites were abandoned.

The remarkable Maya collapse has intrigued scholars for decades. Archaeologists are not yet quite sure *what* happened, let alone *why*. Proposed single-cause explanations, each of them inadequate, include devastation by hurricanes or earthquakes, extreme climatic fluctuations, insect infestations, epidemic diseases, malnutrition, overpopulation, an unbalanced male/female sex ratio, peasant revolts against the elite, and mass migrations. Some scholars have also cited external factors, such as the breakdown of trade relations with the areas that supplied the resource-poor Maya or invasion by peoples from highland Mexico.

Other scholars claim that political instability brought about the collapse (Rice et al., 2001). Cioffi-Revilla and Landman (1999) argue that the Classic Maya city-states collapsed primarily because they failed to integrate into a single unified political system, such as that achieved by the Aztec in central Mexico and the Inka in highland South America. Unlike the people of Egypt or Mesopotamia, the Maya had no Narmer or Sargon to bring unity to their city-states— and those who tried met their match in the insurmountable logistical obstacles presented by the tropical jungles of the lowlands (Cioffi-Revilla and Landman, 1999, pp. 586–588).

The consequences of this turmoil were primarily limited to the southern Maya region, where only much-reduced peasant populations remained in the vicinity of the silent centers. Some northern lowland sites actually expanded and continued to flourish for centuries as a comparatively modest and much modified Postclassic* period Maya culture in Yucatán (Freidel and Sabloff, 1984).

Highland Mexico

The convergence of two mountain ranges in central Mexico forms a great highland of some 3,000 square miles, commonly known as the Valley of Mexico (see Fig. 16–2). Actually an elevated plateau rimmed by mountains and volcanic peaks to the west, south and east, with its rich agricultural soils watered by several rivers and with large lakes at its center, this broad semiarid basin served as a stage for the development of several important Mesoamerican states and civilizations. The earliest city-state to dominate the Valley, **Teotihuacán**, became one of the largest urban centers in the New World up to the nineteenth century (Cowgill, 2000).

TEOTIHUACÁN

The agricultural potential of Mexico's central highland drew early farmers into the region's diverse landscapes. Some used stone axes and fire to open garden plots in the native oak and pine forests that clothed the foothills of the mountains. Others redirected the flow of streams or seeping springs to the roots of their maize plants. Among the marshes that obscured the shoreline of the brackish lakes in the Valley of Mexico appeared fields of yet other kinds: raised ridges and dark beds of muck (known as **chinampas**) dredged from the lake bottom. Nearby, outcrops of volcanic obsidian, glassy and green, fostered stone toolmaking. Farming hamlets rapidly grew into villages and then coalesced into towns as agriculture and trade prospered within the region.

Teotihuacán was one of these expanding communities by some 2,200 ya. With its nearby fields nourished by a system of irrigation canals, Teotihuacán experienced especially rapid growth. Its closest competitor, Cuicuilco (see Fig. 16–2), had a population of around 20,000 at its peak but vanished from the scene around 2,000 ya, when it was buried by a lava flow. This unfortunate event worked to Teotihuacán's advantage, and the community continued to expand for the next six centuries. It soon dominated the Valley of Mexico and, after 1,800–1,700 ya, its presence is archaeologically recognized in many parts of Mesoamerica, as far away as Guatemala (Spencer and Redmond, 2004).

At its height between 1,700 and 1,400 ya, Teotihuacán (Fig. 16–15) had more than 100,000 residents and covered 7.7 square miles. Somewhat in contrast to the Maya centers, Teotihuacán's layout was more orderly and its population more highly concentrated. Built on a grid pattern with a primary north-south axis, its avenues, plazas, major monuments, and homes alike—and even the San Juan River— were aligned to a master plan.

The city's inhabitants lived in some 2,000 residential apartment compounds, arranged into formal neighborhoods based on occupation or social class and ranging from tradespeople to merchants, military officers, and even foreigners. Civic and religious leaders enjoyed more luxurious facilities in the central district (Millon,

Teotihuacán (tay-oh-tee-wah-cahn´)
Earliest city-state to dominate the Valley of Mexico, it became one of the largest urban centers in the New World up to the nineteenth century.

chinampas (chee-nahm´-pahs)
Productive agricultural plots created by dredging up lake-bottom muck to form raised ridges or platforms; also called "floating gardens."

FIGURE **16–15**
Feathered Serpent figure on temple façade at Teotihuacán, Mexico.

*The Postclassic is a Mesoamerican archaeological period that dates to roughly A.D. 900–1520.

1988). Artisans laboring in hundreds of individual household workshops produced ceramic vessels, obsidian blades, shell and jade carvings, fabrics, leather goods, and other practical or luxury items.

An impressive civic-ceremonial precinct covered nearly 0.6–1.0 square miles in the heart of the city. Imaginative Spanish explorers assigned the name Avenida de los Muertos (literally, "Avenue of the Dead") to the main thoroughfare extending northward 2.8 miles to a massive structure, the Pyramid of the Moon. An even greater Pyramid of the Sun, its base equal to that of Khufu's pyramid in Egypt (though it rises only half as high), occupies a central position along the same avenue. Archaeologists have come to recognize that the Teotihuacán rulers built this immense structure to resemble a sacred mountain, and they raised it directly over a natural cave that symbolized the entry to the underworld. Flanking the south end of the Avenida de los Muertos, the Ciudadela was the administrative complex, and the Great Compound served as Teotihuacán's central marketplace.

Unlike Maya art, that of Teotihuacán doesn't show identifiable rulers or personalized representations. There are no Teotihuacán counterparts of Maya stelae commemorating the conquests and lineages of a given king. Artistic expression is both impersonal and repetitive, the same elements or motifs appearing again and again; this pattern is particularly evident in Teotihuacán architecture, whose repetitive nature was relieved mostly by the use of bright colors. Although social differentiation clearly existed, such differences are evident in art mostly in differences of costume, not in representations of the human body (Cowgill, 2000).

Warfare appears to have been endemic among Mesoamerican states, but cultural differences determined how war was expressed artistically (Brown and Stanton, 2003). These differences went unappreciated by archaeologists years ago, and for a long time they believed that Teotihuacán was a relatively peaceful state. Now that researchers better understand Teotihuacán culture, we can see that warfare also was an important part of this early state.

Mention of warfare leads us logically to examining the possible influence that Teotihuacán wielded throughout Mexico's central region and beyond. The society's fine orange-slipped ceramics, architectural and artistic styles, and obsidian products are said to be present at distant contemporary centers such as Monte Albán in Oaxaca; the Maya site of **Kaminaljuyú** in the Guatemalan highlands; and Tikal, Uaxactún, and Becán in the Maya lowlands (Berlo, 1992). Some also argue that Teotihuacán played a large role in the development of Maya states (e.g., Sanders and Michels, 1977; Sanders et al., 1979).

Kaminaljuyú (cam-en-awl-hoo-yoo′) Major prehistoric Maya site located at Guatemala City.

AT A GLANCE — Important Highland Mesoamerican Sites and Regions

Site	Dates (ya)	Comments
Teotihuacán (Mexico)	c. 2,200–1,350	Earliest city-state to dominate the Valley of Mexico, one of the largest urban centers in the New World up to the nineteenth century
Cuicuilco (Mexico)	c. 2,300–2,000	Important early center in the Valley of Mexico; its destruction by a lava flow made it easier for Teotihuacán to take control of the Valley
Kaminaljuyú (Guatemala)	c. 3,000–1,100	Major Maya site located on the outskirts of Guatemala City; similarities of its elaborate tombs and architecture are often cited as evidence of the far-flung influence of Teotihuacán
Tula (Mexico)	c. 1,200–850	Totlec capital in the Valley of Mexico
Chichén Itzá and **Mayapán** (Mexico)	c. 1,100–600	Postclassic Maya centers in the lowlands of northern Yucatán
Tenochtitlán (Mexico)	c. 675–480	Aztec capital city in the Valley of Mexico

As with many—if not most—archaeological generalizations like these, the more we learn, the more complex the picture gets. And, while no one doubts that Teotihuacán interacted with other regions, the precise nature of this interaction is still being explored (Braswell, 2003). At one extreme, we have cases such as the Escuintla region on the Pacific coast of Guatemala, where researchers recently found material evidence of a Teotihuacán colony that established itself at several sites and soon made itself felt throughout this region as well as in southern Chiapas and western El Salvador (Bove and Busto, 2003). At the other extreme are scholars, many of them Maya specialists, who view the whole notion of Teotihuacán "influence" as greatly exaggerated, and in cases where there is indisputable material evidence of contact, they argue it hasn't yet been proven that Teotihuacán had a significant local impact, or that it changed anything (e.g., Iglesias Ponce de Léon, 2003). It's more than likely that the truth lies somewhere in between these strongly opposed views, but precisely where we've yet to discover.

Teotihuacán's demise also remains an archaeological mystery. After six remarkable centuries, the city was not doing well. Physical anthropologists who have examined human remains excavated from the site's later features recognize the common skeletal indicators of nutritional stress and disease as well as high infant mortality rates. Still, population levels remained stable for another century or so before declining rapidly.

The end came, in flames and havoc, about 1,350 ya (Cowgill, 2000). The entire ceremonial precinct blazed as temples were thrown down and their icons smashed, though residential areas remained unscathed. In the frenzy, some of the nobility were seized and dismembered, apparently by their own people. As archaeologist George L. Cowgill (2000, p. 290) puts it, "What ended was not just a dynasty, it was the belief system that had supported the state." The city may even have been abandoned, or nearly so, for a brief period, but researchers still have much to learn about this period of the city's past. Regardless, the destruction ended Teotihuacán's political and religious preeminence, and many of its residents scattered to other communities. We have yet to determine the factors—whether internal or external—that brought this extraordinary city to its knees.

TOLTECS AND POSTCLASSIC MAYA

Teotihuacán's collapse did not leave a political, economic, or religious vacuum in highland Mesoamerica. Of the many groups contending for control over the region during the next several centuries, the **Toltecs** eventually emerged as the most powerful. They established a capital at **Tula**, in the northern region of the Valley of Mexico some 40 miles northwest of Teotihuacán. By 1,200–1,100 ya, the city may have had as many as 50,000–60,000 residents. This city-state covered some 4.5–5.0 square miles and included several pyramids and ball courts in two ceremonial precincts (Healan and Stoutamire, 1989).

Although its more modest ceremonial precincts scarcely rivaled those of Classic period times, Tula does show some artistic and architectural continuities with Teotihuacán (Cowgill, 2000). The Toltecs also briefly guided a commercial and military enterprise that expanded through trade and tribute networks, colonization efforts, and probably conquest (Davies, 1983; Healan, 1989). Toltec prestige reached in several directions. We even recognize their influence in the copper bells, ceremonial ball courts, and other exotic products found on Hohokam sites in the American Southwest, from which the Toltecs acquired their valued blue turquoise stone, probably by making long-distance exchanges (see p. 359).

Within Mesoamerica, the Toltecs' association with the contemporary Postclassic period Maya site of **Chichén Itzá** in northern Yucatán is also intriguing (Fig. 16–16). Even though they were nearly 800 miles apart, Tula and Chichén Itzá shared elements of art style as well as strikingly similar ball courts, skull racks, temple pyramids,

Toltecs Central Mexican highlands people who created a pre-Aztec empire with its capital at Tula in the Valley of Mexico.

Tula (too´-la) Toltec capital in the Valley of Mexico; sometimes known as Tollan.

Chichén Itzá (chee-chen´ eet-zah´) Postclassic Maya site in Yucatán, linked with the Toltecs of Mexico.

FIGURE **16–16**
Temple of the Warriors building complex at Chichén Itzá, Mexico.

Barry Lewis

Barry Lewis

FIGURE **16–17**
Statue of the rain god Tlaloc, which stands at the entrance to the National Museum of Anthropology in Mexico City.

Barry Lewis

FIGURE **16–18**
The rugged Sierra Madre Oriental mountains flank the eastern side of the Mexican altiplano (high plain), down which Native American groups from northern Mexico and the American Southwest traveled to the Valley of Mexico.

and other public architecture. A cult of militarism and human sacrifice to the rain god Tlaloc (Fig. 16–17) pervaded both sites.

Archaeologists are still debating the nature of this relationship. Many who once interpreted the evidence as an indication of Toltec military or political domination now suggest that members of the Mexican and Maya elites may have interacted more or less amiably during a period of extensive contact and trade between Yucatán and highland Mexico (Weaver, 1993). But others hold to the view that the Toltecs were masters of a dual empire, lording over the Maya from their second capital at Chichén Itzá (Coe et al., 1986). Despite research at some of Chichén's more interesting features—including the Sacred **Cenote**, or sacrificial pool, where offerings (including humans) were cast into the deep waters—archaeologists have found no definitive clues to this puzzle.

As Toltec power declined around 850 ya, Chichén Itzá yielded its preeminence to Mayapán, a Maya trading center in northwestern Yucatán (Sabloff and Rathje, 1975). Within Mexico's central highlands, the Toltecs themselves confronted internal dissension and pressure on their frontiers before finally abandoning Tula, leaving its burned temples and palaces in rubble. By then, a prolonged drought was withering many of the farming communities in northern Mexico and the American Southwest, bringing streams of refugees into the Valley of Mexico and throwing the region into chaos once more (Fig. 16–18).

Cenote   (sen-o´-tay) A natural sinkhole or collapsed cavern partly filled with water.

Mexica   (meh-shee´-ka) Original name by which the Aztecs were known before their rise to power.

Aztecs   Militaristic people who dominated the Valley of Mexico and surrounding area at the time of the European conquest.

AZTECS

One of the groups that appeared on the scene at this point was the **Mexica**, better known historically as the **Aztecs** (Smith, 2003). Impoverished and in search of a permanent homeland, like other people in this turbulent era, the Mexica encountered hostility in their wanderings and fought fiercely to gain a territory. After being pushed from place to place, they finally settled a large, easily defended island near shallow Lake Texcoco's western shore, in the very heart of the Valley of Mexico (Fig. 16–19). From this more secure base, they eventually won control of the entire region through strategic military alliances and brutal warfare.

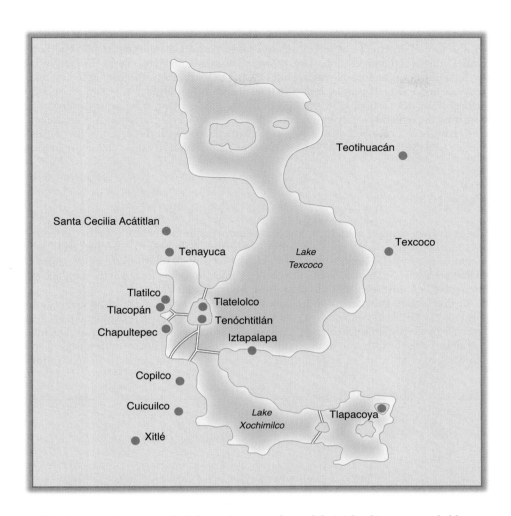

FIGURE **16–19**
Tenochtitlán and neighboring polities of the Lake Texcoco region in the Valley of Mexico.

The Aztecs, as they now called themselves, transformed their island into a remarkable capital they named **Tenochtitlán**. Tied to the mainland only by several narrow causeways, the city itself was sectioned by canals that encouraged canoe transport of goods and people. Its large central plaza encompassed palaces, administrative buildings, and a huge twin-towered temple pyramid for their gods. Between many of the canals, productive *chinampas* yielded an abundance of agricultural foods throughout the year, including maize, beans, tomatoes, and chilies.

The Aztecs incorporated and built on many of the accomplishments of their Mesoamerican predecessors. Their calendar, for instance, was a modification of the one used by the Maya 1,000 years earlier. Aztec religion, with its emphasis on the sun and on war and human sacrifice, derived from Toltec practices and, ultimately, from ancient Teotihuacán. The Aztecs also learned much about social and political organization and economic enterprise from their predecessors. They established a hereditary nobility of several ranks, including a royal lineage from which their highest leaders descended. Free commoners, comprising the vast majority of Aztec society, were organized into about 20 large kin-based groups to work their own communal lands, while slaves labored for the nobles.

More so than any of its predecessors, the Aztec domain was a consolidated and centralized state under the firm rule of a single leader (Clendinnen, 1991; Townsend, 1992). Using a well-trained military force as well as political alliances, aggressive tax collectors, and a state-sponsored corps of professional traders, the Aztecs dominated neighboring peoples and extended their influence well beyond the Valley of Mexico. Tribute in the form of maize, cotton cloth, colored stones, exotic feathers, gold, and slaves flowed into the capital. Many of the war captives seized by the Aztec army were reserved for the periodic bloody sacrifices to the Aztec gods (Fig. 16–20).

FIGURE **16–20**
Aztec rite of human sacrifice, depicted in a sixteenth-century chronicle.

Tenochtitlán (tay-nosh-teet-lahn´)
Aztec capital, built on the future site of Mexico City.

Until the Spanish arrived, Tenochtitlán remained a large and lively urban and religious center, the core of an empire of several million souls. With its magnificent public buildings, houses built over the water, and canoes crowding its canals, the Aztec city in 1519 reminded the Spanish conquistadors of Venice, Italy. One of the soldiers recalled that "so large a market place and so full of people, and so well regulated and arranged, (we) had never beheld before" (Diaz del Castillo, 1956, pp. 218–219). Yet, within a year, these same admirers had destroyed the remarkable city in their quest for wealth and territory. Some of its impressive ruins have been uncovered during subway construction beneath the streets of present-day Mexico City (Moctezuma, 1988), but few traces of Tenochtitlán remain visible aboveground.

Peru

The great **Inka** empire, when encountered by Europeans in the sixteenth century, extended over most of highland and coastal South America from Colombia to Argentina and Chile, including modern-day Peru. In many respects, the Inka civilization was the culmination of all that preceded it in western South America. Its foundations were rooted in the most ancient cultures of Peru (Moseley, 1992; Bruhns, 1994; Silverman, 2004).

At first glance, Peru seems an unlikely region for nurturing agricultural civilizations (Fig. 16–21). Its Pacific shore forms a narrow coastal desert, a dry fringe of land broken at intervals by deeply entrenched river valleys slicing from the Andes to the ocean. The high mountains rise abruptly and dramatically behind the coastal plain, forming a rugged and snowcapped continental spine (Fig. 16–22). These geographical contrasts figured promi-

FIGURE **16–21**
Peruvian sites and locations mentioned in the text.

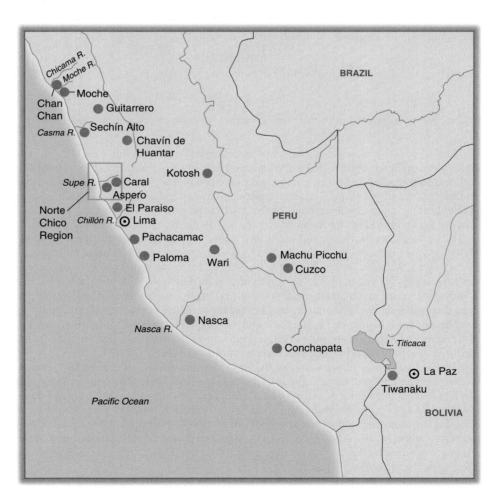

Inka   People whose sophisticated culture dominated Peru at the time of the European arrival; also, the term for that people's highest ruler. (Also spelled *Inca*.)

nently in Peru's prehistory (Bruhns, 1994). In fact, the dynamic tension between coast and highlands—between fishers and farmers—provides a key to understanding the region's cultural past.

As we've seen, humans were active in South America at about the same time as they were in western North America (see Chapter 13). In the central Andes region—that is, Peru and parts of Bolivia and Ecuador—the earliest inhabitants appear to have been broad spectrum foragers who exploited a wide range of animals and marine resources for food (Dillehay et al., 2004). Preserved organic materials on the early sites of Monte Verde, in Chile, and Guitarrero Cave, Peru, hint at the important role of plants as well (see p. 358).

Because of Peru's topographic diversity, the natural distribution of food resources tended to correlate not only with elevation but also with the alternating wet and dry seasons. Some archaeologists have suggested that to effectively exploit a broad spectrum of species, generalized hunters and gatherers needed to move through a series of vertically stacked resource zones between coast and uplands, where various plants, animals, or sea foods were available at different times of the year (Lynch, 1980). We previously referred to this food procurement strategy as *transhumance* (see p. 328). Other archaeologists, however, hypothesize that more intensive use of the varied microenvironments within a single resource zone would have been just as efficient (Keatinge, 1988).

FISHING, FARMING, AND THE RISE OF CIVILIZATION

The role of farming as compared to fishing in the development of Peruvian civilization has generated intense discussion (Moseley, 1975; Wilson, 1981; Bruhns, 1994), since most advanced societies elsewhere were generally agricultural. Archaeologist Michael Moseley points out that the deep, cold Pacific Ocean currents off the Peruvian coast that create the richest fishing waters in the Western Hemisphere are also responsible for the onshore climatic conditions that make this same stretch of the coast one of the world's driest deserts (Moseley, 1992, p. 102). Marine resources surely supported people in this region from the earliest period of human settlement.

Between 6,000 and 4,500 ya, when farming was already under way in a few highland areas, coastal fishing groups settled as permanent residents at sites such as La Paloma (see p. 357). The productive fisheries may have delayed farming in this dry coastal region for some time, until the long-term effects of a stronger, recurring El Niño pattern and other factors promoted the development of a simple form of agriculture. In early farming efforts near the coast, the people planted squash, gourds, and beans in the damp beds of seasonal streams flowing down from the Andes.

Evidence of social differentiation and the intensification of agriculture spread widely in western South America between 5,500 and 3,800 ya and can be found at coastal sites in Ecuador and Peru. For example, the approximately 5,000- to 4,500-year-old coastal site of Aspero, located in the Norte Chico region to the north of Lima (see Fig. 16–21), covers roughly 37 acres and includes six platform mounds. This community depended on marine resources as well as several domesticated food crops, plus cotton. A bit farther to the south, in the Chillón Valley, the preagricultural, marine-resources-focused El Paraiso site had a large population who lived in a community built around an impressive U-shaped ceremonial complex of enormous masonry structures (Haas and Creamer, 2004). Creating this complex may have required as many as 1 million person-days of labor. Both Aspero and El Paraiso are evidence of social differentiation and a certain amount of centralized power in some coastal centers at a very early date.

Recent surveys and excavations at inland sites in the Norte Chico region have revealed more than 20 major preceramic sites with monumental architecture and large residential areas (Fig. 16–23) that existed between 5,000 and 3,800 ya (Haas et al., 2004). For example, the large urban center of Caral in the Supe Valley dates to about 5,200–4,500 ya. This site covers roughly 270 acres and includes sunken circular plazas, large and small platform mounds, and many residential and other building complexes. Although Caral lies 14 miles inland, the faunal remains are all marine animals, principally small fishes such as anchovies and sardines (Haas and Creamer, 2004).

Haas and Creamer (2004) argue that when you consider Norte Chico sites such as Caral and Aspero together, it's evident that a sort of symbiotic economic relationship existed

FIGURE **16–22**
The arid western flank of the Andes Mountains in Peru. Snow-covered and cloud-wrapped peaks can be seen in the distance.

FIGURE 16–23

Platform mounds mark the location of the site of Caballete, one of more than 20 large preceramic sites with monumental architecture in the Norte Chico region of Peru. A parked truck (indicated on the photo by a red arrow) provides a rough scale.

Proyecto Arqueológico Norte Chico

between inland and coastal sites. Coastal sites like Aspero provided the region's main source of animal protein, mostly in the form of anchovies and sardines, and the inland sites provided the main source of plant resources, including cotton for fishnets and gourds for net floats. If this interpretation is true, it strikes Moseley's maritime hypothesis a serious blow. The *inland* sites, not the coastal ones, now appear to have had the upper hand in the emergence of leadership and political power in the region. At the inland sites we find archaeologically identifiable status differences, larger monumental architecture, motifs and features such as sunken circular plazas that appear to be antecedents of pan-Andean patterns, control over agricultural resources, and evidence of agricultural intensification (Haas and Creamer, 2004, pp. 46–47).

Archaeological hallmarks associated with agricultural intensification in coastal Peru include pottery, cotton textiles, and artifacts associated with spinning and weaving. One key to the inland expansion of agriculture was irrigation, which—by channeling streams onto nearby fields—enabled farmers to deliver water to thirsty crops for a longer period each year. Another key was hillside terracing, which gained farmers more space to grow crops. Creating irrigation canals and terraces required the coordinated efforts of relatively large communal workforces, at least periodically. In return, these energy expenditures ensured significant agricultural payoffs.

Peru's coastal regions were wholeheartedly committed to subsistence agriculture after about 3,800 ya. Farming communities are found in river valleys such as the Moche, where irrigation was feasible (see Fig. 16–21). There, local communities organized themselves to excavate canals that would convey water to crops of maize, peanuts, and potatoes, plants originally domesticated in Mexico and the Andean highlands. Staples such as these made farming a worthwhile endeavor, especially considering the periodic unreliability of coastal resources due to El Niño. The success of this first farming period in the lowlands may be measured by the imposing size of ceremonial complexes, such as Sechín Alto on the Casma River, that mark more than two dozen coastal valleys and several upland sites in central and northern Peru.

Sechín Alto and other such sites are early examples of the "corporate construction" projects that became standard in Peru. The huge U-shaped arrangements of temples, platforms, and courtyards—as well as irrigation networks, in many instances—must represent the labors of a large force of people drawn from resident populations as well as the general vicinity. Clearly, sites of this kind were important ceremonial and possibly market centers for several neighboring valleys (Pozorski and Pozorski, 1988).

What inspired the collective efforts that produced the civic architecture and the defined art styles in Peru? Most archaeologists take these developments during the initial farming period to indicate greater social complexity as civil or religious leaders gained more authority. Under their direction, public energies were applied to large-scale projects. But what motivated individuals to participate in these collective enterprises? And what considerations guided their leaders? What was the source of their persuasive or coercive powers? In Peru, as elsewhere, archaeologists have considered militarism, religion, and control of resources, among other motivating forces, in explaining the rise of civilizations; still, they haven't yet come to many definite conclusions (e.g., Haas et al., 1987).

CHAVÍN

Around 3,200–2,850 ya, the peoples of the northern Peruvian highlands and coast came together in a religious fervor that brought some degree of cultural unity to this broad region. Underlying their unity was some form of centralized authority (Kembel and Rick, 2004), with a shared ideology that the people expressed especially through their ritual art. **Chavín de Huantar**, an intriguing civic-ceremonial center set in a high Andean valley, is the most well-known archaeological example of this iconography (Pozorski and Pozorski, 1987; Burger, 1992). There, raised stone tiers flanked sunken courtyards where ceremonies took place in the shadow of an elaborate temple riddled by underground chambers and passageways. Anthropomorphic stone sculptures and other art at the site combined human characteristics with the features of jaguars, snakes, birds of prey, and mythological beings.

While Chavín de Huantar itself may have served as a religious pilgrimage center—possibly the seat of a respected *oracle*, or fortune-teller—and training center for initiates, the Chavín art style was influenced by earlier art and architecture (Kembel and Rick, 2004). Chavín motifs were reproduced most frequently on cotton and camelid wool textiles, but they also appeared on pottery, marine shell, and metal objects. The symbolism and artifacts bestowed prestige upon those who were privileged to acquire them. Although Chavín may have been an agent of widespread cultural change in the region, at least on a stylistic and ideological level, its influence had faded considerably by about 2,500 ya.

Chavín de Huantar Chavín civic-ceremonial center in the northern highlands of Peru.

AT A GLANCE — Important Peruvian Sites and Regions

Site	Dates (ya)	Comments
El Paraiso	c. 4,000	Important preagricultural and preceramic planned settlement in the Chillón Valley
Caral	c. 5,200–4,500	Large preceramic urban centre in the Supe Valley
Chavín de Huantar	c. 2,900–2,500	Civic-ceremonial center in the northern highlands
Nasca	c. 2,000–1,600	Non-state theocracy in south-central Peru near the coast
Moche	c. 1,900–1,300	Early state on Peru's north coast; its capital city (also called Moche) was possibly the earliest true city in the Andes
Wari	c. 1,460–1,100	Early state in the central highlands
Tiwanaku	c. 2,400–1,000	Early state in the southern highlands near Lake Titcaca
Chan Chan	c. 1,000–600	Capital city of the Chimor (Chimú) state
Cuzco	c. 1,000–465	Inka capital city in the southern Peruvian highlands
Pachacamac	c. 1,000–465	Religious pilgrimage center and second capital of the Inka state
Machu Picchu	c. 540	Isolated Inka city in the Andes about 50 miles north of Cuzco

EARLY STATES

Nasca developed between 2,000 and 1,600 ya in south-central Peru, near the coast. Once believed to be an early state, it's now viewed as a non-state **theocracy** (Silverman, 1993). The most mystifying feature of Nasca culture may be the radiating lines, geometric forms, and animal figures "drawn" in gigantic scale on the flat desert tableland of the south coast and fully visible only from the air (Fig. 16–24). These patterns were carefully laid out with the aid of wooden stakes and cordage and then simply swept clear of darkened surface stones to expose the lighter underlying soil (Aveni, 1986, 1990). Interpreted by some as appeals to the gods for water, many of the naturalistic motifs, including a fish, monkey, spider, birds, and plants, appear also on Nasca burial wrappings and decorated ceramic vessels. The much more numerous linear traces functioned as ceremonial pathways, some linking dispersed members of kin-groups to their family lands and others aligning with important streams, sacred mountains, pilgrimage sites, or even astronomical events (Aveni, 2000).

The period just prior to 1,400 ya saw the founding and somewhat parallel development of several regional kingdoms or states, including the **Moche** culture on Peru's north coast, the **Wari** state in the central highlands, and **Tiwanaku** in the south-central Andean high plains (Stanish, 2001). Consistent with their identification as complex societies, these states soon had specialized craftsmen, pyramids, irrigation canals, and public buildings. Elaborate high-status burials and military symbolism, combined with anthropomorphic artistic elements derived from Chavín, hint at the nature and extent of that complexity (Alva and Donnan, 1993).

Between 1,900 and 1,300 ya, Moche rulers consolidated their hold over neighboring valleys initially through warfare and then by greatly expanding irrigated agricultural lands in the conquered areas. The archaeologist Charles Stanish (2001, p. 53) suggests that the Moche capital (of the same name) may have been "the first true city in the Andes." Among its monumental works, the city of Moche's **Huaca del Sol** (Pyramid of the Sun) incorporated some 100 million hand-formed bricks and was one of the largest prehistoric structures in the Americas.

Artistic specialists at each center created remarkable objects that adhered to formally defined local styles. Most of these creations served the elite as status symbols in life and in death. Unique **polychrome** ceramic vessels modeled to represent portraits, buildings, everyday scenes, or imaginative fantasies were a Moche specialty (Fig. 16–25). Metalsmiths hammered, alloyed, and cast beautiful ornaments, ceremonial weapons, and religious paraphernalia from precious gold, silver, and copper. Unlike Old World societies, those in the Americas seldom employed metal for technological purposes, generally reserving it for ornamental use as a badge of social standing.

The contents of excavated tombs of Moche warrior-priests rival those of the rulers of Egypt or Mesopotamia (Alva and Donnan, 1993). These high officials, both male and female, officiated over the human sacrifice ceremony that was an important component of Moche state religion. Upon their own deaths, these officials were dressed in the elaborate and dis-

theocracy A polity governed by religious authorities.

Moche (moh´-chay) Regional state, city, and valley of the same name in northern Peru.

Wari (wah´-ree) Regional state and city of the same name in southern Peru.

Tiwanaku (tee-wahn-ah´-koo) Regional state, city, and valley of the same name near Lake Titicaca, in Bolivia.

Huaca del Sol (wah´-ka dell sole) Massive adobe pyramid built at Moche, in northern Peru.

polychrome Many-colored.

FIGURE 16–24
Nasca ground drawings as seen from the air include both zoomorphic and linear motifs. The monkey is longer than a football field.

Drawings by William Turnbaugh, from photographs

tinctive regalia of their elevated position. Protected by dead attendants, llamas, and dogs, their tombs have yielded a trove of ceremonial accessories, including headdresses, earrings, necklaces, and goblets used for drinking blood.

To the south of the northern coastal area dominated by the Moche, the Wari state emerged in the central highlands at roughly the same time (Cook, 2004). The name derives from the capital of Wari, whose urban core covered roughly 2 square miles in an architectural plan that tends to be repeated in other Wari centers (Stanish, 2001).

Rituals of power and feasting were also important expressions of Wari elite ideologies. At the site of Conchopata, which was second only to the Wari center, oversized face-neck jars appear to have been symbolically killed and buried as part of a ritual. The archaeologist Anita G. Cook argues that such vessels played an important role in ceremonial feasts sponsored by elites (Cook, 2004).

Like Wari, Tiwanaku was a well-organized state that used trade, control of food and labor resources, religion, and military conquest to extend its interests from the Andes to the coast (Isbell and Vranich, 2004). The people of these states shared similar expressions of religious art, and the prominent Staff God deity (Fig. 16–26) shared by both kingdoms can be traced back before Chavín to early representations known from the Norte Chico region around 3,250 ya (Haas and Creamer, 2004, pp. 48–49). Beneath these similarities, however, their architecture, lifeways, and cultural landscapes appear to have been fundamentally different (Isbell and Vranich, 2004).

Tiwanaku's 12,000-foot altitude near the south shore of Lake Titicaca, in Bolivia (Fig. 16–21 and Fig. 16–27), should have made farming a marginal activity there, threatened as it was by frost and an unstable water supply. Undaunted, the people of the city and nearby communities altered their lakeshore environment, creating raised fields with elevated planting platforms in marshy areas and directing water through cultivated areas with aqueducts and canals. Based on these rediscovered principles, farming experiments conducted by archaeologist Alan Kolata proved so productive that modern growers are now adopting some of the ancient methods (Straughan, 1991).

It's important to realize that the rise and fall of highland states was not limited only to Moche, Wari, and Tiwanaku. Peru's north coast, for example, became the center of yet

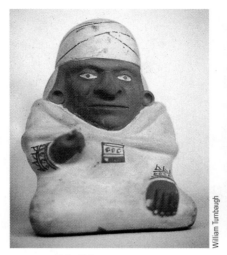

FIGURE 16–25
Moche portrait jar from northern Peru.

FIGURE 16–26
Staff God, Tiwanaku, Bolivia.

FIGURE 16–27
Ruins of the Kalasasaya Temple at Tiwanaku in Bolivia.

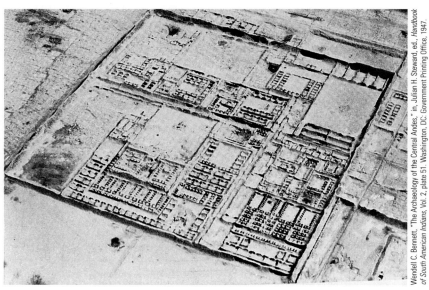

Wendell C. Bennett, "The Archaeology of the Central Andes," in, Julian H. Steward, ed., *Handbook of South American Indians*, Vol. 2, plate 51. Washington, DC: Government Printing Office, 1947.

FIGURE 16–28

Aerial view of one of the royal enclosures at Chan Chan, the Chimor Capital, Peru.

another episode of expansion beginning around 1,100–1,000 ya. This **Chimor** (archaeologically called Chimú) kingdom of the north was rooted in the Moche Valley. The eroded mud-brick architecture of its capital, Chan Chan, still blankets several square miles of coastal desert there. Among the ruins are nearly a dozen walled compounds, each of which served as a grand and secluded palace, storehouse, and tomb for the successive monarchs of ruling lineages (Fig. 16–28). At the end of each reign, the ruler was interred in a burial platform amid prodigious wealth—and sometimes amid his harem of young women—and the compound was sealed. By contrast, the insubstantial quarters of tens of thousands of urban peasants once crammed the spaces below the massive compound walls (Moseley and Day, 1982).

Archaeological field investigations suggest that the extent of the Chimor empire was rather less than the 620 miles of the north coast, as reported in early Spanish accounts (Conlee et al., 2004). Even so, the Chimor dominated and established regional administrative centers over a considerable region to watch over local populations and to coordinate agricultural terracing projects as well as road and canal construction.

INKA

The pattern of conquest and control set by Chimor was not ignored by their rivals and successors—the Inka, the last native empire builders of ancient Peru. From its beginnings in the **Cuzco** area around 1,000 ya, this highland society achieved ascendancy over the southern highlands through bold military initiatives and strategic alliances by 550 ya. The aging Chimor kingdom itself succumbed to Inka conquests on the north coast about A.D. 1470, and the Inka soon consolidated an imperial domain that extended over all of modern Peru and the neighboring region (Lanning, 1967; Mason, 1968). It became the largest polity in the prehispanic Americas (Covey, 2003).

While the Inka army certainly played a major role in expanding the empire, just as important in maintaining the state was an efficient administration that established communication and supply systems to hold the empire together. The absolute power of the divine ruler, or *Inka*, was effectively carried out by subordinates who oversaw tax collection, allotment of communal lands, resettlement of malcontents, and selection of the "chosen women" destined either for marriage to the nobles or for sacrifice to the gods. Inka governors were appointed to rule the many provinces into which the empire was carved, and Quechua was adopted as the administrative language to be used throughout the empire (Trigger, 2003, p. 107). Along with such practices, a key element of Inka success in governing its empire was an enlightened tolerance for local ethnic and cultural diversity among their many subjects. Social, political, and religious customs that did not threaten Inka dominance were permitted to continue.

Cuzco now served as capital of an empire of at least 6 million people, and its rulers proclaimed it "the navel of the universe." But in contrast to the principal cities of most other American civilizations, the Inka's highland town retained its modest character. Cuzco itself was a relatively simple urban center whose core covered possibly 100 acres, set amid residential areas. Beyond this zone were farmlands interspersed with planned settlements of elites and laborers, as well as state storehouses (Trigger, 2003). On an overlooking hill rose **Sacsahuamán** fortress, its massive mortarless walls formed by huge stone blocks expertly dressed and fitted together without the aid of metal tools (Fig. 16–29). This distinctive architectural stonework appeared throughout the Inka realm in religious shrines and other public buildings (Protzen, 1986).

Well-maintained roads led out of Cuzco to the four quarters of the Inka state (Hyslop, 1984; Morris, 1988). Crossing mountains, valleys, and deserts, some 18,750 miles of paved ways tied the far-flung domain together, facilitating official communication by fleet-footed

Chimor   A powerful culture that dominated the northern Peruvian coast between about 1,000 and 500 ya.

Sacsahuamán   (sak-sa-wah-mahn´) Stone fortress and shrine overlooking Cuzco.

couriers, the deployment of army units, and royal processions. Way stations spaced along the primary routes offered comfort to official travelers.

Beyond Cuzco, the only sizable settlements were Pachacamac, a destination of religious pilgrims on Peru's north coast, and Quito, in Ecuador, established as a second capital by the Inka leader **Huayna Capac**. One of the most remarkable and picturesque of Inka sites was the remote citadel of Machu Picchu, high above the upper reaches of the Urubamba River (Fig. 16–30). Situated to facilitate trade in jungle products from the east, the outpost also protected the capital and served as a seasonal retreat for the Inka aristocracy.

The Inka deliberately countered the development of major urban centers, fearing the possibility that large numbers of city dwellers might be a potential source of unrest. Resettlement programs dispersed larger communities in newly conquered areas so that the populace consisted almost entirely of rural peasants. Most grew maize, potatoes, quinoa, and other crops in irrigated valleys or on hillside terraces prepared by state-directed labor. Herders in the highlands tended flocks of domesticated llamas and alpacas, which supplied transport, dung for fuel, wool, objects of religious sacrifices, and food—although the only meat that most people ate was the domesticated guinea pig, a small tailless rodent. The state claimed about two-thirds of the produce, much of which was naturally freeze-dried in high-altitude warehouses and then eventually redistributed to the citizens as they labored on roads and other state-sponsored civic projects. Despite its effective organization and precautions, the Inka empire lasted less than a century. Its rapid demise, like that of the Aztecs in Mexico, was the result of unanticipated challenges from half a world away.

FIGURE **16–29**
Inka stone walls of Sacsahuamán, near Cuzco, Peru.

FIGURE **16–30**
Machu Picchu, Peru.

Huayna Capac (why´-na kah´-pak)
Inka leader whose death precipitated civil war.

425

European Conquest of the New World

Just over 500 years have passed since a Genoese navigator, commissioned by the rulers of Spain to sail westward to the Orient, made his first landfall on a tiny island in the western Atlantic. By the beginning of the sixteenth century, within several years of this event, Europeans generally realized that Columbus had come upon a new world, rather than the new route to the East Indies that he and his sponsors had been seeking.

Most people who had any direct interest in these matters at first expressed only bitter disappointment. But after disillusionment came a determination to make the most of the situation. Spanish, Portuguese, English, Dutch, and French parties set off, each to see what gains they might wring from this "newe found land" that lay across the path to the exotic wealth of the Orient (Fig. 16–31). At the same time, all of them would be searching for any possible way around or through the land they now called America.

The clash of these two worlds, the Old and the New, was unique. Never before and never again would there be such a large-scale confrontation between peoples and cultures that had evolved in isolation over hundreds of generations. In any event, it's unlikely that the painful developments that followed could have been avoided, even if both sides had fully understood the situation.

The Western Hemisphere was populated by tens of millions of people (Dobyns, 1966, estimates 100 million; but many believe that figure is far too high) who exhibited a remarkable range and richness of genetic, cultural, and linguistic diversity. Small bands of hunters and fishers foraged the northernmost and southernmost extremes of the continents. Food collectors and farmers shared most of the middle latitudes. Agricultural chiefdoms held sway in southeastern North America, the Caribbean islands, and northern South America. But as many as a third of all the New World's peoples were subjects of one or the other of the native states that prevailed in Mesoamerica and Peru in the early 1500s.

The Aztec and Inka empires were the major civilizations of America at the time of the first contacts between the Old and New Worlds. Each civilization represented the culmination of centuries of cultural tradition and development. Both achieved extraordinary accomplishments in every dimension—art, social organization, commerce, technology, learning, government, and religion. The Aztec and Inka states commanded the resources, talents, and vigor of vast territories. At the same time, their influence radiated into even larger regions of the two continents. These centers of wealth and power were strong attractions for the Europeans.

FIGURE 16–31

Sixteenth-century woodblock print depicting an early encounter between Europeans and Native Americans.

William Turnbaugh, from a private collection

But these native empires ended with shocking swiftness. In the two decades following 1520, both the Aztecs and the Inka and their domains fell into the hands of Spanish conquerors (Prescott, 1906). Leaving Cuba in 1517, Hernán Cortés and several hundred fellow adventurers pressed through the swampy lowlands of Veracruz and on to the central highlands of Mexico. There, in November 1519, the Aztec ruler **Motecuhzoma Xocoyotzin** (usually known as Moctezuma) received them with some justifiable suspicion. Cortés' arrival coincided remarkably with the divinely foretold return of the Aztec god **Quetzalcoatl**. But the Spaniards' obsession with gold and plunder seemed all too earthly. As Cortés and his soldiers entered Tenochtitlán, they compared it to the principal cities of Europe, which hardly surpassed the Aztec capital in size or grandeur. Their admiration notwithstanding, the newcomers resolved to seize Tenochtitlán. Almost immediately, Moctezuma found himself imprisoned and the Spanish in control. An uprising against the European invaders was quelled with the willing assistance of many thousands of the Aztecs' disenchanted neighbors and former subjects. By 1521, the Spanish were the uncontested successors to the great empire in the heartland of Mexico.

Barely a decade later, the conquest of Peru would take much the same course. An expeditionary force of 180 Spanish soldiers led by Francisco Pizarro entered the Inka domain in 1532, just as **Atahuallpa** claimed victory in a bitter five-year struggle for succession to the throne of his father, Huayna Capac—who had died of smallpox, one of several diseases that accompanied the European invasion of the New World. Pizarro found many disappointed followers of Huascar, Atahuallpa's half brother and rival for the throne, who were eager to assist in deposing the new Inka. Through treachery, the Spanish eliminated both contenders, but not until first amassing a fabulous ransom in gold and silver from the unfortunate Atahuallpa, who was then put to death. Despite some native resistance following these events, the Spanish had firm control of Peru by 1538.

In one brief and tragic—yet remarkable—moment in history, the crowning achievements of half a world were undone. Successive decades would witness the wholesale devastation of peoples and cultures that represented thousands of years of development and adaptation. As the Spanish conquest proceeded outward from the Mexican and Peruvian centers, other Europeans began the process anew in more peripheral areas occupied by farmers and hunter-gatherers.

Armed conflict itself was relatively less destructive than the other cumulative effects of contact. Old World diseases against which native peoples had no natural antibodies—measles, smallpox, chicken pox, the common cold—often decimated populations well before their first direct contact with the newcomers. Epidemics in many areas swept away possibly 75 to 90 percent of the people within months, leaving survivors with little will or ability to resist further social and economic intrusions. Slavery also took its toll; the skeletons of certain Native Americans from this era show signs of increased malnutrition and disease. Columbus himself enslaved local Native Americans to grow sugar on Caribbean islands, and by 1540, the native peoples of that region had died out entirely. Plantation owners then imported African slaves as laborers.

As colonizers invaded the lands they increasingly regarded as their own, they brought with them the agricultural complexes, technological equipment, and social, economic, and religious philosophies that would help them to transform much of the New World into a patchwork of cultures resembling the Old. But as they discovered, it wasn't a one-way street. The Old World too was forever changed by its contact with the New. For example, consider the profound impact that many New World domesticated plants have had on the agriculture and economies of the rest of the world. Still, the cost of the meeting of the two worlds, in human, cultural, and ecological terms, was enormous; we'll never know the extent of it.

Summary

In Mesoamerica, cultivated crops—among which maize was primary—supported stable populations in some parts of the central highlands and along the southern Gulf of Mexico by about 4,000 ya. In western South America, an area characterized by great topographic extremes, the first farming activities were complemented near the coast by fishing and in the highlands by maintaining flocks of camelids. These varied and productive resources served as the economic bases for a series of increasingly complex and sophisticated cultures in each of the regions we considered in this chapter.

Motecuhzoma Xocoyotzin (mo-teh-ca-zooma' shoh-coh-yoh'-seen) Last Aztec ruler, also known as Moctezuma II, whose death at the hands of the Spanish precipitated the destruction of the Aztec empire.

Quetzalcoatl (ket-sal'-kwat-el) Also known as the Feathered Serpent; a deity representing good, worshiped by Aztecs and possibly earlier at Teotihuacán.

Atahuallpa (at-a-wall'-pah) Inka leader defeated by Pizarro.

Site	Dates (ya)	Comments
San Lorenzo (Mexico)	3,150–2,900	Olmec civic-ceremonial center in southern Veracruz
Tikal (Guatemala)	ca. 2,200–1,100	Major Maya center in the Petén region of northern Guatemala
Teotihuacán (Mexico)	ca. 2,200–1,350	Earliest city-state to dominate the Valley of Mexico, one of the largest urban centers in the New World up to the nineteenth century
Tula (Mexico)	ca. 1,200–850	Toltec capital in the Valley of Mexico
Tenochtitlán (Mexico)	675–480	Aztec capital city in the Valley of Mexico
Chavín de Huantar (Peru)	ca. 2,900–2,500	Chavín civic-ceremonial center in the northern highlands of Peru
Cuzco (Peru)	ca. 1,000–465	Inka capital in the southern Peruvian highlands

TABLE 16–1 The Most Significant Archaeological Sites Discussed in This Chapter

In time, some of these societies became states and civilizations. We have focused primarily on the Olmec and Maya in lowland Mesoamerica; Teotihuacán, Toltec, and Aztec in highland Mexico; and a 5,000-year sequence of increasingly integrated and expansive cultures in Peru, culminating in the Inka empire.

While there are some broad similarities in the major features of Old and New World development, especially regarding the connections between agriculture and civilization, we shouldn't overlook the subtle but significant distinctions between these regions. To mention only a few, American civilizations emerged in more ecologically diverse locations; they relied very little on domesticated animals, wheels, or metal for technological purposes; and they tended to move more rapidly from rise to decline. But again, keep in mind that these similarities are broad.

Most archaeologists agree that pre-Columbian transoceanic contact between the Old World and the Americas was at best minimal before the Vikings explored North America around a thousand years ago. Such long-term isolation produced a notable divergence between the populations of the two hemispheres, particularly in their cultures. With the confrontation of Old and New World peoples that took place during the Age of Exploration, biocultural isolation in these regions came to an end. So, very nearly, did the New World societies themselves.

In Table 16–1 you'll find a useful summary of the most important archaeological sites discussed in this chapter.

Critical Thinking Questions

1. What do archaeologists find so intriguing about the relationship between Chichén Itzá and Tula in Mexico? What does this tell you about contacts between populations, as compared to isolation?
2. What made the Aztecs and Inkas so successful? Why do you think the Spanish were able to destroy these civilizations so quickly?
3. How do you think the world would be different, *if*, let's say, the Aztecs had oceangoing vessels and firearms before the Europeans did?

APPENDIX A

Atlas of Primate Skeletal Anatomy

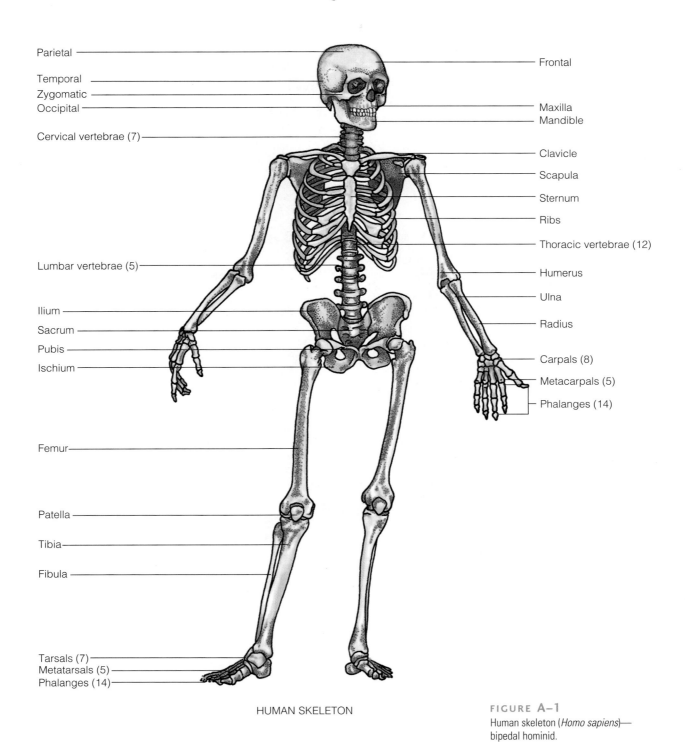

Parietal

Temporal
Zygomatic
Occipital

Cervical vertebrae (7)

Lumbar vertebrae (5)

Ilium
Sacrum
Pubis
Ischium

Femur

Patella

Tibia

Fibula

Tarsals (7)
Metatarsals (5)
Phalanges (14)

Frontal

Maxilla
Mandible

Clavicle
Scapula
Sternum
Ribs
Thoracic vertebrae (12)
Humerus
Ulna
Radius

Carpals (8)
Metacarpals (5)
Phalanges (14)

HUMAN SKELETON

FIGURE A–1
Human skeleton (*Homo sapiens*)—
bipedal hominid.

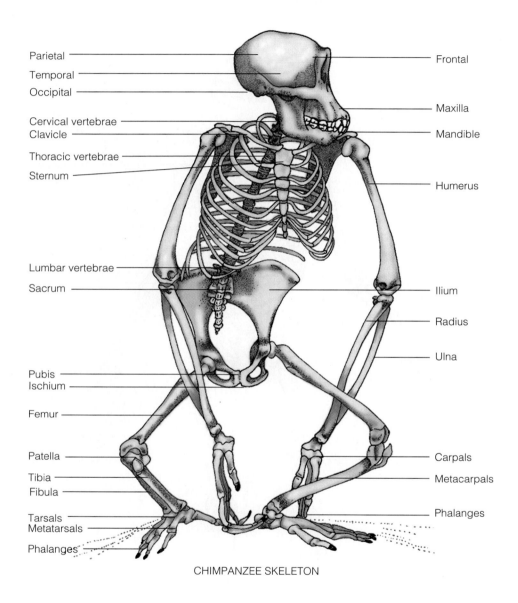

Parietal

Temporal

Occipital

Cervical vertebrae

Clavicle

Thoracic vertebrae

Sternum

Lumbar vertebrae

Sacrum

Pubis

Ischium

Femur

Patella

Tibia

Fibula

Tarsals

Metatarsals

Phalanges

Frontal

Maxilla

Mandible

Humerus

Ilium

Radius

Ulna

Carpals

Metacarpals

Phalanges

CHIMPANZEE SKELETON

FIGURE A–2

Chimpanzee skeleton (*Pan troglodytes*)—
knuckle-walking pongid.

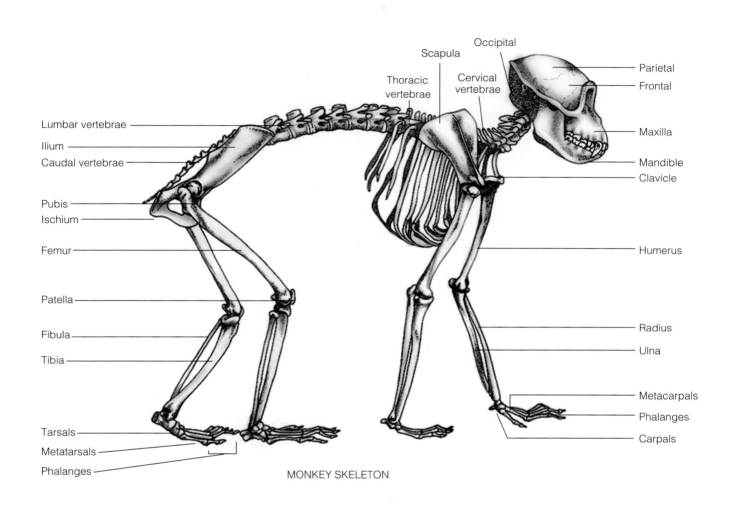

Occipital

Scapula

Cervical
vertebrae

Thoracic
vertebrae

Parietal

Frontal

Maxilla

Mandible

Clavicle

Humerus

Radius

Ulna

Metacarpals

Phalanges

Carpals

Lumbar vertebrae

Ilium

Caudal vertebrae

Pubis

Ischium

Femur

Patella

Fibula

Tibia

Tarsals

Metatarsals

Phalanges

MONKEY SKELETON

FIGURE A–3
Monkey skeleton (rhesus macaque; *Macaca mulatta*)—a typical quadrupedal primate.

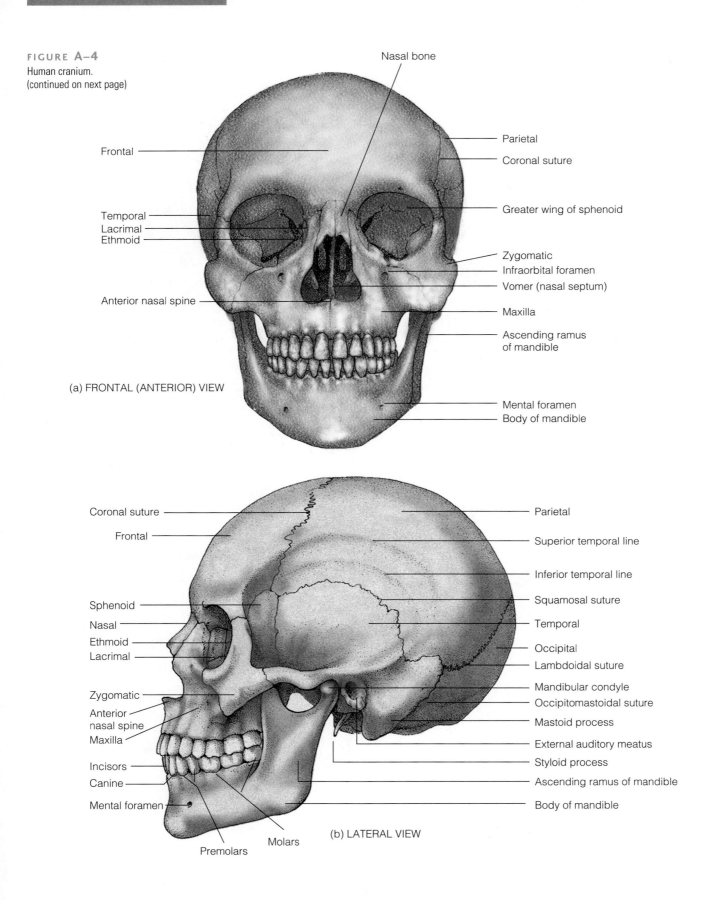

FIGURE A–4
Human cranium.
(continued on next page)

(a) FRONTAL (ANTERIOR) VIEW

Nasal bone

Frontal

Temporal
Lacrimal
Ethmoid

Anterior nasal spine

Parietal
Coronal suture

Greater wing of sphenoid

Zygomatic
Infraorbital foramen
Vomer (nasal septum)
Maxilla
Ascending ramus
of mandible

Mental foramen
Body of mandible

(b) LATERAL VIEW

Coronal suture
Frontal

Sphenoid
Nasal
Ethmoid
Lacrimal

Zygomatic
Anterior
nasal spine
Maxilla

Incisors
Canine

Mental foramen

Premolars
Molars

Parietal
Superior temporal line
Inferior temporal line
Squamosal suture
Temporal
Occipital
Lambdoidal suture
Mandibular condyle
Occipitomastoidal suture
Mastoid process
External auditory meatus
Styloid process
Ascending ramus of mandible
Body of mandible

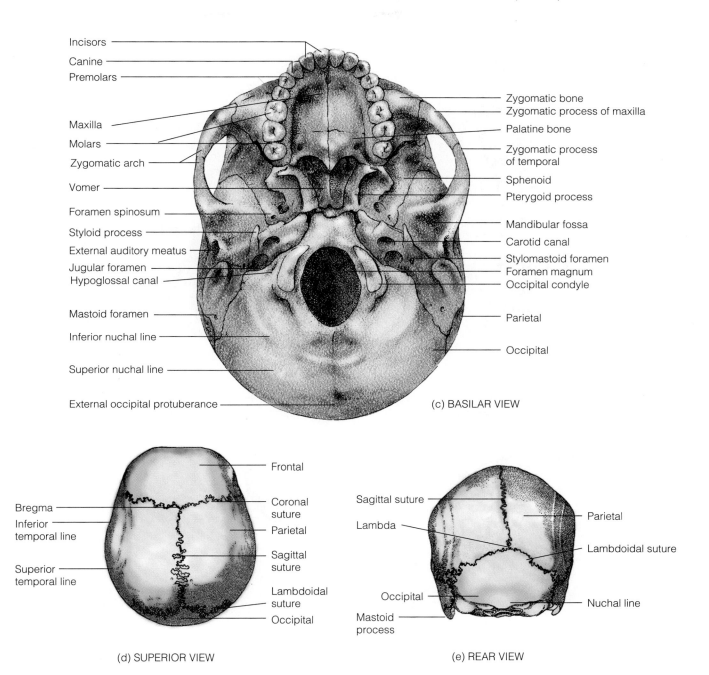

Incisors

Canine

Premolars

Maxilla

Molars

Zygomatic arch

Vomer

Foramen spinosum

Styloid process

External auditory meatus

Jugular foramen

Hypoglossal canal

Mastoid foramen

Inferior nuchal line

Superior nuchal line

External occipital protuberance

Zygomatic bone

Zygomatic process of maxilla

Palatine bone

Zygomatic process
of temporal

Sphenoid

Pterygoid process

Mandibular fossa

Carotid canal

Stylomastoid foramen

Foramen magnum

Occipital condyle

Parietal

Occipital

(c) BASILAR VIEW

Frontal

Coronal
suture

Parietal

Sagittal
suture

Lambdoidal
suture

Occipital

Bregma

Inferior
temporal line

Superior
temporal line

(d) SUPERIOR VIEW

Sagittal suture

Lambda

Parietal

Lambdoidal suture

Occipital

Nuchal line

Mastoid
process

(e) REAR VIEW

433

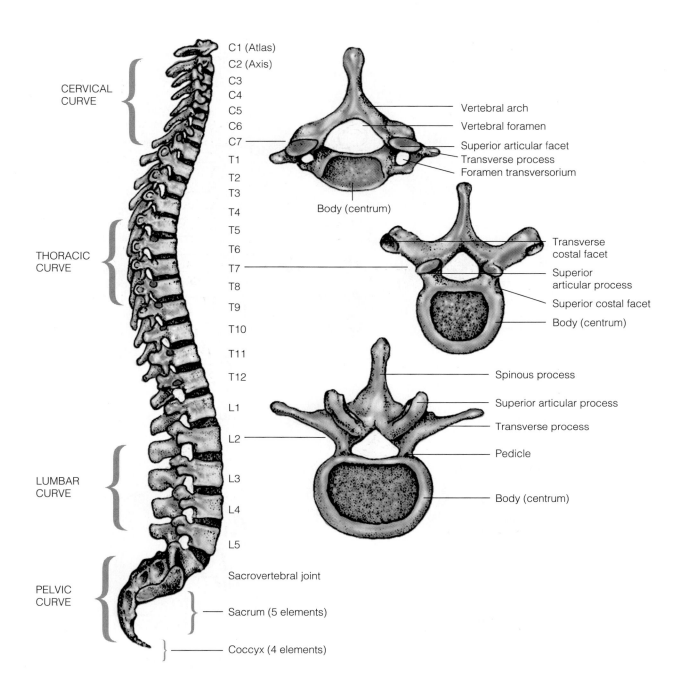

C1 (Atlas)
C2 (Axis)
C3
C4
C5
C6
C7

CERVICAL
CURVE

Vertebral arch
Vertebral foramen
Superior articular facet
Transverse process
Foramen transversorium

Body (centrum)

T1
T2
T3
T4
T5
T6
T7
T8
T9
T10
T11
T12

THORACIC
CURVE

Transverse
costal facet
Superior
articular process
Superior costal facet
Body (centrum)

Spinous process
Superior articular process
Transverse process
Pedicle
Body (centrum)

L1
L2
L3
L4
L5

LUMBAR
CURVE

Sacrovertebral joint

Sacrum (5 elements)

Coccyx (4 elements)

PELVIC
CURVE

FIGURE A–5
Human vertebral column (lateral view) and
representative cervical, thoracic, and lumbar
vertebrae (superior views).

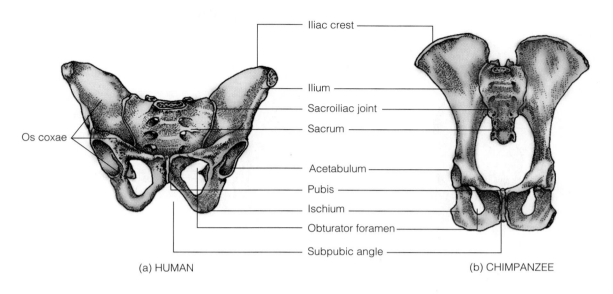

FIGURE **A–6**
Pelvic girdles.

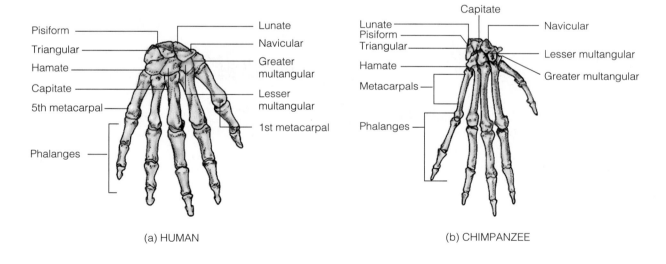

FIGURE **A–7**
Hand anatomy.

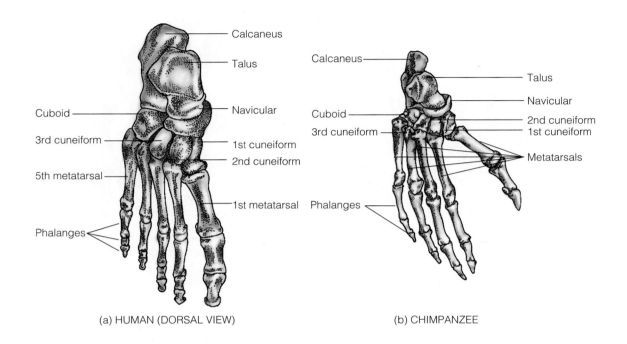

(a) HUMAN (DORSAL VIEW)

Calcaneus
Talus
Cuboid
Navicular
3rd cuneiform
1st cuneiform
2nd cuneiform
5th metatarsal
1st metatarsal
Phalanges

(b) CHIMPANZEE

Calcaneus
Talus
Navicular
Cuboid
2nd cuneiform
3rd cuneiform
1st cuneiform
Metatarsals
Phalanges

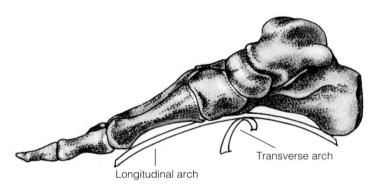

Transverse arch
Longitudinal arch

(c) HUMAN (MEDIAL VIEW)

FIGURE A–8
Foot (pedal) anatomy.

Summary of Early Hominid Fossil Finds from Africa

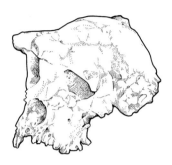

Sahelanthropus
Taxonomic designation:
Sahelanthropus tchadensis

Year of first discovery: 2001

Dating: ~7 mya

Fossil material: Nearly complete cranium, 2 jaw fragments, 3 isolated teeth

Location of finds: Toros-Menalla, Chad, central Africa

Ardipithecus
Taxonomic designation:
Ardipithecus ramidus

Year of first discovery: 1992

Dating: Earlier sites, 5.8–5.6 mya; Aramis, 4.4 mya

Fossil material: Earlier materials: 1 jaw fragment, 4 isolated teeth, postcranial remains (foot phalanx, 2 hand phalanges, 2 humerus fragments, ulna). Later sample (Aramis) represented by many fossils, including up to 50 individuals (many postcranial elements, including at least 1 partial skeleton). Considerable fossil material retrieved from Aramis but not yet published; no reasonably complete cranial remains yet published.

Location of finds: Middle Awash region, including Aramis (as well as earlier localities), Ethiopia, East Africa

Orrorin

Taxonomic designation: *Orrorin tugenensis*

Year of first discovery: 2000

Dating: ~6 mya

Fossil material: 2 jaw fragments, 6 isolated teeth, postcranial remains (femoral pieces, partial humerus, hand phalanx). No reasonably complete cranial remains yet discovered.

Location of finds: Lukeino Formation, Tugen Hills, Baringo District, Kenya, East Africa

Australopithecus anamensis

Taxonomic designation: *Australopithecus anamensis*

Year of first discovery: 1965 (but not recognized as separate species at that time); more remains found in 1994 and 1995

Dating: 4.2–3.9 mya

Fossil material: Total of 22 specimens, including cranial fragments, jaw fragments, and postcranial pieces (humerus, tibia, radius). No reasonably complete cranial remains yet discovered.

Location of finds: Kanapoi, Allia Bay, Kenya, East Africa

Australopithecus afarensis

Taxonomic designation: *Australopithecus afarensis*

Year of first discovery: 1973

Dating: 3.7–3.0 mya

Fossil material: Large sample, with up to 65 individuals represented: 1 partial cranium, numerous cranial pieces and jaws, many teeth, numerous postcranial remains, including partial skeleton. Fossil finds from Laetoli also include dozens of fossilized footprints.

Location of finds: Laetoli (Tanzania), Hadar (Ethiopia), also likely found at East Turkana (Kenya) and Omo (Ethiopia), East Africa

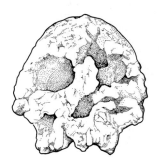

Kenyanthropus

Taxonomic designation:
Kenyanthropus platyops

Year of first discovery: 1999

Dating: 3.5 mya

Fossil material: Partial cranium, temporal fragment, partial maxilla, 2 partial mandibles

Location of finds: Lomekwi, West Lake Turkana, Kenya, East Africa

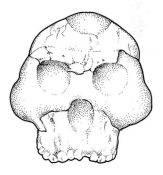

Australopithecus garhi

Taxonomic designation:
Australopithecus garhi

Year of first discovery: 1997

Dating: 2.5 mya

Fossil material: Partial cranium, numerous limb bones

Location of finds: Bouri, Middle Awash, Ethiopia, East Africa

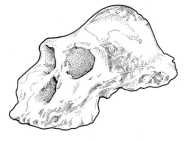

Australopithecus aethiopicus

Taxonomic designation:
Australopithecus aethiopicus
(also called *Paranthropus aethiopicus*)

Year of first discovery: 1985

Dating: 2.4 mya

Fossil material: Nearly complete cranium

Location of finds: West Lake Turkana, Kenya

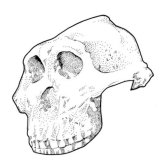

Australopithecus boisei

Taxonomic designation:
Australopithecus boisei (also called *Paranthropus boisei*)

Year of first discovery: 1959

Dating: 2.4–1.2 mya

Fossil material: 2 nearly complete crania, several partial crania, many jaw fragments, dozens of teeth. Postcrania less represented, but parts of several long bones recovered.

Location of finds: Olduvai Gorge and Peninj (Tanzania), East Lake Turkana (Koobi Fora), Chesowanja (Kenya), Omo (Ethiopia)

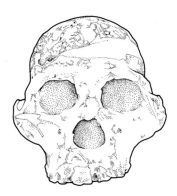

Australopithecus africanus

Taxonomic designation:
Australopithecus africanus

Year of first discovery: 1924

Dating: ~3.3–1.0 mya

Fossil material: 1 mostly complete cranium, several partial crania, dozens of jaws/partial jaws, hundreds of teeth, 4 partial skeletons representing significant parts of the postcranium

Location of finds: Taung, Sterkfontein, Makapansgat, Gladysvale (all from South Africa)

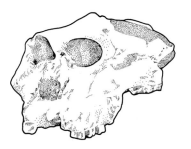

Australopithecus robustus

Taxonomic designation:
Australopithecus robustus (also called *Paranthropus robustus*)

Year of first discovery: 1938

Dating: ~2–1 mya

Fossil material: 1 complete cranium, several partial crania, many jaw fragments, hundreds of teeth, numerous postcranial elements

Location of finds: Kromdraai, Swartkrans, Drimolen, Cooper's Cave, possibly Gondolin (all from South Africa)

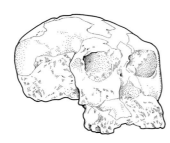

Early *Homo*
Taxonomic designation: *Homo habilis*
Year of first discovery: 1959/1960
Dating: 2.4–1.8 mya
Fossil material: 2 partial crania, other cranial pieces, jaw fragments, several limb bones, partial hand, partial foot, partial skeleton

Location of finds: Olduvai Gorge (Tanzania), Lake Baringo (Kenya), Omo (Ethiopia), Sterkfontein (?) (South Africa)

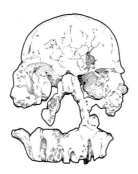

Early *Homo*
Taxonomic designation: *Homo rudolfensis*
Year of first discovery: 1972
Dating: ~1.8 mya
Fossil material: 4 partial crania, 1 mostly complete mandible, other jaw pieces, numerous teeth, a few postcranial elements (none directly associated with crania)

Location of finds: East Lake Turkana (Koobi Fora), Kenya, East Africa

APPENDIX C

Population Genetics

As noted in Chapter 4, the basic approach in population genetics makes use of a mathematical model called the Hardy-Weinberg equilibrium equation. The Hardy-Weinberg theory of genetic equilibrium postulates a set of conditions in a population where *no* evolution occurs. In other words, none of the forces of evolution are acting, and all genes have an equal chance of recombining in each generation (i.e., there is random mating of individuals). More precisely, the hypothetical conditions that such a population would be *assumed* to meet are as follows:

1. The population is infinitely large. This condition eliminates the possibility of random genetic drift or changes in allele frequencies due to chance.
2. There is no mutation. Thus, no new alleles are being added by molecular changes in gametes.
3. There is no gene flow. There is no exchange of genes with other populations that can alter allele frequencies.
4. Natural selection is not operating. Specific alleles confer no advantage over others that might influence reproductive success.
5. Mating is random. There are no factors that influence who mates with whom. Thus, any female is assumed to have an equal chance of mating with any male.

If all these conditions are satisfied, allele frequencies will not change from one generation to the next (i.e., no evolution will take place), and a permanent equilibrium will be maintained as long as these conditions prevail. An evolutionary "barometer" is thus provided that may be used as a standard against which actual circumstances are compared. Similar to the way a typical barometer is standardized under known temperature and altitude conditions, the Hardy-Weinberg equilibrium is standardized under known evolutionary conditions.

Note that the idealized conditions that define the Hardy-Weinberg equilibrium are just that: an idealized, *hypothetical* state. In the real world, no actual population would fully meet any of these conditions. But do not be confused by this distinction. By explicitly defining the genetic distribution that would be *expected* if *no* evolutionary change were occurring (i.e., in equilibrium), we can compare the *observed* genetic distribution obtained from actual human populations. The evolutionary barometer is thus evaluated through comparison of these observed allele and genotype frequencies with those expected in the predefined equilibrium situation.

If the observed frequencies differ from those of the expected model, then we can say that evolution is taking place at the locus in question. The alternative, of course, is that the observed and expected frequencies do not differ sufficiently to state unambiguously that evolution is occurring at a locus in a population. Indeed, frequently this is the result that is obtained, and in such cases, population geneticists are unable to delineate evolutionary changes at the particular locus under study. Put another way, geneticists are unable to reject what statisticians call the *null hypothesis* (where "null" means nothing, a statistical condition of randomness).

The simplest situation applicable to a microevolutionary study is a genetic trait that follows a simple Mendelian pattern and has only two alleles (*A, a*). As you recall from earlier discussions, there are then only three possible genotypes: *AA, Aa, aa.* Proportions of these genotypes (*AA:Aa:aa*) are a function of the *allele frequencies* themselves (percentage of *A* and percentage of *a*). To provide uniformity for all genetic loci, a standard notation is employed to refer to these frequencies:

Frequency of dominant allele (*A*) = *p*
Frequency of recessive allele (*a*) = *q*

Since in this case there are only two alleles, their combined total frequency must represent all possibilities. In other words, the sum of their separate frequencies must be 1:

$$p \quad + \quad q = 1 \text{ (100\% of alleles at the locus in question)}$$

(Frequency of A alleles)   Frequency of a alleles)

To ascertain the expected proportions of genotypes, we compute the chances of the alleles combining with each other in all possible combinations. Remember, they all have an equal chance of combining, and no new alleles are being added.

These probabilities are a direct function of the frequency of the two alleles. The chances of all possible combinations occurring randomly can be simply shown as

$$
\begin{array}{r}
p \; + \; q \\
\times \; p \; + \; q \\
\hline
pq \; + \; q^2 \\
p^2 \; + \; pq \\
\hline
p^2 \; + 2pq \; + \; q^2
\end{array}
$$

Mathematically, this is known as a binomial expansion and can also be shown as

$$(p + q)(p + q) = p^2 + 2pq + q^2$$

What we have just calculated is simply:

Allele Combination	Genotype Produced	Expected Proportion in Population
Chances of A combining with A	AA	$p \times p = p^2$
Chances of A combining with a;	Aa	$p \times q$
a combining with A	aA	$p \times q$ $= 2pq$
Chances of a combining with a	aa	$q \times q = q^2$

Thus, p^2 is the frequency of the AA genotype, $2pq$ is the frequency of the Aa genotype, and q^2 is the frequency of the aa genotype, where p is the frequency of the dominant allele and q is the frequency of the recessive allele in a population.

Calculating Allele Frequencies: An Example

How geneticists use the Hardy-Weinberg formula is best demonstrated through an example. Let us assume that a population contains 200 individuals, and we will use the *MN* blood group locus as the gene to be measured. This gene produces a blood group antigen—similar to *ABO*—located on red blood cells. Because the *M* and *N* alleles are codominant, we can ascertain everyone's phenotype by taking blood samples and observing reactions with specially prepared antisera. From the phenotypes, we can then directly calculate the *observed* allele frequencies. So let us proceed.

All 200 individuals are tested, and the results are shown in Table B–1. Although the match between observed and expected frequencies is not perfect, it is close enough statistically to satisfy equilibrium conditions. Since our population is not a large one, sampling may easily account for the small observed deviations. Our population is therefore probably in equilibrium (i.e., at this locus, it is not evolving). At the minimum, what we can say scientifically is that we cannot reject the *null hypothesis.*

TABLE B-1   Calculating Allele Frequencies in a Hypothetical Population

Observed Data

Genotype	Number of individuals*	Percent	Number of Alleles M	N
MM	80	(40%)	160	0
MN	80	(40%)	80	80
NN	40	(20%)	0	80
Totals	200	(100%)	240 +	160 = 400
		Proportion:	.6 +	.4 = 1

*Each individual has two alleles. Thus, a person who is *MM* contributes two *M* alleles to the total gene pool. A person who is *MN* contributes one *M* and one *N*. Two hundred individuals, then, have 400 alleles for the *MN* locus.

Observed Allele Frequencies

$M = .6(p)$
$N = .4(q)$ ($p + q$ should equal 1, and they do)

Expected Frequencies

What are the predicted genotypic proportions if genetic equilibrium (no evolution) applies to our population? We simply apply the Hardy-Weinberg formula: $p^2 + 2pq + q^2$.

p^2	=	$(.6)(.6)$	= .36
$2pq$	=	$2(.6)(.4) = 2(.24)$	= .48
q^2	=	$(.4)(.4)$	= .16
Total			1.00

There are three possible genotypes (*MM, MN, NN*), and the total of the relative proportions should equal 1; as you can see, they do.

Comparing Frequencies

How do the expected frequencies compare with the observed frequencies in our population?

	Expected Frequency	Expected Number of Individuals	Observed Frequency	Actual Number of Individuals with Each Genotype
MM	.36	72	.40	80
MN	.48	96	.40	80
NN	.16	32	.20	40

GLOSSARY

acclimatization   Physiological responses to changes in the environment that occur during an individual's lifetime. Such responses may be temporary or permanent, depending on the duration of the environmental change and when in the individual's life it occurs. The *capacity* for acclimatization may typify an entire species or population, and because it is under genetic influence, it is subject to evolutionary factors such as natural selection or genetic drift.

Acheulian   (ash´-oo-lay-en) Pertaining to a stone tool industry from the Lower and Middle Pleistocene; characterized by a large proportion of bifacial tools (flaked on both sides). Acheulian tool kits are very common in Africa, Southwest Asia, and western Europe, but they're thought to be less common elsewhere. Also spelled *Acheulean*.

adaptation   Functional response of organisms or populations to the environment. Adaptation results from evolutionary change (specifically, as a result of natural selection).

adaptive niche   The entire way of life of an organism: where it lives, what it eats, how it gets food, how it avoids predators, and so on.

adaptive radiation   The relatively rapid expansion and diversification of life-forms into new ecological niches.

affiliative   Pertaining to amicable associations between individuals. Affiliative behaviors, such as grooming, reinforce social bonds and promote group cohesion.

agriculture   Cultural activities associated with planting, herding, and processing domesticated species; farming.

allele frequency   In a population, the percentage of all the alleles at a locus accounted for by one specific allele.

alleles   Alternate forms of a gene. Alleles occur at the same locus on paired chromosomes and thus govern the same trait. However, because they are different, their action may result in different expressions of that trait. The term *allele* is often used synonymously with *gene*.

alluvial   Deposited by streams, usually during flood stages.

altruism   Behavior that benefits another individual but at some potential risk or cost to oneself.

amino acids   Small molecules that are the components of proteins.

analogies   Similarities between organisms based strictly on common function, with no assumed common evolutionary descent.

Anasazi   (an-ah-saw´-zee) Ancient culture of the southwestern United States, associated with preserved cliff dwellings and masonry pueblo sites.

ancestral (primitive)   Referring to characters inherited by a group of organisms from a remote ancestor and thus not diagnostic of groups (lineages) that diverged after the character first appeared.

anthropoids   Members of a suborder of Primates, the *Anthropoidea* (pronounced "ann-throw-poid´-ee-uh"). Traditionally, the suborder includes monkeys, apes, and humans.

anthropology   The field of inquiry that studies human culture and evolutionary aspects of human biology; includes cultural anthropology, archaeology, linguistics, and physical anthropology.

anthropometry   Measurement of human body parts. When osteologists measure skeletal elements, the term *osteometry* is often used.

anthropomorphic   (*anthro*, meaning "man," and *morph*, meaning "shape") Having or being given humanlike characteristics.

antigens   Large molecules found on the surface of cells. Several different loci governing antigens on red and white blood cells are known. (Foreign antigens provoke an immune response in individuals.)

antiquarian   Relating to an interest in things and texts of the past.

arboreal   Tree-living; adapted to life in the trees.

arboreal hypothesis   The traditional view that primate characteristics can be explained as a consequence of primate diversification into arboreal habitats.

archaeobotany   The analysis and interpretation of the remains of ancient plants recovered from the archaeological record.

Archaic   North American archaeological period that follows the end of the last Ice Age and traditionally ends with the beginning of the use of ceramics; equivalent to the Mesolithic in the Old World.

argon-argon (^{40}Ar/^{39}Ar) method   Working on a similar basis as the potassium-argon method, this approach uses the ratio of argon-40 to argon-39 for dating igneous and metamorphic rocks; it offers precision and temporal range advantages for dating some early hominid sites.

artifacts   Objects or materials made or modified for use by hominids. The earliest artifacts tend to be tools made of stone or, occasionally, bone.

Atahuallpa   (at-a-wall´-pah) Inka leader defeated by Pizarro.

Athabaskan   Largest Native American language family in North America; includes more than 35 languages spoken in western North America.

Aurignacian   Pertaining to an Upper Paleolithic stone tool industry in Europe beginning at about 40,000 ya.

aurochs   European wild oxen, ancestral to domesticated cattle.

australopithecine   (os-tra-loh-pith´-e-seen) The colloquial name for members of the genus *Australopithecus*. The term was first used as a subfamily designation, but it's now most commonly used informally.

autonomic   Pertaining to physiological responses not under voluntary control. An example in chimpanzees would be the erection of body hair during excitement. Blushing is a human example. Both responses convey information regarding emotional states, but neither is deliberate and communication isn't intended.

autosomes   All chromosomes except the sex chromosomes.

Aztecs   Militaristic people who dominated the Valley of Mexico and surrounding area at the time of the European conquest.

Bandkeramik   Literally, "lined pottery"; refers to a Neolithic ceramic ware widely encountered in central Europe and to the culture that produced it.

behavior   Anything organisms do that involves action in response to internal or external stimuli; the response of an individual, group, or species to its environment. Such responses may or may not be deliberate,

445

and they aren't necessarily the results of conscious decision making.

behavioral ecology   The study of the evolution of behavior, emphasizing the role of ecological factors as agents of natural selection. Behaviors and behavioral patterns have been favored because they increase the reproductive fitness of individuals (i.e., they are adaptive) in specific environmental contexts.

Beringia   (bare-in´-jya) The dry-land connection between Asia and America that existed periodically during the Pleistocene epoch.

binocular vision   Vision characterized by overlapping visual fields, provided for by forward-facing eyes. Binocular vision is essential to depth perception.

binomial nomenclature   (*binomial,* meaning "two names") In taxonomy, the convention established by Carolus Linnaeus whereby genus and species names are used to refer to species. For example, *Homo sapiens* refers to human beings.

biocultural evolution   The mutual, interactive evolution of human biology and culture; the concept that biology makes culture possible and that developing culture further influences the direction of biological evolution; a basic concept in understanding the unique components of human evolution.

biological continuum   Refers to the fact that organisms are related through common ancestry and that behaviors and traits seen in one species are also seen in others to varying degrees. (When expressions of a phenomenon continuously grade into one another so that there are no discrete categories, they are said to exist on a continuum. Color is such a phenomenon.)

biological determinism   The concept that phenomena, including various aspects of behavior (e.g., intelligence, values, morals) are governed by biological (genetic) factors; the inaccurate association of various behavioral attributes with certain biological traits, such as skin color.

biological species concept   A depiction of species as groups of individuals capable of fertile interbreeding, but reproductively isolated from other such groups.

biostratigraphy   A relative dating technique based on regular changes seen in evolving groups of animals as well as presence or absence of particular species.

brachiation   A form of locomotion in which the body is suspended beneath the

hands and support is alternated from one forelimb to the other; arm swinging.

breeding isolates   Populations that are clearly isolated geographically and/or socially from other breeding groups.

burins   Small, chisel-like tools with a pointed end; thought to have been used to engrave bone, antler, ivory, or wood.

carrying capacity   In an environment, this is the maximum population of a specific organism that can be maintained at a steady state.

Çatalhöyük   (chaetal´-hae-yook´) A large early Neolithic site in southern Turkey; the name is Turkish for "forked mound."

catastrophism   The view that the earth's geological landscape is the result of violent cataclysmic events. This view was promoted by Cuvier, especially in opposition to Lamarck.

Cenote   (sen-o´-tay) A natural sinkhole or collapsed cavern partly filled with water.

centromere   The constricted portion of a chromosome. After replication, the two strands of a double-stranded chromosome are joined at the centromere.

Cercopithecidae   (serk-oh-pith´-eh-sid-ee) The family designation for all the Old World monkeys.

Cercopithecines   (serk-oh-pith´-eh-seens) The subfamily of Old World monkeys that includes baboons, macaques, and guenons.

charnel house   A building that holds the bones or bodies of the dead.

Chatelperronian   Pertaining to an Upper Paleolithic industry found in France and Spain, containing blade tools and associated with Neandertals.

Chavín de Huantar   Chavín civic-ceremonial center in the northern highlands of Peru.

Chichén Itzá   (chee-chen´ eet-zah´) Postclassic Maya site in Yucatán, linked with the Toltecs of Mexico.

Chimor   A powerful culture that dominated the northern Peruvian coast between about 1,000 and 500 ya.

chinampas   (chee-nahm´-pahs) Productive agricultural plots created by dredging up lake-bottom muck to form raised ridges or platforms; also called "floating gardens."

Chordata   The phylum of the animal kingdom that includes vertebrates.

chromosomes   Discrete structures, composed of DNA and protein, found only in

the nuclei of cells. Chromosomes are visible only under magnification during certain stages of cell division.

cities   A city is an urban center that both supports and is supported by a hinterland of lesser communities.

city-states   An urban center and its supporting territory that forms an autonomous sociopolitical unit. Farmers and other food producers tended to live in the urban center and work their fields on the outskirts of the city.

civilization   The larger social order that includes states related by language, traditions, history, economic ties, and other shared cultural aspects.

clade   A group of organisms sharing a common ancestor. The group includes the common ancestor and all descendents.

cladistics   An approach to classification that attempts to make rigorous evolutionary interpretations based solely on analysis of certain types of homologous characters (those considered to be derived characters).

cladogram   A chart showing evolutionary relationships as determined by cladistic analysis. It is based solely on interpretation of shared derived characters. It contains no time component and does *not* imply ancestor-descendant relationships.

classification   In biology, the ordering of organisms into categories, such as orders, families, and genera, to show evolutionary relationships.

climatic maximum   Episode of higher average annual temperatures that affected much of the globe for several millennia after the end of the last ice age; also known as the *altithermal* in the western United States or *hypsithermal* in the East.

cline   A gradual change in the frequency of genotypes and phenotypes from one geographical region to another.

clones   Plural for clone, an organism that is genetically identical to another organism. The term may also be used to refer to genetically identical DNA segments and molecules.

cloning   The process of producing a clone.

Clovis   Phase of North American prehistory, 13,500–13,000 ya in the West, during which short-fluted projectile points were used in hunting mammoths.

codices   (*sing.,* codex) Illustrated books.

codominance   The expression of two alleles in heterozygotes. In this situation, neither is dominant or recessive, so that both influence the phenotype.

collectors Hunter-gatherers who tend to stay in one place for a long time; task groups may range far afield to hunt and collect food and other resources that are brought back to camp and shared among its inhabitants; valued food resources commonly stored in anticipation of future use.

colobines (kole´-uh-beans) The subfamily of Old World monkeys that includes the African colobus monkeys and Asian langurs.

communication Any act that conveys information, in the form of a message, to another individual. Frequently, the result of communication is a change in the recipient's behavior. Communication may not be deliberate, but may instead be the result of involuntary processes or a secondary consequence of an intentional action.

complementary Referring to the fact that DNA bases form base pairs in a precise manner. For example, adenine can bond only to thymine. These two bases are said to be *complementary* because one requires the other to form a complete DNA base pair.

context The environmental setting where an archaeological trace is found. *Primary* context is the setting in which the archaeological trace was originally deposited. A *secondary* context is one to which it has been moved (e.g., by the action of a stream).

continental drift The movement of continents on sliding plates of the earth's surface. As a result, the positions of large landmasses have shifted drastically during the earth's history.

coprolites Preserved fecal material, which can be studied for what the contents reveal about diet and health.

Cordilleran (cor-dee-yair´-an) Pleistocene ice sheet originating in mountains of western North America.

core area The portion of a home range containing the highest concentration and most reliable supplies of food and water. The core area is usually defended.

craft specialization Economic system that allows individuals to devote full time to certain occupations.

cross-dating Relative dating method that estimates the age of artifacts and features based on their similarities with comparable materials from dated contexts.

cultigen A plant that is wholly dependent on humans; a domesticate.

cultivars Wild plants fostered by human efforts to make them more productive.

culture All aspects of human adaptation, including technology, traditions, language, religion, and social roles. Culture is a set of learned behaviors ; it is transmitted from one generation to the next through learning and not by biological or genetic means.

cuneiform (*cuneus*, meaning "wedge") Wedge-shaped writing of ancient Mesopotamia.

cusps The elevated portions (bumps) on the chewing surfaces of premolar and molar teeth.

cytoplasm The portion of the cell contained within the cell membrane, excluding the nucleus. The cytoplasm consists of a semifluid material and contains numerous structures involved with cell function.

Dalton Late or transitional Paleo-Indian projectile point type that dates between 10,000 and 8,000 ya in the eastern United States.

data (*sing.*, datum) Facts from which conclusions can be drawn; scientific information.

demographic Pertaining to the size or rate of increase of human populations.

dendrochronology Archaeological dating method based on the study of yearly growth rings in ancient wood.

dental caries Erosions in teeth caused by decay; cavities.

deoxyribonucleic acid (DNA) The double-stranded molecule that contains the genetic code. DNA is a main component of chromosomes.

derived (modified) Referring to characters that are modified from the ancestral condition and thus *are* diagnostic of particular evolutionary lineages.

desertification Any process resulting in the formation or growth of deserts.

diffusion The idea that widely distributed cultural traits originated in a single center and were spread from one group to another through contact or exchange.

displays Sequences of repetitious behaviors that serve to communicate emotional states. Nonhuman primate displays are most frequently associated with reproductive or aggressive behavior.

diurnal Active during the day.

Divination Foretelling the future.

domestication A state of interdependence between humans and selected plant or animal species. Intense selection activity induces permanent genetic change, enhancing a species' value to humans.

dominance hierarchies Systems of social organization in which individuals within a group are ranked relative to one another. Higher-ranking animals have greater access to preferred food items and mating partners than do lower-ranking individuals. Dominance hierarchies are sometimes called pecking orders.

dominant Describing a trait governed by an allele that can be expressed in the presence of another, different allele (that is, in heterozygotes). Dominant alleles prevent the expression of recessive alleles in heterozygotes. (This is the definition of *complete* dominance.)

ecofacts Natural materials that give environmental information about a site. Examples include plant and animal remains that were discarded as food waste, and pollen grains preserved in the soil.

ecological Pertaining to the relationships between organisms and all aspects of their environment (temperature, predators, non-predators, vegetation, availability of food and water, types of food, disease organisms, parasites, etc.).

ecological niches The positions of species within their physical and biological environments, together making up the *ecosystem*. A species' ecological niche is defined by such components as diet, terrain, vegetation, type of predators, relationships with other species, and activity patterns, and each niche is unique to a given species.

El Niño Periodic climatic instability, related to temporary warming of Pacific Ocean waters, which may influence storm patterns and precipitation for several years.

empirical Relying on experiment or observation; from the Latin *empiricus*, meaning "experienced."

enculturation The process by which individuals, generally as children, learn the values and beliefs of the family, peer groups, and society in which they are raised.

endemic Continuously present in a population.

endocast A solid impression of the inside of the skull, often preserving details relating to the size and surface features of the brain.

endogamy Mating with individuals from the same group.

endothermic (*endo*, meaning "within" or "internal") Able to maintain internal body

447

temperature through the production of energy by means of metabolic processes within cells; characteristic of mammals, birds, and perhaps some dinosaurs.

enlightenment An eighteenth-century philosophical movement in western Europe that assumed a knowable order to the natural world and the interpretive value of reason as the primary means of identifying and explaining this order.

enzymes Specialized proteins that initiate and direct chemical reactions in the body.

Epipaleolithic (*epi*, meaning "after") Term used primarily in reference to the Near East, designating the time of Middle Stone Age foragers and collectors.

epochs Categories of the geological time scale; subdivisions of periods. In the Cenozoic, epochs include the Paleocene, Eocene, Oligocene, Miocene, and Pliocene (from the Tertiary) and the Pleistocene and Holocene (from the Quaternary).

estrus (ess´-truss) Period of sexual receptivity in female mammals (except humans), correlated with ovulation. When used as an adjective, the word is spelled *estrous.*

ethnoarchaeologists Archaeologists who use ethnographic methods to study modern peoples so that they can better understand and explain patterning in the archaeological record.

ethnocentric Viewing other cultures from the inherently biased perspective of one's own culture. Ethnocentrism often results in other cultures being seen as inferior to one's own.

ethnographies Detailed descriptive studies of human societies. In cultural anthropology, *ethnographies* are traditionally studies of non-Western societies.

eugenics The philosophy of "race improvement" through the forced sterilization of members of some groups and increased reproduction among others; an overly simplified, often racist view that is now discredited.

evolution A change in the genetic structure of a population from one generation to the next. The term is also frequently used to refer to the appearance of a new species.

evolutionary systematics A traditional approach to classification (and evolutionary interpretation) in which presumed ancestors and descendants are traced in time by analysis of homologous characters.

exogamy Mating pattern whereby individuals obtain mates from groups other than their own.

experimental archaeology Research that attempts to replicate ancient technologies and construction procedures to test hypotheses about past activities.

faience (fay-ahnz´) Glassy material, usually of blue-green color, shaped into beads, amulets, and figurines by ancient Egyptians.

features Products of human activity that are usually integral to a site and therefore not portable. Examples include fire hearths and house foundations.

fission-track dating Dating technique based on the natural radiometric decay (fission) of uranium-238 atoms, which leaves traces in certain geological materials.

fitness Pertaining to natural selection, a measure of *relative* reproductive success of individuals. Fitness can be measured by an individual's genetic contribution to the next generation compared to that of other individuals. The terms *genetic fitness, reproductive fitness,* and *differential reproductive success* are also used.

fixity of species The notion that species, once created, can never change; an idea diametrically opposed to theories of biological evolution.

flexed The position of the body in a bent orientation, with arms and legs drawn up to the chest.

fluorine analysis Relative dating method that measures and compares the amounts of fluorine that bones have absorbed from groundwater during burial.

fluted point A biface or projectile point having had long, thin flakes removed from each face to prepare the base for hafting, or attachment to a shaft.

Folsom Phase of southern Great Plains prehistory, around 12,500 ya, during which long-fluted projectile points were used for bison hunting.

foragers Hunter-gatherers who live in small groups that move camp frequently to take advantage of fresh resources as they come into season; few resources stored in anticipation of future use.

forensic anthropology An applied anthropological approach dealing with legal matters. Forensic anthropologists work with coroners and law enforcement agencies in the recovery, analysis, and identification of human remains.

founder effect A type of genetic drift in which allele frequencies are altered in small populations that are taken from, or are remnants of, larger populations.

frugivorous (fru-give´-or-us) Having a diet composed primarily of fruit.

gametes Reproductive cells (eggs and sperm in animals) developed from precursor cells in ovaries and testes.

gene A sequence of DNA bases that specifies the order of amino acids in an entire protein or, in some cases, a portion of a protein. A gene may be made up of hundreds or thousands of DNA bases.

gene flow Exchange of genes between populations.

gene pool The total complement of genes shared by the reproductive members of a population.

genetic drift Evolutionary changes—that is, changes in allele frequencies—produced by random factors. Genetic drift is a result of small population size.

genetics The study of gene structure and action and of the patterns of inheritance of traits from parent to offspring. Genetic mechanisms are the underlying foundation for evolutionary change.

genome The entire genetic makeup of an individual or species. In humans, it is estimated that each person possesses approximately 3 billion DNA nucleotides.

genotype The genetic makeup of an individual. Genotype can refer to an organism's entire genetic makeup or to the alleles at a particular locus.

genus A group of closely related species.

geological time scale The organization of earth history into eras, periods, and epochs; commonly used by geologists and paleoanthropologists.

Gilgamesh Semilegendary king and culture hero of early Uruk; reputed to have had many marvelous adventures.

glaciations Climatic intervals when continental ice sheets cover much of the northern continents. Glaciations are associated with colder temperatures in northern latitudes and more arid conditions in southern latitudes, most notably in Africa.

glyph A carved or incised symbolic figure.

grade A grouping of organisms sharing a similar adaptive pattern. Grade isn't necessarily based on closeness of evolutionary relationship, but it does contrast organisms in a useful way (e.g., *Homo erectus* with *Homo sapiens*).

Great Basin Rugged, dry plateau between the mountains of California and Utah, comprising Nevada, western Utah, and southern Oregon and Idaho.

grooming Picking through fur to remove dirt, parasites, and other materials. Social grooming is common among primates and reinforces social relationships.

habitual bipedalism Bipedal locomotion as the form of locomotion shown by hominids most of the time.

haft To equip a tool or implement with a handle or hilt.

half-life The time period in which one-half the amount of a radioactive isotope is converted chemically (into a daughter product). For example, after 1.25 billion years, half the ^{40}K remains; after 2.5 billion years, one-fourth remains.

Hammurabi (ham-oo-rah´-bee) Early Babylonian king, ca. 1800–1750 B.C.

Harappa (ha-rap´-pa) A fortified city in the Indus Valley of northeastern Pakistan.

Hardy-Weinberg equilibrium The mathematical relationship expressing—under ideal conditions—the predicted distribution of alleles in populations; the central theorem of population genetics.

hemispheres The two halves of the cerebrum that are connected by a dense mass of fibers. (The cerebrum is the large, rounded, outer portion of the brain.)

hemoglobin A protein molecule that occurs in red blood cells and binds to oxygen molecules.

heterodont Having different kinds of teeth; characteristic of mammals, whose teeth consist of incisors, canines, premolars, and molars.

heterozygous Having different alleles at the same locus on members of a chromosome pair.

hieroglyphics (*hiero*, meaning "sacred," and *glyphein*, meaning "carving") The picture-writing of ancient Egypt.

historical archaeology Archaeology supplemented by contemporary written documents.

Hohokam (ho-ho-kahm´) Prehistoric farming culture of southern Arizona.

Holocene The geological epoch during which we now live. The Holocene follows the Pleistocene epoch and began roughly 11,000–10,000 years ago.

home-based foragers Hominids that hunt, scavenge, or collect food and raw materials from the general locality where they habitually live and bring these materials back to some central or home-base site to be shared with other members of their co-residing group.

homeostasis A condition of balance, or stability, within a biological system, maintained by the interaction of physiological mechanisms that compensate for changes (both external and internal).

hominid Colloquial term for member of the family Hominidae, the classificatory group to which humans belong; also includes other, now extinct, bipedal relatives.

Hominoidea The formal designation for the superfamily of anthropoids that includes apes and humans.

Homo habilis (hab´-ih-liss) A species of early *Homo,* well known from East Africa but possibly also found in other regions.

homologies Similarities between organisms based on descent from a common ancestor.

homoplasy (*homo*, meaning "same," and *plasy,* meaning "growth") The separate evolutionary development of similar characteristics in different groups of organisms.

homozygous Having the same allele at the same locus on both members of a chromosome pair.

Hopewell A Middle Woodland archaeological culture centered in the Midwest, but influencing a much wider region through trade and shared bodies of ritual.

hormones Substances (usually proteins) that are produced by specialized cells and that travel to other parts of the body, where they influence chemical reactions and regulate various cellular functions.

horticulture Farming method in which only hand tools are used; typical of most early Neolithic societies.

Huaca del Sol (wah´-ka dell sole) Massive adobe pyramid built at Moche, in northern Peru.

Huayna Capac (why´-na kah´-pak) Inka leader whose death precipitated civil war.

Human Genome Project An international effort aimed at sequencing and mapping the entire human genome.

hunter-gatherers People who make their living by hunting, fishing, and gathering their food, and not by producing it.

hybrids Offspring of mixed ancestry; heterozygotes.

Hylobatidae (high-lo-baht´-id-ee) The family designation of the gibbons and siamangs that live in parts of southeast Asia.

hypothesis (*pl.*, hypotheses) A provisional explanation of a phenomenon. Hypotheses require repeated testing.

hypoxia Lack of oxygen. Hypoxia can refer to reduced amounts of available oxygen in the atmosphere (due to lowered barometric pressure) or to insufficient amounts of oxygen in the body.

index fossils Fossil remains of known age, used to estimate the age of the geological stratum in which they are found. For example, extinct marine arthropods called trilobites can be used as an index fossil of Cambrian and Ordovician geological formations.

Inka People whose sophisticated culture dominated Peru at the time of the European arrival; also, the term for that people's highest ruler. (Also spelled *Inca.*)

intelligence Mental capacity; ability to learn, reason, or comprehend and interpret information, facts, relationships, and meanings; the capacity to solve problems, whether through the application of previously acquired knowledge or through insight.

interglacials Climatic intervals when continental ice sheets are retreating, eventually becoming much reduced in size. Interglacials in northern latitudes are associated with warmer temperatures, while in southern latitudes the climate becomes wetter.

interspecific Between species; refers to variation beyond that seen within the same species to include additional aspects seen between two different species.

intraspecific Within species; refers to variation seen within the same species.

ischial callosities Patches of tough, hard skin on the buttocks of Old World monkeys and chimpanzees.

K-selected Pertaining to an adaptive strategy whereby individuals produce relatively few offspring, in whom they invest increased parental care. Although only a few infants are born, chances of survival are increased for each one because of parental investments in time and energy. Examples of K-selected nonprimate species are birds and canids (e.g., wolves, coyotes, and dogs).

Kaminaljuyú (cam-en-awl-hoo-yoo´) Major prehistoric Maya site located at Guatemala City.

Kebaran Late Pleistocene hunter-gatherers of the eastern Mediterranean region and Levant.

kivas Underground chambers or rooms used for gatherings and ceremonies by pueblo dwellers.

knuckle walking A form of quadrupedal locomotion used by chimpanzees, bonobos, and gorillas wherein, the weight of the upper body is supported on the knuckles rather than on the palms of the hands.

large-bodied hominoids Those hominoids including the great apes (orangutans, chimpanzees, gorillas) and hominids, as well as all ancestral forms back to the time of divergence from small-bodied hominoids (i.e., the gibbon lineage).

Laurentian (lah-ren´-shun) Pleistocene ice sheet centered in the Hudson Bay region and extending across much of eastern Canada and the northern United States.

life history traits Also called life history strategies; characteristics and developmental stages that influence rates of reproduction.

locus (*pl.,* loci) (lo´-kus, lo-sigh´) The position on a chromosome where a given gene occurs. The term is sometimes used interchangeably with *gene.*

loess (luss) Fine-grained soil composed of glacially pulverized rock, deposited by the wind.

Lower Paleolithic A unit of archaeological time that begins >2.5 mya with the earliest identified tools made by hominids and ends around 200,000 B.C.

macaques (muh-kaks´) Group of Old World monkeys comprising several species, including rhesus monkeys. Most macaque species live in India, other parts of Asia, and nearby islands.

macroevolution Changes produced only after many generations, such as the appearance of a new species.

macrofossil Plant parts such as seeds, nutshells, and stems, preserved in the archaeological record and large enough to be clearly visible to the naked eye.

Magdalenian Pertaining to the final phase of the Upper Paleolithic stone tool industry in Europe.

manioc Cassava, a starchy edible root crop of the tropics.

material culture The physical manifestations of human activities, such as tools, art, and structures. As the most durable aspects of culture, material remains make up the majority of archaeological evidence of past societies.

Maya Prehistoric Mesoamerican culture consisting of regional kingdoms and known for its art and architectural accomplishments.

meiosis Cell division in specialized cells in ovaries and testes. Meiosis involves two divisions and results in four daughter cells, each containing only half the original number of chromosomes. These cells can develop into gametes.

Mendelian traits Characteristics that are influenced by alleles at only one genetic locus. Examples include many blood types, such as ABO. Many genetic disorders, including sickle-cell anemia and Tay-Sachs disease, are also Mendelian traits.

Mesoamerica (*meso,* meaning "middle") Geographical and cultural region from central Mexico to northwestern Costa Rica; formerly called "Middle America" in the archaeological literature.

Mesolithic (*meso,* meaning "middle," and *lith,* meaning "stone") Middle Stone Age; period of hunter-gatherers, especially in northwestern Europe.

Mesopotamia (*meso,* meaning "middle," and *potamos,* meaning "river") Land between the Tigris and Euphrates Rivers, mostly included in modern-day Iraq.

metabolism The chemical processes within cells that break down nutrients and release energy for the body to use. (When nutrients are broken down into their component parts, such as amino acids, energy is released and made available for the cell to use.)

Metazoa Multicellular animals; a major division of the animal kingdom.

Mexica (meh-shee´-ka) Original name by which the Aztecs were known before their rise to power.

microevolution Small changes occurring within species, such as a change in allele frequencies.

microfossil Small to microscopic plant remains, most falling in a range of 10–100 microns, or roughly the size of individual

grains of wheat flour in the bag from your grocer's shelf.

middens Archaeological sites or features within sites formed largely by the accumulation of domestic waste.

Middle Pleistocene The portion of the Pleistocene epoch beginning 780,000 ya and ending 125,000 ya.

midline An anatomical term referring to a hypothetical line that divides the body into right and left halves.

millet Small-grained cereal grass native to Asia and Africa.

Mississippian Late prehistoric chiefdoms of the southeastern United States and southern Midwest between roughly 1,100 and 300 ya.

mitochondria (*sing.,* mitochondrion) (my´-tow-kond´-dree-uh) Structures contained within the cytoplasm of eukaryotic cells that convert energy, derived from nutrients, into a form that is used by the cell.

mitochondrial DNA (mtDNA) DNA found in the mitochondria that is inherited only through the maternal line.

mitosis Simple cell division; the process by which somatic cells divide to produce two identical daughter cells.

Moche (moh´-chay) Regional state, city, and valley of the same name in northern Peru.

Mogollon (mo-go-yohn´) Prehistoric village culture of northern Mexico and southern Arizona/New Mexico.

Mohenjo-Daro (mo-henjo-dar´-o) An early Indus Valley city in south-central Pakistan.

molecules Structures made up of two or more atoms. Molecules can combine with other molecules to form more complex structures.

Motecuhzoma Xocoyotzin (mo-teh-ca-zooma´ shoh-coh-yoh´-seen) Last Aztec ruler, also known as Moctezuma II, whose death at the hands of the Spanish precipitated the destruction of the Aztec empire.

morphology The form (shape, size) of anatomical structures; can also refer to the entire organism.

mosaic evolution A pattern of evolution in which the rates of evolution in one functional system vary from those in other systems. For example, in hominid evolution, the dental system, locomotor system, and neurological system (especially the brain) all evolved at markedly different rates.

Mousterian Pertaining to the stone tool industry associated with Neandertals and some modern *H. sapiens* groups. Also called Middle Paleolithic. This industry is characterized by a larger proportion of flake tools than found in Acheulian tool kits.

mutation A change in DNA. Technically, mutation refers to changes in DNA bases as well as changes in chromosome number and/or structure.

multidisciplinary Pertaining to research that involves mutual contributions and cooperation of experts from various scientific fields (i.e., disciplines).

Naj Tunich (nah toon´-eesh) Maya sacred cave in Guatemala.

natal group The group in which animals are born and raised. (*Natal* pertains to birth.)

Natufian Collector-type hunter-gatherers who established sedentary settlements in parts of the Near East after 12,000 ya.

natural selection The most critical mechanism of evolutionary change, first articulated by Charles Darwin; refers to genetic change or changes in the frequencies of certain traits in populations due to differential reproductive success between individuals.

Nebuchadnezzar (neh-boo-kud-neh´-zer) Late Babylonian king, ca. 605–562 B.C.

Neolithic (*neo*, meaning "new," and *lith*, meaning "stone") New Stone Age; period of farmers.

Neolithic Revolution Childe's term for the far-reaching consequences of food production.

neural tube In early embryonic development, the anatomical structure that develops to form the brain and spinal cord.

nocturnal Active during the night.

nuchal torus (nuke´-ul, pertaining to the neck) A projection of bone in the back of the cranium where neck muscles attach; used to hold up the head.

Nucleated settlement A city or village in which houses, administrative facilities, public areas, storehouses, and the like are clumped or clustered close together.

nucleotides Basic units of the DNA molecule, composed of a sugar, a phosphate, and one of four DNA bases.

nucleus A structure (organelle) found in all eukaryotic cells. The nucleus contains chromosomes (nuclear DNA).

oases (*sing.*, oasis) Permanent springs or water holes in an arid region.

Oaxaca (wah-ha´-kah) A southern Mexican state bordering the Pacific Ocean.

obligate bipedalism Bipedalism as the *only* form of hominid terrestrial locomotion. Since major anatomical changes in the spine, pelvis, and lower limb are required for bipedal locomotion, once hominids adapted it, other forms of locomotion on the ground became impossible.

Olmec Prehistoric chiefdoms in the Gulf Coast lowlands of Veracruz and Tabasco, Mexico, with a highly developed art style and social complexity; flourished from 3,200 to 2,400 ya.

omnnivorous Having a diet consisting of many kinds of foods, such as plant materials (seeds, fruits, leaves), meat, and insects.

Ounjougou African hunter-gatherers who made early use of wild cereal grasses on the southern edge of the Sahara between 12,000 and 9,000 ya.

Paleo-Indians (*paleo*, meaning "ancient") In the Americas, early hunter-gatherers, from about 14,000 to 8,000 ya.

paleoanthropology The interdisciplinary approach to the study of earlier hominids—their chronology, physical structure, archaeological remains, habitats, etc.

paleomagnetism Dating method based on the earth's shifting magnetic pole.

paleontologists Scientists whose study of ancient life-forms is based on fossilized remains of extinct animals and plants.

paleopathology The branch of osteology that studies the traces of disease and injury in human skeletal (or, occasionally, mummified) remains.

paleospecies Species defined from fossil evidence, often covering a long time span.

palynologists Scientists who identify ancient plants from pollen samples unearthed at archaeological sites.

pandemic An extensive outbreak of disease affecting large numbers of individuals over a wide area; potentially a worldwide phenomenon.

Paranthropus (par´-an-throw´-puss) A genus of hominid characterized by very large

back teeth and jaws. Frequently, this genus is combined into *Australopithecus*.

pathogens Any agents, especially microorganisms such as viruses, bacteria, or fungi, that infect a host and cause disease.

pharaoh Title of the king or ruler of ancient Egypt.

phenotypes The observable or detectable physical characteristics of an organism; the detectable expressions of genotypes.

phylogenetic tree A chart showing evolutionary relationships as determined by evolutionary systematics. It contains a time component and implies ancestor-descendant relationships.

phylogeny A schematic representation showing ancestor-descendant relationships, usually in a chronological framework.

phytoliths (*phyto*, meaning "plant," and *lith*, meaning "stone") Microscopic silica structures formed in the cells of many plants.

placental A type (subclass) of mammal. During the Cenozoic, placentals became the most widespread and numerous mammals and today are represented by upwards of 20 orders, including the primates.

Plano Great Plains bison-hunting culture of 11,000–9,000 ya, which employed narrow, unfluted points.

plasticity The capacity to change. In a behavioral context, the ability of animals to modify actions in response to differing circumstances.

Pleistocene The epoch of the Cenozoic from 1.8 mya until 10,000 ya. Frequently referred to as the Ice Age, this epoch is associated with continental glaciations in northern latitudes.

Plio-Pleistocene Pertaining to the Pliocene and first half of the Pleistocene, a time range of 5–1 mya. For this time period, numerous fossil hominids have been found in Africa.

polity, polities The political organization of a society or group.

pollen Microscopic grains containing the male gametes of seed-producing plants.

polyandry A mating system wherein a female continuously associates with more than one male (usually two or three) with whom she mates. Among nonhuman primates, polyandry is seen only in marmosets and tamarins. It also occurs in a few human societies.

polychrome Many-colored.

polygenic   Referring to traits that are influenced by genes at two or more loci. Examples of such traits are stature, skin color, and eye color. Many polygenic traits are also influenced by environmental factors.

polygynous   Referring to polygyny, a mating system whereby males have more than one mate.

polymerase chain reaction (PCR)   A method of producing copies of a DNA segment using the enzyme DNA polymerase.

polymorphisms   Loci with more than one allele. Polymorphisms can be expressed in the phenotype as the result of gene action (as in ABO), or they can exist solely at the DNA level within noncoding regions.

polytypic   Referring to species composed of populations that differ with regard to the expression of one or more traits.

Pongidae   (ponj´-id-ee) The traditional family designation of the great apes (orangutans, chimpanzees, bonobos, and gorillas).

population   Within a species, a community of individuals where mates are usually found.

population genetics   The study of the frequency of alleles, genotypes, and phenotypes in populations from a microevolutionary perspective.

postcranial   (*post* meaning "after") In a quadruped, referring to that portion of the body behind the head; in a biped, referring to all parts of the body *beneath* the head (i.e., the neck down).

potassium-argon (K/Ar) method   Dating technique based on accumulation of argon-40 gas as a by-product of the radiometric decay of potassium-40 in volcanic materials; used especially for dating early hominid sites in East Africa.

potlatch   Ceremonial feasting and gift-giving event among Northwest Coast Indians.

prehensility   Grasping, as by the hands and feet of primates.

prehistory   The several million years between the emergence of bipedal hominids and the availability of written records.

primate   A member of the order of mammals Primates (pronounced "pry-may´-tees"), which includes prosimians, monkeys, apes, and humans.

primatologists   Scientists who study the evolution, anatomy, and behavior of nonhuman primates. Those who study

behavior in free-ranging animals are usually trained as physical anthropologists.

primatology   The study of the biology and behavior of nonhuman primates (prosimians, monkeys, and apes).

principle of independent assortment   The distribution of one pair of alleles into gametes does not influence the distribution of another pair. The genes controlling different traits are inherited independently of one another.

principle of segregation   Genes (alleles) occur in pairs (because chromosomes occur in pairs). During gamete production, the members of each gene pair separate, so that each gamete contains one member of each pair. During fertilization, the full number of chromosomes is restored, and members of gene or allele pairs are reunited.

principle of superpositioning   In a stratigraphic sequence, the lower layers were deposited before the upper layers. Or, simply put, the stuff on top of a heap was put there last.

prosimians   Members of a suborder of Primates, the *Prosimii* (pronounced "pro-sim´-ee-eye"). Traditionally, the suborder includes lemurs, lorises, and tarsiers.

protein synthesis   The assembly of chains of amino acids into functional protein molecules. The process is directed by DNA.

proteins   Three-dimensional molecules that serve a wide variety of functions through their ability to bind to other molecules.

protohominids   The earliest members of the hominid lineage, as yet only poorly represented in the fossil record; thus, their structure and behavior are reconstructed largely hypothetically.

public archaeology   A broad term that covers archaeological research conducted for the public good as part of cultural resource management and heritage management programs; a major growth area of world archaeology.

pueblos   Spanish for "town," referring to multiroom residence structures built by village farmers in the American Southwest; also refers collectively to the several cultures that built and lived in such villages.

punctuated equilibrium   The concept that evolutionary change proceeds through long periods of stasis punctuated by rapid periods of change.

Qin Shi Huangdi   (chin-shee-huang-dee) First emperor of a unified China.

quadrupedal   Using all four limbs to support the body during locomotion; the basic mammalian (and primate) form of locomotion.

quantitatively   (quantitative) Pertaining to measurements of quantity and including such properties as size, number, and capacity.

Quetzalcoatl   (ket-sal´-kwat-el) Also known as the Feathered Serpent; a deity representing good, worshiped by Aztecs and possibly earlier at Teotihuacán.

quinoa   (keen-wah´) Seed-bearing member of the genus *Chenopodium*, cultivated by early Peruvians.

r-selected   An adaptive strategy that emphasizes relatively large numbers of offspring and reduced parental care (compared to K-selected species). *K-selection* and *r-selection* are relative terms; for example, mice are r-selected compared to primates but K-selected compared to fish.

rachis   The short stem by which an individual seed attaches to the main stalk of a plant as it develops.

radiocarbon dating   Method for determining the age of organic archaeological materials by measuring the decay of the radioactive isotope of carbon, ^{14}C; also known as ^{14}C dating.

radiometric decay   A measure of the rate at which certain radioactive isotopes disintegrate.

recessive   Describing a trait that is not expressed in heterozygotes; also refers to the allele that governs the trait. For a recessive allele to be expressed, there must be two copies of the allele (that is, the individual must be homozygous).

recombination   The exchange of DNA between paired chromosomes during meiosis; also called *crossing over*.

replicate   To duplicate. The DNA molecule is able to make copies of itself.

reproductive strategies   The complex of behavioral patterns that contributes to individual reproductive success. The behaviors need not be deliberate, and they often vary considerably between males and females.

reproductive success   The number of offspring an individual produces and rears to reproductive age; an individual's genetic contribution to the next generation.

rhinarium (rine-air´-ee-um) The moist, hairless pad at the end of the nose; seen in most mammals. The rhinarium enhances an animal's ability to smell.

ribonucleic acid (RNA) A molecule, similar in structure to DNA. Three single-stranded forms of RNA are essential to protein synthesis.

Sacsahuamán (sak-sa-wah-mahn´) Stone fortress and shrine overlooking Cuzco.

science A body of knowledge gained through observation and experimentation; from the Latin *scientia*, meaning "knowledge."

scientific method A research method whereby a problem is identified, a hypothesis (or hypothetical explanation) is stated, and that hypothesis is tested through the collection and analysis of data. If the hypothesis is tested many times and not rejected, it becomes a theory.

scientific testing The precise repetition of an experiment or expansion of observed data to provide verification; the procedure by which hypotheses and theories are verified, modified, or discarded.

seasonality and resource scheduling Technique of hunter-gatherers to maximize subsistence by relocating in accord with the availability of key resources at specific times and places throughout the year.

sectorial Adapted for cutting or shearing; among primates, refers to the compressed (side-to-side) first lower premolar, which functions as a shearing surface with the upper canine.

sedentism To reside in a single location for most or all of the year; to become sedentary.

selective pressures Forces in the environment that influence reproductive success in individuals.

sensory modalities Different forms of sensation (e.g., touch, pain, pressure, heat, cold, vision, taste, hearing, and smell).

seriation Relative dating method that orders artifacts into a temporal series based on their similar attributes or the frequency of these attributes.

sex chromosomes The X and Y chromosomes. The Y chromosome determines maleness and, in its absence, an embryo develops as a female.

sexual dimorphism Differences in physical characteristics between males and females of the same species. For example, humans are slightly sexually dimorphic for body size, with males being taller, on average, than females of the same population.

sexual selection A type of natural selection that operates on only one sex within a species. It's the result of competition for mates, and it can lead to sexual dimorphism with regard to one or more traits.

shamanism Traditional practices that mediate between the world of humans and the world of spirits.

Shang The Shang or Yin dynasty was the first historic civilization in northern China.

shared derived Relating to specific character states shared in common between two life-forms and considered the most useful for making evolutionary interpretations.

site survey The process of discovering the location of archaeological sites; sometimes called site reconnaissance.

slash-and-burn agriculture A traditional land-clearing practice involving the cutting and burning of trees and vegetation. In many areas, fields are abandoned after a few years and clearing occurs elsewhere.

social stratification Class structure or hierarchy, usually based on political, economic, or social standing.

social structure The composition, size, and sex ratio of a group of animals. Social structures are partly the results of natural selection in specific habitats, and they guide individual interactions and social relationships.

somatic cells Basically, all the cells in the body except those involved with reproduction.

sorghum Cereal grass; some subspecies are grown for food grains, others for their sweet, juicy stalk.

speciation The process by which a new species evolves from a prior species. Speciation is the most basic process in macroevolution.

specialized Evolved for a particular function; usually refers to a specific trait (e.g., incisor teeth), but may also refer to an organism's entire way of life.

species A group of organisms that can interbreed to produce fertile offspring. Members of one species are reproductively isolated from members of all other species (i.e., they can't mate with them to produce fertile offspring).

spina bifida A condition in which the arch of one or more vertebrae fails to fuse and form a protective barrier around the spinal cord.

stelae (sing., stela) (stee´-lee) Upright posts or stones, often bearing inscriptions.

stereoscopic vision The condition whereby visual images are, to varying degrees, superimposed on one another. This trait provides for depth perception, or the perception of the external environment in three dimensions. Stereoscopic vision is partly a function of structures in the brain.

stimulus diffusion In the interaction of two societies, the knowledge of a cultural trait or feature in one society can stimulate the invention of a similar trait or feature in the other.

stratigraphy Study of the sequential layering of deposits.

stratum (*pl.*, strata) A single layer of soil or rock; sometimes called a level.

stress In a physiological context, any factor that acts to disrupt homeostasis; more precisely, the body's response to any factor that threatens its ability to maintain homeostasis.

symbiosis (*syn*, meaning "together," and *bios*, meaning "life") Mutually advantageous association of two different organisms; also known as *mutualism*.

Tamaulipas (tah-mah-leep´-ahs) A Mexican state located on the Gulf Coast south of Texas.

taphonomy (from Greek *taphos*, meaning "dead") The study of how bones and other materials came to be buried in the earth and preserved as fossils. A taphonomist studies the processes of sedimentation, the action of streams, preservation properties of bone, and carnivore disturbance factors.

taro Species of tropical plant with an edible starchy root.

taxonomy The branch of science concerned with the rules of classifying organisms on the basis of evolutionary relationships.

Tehuacán Valley (tay-wah-kahn´) A dry highland region on the boundary of the states of Puebla and Oaxaca in southern Mexico.

tells Mounds of accumulated rubble representing the site of an ancient city. A tell differs in both scale and content from a *midden*.

Tenochtitlán (tay-nosh-teet-lahn´) Aztec capital, built on the future site of Mexico City.

teosinte (taeo-sin´-tae) A native grass of southern Mexico, believed to be ancestral to maize.

Teotihuacán (tay-oh-tee-wah-cahn′) Earliest city-state to dominate the Valley of Mexico, it became one of the largest urban centers in the New World up to the nineteenth century.

territorial state A form of state political organization with multiple administrative centers and one or more capitals. The cities tend to house the elite and administrative classes, and food producers usually lived and worked in the surrounding hinterland.

territories Portions of an individual's or group's home range that are actively defended against intrusion, especially by members of the same species.

theocracy A polity governed by religious authorities.

theory A broad statement of scientific relationships or underlying principles that has been at least partially verified.

thermoluminiscence (TL) (ther-mo-loo-min-ess′-ence) Technique for dating certain archaeological materials, such as ceramics, that release stored energy of radioactive decay as light upon reheating.

Tikal (tee-kal′) Principal Maya city in Guatemala.

till plain Stones, boulders, mud, sand, and silt deposited by glaciers as they melt; a ground moraine.

Tiwanaku (tee-wahn-ah′-koo) Regional state, city, and valley of the same name near Lake Titicaca, in Bolivia.

Toltecs Central Mexican highlands people who created a pre-Aztec empire with its capital at Tula in the Valley of Mexico.

totem An animal or being associated with a kin-group and used for social identification; also, a carved pole representing these beings.

trace-element analysis A chemical technique for measuring the incidence of microminerals, or trace elements, in rocks; applied by archaeologists to identify the source areas of rocks used as raw materials by humans.

transhumance Seasonal migration from one resource zone to another, especially between highlands and lowlands.

transmutation The change of one species to another. The term *evolution* did not assume its current meaning until the late nineteenth century.

Tula (too′-la) Toltec capital in the Valley of Mexico; sometimes known as Tollan.

tundra Treeless plains characterized by permafrost conditions that support the growth of shallow-rooted vegetation such as grasses and mosses.

Tutankhamen (toot-en-cahm′-en) Egyptian pharaoh of the New Kingdom period, who died at age 19 in 1323 B.C.; informally known today as King Tut.

Uaxactún (wash-akh-toon′) Maya urban center in Guatemala.

Ubaid (oo-bide′) Early formative culture of Mesopotamia, 7,500–6,200 ya; predecessor to Sumerian civilization.

uniformitarianism The theory that the earth's features are the result of long-term processes that continue to operate in the present as they did in the past. Elaborated on by Lyell, this theory opposed catastrophism and contributed strongly to the concept of immense geological time.

Upper Paleolithic A cultural period usually associated with modern humans, but also found with some Neandertals, and distinguished by technological innovation in various stone tool industries. Best known from western Europe; similar industries are also known from central and eastern Europe and Africa.

Upper Pleistocene The portion of the Pleistocene epoch beginning 125,000 ya and ending approximately 10,000 ya.

variation (genetic) Inherited differences among individuals; the basis of all evolutionary change.

vasoconstriction Narrowing of blood vessels to reduce blood flow to the skin. Vasoconstriction is an involuntary response to cold and reduces heat loss at the skin's surface.

vasodilation Expansion of blood vessels, permitting increased blood flow to the skin. Vasodilation permits warming of the skin, and it facilitates radiation of warmth in order to cool the skin. Vasodilation is an involuntary response to warm temperatures, various drugs, and even emotional states (blushing).

vectors Agents that serve to transmit disease from one carrier to another. Mosquitoes are vectors for malaria, just as fleas are vectors for bubonic plague.

vertebrates Animals with segmented, bony spinal columns; includes fishes, amphibians, reptiles, birds, and mammals.

Wari (wah′-ree) Regional state and city of the same name in southern Peru.

Xia (shah) Semilegendary kingdom or dynasty of early China.

Younger Dryas A stadial between roughly 13,500 and 11,500 ya; the climate of higher latitudes became colder and drier but did not mark a full return to glacial conditions.

Zhou (chew) Chinese dynasty that followed Shang and ruled between 1122 and 221 B.C.

ziggurat Late Sumerian mud-brick temple-pyramid.

zoonoses (*sing.*, zoonosis) Diseases that can be transmitted to humans from other vertebrates.

zoonotic (zoh-oh-nah′-tic) Pertaining to a zoonosis (*pl.*, zoonoses), a disease that is transmitted to humans through contact with nonhuman animals.

zygote A cell formed by the union of an egg and a sperm cell. It contains the full complement of chromosomes (in humans, 46) and has the potential of developing into an entire organism.

BIBLIOGRAPHY

Acosta, José de
  2002   *Natural and Moral History of the Indies.* Jane E. Mangan
          (ed.). Durham, NC: Duke University Press.
Acsádi, G and J. Nemeskéri
  1970   *History of Human Life Span and Mortality.* Budapest:
          Akadémiai Kiadó.
Adams, Robert McC.
  1981   *Heartland of Cities.* Chicago: University of Chicago Press.
Adcock, Gregory J., Elizabeth S. Snow, Dennis Simon, et al.
  2001   "Mitochondrial DNA Sequences in Ancient Australians:
          Implications for Modern Human Origins." *Proceedings of
          the National Academy of Sciences,* 98:537–542.
Adovasio, James M., J. Donahue, and Robert Stuckenrath
  1990   "The Meadowcroft Rockshelter Radiocarbon Chronology
          1975–1990." *American Antiquity,* 55(2):348–354.
Aitken, M. J., C. B. Stringer, and P. A. Mellars (eds.)
  1993   *The Origin of Modern Humans and the Impact of
          Chronometric Dating.* Princeton: NJ: Princeton University
          Press.
Aldred, Cyril
  1998   *The Egyptians.* (Rev. Ed.) New York: Thames & Hudson.
Allchin, Briget and Raymond Allchin
  1982   *The Rise of Civilization in India and Pakistan.* Cambridge:
          Cambridge University Press.
Alva, Walter and Christopher Donnan
  1993   *Royal Tombs of Sipan.* Los Angeles: Fowler Museum of
          Cultural History, University of California, Los Angeles.
Ames, K. M. and Herbert D. Maschner
  1999   *Peoples of the Northwest Coast: Their Archaeology and
          Prehistory.* New York: Thames & Hudson.
Andrews, Peter
  1984   "An Alternative Interpretation of the Characters Used
          to Define *Homo erectus.*" *Courier Forschungsinstitut
          Senckenberg,* 69:167–175.
Armelagos, George J. and Kristin N. Harper
  2005   "Genomics at the Origins of Agriculture, Part One."
          Evolutionary Anthropology, 14:68–77.
Arnold, Thomas G.
  2002   "Radiocarbon Dates from the Ice-Free Corridor."
          Radiocarbon, 44(2):437–454.
Arsuaga, Juan-Luis, Carlos Lorenzo, and Ana Garcia
  1999   "The Human Cranial Remains from Gran Dolina Lower
          Pleistocene Site (Sierra de Atapuerca, Spain)." *Journal of
          Human Evolution,* 37:431–457.
Arsuaga, J. L., I. Martinez, A. Garcia, et al.
  1997   "Sima de los Huesos (Sierra de Atapuerca, Spain). The Site."
          Journal of Human Evolution, 33:109–127.
Ascenzi, A., I. Biddittu, P. F. Cassoli, et al.
  1996   "A Calvarium of Late *Homo erectus* from Ceprano, Italy."
          Journal of Human Evolution, 31:409–423.
Asfaw, Berhane, W. Henry Gilbert, Yonnas Beyene, et al.
  2002   "Remains of *Homo erectus* from Bouri, Middle Awash,
          Ethiopia." *Nature,* 416:317–320.
Aveni, Anthony F.
  1986   "The Nazca Lines: Patterns in the Desert." *Archaeology,*
          39(4):32–39.

———   2000   "Solving the Mystery of the Nazca Lines." *Archaeology,*
          53(3): 26–35.
———   (ed.)
  1990   "The Lines of Nazca." *Memoirs of the American
          Philosophical Society, 183.*

Badrian, Noel and Richard K. Malenky
  1984   "Feeding Ecology of *Pan paniscus* in the Lomako Forest,
          Zaire." *In: The Pygmy Chimpanzee,* Randall L. Susman (ed.),
          New York: Plenum Press, pp. 275–299.
Bailey, G.
  1975   "The Role of Molluscs in Coastal Economies." *Journal of
          Archaeological Science,* 2:45–62.
Balter, Michael
  2005   *The Goddess and the Bull.* New York: Free Press.
Bar-Oz, Guy
  2004   *Epipaleolithic Subsistence Strategies in the Levant: A
          Zooarchaeological Perspective.* Boston, MA: Brill Academic
          Publishers.
Barnes, G. L.
  1992   *China, Korea, and Japan: The Rise of Civilization in East
          Asia.* New York: Thames & Hudson.
Barnosky, Anthony, Paul L. Koch, Robert S. Feranec, Scott L. Wing,
and Alan B. Shabel
  2004   "Assessing the Causes of Late Pleistocene Extinctions on the
          Continents." *Science,* 306:70–75.
Bartlett, Thad. Q., Robert W. Sussman, and James M. Cheverud
  1993   "Infant Killing in Primates: A Review of Observed Cases
          with Specific References to the Sexual Selection
          Hypothesis." *American Anthropologist,* 95(4):958–990.
Bartstra, Gert-Jan
  1982   "*Homo erectus erectus:* The Search for Artifacts." *Current
          Anthropology,* 23(3):318–320.
Bar-Yosef, Ofer
  1986   "The Walls of Jericho: An Alternative Explanation." *Current
          Anthropology,* 27(2):157–162.

———   1987   "Late Pleistocene Adaptations in the Levant." *In: The
          Pleistocene in the Old World: Regional Perspectives,* Olga
          Soffer (ed.), New York: Plenum, pp. 219–236.

———   1993   "The Role of Western Asia in Modern Human Origins."
          In: M. J. Aitken, et al. (eds.), q.v., pp. 132–147.

———   1994   "The Contributions of Southwest Asia to the Study of the
          Origin of Modern Humans." *In: Origins of Anatomically
          Modern Humans,* M. H. Nitecki and D. V. Nitecki (eds.),
          New York: Plenum Press, pp. 23–66.

———   1998   "The Natufian Culture in the Levant, Threshold to the
          Origins of Agriculture." *Environmental Anthropology,*
          6(5):159–177.

Beadle, George W.
  1980   "The Ancestry of Corn." *Scientific American,* 242:112–119.

Bearder, Simon K.
1987 "Lorises, Bushbabies & Tarsiers: Diverse Societies in Solitary Foragers." *In*: Smuts, et al. (eds.), q.v., pp. 11–24.

Begun, David R.
2003 "Planet of the Apes." *Scientific American*, 289:74–83.

Begun, D. and A. Walker
1993 "The Endocast." *In:* A. Walker and R. E. Leakey (eds), q.v., pp. 326–358.

Beja-Pereira, A., G. Luikart, P. England, et al.
2003 "Gene-Culture Coevolution between Cattle Milk Protein Genes and Human Lactase Genes." *Nature Genetics,* 35:311–313.

Belfer-Cohen, Anna
1991 "The Natufians in the Levant." *Annual Review of Anthropology*, 20:167–186.

Ben Shaul, D. M.
1962 "The Composition of the Milk of Wild Animals." *International Zoo Yearbook,* 4:333–342.

Benz, Bruce F. and Hugh H. Iltis
1990 "Studies in Archaeological Maize I: The 'Wild' Maize from San Marcos Cave Reexamined." *American Antiquity*, 55(3):500–511.

Berger, Thomas and Erik Trinkaus
1995 "Patterns of Trauma Among the Neandertals." *Journal of Archaeological Science,* 22:841–852.

Berlo, Janet (ed.)
1992 *Art, Ideology, and the City of Teotihuacán*. Washington, DC: Dumbarton Oaks.

Bermudez de Castro, J.M., J. Arsuaga, E. Carbonell, et al.
1997 "A Hominid from the Lower Pleistocene of Atapuerca, Spain. Possible Ancestor to Neandertals and Modern Humans." *Science*, 276:1392-1395.

Bermudez de Castro, J. M., M. Martinon-Torres, E. Carbonell, et al.
2004 "The Atapuerca Sites and their Contribution to the Knowledge of Human Evolution in Europe." *Evolutionary Anthropology*, 13:25–41.

Binford, Lewis R.
1968 "Post-Pleistocene Adaptations." In: Binford, S. and L. R. Binford (eds.). *New Perspectives in Archaeology*. Chicago: Aldine, pp. 313–341.

———
1978 *Nunamiut Ethnoarchaeology*. New York: Academic Press.

———
1981 *Bones. Ancient Men and Modern Myths*. New York: Academic Press.

———
1983 *In Pursuit of the Past*. New York: Thames and Hudson.

Binford, Lewis R. and Chuan Kun Ho
1985 "Taphonomy at a Distance: Zhoukoudian, 'The Cave Home of Beijing Man'?" *Current Anthropology*, 26:413–442.

Binford, Lewis R. and Nancy M. Stone
1986a "The Chinese Paleolithic: An Outsider's View." *AnthroQuest*, Fall 1986(1):14–20.

———
1986b "Zhoukoudian: A Closer Look." *Current Anthropology*, 27(5):453–475.

Boaz, N. T. and Russell L. Ciochon
2001 "The Scavenging of *Homo erectus pekinensis*." *Natural History,* 110(2):46–51.

———
1990 "Tool Use and Tool Making in Wild Chimpanzees." *Folia Primatologica*, 54:86–99.

Boesch, C., P. Marchesi, N. Marchesi, et al.
1994 "Is Nut Cracking in Wild Chimpanzees a Cultural Behaviour?" *Journal of Human Evolution*, 26:325–338.

Bogin, Barry
1988 *Patterns of Human Growth*. Cambridge: Cambridge University Press.

Bogucki, Peter
1988 *Forest Farmers and Stockherders: Early Agriculture and Its Consequences in North Central Europe*. Cambridge: Cambridge University Press.

Bokonyi, S.
1969 "Archaeological Problems and Methods of Recognizing Animal Domestication." *In: The Domestication and Exploitation of Plants and Animals*, P. J. Ucko and G. W. Dimbleby (eds.), Chicago: Aldine, pp. 207–218.

Bordaz, Jacques
1970 *Tools of the Old and New Stone Age*. Natural History Press, Garden City.

Borries, C., et al.
1999 "DNA Analyses Support the Hypothesis that Infanticide is Adaptive in Langur Monkeys." *Proceedings of the Royal Society of London*, 266:901–904.

Boserup, Ester
1965 *The Conditions of Agricultural Growth*. Chicago: Aldine.

Bove, Frederick J. and Sonia Medrano Busto
2003 "Teotihuacan, Militarism, and Pacific Guatemala." *In:* Braswell (ed.), q. v., pp. 45–79.

Brace, C. L. and Ashley Montagu
1977 *Human Evolution* (2nd Ed.). New York: Macmillan.

Brace, C. Loring, H. Nelson, and N. Korn
1979 *Atlas of Human Evolution* (2nd Ed.). New York: Holt, Rinehart & Winston.

Brace, C. Loring, A. Russell Nelson, Noriko Seguchi, et al.
2001 "Old World Sources of the First New World Human Inhabitants: A Comparative Craniofacial View." *Proceedings of the National Academy of Science*, 98(4):10017–10022.

Bradley, Bruce and Dennis Stanford
2004 "The North Atlantic Ice-Edge Corridor: A Possible Palaeolithic Route to the New World." *World Archaeology* 36(4):459–478.

Brady, James E. and Andrea Stone
1986 "Naj Tunich: Entrance to the Maya Underworld." *Archaeology*, 39(6):18–25.

Braidwood, Robert J. and Bruce Howe
1960 *Prehistoric Investigations in Iraqi Kurdistan*. Studies in Ancient Oriental Civilization, No. 31. Chicago: Oriental Institute.

Braswell, Geoffrey E. (ed.)
2003 *The Maya and Teotihuacan: Reinterpreting Early Classic Interaction*. Austin: University of Texas Press.

Breuer, T. M.
2005 "First Observation of Tool Use in Wild Gorillas." *PLoS Biology*, 3(11):3380.

Bromage, Timothy G. and Christopher Dean
1985 "Re-evaluation of the Age at Death of Immature Fossil Hominids." *Nature*, 317:525–527.

Brooks, Alison, et al.
1995 "Dating and Context of Three Middle Stone Age Sites with Bone Points in the Upper Semliki Valley, Zaire." *Science*, 268:548–553.

Brown, Ian
1994 "Recent Trends in the Archaeology of the Southeastern United States." *Journal of Archaeological Research*, 2(1):45–111.

Brown, M. Kathryn and Travis W. Stanton (eds.)
2003 *Ancient Mesoamerican Warfare*. Walnut Creek, CA: Altamira Press.

Brown, P., T. Sutiikna, M. K. Morwood, et al.
2004 "A New Small-Bodied Hominin from the Late Pleistocene of Flores, Indonesia." *Nature*, 431:1055–1061.

Brown, T. M. and K. D. Rose
1987 "Patterns of Dental Evolution in Early Eocene Anaptomorphine Primates Omomyidae from the Bighorn Basin, Wyoming." *Journal of Paleontology*, 61:1–62.

Brubaker, L. B., P. M. Anderson, M. E. Edwards, and A. V. Lozhkin
2005 "Beringia as a Glacial Refugium for Boreal Trees and Shrubs: New Perspectives from Mapped Pollen Data." *Journal of Biogeography*, 32(5):833–848.

Bruhns, Karen Olsen
1994 *Ancient South America*. Cambridge: Cambridge University Press.

Brunet, M., F. Guy, D. Pilbeam, et al.
2002 "A New Hominid from the Upper Miocene of Chad, Central Africa." *Nature*, 418:145–151.

Bryan, Alan L. and Ruth Gruhn
2003 "Some Difficulties in Modeling the Original Peopling of the Americas." *Quaternary International*, 109–110:175–179.

Bryant, Vaughn M.
2003 "Invisible Clues to New World Plant Domestication." *Science*, 299:1029–1030.

Buchan, J. C., S. C. Alberts, J. B. Silk, and J. Altmann
2003 "True Paternal Care in a Multi-male Primate Society." *Nature*, 425:179–180.

Burger, Richard L.
1992 *Chavín and the Origins of Andean Civilizations*. New York: Thames & Hudson.

Butler, Declan
2006 "Yes But Will It Jump?" News. *Nature*, 439:124–125.

Butzer, Karl W.
1984 "Long-term Nile Flood Variation and Political Discontinuities in Pharaonic Egypt." *In:* Clark and Brandt (eds.), q.v., pp. 102–112.

Byers, Douglas S. (ed.)
1967 *The Prehistory of the Tehuacán Valley. Vol. 1: Economy and Subsistence*. Austin: University of Texas Press.

Cannon, Michael D. and David J. Meltzer
2004 "Early Paleoindian Foraging: Examining the Faunal Evidence for Large Mammal Specialization and Regional Variability in Prey Choice." *Quaternary Science Reviews*, 23:1955–1987.

Caramelli, David, Carlos Lalueza-Fox, Cristiano Vernesi, et al.
2003 "Evidence for Genetic Discontinuity Between Neandertals and 24,000-year-old Anatomically Modern Humans." *Proceedings of the National Academy of Sciences*, 100:6593–6597.

Carrol, Robert L.
1988 *Vertebrate Paleontology and Evolution*. New York: W. H. Freeman and Co.

Carter, Howard and A. C. Mace
1923 *The Tomb of Tutankhamen*. London: Cassell and Co., Ltd.

Cartmill, Matt
1972 "Arboreal Adaptations and the Origin of the Order Primates." *In: The Functional and Evolutionary Biology of Primates*, R. H. Tuttle (ed.), Chicago: Aldine-Atherton, pp. 97–122.

_____ 1992 "New Views on Primate Origins." *Evolutionary Anthropology*, 1:105–111.

Casson, Lionel
2001 *Everyday Life in Ancient Egypt*. Baltimore: Johns Hopkins University Press.

Catto, Norm and Gail Catto
2004 "Climate Change, Communities, and Civilizations: Driving Force, Supporting Player, or Background Noise?" *Quaternary International*, 123–125:7–10.

Cauvin, Jacques
2000 *The Birth of the Gods and the Origins of Agriculture*. Cambridge: Cambridge University Press.

Cavalli-Sforza, L. L., A. Piazza, P. Menozzi, and J. Mountain
1988 "Reconstruction of Human Evolution: Bringing Together Genetic, Archaeological, and Linguistic Data." *Proceedings of the National Academy of Sciences*, 85:6002–6006.

Chang, Kwang-chih
1980 *Shang Civilization*. New Haven: Yale University Press.

_____ 1986 *The Archaeology of Ancient China* (4th Ed.). New Haven: Yale University Press.

_____ 2000 "Ancient China and Its Anthropological Significance." *In*: Lamberg-Karlovsky (ed.), q.v., pp. 1–11.

Charteris, J., J. C. Wali, and J. W. Nottrodt
1981 "Functional Reconstruction of Gait from Pliocene Hominid Footprints at Laetoli, Northern Tanzania." *Nature*, 290:496–498.

Chatters, James C.
2001 *Ancient Encounters : Kennewick Man and the First Americans*. New York: Simon & Schuster.

_____ 2004 "Kennewick Man: A Paleoamerican Skeleton from the Northwestern U.S." In: *New Perspectives on the First Americans*, Bradley T. Lepper and Robson Bonnichsen (ed.), College Station, TX: Center for the Study of First Americans, pp. 129–135.

Childe, V. Gordon
1928 *The Most Ancient East*. London: Routledge and Kegan Paul.

_____ 1934 *New Light on the Most Ancient East*. London: Kegan Paul, Trench, Trubner.

_____ 1951 *Man Makes Himself* (Rev. Ed.). New York: New American Library.

Chrisman, Donald, Richard S. MacNeish, Jamshed Mavalwala, and Howard Savage
1996 "Late Pleistocene Human Friction Skin Prints from Pendejo Cave, New Mexico." *American Antiquity*, 61(2):357–376.

Chrisman, Donald, J. Mavalwala, H. Savage, and A. Tessarolo
2003 "Friction-Skin Imprints and Hair." In: MacNeish and Libby, q.v., pp. 417–430.

Ciochon, Russell L. and Robert S. Corruccini (eds.)
1983 *New Interpretations of Ape and Human Ancestry*. New York: Plenum Press.

457

Cioffi-Revilla, Claudio and Todd Landman
1999 "Evolution of Maya Polities in the Ancient Mesoamerican System." *International Studies Quarterly*, 43:559–598.

Clark, Grahame
1972 *Star Carr: A Case Study of Bioarchaeology.* Reading, MA: Addison-Wesley.

———
1979 *Mesolithic Prelude.* Edinburgh: Edinburgh University Press.

Clark, J. Desmond
1976 "Prehistoric Populations and Resources Favoring Plant Domestication in Africa." *In: Origins of African Plant Domestication*, J. R. Harlan, J. DeWet, and A. Stemler (eds.), The Hague: Mouton, pp. 69–84.

Clark, J. Desmond and Steven A. Brandt (eds.)
1984 *From Hunters to Farmers.* Berkeley and Los Angeles: University of California Press.

Clarke, R. J.
1985 "*Australopithecus* and Early *Homo* in Southern Africa." *In: Ancestors: The Hard Evidence*, E. Delson (ed.), New York: Alan R. Liss, pp. 171–177.

———
1998 "First Ever Discovery of a Well-Preserved Skull and Associated Skeleton of an Australopithecine." *South African Journal of Science*, 94:460.

Clarke, Ronald J. and Phillip V. Tobias
1995 "Sterkfontein Member 2 Foot Bones of the Oldest South African Hominid." *Science*, 269:521–524.

Clendinnen, Inga
1991 *Aztecs.* Cambridge: Cambridge University Press.

Cleveland, J. and C. T. Snowdon
1982 "The Complex Vocal Repertoire of the Adult Cotton-top Tamarin (*Saguinus oedipus oedipus*)." *Zeitschrift Tierpsychologie*, 58:231–270.

Coe, Michael D.
1992 *Breaking the Maya Code.* New York: Thames & Hudson.

———
1994 *Mexico: From the Olmecs to the Aztecs.* New York: Thames & Hudson.

———
1999 *The Maya* (6th Ed.). New York: Thames & Hudson.

Coe, Michael D., Dean Snow, and Elizabeth Benson
1986 *Atlas of Ancient America.* New York: Facts on File Publications.

Cohen, Mark N.
1977 *The Food Crisis in Prehistory.* New Haven: Yale University Press.

———
1989 *Health and the Rise of Civilization.* New Haven, CT: Yale University Press.

Cohen, M. N. and G. J. Armelagos (eds.)
1984 *Paleopathology at the Origins of Agriculture.* Orlando: Academic Press.

Coil, James, Alejandra Korstanje, Steven Archer, Christine A. Hastorf
2003 "Laboratory Goals and Consideration for Multiple Microfossil Extraction in Archaeology." *Journal of Archaeological Science*, 30:991–1008.

Colinvaux, Paul A.
1979 *Why Big Fierce Animals Are Rare: An Ecologist's Perspective.* Princeton, NJ: Princeton University Press.

Colledge, Sue, James Conolly, and Stephen Shennan
2004 "Archaeobotanical Evidence for the Spread of Farming in the Eastern Mediterranean." *Current Anthropology*, 45(supplement):S35–S58.

Colwell, Rita R.
1996 "Global Climate and Infectious Disease: The Cholera Paradigm." *Science*, 274(5295):2025–2031.

Conkey, M.
1987 "New Approaches in the Search for Meaning? A Review of the Research in 'Paleolithic Art.'" *Journal of Field Archaeology*, 14:413–430.

Conlee, Christina A., Jalh Dulanto, Carol J. Mackey, and Charles Stanish
2004 "Late Prehispanic Sociopolitical Complexity." *In*: Silverman (ed.), q.v., pp. 209–236.

Conneller, Chantal
2004 "Hunter-Gatherers 'on the move'?" *Antiquity*, 78(302):916–922.

Conroy, Glenn C.
1997 *Reconstructing Human Origins. A Modern Synthesis.* New York: Norton.

Conroy, G. C., M. Pickford, B. Senut, J. van Couvering, and P. Mein
1992 "*Otavipithecus namibiensis*, First Miocene Hominoid from Southern Africa." *Nature*, 356:144–148.

Cook, Anita G.
2004 "Wari Art and Society." *In*: Silverman (ed.), q.v., pp. 146–166.

Cooper, Alan, Andrew Rambaut, Vincent Macaulay, et al.
2001 "Human Origins and Ancient DNA." Letter to *Science*, 282:1655–1656.

Cordell, Linda S.
1998 *Prehistory of the Southwest.* (2nd Ed.). Orlando, FL: Academic Press.

Corruccini, Robert S. and Russell L. Ciochon (eds.)
1994 *Integrative Paths to the Present; Paleoanthropological Advances in Honor of F. Clark Howell.* Englewood Cliffs, NJ: Prentice-Hall.

Covey, R. Alan
2003 "A Processual Study of Inka State Formation." *Journal of Anthropological Archaeology*, 22:333–357.

Cowgill, George L.
2000 "The Central Mexican Highlands from the Rise of Teotihuacan to the Decline of Tula." *In: The Cambridge History of the Native Peoples of the Americas, Vol. II: Mesoamerica, Part I*, Richard E. W. Adams and Murdo J. MacLeod (eds.). Cambridge, UK: Cambridge University Press, pp. 250–317.

———
2004 "Origins and Development of Urbanism: Archaeological Perspectives." *Annual Review of Anthropology*, 33:525–549.

Crawford, Gary W. and Chen Shen
1998 "The Origins of Rice Agriculture: Recent Progress in East Asia." *Antiquity*, 72: 858–867.

Crawford, Harriet
2004 *Sumer and the Sumerians.* (2nd Ed.). Cambridge, UK: Cambridge University Press.

Crown, Patricia L.
1991 "Hohokam: Current Views of Prehistory and the Regional System." *In: Chaco and Hohokam Prehistoric Regional Systems in the American Southwest*, Patricia L. Crown and W. James Judge (eds.), Santa Fe: School of American Research Press, pp. 135–157.

Cummings, Michael
   2000   *Human Heredity. Principles and Issues* (5th Ed.). St. Paul: Wadsworth/West Publishing Co.

Currat, M., G. Trabuchet, D. Rees, et al.
   2002   "Molecular Analysis of the Beta-Globin Gene Cluster in the Niokholo Mandenka Population Reveals a Recent Origin of the Beta S Senegal Mutation." *American Journal of Human Genetics,* 70:207–223.

Curtin, Phillip D.
   2002   "Overspecialization and Remedies." *In:* R. H. Steckel and J. C. Rose (eds.), q.v., pp. 603–608.

Curtin, R. and P. Dolhinow
   1978   "Primate Social Behavior in a Changing World." *American Scientist,* 66:468–475.

Dalton, Rex
   2005   "Scientists Finally Get Their Hands on Kennewick Man." *Nature,* 436(7047):10.

Dart, Raymond
   1959   *Adventures with the Missing Link.* New York: Harper & Brothers.

Darwin, Charles
   1859   *On the Origin of Species.* A Facsimile of the First Edition, Cambridge, MA: Harvard University Press (1964).

Darwin, Francis (ed.)
   1950   *The Life and Letters of Charles Darwin.* New York: Henry Schuman.

Davies, Nigel
   1983   *The Ancient Kingdoms of Mexico.* New York: Penguin.

Davis, S. and F. R. Valla
   1978   "Evidence for Domestication of the Dog 12,000 Years Ago in the Natufian of Israel." *Nature,* 276:608–610.

Day, M. H. and E. H. Wickens
   1980   "Laetoli Pliocene Hominid Footprints and Bipedalism." *Nature,* 286:385–387.

D'Azevedo, Warren (ed.)
   1986   *Handbook of North American Indians,* vol. 11: Great Basin. Washington, DC: Smithsonian Institution Press.

Dean, Christopher, Meave G. Leakey, Donald Reid, et al.
   2001   "Growth Processes in Teeth Distinguishing Modern Humans from *Homo erectus* and Earlier Hominins." *Nature,* 414:628–631.

Dean, M., M. Carring, C. Winkler, et al.
   1996   "Genetic Restriction of HIV-1 Infection and Progression to AIDS by a Deletion Allele of the CKR5 Structural Gene." *Science,* 273:1856–1862.

Defleur, A, T. White, P. Valensi, et al.
   1999   "Neanderthal Cannibalism at Moula-Guercy, Ardèche, France." *Science,* 286:128–131.

de Heinzelin, Jean, J. Desmond Clark, Tim White, et al.
   1999   "Environment and Behavior of 2.5-Million-Year-Old Bouri Hominids." *Science,* 284:625–629.

De la Torre, Ignacio and Rafael Mora
   2005   "Unmodified Lithic Material at Olduvai Bed I: Manuports or Ecofacts?" *Journal of Archaeological Science,* 32 (2):273–285.

Delcourt, Hazel R. and Paul A. Delcourt
   1991   *Quaternary Ecology: A Paleoecological Perspective.* London: Chapman & Hall.

de Lumley, Henry and M. de Lumley
   1973   "Pre-Neanderthal Human Remains from Arago Cave in Southeastern France." *Yearbook of Physical Anthropology,* 16:162–168.

Dene, H. T., M. Goodman, and W. Prychodko
   1976   "Immunodiffusion Evidence on the Phylogeny of the Primates." *In: Molecular Anthropology,* M. Goodman, R. E. Tashian, and J. H. Tashian (eds.), New York: Plenum Press, pp. 171–195.

Dennell, Robin
   1983   *European Economic Prehistory: A New Approach.* New York: Academic Press.

Dennell, Rubin and Wil Roebroeks
   2005   "An Asian Perspective on Early Human Dispersal from Africa." *Nature,* 438:1099–1104.

Desmond, Adrian and James Moore
   1991   *Darwin.* New York: Warner Books.

de Waal, Frans
   1989   *Peacemaking among Primates.* Cambridge: Harvard University Press.

———
   1999   "Cultural Primatology Comes of Age." *Nature,* 399:635–636.

Diamond, Jared
   1987   "The Worst Mistake in the History of the Human Race." *Discover,* 8(5):64–66.

———
   1989   "The Accidental Conqueror." *Discover,* 10(12):71–76.

Diaz del Castillo, Bernal
   1956   *The Discovery and Conquest of Mexico.* New York: Farrar, Straus & Cudahy.

Diehl, Richard
   2004   *The Olmecs: America's First Civilization.* New York: Thames & Hudson.

Diehl, Richard A. and Janet C. Berlo (eds.)
   1989   *Mesoamerica after the Decline of Teotihuacán, A.D. 700–900.* Washington, DC: Dumbarton Oaks.

Diehl, Richard A. and Michael D. Coe
   1996   "Olmec archaeology." *In: The Olmec World,* by M. D. Coe, R. A. Diehl, D. A. Freidel, P. T. Furst, F. K. Reilly III, L. Schele, C. E. Tate, and K. A. Taube. Princeton: The Art Museum, Princeton University, pp. 2–25.

Dillehay, Thomas D.
   1989   *Monte Verde: A Late Pleistocene Settlement in Chile, Vol. 1: Paleoenvironment and Site Context.* Washington, DC: Smithsonian Institution Press.

———
   1997   *Monte Verde: A Late Pleistocene Settlement in Chile, Vol. 2: The Archaeological Content and Interpretation.* Washington, DC: Smithsonian Institution Press.

———
   2000   *The Settlement of the Americas: A New Prehistory.* New York: Basic Books.

Dillehay, Tom D., Duccio Bonavia, and Peter Kaulicke
   2004   "The First Settlers." *In:* Silverman (ed.), q.v., pp. 16–34.

Dincauze, Dena
   1997   "Regarding Pendejo Cave: Response to Chrisman et al." *American Antiquity,* 62(3):554–555.

DiPeso, Charles C.
   1974   *Casas Grandes, A Fallen Trading Center of the Gran Chichimeca.* Flagstaff: Northland Press.

Dixon, E. James
1999　*Bones, Boats, and Bison: Archaeology and the First Colonization of Western North America.* Albuquerque: University of New Mexico.

Dobyns, Henry F.
1966　"Estimating Aboriginal American Population: An Appraisal of Techniques with a New Hemisphere Estimate." *Current Anthropology,* 7:395–449.

Doebley, J.
1994　"Morphology, Molecules, and Maize." *In: Corn and Culture in the Prehistoric New World,* S. Johannessen and C. A. Hastorf, (eds.), Boulder, CO: Westview Press, pp. 101–112.

Domínguez-Rodrigo, Manuel
2002　"Hunting and Scavenging by Early Humans: The State of the Debate." *Journal of World Prehistory,* 16(1):1–54.

Domínguez-Rodrigo, Manuel and Travis Rayne Pickering
2003　"Early Hominid Hunting and Scavenging: A Zooarchaeological Review." *Evolutionary Anthropology,* 12:275–282.

Doran, D. M. and A. McNeilage
1998　"Gorilla Ecology and Behavior." *Evolutionary Anthropology,* 6(4):120–131.

Duarte, C., J. Mauricio, P. B. Pettitt, et al.
1999　"The Early Upper Paleolithic Human Skeleton from the Abrigo do Lagar Velho (Portugal) and Modern Human Emergence in Iberia." *Proceedings of the National Academy of Sciences,* 96:7604–7609.

Dunnell, Robert C.
1982　"Science, Social Science, and Common Sense: The Agonizing Dilemma of Modern Archaeology." *Journal of Anthropological Research,* 38:1–25.

Durham, William
1981　Paper presented to the Annual Meeting of the American Anthropological Association, Washington, D.C., Dec. 1980. Reported in *Science,* 211:40.

Edmonds, M.
1999　*Ancestral Geographies of the Neolithic: Landscape, Monuments, and Memory.* London: Routledge.

Edwards, Mike
2000　"Indus Civilization: Clues to an Ancient Puzzle." *National Geographic,* 197(6):108–131.

Ehret, C.
1984　"Historical/Linguistic Evidence for Early African Food Production." *In:* J. D. Clark and S. A. Brandt (eds.), q.v., pp. 26–35.

Emerson, Thomas E. and R. Barry Lewis (eds.)
2000　*Cahokia and the Hinterlands.* Urbana: University of Illinois Press.

Enard, W., M. Przeworski, S. E. Fisher, et al.,
2002　"Molecular Evolution of FOXP2, a Gene Involved in Speech and Language." *Nature,* 418:869–872.

Erlandson, Jon M.
1988　"The Role of Shellfish in Prehistoric Economies: A Protein Perspective." *American Antiquity,* 53:102–109.

———　2002　"Anatomically Modern Humans, Maritime Voyaging, and the Pleistocene Colonization of the Americas." *In:* "The First Americans, The Pleistocene Colonization of the New World," N. G. Jablonski (ed.), *Memoirs of the California Academy of Sciences,* 27:59–92.

Etler, Dennis A. and Li-Tianyuan
1994　"New Archaic Human Fossil Discoveries in China and Their Bearing on Hominid Species Definition During the Middle Pleistocene." *In:* R. Corruccini and R. Ciochon (eds.), q.v., pp. 639–675.

Ezzo, Joseph A.
1993　"Human Adaptation at Grasshopper Pueblo, Arizona: Social and Ecological Perspectives." *International Monographs in Prehistory, Archaeological Series, 4.* Ann Arbor.

Fagan, Brian M.
1993　"Taming the Aurochs." *Archaeology,* 46(5):14–17.

Falgeres, Christophe, Jean-Jacques Bahain, Yugi Yokoyama, et al.
1999　"Earliest Humans in Europe: The Age of TD6 Gran Dolina, Atapuerca, Spain." *Journal of Human Evolution,* 37:345–352.

Falk, Dean
1989　"Comments." *Current Anthropology,* 30:141.

Fedigan, Linda M.
1983　"Dominance and Reproductive Success in Primates." *Yearbook of Physical Anthropology,* 26:91–129.

Fiedel, Stuart J.
1999a　"Artifact Provenience at Monte Verde: Confusion and Contradictions." *In:* "Special Report: Monte Verde Revisited," *Discovering Archaeology,* 1(6):1–23 (separate insert).

———　1999b　"Older Than We Thought: Implications of Corrected Dates for Paleoindians." *American Antiquity,* 64(1):95–116.

———　2004　"The Kennewick Follies: 'New' Theories about the Peopling of the Americas." *Journal of Anthropological Research,* 60:75–110.

Fiedel, Stuart J. and G. Haynes
2004　"A premature burial: comments on Grayson and Meltzer's 'requiem for overkill'." *Journal of Archaeological Science,* 31:121–131.

Fischer, Anders (ed.)
1995　"Man and Sea in the Mesolithic: Coastal Settlement Above and Below Present Sea Level." *Oxbow Monograph 53.* Oxford, England: Oxbow Books.

Fischman, Josh
2005　"Family Ties." *National Geographic,* 207(April):16–27.

Fitzgerald, Patrick
1978　*Ancient China.* Oxford: Elsevier Phaidon.

Fleagle, John
1983　"Locomotor Adaptations of Oligocene and Miocene Hominoids and their Phyletic Implications." *In:* R. L. Ciochon and R. S. Corruccini (eds), q.v., pp. 301–324.

———　1988/1999　*Primate Adaptation and Evolution.* New York: Academic Press. (2nd Ed.), 1999.

———　1994　"Anthropoid Origins." *In:* R. S. Corruccini and R. L. Ciochon (eds.), q.v., pp. 17–35.

Flannery, Kent V.
1972　"The Origins of the Village As a Settlement Type in Mesoamerica and the Near East: A Comparative Study." *In: Man, Settlement and Urbanism,* P. J. Ucko, R. Tringham, and G. W. Dimbleby (eds.), London: Duckworth, pp. 23–53.

———
1973   "The Origins of Agriculture." *Annual Review of Anthropology,* 2:217–310.

———
1986   *Guila Naquitz: Archaic Foraging and Early Agriculture in Oaxaca, Mexico.* New York: Academic Press.

Flannery, Kent V. (ed.)
1982   *Maya Subsistence: Studies in Memory of Dennis E. Puleston.* New York: Academic Press.

Flannery, Kent V. and Joyce Marcus
2000   "Formative Mexican Chiefdoms and the Myth of the 'Mother Culture.'" *Journal of Anthropological Archaeology,* 19: 1–37.

Fleischer, R. F. and H. R. Hart, Jr.
1972   "Fission Track Dating Techniques and Problems." *In: Calibration of Hominid Evolution,* W. W. Bishop and J. A. Miller (eds.). Edinburgh: Scottish Academic Press, pp. 135–170.

Foley, R. A.
1991   "How Many Species of Hominid Should There Be?" *Journal of Human Evolution,* 30: 413–427.

Foley, R. A. and M. M. Lahr
1997   "Mode 3 Technologies and the Evolution of Modern Humans." *Cambridge Archaeological Journal:* 7:3–36.

Foley, Robert
2002   "Adaptive Radiations and Dispersals in Hominin Evolutionary Ecology." *Evolutionary Anthropology,* 11(Supplement 1):32–37.

Formicola, Vincenzo and Alexandra P. Buzhilova
2004   "Double Child Burial from Sunghir (Russia): Pathology and Inferences for Upper Paleolithic Funerary Practices." *American Journal of Physical Anthropology,* 124:189–198.

Freidel, David A. and Jeremy A. Sabloff
1984   *Cozumel: Late Maya Settlement Patterns.* New York: Academic Press.

Freidel, David, Linda Schele, and Joy Parker
1993   *Maya Cosmos: Three Thousand Years on the Shaman's Path.* New York: William R. Morrow.

Fried, Morton H.
1967   *The Evolution of Political Society: An Essay in Political Anthropology.* New York: Random House.

Friedman, Florence Dunn (ed.) et al.
1998   *Gifts of the Nile: Ancient Egyptian Faience.* New York: Thames & Hudson.

Frisancho, A. Roberto
1993   *Human Adaptation and Accommodation.* Ann Arbor: University of Michigan Press.

Frisch, Rose E.
1988   "Fatness and Fertility." *Scientific American,* 258:88–95.

Frison, George C.
1978   *Prehistoric Hunters of the High Plains.* New York: Academic Press.

Fritz, Gayle J.
1994   "Are the First American Farmers Getting Younger?" *Current Anthropology,* 35(3):305–309.

———
1999   "Gender and the Early Cultivation of Gourds in Eastern North America." *American Antiquity,* 64(3):417–429.

Fuller, Dorian, Ravi Korisettar, P. C. Venkatasubbaiah, Martin K. Jones
2004   "Early Plant Domestications in Southern India: Some Preliminary Archaeobotanical Results." *Vegetation History and Archaeobotany,* 13:115–129.

Galik, K., B. Senut, M. Pickford, et al.
2004   "External and Internal Morphology of the Bar1002'00 *Orrorin tugenensis* Femur." *Science,* 305:1450–1453.

Gao, Feng, Elizabeth Bailes, David L. Robertson, et al.
1999   "Origin of HIV-1 in the Chimpanzee *Pan troglodytes troglodytes.*" *Nature,* 397:436–441.

Gardner, R. Allen, B. T. Gardner, and T. T. van Cantfort (eds.)
1989   *Teaching Sign Language to Chimpanzees.* Albany: State University of New York Press.

Gebo, Daniel L., Marian Dagosto, K. Christopher Beard, and Tao Qi
2000   "The Smallest Primates." *Journal of Human Evolution,* 38:585–594.

Gibson, Jon L.
2001   *The Ancient Mounds of Poverty Point.* Gainesville, FL: University Press of Florida.

Gillespie, B. and R. G. Roberts
2000   "On the Reliability of Age Estimate for Human Remains at Lake Mungo." *Journal of Human Evolution,* 38:727–732.

Gingerich, Phillip D.
1985   "Species in the Fossil Record: Concepts, Trends, and Transitions." *Paleobiology,* 11:27–41.

Glantz, M. M. and T. B. Ritzman
2004   "A Re-Analysis of the Neandertal Status of the Teshik-Tash Child." *American Journal of Physical Anthropology, Supplement* 38:100–101 (Abstract).

Glassow, Michael A.
1996   *Purisimeño Chumash Prehistory.* New York: Harcourt Brace.

Goebel, Ted, Michael R. Waters, and Margarita Dikova
2003   "The Archaeology of Ushki Lake, Kamchatka, and the Pleistocene Peopling of the Americas." *Science,* 301:501–505

Gollings, John, John M. Fritz and George Michell
1991   *City of Victory: Vijayanagara, the Medieval Hindu Capital of Southern India.* New York: Aperture Press.

Goodall, Jane
1986   *The Chimpanzees of Gombe.* Cambridge: Harvard University Press.

Goodman, M., C. A. Porter, J. Czelusniak, et al.
1998   "Toward a Phylogenetic Classification of Primates Based on DNA Evidence Complemented by Fossil Evidence." *Molecular Phylogenetics and Evolution,* 9:585–598.

Gossett, Thomas F.
1963   *Race, the History of an Idea in America.* Dallas: Southern Methodist University Press.

Gould, Richard A.
1977   "Puntutjarpa Rockshelter and the Australian Desert Culture." *Anthropological Papers of the American Museum of Natural History,* 54(1).

Gould, Stephen Jay
1981   *The Mismeasure of Man.* New York: W. W. Norton.

———
1985   "Darwin at Sea—and the Virtues of Port." *In:* Stephen Jay Gould, *The Flamingo's Smile. Reflections in Natural History.* New York: W. W. Norton, pp. 347–359.

———
1987   *Time's Arrow, Time's Cycle.* Cambridge: Harvard University Press.

———
1989   *Wonderful Life: The Burgess Shale and the Nature of History.* New York: W. W. Norton.

Gould, S. J. and N. Eldredge
1977   "Punctuated Equilibria: The Tempo and Mode of Evolution Reconsidered." *Paleobiology,* 3:115–151.

Gramly, Richard Michael
1992   *Guide to the Palaeo-Indian Artifacts of North America.* (2nd Ed.). Buffalo, NY: Persimmon Press.

Grant, B. S. and L. L. Wiseman
2002   "Recent History of Melanism in American Peppered Moths." *The Journal of Heredity,* 93(2):86–90.

Grant, Peter R. and B. Rosemary Grant
2002   "Unpredictable Evolution in a 30-year Study of Darwin's Finches." *Science,* 296:707–711.

Grayson, Donald K. and David J. Meltzer
2002   "Clovis Hunting and Large Mammal Extinction: A Critical Review of the Evidence." *Journal of World Prehistory,* 16(4):313–359.

——————
2003   "A Requiem for North American Overkill." *Journal of Archaeological Science,* 30:585–593.

——————
2004   "North American Overkill Continued?" *Journal of Archaeological Science,* 31:133–136.

Green, T. J., B. Cochran, T. W. Fenton, et al.
1998   "The Buhl Burial: A Paleoindian Woman from Southern Idaho." *American Antiquity,* 43(4):437–456.

Greenberg, Joseph
1987   *Language in the Americas.* Palo Alto: Stanford University Press.

Greene, John C.
1981   *Science, Ideology, and World View.* Berkeley: University of California Press.

Greenwood, B. and T. Mutabingwa
2002   "Malaria in 2000." *Nature,* 415:670–672.

Gregg, Susan Alling
1988   *Foragers and Farmers: Population Interaction and Agricultural Expansion in Prehistoric Europe.* Chicago: University of Chicago Press.

Gregory, J. M., P. Huybrechts, and S. C. B. Raper
2004   "Threatened Loss of the Greenland Ice Sheet." *Nature,* 428:616.

Grine, Frederick E.
1988   *Evolutionary History of the 'Robust' Australopithecines.* New York: Aldine de Gruyter.

Grove, David C.
1989   "Olmec, What's in a Name?" *In: Regional Perspectives on the Olmec,* R. J. Sharer and D. C. Grove (eds.), Cambridge University Press, Cambridge, UK, pp. 8–14.

——————
1996   "The Formative Period in Mesoamerica." *In: The Oxford Companion to Archaeology,* Brian M. Fagan (ed.), Oxford, Oxford University Press, pp. 444–445.

Groves, Colin P.
2001   *Primate Taxonomy.* Washington, DC: Smithsonian Institution Press.

Guidon, N., A.-M. Pessis, Fabio Porenti, et al.
1996   "Nature and Age of the Deposits in Pedra Furada, Brazil: Reply to Meltzer, Adovasio, and Dillehay." *Antiquity,* 70:408–421.

Haas, Jonathan, and Winifred Creamer
2004   "Cultural Transformations in the Central Andean Late Archaic." *In:* Silverman (ed.), q.v., pp. 35–50.

Haas, Jonathan, Winifred Creamer, and Alvaro Ruiz
2004   "Dating the Late Archaic Occupation of the Norte Chico Region in Peru." *Nature,* 432:1020–1023.

Haas, Jonathan, Shelia Pozorski, and Thomas Pozorski (eds.)
1987   *The Origins and Development of the Andean State.* New York: Cambridge University Press.

Haile-Selassie, Yohannes Gen Suwa and Tim D. White
2004   "Late Miocene Teeth from Middle Awash, Ethiopia, and Early Hominid Dental Evolution." *Science,* 303:1503–1505.

Harbottle, Garman and Phil C. Weigand
1992   "Turquoise in Pre-Columbian America." *Scientific American,* 226(2):78–85.

Harlan, Jack R.
1992   *Crops and Man* (2nd Ed.). Madison, WI: American Society of Agronomy and Crop Science Society of America.

Harlow, Harry F. and Margaret K. Harlow
1961   "A Study of Animal Affection." *Natural History,* 70:48–55.

Harris, Edward
1989   *Principles of Archaeological Stratigraphy.* (2nd Ed.). New York: Academic Press.

Harrison, Richard J.
1985   "The 'Policultivo Ganadero,' or Secondary Products Revolution in Spanish Agriculture, 5000–1000 B.C." *Proceedings of the Prehistoric Society,* 51:75–102.

Hart, John P. and C. Margaret Scarry
1999   "The Age of Common Beans (*Phaseolus vulgaris*) in the Northeastern United States." *American Antiquity,* 64(4):653–658.

Haury, Emil W.
1976   *The Hohokam, Desert Farmers and Craftsmen: Excavations at Snaketown, 1964–1965.* Tucson: University of Arizona Press.

Hawass, Zahi and Mark Lehner
1994   "The Sphinx: Who Built It, and Why?" *Archaeology,* 47(5):30–41.

Haynes, C. Vance
1993   "Clovis-Folsom Geochronology and Climatic Change." *In:* Soffer and Praslov (eds.), q.v., pp. 219–236.

——————
1999   "Bad Weather and Good Hunters." *Discovering Archaeology,* 1(5):52).

Hays, T. R.
1984   "A Reappraisal of the Egyptian Predynastic." *In:* J. D. Clark and S. A. Brandt (eds.), q.v., pp. 65–73.

Healan, Dan M. (ed.)
1989   *Tula of the Toltecs.* Iowa City, IA: University of Iowa Press.

Healan, Dan M. and James W. Stoutamire
1989   "Surface Survey of the Tula Urban Zone." *In:* Healan (ed.), q.v., pp. 203–236.

Henry, David O.
1989   *From Foraging to Agriculture: The Levant at the End of the Ice Age.* Philadelphia: University of Pennsylvania Press.

Henzi, P. and L. Barrett
2003   "Evolutionary Ecology, Sexual Conflict, and Behavioral Differentiation Among Baboon Populations." *Evolutionary Anthropology,* 12(5):217–230.

Herre, Wolf
1969   "The Science and History of Domestic Animals." *In: Science in Archaeology,* D. Brothwell and E. Higgs (eds.), New York: Frederick A. Praeger, pp. 257–272.

Hetherington, Renée, J. Vaughn Barrie, Robert G. B. Reid, et al.
2003 "Late Pleistocene Coastal Paleogeography of the Queen Charlotte Islands, British Columbia, Canada, and Its Implications for Terrestrial Biogeography and Early Postglacial Human Occupation." *Canadian Journal of Earth Science*, 40:1755–1766.

Higham, Charles and Tracey L.-D. Lu
1998 "The Origins and Dispersal of Rice Cultivation." *Antiquity*, 72:867–877.

Higham, Tom, Christopher Bronk Ramsey, Ivor Karavanic, et al.
2006 "Revised Direct Radiocarbon Dating of the Vindija G$_1$ Upper Paleolithic Neandertals." *Proceedings of the National Academy of Sciences*, 103:553–557.

Hodder, Ian
1990 *The Domestication of Europe*. Oxford, Blackwell.

1996 *On the Surface: Çatalhöyük, 1993–95*. London: David Brown. (ed.)

2001 "Symbolism and the Origins of Agriculture in the Near East." *Cambridge Archaeological Journal*, 11(1):107–112.

Hoffman, Michael A.
1991 *Egypt Before the Pharaohs* (Rev. Ed.). Austin: University of Texas Press.

Holloway, Ralph L.
1983 "Cerebral Brain Endocast Pattern of *Australopithecus afarensis* Hominid." *Nature*, 303:420–422.

1985 "The Poor Brain of *Homo sapiens neanderthalensis*." *In: Ancestors, The Hard Evidence*, E. Delson (ed.). New York: Alan R. Liss, pp. 319–324.

Holmes, C. E.
1996 "Broken Mammoth." *In:* West and West (eds.), q.v., pp. 312–318.

Houston, Stephen D., David Stuart, Oswaldo Chinchilla Mazariegos (eds.)
2001 *The Decipherment of Ancient Maya Writing*. Oklahoma City: University of Oklahoma Press.

Howell, F. C.
1999 "Paleo-demes, Species, Clades, and Extinctions in the Pleistocene Hominin Record." *Journal of Anthropological Research*, 55:191–243.

Howell, John H.
1987 "Early Farming in Northwestern Europe." *Scientific American*, 257(5):118–126.

Hrdy, Sarah Blaffer
1977 *The Langurs of Abu*. Cambridge, MA: Harvard University Press.

Hrdy, Sarah Blaffer, Charles Janson, and Carel van Schaik
1995 "Infanticide: Let's Not Throw Out the Baby with the Bath Water." *Evolutionary Anthropology*, 3(5):151–154.

Hu, Dale J., Timothy J. Dondero, Mark A. Rayfield, et al.
1996 "The Emerging Genetic Diversity of HIV. The Importance of Global Surveillance for Diagnostics, Research, and Prevention." *Journal of the American Medical Association*, 275(3):210–216.

Huysecom, E., S. Ozainne, F. Raeli, A. Ballouche, M. Rasse, and S. Stokes
2004 "Ounjougou (Mali): A History of Holocene Settlement at the Southern Edge of the Sahara." *Antiquity*, 78(301):579–593.

Hyslop, John
1984 *The Inka Road System*. Orlando: Academic Press.

Iglesias Ponce de Léon, María
2003 "Problematical Deposits and the Problem of Interaction: The Material Culture of Tikal during the Early Classic Period." *In*: Braswell (ed.), q.v., pp. 167–198.

The International SNP Map Working Group
2001 "A Map of Human Genome Sequence Variation Containing 1.42 Million Single Nucleotide Polymorphisms." *Nature*, 409:928–933.

Isbell, William H. and Alexei Vranich
2004 "Experiencing the Cities of Wari and Tiwanaku." *In*: Silverman (ed.), q.v., pp. 167–182.

Iseminger, William R.
1996 "Mighty Cahokia." *Archaeology*, 49:(3):30–37.

Issar, Arie S., and Mattanyah Zohar
2004 *Climate Change—Environment and Civilization in the Middle East*. Berlin, Germany: Springer-Verlag.

Izawa, K. and A. Mizuno
1977 "Palm-Fruit Cracking Behaviour of Wild Black-Capped Capuchin (*Cebus apella*)." *Primates*, 18:773–793.

Jablonski, Nina
1992 "Sun, Skin Colour, and Spina Bifida: An Exploration of the Relationship between Ultraviolet Light and Neural Tube Defects." *Proceedings of the Australian Society of Human Biology*, 5:455–462.

Jablonski, Nina G. and George Chaplin
2000 "The Evolution of Skin Coloration." *Journal of Human Evolution*, 39:57–106.

Jantz, R. L. and D. W. Owsley
2001 "Variation Among North American Crania. *American Journal of Physical Anthropology*, 114:146–55.

Jarrige, Jean-Francois and Richard H. Meadow
1980 "The Antecedents of Civilization in the Indus Valley." *Scientific American*, 243(2):122–133.

Jia, Lan-po
1975 *The Cave Home of Peking Man*. Peking: Foreign Language Press.

Jia, L. and Huang Weiwen
1990 *The Story of Peking Man*. New York: Oxford University Press.

Jochim, Michael A.
1976 *Hunting-Gathering Subsistence and Settlement: A Predictive Model*. New York: Academic Press.

1998 *A Hunter-Gatherer Landscape: Southwest Germany in the Late Paleolithic and Mesolithic*. New York: Plenum.

Jonaitas, Aldona
1988 *From the Land of the Totem Poles*. Seattle: University of Washington Press.

Judge, W. James
1984 "New Light on Chaco Canyon." *In: New Light on Chaco Canyon*, David Noble (ed.), Santa Fe: School of American Research, pp. 1–12.

Kano, T.
1992 *The Last Ape. Pygmy Chimpanzee Behavior and Ecology*. Stanford: Stanford University Press.

Kantner, John
1999 "Anasazi Mutilation and Cannibalism in the American Southwest." *In: The Anthropology of Cannibalism*, Laurence R. Goldman, (ed.), Westport, CT: Bergin and Garvey, pp. 75–104.

Keatinge, Richard W.
1988 *Peruvian Prehistory.* Cambridge: Cambridge University Press.

Kelly, Robert L.
1995 *The Foraging Spectrum: Diversity in Hunter-Gatherer Lifeways.* Washington, DC: Smithsonian Institution Press.

_____
2003 "Maybe we do know when people first came to North America; and what does it mean if we do?" *Quaternary International*, 109–110:133–145.

Kembel, Silvia Rodriguez and John W. Rick
2004 "Building Authority at Chavín de Huántar: Models of Social Organization and Development in the Initial Period and Early Horizon." *In:* Silverman (ed.), q.v., pp. 51–76.

Kennedy, Kenneth A. R. and S. U. Deraniyagala
1989 "Fossil Remains of 28,000-Year-Old Hominids from Sri Lanka." *Current Anthropology*, 30:397–399.

Kenoyer, Jonathan Mark
1998 *Ancient Cities of the Indus Valley Civilization.* Oxford: Oxford University Press.

Kent, Jonathan D.
1987 "The Most Ancient South: A Review of the Domestication of the Andean Camelids." *In: Studies in the Neolithic and Urban Revolutions: The V. Gordon Childe Colloquium, Mexico, 1986*, Linda Mazanilla (ed.), Oxford: B.A.R., pp. 169–184.

Kenyon, Kathleen M.
1981 *Excavations at Jericho*, Vol. 3. Jerusalem: British School of Archaeology.

Keynes, Randal
2002 *Darwin, His Daughter and Human Evolution.* New York: Riverhead Books.

Keyser, André W.
2000 "New Finds in South Africa." *National Geographic*, (May):76–83.

King, Barbara J.
1994 *The Information Continuum.* Santa Fe: School of American Research.

Kislev, Mordechai, Ehud Weiss, and Anat Hartmann
2004 "Impetus for Sowing and the Beginning of Agriculture: Ground Collecting of Wild Cereals." *Proceedings of the National Academy of Sciences*, 101(9):2692–2695.

Klein, Richard G.
1989/ *The Human Career. Human Biological and Cultural*
1999 *Origins.* Chicago: University of Chicago Press. (2nd Ed.).

Klein, Richard G. and Blake Edgar
2002 *The Dawn of Human Culture.* New York: John Wiley & Sons.

Kraeling, Carl H. and Robert McC. Adams (eds.)
1960 *City Invincible.* Chicago: University of Chicago Press.

Kramer, Andrew
1993 "Human Taxonomic Diversity in the Pleistocene: Does *Homo erectus* Represent Multiple Hominid Species?" *American Journal of Physical Anthropology*, 91:161–171.

Krings, Matthias, Cristen Capelli, Frank Tscentscher, et al.
2000 "A View of Neandertal Genetic Diversity." *Nature Genetics*, 26:144–146.

Krings, Matthias, Anne Stone, Ralf W. Schmitz, et al.
1997 "Neandertal DNA Sequences and the Origin of Modern Humans." *Cell*, 90:19–30.

Kulikov, Eugene E., Audrey B. Poltaraus, and Irina A. Lebedeva
2004 "DNA Analysis of Sunghir Remains: Problems and Perspectives." Poster Presentation, European Paleopathology Association Meetings, Durham, U.K, August 2004.

Lack, David
1966 *Population Studies of Birds.* Oxford: Clarendon.

Lahdenperä, M., S. Lummaa, S. Helle, et al.
2004 "Fitness Benefits of Prolonged Post-reproductive Lifespan in Women." *Nature*, 428:178–181.

Lahr, Marta Mirazon and Robert Foley
1998 "Towards a Theory of Human Origins: Geography, Demography, and Diversity in Recent Human Evolution." *Yearbook of Physical Anthropology*, 41:137–176.

Lalani, A. S., J. Masters, W. Zeng, et al.
1999 "Use of Chemokine Receptors by Poxviruses." *Science*, 286:1968–71.

Lamberg-Karlovsky, Martha (ed.)
2000 "The Breakout: The Origins of Civilization." *Peabody Museum Monographs 9.* Cambridge, MA: Harvard University.

Lamberg-Karlovsky, C. C. and Jeremy A. Sabloff
1995 *Ancient Civilizations: The Near East and Mesoamerica.* Prospect Heights, IL: Waveland.

Lambert, Joseph
1997 *Traces of the Past: Unraveling the Secrets of Archaeology through Chemistry.* New York: Addison-Wesley Longman.

Lanning, Edward P.
1967 *Peru Before the Incas.* Englewood Cliffs, NJ: Prentice-Hall.

Larsen, Clark Spencer
1995 "Biological Changes in Human Populations with Agriculture." *Annual Reviews of Anthropology*, 24:185–213.

_____
1997 *Bioarchaeology: Interpreting Behavior From the Human Skeleton.* Cambridge: Cambridge University Press.

Leakey, M. D. and R. L. Hay
1979 "Pliocene Footprints in Laetolil Beds at Laetoli, Northern Tanzania." *Nature*, 278:317–323.

Leakey, M. G., F. Spoor, F. H. Brown, et al.
2001 "New Hominin Genus from Eastern Africa Shows Diverse Middle Pliocene Lineages." *Nature*, 410:433–440.

Lederberg, Joshua
1996 "Infection Emergent." *Journal of the American Medical Association*, 275(3):243–245.

Legge, Anthony J.
1972 "Prehistoric Exploitation of Gazelle in Palestine." *In: Papers in Economic Prehistory*, E. S. Higgs (ed.), Cambridge: Cambridge University Press, pp. 119–124.

Legge, Anthony J. and Peter A. Rowley-Conwy
1987 "Gazelle Killing in Stone Age Syria." *Scientific American*, 257(2):88–95.

Lehner, Mark
1997 *The Complete Pyramids.* New York: Thames & Hudson.

Lerner, I. M. and W. J. Libby
1976 *Heredity, Evolution, and Society.* San Francisco: W. H. Freeman.

Lewis, R. Barry and Charles Stout (eds.)
1998   *Mississippian Towns and Sacred Spaces: Searching for An Architectural Grammar.* Tuscaloosa: University of Alabama Press.

Li, K. S., Y. Guan, J. Wang, et al.
2004   "Genesis of a Highly Pathogenic and Potentially Pandemic H5N1 Influenza Virus in Eastern Asia." *Nature,* 430:209–213.

Linnaeus, C.
1758   *Systema Naturae.*

Lordkipanidze, David, Abesalom Vekua, Reid Ferring, et al.
2005   "The Earliest Toothless Hominin Skull. *Nature,* 434:717–718.

Lowe, Gareth W.
1989   "The Heartland Olmec: Evolution of Material Culture." *In:* R. J. Sharer and D. C. Grove (eds.), q.v., pp. 33–67.

Loy, Thomas H. and E. James Dixon
1998   "Blood Residues on Fluted Points from Eastern Beringia." *American Antiquity,* 63(1): 21–46.

Lucero, Lisa. J.
1999   "Classic Lowland Maya Political Organization: A Review." *Journal of World Prehistory,* 13(2):211–263.

_____
2003   "The Politics of Ritual: The Emergence of Classic Maya Rulers." *Current Anthropology,* 44(4):523–558.

Lynch, Thomas F.
1983   "The Paleo-Indians." *In: Ancient South Americans,* J. D. Jennings (ed.), San Francisco: W. H. Freeman, pp. 87–137.

_____ (ed.)
1980   *Guitarrero Cave.* New York: Academic Press.

MacKinnon, J. and K. MacKinnon
1980   "The Behavior of Wild Spectral Tarsiers." *International Journal of Primatology,* 1:361–379.

MacNeish, Richard S.
1964   "Ancient Mesoamerican Civilization." *Science,* 143:531–537.

_____
1967   "A Summary of the Subsistence." *In:* D. S. Byers (ed.), q.v., pp. 290–310.

_____
1978   *The Science of Archaeology?* North Scituate, MA: Duxbury Press.

MacNeish, Richard S. and Jane G. Libby
2003   *Pendejo Cave.* Albuquerque: University of New Mexico Press.

MacNeish, Richard S., et al.
1972   *The Prehistory of the Tehuacán Valley. Vol. 5: Excavations and Reconnaissance.* Austin: University of Texas Press.

Maisels, C. K.
1999   *Early Civilizations of the Old World: The Formative Histories of Egypt, the Levant, Mesopotamia, India, and China.* London: Routledge.

Malm, Torben
1995   "Excavating Submerged Stone Age Sites in Denmark— The Tybrind Vig Example." *In:* A. Fischer (ed.), q.v., pp. 385–396.

Manson, J. H. and R. Wrangham
1991   "Intergroup Aggression in Chimpanzees and Humans." *Current Anthropology,* 32:369–390.

Manzi, G., F. Mallegni, and A. Ascenzi
2001   "A Cranium for the Earliest Europeans: Phylogenetic Position of the Hominid from Ceprano, Italy." *Proceedings of the National Academy of Sciences,* 98:1011–1016.

Marcus, Joyce
1993   *Mesoamerican Writing Systems: Propaganda, Myth, and History in Four Ancient Civilizations.* Princeton, NJ: Princeton University Press.

Marlar, Jennifer E. and Richard A. Marlar
2000   "Cannibals at Cowboy Wash; Biomolecular Archaeology Solves a Controversial Puzzle." *Discovering Archaeology,* 2(5):30–36.

Martin, Paul S.
1967   "Prehistoric Overkill." *In: Pleistocene Extinctions: The Search for a Cause,* P. S. Martin and H. E. Wright, Jr. (eds.), New Haven: Yale University Press, pp. 75–120.

_____
1982   "The Pattern of Meaning of Holarctic Mammoth Extinction." *In: Paleoecology of Beringia,* D. Hopkins, J. Matthews, C. Schweger, and S. Young (eds.), New York: Academic Press, pp. 399–408.

_____
1999   "The Time of the Hunters." *Discovering Archaeology,* 1(5):40–47.

Masataka, N.
1983   "Categorical Responses to Natural and Synthesized Alarm Calls in Goeldi's Monkeys (*Callimico goeldi*)." *Primates:* 24:40–51.

Mason, J. Alden
1968   *The Ancient Civilizations of Peru* (Rev. Ed.). London: Penguin Books.

Mayr, Ernst
1970   *Population, Species, and Evolution.* Cambridge: Harvard University Press.

McGhee, Robert
1996   *Ancient People of the Arctic.* Vancouver: University of British Columbia Press.

McGovern, Patrick E., Juzhong Zhang, Jigen Tang, et al. (eds.)
1985   *Shawnee-Minisink: A Stratified Paleoindian-Archaic Site in the Upper Delaware Valley.* Orlando: Academic Press.

McGrew, W. C.
1992   *Chimpanzee Material Culture. Implications for Human Evolution.* Cambridge: Cambridge University Press.

_____
1998   "Culture in Nonhuman Primates?" *Annual Review of Anthropology,* 27:301–328.

McHenry, Henry
1988   "New Estimates of Body Weight in Early Hominids and Their Significance to Encephalization and Megadontia in 'Robust' Australopithecines." *In:* F. E. Grine (ed.), q.v., pp. 133–148.

_____
1992   "Body Size and Proportions in Early Hominids." *American Journal of Physical Anthropology,* 87:407–431.

McKusick, V. A. (with S. E. Antonarakis, et al.)
1998   *Mendelian Inheritance in Man.* (12th Ed.). Baltimore: Johns Hopkins University Press.

Meehan, Betty
1982   *Shell Bed to Shell Midden.* Canberra: Australian Institute of Aboriginal Studies.

Mellars, Paul and Petra Dark
1999   *Star Carr in Context: New Archaeological and Palaeoecological Investigations at the Early Mesolithic Site of Star Carr, North Yorkshire.* McDonald Institute Monographs. London: David Brown.

Mellars, P. and C. Stringer (eds.),
1989   *The Human Revolution.* Princeton, NJ: Princeton University Press.

Meltzer, David J.
1993a   "Is There a Clovis Adaptation?" *In:* Soffer and Praslov (eds.), q.v., pp. 293–310.

———
1993b   *Search for the First Americans.* Washington, DC: Smithsonian Books.

Meltzer, David, James Adovasio, and Tom D. Dillehay
1994   "On a Pleistocene Human Occupation at Pedra Furada, Brazil." *Antiquity,* 68:695–714.

Meltzer, David J. et al.
1997   "On the Pleistocene Antiquity of Monte Verde, Southern Chile." *American Antiquity,* 62(4): 659–663.

Merriwether, D. Andrew, Francisco Rothhammer, and Robert E. Ferrell
1995   "Distribution of the Four Founding Lineage Haplotypes in Native Americans Suggests a Single Wave of Migration for the New World." *American Journal of Physical Anthropology,* 98(4): 411–430.

Mihlbachler, M. C., C. A. Hemmings, S. D. Webb
2000   "Reevaluation of the Alexon Bison Kill Site, Wacissa River, Jefferson County, Florida." *Current Research in the Pleistocene,* 17:55–57.

Miles, H. Lyn Whire
1990   "The Cognitive Foundations for Reference in a Signing Orangutan." *In:* Parker, S. T. and K. R. Gibson (eds.) *Language and Intelligence in Monkeys and Apes: Comparative Developmental Perspectives.* New York: Cambridge University Press, pp. 511–539.

Millon, René
1988   "The Last Years of Teotihuacán Dominance." *In: The Collapse of Ancient States and Civilizations.* N. Yoffee and G. Cowgill (eds.), Tucson: University of Arizona Press, pp. 102–164.

Milner, George R.
1998   *Cahokia Chiefdom: The Archaeology of a Mississippian Society.* Washington, DC:Smithsonian Institution Press.

Moctezuma, Eduardo Matos
1988   *The Great Temple of the Aztecs.* New York: Thames & Hudson.

Molnar, Stephen
1983   *Human Variation. Races, Types, and Ethnic Groups* (2nd Ed.). Englewood Cliffs: Prentice-Hall.

Montet, Pierre
1981   *Everyday Life in Egypt in the Days of Ramesses the Great.* Philadelphia: University of Pennsylvania Press.

Moore, Andrew M. T.
1985   "The Development of Neolithic Societies in the Near East." *Advances in World Archaeology,* 4:1–69.

Moore, Andrew M. T., G. C. Hillman, and A. J. Legge
2000   *Village on the Euphrates: From Foraging to Farming at Abu Hureyra.* New York: Oxford University Press.

Moore, Lorna G., et al.
1994   "Genetic Adaptation to High Altitude." *In:* Stephen C. Wood and Robert C. Roach (eds.), *Sports and Exercise Medicine.* New York: Marcel Dekker, Inc., pp. 225–262.

Moore, L. G., S. Niermeyer, and S. Zamudio
1998   "Human Adaptation to High Altitude: Regional and Life-Cycle Perspectives." *American Journal of Physical Anthropology,* Suppl. 27:25–64.

Moratto, Michael J.
1984   *California Archaeology.* New York: Academic Press.

Morris, Craig
1988   "A City Fit for an Inka." *Archaeology,* 41(5):43–49.

Morwood, M. J., P. Brown, T. Jatmiko, et al.
2005   "Further Evidence for Small-Bodied Hominins from the Late Pleistocene of Flores, Indonesia." *Nature,* 437:1012–1017.

Morwood, M. J., R. P. Suejono, R. G. Roberts, et al.
2004   "Archaeology and Age of a New Hominin from Flores in Eastern Indonesia." *Nature,* 431:1087–1091.

Moseley, Michael E.
1975   *The Maritime Foundations of Andean Civilization.* Menlo Park: Cummings Publishing Company.

———
1992   *The Incas and Their Ancestors.* New York: Thames & Hudson.

Moseley, Michael E. and Kent Day (eds.)
1982   *Chan Chan: Andean Desert City.* Albuquerque: University of New Mexico Press.

Moura, A. C. de A., and P. C. Lee
2004   "Capuchin Stone Tool Use in Caatinga Dry Forest." *Science,* 306:1909.

Munro, Natalie D.
2004   "Zooarchaeological Measures of Hunting Pressure and Occupation Intensity in the Natufian: Implications for Agricultural Origins." *Current Anthropology,* 45(supplement):S5–S33.

Murdock, George Peter
1959   *Africa: Its Peoples and Their Culture History.* New York: McGraw-Hill.

Napier, John
1967   "The Antiquity of Human Walking." *Scientific American,* 216:56–66.

Neese, R. M. and G. C. Williams
1994   *Why We Get Sick.* New York: Times Books.

Neves, Walter A., Rolando González-José, Mark Hubbe, et al.
2004   "Early Holocene Human Skeletal Remains from Cerca Grande, Lagoa Santa, Central Brazil, and the Origins of the First Americans." *World Archaeology,* 36(4):479–501.

Ni, Xijun, Yuanqing Wang, Yaoming Hu, and Chuankui Li
2004   "A Euprimate Skull from the Early Eocene of China." *Nature,* 427:65–68.

Nishida, T.
1991   Comments. *In:* J. H. Manson and R. Wrangham, q.v., pp. 381–382.

Nishida, T., M. Hiraiwa-Hasegawa, T. Hasegawa, and Y. Takahata
1985   "Group Extinction and Female Transfer in Wild Chimpanzees in the Mahale National Park, Tanzania." *Zeitschrift Tierpsychologie,* 67:284–301.

Nishida, T., H. Takasaki, and Y. Takahata
1990 "Demography and Reproductive Profiles." *In: The Chimpanzees of the Mahale Mountains*, T. Nishida (ed.), Tokyo: University of Tokyo Press, pp. 63–97.

Nishida, T., R. W. Wrangham, J. Goodall, and S. Uehara
1983 "Local Differences in Plant-feeding Habits of Chimpanzees between the Mahale Mountains and Gombe National Park, Tanzania." *Journal of Human Evolution*, 12:467–480.

Nissen, Hans J.
1988 *The Early History of the Ancient Near East, 9000–2000 B.C.* Chicago: University of Chicago Press.

———
2001 "Cultural and Political Networks in the Ancient Near East during the Fourth and Third Millennia B.C." *In: Uruk Mesopotamia and Its Neighbors*. Mitchell S. Rothman (ed.). Santa Fe: School of American Research Press, pp. 149–179.

Nitecki, M. H. and D. V. Nitecki (eds.)
1994 *Origins of Anatomically Modern Humans*. New York: Plenum Press

Normille, D.
1997 "Yangtze Seen As Earliest Rice Site." *Science*, 275:309.

Nowak, Ronald M.
1999 *Walker's Primates of the World*. Baltimore: Johns Hopkins University Press.

Oakley, Kenneth
1963 "Analytical Methods of Dating Bones." *In: Science in Archaeology*, D. Brothwell and E. Higgs (eds.). New York: Basic Books, Inc.

Oates, John F., Michael Abedi-Lartey, W. Scott McGraw, et al.
2000 "Extinction of a West African Red Colobus Monkey." *Conservation Biology*, 14(5):1526–1532.

O'Connell, J. F., K. Hawkes, K. D. Lupo, N. G. Burton-Jones
2002 "Male Strategies and Plio-Pleistocene Archaeology." *Journal of Human Evolution*, 43:831–872.

Odell, George H.
1998 "Investigating Correlates of Sedentism and Domestication in Prehistoric North America." *American Antiquity*, 63(4):553–571.

Olsen, Stanley J.
1985 *Origins of the Domestic Dog: The Fossil Record*. Tucson: University of Arizona Press.

Ovchinnikov, Igor V., Anders Gotherstrom, Galina P. Romanova, et al.
2000 "Molecular Analysis of Neanderthal DNA from the Northern Caucasus." *Nature*, 404:490–493.

Owsley, Douglas W. and Richard L. Jantz
2000 "Biography in the Bones." *Discovering Archaeology*, 2(1):56–58.

Pagel, Mark and Ruth Mace
2004 "The Cultural Wealth of Nations." *Nature*, 428:275–278.

Parés, Josef M. and Alfredo Pérez-González
1995 "Paleomagnetic Age for Hominid Fossils at Atapuerca Archaeological Site, Spain." *Science*, 269:830–832.

Parfit, Michael
2000 "Hunt for the First Americans." *National Geographic*, 198(6):40–67.

Parfitt, Simon A., René W. Barendregt, Marzia Breda, et al.
2005 "The Earliest Record of Human Activity in Europe." *Nature*, 433:1003–1012.

Parpola, Asko
1994 *Deciphering the Indus Script*. Cambridge: Cambridge University Press.

Pauketat, Timothy R. and Rita P. Wright
2004 *Ancient Cahokia and the Mississippians*. Cambridge: Cambridge University Press.

Pearsall, Deborah M.
2000 *Paleoethnobotany: A Handbook of Procedures*. (2nd Ed.). San Diego, CA: Academic Press.

Peres, C. A.
1990 "Effects of Hunting on Western Amazonian Primate Communities." *Biological Conservation* 54:47–59.

Perlès, C.
2001 *The Early Neolithic in Greece*. Cambridge: Cambridge University Press.

Phillips, K. A.
1998 "Tool Use in Wild Capuchin Monkeys." *American Journal of Primatology*, 46(3):259–261.

Phillipson, David W.
1984 "Early Food Production in Central and Southern Africa." *In*: J. D. Clark and S. A. Brandt (eds.), q.v., pp. 272–280.

Pickford, Martin and Brigitte Senut
2001 "The Geological and Faunal Context of Late Miocene Hominid Remains from Lukeino, Kenya." *C. R. Acad. Sci. Paris, Sciences de la Terre et des Planètes*, 332:145–152.

Pinner, Robert W., Steven M. Teutsch, Lone Simonson, et al.
1996 "Trends in Infectious Diseases Mortality in the United States." *Journal of the American Medical Association*, 275(3):189–193.

Piperno, Dolores R.
1988 *Phytolith Analysis: An Archaeological and Geological Perspective*. New York: Academic Press.

Piperno. Dolores and Deborah M. Pearsall
1998 *The Origins of Agriculture in the Lowland Neotropics*. San Diego: Academic Press.

Piperno, Dolores, and Karen E. Stothert
2003 "Phytolith Evidence for Early Holocene Cucurbita Domestication in Southwest Ecuador." *Science*, 299:1054–1057.

Piperno, Dolores R., Ehud Weiss, Irene Holst, and Dani Nadel
2004 "Processing of Wild Cereal Grains in the Upper Paleolithic Revealed by Starch Grain Analysis." *Nature*, 430:670–673.

Pitulko, V. V., P. A. Nikolsky, E. Yu. Girya, et al.
2004 "The Yana RHS Site: Humans in the Arctic Before the Last Glacial Maximum." *Science*, 303:52–56.

Plog, Stephen
1997 *Ancient People of the American Southwest*. New York: Thames & Hudson.

Pohl, Mary, E. E., Kevin O. Pope, and Christopher von Nagy
2002 "Olmec Origins of Mesoamerican Writing." *Science*, 298:1984–1987.

Pope, Kevin O., Mary E. D. Pohl, John G. Jones, et al.
2001 "Origin and Environmental Setting of Ancient Agriculture in the Lowlands of Mesoamerica." *Science*, 292:1370–1373.

Possehl, Gregory L.
1990 "Revolution in the Urban Revolution: The Emergence of Indus Urbanization." *Annual Review of Anthropology*, 19:261–282.

———
1996 *Indus Age: The Writing System*. Philadelphia: University of Pennsylvania Press.

1999 *Indus Age: The Beginnings*. Philadelphia: University of Pennsylvania Press.

2002 *The Indus Civilization: A Contemporary Perspective.* Walnut Creek, CA: Altamira Press.

Potts, Richard
1988 *Early Hominid Activities at Olduvai.* New York: Aldine.

1991 "Why the Oldowan? Plio-Pleistocene Toolmaking and the Transport of Resources." *Journal of Anthropological Research*, 47:153–176.

1993 "Archeological Interpretations of Early Hominid Behavior and Ecology." *In: The Origin and Evolution of Humans and Humanness*, D. T. Rasmussen (ed.), q.v., pp. 49–74.

Powell, K. B.
2003 "The Evolution or Lactase Persistence in African Populations." *American Journal of Physical Anthropology*, Supplement 36:170 (Abstract).

Powell, Marvin
1985 "Salt Seed and Yields in Sumerian Agriculture." *Zeitschift für Assyriologie*, 75:7–38.

Pozorski, Shelia and Thomas Pozorski
1988 *Early Settlement and Subsistence in the Casma Valley, Peru.* Iowa City, IA: University of Iowa Press.

Pozorski, Thomas and Shelia Pozorski
1987 "Chavín, the Early Horizon, and the Initial Period." *In:* J. Haas et al. (eds.), q.v., pp. 36–46.

Prescott, William H.
1906 *History of the Conquest of Peru.* New York: Everyman's Library.

Price, T. Douglas
1995 "Social Inequality at the Origins of Agriculture." *In: Foundations of Social Inequality*, T. Douglas Price and Gary M. Feinman (eds.), New York: Plenum, pp. 129–151.

1987 "A Mesolithic Camp in Denmark." *Scientific American*, 265(3):113–121.

Proctor, Robert
1988 "From Anthropologie to Rassenkunde." *In: Bones, Bodies, Behavior. History of Anthropology* (Vol. 5), W. Stocking, Jr. (ed.), Madison: University of Wisconsin Press, pp. 138–179.

Protzen, Jean-Pierre
1986 "Inca Stonemasonry." *Scientific American*, 254(2):94–105.

Pusey, A., J. Williams, and J. Goodall
1997 "The Influence of Dominance Rank on the Reproductive Success of Female Chimpanzees." *Science*, 277:828–831.

Rak, Y.
1983 *The Australopithecine Face.* New York: Academic Press.

Rasmussen, D. T. (ed.)
1993 *The Origin and Evolution of Humans and Humanness.* Boston: Jones and Bartlett.

Redman, Charles L.
1978 *The Rise of Civilization.* San Francisco: W. H. Freeman.

Reinhard, K. I. and Vaughan M. Bryant
1992 "Coprolite Analysis." *Archaeological Method and Theory*, 14:245–288.

Relethford, John H.
2001 *Genetics and the Search for Modern Human Origins."* New York: Wiley-Liss.

Renne, P. R., W. D. Sharp, A. L. Deino, et al.
1997 "^{40}Ar/^{39}Ar Dating into the Historic Realm: Calibration Against Pliny the Younger." *Science*, 277:1279–1280.

Reno, Phillip L., Richard S Meindl, Melanie A. McCollum, and C. Owen Lovejoy
2003 "Sexual Dimorphism in *Australopithecus afarensis* Was Similar to that of Modern Humans." *Proceeding of the National Academy of Sciences*, 100:9404–9409.

Rice, Don S. and T. Patrick Culbert
1990 "Historical Contexts for Population Reconstruction in the Maya Lowlands." *In: Precolumbian Population History in the Maya Lowlands*, T. P. Culbert and D. S. Rice (eds.), Albuquerque: University of New Mexico Press, pp. 1–36.

Rice, Don, Arthur A. Demarest, and Prudence M. Rice
2001 *The Terminal Classic in the Maya Lowlands: Collapse, Transition, and Transformation.* Boulder, CO: Westview Press.

Riddle, Robert D. and Clifford J. Tabin
1999 "How Limbs Develop." *Scientific American*, 280(2):74–79.

Ridley, Mark
1993 *Evolution.* Boston: Blackwell Scientific Publications.

Rightmire, G. P.
1981 "Patterns in the Evolution of *Homo erectus.*" *Paleobiology*, 7:241–246.

1998 "Human Evolution in the Middle Pleistocene: The Role of *Homo heidelbergensis.*" *Evolutionary Anthropology*, 6:218–227.

2004 "Affinities of the Middle Pleistocene Crania from Dali and Jinniushan, China. *American Journal of Physical Anthropology*, Supplement 38:167 (Abstract).

Rindos, David
1984 *The Origins of Agriculture: An Evolutionary Perspective.* Orlando: Academic Press.

Roaf, Michael
1996 *Cultural Atlas of Mesopotamia and the Ancient Near East.* New York: Facts on File.

Roberts, Charlotte A. and Jane E. Buikstra
2003 *The Bioarchaeology of Tuberculosis: A Global Perspective on a Re-emerging Disease.* Gainsville: University Press of Florida.

Roberts, D. F.
1973 *Climate and Human Variability.* An Addison-Wesley Module in Anthropology, No. 34. Reading, MA: Addison-Wesley.

Robinson, J. T.
1972 *Early Hominid Posture and Locomotion.* Chicago: University of Chicago Press.

Robinson, William J.
1990 "Tree-Ring Studies of the Pueblo de Acoma." *Historical Archaeology*, 24(3):99–106).

Rollefson, Gary O.
2001 "2001: An Archaeological Odyssey." *Cambridge Archaeological Journal*, 11(1):112–114.

Roosevelt, Anna C. et al.
1996 "Paleoindian Cave Dwellers in the Amazon: The Peopling of the Americas." *Science*, 272 (19 April): 373–384.

Rose, M. D.
1991   "Species Recognition in Eocene Primates." *American Journal of Physical Anthropology*, Supplement 12, p. 153.

Rothschild, Nan A.
1979   "Mortuary Behavior and Social Organization at Indian Knoll and Dickson Mounds," *American Antiquity*, 44:658–675.

Rowe, Marvin W. and Karen L. Steelman
2003   "Comment on 'Some Evidence of a Date of First Humans to Arrive in Brazil.'" *Journal of Archaeological Science*, 30(10):1349–1351.

Rowley-Conwy, Peter
2004   "How the West Was Lost: A Reconsideration of Agricultural Origins in Britain, Ireland, and Southern Scandinavia." *Current Anthropology*, 45(supplement):S83–S113.

Rudran, R.
1973   "Adult Male Replacement in One-Male Troops of Purple-Faced Langurs (*Presbytis senex senex*) and its Effect on Population Structure." *Folia Primatologica*, 19:166–192.

Ruff, C. B. and H. M. McHenry
2004   "Can Sexual Dimorphism in Skeletal Size Be Used to Assess Sexual Dimorphism in Body Size?" *American Journal of Physical Anthropology*, Supplement 38:171 (Abstract).

Ruff, C. B. and Alan Walker
1993   "The Body Size and Shape of KNM-WT 15000." *In*: A. Walker and R. Leakey (eds.), q.v., pp. 234–265.

Ruhlen, M.
1994   "Linguistic Evidence for the Peopling of the Americas." *In*: *Method and Theory for Investigating the Peopling of the Americas*, Robson Bonnichsen and D. Gentry Steele (eds.), Corvallis, OR: Oregon State University, pp. 177–188.

Sabloff, Jeremy A. and William L. Rathje
1975   "The Rise of a Maya Merchant Class." *Scientific American*, 233(4):72–82.

Sadr, Karim
2003   "The Neolithic of Southern Africa." *The Journal of African History*, 44(2):195-209.

Samson, M., F. Libert, B. J. Doranz, et al.
1996   "Resistance to HIV-1 Infection in Caucasian Individuals Bearing Mutant Alleles of the CCR-5 Chemokine Receptor Gene." *Nature* 382(22):722–725.

Samuels, Stephen R. (ed.)
1991   *Ozette Archaeological Project Research Reports*. Pullman, WA: Washington State University.

Sanders, William T. and Joseph Michels (eds.)
1977   *Teotihuacan and Kaminaljuyu: A Study in Prehistoric Culture Contact*. College Park: Pennsylvania State University Press.

Sanders, William T., Jeffrey R. Parsons, and Robert S. Santley
1979   *The Basin of Mexico: Ecological Processes in the Evolution of a Civilization*. New York: Academic Press.

Sandweiss, D. H., et al.
1996   "Geoarchaeological Evidence from Peru for a 5000 Years B.P. Onset of El Niño." *Science*, 273:1531–1533.

Santos, G. M., M. I. Bird, F. Parenti, et al.
2003   "A Revised Chronology of the Lowest Occupation Layer of Pedra Furada Rock Shelter, Piauí, Brazil: The Pleistocene Peopling of the Americas." *Quaternary Science Reviews*, 22(21–22):2303–2310.

Sauer, Jonathan D.
1994   *Historical Geography of Crop Plants: A Select Roster*. Boca Raton: CRC Press.

Saunders, Joe W. et al.
1997   "A Mound Complex in Louisiana at 5400-5000 Years Before Present." *Science*, 277:1796–1799.

Savage-Rumbaugh, S.
1986   *Ape Language: From Conditioned Responses to Symbols*. New York: Columbia University Press.

Savolainen, P.
2002   "Genetic Evidence for an East Asian Origin of Domestic Dogs." *Science*, 298:1610–1613.

Schele, Linda and David Freidel
1990   *A Forest of Kings*. New York: William R. Morrow.

Schele, Linda and Mary Ellen Miller
1986   *The Blood of Kings: Dynasty and Ritual in Maya Art*. Fort Worth: Kimbell Art Museum.

Schmitz, Ralf W., David Serre, Georges Bonani, et al.
2002   "The Neandertal Type Site Revisited: Interdisciplinary Investigations of Skeletal Remains from the Neander Valley, Germany. *Proceedings of the National Academy of Sciences*, 99:13342–13347.

Schoeninger, Margaret J.
1981   "The Agricultural 'Revolution': Its Effect on Human Diet in Prehistoric Iran and Israel." *Paléorient*, 7:73–92.

Schoeninger, M. J., M. J. Deniro, and H. Tauber
1983   "Stable Nitrogen Isotope Ratios of Bone Collagen Reflect Marine and Terrestrial Components of Prehistoric Human Diet." *Science*, 220:1381–1383.

Schurr, Theodore G.
2000   "The Story in the Genes." *Discovering Archaeology*, 2(1):59–60.

––––––
2004   "The Peopling of the New World: Perspectives from Molecular Anthropology." *Annual Review of Anthropology*, 33:551–583.

Schurr, Theodore G. and Stephen T. Sherry
2004   "Mitochondrial DNA and Y Chromosome Diversity and the Peopling of the Americas: Evolutionary and Demographic Evidence." *American Journal of Human Biology*, 16:420–439.

Schurr, T. G. et al.
1990   "Amerindian Mitochondrial DNAs Have Rare Asian Mutations at High Frequencies Suggesting a Limited Number of Founders." *American Journal of Human Genetics*, 46:613–623.

Scriver, Charles R.
2001   "Human Genetics: Lessons from Quebec Populations." *Annual Review of Genomics and Human Genetics*, 2:69–101.

Sebastian, Lynne
1992   *The Chaco Anasazi: Sociopolitical Evolution in the Prehistoric Southwest*. Cambridge: Cambridge University Press.

Seiffert, Erik, Elwyn Simons, William C. Clyde, et al.
2005   "Basal Anthropoids from Egypt and the Antiquity of Africa's Higher Primate Radiation." *Science*, 310:300–304.

Semaw, S., P. Renne, W. K. Harris, et al.
1997   "2.5-million-year-old Stone Tools from Gona, Ethiopia." *Nature*, 385:333–336.

Senut, Brigitte, Martin Pickford, Dominique Grommercy, et al.
2001   "First Hominid from the Miocene (Lukeino Formation, Kenya)." *C. R. Acad. Sci. Paris, Sciences de la Terre et des Planètes*, 332:137–144.

469

Serre, David, André Langaney, Marie Chech, et al.
2004   "No Evidence of Neandertal mtDNA Contribution to Early Modern Humans." *PloS Biology*, 2:313–317.

Seyfarth, Robert M.
1987   "Vocal Communication and Its Relation to Language." *In:* Smuts, et al. (eds.), q.v., pp. 440–451.

Seyfarth, Robert M., Dorothy L. Cheney, and Peter Marler
1980a   "Monkey Responses to Three Different Alarm Calls." *Science,* 210:801–803.

_____ 1980b   "Vervet Monkey Alarm Calls." *Animal Behavior,* 28:1070–1094.

Shaffer, Brian S. and Barry W. Baker
1997   "How Many Epidermal Ridges Per Linear Centimeter: Comments on Possible Pre-Clovis Human Friction Skin Prints from Pendejo Cave." *American Antiquity,* 62(3):559–560.

Sharer, Robert J.
1996   *Daily Life in Maya Civilization.* Westport, CT: Greenwood Press.

Sharer, Robert J. and David C. Grove (eds.)
1989   *Regional Perspectives on the Olmec.* Cambridge: Cambridge University Press.

Shea, John J.
1998   "Neandertal and Early Modern Human Behavioral Variability." *Current Anthropology,* 39 (Supplement):45–78.

Sheets, Payson D.
2006   *The Ceren Site: An Ancient Village Buried by Volcanic Ash in Central America.* Second Edition. Belmont, CA: Thomson Wadsworth.

_____ (ed.)
2002   *Before the Volcano Erupted: The Ancient Cerén Village in Central America.* Austin: University of Texas Press.

Sherratt, A.
1981   "Plough and Pastoralism: Aspects of the Secondary Products Revolution." *In:* Ian Hodder, Glynn L. Isaac, and Norman Hammond (eds.), *Patterns of the Past: Studies in Honour of David Clarke.* Cambridge: Cambridge University Press, pp. 261–305.

Shublin, Nell, Cliff Tabin, and Sean Carroll
1997   "Fossil Genes, and the Evolution of Animal Limbs." *Nature,* 388:639–648.

Silverman, Helaine
1993   *Cahuachi in the Ancient Nasca World.* Iowa City: University of Iowa Press.

_____ (ed.)
2004   *Andean Archaeology.* Malden, MA: Blackwell Publishing.

Simmons, Alan H.
1986   "New Evidence for the Use of Cultigens in the American Southwest." *American Antiquity,* 51:73–89.

Simons, E. L.
1972   *Primate Evolution.* New York: Macmillan.

Smith, Andrew
1992   "Pastoralism in Africa." *Annual Review of Anthropology,* 21:125–141.

Smith, Andrew, Penny Berens, Candy Malherbe, and Matt Guenther
2000   *The Bushmen of Southern Africa: A Foraging Society in Transition.* Athens, OH: Ohio University Press.

Smith, Bruce D.
1985   "The Role of *Chenopodium* As a Domesticate in Pre-Maize Garden Systems of the Eastern United States." *Southwestern Archaeology,* 4:51–72.

_____ 1989   "Origins of Agriculture in Eastern North America." *Science,* 246:1566–1571.

_____ 1992   *Rivers of Change: Essays on Early Agriculture in Eastern North America.* Washington, DC: Smithsonian Institution.

_____ 1995   *Emergence of Agriculture.* New York: Scientific American Library.

_____ 1997   "Reconsidering the Ocampo Caves and the Era of Incipient Cultivation in Mesoamerica." *Latin American Antiquity,* 8: 342–383.

Smith, Christopher
1998   *Late Stone Age Hunters of the British Isles.* London: Routledge.

Smith, Fred H.
1984   "Fossil Hominids from the Upper Pleistocene of Central Europe and the Origin of Modern Europeans." *In:* F. H. Smith and F. Spencer (eds.), *The Origins of Modern Humans.* New York: Alan R. Liss, pp. 187–209.

_____ 2002   "Migrations, Radiations and Continuity: Patterns in the Evolution of Late Pleistocene Humans. *In* W. Hartwig (ed.), *The Primate Fossil Record.* Cambridge: Cambridge University Press, pp.437–456.

Smith, Fred H., A. B. Falsetti, and S. M. Donnelly
1989   "Modern Human Origins." *Yearbook of Physical Anthropology,* 32:35–68.

Smith, Fred H., Ivor Jankovic, and Ivor Karavanic
2005   "The Assimilation Model, Modern Human Origins in Europe, and the Extinction of Neandertals." *Quaternary International,* 137:7–19.

Smith, Fred H., Erik Trinkaus, Paul B. Pettitt, et al.
1999   "Direct Radiocarbon Dates for Vindija G1 and Velika Pécina Late Pleistocene Hominid Remains." *Proceedings of the National Academy of Sciences,* 96:12281–12286.

Smith, Michael E.
2003   *The Aztecs.* (2nd Ed.). Malden, MA: Blackwell Publishing.

Smith, Patricia, Ofer Bar-Yosef, and Andrew Sillen
1984   "Archaeological and Skeletal Evidence for Dietary Change During the Late Pleistocene/Early Holocene in the Levant." *In:* Cohen and Armelagos (eds.), q.v., pp. 101–136.

Smuts, B. et al. (eds.)
1987   *Primate Societies.* Chicago: University of Chicago Press.

Snow, C. P.
1965   *Two Cultures and the Scientific Revolution,* (2nd Ed.). Cambridge: Cambridge University Press.

Snow, Dean R.
1980   *The Archaeology of New England.* New York: Academic Press.

Soffer, Olga, and N. D. Praslov (eds.)
1993   *From Kostenki to Clovis: Upper Paleolithic—Paleo-Indian Adaptations.* New York: Plenum Press.

Spencer, Charles S. and Elsa M. Redmond
2004   "Primary State Formation in Mesoamerica." *Annual Review of Anthropology,* 33:173–199.

Stanish, Charles
2001   "The Origin of State Societies in South America." *Annual Review of Anthropology,* 30:41–64.

Steckel, Richard H. and Jerome C. Rose
2002   *The Backbone of History: Health and Nutrition in the Western Hemisphere*. New York: Cambridge University Press.

Steele, D. Gentry
2000   "The Skeleton's Tale." *Discovering Archaeology*, 2(1): 61–62.

Steele, D. Gentry and J. F. Powell
1999   "Peopling of the Americas: A Historical and Comparative Perspective." *In:* Bonnichsen R, (ed.). *Who Were the First Americans?* Corvallis, OR: Center for the Study of the First Americans, Oregon State University, pp. 97–126.

Stein, Burton
1994   *Vijayanagara.* Cambridge, UK: Cambridge University Press.

Steklis, Horst D.
1985   "Primate Communication, Comparative Neurology, and the Origin of Language Reexamined." *Journal of Human Evolution,* 14:157–173.

Stelzner, J. and K. Strier
1981   "Hyena Predation on an Adult Male Baboon." *Mammalia,* 45:106–107.

Stokstad, Erik
2002   "Oldest New World Writing Suggests Olmec Innovation." *Science,* 298:1872–1874.

Straughan, Baird
1991   "The Secrets of Ancient Tiwanaku Are Benefiting Today's Bolivia." *Smithsonian,* 21(11):38–49.

Strier, Karen B.
2003   *Primate Behavioral Ecology.* (2nd Ed.). Boston: Allyn and Bacon.

Struhsaker, T. T.
1967   "Auditory Communication among Vervet Monkeys (*Cercopithecus aethiops*)." *In: Social Communication Among Primates*, S. A. Altmann (ed.), Chicago: University of Chicago Press.

_____
1975   *The Red Colobus Monkey.* Chicago: University of Chicago Press.

Struhsaker, Thomas T. and Lysa Leland
1987   "Colobines: Infanticide by Adult Males." *In:* Smuts, et al. (eds.), q.v., pp. 83–97.

Surovell, Todd A.
2003   "Simulating Coastal Migration in New World Colonization." *Current Anthropology*, 44(4):580–591.

Surovell, Todd A., Nicole Waguespack, and P. Jeffrey Brantingham
2005   "Global Archaeological Evidence for Proboscidean Overkill." *Proceedings of the National Academy of Sciences,* 102(17):6231–6236.

Susman, Randall L. (ed.)
1984   *The Pygmy Chimpanzee. Evolutionary Biology and Behavior.* New York: Plenum.

Susman, Randall L., Jack T. Stern, and William L. Jungers
1985   "Locomotor Adaptations in the Hadar Hominids." *In: Ancestors: The Hard Evidence*, E. Delson (ed.), New York: Alan R. Liss, pp.184–192.

Sussman, Robert W.
1991   "Primate Origins and the Evolution of Angiosperms." *American Journal of Primatology*, 23:209–223.

Sussman, Robert W., James M. Cheverud, and Thad Q. Bartlett
1995   Infant Killing as an Evolutionary Strategy: Reality or Myth?" *Evolutionary Anthropology*, 3(5):149–151.

Swisher, C. C., W. J. Rink, S. C. Anton, et al.
1996   "Latest *Homo erectus* of Java: Potential Contemporaneity with *Homo sapiens* in Southwest Java." *Science,* 274:1870–1874.

Szalay, Frederick S. and Eric Delson
1979   *Evolutionary History of the Primates.* New York: Academic Press.

Tagg, Martyn D.
1996   "Early Cultigens from Fresnal Shelter, Southeastern New Mexico." *American Antiquity,* 61(2): 311–24.

Tattersall, Ian, Eric Delson, and John Van Couvering
1988   *Encyclopedia of Human Evolution and Prehistory.* New York: Garland Publishing.

Taylor, R. E. and M. J. Aitken
1997   *Chronometric Dating in Archaeology.* New York: Plenum.

Tenaza, R. and R. Tilson
1977   "Evolution of Long-Distance Alarm Calls in Kloss' Gibbon." *Nature,* 268:233–235.

Teresi, Dick
2002   *Lost Discoveries. The Ancient Roots of Modern Science – from the Babylonians to the Maya.* New York: Simon and Schuster.

Thieme, Hartmut
1997   "Lower Palaeolithic Hunting Spears from Germany." *Nature,* 385:807–810.

Thomas, Julian
1988   "Neolithic Explanations Revisited: The Mesolithic-Neolithic Transition in Britain and South Scandinavia." *Proceedings of the Prehistoric Society* 54:59–66.

Thorne, A., R. Grün, G. Mortimer, et al.
1999   "Australia's Oldest Human Remains: Age of the Lake Mungo 3 Skeleton." *Journal of Human Evolution,* 36:591–612.

Tiemel, Chen, Yang Quan, and Wu En
1994   "Antiquity of *Homo sapiens* in China." *Nature,* 368:55–56.

Tobias, Phillip
1971   *The Brain in Hominid Evolution.* New York: Columbia University Press.

_____
1983   "Recent Advances in the Evolution of the Hominids with Especial Reference to Brain and Speech." Pontifical Academy of Sciences, *Scrita Varia,* 50:85–140.

Townsend, Richard F.
1992   *The Aztecs.* New York: Thames & Hudson.

Trigger, Bruce G.
2003   *Understanding Early Civilizations.* Cambridge, UK: Cambridge University Press.

Trigger, Bruce G., Barry J. Kemp, David O'Connor, and Alan B. Lloyd
1983   *Ancient Egypt: A Social History.* Cambridge: Cambridge University Press.

Tringham, Ruth
1971   *Hunters, Fishers, and Farmers of Eastern Europe, 6000–3000 B.C.* London: Hutchinson University Library.

Trinkaus, Erik and Pat Shipman
1992   *The Neandertals.* New York: Alfred A. Knopf.

Turner, Christy G.
1987   "Telltale Teeth." *Natural History,* 96(1):6–10.

Turner, Christy G. and Jacqueline A. Turner
1999   *Man Corn: Cannibalism and Violence in the American Southwest and Mexico.* Salt Lake City: University of Utah Press.

Van der Merwe, Nikolaas J.
1969   *The Carbon-14 Dating of Iron*, Chicago and London: University of Chicago Press.

Van Noten, Francis and Jan Raymaekers
1987   "Early Iron Smelting in Central Africa." *Scientific American*, 258(6):104–111.

van Schaik, C. P., M. Ancrenaz, G. Bogen, et al.
2003   "Orangutan Cultures and the Evolution of Material Culture." *Science*, 299:102–105.

Vavilov, N. I.
1992   *The Origin and Geography of Cultivated Plants*. Cambridge: Cambridge University Press.

Vekua, Abesalom, David Lorkipanidze, G. Phillip Rightmire et al.
2002   "A New Early *Homo* from Dmanisi, Georgia." *Science*, 297:85–89.

Verhoeven, Marc
2004   "Beyond Boundaries: Nature, Culture and a Holistic Approach to Domestication in the Levant." *Journal of World History*, 18(3):179–281.

Vignaud, P., P. Duringer, H. MacKaye, et al.
2002   "Geology and Palaeontology of the Upper Miocene Toros-Menalla Hominid Locality, Chad." *Nature*, 418:152–155.

Villa, Paola
1983   *Terra Amata and the Middle Pleistocene Archaeological Record of Southern France*. University of California Publications in Anthropology, Vol. 13. Berkeley: University of California Press.

Visalberghi, E.
1990   "Tool Use in Cebus." *Folia Primatologica*, 54:146–154.

Wagner, Daniel P. and Joseph M. McAvoy
2004   "Pedoarchaeology of Cactus Hill, a Sandy Paleoindian Site in Southeastern Virginia, U.S.A." *Geoarchaeology: An International Journal*, 19(4):297–322.

Walker, A.
1976   "Remains Attributable to *Australopithecus* from East Rudolf." *In: Earliest Man and Environments in the Lake Rudolf Basin*, Y. Coppens, et al. (eds.), Chicago: University of Chicago Press, pp. 484–489.

———
1991   "The Origin of the Genus *Homo*." *In:* S. Osawa and T. Honjo (eds.), *Evolution of Life*. Tokyo: Springer-Verlag, pp. 379–389.

———
1993   "The Origin of the Genus *Homo*." *In:* D. T. Rasmussen (ed.), q.v., pp. 29–47.

Walker, Alan and R. E. Leakey
1993   *The Nariokotome* Homo erectus *Skeleton*. Cambridge: Harvard University Press.

Walsh, P. D., K. A. Abernathy, M. Bermejo, et al.
2003   "Catastrophic Ape Decline in Western Equatorial Africa." *Nature*, 422:611–614.

Ward, Peter
1994   *The End of Evolution*. New York: Bantam.

Washburn, S. L.
1963   "The Study of Race." *American Anthropologist*, 65:521–531.

Weaver, Muriel Porter
1993   *The Aztecs, Maya, and Their Predecessors: Archaeology of Mesoamerica* (3rd Ed.). San Diego: Academic Press.

Webster, David, AnnCorinne Freter, and Nancy Gonlin
2000   *Copán: The Rise and Fall of an Ancient Maya Kingdom*. Belmont, CA: Thomson Wadsworth.

Webb, William S.
1974   *Indian Knoll*. University of Tennessee Press, Knoxville.

Weeks, Kent R.
2001   *KV5: A Preliminary Report on the Excavation of the Tomb of the Sons of Ramesses II in the Valley of the Kings*. Cairo, Egypt: American University in Egypt Press.

Weiner, J. S.
1955   *The Piltdown Forgery*. London: Oxford University Press.

Weiner, Steve, Qinqi Xu, Paul Goldberg, Jinyi Liu, and Ofer Bar-Yosef
1998   "Evidence for the Use of Fire at Zhoukoudian, China." *Science*, 281:251–253.

Weiss, Ehud, Wilma Wetterstrom, Dani Nadel, and Ofer Bar-Yosef
2004a   "The Broad Spectrum Revisited: Evidence from Plant Remains." *Proceedings of the National Academy of Science*, 101(26):9551–9555.

Weiss, Ehud, Mordechai E. Kislev, Orit Simchoni and Dani Nadel.
2004b   "Small-Grained Wild Grasses as Staple Food at the 23,000-Year-Old Site of Ohalo II, Israel." *Economic Botany*, 58(supplement): S125–S134.

Weiss, Robin A. and Richard W. Wrangham
1999   "From *Pan* to Pandemic." *Nature*, 397:385–386.

Weiss, U.
2002   "Nature Insight: Malaria." *Nature*, 415:669.

Wendorf, Fred and Romuald Schild
1989   *The Prehistory of Wadi Kubbaniya*. Dallas, TX: Southern Methodist University.

———
1994   "Are the Early Holocene Cattle in the Eastern Sahara Domestic or Wild?" *Evolutionary Anthropology*, 3:118–128.

Wenke, Robert J.
1990   *Patterns in Prehistory : Humankind's First Three Million Years*. (3rd Ed.). New York: Oxford University Press.

West, Frederick Hadleigh and Constance West (eds.)
1996   *American Beginnings: The Prehistory and Palaeoecology of Beringia*. Chicago: University of Chicago Press.

Wheat, Joe Ben
1972   "The Olsen-Chubbuck Site: A Paleo-Indian Bison Kill." *American Antiquity*, 37:1–180.

White, Tim D.
1992   *Prehistoric Cannibalism at Mancos SMTUMR-2346*. Princeton, NJ: Princeton University Press.

White, T. D., Berhane Asfaw, David DeGusta, et al.
2003   "Pleistocene *Homo sapiens* from Middle Awash Ethiopia." *Nature*, 433:742–747.

White, Tim D., Gen Suwa, and Berhane Asfaw
1994   "*Australopithecus ramidus*, a New Species of Early Hominid from Aramis, Ethiopia." *Nature*, 371:306–312.

———
1995   Corrigendum (White, et al., 1994). *Nature*, 375:88.

Whiten, A., J. Goodall, W. C. McGrew, et al.
1999   "Cultures in Chimpanzees." *Nature*, 399:682–685.

Whittle, Alasdair
1985   *Neolithic Europe: A Survey*. Cambridge: Cambridge University Press.

Wicklein, John
1994   "Spirit Paths of the Anasazi." *Archaeology*, 47(1):36–41.

Wildman, Derek E., Monica Uddin, Guozhen Liu, et al.
2003   "Implications of Natural Selection in Shaping 99.4% Nonsynonymous DNA Identity Between Humans and Chimpanzees: Enlarging Genus *Homo*." *Proceedings of the National Academy of Sciences*, 100:7181–7188.

Williams, M. A. J.
1984   "Late Quaternary Prehistoric Environments of the Sahara." *In:* J. D. Clark and S. A. Brandt (eds.), q.v., pp. 74–83.

Wills, W. H.
1989   *Early Prehistoric Agriculture in the American Southwest*. Santa Fe: School of American Research Press.

Wilmut, I., A. E. Schnieke, et al.
1997   "Viable Offspring Derived from Fetal and Adult Mammalian Cells." *Nature*, 385:810–813.

Wilson, David J.
1981   "Of Maize and Men: A Critique of the Maritime Hypothesis of State Origins on the Coast of Peru." *American Anthropologist*, 83:931–940.

Wilson, Edward O.
1992   *The Diversity of Life*. Cambridge, MA: Harvard University Press.

Winslow, D. L. and J. R. Wedding
1997   "Spirit Cave Man." *American History*, 32 (March/April): 74.

Wolpoff, Milford H.
1983b   "*Ramapithecus* and Human Origins. An Anthropologist's Perspective of Changing Intepretations." *In:* R. L. Ciochon and R. S. Corruccini (eds.), q.v., pp. 651–676.

———
1984   "Evolution in *Homo erectus:* The Question of Stasis." *Paleobiology*, 10:389–406.

———
1989   "Multiregional Evolution: The Fossil Alternative to Eden." *In:* P. Mellars and C. Stringer, (eds.) q.v., pp. 62–108.

———
1999   *Paleoanthropology*. (2nd Ed.). New York: McGraw-Hill.

Wolpoff, M., et al.
1994   "Multiregional Evolutions: A World-Wide Source for Modern Human Populations." *In:* M. H. Nitecki and D. V. Nitecki (eds.), q.v., pp. 175–199.

Wolpoff, M. H., J. Hawks, D. Frayer, and K. Hunley
2001   "Modern Human Ancestry at the Peripheries: A Test of the Replacement Theory." *Science*, 291:293–297.

Wolpoff, Milford H., Brigitte Senut, Martin Pickford, and John Hawks
2002   "Paleoanthropology (Communication Arising): *Sahelanthropus* or '*Sahelpithecus*'?" *Nature*, 419:581–582.

Wood, Bernard
1991   *Koobi Fora Research Project IV: Hominid Cranial Remains from Koobi Fora*. Oxford: Clarendon Press.

———
1992   "Origin and Evolution of the Genus *Homo*." *Nature*, 355:783–790.

———
2002   "Hominid Revelations from Chad." News and Views, *Nature*, 418:133–135.

Wood, Bernard and Mark Collard
1999a   "The Human Genus." *Science*, 284:65–71.

———
1999b   "The Changing Face of Genus *Homo*." *Evolutionary Anthropology*, 8:195–207.

Wood, B. and B. G. Richmond
2000   "Human Evolution: Taxonomy and Paleobiology." *Journal of Anatomy*, 197:19–60.

Woolley, Leonard
1929   *Ur of the Chaldees*. London: Ernest Benn.

Wright, H. E.
1993   "Environmental Determinism in Near Eastern Prehistory." *Current Anthropology*, 34:458–469.

Wu, Rukang and Xingren Dong
1985   "*Homo erectus* in China." *In: Palaeoanthropology and Palaeolithic Archaeology in the People's Republic of China,* R. Wu and J. W. Olsen (eds.), New York: Academic Press, pp. 79–89.

Wuehrich, Bernice
1998   "Geological Analysis Damps Ancient Chinese Fires." *Science*, 28:165–166.

Wurm, Stephen
1994   "Australasia and the Pacific." *In: Atlas of the World's Languages,* Christopher Moseley, R. E. Asher, and Mary Tait (eds.), London: Routledge, pp. 25–46.

Yamei, Hon, Richard Potts, Yaun Baoyin, et al.
2000   "Mid-Pleistocene Acheulean-like Stone Technology of the Bose Basin, South China." *Science*, 287:1622–1626.

Yan, Wenming
1999   "Neolithic Settlements in China: Latest Finds and Research." *Journal of East Asian Archaeology*, 1:131–147.

Yellen, John E.
1980   *Archaeological Approaches to the Present*. New York: Academic Press.

Yellen, John E., et al.
1995   "A Middle Stone Age Worked Bone Industry from Katanda, Upper Semliki Valley, Zaire." *Science*, 268:553–556.

Yoffee, Norman
2005   *Myths of the Archaic State: Evolution of the Earliest Cities, States, and Civilizations*. Cambridge, UK: Cambridge University Press.

Young, Biloine Whiting and Melvin L. Fowler
2000   *Cahokia: The Great Native American Metropolis*. Urbana: University of Illinois Press.

Young, David
1992   *The Discovery of Evolution*. Cambridge: Natural History Museum Publications, Cambridge University Press.

Yudkin, J.
1969   "Archaeology and the Nutritionist." *In: The Domestication and Exploitation of Plants and Animals*, P. J. Ucko and G. W. Dimbleby (eds.), Chicago: Aldine, pp. 547–554.

Zeder, Melinda
1997   "The American Archeologist: Results of the 1994 SAA Census." *SAA Bulletin*, 15:12–17.

PHOTO CREDITS

Digging Deeper, Christopher Messer/iStockphoto; **1**, Chapter opener, Juan Rodriguez/iStockphoto; **3**, Fig. 1–1a–c, Lynn Kilgore; Fig. 1–1d, Robert Jurmain; **6**, Fig. 1–2, © Russell L. Ciochon, University of Iowa; **7**, Fig. 1–3, Lynn Kilgore; Fig. 1–4, Judith Regensteiner; Fig. 1–5, Kathleen Galvin; **8**, Fig. 1–6, Robert Jurmain; Fig. 1–7, Bonnie Pedersen/Arlene Kruse; **9**, Fig. 1–8a and b, Lynn Kilgore; Fig. 1–9, Lorna Pierce/Judy Suchey; **10**, Fig. 1–10, Linda Levitch; **11**, Fig. 1–11, Whitney Powell-Cummer; Fig. 1–12, Gordon P. Watts, Jr.; **12**, Fig. 1–13, Illinois Transportation Archaeological Research Program, University of Illinois; Fig. 1–14, William Turnbaugh; painting by Gilbert Stuart; **13**, Fig. 1–15, Barry Lewis; **14**, Fig. 1–16, Illinois Transportation Archaeological Research Program, University of Illinois; **19**, Chapter opener, Mark Evans/Brian Huffman/iStockphoto; **22**, Fig. 2–1, Dept. of Library Services, American Museum of Natural History; **23**, Fig. 2–2, Dept. of Library Services, American Museum of Natural History; Fig. 2–3, © Michael Nicholson/CORBIS; Fig. 2–4, © Bettmann/CORBIS; **24**, Fig. 2–6, Dept. of Library Services, American Museum of Natural History; **25**, Fig. 2–7, Dept. of Library Services, American Museum of Natural History; Fig. 2–8, Dept. of Library Services, American Museum of Natural History; **26**, Fig. 2–9, © Bettmann/CORBIS; **27**, Fig. 2–12, Wolf: John Giustina/Getty Images; Dogs surrounding wolf: Lynn Kilgore and Lin Marshall; **28**, Fig. 2–13, Down House and The Royal College of Surgeons of England; **29**, Fig. 2–14a, Michael Tweedie/Photo Researchers; Fig. 2-14b, Breck P. Kent/Animals Animals; **35** Chapter opener, Mark Evans/Brian Huffman/iStockphoto; **42**, Fig. 3–5, Biophoto Associates/Science Source/Photo Researchers; **47**, Fig. 3–10, Raychel Ciemma and Precision Graphics; **54**, Fig. 3–16a–f, Lynn Kilgore; Fig. 3–16g, Robert Jurmain; **56**, Fig. 3–17, Cellmark Diagnostics, Abingdon, UK; **61**, Fig. 3–19, Lynn Kilgore; Fig. 3–20a, b, © Dr. Stanley Flegler/Visuals Unlimited; **66**, Fig. 1, Margaret Maples; Fig. 1 inset, © Bettmann/CORBIS; **68**, Fig. 2, Craig King, Armed Forces DNA Identification Laboratory; **69**, Chapter opener, Mark Evans/Brian Huffman/iStockphoto; **75**, Fig. 4–1a, b, Robert Jurmain; **79**, Fig. 4–4, © Michael S. Yamashita/CORBIS; **81**, Fig. 4–5, Norman Lightfoot/Photo Researchers; **82**, Fig. 4–6, © Biophoto Associates/Photo Researchers, Inc.; **84**, Fig. 4–8a, Renee Lynn/Photo Researchers; Fig. 4–8b, George Holton/Photo Researchers; **86**, Fig. 4–9a, William Pratt; Fig. 4–9b, L. G. Moore; **90**, Fig. 4–10, Karl Ammann; **94**, Chapter opener, Mark Evans/Brian Huffman/iStockphoto; **108**, Fig. 5–9, J. C. Stevenson/Animals Animals; **112**, Chapter opener, Daniel Tang/iStockphoto; **114**, Fig. 6–1a–e, Lynn Kilgore; **116**, Fig. 6–3 a, b, Lynn Kilgore; Fig. 6–4, Lynn Kilgore; **118**, Fig. 6–5 (Howler species), Raymond Mendez/Animals Animals; (Spider monkeys and muriquis), Robert L. Lubeck/Animals Animals; (Prince Bernhard's titi), Marc van Roosmalen; (Marmosets and tamarins), © Zoological Society of San Diego, photo by Ron Garrison; (Muriqui), Andrew Young; (White-faced capuchins), © Jay Dickman/CORBIS; (Squirrel monkeys), © Kevin Schafer/CORBIS; (Uakari), R. A. Mittermeier/ Conservation International; **119**, Fig. 6–5 (Baboon species), Bonnie Pedersen/Arlene Kruse; (Macaque species), Jean De Rousseau; (Gibbons and siamangs), Lynn Kilgore; (Tarsier species), David Haring, Duke University Primate Zoo; (Orangutans), © Tom McHugh/Photo Researchers, Inc.; (Colobus species) Robert Jurmain; (Galagos), Bonnie Pedersen/Arlene Kruse; (Chimpanzees and bonobos), Arlene Kruse/Bonnie Pedersen; (Mountain and lowland gorillas), Lynn Kilgore; (*Cercopithecus* species), Robert Jurmain;

(Loris species), San Francisco Zoo; (Langur species), Joe MacDonald/Animals Animals; (Lemurs), Fred Jacobs; **120**, Fig. 6–6, © Russell L. Ciochon, University of Iowa; **121**, Fig. 6–7a–d, Redrawn from original art by Stephen D. Nash in John G. Fleagle, *Primate Adaptation and Evolution*, 2nd ed., 1999. Reprinted by permission of publisher and Stephen Nash; **125**, Fig. 6–12, Fred Jacobs; Fig. 6–13, Fred Jacobs; **126**, Fig. 6–14, San Francisco Zoo; Fig. 6–15, Bonnie Pedersen/Arlene Kruse; Fig. 6–16, David Haring, Duke University Primate Zoo; **127**, Fig. 6–18, (Muriqui), Andrew Young; (Squirrel monkeys), © Kevin Schafer/CORBIS; (Prince Bernhard's titi), Marc van Roosmalen; (Uakari), R. A. Mittermeier/Conservation International; (White-faced capuchins), © Jay Dickman/CORBIS; **128**, Fig. 6–19, © Zoological Society of San Diego, photo by Ron Garrison; Fig. 6–20, Raymond Mendez/Animals Animals; **129**, Fig. 6–22, Robert L. Lubeck/Animals Animals; **129**, Fig. 6–24, Robert Jurmain; **130**, Fig. 6–25a, b, Bonnie Pedersen/Arlene Kruse; Fig. 6–26, Lynn Kilgore; **131**, Fig. 6–28, Lynn Kilgore; **132**, Fig. 6-29a, b, Noel Rowe; Fig. 6–31a, b, Lynn Kilgore; **133**, Fig. 6–32a, b, Lynn Kilgore; **134**, Fig. 6–33a, b, Robert Jurmain, photo by Jill Matsumoto/Jim Anderson; **135**, Fig. 6–34, Ellen Ingmanson; **136**, Fig. 6–35, John Oates; **137**, Fig. 6–36, Karl Ammann; **139**, Fig. 1, Jim Moore/Anthro Photo; **140**, Fig. 2, Robert Jurmain; **142**, Chapter opener, Daniel Tang/iStockphoto; **144**, Fig. 7–1, © Russ Mittermeir; **145**, Fig. 7–2, Lynn Kilgore; **147**, Fig. 7–3, Time Life Pictures/Getty Images; **148**, Fig. 7–4, Lynn Kilgore; Fig. 7–5, Lynn Kilgore; **149**, Fig. 7–6, Lynn Kilgore; **151**, Fig. 7–8a, Robert Jurmain; Fig. 7–8b, Meredith Small; Fig. 7–8c, d, Arlene Kruse/Bonnie Pedersen; **152**, Fig. 7–9, Lynn Kilgore; **153**, Fig. 7–10, Joe MacDonald/Animals Animals; **155**, Fig. 7–11a, David Haring, Duke University Primate Center; Fig. 7–11b, Arlene Kruse/Bonnie Pedersen; Fig. 7–11c, Robert Jurmain; Fig. 7–11d, © Tom McHugh/Photo Researchers, Inc.; Fig. 7–11e, Robert Jurmain; **156**, Fig. 7–12, Lynn Kilgore; **157**, Fig. 7–13a, Lynn Kilgore; Fig. 7–13b, Manoj Shah/The Image Bank; **158**, Fig. 7–14, Tetsuro Matsuzawa; **159**, Fig. 7–15, Lynn Kilgore; **160**, Fig. 7–16, Rose A. Sevcik, Language Research Center, Georgia State University; photo by Elizabeth Pugh; **161**, Fig. 7–17, Lynn Kilgore; **164**, Chapter opener, Lanica Klein/iStockphoto; **171**, Fig. 8–3, Barry Lewis; **172**, Fig. 8–4, Barry Lewis; Fig. 8–5, Michael L. Hargrave; **173**, Fig. 8–6, Barry Lewis; **174**, Fig. 8–7, Barry Lewis; Fig. 8–8, Illinois Transportation Archaeological Research Program, University of Illinois; Fig. 8–9, Barry Lewis; **175**, Fig. 8–10, Barry Lewis; Fig. 8–11, Dr. Colin Betts, Luther College; **176**, Fig. 1, William L. Rathja; Fig. 2, William L. Rathja; **177**, Fig. 8–12, Richard VanderHoek; Fig. 8–13, William Turnbaugh; **180**, Fig. 8–14, William Turnbaugh; **183**, Fig. 8–16, Beta Analytic, Inc., Darden Hood, president; **184**, Fig. 8–17, William Turnbaugh; **186**, Fig. 8–19, L.S.B. Leakey Foundation; Fig. 8–20, Robert Jurmain; **187**, Fig. 8–21, Harry Nelson; **188**, Fig. 8–22, Robert Jurmain; **191**, Fig. 1, Clark Larsen, © Çatalhöyük Archaeological Project; **192**, Fig. 2, From Copley, M. S. et al. 2004. *Antiquity* 79:904; **193**, Chapter opener, Lanica Klein/iStockphoto; **197**, Fig. 9–4, © The Natural History Museum, London; **198**, Fig. 9–5, David Pilbeam; **203**, Fig. 9–9, © Mission Paléoanthropologique Franco-Tchadienne; **205**, Fig. 9–11, Lynn Kilgore; Fig. 9–12, Peter Jones; **206**, Fig. 9–13, Institute of Human Origins; Fig. 9–14, Robert Jurmain; **208**, Fig. 9–15, Reproduced with permission of the National Museums of Kenya, copyright reserved, courtesy of Alan Walker; **209**, Fig. 9–16a, b, Reproduced with permission of the National Museums of Kenya, copyright reserved; **210**, Fig. 9–17, Raymond Dart; photo by Alun Hughes; Fig. 9–18, Alun Hughes, reproduced by permission of Professor P. V. Tobias; **211**, Fig. 9–19, AP/Wide World Photos; **212**, Fig. 9–20, Robert Jurmain; Fig. 9–21, © Russell L. Ciochon, University of Iowa; **213**, Fig. 9–22, (Toros-Menalia) © Mission Paléoanthropologique Franco-Tchadienne; (WT 17000), Reproduced with permission of the National Museums of Kenya, copyright reserved, courtesy Alan Walker; (Lucy), Robert Jurmain; (SK 48), © Russell L. Ciochon, University of Iowa; (Sts 5), © Russell L.

INDEX